T5-CCM-554

THE HYMNAL 1982 COMPANION

Raymond F. Glover

GENERAL EDITOR

Volume Three B

HYMNS 385 THRU 720

CALVARY EPISCOPAL CHURCH
102 N. SECOND
MEMPHIS, TENNESSEE

The
CHURCH HYMNAL CORPORATION
New York

Copyright © 1994
The Church Pension Fund
All rights reserved.
The Church Hymnal Corporation
445 Fifth Avenue
New York, NY 10016

385 *Many and great, O God, are thy works*

Music: **DAKOTA INDIAN CHANT (LACQUIPARLE)**

This Native American hymn is deeply rooted in the tradition of the Dakota Indians of South Dakota. Its place in the history of their faith and persecution is one of great importance. Like the text of Dietrich Bonhoeffer, "By gracious powers" [695/696], it gives witness to an unwavering faith in a loving God in spite of great tribulation.

Words:

1. Wakantanka taku nitawa
   Tankaya qa ota;
Maȟpiya kin eyahnake ça.
Maka kin he duowanca;
Muniowanca śbeya wanke cin,
   Hena oyakihi.

2. Nitawacin waśaka, wakan,
   On wawicaȟyaye;
Woyute qa wokayake kin,
Woyatke ko iyacinyan,
Anpetu kin otoiyohi
   Wawiyohiyaye.

3. Adam ate unyanpi kin he,
   Woope wan yaqu;
Woope kin awaȟtani qon,
Miye dehan teȟiya waun,
Jesus onśimayakida qa
   Miyecicajuju.

4. Anpetu wan en yahi kin he
   Wootanin tanka,
Oyate kin hiyeye cin he
Iyoyanpa wicayaya;
Jesus waonśiyakida kin
   Unniyatanpi kta.

5. Wicoȟan wan unyaqupi kin
   Jesus amatonwan;
Woyute wan woyatke ahna

Mayaqu kin yuwaśte wo;
Unnaġipi untancanpi ko
Unyuecetu po.

6. Micehpi kin woyute yapi
Itancan kin dee,
Mawe kin he woyatke wakan,
Ehe ciqon, wacinwaye:
Nitatiyopa kin he wacin,
Jesus onśimada.

7. Woehdaku nitawa kin he
Minaġi kin qu wo;
Maȟpiya kin iwankam yati,
Wocowaśte yuha nanka,
Wiconi kin he mayaqu nun,
Owihanke wanin.

This text, based on Jer. 10:12–13, first appeared in *Dakota Dowanpi Kin (Odowan Wowapi)* (Boston, 1846), the supplement to the 1842 words-only edition of *Dakota Odowan* (Dakota Hymns). The 1846 supplement prints the text with the initials "J.R." which have been identified as those of Joseph Renville.

A contemporary translation by Sydney H. Byrd, a member of the Dakota Presbytery and of the Dakota tribe follows:

1. Great Spirit God, the things which are Thine,
Are great and numerous.
The heavens above Thou didst set in place,
And earth received its form by Thy hands.
The ocean depths respond to Thy will,
For thou canst do all things.

2. Thy will, so strong and mysterious,
Brings growth to all the earth.
Food for our souls and clothing to wear,
Are likened to Thy cup that fulfills.
Provide for us each day of our lives,
Sufficient for our needs.

3. Adam the father of humankind,
To him you gave Thy law.

That law I disobeyed with my sin.
And now I suffer pain and disgrace.
Jesus express Thy mercy to me,
And pay for all my sins.

4. The day Thou didst come to dwell on earth,
Was tidings of great joy!
The nations scattered about the world,
To them you gave the light of Thy life.
O Jesus, Thou compassionate One,
We render praise to Thee.

5. Thy Sacrament entrusted to us,
Jesus attend with me.
Thy bread of life and drink for our souls,
which Thou didst offer, no purify,
Cleanse Thou our souls and all human flesh,
Restoring us in love.

6. Thy plan for our salvation O Lord,
Grant to my sinful soul,
Thy abode is beyond the heavens,
All goodness is secure in Thy hands.
This divine life which Thou didst give me
Is one that has no end.

© 1990, S. H. Byrd. Used by permission.

The importance of this hymn in the lives of Native Americans, especially those of the Dakota or Sioux Indians, is related in a letter of November 7, 1986 by Mr. Byrd to Mrs. Lois C. Willand, a Minnesota writer who has done extensive research on this hymn. Mr. Byrd writes:

> One of the most moving sermons I have ever heard was given by an old Presbyterian missionary, the Rev. Abraham Crawford, at First Presbyterian Church in Flandreau, South Dakota, many years ago. He was pastor of the church at that time.
>
> He told of the hanging at Mankato of Dakota Indians by orders of a military court on December 26, 1862, in the largest mass

execution in American history! The Dakotas had no legal counsel and testified in their own behalf. Nearly all of them were found guilty and condemned to death.

Missionaries had been in the prison compounds ministering to the Indians. They were also engaged in teaching the prisoners to read and write in their own language. A remarkable change began taking place! There were mass conversions to Christianity. The missionaries also appealed to President Lincoln to show leniency to the prisoners. After personally reviewing all the records, the President commuted the sentence of all but 38 of the condemned men.

The execution date was originally set for December 19, 1862, but for some strange reason, it was changed to December 26. On that fateful day, the 38 prisoners were led out of the compound. They were chained together as they shuffled forward. The women began wailing.

One of the men cried in a loud voice, "Mitakuyapi, nanmahon po!" (Hear me, my people!) "Today is not a day of defeat. It is indeed a day of victory. For we have made our peace with our Creator and now go to be with Him forever. Remember this day. Tell our children so they can tell their children, that we are honorable men who die for a noble cause." Then he lifted up his voice to lead the condemned prisoners in a hymn of praise (Dakota Odowan 141). The trapdoor was sprung and the 38 Dakotas went to be with their Creator forever.

Rev. Crawford concluded his sermon by saying in an emotional voice, "And one of those who went to be with his Creator was my grandfather!" The stillness in that old historic church at Flandreau was a divine moment of reverence for all of us. Not a single person was excluded from the unity we all felt as an extended family. We were all somehow related to those who gave their lives at Mankato many years ago. We concluded the service by singing Dakota Odowan 141. Many sang with tears in their eyes.

The text, with a Dakota native air, was published by the American Missionary Association and the Presbyterian Board of Foreign Missions in the 1879 edition of the *Odowan*, a collection that has gone through five revisions and continues in use today. In the early decades of the century, the text and tune had gained such popularity with YWCA and other young peoples' groups that, in 1929, the Music Committee of the national YWCA asked Philip Frazier, a third-generation full-blooded Dakota (Sioux) Congregational minister and missionary to produce a version in English. Frazier paraphrased the first and last stanzas of the original and presented it to the 1930 national convention of the YWCA. Frazier and his wife, Susie Meek Frazier, through their concert-lectures, then spread the English-language version across the country. The *Methodist Hymnal* (Nashville, 1964) was the first major hymnal to include it. *More Hymns and Spiritual Songs* introduced it to Episcopalians. The only alteration in the text appears in the first line, where the word "works" replaces "things."

Music: The tune DAKOTA INDIAN CHANT (Lacquiparle) is identified as a native Dakota air to which Joseph Renville attached his text. The text and tune were published in the 1879 *Dakota odowan*, where they appear with a harmonization by James Ramsey Murray of Andover, MA (see Example 1).

Example 1

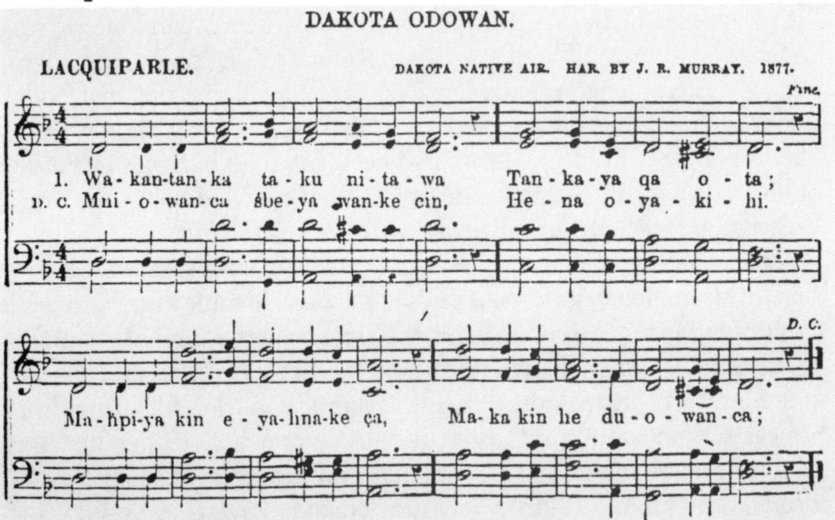

The tune is ABA in form, and each of its two parts shares a common basic structure. The A phrase opens with three repeated C's followed by a leap of a fifth (the *H82* version is transposed down a step to C).

In the B phrase, after the repeated C's, the melody leaps an octave. The melody, with a one-measure extension, then follows in a pattern which is very similar to that of the A phrase. In keeping with a unison performance practice, the editors of *H82* have suggested the use of a simple accompaniment on a percussion instrument. "Lac qui parle" is translated as "lake that speaks."

HCB/RG

386 We sing of God, the mighty source

Music: **CORNWALL**

This profound and mystic text by one of the great British poets of the eighteenth century is a superb example of how a text intended for reading can, under the care of a sensitive editor, become a fine hymn. It is matched here with a tune by Samuel Sebastian Wesley that appears in the *Hymnal* for the first time.

Words: This cento* from Christopher Smart's grand poem *A Song of David* (London, 1763) uses sts. 18, 40, 84, and 86 of that eighty-six-stanza work. The particular selection of stanzas was made for *H82*; however, all but st. 40 appeared in *H40* where Smart's st. 21 was the second stanza. (The Text Committee for *H82* proposed a five-stanza version including st. 21 to General Convention, but that body chose to delete the stanza.) The four *H40* stanzas were chosen from the five (18, 84, 21, 76, 78) that had been gathered in *Songs of Praise* (London, 1926) in the first attempt to shape a modern hymn from Smart's magnificent but unwieldy work.

This collection of stanzas retains the *Songs of Praise* alteration of the first line from one that describes David's actions in some indefinite past ("He sung") to one that engages the singers at the present moment ("We sing"). Other changes include: "the Lord God" in st. 2, line 1 has been substituted for Smart's "Jehova"; in the following line "on earth" (apparently referring to Moses) makes an easier line for singing but obscures Smart's original and stronger wording "earth heard"; the phrase "Mary's son" (an emendation made by General Convention) at st. 4, line 3 replaces Smart's "called Thy son" (altered to "called man's son" in *H40*) and "Seers that" in st. 4, line 4 has since *H40* replaced the rather problematical original "Thou at."

In many ways the opening line of Smart's st. 18 (from his catalogue of the subjects of David's poetry)—"He sung of God" — could be applied to himself. He regularly competed for, and often won, the Seatonian Prize, awarded for a poem on the attributes of the Supreme Being. *A Song of David* seems to have been written during one of his periods of confinement for mental instability. Although the exact chronology remains unclear, it belongs among a cluster of works including his celebrated *Jubilate Agno* (written between 1758 and 1763) and his *Translation of the Psalms of David* (London, 1765). *A Song of David* was first published separately in 1763 and was reprinted at the end of the *Psalms* in 1765.

Although many scriptural parallels could be suggested for various phrases, the first stanza printed here may be intended to echo parts of Pss. 96 and 98. The first part of st. 2 alludes to Moses' encounter with God at the burning bush (Example 3:1–15, especially 14), and the latter half seems to echo Ps. 19:3–4. Possible allusions in the third stanza would include Pss. 19:5, 148:3, 98:7, 136:12, and 93:4. The opening of the fourth stanza may draw on Phil. 2:5–11 (cf. Smart's Christmas hymn at 491), and the revised fourth line may be read as an allusion either to the coming of the Magi (Mt. 2:1–12) or to the ecstatic responses of Simeon and Anna (Lk. 2:25–38). Whatever his sources or intended allusions, Smart concludes his poem with a resounding affirmation effectively reinforced by alliteration: "the marvelous deed's . . . determined, dared, and done."

Music: CORNWALL first appeared in Samuel Sebastian Wesley's *The European Psalmist* (London, 1872), his great "scrapbook" of church music. It was written for his grandfather Charles's text "Thou God of glorious majesty." Routley describes it as typical of Wesley's difficulty combining "real inspiration with congregational accessibility," citing the striking move to the mediant minor in measures 3 through 6.[1] Nevertheless, the tune gained popularity after its appearance in the 1916 edition of *HA&M*. This marks its first appearance in the *Hymnal*.

---

1. E. Routley, *The Music of Christian Hymns* (Chicago, 1981), 106a.

CPD/WTJ

387 *We sing of God, the mighty source*

Music: **MAGDALEN COLLEGE**

It was with this tune by William Hayes, a composer living in England at the same time as the poet, that this text by Christopher Smart appeared in *H40*. This matching by the editors of *Songs of Praise* (London, 1926) is one of pure genius, for the soaring lines and rhythmic vitality of the melody elegantly support and illuminate the text.

Words: See hymn 386.

Music: This tune was composed by Dr. William Hayes, Professor of Music at the University of Oxford and organist of Magdalen College. The date of composition is not known, but Hayes printed the tune in *Sixteen Psalms Selected from the Revd Mr Merrick's New Version; Set to Music for the Use of Magd: Coll. Chapel in Oxford* (Oxford: for the author: Sold by Wm Randal in Catherine Street in the Strand, . . . London, n.d.).[1]

Hayes set the tune to James Merrick's Ps. 122, "The festal Morn, my God, is come," which happens to have an "ascending" feature in the second line of all three stanzas ("That calls me to thy honour'd Dome," st. 1; "Fair Sion's tow'rs in prospect rise," st. 2; "The Heav'n-protected Tribes ascend" st. 3), providing an unusually complete justification for the striking upward scale in the second phrase. Hayes's D-major setting is for SATB and organ, but with a low alto part suited to countertenors. The harmonies are approximately the same as in *H82*, but the spacing has been adjusted at some point in their history. Hayes used half notes rather than quarter notes and barred the tune in 2/2 so that it had twice as many measures. It is not at all clear that the stress should come at the points suggested by the modern bar lines; the first two phrases, moreover, began on an upbeat. Hayes provided an organ prelude (see Example 1) for the first verse only and a short interlude and postlude to be played after the second and fourth phrases of every verse.

Only six printings have been found before 1820, including one in the United States, in Samuel Holyoke's *The Christian Harmonist* (Salem, MA, 1804) where it is still set to Merrick's psalm. For Episcopalians, the tune was first included in the Tucker music edition, *The Hymnal with Tunes Old and New* (New York, 1874).

Example 1

1. Randall died in January 1776, but his 1776 catalogue (London, British Library, Hirsch IV.1113.[12].), possibly issued late in 1775, does not list the book, whereas his widow's, published a few years later, does. Therefore the date of publication must have been early in 1776.

NT

388 O worship the King, all glorious above!

Music: **HANOVER**

This text/tune matching, which for Episcopalians first appeared in the J. Ireland Tucker music edition of the 1871 *Hymnal*, is of such stature in the minds of most congregations as to be thought of as a "classic." In the Tucker edition the tune was attributed to G. F. Handel as was the case in other earlier publications of hymnals and tunebooks.

Words: This metrical version of Ps. 104 was written by Sir Robert Grant. It first appeared in *Christian Psalmody: A Collection of above 700 Psalms, Hymns and Spiritual Songs, Selected and Arranged for Public, Social, Family and Private Worship* (London, 1833), edited by Edward Bickersteth. It comprised six stanzas, the sixth being omitted from *H82*:

O Lord of all might, how boundless thy love!
While angels delight to hymn thee above,

The humbler creation, though feeble their lays,
With true adoration shall lisp to thy praise.

The second line of the first stanza originally began "O gratefully sing his unchangeable love," and the earliest form of st. 3, line 4 had "girdle" instead of the later "mantle." The hymn, in a slightly revised form, appeared in the posthumous collection of Grant's religious verse: *Sacred Poems by the late Rt. Hon. Sir Robert Grant* (London, 1839). Minor modifications appeared over the next thirty years until it reached its commonly accepted form in *The Hymnal Companion to the Book of Common Prayer* (London, 1870), edited by Bickersteth's son, Edward Henry Bickersteth.

John Julian, in his normally reliable *Dictionary of Hymnology*, introduced a red herring regarding the origin of this text, misleading numerous editors of hymnal companions, among others. Julian makes the statement that:

> This version of Ps. civ is W. Kethe's rendering of the same psalm in the Anglo-Genevan *Psalter* of 1561, reset by Sir R. Grant in the same metre but in a less quaint and much more ornate style (*Julian*, 854).

Julian goes on to cite sts. 1 and 3 of Kethe's version to "prove" his point. The similarities, however, are in fact extremely slight and are due to the content of the same biblical psalm on which the two metrical versions are based. Julian entirely confused the connections between the two versions, which are musical rather than verbal. As John Wilson has demonstrated, Grant did not rewrite Kethe but independently created his own version of Ps. 104. What the two texts have in common is the metre, that of the traditional 104th Psalm tune.[1] The hymn has been in the *Hymnal* since 1871.

---

1. See further, J. Wilson, "Julian and 'O Worship the King,'" *The Hymn Society of Great Britain and Ireland Bulletin*, 12 (October, 1989), 155.

Music: This rousing tune, long attributed to William Croft and before that to Handel, must now be regretfully consigned to the "Anonymous" list.

It was among the distinguished group of new tunes published, without attribution, in the sixth edition of *A Supplement to the New Version of Psalms* (London, 1708). Leonard Ellinwood stated that Croft "is generally regarded as the editor of that collection" and on that basis several of its new tunes have been ascribed to him by modern editors (*H40*c, 312). One, indeed—ST. ANNE [680]—is attributed to him by two of his contemporaries and associates, Philip Hart and John Church.

HANOVER had appeared in more than fifty collections, however, before Croft's name was mentioned in John Barker's *A Select Number of the Best Psalm Tunes, Extant* (Birmingham, ca. 1750), where the tune is marked "set by D. C.". This is explained on the title page, which mentions "Twelve *Psalm Tunes*, never before in Score, most of them (if not all) Set by the late Dr. CROFT." At first sight this might seem a promising source of information, for Barker had been a Chapel Royal chorister under Croft and evidently possessed manuscripts of some of his compositions, including four charity hymns that he now published in this same volume.[1] Closer inspection, however, casts doubt on Barker's reliability. All the twelve tunes "set by Dr. Croft" come from the 1708 *Supplement*, but only one, ST. ANNE, is known from other evidence to be by Croft, and three of them certainly are not; two had even appeared before he was born.

The most likely explanation is that Barker had a manuscript in the hand of his former master of four-part settings of twelve tunes that were also in the 1708 *Supplement* and concluded that these were Croft's own harmonizations. He may have been wrong: the published setting of HANOVER (Example 1) seems too full of consecutive fifths for a learned composer of Croft's stature. The bass is the same as in the *Supplement*, except for the first note, where a dominant has been substituted for the original tonic.

Even if the harmonies are Croft's, however, we are no nearer to establishing his authorship of the tune.

The only other eighteenth-century source attributing HANOVER to Croft is *A Collection of Twenty-Eight Psalm Tunes* by Michael Broome, a Birmingham associate of Barker's and the printer of his collection. Beginning with William Riley's *Psalms and Hymns, for the Use of the Chapel of the Asylum, or House of Refuge for Female Orphans* (London, 1767), attribution to Handel become more and more frequent. In 1803 William Crotch, in *Tallis's Litany . . . A Collection of Old Psalm Tunes . . . and Tallis's 'Come Holy Ghost'* (Oxford, 1803), assigned the tune to "Handel or more probably Dr. Croft," and it may have been on his authority that Croft's name gradually ousted Handel's in the later nineteenth century. While Handel certainly did not write the tune, we do not really know who did.

Example 1

The original words were "Our God, bless us all/with mercy and love" (Ps. 67, in peculiar metre, from the 1700 edition of Tate & Brady's *Supplement*). Alternative psalms were suggested: 149, New Version, and 104, Old Version. In fact, these two ("O praise ye the

Lord" and "My soul, praise the Lord") soon became the favored texts. The name HANOVER is first found in the second edition of William Lawrence's *A Collection of Tunes* (London, 1722) and was presumably an expression of loyalty to the new dynasty of George I. As early as 1725 the tune was printed in America in the fifth edition of John Tufts's *Introduction to Music* with the title PSALM 149, and from 1737 it was in the Supplement to the *Bay Psalm Book*, which also had a version of Ps. 149 in this metre.

The popularity of this tune has been phenomenal throughout its history. Since about 1750 it has been in almost every major hymnbook in the English-speaking world. It was the sixth most frequently printed sacred piece in American tunebooks up to the year 1810 (*CREAP*, lxxvii). Second only to OLD 100TH, it was the tune most frequently found on English organ barrels in the period of their widespread use (ca. 1790 to 1860). Abraham Milner in 1761 composed a LM tune based on HANOVER that was later called A(Y)LIFF STREET or AIRLIE STREET, a name that sometimes spreads to the original tune.

The harmonies in *H82* are very similar to those in *HA&M* except for the first part of the last line, with its accentual ninth chord on the subdominant, perhaps originating in *EH*. J. Ireland Tucker included the tune matched with this text in his *The Hymnal with Tunes New and Old* (New York, 1874), where the tune was credited to Handel.

---

1. See N. Temperley, "Croft and the Charity Hymn," *The Musical Times* 119 (1978), 539–41.

RAL/NT

389 Let us, with a gladsome mind

Music: **MONKLAND**

A quality of almost naive joy permeates this hymn, a paraphrase of Ps. 136 by a youthful John Milton set to an eighteenth-century tune of unusual buoyancy.

Words: This hymn is composed of selected stanzas from a paraphrase of Ps. 136 written by Milton at the age of fifteen and first published in *Poems of Mr. John Milton, Both English and Latin,*

389 · Let us, with a gladsome mind (732

Compos'd at several times (London, 1645). Imitating the repetition of "for his mercy endures for ever" as the second half of each verse of the psalm, Milton's paraphrase employs a recurring refrain in each stanza. In its full form the poem reads as follows:

1. Let us with a gladsome mind
Praise the Lord, for he is kind,
For his mercies aye endure,
Ever faithful, ever sure.

2. Let us blaze his Name abroad,
For of gods he is the God;
For, etc.

3. O let us his praises tell,
That doth the wrathful tyrants quell.
For, etc.

4. That with his miracles doth make
Amazed Heav'n and Earth to shake.
For, etc.

5. That by his wisdom did create
The painted Heav'ns so full of state.
For, etc.

6. That did the solid Earth ordain
To rise above the wat'ry plain.
For, etc.

7. That by his all-commanding might,
Did fill the new-made world with light.
For, etc.

8. The floods stood still like Walls of Glass,
While the Hebrew Bands did pass.
For, etc.

9. But full soon they did devour
The Tawny King with all his power.
For, etc.

10. His chosen people he did bless
In the wasteful Wilderness.
For, etc.

11. In bloody battle he brought down
Kings of prowess and renown.
For, etc.

12. He foil'd bold Seon and his host,
That rul'd the Amorrean coast.
For, etc.

13. And large-limb'd Og he did subdue,
With all his over-hardy crew.
For, etc.

14. And to his servant, Israel,
He gave their Land therein to dwell.
For, etc.

15. And caus'd the Golden-tressed Sun,
All the day long his course to run.
For, etc.

16. The horned Moon to shine by night,
Amongst her spangled sisters bright.
For, etc.

17. He with his thunder-clasping hand,
Smote the first born of Egypt Land.
For, etc.

18. And in despite of Pharoah fell,
He brought from thence his Israel.
For, etc.

19. The ruddy waves he cleft in twain,
Of the Erythracean main.
For, etc.

20. He hath with a piteous eye
Beheld us in our misery.
For, etc.

21. And freed us from the slavery
Of the invading enemy.
For, etc.

22. All living creatures he doth feed,
And with full hand supplies their need.
For, etc.

23. Let us therefore warble forth
His mighty Majesty and worth.
For, etc.

24. That his mansion hath on high
Above the reach of mortal eye.
For his mercies aye endure,
Ever faithful, ever sure.

As comparison of the original text and the *Hymnal* version reveals, the youthful poet's stanzas have required some tidying in order to make them regular enough for singing, and the first stanza has been repeated to provide an effective conclusion. Both the selection and editing of stanzas printed here (and in *H40*, when the text first entered the Episcopal *Hymnal*) derive from *Songs of Praise* (London, 1926), which in turn followed the lead of *EH* with the deletion of its two optional stanzas. (For the sake of precision, the text credit in *H82* really ought to have an "alt." appended [like the one in *H40*] to reflect these editorial emendations.)

In view of what has been changed in this text, it is important to note what has not been altered, especially in the fourth and fifth stanzas of the *Hymnal* version. By employing these rather conventional attributes of the "golden-tressèd" sun-god Apollo and the "hornèd" (i.e. crescent) moon of the goddess Diana, Milton is demonstrating the affirmation of the second stanza, "for of gods he is the God." In doing so, he had excellent precedent, for such is the very intention of the creation narrative in the opening chapters of Genesis. By creating and/or naming something, the one true God of Israel is in effect being portrayed as superior to the lesser deities of other peoples. Milton was similarly writing in the afterglow of the Renaissance with the confidence of a Christian Humanist who could requisition pagan mythology to adorn and support his faith.

Though this idiom may seem farfetched to present-day congregations, it is no more extreme than much visual art that is accepted without question, such as the classically derived "putti" hovering in many a painting and stained-glass window. Retaining this archaic imagery is much to be preferred to the flattening this text has suffered in other places (e.g., "silver moon . . . with gentle light" in H. W. Baker's version ([*Julian*, 673]).

Music: The origin of this tune has for decades been shrouded in mystery. The *Hymnal 1940 Companion* editors traced the source to an English Moravian collection, *Hymn Tunes of the United Brethren* (Manchester, 1824), edited by John Lees (Example 1). Notice was also made of the first appearance of the tune in *HA&M* (1861) set to "Praise, O praise our God and King" by Henry Williams Baker, an editor of the collection.

Example 1

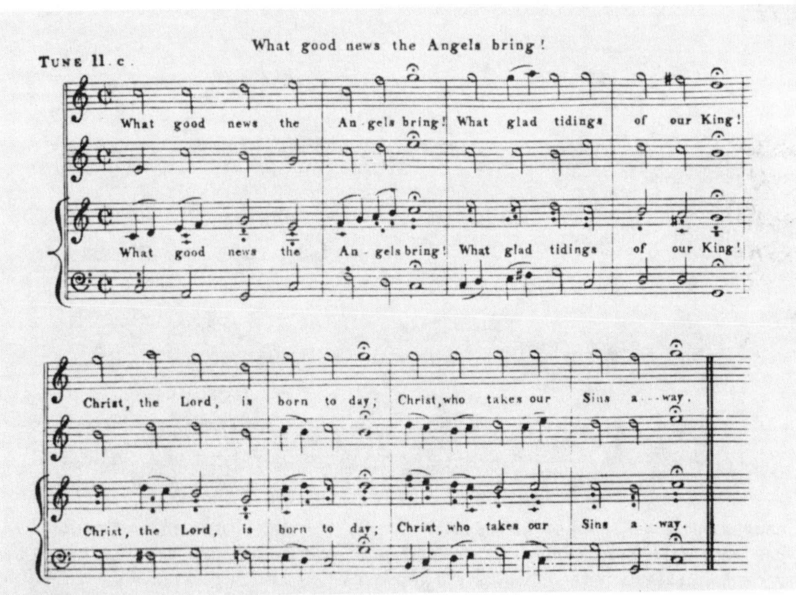

From *The Hymn Tunes of the Church of the Brethren* (Manchester, 1824), compiled by John Lees of the Moravian Settlement at Fairfield, Manchester, showing one of the 'new compositions' referred to in his Preface. The names of the composers were not given. Reproduced by permission of The Hymn Society of Great Britain and Ireland.

Fortunately, John Wilson brings the story up to date. The author tells us that in December 1960 Miss Frances Blandford of the Bristol Moravian Church, in her work on the archives of the Moravian Church in England, recognized two important manuscripts in the autograph of John Antes, an American-born eighteenth-century amateur Moravian composer. The first was a notebook entitled *A Collection of Hymn Tunes chiefly composed for private amusement by Jn Antes*. Second is a later fair copy book of fifty tunes including thirty-nine found in the notebook. Here no. 11 is the tune we call MONKLAND printed with melody, figured bass and, in small note heads, two inner parts (Example 2). Antes used a text from a 1789 Moravian words book that Wilson concludes dates the tune from Antes's years in Fulneck, Yorkshire, where he worked as a business manager of the Moravian community from 1785 to 1808.[1]

Example 2

From the Autograph MS of 50 original hymn tunes by John Antes (1740–1811), American-born Moravian minister and a notable amature composer. The MS dates from his later years and was not brought to light until 1960. Reproduced by permission of The Hymn Society of Great Britain and Ireland.

Bernard Massey in *Bulletin 174* of the Hymn Society points out that the John B. Wilkes who is credited as arranger of the 1861 *HA&M*

version is John Wilkes, a Moravian musician who as a young man probably discovered the tune in an 1824 Moravian tunebook that may have been used in the Leominster chapel he attended (see Example 2). He was probably organist of the Monkland parish from perhaps 1851 to 1854, and there knew H. W. Baker.[2]

Wilkes made only minor alterations in the Antes tune, removing passing notes from the melody in the third and fourth phrases, leaving the bass line and the harmony virtually unaltered. For this reason John Wilson suggests that Wilkes is more accurately thought of as editor of the tune rather than its arranger. The text and tune were introduced to the Episcopal *Hymnal* in the 1940 edition.

---

1. J. Wilson, "The Tune 'Monkland' and John Antes," *The Hymn Society of Great Britain and Ireland Bulletin*, 173 (October, 1987), 260–264.
2. B. Massey, "John Wilkes Again," *The Hymn Society of Great Britain and Ireland Bulletin*, 174 (January, 1988), 6.

CPD/RG

390 Praise to the Lord, the Almighty

Music: **LOBE DEN HERREN**

In an August 1978 survey of congregations across the country sponsored by the SCCM to ascertain the use of materials in *H40*, this hymn was rated as one of those used most often. Although its popularity came as no great surprise, it was an item of real news to many when they discovered that the hymn did not enter the *Hymnal* until the 1940 edition!

Words: This hymn, one of the most popular and well-loved of all hymns of praise, was written by Joachim Neander and first published in the author's *Glaub- und Liebesübung: Aufgemuntert durch Einfältige Bundes-Lieder und Danck-Psalmen* (Bremen, 1680) in five stanzas in a metre taken from a secular source (see commentary on the tune below). Catherine Winkworth translated the hymn, omitting st. 3, for *The Chorale Book for England* (London, 1863), thus forming the basis for the most widely used version of the hymn in English. The original German of these stanzas is as follows:

1. Lobe den herren, den mächtigen König der Ehren,
meine geliebete Seele, das ist mein Begehren.
  Kommet zuhauf,
  Psalter und Harfe, wacht auf,
lasset die Musicam hören!

2. Lobe den Herren, der alles so herrlich regieret,
der dich auf Adelers Fittichen sicher geführet,
  Der dich erhält,
wie es dir selber gefällt;
hast du nicht dieses verspüret?

4. Lobe den Herren, der deinen Stand sichtbar gesegnet,
der aus dem Himmel mit Strömen der Liebe geregnet.
  Denke daran,
  Was der Allmächtige kann,
der dir mit Liebe begegnet.

5. Lobe den Herren, was in mir ist, lobe den Namen.
Alles, was Odem hat, lobe mit Abrahams Samen.
  Er ist dein Licht,
  Seele, vergiss es ja nicht.
Lobende, schliesse mit Amen.

The version in *H82* is a revision of Catherine Winkworth's translation. A major weakness in both Miss Winkworth's translation and its revised form is that the powerful biblical imagery of st. 5, line 2—literally "all that hath breath praise with Abraham's seed" — that links Ps. 150:6 with Gen. 17:7 is omitted.

Music: The tune now known as LOBE DEN HERREN occurs in a wide variety of forms, which suggests that it has folk song origins. The fact that one variant occurs in a manuscript collection of largely secular songs would seem to confirm such an origin. The earliest printed version of the melody appeared in *Ander Theil des Erneuerten Gesangbuch* (Stralsund, 1665), associated with the text "Hast du denn, Liebster, dein Angesicht" (*Zahn* 1912a; A in Example 1). Within two years the same text appeared, but with another variant of the melody, in *Praxis Pietatis Melica* (Frankfurt, 1667) (*Zahn* 1912b; B in Example 1). The manuscript referred to above was compiled in Dresden by a

Example 1

A
Stralsund 1665
B
Frankfurt 1667
C
Dresden 1679
D
Bremen 1680
A
B
C
D
A
B
C
D

student named Johann Heck, who inscribed the title: *Cantiones hae sunt descritae a me Johanne Heckio*. Here another variant of the melody is found (Not in *Zahn*; C in Example 1), but associated with the secular text "Seh' ich nicht blinckende," probably a parody of a poem by Johann Rist. Most of the songs in Heck's manuscript were transcribed in the year 1679, but the evidence suggests that he copied from other sources. Whether or not this variant in the Heck manuscript therefore predates the earliest printed form of 1665, when the melody appeared as a hymn tune, is an open question. Nevertheless, it does at least point to a secular origin of the melody. When the melody was first associated with Neander's "Lobe den Herrn, den mächtigen König der Ehren," in *A Und O: Joachim Neandri Glaub- und Liebesübung* (Bremen, 1680), it appeared in yet another form (*Zahn* 1912c; D in Example 1 on following page). Other variants followed—one or two appearing in the early 1690s with the now familiar repeated tonic before rising to the dominant at the beginning of the tune—until it reached the generally accepted form around 1700. The harmonization in *H82* was taken over from *H40* with note values halved. It is based on the harmonization provided by the musical editors, William Sterndale Bennett and Otto Goldschmidt, of *The Chorale Book for England* (London, 1863).

RAL

391 Before the Lord's eternal throne

Music: **WINCHESTER NEW**

This text by Isaac Watts first appeared in the *Hymnal* in 1808. It is an indication of the more liberal attitude of Anglicans in the United States toward hymns of "human composure" than was the case with their contemporaries in England. The text has been matched with this tune since *H40*.

Words: The text given in *H82* is an interesting set of revisions from Isaac Watts's original paraphrase of Ps. 100, "Sing to the Lord with joyful voice," first printed in his *Psalms of David Imitated in the Language of the New Testament and Applied to the Christian State and Worship* (London, 1719). Watts's original first two stanzas were:

1. Sing to the Lord with joyful voice;
   Let every land his name adore;
   The British Isles shall send the noise
   Across the ocean to the shore.

2. Nations attend before his throne,
   With solemn fear, with sacred joy:
   Know that the Lord is God alone:
   He can create, and he destroy.

Erik Routley points out that John Wesley, in his *Collection of Psalms and Hymns* (Charleston, SC, 1737) "wrote his own first two lines, then used lines 3 and 4 of Watts's st. 2.":

Before Jehovah's awful throne
Ye nations bow with sacred joy.
Know that the Lord is God alone:
He can create, and he destroy. [1]

The editors of *H82*, in their desire to clarify the meaning of texts through the deletion of archaic language, further revised the opening line to "Before the Lord's eternal throne." This eliminates confusion with contemporary usage of the word "awful." Other hymnal editors have revised the same line to "Before Jehovah's awesome throne," or, as in *H40*, to "Before the Lord Jehovah's throne."

Revisions were also made in st. 2 which originally read:

His sovereign power, without our aid,
Made us of clay, and formed us men;
And when like wandering sheep we stray'd,
He brought us to his fold again.

---

1. See E. Routley, *An English-Speaking Hymnal Guide* (Collegeville, MN, 1979), 71.

Music: See hymn 76.

TAR

392 Come, we that love the Lord

Music: **VINEYARD HAVEN**

The matching of this text and tune was suggested by Erik Routley to Russell Schulz-Widmar who included it in his hymnal supplement *Songs of Thanks and Praise* (Chapel Hill, NC, 1980).

Words: Originally in ten stanzas, this Isaac Watts hymn has been the subject of considerable variation in both text and stanza arrangement. Watts first published it in his *Hymns and Spiritual Songs*, Book II (London, 1707). John Wesley later selected eight stanzas for use in his *Collection of Psalms and Hymns* (Charleston, SC, 1737). It first appeared in an Episcopal hymnal in 1871, where all but sts. 2 and 5 of Watts's original were included, but it was dropped in the 1892 *Hymnal* and not restored until *H82*. The version of the hymn used in *H82* makes use of Watts's sts. 1, 3, 8, and 10 with slight alterations. The use of the tune VINEYARD HAVEN necessitated the inclusion of the refrain, "Hosanna, hosanna! Rejoice, give thanks and sing" (see hymn 557). The original Watts text is:

1. Come, we that love the Lord,
   And let our joys be known,
Join in a song with sweet accord,
   And thus surround the throne.

2. The sorrows of the mind
   Be banisht from the place!
Religion never was design'd
   To make our pleasures less.

3. Let those refuse to sing
   That never knew our God,
But favorites of the heavenly King
   May speak their joys abroad.

4. The God that rules on high,
   And thunders when he please,
That rides upon the stormy sky,
   And manages the seas.

5. This awful God is ours,
   Our Father and our love,

He shall send down his heav'nly pow'rs
To carry us above.

6. There we shall see his face,
And never, never sin,
There from the rivers of his grace
Drink endless pleasures in.

7. Yes, and before we rise
To that immortal state,
The thoughts of such amazing bliss
Should constant Joys create.

8. The men of grace have found
Glory begun below,
Celestial fruits on earthly ground
From faith and hope may grow.

9. The hill of Zion yields
A thousand sacred sweets,
Before we reach the heavenly fields,
Or walk the golden streets.

10. Then let our songs abound,
And every tear be dry,
We're marching thro' Immanuel's ground
To fairer worlds on high.

Music: See hymn 557.

TAR

393 Praise our great and gracious Lord

Music: **MAOZ ZUR**
Both the text and tune of this hymn have deep roots in Judaism; the text that tells of God's leading of his people into the Promised Land is matched with MAOZ ZUR (Rock of Ages), a Chanukah hymn.

Words: Henrietta (Harriet) Auber is the author of this text. Her work is known today principally through her collection *Spirit of the*

Psalms (London, 1829). She is probably best recognized for her hymn "Our blest Redeemer, ere he breathed."

This text is an adaptation of Auber's paraphrase of Ps. 78, "O praise our great and gracious Lord." The text, originally 86. 86. 86. 86, was altered to match it with the 77. 77. 67. 67 metre of the tune. The poet's original sts. 1 and 2 were:

1. O praise our great and gracious Lord,
   And call upon His name;
   To strains of joy tune every chord,
   His mighty acts proclaim.
   Tell how He led His chosen race
   To Canaan's promised land;
   Tell how His covenant of grace,
   Unchanged shall ever stand.

2. He gave the shadowing cloud by day,
   The moving fire by night;
   To guide His Israel on their way,
   He made their darkness light.
   And have we not a sure retreat,
   A Saviour ever nigh?
   The same clear light to guide our feet,
   The day-spring from on high?

Music: This hymn is sung at the kindling of the Chanukah lights, originally only in the home, but later in the synagogue as well. The original text is written by an unidentified poet of the thirteenth century called Mordechai. Musicologist Eduard Birnbaum (1855–1920) first traced its origins to two non-Jewish sources,[1] while Eric Werner identi-

Example 1

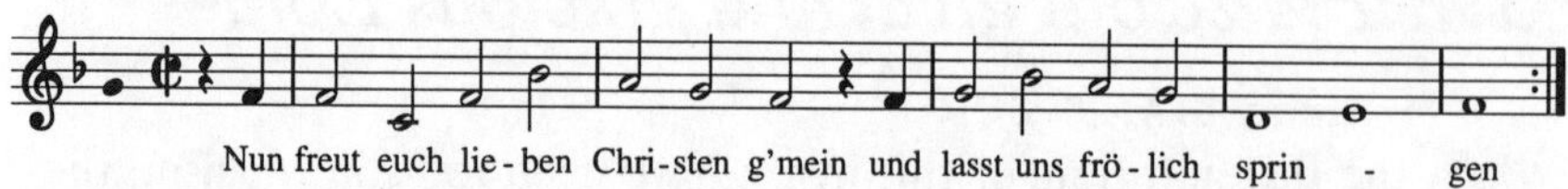
Nun freut euch lie - ben Chri - sten g'mein und lasst uns frö - lich sprin - gen

Example 2

etc.
So weiss ich eins das mich er - freut

fied a third possible source.[2] Its opening phrase is identical to Luther's "Nun freut euch lieben Christen g'mein," (Wittenberg, 1524; Example 1), which is based upon the German folk song "So Weiss ich eins was mich erfreut, das plumlein auf preyer heyde" (Example 2); the third phrase would appear to be borrowed from the refrain of the popular song "Ich weiss mir ein Meidlein huebsch und fein" (Example 3).

Example 3

Hüt du dich, ver - trau ihr nicht, sie nar - ret dich, sie nar - ret dich

The turn at the end of the second phrase betrays the influence of Late Baroque and Rococo instrumental music. The first complete notation of the present tune is given in Isaac Nathan's 1824 setting of Lord Byron's "On Jordan's Bank" (Example 4).[3] A very different modal tune sung by Tedesco (German-Italian) Jews was notated by Benedetto Marcello (Example 5).[4]

Example 4

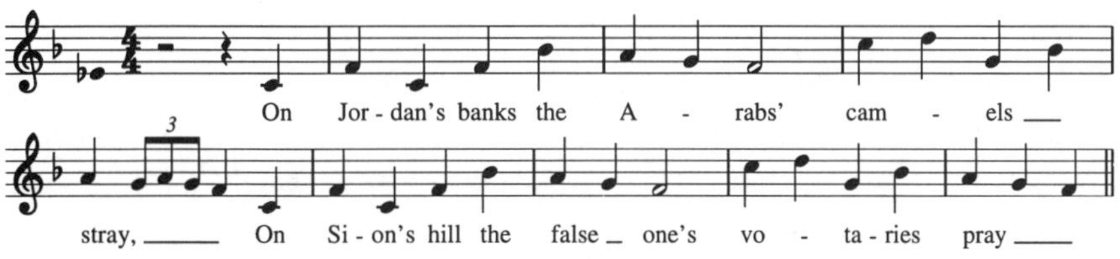
On Jor - dan's banks the A - rabs' cam - els
3
stray, On Si - on's hill the false one's vo - ta - ries pray

Example 5

Ma - 'oz tsur ye - shu - 'a - ti le - kha na - 'eh le - sha - be - ah

Birnbaum suggested that the standard melody originally belonged not to Mordechai's text but to another "piyyut" (liturgical hymn), "Shenei Zeitim," for the (first) Sabbath of Chanukah, whose metre and syllabic stress fits this tune better. Whereas "Shenei Zeitem" was rendered by the cantor alone, "Maoz Tsur" is sung by the congregation or by the family at home. The popularity of the tune led to its adaptation as a synagogal musical leitmotif for the Festival of Chanukah: it is sung to several prose liturgical texts associated with the festival. The concluding hymn, "Adon olam," is also often adapted to this melody. English Jews frequently modulate to the dominant in the repeat of the first phrase, while American Jews now frequently repeat the last phrase.[5]

---

1. E. Birnbaum, *Chanuca-Melodie "Maoz Zur"* (Konigsberg, 1889), introduction.
2. E. Werner, *A Voice Still Heard* (University Park, PA, 1976), 90–93.
3. I. Nathan and Lord Byron, *A Selection of Hebrew Melodies, Ancient and Modern*, ed. F. Burwick and P. Douglas (Tuscaloosa, 1988), 79.
4. B. Marcello, *Estro poetico harmonico*, vol. 3 (Venice, 1724), 11.
5. I. L. Mombach, *Ne'im Zemirot Yisrael* (London, 1881), 142.

TAR/JGo

394 Creating God, your fingers trace

Music: **WILDERNESS**

The psalm paraphrase, long a popular poetic form for hymn writers, lives on with strength in the works of contemporary writers such as the author of this text (see the essay, "English Metrical Psalmody," vol. 1, 321). This text, a paraphrase of Ps. 148, is matched here with an expansive tune, written early in this century by an English composer, that appeared in *H40*.

Words: "Creating God, your fingers trace," written in 1974 by Jeffery Rowthorn, illustrates the ongoing vitality of the psalm paraphrase as a hymn form. In rich and vivid language, the poet has recast this ancient Old Testament hymn in a form that speaks directly to the modern worshiper while retaining the spirit and intent of the original. The fourteen-verse psalm is set as an LM hymn of four stanzas, each stanza opening with an address to God, who is "creating," "sustaining," "redeeming," and "indwelling."

The sense of awe and mystery of God is captured in sts. 1 and 2 in a manner that enhances and freshly illuminates the psalmist's theme. Stanza 3 not only recasts but expands the original text to include among God's creatures those who are "despised for creed or race." The stanza ends with a prayer: "Let peace, descending like a dove, make known on earth your healing love."

Like Isaac Watts before him, Jeffery Rowthorn has, in his paraphrase, made the psalm universal. For example, the BCP translation of Ps. 148 at verse 14 reads "children of Israel." In this paraphrase, we sing of "one family with a billion names." This hymn was one of two winning texts in the 1979 Hymn Society of America's "New Psalms for Today" competition.

This is the first appearance of this text in the Episcopal *Hymnal*.

Music: See hymn 39.

RG

395 Creating God, your fingers trace

Music: **KING**

A contemporary tune has been matched with this contemporary psalm paraphrase for its second appearance in *H82*.

Words: See hymn 394.

Music: The hymn tune KING was composed in 1976 by Dr. David Hurd, Professor of Music and Chapel Organist, General Theological Seminary, New York City, for use with the text attributed to St. Patrick, "I sing as I arise today." A unison hymn tune with a particularly graceful melodic line, this setting utilizes a four-bar introduction/interlude that skillfully anticipates the structure and mood of the hymn. The initial phrase of the melody is distinctive for the sweep of its ascending movement from treble D♭ to its upper octave. It is answered by a carefully balanced descending second phrase. Phrases 3 and 4 echo melodic and rhythmic elements of the opening lines while the fourth is extended through the use of a syncopated rhythmic figure and a gently undulating cadential passage. An accompaniment of harmonic richness utilizing moving inner parts, especially at moments of repose in the melody, supports the melody with particular effectiveness. The tune honors Dr. Larry King (1932–1990), Director of Music, Trinity Church, Wall Street, New York.

RG

396/397 *Now thank we all our God*

Music: **NUN DANKET ALLE GOTT**

This "German Te Deum," as it has been called, has become the classic thanksgiving hymn that transcends all national, language and denominational boundaries. For example, it had become so familiar in the English-speaking world that no one in 1944–1945 ever questioned the protocol of celebrating victory over Hitler's Germany by singing this *German* hymn. Paradoxically, it originated within the havoc and ruin of the Thirty Years War and was appropriately sung to celebrate the Peace of Westphalia, December 10, 1648, that brought that war to an end. The hymn, however, had more humble origins. It has been matched with this tune since the mid-seventeenth century.

Words: "Now thank we all our God" did not originate as a hymn of national thanksgiving, but rather as a hymn for family table-grace. Its author was Martin Rinckart, archdeacon in Eilenburg, Saxony. In the late nineteenth century it was reported that an original manuscript of the hymn, owned by a descendant of Rinckart, indicated that the hymn was written by Rinckart for his children to sing and dated 24 June 1630; its location is now unknown. In *Die Meisnische Thränen-Saat* (Leipzig, 1637), Rinckart records that his "Danck-Psälmlein und Catechismus-Liedern" were completed six or seven years earlier, that is, around 1630. Thus, the veracity of the misplaced manuscript appears confirmed. The text first appeared in print in the long-lost first edition of Rinckart's *Jesu Herz-Büchlein* (Leipzig, 1636). The later 1663 edition reveals that the hymn was included under the rubric "Prayers after Meals." After its first appearance in 1636, it was included in Johann Crüger's *Praxis Pietatis Melica* (Berlin, 1647), together with Crüger's incomparable tune for it (see commentary below). The first two stanzas are based on Ecclus. 50:22–24; the third is doxological:

1. Nun danket alle Gott
   mit Herzen, Mund und Händen
der grosse Dinge tut
   an uns und allen Enden,
der uns von Mutterleib
   und Kindesbeinen an
unzählig viel zugut
   und noch jetzund getan.

2. Der ewigreiche Gott
 woll uns bei unserm Leben
ein immer fröhlich Herz
 und edlen Frieden geben
und uns in seiner Gnad
 erhalten fort und fort
und uns aus aller Not
 erlösen hier und dort.

3. Lob, Ehr und Preis sei Gott,
 dem Vater und dem Sohne
und dem, der beiden gleich
 im höchsten Himmelsthrone
dem dreimal einen Gott,
 wie es ursprünglich war
und ist und bleiben wird
 jetzund und immerdar.

The translation is based on Catherine Winkworth's, which first appeared in her *Lyra Germanica, Second Series* (London, 1858). The hymn has been in Episcopal *Hymnals* since 1871.

Music: The tune NUN DANKET ALLE GOTT (*Zahn* 5142) first appeared in Johann Crüger's *Praxis Pietatis Melica*, 3rd ed. (Berlin, 1647), where it was set to Martin Rinckart's text "Nun danket alle gott." While sometimes attributed to Martin Rinckart, the 5th edition of *Praxis Pietatis Melica* (Berlin, 1653) clearly identifies Crüger as the composer. The tune appears here in both the rhythmic form [396] in a harmonization by Johann Crüger and in the isorhythmic form [397] based on the harmonization by Felix Mendelssohn in his *Lobgesang* (Hymn of Praise) (1840).

RAL/CS

398 I sing the almighty power of God

Music: **FOREST GREEN**

This text by Isaac Watts first appeared for use by Episcopalians in the 1874 edition of the *Hymnal*. It was dropped from subsequent editions until its restoration in *H82*. Here the SCCM followed a precedent established by the editors of *The Methodist Hymnal* (Nashville, 1964) by including it as a CMD text matched with a much-loved English folk melody.

Words: Written as a song for children, this text of Isaac Watts was printed in his *Divine Songs attempted in Easy Language for the use of Children* (London, 1715) under the heading "Praise for Creation and Providence." (The title of the collection was changed to *Divine and Moral Songs* in 1795.) Although its original eight four-line stanzas are almost never used in their entirety, the hymn in altered forms is found in many English-language hymnals. (For example, in some cases, the first line of the text is rendered in a plural form, "We sing the almighty power of God.") The 1874 edition of the *Hymnal* used sts. 1, 2, 4, 5, and 6 of the CM original. *The Hymnal 1982* follows the order of the *Methodist Hymnal* (Nashville, 1964) in its use of sts. 1, 3, and 5 of the original as a three-stanza CMD text, but with alterations in Watts's original. The original st.5 read:

Creatures (as numerous as they be)
  Are subject to thy care;
There's not a place where we can flee,
  But God is present there.

The omitted sts. 7 and 8 are:

In heaven he shines with beams of love,
  With wrath in hell beneath,
'Tis on his earth I stand or move,
  And 'tis his air I breathe.

His hand is my perpetual guard,
  He keeps me with his eye;
Why should I then forget the Lord
  Who is for ever nigh?

In the *Methodist Hymnal* st. 3:7 reads "And everywhere that man can be." This has been altered in *H82* in support of the SCCM's commitment to use inclusive language whenever possible.

Music: See hymn 78. The first appearance of this tune matched with this Watts text was in the *Methodist Hymnal* (Nashville, 1964).

TAR, RFG, and CAD

399 To God with gladness sing

Music: **CAMANO**

In these recent decades of liturgical renewal throughout the Church, there has been a resurgence in the creation and use of metrical settings of canticles and psalms. (See the essay "English Metrical Psalmody," vol. 1, 321.) Here we have a paraphrase of Ps. 95 (Venite) matched with a tune by a contemporary American composer.

Words: "To God with gladness sing," a paraphrase of Ps. 95 (Venite), was first published by the author in *New Hymns for All Seasons* (London, 1969). It is the work of James Quinn, S. J., a gifted Scottish Roman Catholic priest, deeply concerned about practical congregational song. This three-stanza hymn in a 66. 66. 44. 44. metre opens with two balanced phrases in an ABAB rhyme scheme. The pattern for the next four shorter phrases, however, is a different pattern, ABBA. Together they form a fresh, engaging text, rich in the creative use of language. This text first appeared in an Episcopal hymnal in *Hymns III*.

For use in *H82*, the text in st. 1, line 3 was altered. The original read:

within his temple bring your songs.

Music: The tune CAMANO by Richard Proulx was commissioned by Russell Schulz-Widmar for use with the James Quinn paraphrase of Ps. 95, "To God with gladness sing," for inclusion in Dr. Schulz-Widmar's hymnal supplement *Songs of Thanks and Praise* (Chapel Hill, NC, 1980). Mr. Proulx's hymn tunes reflect his lifelong immersion in the study and use of plainsong, the historic chant of the Church. The melodies are basically diatonic in structure with a rhythmic freedom that supports the metrical structure of the texts to which they are set. For example, at the ending of word phrases in the tune CAMANO, the composer introduces a measure of three beats after a measure or measures in 4/4 time. This gives the tune a sense of forward thrust and a quality that sets it apart from the ordinary. The tune name honors Camano, the island in Puget Sound, WA, where the composer has a residence. An optional descant by Mr. Proulx is available for use with st. 3 of the text.

RG

400 All creatures of our God and King

Music: **LASST UNS ERFREUEN**

This much-loved text that enjoys wide ecumenical usage did not appear in an official Episcopal publication until *Hymns III*, where it is matched with the equally popular tune LASST UNS ERFREUEN.

Words: St. Francis's "Canticle of brother sun and of all creatures," ("Cantico di fratre sole, laude della creatur,") is often referred to as the first genuine religious poem in Italian. It is certainly an early example of Italian vernacular religious song, the *Laude spirituale* that flourished in the early thirteenth century (see the articles "The Development of Plainchant to the Counter Reformation," vol. 1, 171-172; "Popular Religious Song," vol. 1, 16-17 and hymn entries 406/407). There is a tradition that the canticle was written by St. Francis during the final year of his life, 1225 to 1226, a period of intense pain and suffering.[1]

1. Altissimu, omnipotente, bonsignore,
tue sono le laude,
la gloria elhonore
et omne benedictione.

2. Ad te solo, Altissimo, se Konfano
et nullu homo enne dignu
te mentovare.

3. Laudato se, misignore, com tucte le tue creature,
spetialmente messer lo frate sole,
loquale iorno et allumini noi par loi.

4. Et ellu ebellu eradiante cum grande splendore:
de te, Altissimo, porta significatione.

5. Laudato si, misignore, per sora luna ele stelle:
in celu lai formate clarite
et pretiose et belle.

6. Laudato si, misignore, per frate vento,
et per aere et nubilo
et sereno et omne tempo
per loquale a le tue creature
dai sustentatamento.

7. Laudato si, misignore, per sor aqua,
laquale e multo utile et humile
et pretiosa et casta.

8. Laudato si, misignore, per frate focu,
per loquale ennalumini la nocte:
edello ebello et iocundo
et robustoso et forte.

9. Laudato si, misignore, per sora nostra matre terra,
laquale ne sustenta et governa,
et produce diversi fructi
con coloriti flori et herba.

10. Laudato si, misignore, per quelli ke perdonano
per lo tuo amore
et sostengo infirmitate
et tribulatione.

11. Beate quelli kel sosterrano in pace,
ka da te, Altissimo,
sirano incoronati.

12. Laudato si, misignore, per sora nostra
morte corporale,
da laquale nullu homo
vivente poskappare.

13. Gai acqueli ke morrano
ne le peccato mortali!

14. Beati quelli ke trovarane
le tue sanctissime voluntati
ke la morte secunda
nol farra male.

15. Laudate et benedicite, misignore,
et rengratiate et servaite li
cum grande humilitate.[2]

The hymn version was "written during the time (1899-1919) when Mr. [William H.] Draper was Rector of Adel, Yorkshire, for a Schoolchildren's Whitsuntide Festival at Leeds, the exact year of which he does not remember. The hymn shapes the thoughts of the Canticle into a fine musical form for singing, omitting, however, the 'brother' and 'sister' element."[3] Draper picks up the ambiguity of the Italian "per," which means "for" or "from," and instead of expressing the praise of God *for* the creatures of God, it is the creatures themselves that articulate their own praises. This English text was written in the metre of LASST UNS ERFREUEN and was first published with the tune in *The Public School Hymn Book* (London, 1919). Thereafter it appeared in numerous hymnals (though not *H40*), often in an abbreviated form. For *H82* the text was lightly revised and altered into a "you" form.

---

1. See *Francis of Assisi: Writings and Early Biographies*, ed. M. A. Habig, 4th ed. (Chicago 1983), 1020-1024. Among recent studies on the text, the following are important: E. Leclerc, *The Canticle of Creatures, Symbols of Union: An Analysis of St. Francis of Assisi* (Chicago 1974); E. W. Platzeck, *Das Sonnenlied des heiligen Franziskus von Assisi* (Werl, Westphalia 1984); see also Habig, op. cit., 1917-1923.
2. A literal translation is found in V. Kybal, *Francis of Assisi* (Notre Dame 1984), 176-177.
3. P. Dearmer, *Songs of Praise Discussed* (London 1933), 234.

Music: The popularity of this tune in the English-speaking world is directly attributable to *EH* and its musical editor, Ralph Vaughan Williams (see the article "British Hymnody 1900 to 1950," vol. 1, 487).[1] The origins of the tune, however, date from a much earlier period. The opening phrase of the massive Strassburg melody ES SIND DOCH SELIG ALLE (*Zahn* 8303), published in 1525 (see commentary on OLD 113TH [429]), inspired Catholic musicians in Cologne at the beginning of the seventeenth century to compose a new tune: LASST UNS ERFREUEN. It first appeared in *Auserlesene, Catholische, Geistlische Kirchengesäng . . . . durch das gantze Jahr zu singen* (Cologne, 1623).

Example 1

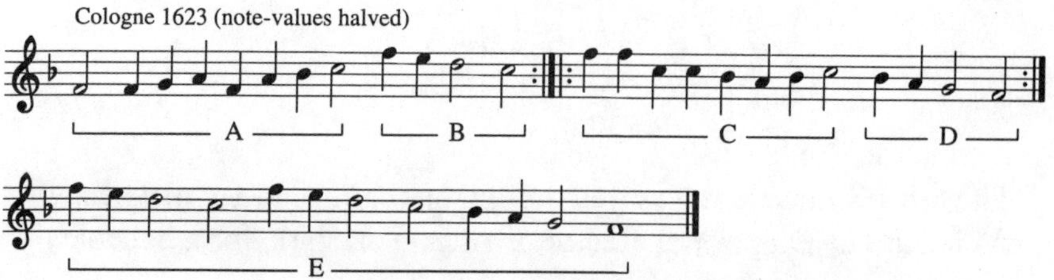

755)

The only known copy is now no longer extant; however, in the late nineteenth century, Wilhelm Bäumker had the opportunity to examine it and to transcribe this melody (see Example 1).[2]

Example 2

The form ABABCDCDE is somewhat different from its later manifestation. Two years later, in *Catholische Kirchen Gesäng, auff die Fürnembste Fest des gantzen Jahrs . . .* (Cologne, 1625), the same melodic elements were given its now-familiar form: AABBCCDDE (Example 2, tune 1). Both forms of the tune circulated side by side, although Catholic hymnals in the nineteenth and twentieth centuries favored the earlier form. A version of the later form appeared in

Henrich Reimann's *Das Deutsche Geistliche Lied* (Berlin, 1895). The note values were halved; the final note of the first melodic phrase (measure 5) was elongated to allow for the repetition of the phrase in the accompaniment; other editorial adjustments were made and the melody was marked *Allegro*, almost doubling the seventeenth-century tempo (Example 2, tune 2.) Reimann's collection of tunes was known to Vaughan Williams, who acknowledged it as his source, for example, for the melody MIT FREUDEN ZART in *EH*, no. 604, to which the following note was added: "By permission of Messrs. Schott & Simrock, from Reimann's 'Das Deutsche Geistliche Lied' " (see hymn 408). As John Wilson has cogently argued, Reimann was almost certainly Vaughan Williams's source for LASST UNS ERFREUEN (see Example 2, tune 3):

> Vaughan Williams, in supplying his own sturdy harmonies for a slower tempo, could dispense with Reimann's fourth bar; and he introduced a new symmetry by starting the third and fourth lines with long notes, to match the rhythm of the first and second. Less convincingly, he imposed a 3/2 time signature throughout, retaining Reimann's long penultimate note, which at the *EH* metronome rate of 100, had now to last for 3.6 seconds . . . . The *EH* version, if not 'authentic,' was an imaginative gesture, and has become a classic in its own right.[3]

---

1. See the substantial article by J. Wilson, "The Tune 'Lasst uns erfreuen' As We Know It," *The Hymn Society of Great Britain and Ireland Bulletin*, 9 (January, 1981), 194-200.
2. See W. Bäumker, *Das Katholische deutsche Kirchenlied in seinen singweisen* (Freiburg, 1886), vol. 1, no. 28.
3. See J. Wilson, "The Tune 'Lasst uns erfreuen' . . . ", 194-200.

RAL

401 The God of Abraham praise

***Music:* LEONI**

This is one of the two English paraphrases in *H82* of the Yigdal, the Jewish articles of faith written down in the twelfth century and put into verse about three hundred years later. The other is "Praise to the living God" [372] which, like this, is matched in *H82* with LEONI, its proper historic tune.

Words: "The God of Abraham praise" was written by Thomas Olivers, possibly around 1763. After hearing the Yigdal chanted in the Great Synagogue in London Olivers was moved to arrange it as an English hymn. He found it a source of inspiration, however, beyond merely versifying the material at hand. Not only did he Christianize it, but his complete version comprises twelve stanzas divided into three parts of four stanzas each. Olivers published the hymn in a circular with copious scripture references and even performance indications. It is headed "A Hymn to the God of Abraham: In Three Parts: adapted to a celebrated Air, sung by the Priest, Signior Leoni, &c., at the Jews' Synagogue, in London" (*Julian*, 1150).[1]

Six stanzas of the original first version appeared in the *Hymnal* in 1826. The version in *H82* uses sts. 1, 4, 7, 10, and 12. The succession of alterations culminating in *H82* is minor: "The Lord, the great I AM" for "Jehovah, Great I AM" in st. 1; "we" for "I" throughout st. 2; "his kingdom he maintains" for "his kingdom still maintains" in st. 3; "eternal Father" for "Jehovah, Father" in st. 4; "hail, Abraham's Lord divine" for "hail, Abraham's God and mine," and "With heaven our songs we raise" for "I join the heavenly lays" in st. 5. The alterations in st. 4 were made in an attempt to avoid an individualistic possession of God.

It should be noted that some hymnals have taken Olivers's first line, "The God of Abraham praise" and grafted it onto the Landsberg/Mann paraphrase of the Yigdal, "Praise to the living God" (see hymn 372).

---

1. Olivers's full original version may be found in E. Routley's *A Panorama of Christian Hymnody* (Collegeville, MN, 1979), 33-34.

Music: See hymn 372.

WTJ

402 Let all the world in every corner sing

Music: **AUGUSTINE**

This classic text of the great mystic priest and poet George Herbert appeared in *H40*, where it was wed to two tunes that were never well received by American congregations. The two tunes by contemporary composers used in *H82* provide this strong poetry with settings that both enhance the meaning of the text and are accessible to a congregation.

Words: In George Herbert's posthumously published collection of poems, *The Temple* (Cambridge, 1633), this poem is the first of two titled "Antiphon." Its presentation on the printed page clearly indicates that it was intended to be sung, though no original music for it has been identified. The two-line rhymed 10.4 antiphon, which is printed before, between, and after the two-couplet 66. 66 stanzas, is each time labeled "Cho[rus]," and the stanzas are each prefixed by "Vers[e]." In the printing of the antiphon the phrase "My God and King" appears on a separate line and in italics, which was the convention of the time to indicate quotation; in present-day hymnals this intention should probably be conveyed by enclosing the phrase in quotation marks.

Although it would be unwise to seek too direct an inspiration for this poem, there are some significant echoes here of various psalms, especially Ps. 96 as translated in the Psalter of the *BCP*. The antiphon, for example, may echo verses 1 and 10a: "O sing unto the Lord a new song; sing unto the Lord, all the whole earth . . . Tell it out among the heathen, that the Lord is King, and that he hath made the round world so fast that it cannot be moved." The first stanza similarly bears a resemblance to verse 11a: "Let the heavens rejoice, and let the earth be glad." The second stanza may be a reflection of sts. 6 and 8: "Glory and worship are before him; power and honor are in his sanctuary . . . Ascribe unto the Lord the honour due unto his Name; bring presents, and come into his courts." The second line of the second stanza may also be an allusion to the sometimes controversial issue of singing psalms in church (see the essay "English Metrical Psalmody," vol. 1, 321-348).

Herbert was a great lover of music both sacred and secular. He regularly attended Evensong at Salisbury Cathedral twice weekly and joined in private musical gatherings afterward.[1] Like his brother Edward (whose lute book is in the Fitzwilliam Museum in Cambridge), George Herbert was an accomplished lutenist and also played the viol. He grew up in a household where there was frequent psalm-singing and where musicians of the stature of John Bull and William Byrd were often guests.

Some hint of Herbert's musical keenness can be detected in this text in the implicit structure of the stanzas. The references to "high" and "low" in the first stanza may indicate that he conceived of the first couplet as being sung by treble voices, the second by bass voices. This pattern would also fit the second stanza, particularly if "longest part" is construed as an allusion to the cantus firmus or ground bass often found in music of this era.

Although this hymn was generally overlooked in the eighteenth century, it is notable that it was quoted in full in the Preface to John Playford's *Psalms and Hymns in Solemn Musick* (London, 1671). It is printed there with the stanzas side by side in two columns, with the antiphon bridging above and below them. This form might account for the fact that a number of nineteenth- and twentieth-century hymnals have printed the antiphons as the opening and closing lines of the stanzas, as did *H40* when this text entered the Episcopal *Hymnal* in that edition.

---

1. See A. M. Charles, *A Life of George Herbert* (Ithaca, 1977), 163-166.

Music: AUGUSTINE was written by Erik Routley in 1960 in response to his children's dissatisfaction with Basil Harwood's LUCKINGTON, almost universally sung in England as *the* tune for the Herbert text. "I facetiously remarked," commented Routley, "that I would try to replace that jubilant piece with one in B flat minor!"[1] He was also concerned with writing a tune for the text as Herbert wrote it, with the antiphon at the beginning, middle, and end, instead of the then-usual two-stanza form. The new tune was duly written, given the name AUGUSTINE after Augustine-Bristo Congregational Church, Edinburgh, where Routley then was minister, and was sung by that congregation from 1962 onward. It was published in *Hymns for Church and School* (London, 1964), and then appeared in *The Church Hymnary, Third*

Edition (Oxford, 1973); "but there a bone-headed sub-editor altered it to the two-stanza form—an insult which was corrected in the second printing after the damage had been done."[2] It was first published in America in *Westminster Praise* (Chapel Hill, NC, 1977), edited by Erik Routley.

The tune has an ABABA form, appropriately matching the structure of the text. Routley made the comment later in life: "In my twenties I should have been afraid to write the middle (B) section of AUGUSTINE—I should have thought it trite; but in practice I think it probably works."[3] Sir David Willcocks pointed out to the composer that there is more than a slight resemblance between the phrase and harmonization at the words "My God and King" in the A section of the hymn tune and Vaughan Williams's setting of the same words in his *Five Mystical Songs* (1911). Routley reports his somewhat tongue-in-cheek answer to Willcocks: "Then I am in the best of company."[4] This reply, however, conceals as much as it reveals, and leaves the question open as to whether the similarity was accidental or deliberate. The present writer, however, believes that it was an act of deferential homage to Vaughan Williams, the most influential English hymn tune composer and arranger of this century and therefore was a self-conscious quotation (see Example 1 below).

Example 1

From Vaughan Williams's *Five Mystical Songs* no. 5, *Antiphon*, mm 118-120 (transposed from D).

---

1. See C. R. Young, ed., *Our Lives Be Praise: the Texts, Tunes and Carols of Erik Routley* (Carol Stream, IL, 1990), xviii.
2. Ibid., xix.
3. Ibid.
4. E. Routley, *Companion to Westminster Praise* (Chapel Hill, NC, 1977), no. 5.

CPD/RAL

403 *Let all the world in every corner sing*

Music: **MACDOUGALL**

Calvin Hampton was an American composer whose hymn tunes are extolled because of the freshness of his approach to melodic and accompaniment writing. He composed the tune MACDOUGALL in 1974 for use with this George Herbert text. First appearing in *Hymnal Supplement II* prepared by the SCCM in 1975, it is an ideal example of his skills.

Words: See hymn 402.

Music: As a setting for the George Herbert text "Let all the world in every corner sing," the melody line of MACDOUGALL, less than an octave in compass, fits very well into the range of the average singer in a congregation. Composed in AA^1BA^2 song form, the melody line of each A phrase, which is always set to the opening antiphon of the text, outlines the chord of E^b and opens with a half note on the word "let." When sung with a slight crescendo to the word "all," the melody gains a forward thrust to its climax on the words "my God and King!" The accompaniment has a trio sonatalike texture in which each of the three voices is an independent part. The inner voice is distinguished by its almost uninterrupted pattern of sixteenth notes. The appearance of the B theme at the words "The heavens are not too high" is answered canonically in the lower voice of the pedal at the distance of one measure. In its first printing, the composer marked the first A phrase to be sung by Men (indicated by "I" in *H82*) and the second A by Women or Trebles (indicated by "II" in *H82*). This division could be continued at the B theme marked "Full" by having the men sing the lower voice of the canon. The final A phrase should be sung full. The tune name honors Jeffrey MacDougall, a friend of the composer.

A two-part version of MACDOUGALL appears in *The Calvin Hampton Hymnary* (Chicago, 1980). In the Foreword, the composer writes:

> When sung as an anthem, the accompaniment can be played by hands alone omitting the vocal line. The accompaniment figure could be played on the guitar, piano, or harpsichord.[1]

The arrangement of the tune in this collection contains a six-measure expansion of both the opening introduction and the second ending. In the latter, the Amen has been deleted and is replaced by an arpeggiated chord of E^b major in the right hand (see Example 1).

Example 1

© 1980 by GIA Publ. Inc., Chicago, Il. All rights reserved.

1. *The Calvin Hampton Hymnary* (Chicago, 1980), foreword.

RG

404 We will extol you, ever-blessed Lord

Music: **OLD 124TH**

This metrical version of Ps. 145 not only provides an alternative to the paraphrase at 414 but also assures congregations of continued use of this popular Genevan psalter tune.

Words: This text is a metrical version of Ps. 145 and is found in *The Scottish Psalter of 1650: A Revision* (Edinburgh, 1940) by Nichol Grieve (referred to as J. Nichol Grieve in *H82*). It is set in four five-line stanzas with st. 4 being a repetition of the first. Stanzas 1 through 3 were included in the Revised *HA&M* (1950) and set to OLD 124TH. This was the source used by the editors of *H82*, who modernized the text from a "thee" form into a "you" form and made several other verbal substitutions.

Music: See 149.

RAL

405 All things bright and beautiful

Music : **ROYAL OAK**

The extensive catalogue of hymns for children by the British poet Cecil Frances Alexander is the source of several texts included in *H82* that have found a place in the singing tradition of people of all ages, among them "Once in Royal David's city" and this text, set to a popular seventeenth-century tune.

Words: In this text Cecil Frances Alexander provides an illustration of the second article of the Apostles' Creed: "God the Father, maker of heaven and earth." It is one of a series of her hymns for children on the articles of the Creed; others appear at nos. 102 and 167. Published in *Hymns for Little Children* (London, 1848), the text first appeared in an Episcopal hymnal in the Catechism section of *H16*.

It has been pointed out that the verb "to make" is the key to this hymn; it occurs seven times in the original seven stanzas.[1] The omitted stanzas, nos. 3 and 6, read:

3. The rich man in his castle
   the poor man at his gate,

God made them, high or lowly
and ordered their estate.

6. The tall trees in the greenwood,
the meadows where we play,
the rushes by the water
we gather every day.

The first of these omitted stanzas is deleted from modern hymnals and widely disparaged as "infamous." Bailey, for example, says "Here the Tory stratification of society is given the sanction of God Almighty. Belief in such a divine Order would make social and economic change impossible and would confine all philanthropic work to 'medicating the symptoms,' rather than eradicating the causes of poverty, crime and oppression."[2] It is perhaps kinder to think that Mrs. Alexander was assembling a wide spectrum of images of creation that would fall within a child's experience and placing them all under the domain of God; observations of the society of her day were treated like those of natural order, as they would be by the uncritical eye of a child. In our day, however, we appreciate the simplicity and charm of the remaining text better for the offending stanza's omission. Stanza 6, also universally omitted, paints a bucolic picture of life experienced by few people in our contemporary world.

The four lines of the first stanza have found their way into popular culture as a result of their use as titles of four books of reminiscences (published from 1972 to 1981) by James Herriot, a veterinarian in the north of England; these were in turn adapted for television and received much attention.

Scripture references include the creation story, Gen. 1:1-2:3, and Prov. 16:4.

---

1. F. Colquhoun, *A Hymn Companion* (London and Wilton, CT, 1985), 30.
2. A. E. Bailey, *The Gospel in Hymns* (New York, 1950), 354.

Music: The tune ROYAL OAK was adapted by Martin Shaw for this text in *Song Time* (London, 1915), a collection that he edited with Percy Dearmer. Robert McCutchan suggests that the name of the melody is derived from the "Royal Oak," a tree in Boscobel, Shropshire, in which Charles II hid himself during his escape following the Battle of Worcester in 1651. McCutchan gives the source of the tune as "The Twenty-ninth of May," a loyalist song celebrating the restoration of Charles II on May 29, 1660. Another name by which the tune is known is "The Jovial Crew."[1]

---

1. R. G. McCutchan, *Hymn Tune Names, Their Sources and Significance* (New York and Nashville, 1957), 127.

MD/CAD

406 Most High, omnipotent, good Lord

Music: **ASSISI**

This translation of a much-loved text by Francis of Assisi and this tune, written for use with it, first appeared in an Episcopal hymnal in *H40*.

Words: (See hymn 400). This text is a translation by Howard Chandler Robbins of the Italian religious poem "Cantico di fratre sole, laude della creatur" attributed to St. Francis of Assisi. The translation was first published in Robbins's *Family Devotions* (New York, 1927) and then revised to its form found in *H40* in his *Way of Light* (New York, 1933). The following sections of text have been altered in *H82* to comply with the SCCM's desire to use inclusive language whenever possible:

st. 1:5	no man
st. 5:3	for man's life
st. 7:2	from whom no man

Music: ASSISI was composed in 1942 by Alfred M. Smith, an Episcopal priest, for use in *H40* with Howard Chandler Robbins's translation of the Hymn of St. Francis "Most High, omnipotent, good Lord." The melody of this unison modal tune encompassing a range of five notes, F to C, is chantlike in nature. This is conveyed not only by the style and shape of the melody, but by its irregular rhythm that fluctuates between groups of two and three notes. To support his melody the composer has created a simple chordal accompaniment, sensitive to the metre and tonality of the tune.

MBJ/RG

407 Most High, omnipotent, good Lord

***Music:* LUKKASON**

This translation of verses from the Hymn to the Sun attributed to Francis of Assisi has called forth from Calvin Hampton a gentle and reflective unison tune. His gifts as a composer of finely crafted lyric lines are clearly evident in LUKKASON.

Words: See hymn 406.

Music: LUKKASON, composed for a theological student in 1973 for use with the text "Most High, omnipotent, good Lord" is one of Calvin Hampton's tunes that fulfills Erik Routley's description of a "strophic song."[1] In this case, however, the style is less that of one of the classic writers of lieder and more like that of one of many contemporary American song writers. LUKKASON's lyric melody moves basically in a stepwise fashion with occasional punctuation by skips of a third. There is also a consistency in the rhythmic structure of the tune: the resulting sense of lift that occurs at the beginning of each phrase gives a particular forward thrust to the tune and invariably imparts weight to important syllables or words. An accompaniment whose inner voices maintain a constant eighth note movement provides sympathetic support for the melody. Performance of stanzas by alternating groups, with all singing the first and last, adds an element of variety to this long hymn.

After use in manuscript form, this tune was first published in the Roman Catholic hymnal *Worship II* (Chicago, 1975). For its inclusion in the *Calvin Hampton Hymnary* (Chicago, 1980) the composer made extensive changes in the last phrase of the tune and added the three-bar introduction and the three-bar conclusion. Although these changes were in part caused by the deletion of the Amen at the end of the hymn, they also reflect Mr. Hampton's feeling that congregational song should first be shaped through use by a congregation who, by basic intuition, will iron out places that are awkward or unnatural. Only after a tune had been subjected to this refining process did he feel that it should be "cast in stone" as a published work. It is this revised form of LUKKASON that appears in *H82* transposed down a half-step.

The earlier version of the original closing phrase is as follows (see Example 1).

Example 1

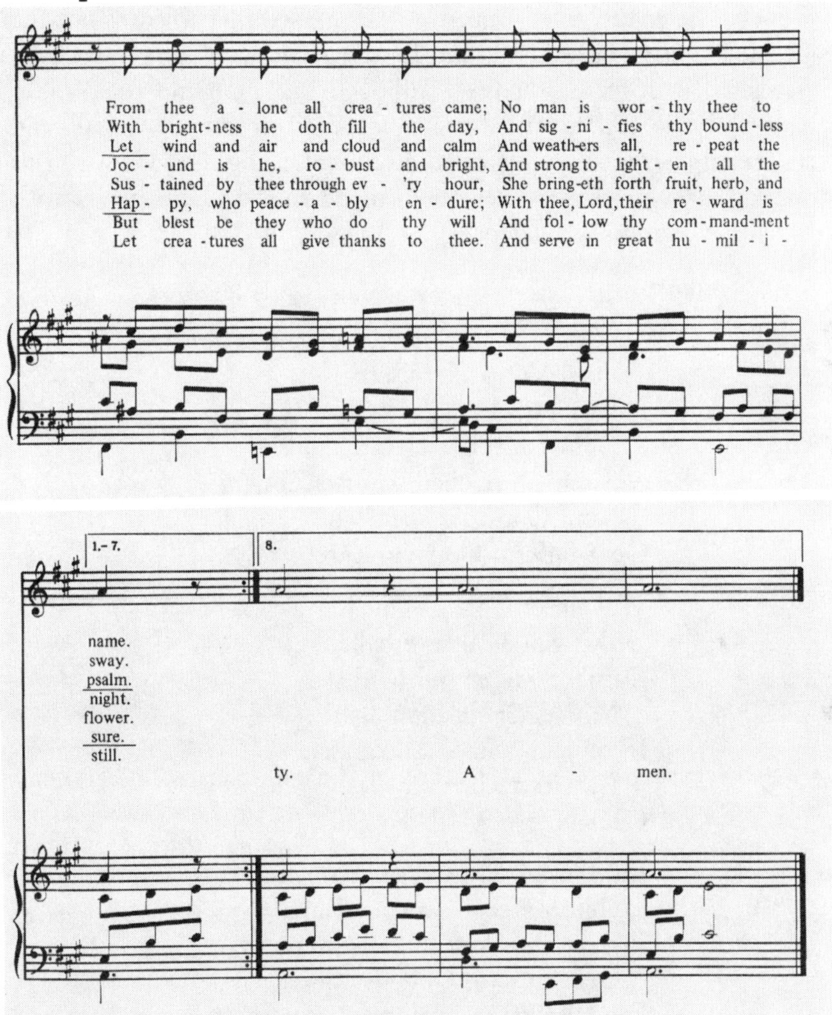
From thee a - lone all crea - tures came; No man is wor - thy thee to
With bright-ness he doth fill the day, And sig - ni - fies thy bound-less
Let wind and air and cloud and calm And weath-ers all, re - peat the
Joc - und is he, ro - bust and bright, And strong to light - en all the
Sus - tained by thee through ev - 'ry hour, She bring-eth forth fruit, herb, and
Hap - py, who peace - a - bly en - dure; With thee, Lord, their re - ward is
But blest be they who do thy will And fol - low thy com-mand-ment
Let crea - tures all give thanks to thee. And serve in great hu - mil - i -
1.–7.
8.
name.
sway.
psalm.
night.
flower.
sure.
still.
ty.
A - men.

© 1980 GIA Publ. Inc., Chicago, Il. All rights reserved.

1. E. Routley, *The Music of Christian Hymns* (Chicago, 1987), 175.

RG

408 Sing praise to God who reigns above

***Music:* MIT FREUDEN ZART**

MIT FREUDEN ZART appeared in *H40* under the tune name BOHEMIAN BRETHREN, matched with the text "Lord Christ, when first thou cam'st to men." Over the years concern was expressed that this was not the ideal relationship of text and tune, for MIT FREUDEN ZART is historically associated with an Easter text. Although this tune and the Walter Russell Bowie text are now firmly matched in many hymnals and continued in *H82*, Episcopalians can now also sing the tune with this doxological song of praise, closer in mood to the German text with which it was initially related.

Words:

Sei Lob und Ehr' dem höchsten Gut.
Dem Vater aller Güte.
Dem Gott, der alle Wunder tut,
Dem Gott, der mein Gemüthe.
Mit seinem reichen Trost erfüllt,
Dem Gott, der allen Jammer stillt.
Gebt unserm Gott die Ehre!

Was unser Gott Geschaffen hat,
Das will er auch erhalten,
Darüber will er früh und spat
Mit seiner Gnade walten.
In seinem ganzen Königreich
Ist alles recht und alles gleich.
Gebt unserm Gott die Ehre!

Ihr, die ihr Christi Namen nennt,
Gebt unserm Gott die Ehre!
Ihr, die ihr Gottes Macht bekennt,
Gebt unserm Gott die Ehre:
Die falschen Götzen macht zu Spott.
Der Herr is Gott! der Herr ist Gott!
Gebt unserm Gott die Ehre!

Described by the German hymnologist Eduard Emil Koch "as outweighing many hundred others; and a classical hymn, which from its first appearance attracted unusual attention" (*Julian*, 1018), this buoyant hymn of Johann Jakob (Jacob in *H82*) Schütz is found in nearly every German hymnal and translated into many English service books. The text appeared for the first time in a tract by Schütz entitled *Christliches Gedenkbüchlein zur Beforderung eines anfangendes neues Lebens* (Frankfurt-am-Main, 1675) ("A Little Christian Devotional Book for the Promotion of a New Life"). Deuteronomy 32:3 provides the scriptural basis for the nine stanzas of the hymn. *The Hymnal 1982* makes use of sts. 1, 3, and 8 from a translation by Frances Elizabeth Cox first published in *Lyra Eucharistica* (London, 1864) and her *Hymns from the German* (London, 1864). Cox's translation appears intact in *H82* with only slight revisions in the third stanza of *H82*.

Johann Schütz is interesting in that he was, in addition to being a lawyer, heavily involved in the German Pietistic movement. A friend of two major Pietistic figures, Philipp Spener and Johann Wilhelm Peterson, he was instrumental in encouraging Spener to begin his influential *Collegia Pietatis*. Under the influence of Peterson, Schütz became a Separatist and severed all ties with the Lutheran Church. The present hymn, however, is surprisingly devoid of the intensely personal and decision-oriented devotional content of most pietistic hymnody. This vigorous text with its psalmlike refrain is further strengthened in *H82* by its matching with the tune MIT FREUDEN ZART. This relationship finds precedent in the *Pilgrim Hymnal* (Boston, 1958) and *The Methodist Hymnal* (Nashville, 1964).

Music: The tune MIT FREUDEN ZART (*Zahn* 8186) first appeared in the hymnal of the Bohemian Brethren, *Kirchengeseng darinnen die Heubtartickel des Christlichen glaubens kurtz gefasset* ([Ivančice], 1566), where it was set to the text "Mit Freuden zart zu dieser Fahrt" by Georg Vetter. Similarities between this tune and that given with Ps. 138, "Il faut que de tous mes esprits," in *Trente quatre pseumes de David* (Geneva, 1551) have been noted (see Example 1), as well as to a French secular song "Une pastourelle gentille" published by Pierre Attaingnant ca. 1529-1530. The harmonization in *H82* is by Ralph Vaughan Williams after Heinrich Reimann (1850-1906) from *EH*. It was introduced to Episcopalians in *H40*, where it was known as BOHEMIAN BRETHREN.

Example 1

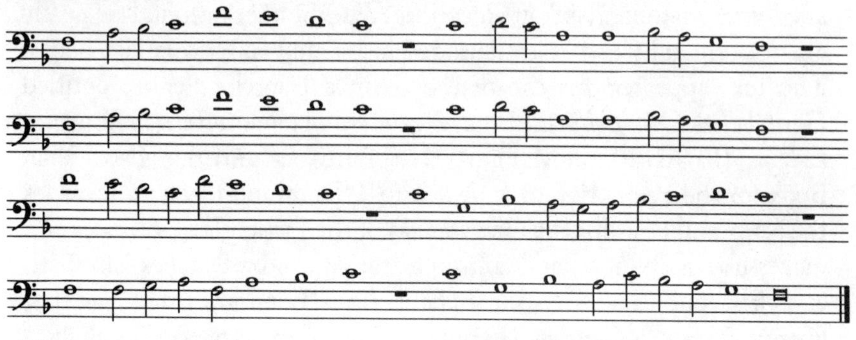

TAR/CS

409 *The spacious firmament on high*

Music: **CREATION**

This hymn is an adaptation of the chorus "The heavens are telling" from Haydn's oratorio *The Creation*. The work, composed in 1797-1798, was first performed at the Palais Schwarzenberg, Vienna, on April 29, 1798. The text of the oratorio chorus was a paraphrase of Ps. 19:1-2. Nothing could be more suitable, therefore, than to adapt the chorus to Addison's splendid paraphrase of verses 1-6 of this psalm, which has the same enlightenment or even deistic flavor as the oratorio itself.

Words: This celebrated paraphrase by Joseph Addison of Ps. 19:1-6 has appeared unaltered in every edition of the *Hymnal* since the first edition of 1789. The full text was originally published at the conclusion of *The Spectator*, no. 465 (August 23, 1712), exactly two weeks after another essay had ended with "When all thy mercies, O my God" (see 415).

This poem is the capstone of Addison's discussion of "the proper Means of strengthening and confirming [Faith] in the Mind of Man." After examining the difficulties of remaining steadfast to those principles that first brought conviction and the desirability of committing such arguments to memory, Addison maintains that faith is strengthened by morality. Even more effective, he then acknowledges, is "an habitual Adoration of the Supreme Being." This latter attitude is nourished by "frequent Retirement from the World, accompanied with religious Meditation." In enumerating ways of reducing the distractions of everyday life, Addison specifically mentions "the Silence and Darkness of the Night" as helpful means of concentrating the mind on higher concerns. Among the illustrations supporting his argument, he cites Ps. 19:1-4 (in the translation of the *Prayer Book* psalter) and, noting that "such a bold and sublime Manner of Thinking furnishes very noble Matter for an Ode," offers these three stanzas of a LMD paraphrase of the opening section of the psalm.

Of the five hymns Addison appended to his *Spectator* essays, this is easily the best-known, having appeared for over two centuries in countless hymnals in many languages all around the world. Its standing as a classic hymn can be inferred from its frequently being annexed to printings in Tate and Brady's *New Version* of the psalter, as well as by its being one of the five hymns appended to the *Scottish Paraphrases* of 1781.

Addison's poem—which never uses the word "God"—is a quintessential expression of what is known as "natural theology" as distinguished from "revealed theology." According to this differentiation, worked out at great length in the Middle Ages (with reference to passages such as Rom. 1:18-23), certain religious truths can be deduced by human beings by applying their natural powers of discursive thought. The First Vatican Council (1869-1870) affirmed that such knowledge is possible because of the dependence of the creature upon God, but post-Reformation theology has generally rejected the competence of fallen humanity to engage in natural theology. Because it is primarily concerned with God as known through creation, with natural law, and with the human soul (particularly its freedom and immortality), discussions of natural theology are now frequently regarded as the province of the philosophy of religion rather than as a branch of theology per se. Even in his own day, Addison's language and imagery (especially his references to an earth-centered universe) would have seemed archaic. This very artifice of antique formality, however, appeals to an ageless human longing for an ordered creation overseen by a benevolent Creator and accounts for much of the enduring popularity of this hymn.

Music: This adaptation of the Haydn chorus was made by Bishop Simms, organist of St. Philip's Church, Birmingham, England, and published as sheet music about 1810. In this original version,[1] the second and third phrases of the tune are reversed; the text is the same as here. The present variant, according to Leonard Ellinwood, first appeared in Isaac B. Woodbury's *Dulcimer, or New York Collection of Sacred Music* (1850) (*H40c*, 201); it is found in *Episcopal Common Praise* (New York, 1868), in B^{b} labeled "For the choir," and in many subsequent Episcopal hymnals. It has not been in common use in the Church of England at any recent period.

Haydn's chorus is not itself very hymnlike after the first two phrases. Its use as a hymn, however, was partially anticipated by Haydn himself in a tune he wrote for William Tattersall's *Improved Psalmody* (London, 1794). That tune, but more particularly its last phrase, is strongly prophetic of "The heavens are telling."

---

1. Reproduced in N. Temperley, *The Music of the English Parish Church*, II (Cambridge, 1979), Example 54.

CPD/NT

410 Praise, my soul, the King of heaven

***Music:* LAUDA ANIMA**

The popularity of this hymn is reflected in the request of Queen Elizabeth II that it be sung as the processional hymn at her wedding on November 20, 1947, coincidentally the hundredth anniversary of the death of its author, Henry Francis Lyte.

Words: A free paraphrase of Ps. 103, this text first appeared in Lyte's *The Spirit of the Psalms* (London, 1834), which contained over 280 paraphrases. It is the second of two settings of that psalm.

When the hymn appeared in the first edition of *HA&M*, the refrain "Praise him! Praise him!" had been replaced with "Alleluia! alleluia!" Both versions continue in common use. In the original, st. 1, line 4 read: "Who like me his praise should sing?" Line 6 of st. 3 read: "Widely as his mercy flows!" A fourth stanza, which was bracketed for omission, read:

Frail as summer's flower we flourish;
Blows the wind, and it is gone;

But while mortals rise and perish,
God endures unchanging on.
Praise him! Praise him!
Praise the high eternal One!

The hymn first appeared in the *Hymnal* in 1874.

Music: Known also as PRAISE MY SOUL, LAUDA ANIMA was composed for Lyte's paraphrase of Ps. 103 and appeared for the first time in R. Brown-Borthwick's *Supplemental Hymns and Tune Book, compiled by the Rev. R. Brown-Borthwick, 3rd ed.* (London, 1869). In its original form it was written for voices in unison with a varied organ accompaniment for each of its five stanzas; a separate four-part setting in the key of E was also included. This latter version, transposed to D, is used here for st. 2 and is the standard harmonization found in many hymnals. This expanded form appears for the first time in an American Episcopal hymnal. The tune is immensely popular in Great Britain and is frequently sung at weddings, including several of the royal family's. Its festive character is heightened by the use of C. S. Lang's descant, which is included in *20 Hymntune Descants* (London, 1953).

MS

411 O bless the Lord, my soul

Music: **ST. THOMAS (WILLIAMS)**

This psalm paraphrase by James Montgomery, with its confident trust in a loving and forgiving God, is matched with a tune that conveys similar qualities of assurance and joyfulness.

Words: This hymn is a paraphrase of Ps. 103:1-5 and first appeared in the eighth edition of Cotterill's *Selection of Psalms and Hymns* (London, 1819). It draws heavily on phrases of Coverdale's translation of the psalm found in editions of the *BCP* prior to 1979. Possibly Montgomery considered it an edition of that work rather than his original. He did not include it in his collection of psalm paraphrases, *Songs of Zion* (London, 1822), nor among his *Original Hymns* (London, 1853), his summary collection of all his psalms and hymns. He did include in both of these another hymn of seven stanzas of six lines each, based on Ps. 103. The present text, without alteration, has been in the *Hymnal* since 1826.

Music: Aaron Williams published a sixteen-line tune in G for Wesley's hymn "Soldiers of Christ, arise" in *the Universal Psalmodist* (London, 1763) under the name HOLBORN. He may well have composed it himself. It had the drawback that each four-line section ended on the tonic, but nevertheless it was adopted by the American compilers Flagg, Bayley and Stickney during the following decade.

It was then discovered that the second section, taken by itself, made an excellent tune. Maurice Frost thought that Williams himself was responsible for this discovery, and Williams certainly published the short version in *The New Universal Psalmodist* of 1770.[1]

But he may have been anticipated by Thomas Knibb in *The Psalm Singer's Help.* There were five unnumbered and undated editions of this work, which was primarily designed for use with Watts's psalms and hymns and Whitefield's *Hymns for Social Worship.* The fourth edition, probably dating from 1769, contains the present tune under the name WILLIAMS'S, and this was most probably the first printing of the tune in its short form. Knibb set it to Watts's Psalm 19, "Behold the lofty sky/declares its maker God".

When Williams reprinted it in 1770 he christened it ST. THOMAS' and substituted Watts's Ps. 48 ("Great is the Lord our God"). It was quickly taken up by Andrew Law in *Select Harmony* (Cheshire, CT, 1778) and was reprinted in dozens of American tunebooks before 1820. Later it found a place in Southern shape-note books such as William Walker's *Christian Harmony* (New Haven, CT, 1866). The name HOLBORN was revived in some Scottish sources, but ST. THOMAS or ST. THOMAS'S remained the most usual designation, with WILLIAMS added later to avoid confusion with Wade's tune of the same name [58]. This tune matched with this text appears in J. Ireland Tucker's *The Hymnal with Tunes Old and New* (New York, 1874).

---

1. M. Frost, *Historical Companion to Hymns Ancient and Modern* (London, 1962), 154.

HLW/NT

412 *Earth and all stars*

Music: **EARTH AND ALL STARS**

This exuberant contemporary Benedicite, omnia opera Domini brings into our repertoire of songs of praise traditional images as well as those that are very much a part of our present-day experience of God's creation. A tune of similar vitality lifts the text to heights of pure and almost uninhibited joyfulness.

Words: Herbert Brokering wrote this text for the ninetieth anniversary of St. Olaf College in Northfield, MN, in 1964. It was originally published in the collection *Twelve Folksongs and Spirituals* (Minneapolis, 1968) and in *Contemporary Worship I* (Minneapolis, 1969). The author's own commentary on "Earth and all stars" is "I tried to gather into a hymn of praise the many facets of life which merge in the life of community. So there are the references to building, nature, learning, family, war, festivity."[1]

The hymn is a series of calls to creation, humanity, music, and human endeavor to "sing to the Lord a new song!" Its structure is that of a call and response song with an expansive melodic refrain. Opportunities for singing the stanzas of this hymn in alternation are limited only by the imagination of the congregations singing it. The text, thoroughly grounded in contemporary experience, forces its singers in every aspect of their lives to see that all that is made, seen, heard, and accomplished—either by Godly or human hands—is done to the glory of God. Herbert Brokering notes the following about his writing:

> Many of the images through which I visualize the rhyme and rhythm of the gospel came to me in Nebraska and Iowa. Season, emotions, death and resurrection, bread, wine, water, wind, sun, spirit—have made great impressions on my imagination. Words want to be seen. Words have their roots in visuals and images. We see what we know. We imagine the language of faith. The image power we have is an enormous gift from God. We are in God's image.[2]

---

1. M. Stulken, *Hymnal Companion to the LBW* (Philadelphia, 1981), 563.
2. Ibid, 564.

Music: The jubilant, exuberant tune EARTH AND ALL STARS was written by David N. Johnson for use with the Herbert F. Brokering text whose first line is also the tune name. The setting of the verses for this unison tune outlines the notes of the tonic chord of A^b, C, E^b. The refrain uses a wonderfully expansive phrase on the word "marvelous" which not only conveys, but expands its meaning. The accompaniment is by Jan Bender. Noteworthy is the use of the hemiola* of the accompaniment on the words "Lord a new song." This harmonic/rhythmic device appears twice in each stanza before the refrain. At that point the tune moves in two measures of 3/4 over an accompaniment that is really one measure of 3/2. The text and tune first appeared in *Twelve Folksongs and Spirituals* (Minneapolis, 1968) and in *Contemporary Worship I* (Minneapolis, 1969). In both these collections, the rhythm at "Sing to the Lord . . . " is as follows (see Example 1).

Example 1

In the first line of the refrain it is as in Example 2.

Example 2

The altered form of the setting found in *H82* using a rhythm in the first measure that is much closer to the spoken rhythm of the words first appeared in the *LBW*.

RG

413 New songs of celebration render

Music: **RENDEZ À DIEU**

Psalm 98, an oft-quoted and much-loved psalm, has been beautifully paraphrased in this text by Dr. Erik Routley. It is appropriately matched by the author to a Genevan Psalter tune attributed to Louis Bourgeois.

Words: This 1972 paraphrase of Ps. 98 by the late Dr. Erik Routley, whose impact on hymn singing, editing, and writing in the last quarter of this century is probably greater than that of any other person, continues the heritage of the Reformed Protestant tradition. Based on a 1970 revision of the French Psalter for inclusion in *Cantate Domino* (Oxford, 1980), an ecumenical hymnal published on behalf of the World Council of Churches, it was also included in *Ecumenical Praise* (Carol Stream, 1977). This hymn is not a slavish copy, but a fresh interpretation of the psalm, one bursting with dynamic energy. For example, resonance and vitality stand out in his use of words: "joyfully, heartily, resounding"; "rivers and seas and torrents roaring," and "peal out the praise of grace abounding." Dr. Routley has captured in contemporary language the spirit of the psalmist with whom we join in praising God as Creator, Savior, and Judge.

The French version by Roger Chapal (1970) is:

1. Entonnons un nouveau cantique
pour célébrer le Dieu sauveur;
ce qu'il a fait est magnifique
levant pour nous un bras vainqueur.
Le salut de Dieu se révèle
et tous les yeux l'ont reconnu;
de proche en proche la nouvelle
jusqu'au bout du monde a couru.

2. Chantez pour lui vos chants de fête;
psalmodiez! criez de joie!
Au son du cor et des trompettes,
acclamez tous le Roi des rois.
Le Seigneur vient juger la terre,
sa vérité va s'imposer.
Que tous les peuples qui espérent
en l'apprenant soient apaisés.

3. Que tous les océans mugissent;
fleuves aussi, battez des mains:
et que les montagnes bondissent
pour acclamer le Roi qui vient.
Le Seigneur ve juger le monde

avec droiture et vérité,
et partout sa justice fonde
son éternelle royauté.

The text, which first appeared in the United States in *Ecumenical Praise* (Carol Stream, IL, 1977), was included in *Hymns III* and is now included in most major English-language hymnals around the world.

Music: See the commentary on no. 301. This four-part setting by Erik Routley first appeared with this text in *Ecumenical Praise*, was taken over in *Hymns III* two years later, and then appeared in *H82*. Alternative harmonizations are given at nos. 301 and 302.

RG/RAL

414 God, my King, thy might confessing

Music: **STUTTGART**

The writing of psalm paraphrases for singing at home and in the parish church has a long tradition for Anglicans (see the essay, "English Metrical Psalmody," vol. 1, 321). This text is the work of an Irish prelate who was also a prolific translator and writer of hymns. It has been matched with this tune since the Hutchins music edition of the 1892 *Hymnal*.

Words: Richard Mant's paraphrase of Ps. 145 first appeared in fourteen stanzas in the author's *Metrical Version of the Psalms* (London, 1824). It was included in full in *Psalms, in Metre Selected from the Psalms of David; Suited to the Feasts and Fasts of the Church* (New York, 1832), and retained its place in later hymnals of the Episcopal Church. *The Hymnal 1982* includes the first six stanzas. The omitted stanzas are:

7. They thy might, all might excelling,
   Shall to all mankind make known;
   And the brightness of thy dwelling,
   And the glories of thy throne.

8. Ever, God of endless praises,
   Shall thy royal might remain;

Evermore thy brightness blazes,
Ever lasts thy righteous reign.

9. Them that fall the Lord protecteth,
He sustains the bow'd and bent;
Every eye from thee expecteth,
Fix'd on thee, its nourishment.

10. Thou to all, great God of nature,
Giv'st in season due their food;
Spread'st thy hand, and every creature
Satisfiest still with good.

11. God is just in all he doeth,
Kind is he in all his ways;
He his ready presence showeth,
When a faithful servant prays.

12. Who sincerely seek and fear him,
He to them their wish will give;
When they call, the Lord will hear them,
He will hear them and relieve.

13. From Jehovah, all who prize him
Shall his saving health enjoy;
All the wicked, who despise him,
He will in their sin destroy.

14. Still, Jehovah, thee confessing,
Shall my tongue thy praise proclaim;
And may all mankind with blessing
Ever hail thy holy Name.

Mant was clearly inspired by the vocabulary and style of Charles Wesley's verse. "Thy might, all might excelling" recalls Wesley's "Love divine, all loves excelling," and the emphatic repetitions at the beginning of lines 3 and 4 of sts. 7 and 8 are typical of Wesley's poetry:

And the brightness *of thy* dwelling,
And the glories *of thy* throne . . .

*Ever*more *thy* bright*ness* blazes,
Ever lasts *thy* right*eous* reign.

Music: See hymn 66.

RAL

415 When all thy mercies, O my God

Music: **DURHAM**

This text, one of the eight that appeared in the original Episcopal *Hymnal* of 1789, is continued in this most recent revision (see the essay, "The Publication of the Hymnal of the Episcopal Church," vol. 1, 49). It is matched with a psalm tune with which it appeared in *H40*.

Words: At the conclusion of Joseph Addison's essay on gratitude in *The Spectator*, no. 453 (August 9, 1712) appeared thirteen stanzas of CM verse, of which the present text supplied the first, second, tenth, twelfth, and thirteenth. Stanzas 3 through 9 and 11 read:

3. Thy Providence my Life sustain'd
   And all my Wants redrest,
When in the silent Womb I lay,
   And hung upon the Breast.

4. To all my weak Complaints and Cries,
   Thy Mercy lent an Ear,
Ere yet my feeble Thoughts had learnt
   To form themselves in Pray'r.

5. Unnumber'd Comforts to my Soul
   Thy tender Care bestow'd,
Before my Infant Heart conceiv'd
   From whom these comforts flow'd.

6. When in the slipp'ry Paths of Youth
   With heedless steps I ran,
Thine Arm unseen convey'd me safe
   And led me up to Man;

7. Through hidden Dangers, Toils, and Deaths,
   It gently clear'd my Way,
And through the pleasing Snares of Vice,
   More to be fear'd than they.

8. When worn with Sickness, oft hast thou
   With health renew'd my Face,
And when in Sins and Sorrows sunk
   Revived my Soul with Grace.

9. Thy bounteous Hand with worldly Bliss
   Has made my Cup run o'er,
And in a kind and faithful Friend
   Has doubled all my store.

11. Through ev'ry Period of my Life
   Thy Goodness I'll pursue,
And after Death in distant Worlds
   The glorious Theme renew.

Although the number and selection of stanzas have varied, some form of this text has been in every Episcopal *Hymnal* since the first edition in 1789 (as is also true of the Addison text at 409). The only alteration in the stanzas printed here is that "fervent heart" replaces "ravished heart" in the third line of st. 2.

Such continual use in the *Hymnal* is reflective of the widespread popularity this text has long enjoyed. John Wesley included nine stanzas of it (under the title "Thanksgiving for God's particular Providence") in his *Collection of Psalms and Hymns* (Charleston, 1737). In the early nineteenth century it was added by the university printers to editions of the Tate and Brady "New Version" of the Psalter, and it was the first of the five hymns added to the *Scottish Paraphrases* in 1781. For the past two centuries nearly every significant hymn collection has included some part of it.

The heart of Addison's essay, and its primary link to the subsequent poem, comes in the second paragraph:

> If Gratitude is due from Man to Man, how much more from Man to his Maker! The Supreme Being does not only confer on us those Bounties which proceed more immediately from his Hand,

but even those Benefits which are conveyed to us by others. Every Blessing we enjoy, by what Means soever it may be derived upon us, is the gift of him who is the great Author of Good, and Father of Mercies.

The final sentence of this paragraph (with its echoes of James 1:17) both expresses the primary motive of the poem and provides a rationale for its autobiographical structure (which has ample antecedents in the Psalms, e.g., 63, 71, 90, 139).

This is a text that also has both backward and forward links with other hymns. The final two lines of Addison's text are indebted to the final two of George Herbert's "King of Glory, King of Peace" [382] and the last two lines of the first stanza here are echoed at the close of Charles Wesley's "Love divine, all loves excelling" [657].

Music: DURHAM is from Thomas Ravenscroft's *Whole Booke of Psalmes* (London, 1621), where it is claimed there as the compiler's own work. It is among what Ravenscroft calls the "Northern tunes," but these geographical classifications seem to have been largely a fiction, designed to justify the tune names, which were, with few exceptions, those of cathedrals and choral foundations. The original key was F, and the setting was, as usual, for four voices with the tune in the tenor, to Pss. 28 and 76 in the Old Version. It enjoyed a moderate esteem in England for a hundred years. Then, after dropping out of use for a time, it was revived in Richard Garbett's *Sacred Harmony* (Exeter, ca. 1818). It was not printed in America before 1820. It appeared in the 1861 edition of *HA&M* but was later dropped from that collection. It was included in *H40*. The present harmonies are Ravenscroft's, with the tenor and cantus interchanged and a few minor modifications.

CPD/NT

416 For the beauty of the earth

Music: **LUCERNA LAUDONIAE**

This popular hymn text, originally published as a hymn of praise, has strong associations in the United States with Thanksgiving Day. It is matched with a tune written for use with it early in this century. This tune, which is new to the *Hymnal*, is gaining in acceptance.

Words: "For the beauty of the earth" was written by Folliot Sandford Pierpoint and published in Orby Shipley's *Lyra Eucharistica* (London, 1864), where, although intended for use at the Eucharist, it was included among the miscellaneous hymns with the heading "The sacrifice of praise." It first appeared in an Episcopal hymnal in 1916. *The English Hymnal* uses all eight stanzas of the hymn and places it among the Eucharistic hymns. Widely used as a children's hymn, this text became a favorite for flower services in England. At these services, held on the afternoon of the fourth Sunday in Lent ("mothering Sunday"), children would present their mothers with bouquets of wildflowers picked the day before.

The refrain of the hymn, which is taken from the Eucharistic prayer in the BCP, has been subject to a variety of alterations. In the 1916 and 1940 editions of the *Hymnal*, the text read "Lord of all, to thee we raise, This our hymn of grateful praise," while *H82* restores the author's original "Christ our God, to thee we raise. . . ." In addition, the 1916 and 1940 editions included only the first five stanzas of the text. The present st. 5 was added in *H82*, and the order of the original fifth and sixth stanzas is reversed.

The omitted seventh and eighth stanzas are as follows:

7. For thy martyrs' crown of light,
For thy prophets' eagle eye,
For thy bold confessors' might,
For the lips of infancy:
Refrain.

8. For thy virgins' robes of snow,
For thy maiden Mother mild,
For thyself, with hearts aglow,
Jesu, Victim undefiled,
Offer we at thine own shrine
Thyself, sweet Sacrament Divine.

Alterations appear in sts. 2, 4, and 6. The original lines are:

st. 2:2 For the heart and brain's delight
st. 4:1 For Thy Bride that evermore
4 This Pure sacrifice of Love
st. 6:2 To our race so freely given,
3 Graces human and Divine,
4 Flowers of earth and buds of Heaven.

Music: This tune by David Evans was composed for use with this text in the *Revised Church Hymnary* (London, 1927), of which the composer was the chief musical editor. It appeared there with an attribution to Edward Arthur, a pseudonym for the composer. It sings with a winsome appeal in its use of subtle discords on accented notes and its fluent changing rhythmic patterns. Each of the three lines could itself have grown into a hymn tune, and together they constitute a work of tremendous attractiveness. The music is cheerful and positive with a strong descending bass line at the beginning of the first and third lines. This is its first appearance in the *Hymnal*, where it is paired with two texts: "For the beauty of the earth" [416] and "God of mercy, God of grace" [538]. The editors of *A Companion to Hymns and Psalms* (Peterborough, England, 1988) write of the tune name:

> The name means 'Lantern of the Lothians,' referring either to a Franciscan monastery at Haddington, East Lothian, destroyed in 1355, or to the fifteenth-century church which replaced it. The nave of the latter survives as part of St. Mary's Church, of which in 1927 the minister was the Rev. G. Wauchope Stewart, a member of the editorial committee of the *Revised Church Hymnary*.[1]

---

1. R. Watson and K. Trickett, eds., *Companion to Hymns and Psalms* (Peterborough, England), 215.

TAR/AW

417 This is the feast of victory for our God

Music: **FESTIVAL CANTICLE**

The presence in *H82* of this hymn, which is also included in the *LBW*, is another symbol of the strong ecumenical ties between the Episcopal and the Lutheran Churches. It also is included in *Worship III: A Hymnal and Service Book for Roman Catholics* (Chicago, 1986). The text first appeared in an Episcopal publication in *Songs for Celebration* (New York, 1980) with the tune YLVISAKER by John Ylvisaker, arranged by Betty Pulkingham.

Words: Oral history has it that "This is the feast . . . " was first used in 1962 at a Lutheran Student Ashram in Williams Bay, WI. From the documents available, however, this is difficult to prove. It is more likely that it was written while John Arthur was a member of the Liturgical Texts Committee of the ILCW (Inter-Lutheran Commission on Worship). This Song of Praise, a paraphrase of Rev. 5:12-13, was written to take the place of the traditional Gloria in excelsis. Its form is that of a responsorial psalm: the stanzas are always followed by the antiphon.

Arthur's text proved to be popular and was used in *Contemporary Liturgy II* (Minneapolis, Philadelphia, St. Louis, 1969) by the ILCW. In that collection of four musical settings for the service of Holy Communion, Arthur's text was set as an alternate to the Gloria. The booklet suggested that its use "during Eastertide is an effort to break the predictability of the Gloria" (p. xii). When the *LBW* was published, the text was used in all three settings of the liturgy. Since then, many pastors and organists have decided that it should be used exclusively for Sunday services in which the Holy Communion is celebrated. Since few Lutheran congregations celebrate the Lord's Supper every Sunday, but do use the Holy Communion service as an Ante-communion service, it signifies communion for many Lutherans when they hear it. The "Canticle Use Chart" in *H82 a1* suggests its use as an alternate for the Gloria during Easter.

Music: FESTIVAL CANTICLE by Richard Hillert was composed for use with this text in 1969[1] and was included with other settings by Daniel Moe, Gerard Cartford, and John Ylvisaker in *Contemporary Liturgy II*. In 1976 it was published separately as a setting for choirs, instruments, and congregation, and in 1978 was included with settings by Cartford and Ronald Nelson in the *LBW*.

In *H82* the setting is arranged as a congregational hymn that, through the use of its antiphons, affords opportunity for responsorial performance, the stanzas being sung by cantors or choir and the antiphons by the congregation and choir.

Richard Hillert's jubilant setting supports the sense of the text, celebrating Christ's victory over death. The rhythmically vital antiphon is very accessible for a congregation and stands in effective contrast to the more lyric style of the verses. Due to the irregular metre of the verses, careful preparation of a congregation is necessary for its accurate performance.

---

1. The opening two measures are almost exactly the same as a bridge passage in the Gloria of Geoffrey Beaumont's *Twentieth Century Folk Mass* (London, 1957; see vol. 1, "British Hymnody Since 1950," 558); see further R. A. Leaver, "Renewal in Hymnody," *Lutheran Quarterly*, vol. 6, (1992), 361–362.[n].

GG/RG

418 This is the feast of victory for our God

Music: **RAYMOND**

When preparing the music edition of *H82*, the Hymn Music Committee of the SCCM felt that two tunes should be available for use with this text. In 1984 they therefore commissioned this tune by Peter Hallock for use with it.

Words: See hymn 417.

Music: Composed by Peter R. Hallock, Organist/Choirmaster, St. Mark's Cathedral, Seattle, the tune RAYMOND is ideally suited for responsorial performance, the stanzas being sung by a cantor or by the choir and the antiphon by the congregation. In support of this concept, the composer writes, "I have imagined the accompaniment for the antiphon to be played on one manual, . . . the acompaniment for the verses to be on a separate manual."[1] The entire setting is declamatory in style, using speech rhythms that duplicate the careful, natural enunciation of the text, a quality that reflects the composer's profound understanding and use of chant in liturgy. A three-note figure in a ♩. ♬ ♪ rhythm on the first syllable of the second Alleluia of the antiphon expands the jubilant declamation of the word and the antiphon itself. Mr. Hallock sets the text to a melody that, with a few minor modifications, is repeated for each stanza. The problems created by the very irregular metrical structure of the verses are transcended through the composer's sensitive translation of the syllabic structure of the text to declamation with pitch. The keyboard accompaniment of these sections is a series of detached parallel sixths that continue to the penultimate measure of each verse. The tune name RAYMOND honors the General Editor of *H82* and *H82c*, Raymond F. Glover.

1. Hallock to Glover, April, 1984. Church Hymnal Corporation Papers, New York, NY.

RG

419 Lord of all being, throned afar

Music: **MENDON**

Although created in 1859 as a part of a longer prose text intended for reading, this poem by Oliver Wendell Holmes was included the following year in two American hymnals. The text matched with this tune first appeared in the Hutchins edition of the 1892 *Hymnal*. Dropped from the 1916 edition, this text and tune were restored in *H40* and continued here.

Words: This hymn is introduced in the author's "Professor at the Breakfast Table" published in the *Atlantic Monthly* in December 1859:

> And so my year's record is finished. The Professor has talked less than his predecessor ("The Autocrat of the Breakfast Table") but he has heard and seen more. Thanks to all those friends who from time to time have sent their messages of kindly recognition and fellow-feeling. Peace to all such as may have been vexed in spirit by any utterance the pages have repeated. They will doubtless forget for the moment the difference in the lines of truth we look at through our human prisms, and join in singing (inwardly) this hymn to the Source of the light we all need to lead us, and the warmth which can make us all brothers.

This is followed by "A Sun-day Hymn," which Holmes later stated had been written eleven years earlier. In the following year, Holmes's hymn appeared in two hymnals: *A Collection of Hymns for the Sanctuary* (Boston and Cambridge, 1860) and *Hymn Book of the Methodist Protestant Church* (Springfield, OH, 1860). All five stanzas of this text appeared in the 1892 and 1940 editions of the *Hymnal*. The third stanza of its original five has been omitted from *H82*:

Our midnight is thy smile withdrawn;
Our noontide is thy gracious dawn;
Our rainbow arch, thy mercy's sign;
All, save the clouds of sin, are thine.

Music: According to Robert Guy McCutchan, the tune MENDON was first published in the *Methodist Harmonist* of 1821.[1] McCutchan implied that that publication used the name MENDON for the tune, but this seems unlikely, since later editions of the book (e.g., 1829), as well as other collections, called it GERMAN AIR. The name MENDON appears to have been given to the tune by Lowell Mason, who printed it under that title as early as the tenth edition of *The Boston Handel and Haydn Society Collection of Church Music* (Boston, 1831). Mendon is the name of a town in Worcester County, Massachusetts. Titled GERMAN AIR, the melody was published in the key of B^{b} in the Episcopal *Tune Book* (New York, 1858), set to three LM hymn texts. No German antecedent for the tune has been discovered.

---

1. See *Hymn Tune Names: Their Sources and Significance* (New York, 1957), 101.

HE/DWM

420 When in our music God is glorified

Music: **ENGELBERG**

Of the many English-language hymn texts written in the last twenty years, this is one that has gained almost immediate and international acceptance and use. Written for use with this tune, it is included in most major English-language hymnals published since 1978.

Words: "When in our music God is glorified" was written by Fred Pratt Green in 1972 at the request of John Wilson, who asked for new words for Stanford's festive tune ENGELBERG. That tune had been written in 1904 for use with the words "For all the saints," but it was eclipsed almost immediately by Vaughan Williams's SINE NO-

MINE [287]. Although matched in *H40* with "All praise to thee" [477], it was not until matched with "When in our music God is glorified" that this tune attained extensive usage. Although securely matched with ENGELBERG, this text has also generated additional new tunes.

The hymn is based loosely on Ps. 150, Mk. 14:26, and Mt. 26:30. It was originally entitled "Let the People Sing!" and the first published form of the opening line was "When in man's music, God is glorified."

History suggests that it is very difficult to write a real hymn on the subject of congregational music-making. Usually there is insufficient weight and development to support the effusiveness that this theme seems to generate. Here, however, we have an honest hymn of substance and scope that is never self-congratulatory or platitudinous and is always grateful and worthy.

Music: See hymn 296.

RG

421 All glory be to God on high

Music: **ALLEIN GOTT IN DER HÖH**

This translation of the sixteenth-century German paraphrase by Nikolaus Decius of the Gloria in excelsis matched with Decius's tune makes this an excellent metrical song of praise for use at the Eucharist during the Liturgy of the Word.

Words: The root of this translation by the Rev. Dr. F. Bland Tucker of the canticle Gloria in excelsis is the German paraphrase by Nikolaus Decius, "Allein Gott in der Höh' sei Ehr." Decius's hymn, originally written in Low German, was sung to its adapted plainsong melody for the first time on Easter Day, April 5, 1523, in Brunswick.[1] The Low German version first appeared in print in Joachim Slüter's words-only *Gesang Buch* (Rostock, 1525). The High German version appeared with its associated melody in Valentine Schumann's *Geistliche Lieder auffs new gebessert und gemehrt* (Leipzig, 1539):

1. Allein Gott in der Höh sei Ehr
 und Dank für seine Gnade,
darum daß nun und nimmermehr
 uns rühren kann kein Schade.

Ein Wohlgefallen Gott an uns hat;
  nun ist groß Fried ohn Unterlaß,
All Fehd hat nun ein Ende.

2. Wir loben, preisen, anbeten dich;
  für deine Ehr wir danken,
daß du, Gott Vater, ewiglich
  regierst ohn alles Wanken.
Ganz ungemessen ist deine Macht,
  fort geschieht, was dein Will hat bedacht.
Wohl uns des feinen Herran!

3. O Jesu Christ, Sohn eingeborn
  deines himmlischen Vaters,
Versöhner der', die warn verlorn,
  du Stiller unsers Haders,
Lamm Gottes, heil'ger Herr und Gott:
  nimm an die Bitt von unsrer Not,
erbarm dich unser aller.

4. O Heilger Geist, du höchstes Gut,
  du allerheilsamster Tröster:
vor Teufels Gewalt fortan behüt,
  die Jesus Christ erlöset
durch groß Marter und bittern Tod;
  abwend all unsern Jammer und Not!
Darauf wir uns verlassen.

Dr. Tucker's translation, which carefully retains the spirit and metre of the original, first appeared in *Hymns III*. Two revisions were made by the author between that first appearance and the present collection; the original readings were:

st. 1:4: to all mankind be given
st. 3:4: the firstborn of creation.

---

1. See M. Jenny, "'Allein Gott in der Höh sei Ehr': Zur genauen Datierung und zu den fruhesten Quellen des altesten evangelischen Kirchenliedes" *IAH Bulletin*, 13 (1985), 26-34.

Music: The tune ALLEIN GOTT IN DER HÖH (*Zahn* 4457) is an adaptation by Nikolaus Decius of a tenth-century plainsong Gloria in excelsis for the Easter season. This Low German versification of the Gloria first appeared in Slüter's *Gesang Buch* (Rostock, 1525). It clearly must have been sung to the adapted melody at this time, though

Example 1

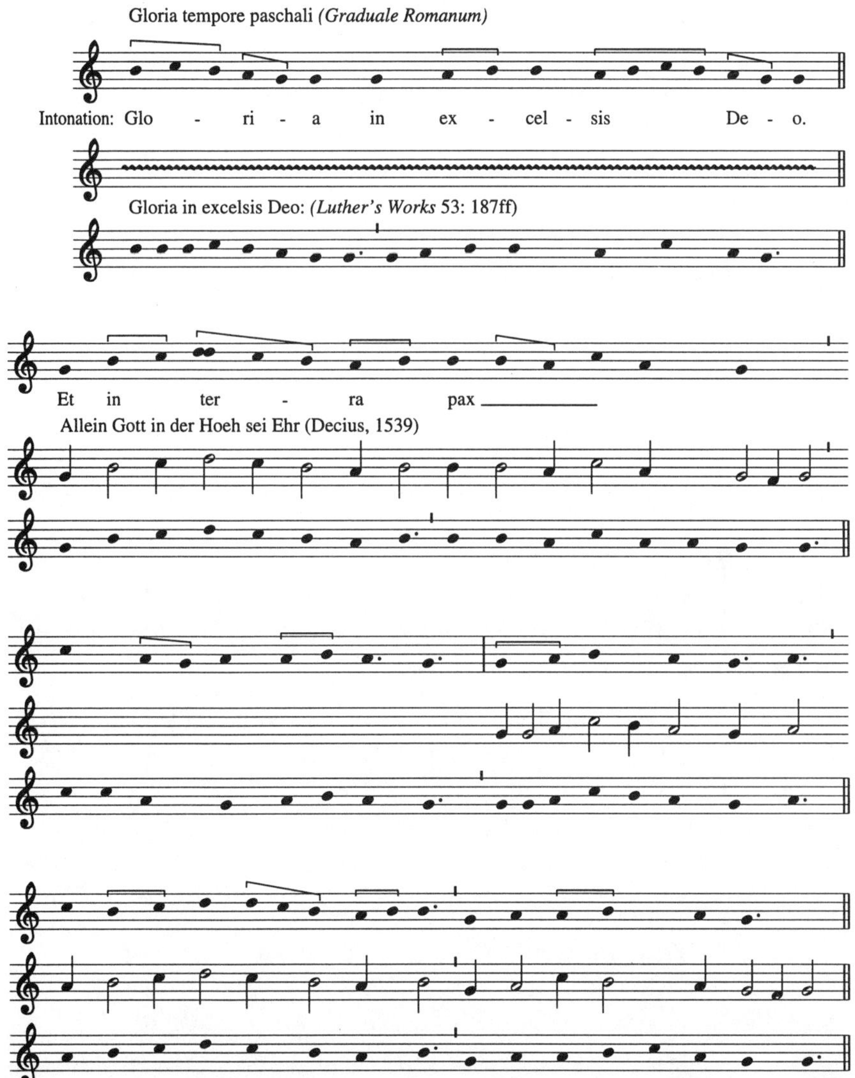

no source dating from this period has been discovered. Its first appearance in a German collection was in Valentin Schumann's *Geistliche Lieder auffs new gebessert und gemehrt* (Leipzig, 1539), with the High German version of the text. The earliest appearance in print, however, was in the English collection of mainly translated German hymns: Miles Coverdale's *Goostly Psalmes* (London, 1535).[1] Two rhymed versions of the Gloria were current in the early Reformation period, one by Luther, the other this version of Decius, both with melodies created from the same plainsong Gloria. Ultimately Decius's version won out and enjoyed widespread popularity in the various German church orders (see Example 1 on previous page). The harmonization given here is by Hieronymous Praetorius and is taken from *Hymns III*.

---

1. See R. A. Leaver, "The Date of Coverdale's *Goostly Psalmes*," *IAH Bulletin*, 9, (May 1981), 58-63.

RG/CS

422 Not far beyond the sea, nor high

Music: **CORNWALL**

Both this text by a contemporary British poet and the tune by a nineteenth-century British composer with which it is matched appear in the *Hymnal* for the first time.

Words: "Not far beyond the sea" was written by George B. Caird around 1945 and used privately at Mansfield College, Oxford. It was not published until 1962. It appeared with the present tune in *100 Hymns for Today* (London, 1969) and was taken from there into *H82*, where the second stanza was omitted:

2. Rooted and grounded in thy love,
With saints on earth and saints above
we join in full accord.
To grasp the breadth, length, depth and height,

The crucified and risen might
of Christ, the Incarnate Word.

The starting point of the hymn is Deut. 30:11-14 and a line from Pastor John Robinson's farewell address to the Pilgrims who were about to set sail for the New World on the Mayflower in 1620. ("We limit not the truth of God" [629] is another hymn based on Robinson's words.) One of the Pilgrims recalled the scene:

> We were now ere long to part asunder, and the Lord knoweth whether ever he [Robinson] should live to see our faces again . . . . [He] charged us . . . if God should reveal anything to us by any other instrument of his, to be ready to receive it as ever we were to receive any truth by his [Robinson's] ministry. For he was very confident that the Lord had more light and truth yet to break forth out of his holy word (*Julian*, 1243).

Music: See hymn 386.

RS-W

423 Immortal, invisible, God only wise

Music: **ST. DENIO**

In *EH* Ralph Vaughan Williams's great skills as its music editor are apparent in many ways. One of them is his uncanny ability to create matchings of words and music that are truly inspired (see the essay "British Hymnody, 1900-1950," vol. 1, 474). The matching of this text to ST. DENIO is an example of his masterful gift.

Words: "Now to the King eternal, immortal, invisible, the only wise God, be honour and glory for ever and ever. Amen." (1 Tim. 1:17) is the inspiration for this very popular hymn of Walter Chalmers Smith. It first appeared in Smith's *Hymns of Christ and the Christian Life* (London, 1867). Percy Dearmer used the first three of the text's six original stanzas and combined the first two lines of sts. 5 and 6 to form the fourth stanza for *EH*. This is the standard form used in modern hymnals. Erik Routley in *An English-Speaking Hymnal*

Guide, however, argues that this configuration alters the theological impact of Smith's hymn. Smith's final stanzas are:

Today and tomorrow with thee still are now;
Nor trouble, nor sorrow, nor care, Lord, hast thou;
Nor passion doth fever, nor age can decay,
The same God for ever as on yesterday.
(This stanza is omitted in contemporary use.)

Great Father of glory, Father of light,
Thine angels adore thee, veiling their sight;
But of all thy good graces this grace, Lord, impart—
Take the veil from our faces, the veil from our heart.

All laud we would render; O help us to see,
'Tis only the splendor of light hideth thee;
And now let thy glory to our gaze unroll
Through Christ in the story, and Christ in the soul.

The SCCM, in support of their intent to use inclusive language whenever possible in *H82*, further altered the final stanza:

Thou reignest in glory, thou rulest in light,
Thine angels adore thee, etc.

Music: This melody, of uncertain origin, first appeared as a hymn tune in *Caniadau y Cyssegr* ("Songs of the Sanctuary") (Denbigh, 1839), edited by John Roberts. The most-favored suggestion is that it comes possibly, like many other hymn tunes, from the carol and ballad tradition. The discussion in the *Journal of the Welsh Folk Song Society*, 1/ii (1911), points to the ballad "Can mlynedd i 'nawr' " ("A hundred years from now") which has similarities to a secular ballad in the John Jenkins, Ceri, manuscripts "Can mlynedd yn ol' " ("A hundred years back") (see the essay "The Welsh Hymn Tune," vol. 1, 310). Although it is known in Wales as JOANNA, the tune first appeared as PALESTRINA. None of the names appear to have any particular significance.

The tune gives the lie to the generally held view that the typical Welsh tune is in the minor, while being itself typically Welsh in its insistence on the notes of the chords of the key. It is strange, however, in that it does not open with the notes of the key chord, but of the subdominant.

Vaughan Williams used ST. DENIO as the theme of the second movement, the *scherzo*, in his *Household Quartet: Three Preludes on Welsh Hymn Tunes* (1942, published 1944) for string quartet or any combination of instruments that could be assembled in a household.

TAR/AL

424 For the fruit of all creation

Music: **EAST ACKLAM**

"For the fruit of all creation" was written by Fred Pratt Green in 1970 expressly for this tune. Francis Jackson's EAST ACKLAM, written thirteen years earlier, had been written for use with Heber's text "God, that madest earth and heaven," but that matching never caught on. John Wilson, the British hymnologist and editor, knew of Jackson's unattached music and suggested to Pratt Green that he give it a new text, preferably one on a harvest theme since new hymns on that subject were in short supply.

Words: This is a brilliant hymn about harvests and modern issues connected with them. The words were written to match the music and the 84. 84. 888. 4 metre. In it, the composer Francis Jackson had given the three short lines of four syllables a single melodic shape, so Pratt Green threaded the lines into an interior refrain with the words "Thanks be to God" (or in st. 2, "God's will be done"). For the three consecutive lines of eight syllables, Jackson had constructed a trio of phrases that mount ever higher and reach a climax just before returning to the refrain motif. Pratt Green wrote three lines that grow similarly to fit this melodic pattern. This is seen most clearly in st. 3 where the unusual rhyme words (astound us/confound us/has found us) define very clear and attractive closures and where the word "love" is placed on the highest note.

Slight changes have been made in the text. In st. 1, the fifth word originally was "his," and the refrain in st. 2 was originally "God's will is done."

Many hymnologists consider this hymn one of the masterworks of the present renaissance in hymn writing.

Music: Francis Jackson wrote EAST ACKLAM and named it after the village in which he lived while organist at York Minster. He intended it for "God, that madest earth and heaven," and it was presented with this text later that year at a reunion service for retired choristers. Since these words were already attached firmly to the Welsh folk song AR HYD Y NOS, Jackson's tune never achieved acceptance. The tune was little used until 1970, when the present words were written for it by Fred Pratt Green. The tune is basically diatonic in structure and makes liberal use of sequential patterns.

RS-W

425 Sing now with joy unto the Lord

Music: **ADON OLAM**

This text based on lines from Canticle 8, The Song of Moses, and a tune from Jewish liturgical sources appear together in the *Hymnal* for the first time. They make a strong witness to the ecumenical ties between Jews and Christians.

Words: While on sabbatical leave at St. John's Abbey and University, Collegeville, MN, during the academic year of 1975/1976, the Rev. Dr. Marion Hatchett, Chair of the Text Committee of the SCCM, was introduced to this text at worship in the chapel there. No additional information on the source of the text was given in the chapel bulletin than that found in *H82*. This text first appeared in an Episcopal hymnal in *Hymns III*, where it was matched with THE EIGHTH TUNE (TALLIS' CANON) [25, 43]. This text in the Jewish liturgy is very popular. Its author is unknown, although it has been attributed to Solomon ibn Gabirol (eleventh century). Perhaps originally written for the Night Prayers, the "Adon Olam" first appeared as part of the liturgy of the German Jews in the fourteenth century.

Music: Except on the High Holidays, where melodies were often adapted to the *nusah* (customary melodic formulae) of the section of the service where it was incorporated, the "Adon Olam" in the

Ashkenazi rites had few traditional tunes, a surprising fact considering the number of melodies to which it is sung. The melody adapted as ADOM OLAM in *H82* comes from the setting of the text "Adon Olam" by Eliezer Gerovitch, who officiated as cantor-composer in St. Petersburg and Rostov-on-the-Don (Example 1).

Example 1

He describes the melody as "alte Weise," that is to say, traditional. It is unknown whether the melody originated in the synagogue or as a folk melody; nor is it certain whether Gerovitch's setting is the original version or an improvisation. A slightly different version is found in the *Evreiskaia Entsiklopedia*, vol. 1 (St. Petersburg, 1900), where the mode is pure aeolian (Example 2).

Example 2

The melody is strictly Eastern European; it was unknown elsewhere in Europe. The first American notation of the melody appeared in Israel and Samuel Goldfarb's *Friday Evening Melodies* (New York, 1918); however, it is simply called "traditional" and not attributed to Gerovitch. A simpler version, which is that sung by most American Jews today, was included in Abraham Z. Idelsohn's *Jewish Song Book* (Cincinnati, 1928), where Idelsohn describes it as a folk tune (Example 3).

Example 3

The second part of Idelsohn's version agrees with that of the *Evreiskaia Entsiklopedia*. The simpler version bears a loose affinity to the synagogal mode named *Magen 'Avot*, built upon the aeolian scale.

RG/JGo

426 Songs of praise the angels sang

Music: **NORTHAMPTON**
This text by James Montgomery proclaims in its first three stanzas important tenets of the Christian faith: Creation, Incarnation, Resurrection, and the Last Judgment. The last three stanzas are the Christian's response through praise, faith, and love, and belief in life after death. It was first matched with this tune in *Hymnal Supplement II*, the second supplement to *H40* (New York, 1976).

Words: This hymn by James Montgomery was first published in Cotterill's *Selection of Psalms and Hymns* (London, 1819) and included in Montgomery's *Christian Psalmist* (Glasgow and London, 1825) with the title "Glory to God in the highest" and a reference to Lk. 2:13. It first appeared in the *Hymnal* in 1826 and continued without alteration until *H82*, when changes were made in sts. 1 and 4. The original words were:

st. 1:3: When Jehovah's work begun,
4: When He spake and it was done.

st. 4:1 And can man alone be dumb,
2 Till that glorious kingdom come?

Music: Charles John King, the composer of this tune, was the first organist and choirmaster of St. Matthew's Church in Northampton, England, where he remained for thirty-five years. More recently, when Walter Hussey was rector of St. Matthew's, it became a center for the commissioning of contemporary art in all forms. It was then that Benjamin Britten wrote *Rejoice in the Lamb* for the choir of that parish. This tune, composed before 1905 for use with this text, is cheerful and positive with a strong descending bass line at the beginning of the first and third lines.

HLW/AW

427 When morning gilds the skies

Music: **LAUDES DOMINI**

This text, limited too often to use only as a morning hymn, has a fascinating history of development from its German roots and various translations and paraphrases to its place today, matched with this tune, as a very much-loved hymn.

Words: "Beim frühen Morgenlicht" is the original German first line of this hymn dating from the nineteenth century. Its first printed appearance is in the *Katholisches Gesangbuch für den öffentlich Gottesdienst im Biszthume* (Würzburg, 1828). Although no author is cited, it is believed to be Franconian in origin (*Julian*, 132). A second appearance, in a different form, was in F. W. von Ditfurth's *Frankische Völkslieder* (Leipzig, 1855).

Two popular English translations were made by Edward Caswall, ca. 1854 and 1858. It is the 1858 version, used in an altered form in the 1892 and 1916 *Hymnals* and still used extensively in England, to which Robert Bridges refers in the "Notes on the Words and Music" in the *Yattendon Hymnal* (Oxford, 1899):

> It is of great merit, and I have tried to give a better version of it than the current one, keeping the original metre, preserving the first lines of the old translation, since it is by them that the hymn is known.

Bridges's 66. 7.6 67. D text, which replaced the Caswall translation in *H40*, may be more accurately described as a paraphrase rather than a translation. Although there are five stanzas in the *Yattendon Hymnal*, where Bridges's paraphrase first appeared, the tune is twice as long as that provided for the *H40* and *H82* cento*. Consequently, a large part has been omitted as may be seen in the material formerly following st. 2:

To Him my High'st and Best
Sing I when love-possest, may . . .
Whate'er my hands begin
This blessing breaketh in, may . . .
By night my heart will sigh
If sleepless then I lie, may . . .
Yea ev'n if heart sh d break
Then soul for heart w d speak, may . . .

This greeting of great joy
I ne'er have found it cloy, may . . .
When sorrow w d molest
Then sing I undistresst, may . . .
When worldly things I rue
This hymn doth hope renew, may . . .
Thro' sickness, pain & want
'Tis still my happy chant, may . . .

Hell's might doth flee away
For dread of this fair lay, May . . .
My sin casts off its shame
Call I on Jesu's name, May . . .

(The latter half of this stanza begins: "No lovelier antiphon.")

Included for comparison is st. 1 of the German original and the 1873 Caswall translation as it appeared in the 1892 edition of the *Hymnal* and since 1868 in *HA&M*:

Beim frühen Morgenlicht	When morning gilds the skies,
Erwacht mein Herz und spricht	My heart awaking cries,
Gelobt sei Jesus Christus!	May Jesus Christ be praised;
So sing ich früh und spät,	Alike at work and prayer
Bei Arbeit und Gebet,	To Jesus I repair;
Gelobt sei Jesus Christus!	May Jesus Christ be praised.

Music: LAUDES DOMINI was composed by Joseph Barnby for use with this text in the Appendix to the first edition of *HA&M* (1868). The tune, composed in the style of a nineteenth-century part-song, is constructed on two musical themes. The second is repeated three times, the last time being a coda, a variant in long notes of the first three notes of the theme. Harmonically, the setting reflects a modest use of chromaticism until the last three measures, when the bass line descends an octave from G with an unexpected B^b just before the final cadence.

MS/RG

428 O all ye works of God, now come

Music: **IRISH**

The presence in *H82* of Canticle 12, A Song of Creation, in a metrical form provides an additional option of performance to congregations using the Offices and immediate accessibility to those for whom a chant setting may be too difficult. It is matched here with a robust eighteenth-century tune.

Words: Work on this metrical version of the canticle "A Song of Creation, Benedicite, omnia opera Domini" was begun by F. Bland Tucker in late 1977 or early 1978 in response to an invitation from the members of the SCCM, who were preparing *Hymns III* for publication. The initial form of the text was a work of six stanzas in common metre.

1. O all you works of God give thanks
   And praise him and adore;
   O angels bless the Lord in heaven
   And praise him evermore.

2. O sun and moon and stars of light
   Your endless praise outpour:
   O changing seasons bless the Lord
   And praise him evermore.

3. O heat and cold, O night and day,
   O storms and thunder's roar,

O fields and forests bless the Lord
And praise him evermore.

4. O earth and sea, O all that live
In water or on shore,
O birds and beasts and humankind (O beasts and birds)
Come praise him evermore.

5. O let his people bless the Lord,
And saints in heaven adore,
And holy humble men of heart
All praise him evermore.

6. O let us glorify and bless (thank)
The God we bow before,
The Father, Son, and Holy Ghost, (The Father, Holy Spirit, Son)
And praise him evermore.

In continuing work with the SCCM Text Committee, an additional stanza was prepared:

O frost and ice and snow
and clouds with rain in store,
O springs and rivers bless the Lord
And praise him evermore.

For final use in *Hymns III*, Dr. Tucker revised the text to its present six-stanza form. Also, to bring it into closer conformity with the BCP text (see BCP, 47-49) where all the invocations are followed by the directive "bless ye the Lord" he added, in sts. 1 through 4, the phrase "and bless the Lord."

A further revision was made by Dr. Tucker for use of the text in *H82* in support of the SCCM's desire to use, whenever possible, inclusive language. Stanza 5, line 4, originally "let holy, humble men of heart" was altered to "let those of holy, humble heart."

Music: The book that launched this anonymous tune, *A Collection of Hymns and Sacred Poems* (Dublin, 1749), was printed in movable type by S. Powell. We do not know the name of the compiler or even the publisher of this book of 295 hymn texts, mostly by Watts and the

Wesleys, and 22 tunes, four of them new. The book would have been lost to history if a single copy had not been preserved at Pittsburgh Theological Seminary. Besides being rare in itself, it is one of a mere handful of printed relics of eighteenth-century Irish Protestant hymnody.

It is remarkable that this obscure source produced a tune of such strength and individuality. The first half keeps to the "plagal" range of the major mode (dominant to dominant) while the second half rises boldly to the "authentic" range so that, for instance, the rising fourth in the first phrase is answered a whole octave higher in the third and fourth phrases—surely a rare feature in hymn tunes of any period.

Example 1

The tune was originally in G (Example 1) and was set to a Watts hymn containing a simile drawn from American experience, the Indian arrow. It was later adopted by the Rev. Caleb Ashworth's Independent congregation at Daventry, Northhamptonshire, and printed by him in a four-voice setting in his *Collection of Tunes* (London, 1761), with the name IRISH. From there it was taken into Josiah Flagg's *Collection of the Best Psalm Tunes* (Boston, 1764), with acknowledgement to

Ashworth, and from then on was one of the most popular tunes in English dissenting and American circles. In some later Anglican sources the third note was altered to the supertonic, to reduce the range to little more than an octave; of course, this greatly weakened the tune's character.

A curious feature of the notation in Example 1 is the lack of dots where one would expect them, after the quarter notes in measures 10, 12, and 13. Similar quarter-eighth pairs are found throughout the book. It is possible that this was an Irish peculiarity, an anomalous survival of mensural notation implying a triplet group. A more mundane explanation is that Powell lacked the piece of type necessary to print a dot (a narrow slice of five-line stave with a dot in one of the spaces).

RG/NT

429 I'll praise my maker while I've breath

***Music:* OLD 113TH**

This glorious doxological hymn of praise by Isaac Watts first appeared for use by Episcopalians in the *Hymnal* of 1832 among the metrical psalms. It was subsequently included in *A Tunebook Proposed For the Use of Congregations of the Protestant Episcopal Church* compiled by a committee of the House of Bishops in 1858 and published in New York in 1859, which included sts. 1, 2, 3, 4, and a doxological fifth stanza. This form of the text was continued in *Episcopal Common Praise*, licensed by the General Convention of 1865 and published in New York in 1867, and in a two-stanza version with a Gloria Patri in the 1871 *Hymnal*. It was deleted in the 1892 edition and restored in 1982. In *H82* it is matched with a sixteenth-century German psalm tune.

Words:

Psalm CXLVI. *as the 113th* Psalm [Tune]
Praise God for his Goodness and Truth

1. I'll praise my Maker with my Breath;
And when my Voice is lost in Death
Praise shall employ my nobler Powers:

My Days of Praise shall ne'er be past
While Life and Thought and Being last,
  Or Immortality endures.

2. Why should I make a Man my Trust?
Princes must die and turn to Dust;
  Vain is the Help of Flesh and Blood;
Their Breath departs, their Pomp & Power
And Thoughts all vanish in an Hour,
  Nor can they make their Promise Good.

3. Happy the Man whose Hopes rely
On *Isral's* [sic] God: He made the Sky,
  And Earth and Seas with all their Train:
His Truth for ever stands secure;
He saves th'Opprest, he feeds the Poor,
  And None shall find his Promise vain.

4. The Lord hath Eyes to give the Blind;
The Lord supports the sinking Mind;
  He sends the labouring Conscience Peace:
He helps the Stranger in Distress,
The Widow and the Fatherless,
  And grants the Prisoner sweet Release.

5. He loves his Saints; he knows them well,
But turns the Wicked down to Hell:
  Thy God O *Zion* ever reigns:
Let every Tongue, let every Age
In this exalted Work engage;
  Praise him in everlasting Strains.

6. I'll praise him while he lends me Breath,
And when my Voice is lost in Death
  Praise shall then employ my nobler Powers:
My Days of Praise shall ne'er be past
While Life and Thought and Being last,
  Or Immortality endures.

Based on Ps. 146, Isaac Watts first published this text in his *Psalms of David* (London, 1719) under the heading "Praise to God for his

Goodness and Truth." The first line of the hymn was originally "I'll praise my maker with my breath" and was altered to its present textual form by John Wesley, who published four of the six stanzas in his *Collection of Psalms and Hymns* (Charleston, SC, 1736-1737). Wesley made additional alterations to Watts's fourth stanza. Watts's read: "The Lord hath eyes to give the blind" with Wesley altering it to "The Lord pours eye-sight on the blind." *The Hymnal 1982* uses the Wesley version of the hymn with some revisions to st. 2. The Watts/ Wesley version includes:

st. 2:1	Happy the man whose hopes rely
2	On Israel's God: He made the Sky
4	His truth
5	He saves

Music: In its original form, a massive 887. 887. D. metre, this tune is one of the most important and influential of those composed during the earliest period of hymn writing in the sixteenth century. It was almost certainly composed by Matthaus Greiter, Cantor in Strassburg, for his own metrical version of Ps. 119, ES SIND DOCH SELIG ALLE (*Zahn* 8303). The text and tune were first published in *Das Dritt theil Strasburger kirchen ampt* (Strassburg, 1525). Although it is among the longest of all congregational hymn tunes, it is skillfully written in such a way that it becomes memorable almost at first singing. The beginning of the repeated A section (*stollen*) of its barform structure progresses upward in a stepwise fashion, with resting points on the pitches of the basic triad, moving from the tonic to the dominant ("*a*" in Example 1); this is then followed by a largely stepwise descent and ascent, reiterating the dominant ("*b*" in Example 1); and the *stollen* is concluded by a return to the tonic ("*c*" in Example 1). After the repeated *stollen,* the B section *(abgesang)* begins at the octave, giving an intensity to the lengthy melody at its midway point, which is emphasized by the repetition (apart from one note) of the melodic phrase ("d" and "*e*" in Example 1) and ends on the dominant. After a phrase centering on the mediant ("*f*" in Example 1), the tune concludes with a sequential repetition of the same melodic phrase ("*g,*" "*h*" and "*i*" in Example 1). It is a truly remarkable tune and its significance can hardly be overemphasized.

In the development of the French Genevan psalter tune, this melody has a primary place. It was one of the tunes that John Calvin encountered in Strassburg in 1538, and he included it within his metrical psalter, issued in Strassburg in 1539, where it was assigned to his own metrical version of Ps. 36 (*Pidoux* 36a). The tune clearly influenced the emerging style of the French Genevan psalm tune. Its majestic and stately form and its two basic note values (long and short) became distinctive features of the psalm tunes included in Calvin's Genevan psalters.

The tune was also influential, however, in the emerging chorale tradition in Lutheran Germany. Sebald Heyden, Cantor in Nuremberg in the same year that Greiter published his Ps. 119 tune, 1535, wrote what was to become a classic Lutheran passion hymn, "O Mensch, bewein dein Sünde gross." Heyden's text was in the same massive metre as Greiter's psalm tune, and the two were soon inseparably associated in Lutheran usage. Among others, Johann Sebastian Bach made organ and choral arrangements of the tune, particularly the strikingly poignant chorale prelude in the *Orgelbüchlein* (BWV 622) and the marvelous chorale fantasia that ends the first part of the *St. Matthew Passion* (BWV 244).

Catholic musicians in Cologne at the beginning of the seventeenth century were so impressed with the tune that they took the opening phrase and its general characteristics and created a new tune, LASST UNS ERFREUEN [400].

The tune entered into English usage, slightly modified in a metre of twelve eights, in the Anglo-Genevan psalter of 1560 (*Frost*, 125). It then appeared in *The Whole Booke of Psalms* (London, 1562) and thereafter in subsequent psalters and tunebooks.

Isaac Watts wrote his version of Ps. 146, "I'll praise my Maker with my breath," with this tune in mind (see his original heading cited above.) This complete twelve-line form of the tune continued in circulation for at least the generation after Watts. It was included, for example, in John Wesley's *Foundery Collection* (London, 1742) and Thomas Butts's *Harmonia Sacra* (London, ca. 1760). Sometime during the later eighteenth century, however, a shortened form of OLD 113TH appeared. Its metrical structure was halved by eliminating the repeat of the opening A section and omitting phrases "*f*," "*g*" and "*h*" (see Example 1). This is the form of the tune that is included in *H82* and other contemporary hymnals.

The tune, with Watts's text, was a favorite of John Wesley; indeed, it was the hymn he sang just before his death.

Example 1

TAR/RAL

430 Come, O come, our voices raise

***Music:* SONNE DER GERECHTIGKEIT**

The name of George Wither is important in the history of Anglican church music, if only for the association this seventeenth-century poet had with the great composer Orlando Gibbons, who wrote a set of tunes for inclusion in Wither's *Hymns and Songs of the Church* (London, 1623) (see the essays "English Metrical Psalmody," vol. 1, 321 and "The Tunes of Congregational Song in Britain from the Reformation to 1750," vol. 1, 349). Today, few of Wither's texts remain in use. His paraphrase of Ps. 148 as edited, made for use in *H82* by members of the SCCM Text Committee, is matched here with a sixteenth-century melody.

Words: Although it is new to the *Hymnal*, this paraphrase of Ps. 148 by George Wither dates from its initial appearance as the opening hymn in his *Haleluia or, Britain's second Remembrancer* (London, 1641). As printed there, the text was entitled "A generall Invitation to praise God" and was arranged in five stanzas, each containing five couplets of seven-syllable lines. Because of the considerable rearrangement and revision the original form has undergone, it will be helpful to print it in full with some indication of what has been retained.

1. (1:1) Come, Oh come in pious *Laies*,
(2) Sound we *God-Almighti's* praise.
(3) Hither bring in one Consent,
(4) Heart, and Voice and Instrument.
Musicke adde of ev'ry kinde;
(2:1a) Sound the Trump, the Cornet winde.
(1b) Strike the Violl, touch the Lute.
(2) Let nor Tongue, nor String be mute:
(3) Nor a Creature dumb be found,
(4) That hath neither Voice nor Sound.

2. Let those Things which do not live
In *Still-Musick*, praises give.
Lowly pipe, ye *Wormes* that creep,
On the *Earth*, or in the *Deep*,
Loud-aloft, your Voices strain,
Beasts, and *Monsters* of the *Main*.

Birds, your warbling *Treble* sing.
Clouds, your *Peales of Thunders* ring.
Sun and *Moon*, exalted higher,
And bright *Stars*, augment this *Quire*.

3. (3:1) Come ye *Sons* of *Humane-Race*,
(2) In this *Chorus* take a place;
(3) And, amid the mortall-Throng,
(4) Be your *Masters of the Song*.
Angels, and supernall Pow'rs,
Be the noblest *Tenor* yours.
(4:1) Let in praise of *God*, the sound
(2) Run a *never-ending Round;*
(3) That our *Song of praise* may be
(4) *Everlasting* as is *He*.

4. From *Earths* vast and hollow wombe,
Musicks deepest *Base* may come.
Seas and *Flouds*, from shore to shoare,
Shall their *Counter-Tenors* roare.
To this *Consort*, (when we sing)
Whistling *Winds* your *Descants* bring.
(6:1) That our song may over clime,
(2) All the Bounds of *Place* and *Time*.
And ascend from *Sphere* to *Sphere*,
To the great *All-mightie's* eare.

5. So, from Heaven, on Earth, he shall
Let his gracious Blessings fall:
(5:1) And this huge wide *Orbe*, we see
(2) Shall one *Quire*, one *Temple* be;
(3) Where, in such a *Praise*, full Tone
(4) We will sing, what he hath done,
That the cursed *Fiends* below,
Shall thereat impatient grow.
(6:3) Then, oh Come, in pious *Laies*,
(4) Sound we *God-Almighties* praise.

The division of the present text into six stanzas of two couplets plus an "alleluia" was made to accommodate the music chosen for it. As reported to General Convention in 1982, each current pair of stanzas was grouped to form three stanzas of 77. 77 D. That three-stanza form was derived from sts. 1, 3, and 4 of the version of this hymn found in *Congregational Praise* (London, 1951).

Though "pious" is a word that tends to stick in the modern throat, Wither's original opening line accurately conveyed his purpose in compiling his collection of hymns. He intended for these sacred songs to replace what he regarded as the immoral lyrics of the secular songs of his day. Although Wither can be an uneven poet, "Come, O come" is certainly one of his best texts, earning approval from no less an authority than Julian as "a noble lyric" (see *Julian*, 347). Given Wither's significance in this history of English hymnody (see the essay "British Hymnody from the Sixteenth through the Eighteenth Centuries," vol. 1, 370-373), it is especially fitting to have his hymn of universal celebration incorporated into this *Hymnal*.

Music: See hymn 224.

CMD

431 The stars declare his glory

Music: **ALDINE**

One of the important aspects of the liturgical movement in the twentieth century is the restoration of the Psalter to its historic place as a reading in the Eucharist. A side effect of this is the impetus it has given poets for the creation of metrical forms of the psalms (see the essay "English Metrical Psalmody," vol. 1, 321). This contemporary paraphrase of Ps. 19 is matched here with a tune written for use with it.

Words: This text based on Ps. 19, "The stars declare his glory," is the work of Timothy Dudley-Smith, a bishop of the Church of England and a major force among contemporary British hymn writers. Written in Sevenoaks, Kent, on April 7, 1970, the text first appeared in *Psalm Praise* (London, 1973). It ranks as one of the poet's favorite works, primarily because, in his opinion, it contains particularly satisfying solutions to several technical problems.

Of this text Bishop Dudley-Smith writes:

> The Psalm itself combines the two themes of the eloquence of nature and the clarity of scripture . . . . The thought of "order" in the final verse may be going beyond the immediate meaning of the psalmist; but it is not, I think, inconsistent to ask that he who orders the heavens and gives the stars their laws will also direct and order (within the bounds of their own freedom) the lives of his children, according to the laws he makes for them.[1]

As in his other text in this hymnal, "Tell out, my soul, the greatness of the Lord!" [437], Bishop Dudley-Smith has relied on the New English Bible for several important words in this paraphrase.

This is its first appearance in the *Hymnal* of the Episcopal Church.

---

1. T. Dudley-Smith, *Lift Every Heart* (London and Carol Stream, IL, 1984), 264.

Music: The unison tune ALDINE was written in 1983 by Richard Proulx for use in *H82* with this text. Very songlike in nature, Mr. Proulx's modal melody consists of three balanced phrases. The third phrase is distinguished by a three-note motif in a ♫ ♩ pattern. It appears at the very beginning of the phrase and in the middle at a wonderful climactic moment that coincides with the peak of the textual line. The composer uses it a third time at the end of the tune. The setting is further distinguished by a flowing accompaniment of harmonic richness. The final cadence shows indebtedness to the work of the American composer George Gershwin. The tune name honors the street in Chicago where Mr. Proulx resides.

RG

432 O praise ye the Lord!

Music: **LAUDATE DOMINUM**

This psalm paraphrase, long popular in the Church both in England and Canada, makes its first appearance in the *Hymnal* of the Episcopal Church matched with a stunning and popular tune written for use with it.

Words: This text by Sir Henry Williams Baker is based on Pss. 148 and 150. It was first included in the revised edition of *HA&M*

(1875), for which Baker served as editor and chairman of the proprietors. It is interesting to note that the hymn was omitted from the 1904 edition of that collection and was not included in the first edition of *EH*. No doubt a large measure of the hymn's popularity goes to the tune by C. Hubert H. Parry.

The second line of st. 2 originally read: "Ye sons of new birth."

Music: This quintessentially British hymn tune, whose opening phrase echoes the chime of countless parish and town clocks, is the work of C. Hubert H. Parry, one of the prime movers in the renaissance of English music at the turn of the century. The tune originally appeared at the closing of his anthem "Hear my words" (1894) set to this paraphrase of Pss. 148 and 150 and was composed for the Salisbury Diocesan Festival Association. In 1916 the tune was included in *HA&M* with Parry's unison setting of st. 4 with its florid organ part. As it was the custom in that period to end hymns with an amen, this arrangement includes a festive twofold setting (see Example 1). Also in that edition, the composer has marked the last phrase "Allargando."

Example 1

Parry's tune is basically AA[1]BB[1] in form. Both of the A statements open with an upward leap of a sixth, the first moving on to outline the chord of B^b while the second outlines the tune's almost immediate modulation to F. The B phrases, which move sequentially upward, are marked by rich harmonies.

MS/RG

433 *We gather together to ask the Lord's blessing*

***Music:* KREMSER**

This text and tune are quintessentially associated in the minds of Americans with Thanksgiving Day. The hymn first appeared in *H40* and continues in *H82* among the General Hymns under the heading "Praise to God." In this way its use is not restricted to the national holiday.

Words:

Wilt heden nu treden voor God den Heere
  Hem boven al loven van herten seer,
End' maken groot sijns lieven naemens eere,
  Die daer nu onsen vijant slaet ter neer.

Ter eerens ons Heeren wilt al u dagen
  Dit wonder bijsonder gedencken toch;
Maeckt u, o mensch! voor God steeds wel te dragen,
  Doet ijder recht en wacht u voor bedrog.

Bid, waken end' maket dat g'in bekoring
  End' 't quade met schade toch niet en valt.
U vroomheijt brengt de vijand tot verstoring,
  Al waer sijn rijck noch eens soo sterck bewalt.

The text of this famous hymn was first published in a collection of Dutch patriotic songs, *Nederlandtsch Gedenckclanck* (Haarlem, 1626). Compiled by Adriaan Valerius, these songs were published posthumously to celebrate the end of Spanish domination in the Netherlands. The text is full of references to psalmlike language of retribution of God against a repressive enemy, like: "he chastens and hastens his will to make known; the wicked oppressing now cease from distressing:"; "so from the beginning the fight we were winning:", and "Let thy congregation escape tribulation."

The English translation by Theodore Baker first appeared in *Dutch Folk Songs* (New York, 1917) compiled by Coenraad V. Bos, with minor alterations.

Music: Valerius's *Nederlandtsch Gedenckclanck* (Haarlem, 1626) is the source of the tune KREMSER. *Gedenckclanck* contains seventy-six popular songs with accompaniments written in lute tablature. KREMSER is based on the folk song "Heij wilder dan wild" contained in Valerius's collection. Valerius notated the melodies in his collection exactly as they were sung.

Edward Kremser, a Viennese composer and conductor of the Männergesangverein, published a collection of Dutch songs all from the *Gedenckclanck* entitled *Sechs Altniederlandische Volkslieder* (Vienna, 1878) for his men's chorus. Because of his choir's use of this melody in its repertoire, the tune became familiar to a much wider audience, and the tune eventually became known by the name KREMSER.

Had Kremser not popularized this melody it may not have made its way into our hymnals, because the Dutch Reformed Church uses Genevan psalm tunes as the center of its congregational music. Another Dutch tune from the same period is the harvest melody VRUECHTEN, associated with the Easter text "This joyful Eastertide" [192].

TAR

434 Nature with open volume stands

***Music:* ELTHAM**

This text, long neglected by hymnal editors, is an example of the work of Isaac Watts at his artistic finest. Erik Routley writes of it "as the greatest of all hymns on the atonement . . . since the reformation."[1] Its matching here with an eighteenth-century tune has in recent years become the accepted standard usage.

1. E. Routley, *Hymns Today and Tomorrow* (Nashville, 1964), 68.

Words: Isaac Watts first published this hymn in his *Hymns and Spiritual Songs* (London, 1707) under the heading "Christ crucified, the wisdom and power of God." It appears in *H82* unaltered except for the omission of the fourth of Watts's original six stanzas:

Here I behold his inmost heart,
  Where grace and vengeance strangely join;[1]
Piercing his Son with sharpest smart,
  To make the purchas'd pleasures mine.

Erik Routley calls this "a text of equal theological and literary merit with 'When I survey.' "[2] Its inclusion in the "Jesus Christ our Lord" section allows for its use in a wide variety of liturgical settings. For example, with its strong emphasis on both atonement and praise, it would be an excellent hymn for Sundays during Lent.

---

1. In eighteenth-century pronunciation, this would be an exact rhyme with "mine."
2. E. Routley, *Companion to Westminster Praise* (Chapel Hill, NC, 1977), 46.

Music: The tune ELTHAM comes from Nathaniel Gawthorn's *Harmonia Perfecta* (London, 1730), a collection published for a Presbyterian singing society that had met at the Weigh House, Little Eastcheap, London, from the early years of the century.[1] Although *H82* attributes this tune to Gawthorn, there is actually no way of definitely identifying the composer. Gawthorn says in his preface that in compiling his collection he consulted Ravenscroft, Lawrence, Playford, and others: "to these I have made Additions entirely New, gather'd elsewhere." The text was Isaac Watts's hymn "Had I the tongues of Greeks and Jews." The tune was in g, competently harmonized in four parts with the melody in the tenor. Each of the four lines ended with a half note and quarter rest.

ELTHAM remained in oblivion until it was discovered by Samuel Sebastian Wesley, who transposed it into f# and published it with his own remarkable harmonization in *The European Psalmist* (London, 1872). Apart from appearing in the ill-fated 1904 *HA&M*, it was neglected for almost another century until Erik Routley recognized it as an extraordinary example of Wesley's genius as a harmonist. He discussed it in the *Bulletin* of the Hymn Society of Great Britain and Ireland (no. 42, January 1948) and in his book *The Musical Wesleys* (Chicago, 1968); it has only now begun to enter the mainstream of hymnody.

Eltham, now a suburb of London, was in Gawthorn's time a small village in Kent.

1. This society and its hymnody are described in L. F. Benson, *The English Hymn* (Richmond, 1915), 89-90.

TAR/NT

435 At the Name of Jesus

Music: **KING'S WESTON**

Although this text entered the *Hymnal* in 1892, it has gained its greatest popularity and use through its matching with the Ralph Vaughan Williams tune KING'S WESTON in *Songs of Praise* (London, 1925) and for Episcopalians in *H40*.

Words: Caroline Maria Noel, the author of this text, spent her adult years as an invalid, experiencing great suffering. It was from that perspective that she wrote the *Name of Jesus, and other Verses for the Sick and Lonely* (London, 1861). It was first published in 1861; in the revised and expanded edition of 1870 was the text "In the Name of Jesus," a processional hymn for Ascension Day based on Phil. 2:9-10. The opening line was altered to "At the Name of Jesus" when it appeared in *HA&M* (1875), but in the 1903 edition of *Church Hymns* (London), it was restored to its original reading "*In* the Name of Jesus" at the request of Noel's family (*Julian*, 1607). The second stanza, which has been omitted, read:

At his voice creation
  Sprang at once to sight,
All the angel faces,
  All the hosts of light,
Thrones and dominations,
  Stars upon their way,
All the heavenly orders,
  In their great array.

The first two lines of the current fourth stanza read:

Name him, brothers, name him,
With love as strong as death

and the following line began with "but" rather than "name." The fourth line of the last stanza read "With his angel train."

Music: Ralph Vaughan Williams composed this tune for *Songs of Praise* (London, 1925) for use with these words. It is a tune with a very solid rhythm, the pattern of which is strongly established in the first six lines, only to be broken in a manner typical of the composer in the last two. It is also unusual in being mainly harmonized in a sparse three-part texture. The tune name is that of a village and country house near Bristol.

MS/AL

436 Lift up your heads, ye mighty gates

Music: **TRURO**

This text, originally intended for use on the first Sunday of Advent, has been in the *Hymnal* since 1892 and in the various editions has been included either among the hymns for the Ascension or as in *H82* among the general hymns. In this latter placement, the text is available for broader use. The matching of the text and tune can be traced to *H16*.

Words: The German hymn "Macht hoch die Tür," based on Ps. 24, was written by Georg Weissel to be sung on the First Sunday in Advent. It was first published in the first part of the *Preussische Fest-Lieder* (Elbing, 1642) and later included in the tenth edition of *Praxis Pietatis Melica* (Berlin, 1661) with a new tune specifically composed for it by Johann Crüger (*Zahn* 5845a). The hymn was translated by Catherine Winkworth, being first published in the first series of her *Lyra Germanica* (London, 1855). Miss Winkworth then reworked it for inclusion in *The Chorale Book for England* (London, 1863) with the associated Crüger tune. In the *Hymnal* of 1892 the hymn appears in abbreviated stanzaic form: LM instead of the original 88. 88. 88. 66. In *H82* the first four stanzas each comprise the first four lines of sts. 1, 3, 4, and 5 of the English translation of the German. Stanza 5 is constructed from couplets found in Catherine Winkworth's version of sts. 4 and 5. The original German stanzas follow, with Miss Winkworth's 1863 translation of them given in full; the couplets that make up the composite st. 5 in *H82* are given in italics.

1. Macht hoch die Tür, die Tor' macht weit	Lift up your heads, ye mighty gates!
Es Kommt der Herr der Herrlichkeit,	Behold, the King of glory waits;
Ein König all Konigreich',	The King of kings is drawing near,
Ein Heiland all Welt zugleich,	The Savior of the world is here.
Der Heil und Leben mit sich bringt;	Life and salvation he doth bring,
Derhalben jauchzt, mit Freuden singt:	Wherefore rejoice and gladly sing:
Gelobet sei mein Gott,	We praise thee, Father, now,
Mein Schöpfer, reich von Rat!	Creator, wise art thou!
3. O wohl dem Land, O wohl der Stadt,	O blest the land, the city blest,
So diesen König bei sich hat!	Where Christ the ruler is confessed!
Wohl allen Herzen insgemein,	O happy hearts and happy homes
Da dieser König ziehet ein!	To whom this King in triumph comes!
Er ist die rechte Freudensonn',	The cloudless Sun of joy he is,
Bringt mit sich lauter Freud' und Wonn'	Who bringeth pure delight and bliss.
Gelobet sei mein Gott,	We praise thee, Spirit, now,
Mein Tröster, früh and spat!	Our Comforter art thou!
4. Macht hoch die Tür, die Tor' macht weit,	Fling wide the portals of your heart;
Eu'r Herz zum Tempel zubereit't,	Make it a temple set apart
Die Zwieglein der Gottseligkeit	From earthly use for heaven's employ,
Steckt auf mit Andacht, Lust und Freud'!	Adorned with prayer and love and joy.
So kommt der König auch zu euch,	*So shall you Sovereign enter in*
Ja Heil und Leben mit zugleich.	*And new and noble life begin.*
Gelobet sei mein Gott,	To thee, O God, be praise
Voll Rat, voll Rat, voll Gnad'	For word and deed and grace!
5. Komm, O mein Heiland Jesu Christ,	Redeemer, come! I open wide
Mein's Herzens Tür dir offen ist!	My heart to thee; here, Lord, abide!
Ach zeuch mit deiner Gnade ein,	Let me thy inner presence feel,
Dein' Freundlichkeit auch uns erschein',	*Thy grace and love in me reveal;*

Dein Heil'ger Geist uns führ und leit'
Den Weg zur ew'gen Seligkeit!
Dem Namen dein, O Herr,
Sei ewig Preis und Ehr'!

Thy Holy Spirit guide us on,
Until our glorious goal is won.
Eternal praise and fame
we offer to thy Name.

The last lines of the first three stanzas of the original German comprise a Trinitarian sequence: "Mein Schöpfer . . . Mein Heiland . . . Mein Tröster" ("My Creator . . . My Savior . . . My Comforter"), which is lost in the H82 version. Notice also that in the German, the general door (die Tür) of st. 1 becomes the particular "door of my heart" (Mein's Herzens Tür) in st. 5.

Music: See hymn 182.

RAL

437 *Tell out, my soul, the greatness of the Lord*

Music: **BIRMINGHAM**

Since its first publication in 1965, this text has found such extensive acceptance and use that it is now found in almost every major English-language hymnal around the world. For Episcopalians, it first appeared in *Hymns III*, where it was matched with this tune.

Words: The text "Tell out, my soul, the greatness of the Lord" was composed in May of 1961 by Timothy Dudley-Smith while he was serving the Church Pastoral Aid Society, a home missionary society of the Church of England. Written at a time when many were arguing that contemporary translations of the Bible were unsingable, this work, based on the Magnificat as found in the New Testament (published 1961) of *The New English Bible*, proved otherwise (see the essay "British Hymnody since 1950," vol. 1, 555). Although the text, one of the author's earliest poems, was not published until 1965 in the *Anglican Hymnbook* (London), it is important to note that Dudley-Smith wrote it before the influential Dunblane Conference of 1962-1967 produced many fresh hymn texts and tunes and established new standards of literary excellence.

The author describes his inspiration for this work, based on the Song of Mary, Lk. 1:46-55: "I was reading a review copy of *The New English Bible, New Testament*, in which the line, 'Tell out my soul the greatness of the Lord' appears . . . I saw in it the first line of a poem, and speedily wrote the rest."[1] The text faithfully encompasses the spirit of the Gospel canticle. Repetition of the cry "Tell out my soul" as the opening statement of each stanza creates unity throughout.

---

1. T. Dudley-Smith, *Lift Every Heart* (London and Carol Stream, IL, 1984), 12.

Music: This tune was first published in Edward Miller's *Sacred Music* (London, 1800) where it was called BREWER and was noted "alter'd from Iohn Hall" (sic). It was arranged for two voices with the bass entering one measure later than the melody at the beginning of the first and third phrases and was printed with an LM text, "Hail, sov'reign Love, that first began" (see Example 1).

Example 1

Reproduced from *Sacred Music* (London, 1800), courtesy of the Library of the University of Illinois.

The tune was next published in James Steven's *A Selection of Sacred Music*, Vol. II (Glasgow, 1805), where it was called BIRMINGHAM. In that variation the tune was in four parts entering simultaneously with the melody in the tenor. The tune was matched in that book with the LM text "When shall I mount and soar away." The third publication of the tune was in Andrew Law's *Harmonic Companion* (Philadelphia, 1807). Law used a peculiar four-shape shape-note system, with notes printed in relation to each other as if on a staff but with no staff lines. Law took the treble and bass parts from Miller's book, added a counter part (which entered with the treble) and a tenor part (which entered with the bass) and linked the tune with the text "Thou whom my soul admires above All earthly joy and earthly love." Law's version, but with the melody in the tenor, was included in several of the four-shape shape-note books that made use of another system first set forth in William Little and William Smith's *Easy Instructor* (Philadelphia,1801) (see the essay "Psalmody in America to the Civil War," vol. 1, 409-411).[1]

A different harmonization was printed with the text "Now to the pow'r of God supreme" in a unique four-shape shape-note system in Charles Woodward's *Ecclesiae Harmonia* (Philadelphia, 1809). This version was converted into Little and Smith's system in *Wyeth's Repository of Sacred Music: Part Second* (Harrisburg, PA, 1813) and was published, with a wide variety of texts, in several later four-shape shape-note books and, with variations in the parts, in some other books, including *The Methodist Harmonist* (New York, 1821).

Other harmonizations of the tune were included in a number of books. The tune apparently remained popular in this country throughout much of the nineteenth century and was included in several denominational hymnals including Thomas Hastings's *Presbyterian Psalmodist* (Philadelphia, 1852), *Hymns for the Use of the Methodist Episcopal Church* (New York, 1857), the Northern Presbyterian *Hymnal of the Presbyterian Church* (Philadelphia, 1867), the Mennonite *Brethren's Tune and Hymn Book* (Dade City, PA, 1874) and the Southern Presbyterian *Book of Hymns and Tunes* (Richmond, VA, 1874). In nineteenth-century American printings it was always linked with LM texts and, as in early English printings, was titled BREWER rather than BIRMINGHAM, the name used in Scottish printings.

The tune first entered an American Episcopal hymnal in *H40*. It was printed under the title BIRMINGHAM with a text in 10 10. 10 10 metre, "O valiant hearts, who to your glory came," and attributed to Francis Cunningham's *A Selection of Psalm Tunes* (London, 1834), where it was matched with the LM text "Come, gracious Spirit, heav'nly Dove" and was printed on two staffs with the melody in the treble (see Example 2 on following page). The tune had not appeared in the 1826 edition of that book. The version from the first Scottish printing of the tune, Steven's *A Selection of Sacred Music* (Glasgow, 1805), was printed on four staffs in Andrew Thomason and Robert Archibald Smith's *Sacred Harmony* (Edinburgh, 1820). In that book the two bottom staffs constituted a score for an accompanist as well as containing the vocal melody and bass parts. Putting them next to each other made it easier for a keyboard player, who might not be competent at reading four staffs at once, to accompany. The second staff from the bottom contained the melody line as the uppermost notes of chords that incorporated the counter part. The version in Cunningham's *A Selection of Psalm Tunes* was simply the bottom two staffs, the accompanist's score, from Thomason and Smith's *Sacred Harmony*. The harmonization printed in *H40* is different from that in Cunningham's book, and the melody line incorporates minor changes: consecutive quarter notes replaced a dotted quarter followed by an eighth in the third measure, and the grace note preceding the last note in the third phrase was omitted.

The version of the tune printed in *H40* had appeared, with an attribution to "F. Cunningham's *A Selection of Psalm Tunes*, 1834," in the enlarged version of *Songs of Praise* (London, 1931). In that edition, however, copyright for the arrangement was neither claimed nor acknowledged. Between its appearance in *Songs of Praise* and its appearance in *H40*, this arrangement, attributed to Cunningham's *A Selection of Psalm Tunes*, had been included in several other books, including the 1933 revision of *EH*, the British *Methodist Hymnbook* (London, 1933) and the 1938 revision of *The Book of Common Praise* (Oxford and Toronto), the hymnal of the Anglican Church of Canada. This arrangement had also appeared in the earlier 1925 edition of *Songs of Praise*. In that edition Cunningham's book was not given as the source. Instead the tune was said to be a "Welsh Hymn Melody," and "Messrs. Gee & Sons" were acknowledged as the owners of the

Example 2

Reproduced from *A Selection of Psalm Tunes* (London, 1834), courtesy of Special Collections, University of Vermont Library.

copyright. In all of these books the tune was associated with texts in a 10 10. 10 10 metre.

It was in *Hymns III* that the tune was first matched with Timothy Dudley-Smith's text "Tell out, my soul, the greatness of the Lord!"

---

1. See "*The Easy Instructor* (1798-1831): A History and Bibliography of the First Shape-Note Tune-Book," in I. Lowens *Music and Musicians in Early America* (New York, 1964), 115-137, 292-310.

RG/MH

438 Tell out, my soul, the greatness of the Lord

***Music:* WOODLANDS**

In an increasing number of contemporary hymnals, the matching of this text with the tune WOODLANDS is becoming the standard practice.

Words: See hymn 437.

Music: WOODLANDS, a stirring unison tune, first appeared in the *Public School Hymnbook* (London, 1919). The tune is named after one of the school houses at Gresham's School, Norfolk, England, where the composer, Walter Greatorex, was Director of Music. (One of the distinguished pupils of Gresham's School in the early part of this century was Benjamin Britten.) It appeared in *H40* with the Addison text "Rise, crowned with light, imperial Salem, rise." The opening four-note figure of the tune  is ideally suited to the declamatory opening of each line of the text, "Tell out, my soul."

AW

439 What wondrous love is this

***Music:* WONDROUS LOVE**

This well-known American folk hymn, matched with its proper tune, appears for the first time in the *Hymnal*, where it makes a welcome addition to the General Hymns appropriate to Jesus Christ our Lord. *The Hymnal 1982* offers three possible performance practices, including the singing of the tune as it first appeared in its three-part form.

Words: This anonymous text appeared in print at least as early as the second enlarged edition of *A General Selection of the Newest and Most Admired Hymns and Spiritual Songs Now in Use. By the Rev. Stith Mead, preacher of the Gospel, M. E. C.* [*Methodist Episcopal Church*] . . . . *Published by permission of the Virginia Conference* . . . . (Lynchburg, VA, 1811). That version is reproduced below from a transcription:

What wond'rous love is this
O my soul! O my soul!
What wond'rous love is this!
  O my Soul!

What wondrous love is this!
That caus'd the Lord of bliss!
To send this precious peace,
To my soul, to my soul!
To send this precious peace, etc.

When I was sinking down,
Sinking down, sinking down,
When I was sinking down,
  Sinking down
When I was sinking down,
Beneath God's righteous frown,
Christ laid aside his Crown,
For my soul, for my soul!
Christ laid aside his crown, etc.

Ye winged Seraphs, fly,
Bear the news, bear the news;
Ye winged seraphs, fly,
  Bear the news:—
Ye winged seraphs, fly
Like Comets thro' the sky,
Fill vast eternity!

With the news! with the news!
Fill vast eternity, etc.

Ye friends of Zion's King,
Join his praise, join his praise,
Come, friends of Zion's King,
  Join his praise.—
Ye friends of Zion's King,
With hearts and voices sing,
And strike each tuneful string,
In his praise, in his praise!
And strike, etc.

To God, and to the Lamb,
I will sing, I will sing;
To God and to the Lamb,
  I will sing—
To God, and to the Lamb,
Who is the great I AM,
While millions join the theme,
I will sing, I will sing!
While millions, etc.

And while from death I'm free,
I'll sing on, I'll sing on,
And while from death I'm free,
  I'll sing on.
And while from death I'm free,
I'll sing and joyful be,
And through Eternity,
I'll sing on, I'll sing on,
And through eternity, etc.

A variant form of this text was probably printed in the no-longer-extant first edition of another book published the same year, *Hymns and Spiritual Songs, Original and Selected* (Frankfort, KY, 1811) by a Baptist clergyman, the Rev. Starke Dupuy.[1] The text reproduced below is from the third edition of that work (1818), where sts. 4 and 5 are reversed, there is an additional stanza and alterations are made in the text (indicated here in italics):

What wond'rous love is this, O my soul, O my soul,
What wond'rous love is this, O my Soul;
What wondrous love is this, that caus'd the Lord of bliss
To bear the dreadful curse, for my soul, *for* my soul,
To bear the dreadful curse for my soul.

When I was sinking down, sinking down, sinking down,
  When I was etc.
When I was sinking down beneath God's righteous frown,
Christ laid aside his crown, for my soul, for my soul,
  Christ, etc.

Ye winged Seraphs fly, bear the news, bear the news;
  Ye winged, etc.
Ye winged seraphs fly, like Comets thro' the sky,
Fill vast eternity, with the news, with the news,
  Fill, etc.

To God and to the Lamb, I will sing, I will sing;
  to God, etc.
To God and to the Lamb, *and to* the great I AM
While millions join the theme, I will sing, I will sing,
  While, etc.

Ye *sons* of Zion's King, join *the* praise, join *the* praise,
  Ye *sons*, etc.
Ye *sons* of Zion's King, with hearts and voices sing,
And strike each tuneful string, in his praise, in his praise,
  And strike, etc.

And *when* from death *we're* free, *we'll* sing on, *we'll* sing on,
  And *when*, etc.
And *when* from death *we're* free, *we'll* sing and joyful be,
And *in* eternity *we'll* sing on, *we'll* sing on,
  And *in*, etc

And when to that bright world we arrive, we arrive,
  and when, etc.,
when to that world we go, free from all pain and woe,
We'll join the happy throng, and sing on, and sing on,
We'll join the happy throng, and sing on.

Some later printings seem to have descended from Mead's version, but most are from Dupuy's.

The text is in an uncommon metre and stanzaic structure, sometimes referred to as the "Captain Kidd" metre because of its use in a ballad "My name was Robert Kidd, when I sailed, when I sailed," which is about the famous pirate executed in 1701.

This text first appeared in an Episcopal hymnal in *MHSS* in the same form as in *The Mennonite Hymnal* (Scottdale, PA, 1969). That form consisted of sts. 1, 2, 4, and 6 from Dupuy's version, except that in st. 6 "I'll sing on" was used rather than "we'll sing on" and "through eternity" rather than "in eternity." In *Hymns III* the text was abbreviated to three stanzas, st. 1 being constructed from sts. 1 and 2 of earlier versions. Scriptural allusions include Phil. 2:6-11, 1 Jn. 4:9; Rev. 5:6-14, 14:1-8, 19:1-9; Ex. 3:13-14, and Jn. 8:58.

---

1. W. J. Reynolds, *Companion to the Baptist Hymnal* (Nashville, 1976), 239.

Music: A three-part version of the hexatonic tune WONDROUS LOVE first appeared in print among the additional tunes in the 1840 printing of *The Southern Harmony* (New Haven, CT), compiled by William Walker (see Example 1). The tune, linked with the text "What wondrous love is this, O my soul," was attributed to "Christopher." In Walker's later book *Christian Harmony* (Philadelphia, 1867), James Christopher of Spartanburg, South Carolina is identified as the arranger of the tune.

This tune and text were soon picked up by several other shape-note books. In some of these books the bass line of the antepenultimate measure was brought into conformity with the bass line of the first full measure of the second phrase. Walker added a counter part in *Christian Harmony* and an "alto by S. M. Denson" was added in J. S. James's *Original Sacred Harp* (Cullman, AL, 1911). A four-part arrangement on two staffs in C. H. Cayce's *The Good Old Songs* (Thornton, AK, 1913), which is still used among Primitive Baptists, incorporates yet another alto part.

A different arrangement of the tune is included in William Hauser's *Olive Leaf* (Wadley, GA, 1878). This version is printed on two staffs with the melody in the treble in a book still used among Primitive

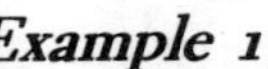

252 WONDROUS LOVE. 12, 9, 6, 6, 12, 9 *Christopher.*

What won-drous love is this, oh! my soul! oh! my soul! What won-drous love is this, oh! my soul! What won-drous love is this! That

caused the Lord of bliss, To bear the dread-ful curse for my soul, for my soul, To bear the dread-ful curse for my sou.

Reproduced from *The Southern Harmony & Musical Companion* by William Walker. Edited by Glenn C. Wilcox © 1987, 1993 by The University Press of Kentucky.

Baptists, John R. and J. Harvey Daily's *Primitive Baptist Hymn and Tune Book* (Indianapolis, 1902). A harmonization that is somewhat close to this was included in the "Supplement" in the Southern Methodist *Hymn and Tune Book* (Nashville, 1889).

WONDROUS LOVE first entered an Episcopal hymnal in *MHSS* where it was printed with an accompaniment by Carlton R. Young from the *Methodist Hymnal* (Nashville, 1964). In *Hymns III* it was printed with an accompaniment by Alastair Cassels-Brown and with the three-part harmonization, with the melody in the tenor, from William Walker's *Southern Harmony*. In *H82* the rhythm of measure seven has been altered from a whole note followed by a half rest as found in most older sources of this tune, including *Southern Harmony*. *The Hymnal 1982* prints both William Walker's harmonization and the accompaniment by Carlton R. Young. Guitar chords are also provided.

MH

440 Blessed Jesus, at thy word

Music: **LIEBSTER JESU**

The tune to which this text is matched was originally associated with a baptismal text with the same opening line, "Liebster Jesu, wir sind hier." Its translation first appeared in an Episcopal publication in *H40* matched with this tune.

Words: The German hymn "Liebster Jesu, wir sind hier" written by Tobias Clausnitzer was first published (anonymously) in *Frommer Christen Betendes Hertz und Singender Mund* (Altdorf, 1663) under the title "Before the Sermon." Clausnitzer's point of departure is found in the words of Cornelius to Peter in Acts 10:33: "So now all of us are here in the presence of God to listen to all that the Lord has commanded you to say" (NRSV). There is also an allusion to the Sursum corda in the first stanza, "dass die Herzen von der Erden/Ganz zu dir gezogen werden" ("that our hearts from the earth are wholly drawn to thee"), which is lost in the English version. In the second line of st. 3 there is a more direct quotation from the Nicene Creed. The translation is substantially that of Catherine Winkworth, which first appeared in the second series of her *Lyra Germanica* (London, 1858) and was then included in *The Chorale Book for England* (London, 1863) with its associated melody.

1. Liebster Jesu, wir sind hier,
 Dich und dein Wort anzühoren;
Lenke Sinnen und Begier
 Auf die süssen Himmelslehren,
Dass die Herzen von der Erden
Ganz zu dir gezogen werden.

2. Unser Wissen und Verstand
 Ist mit Finsternis umhüllet,
Wo nicht deines Geistes Hand
 Uns mit hellem Licht erfüllet.
Gutes denken, Gutes dichten
 Musst du selbst in uns verrichten.

3. O du Glanz der Herrlichkeit,
 Licht vom Licht aus Gott geboren,
Mach uns allesamt bereit,
 Öffne Herzen, Mund und Ohren!
Unser bitten, Flehn und Singen
 Lass, Herr Jesu, wohl gelingen.

Clausnitzer's hymn was parodied by Benjamin Schmolk, who utilized the same opening line, "Liebster Jesu, wir sind hier," and with its associated melody (see the commentary below) created a baptism hymn that appeared in print some time between 1704 and 1706. One stanza of this hymn by Schmolk was included in *H40*, as translated by Winfred Douglas.

Music: The tune LIEBSTER JESU (*Zahn* 3498a), composed by Johann Rudolph Ahle, first appeared in Ahle's *Neue Geistliche Aug die Sonntage . . . Andachten* (Mülhausen, 1664) with the Advent hymn of Franz Burmeister, "Ja, er ist's, das Heil der Welt." The melody was later reconstructed and appeared with the text of Tobias Clausnitzer, "Liebster Jesu, wir sind hier," in *Das grosse Cantional, Oder Kirchen-Gesangbuch* (Darmstadt, 1687) (*Zahn* 3498b). The harmonization that first appeared in *H40* is that of George Herbert Palmer from George Woodward's *Songs of Syon* (London, 1910).

RAL/CS

441 In the cross of Christ I glory

Music: **RATHBUN**

This much-loved text has been matched for use in the Episcopal church with RATHBUN, the tune written for it, since its appearance in the Hutchins music edition of the 1892 *Hymnal*.

Words: Widely considered John Bowring's best hymn, "In the cross of Christ I glory" is based on Gal. 6:14. (This text was also the inspiration for the equally well-known and beloved Isaac Watts hymn "When I survey the wondrous cross.") Erik Routley records the following story related to this hymn:

> The first thing you see as you approach Macao (Island near Hong Kong) is the great white church of Our Lady of Fatima, perched on the island's highest hill. In a revolution the church was destroyed, save for the great west front. This west wall still stands and crowning the topmost point is a great metal cross, which (in repeated attacks) has survived destruction. It was this cross, blackened with smoke, that inspired John Bowring's hymn.[1]

The text was published in the collection *Hymns: as a Sequel to Matins* (London, 1825) and is printed here in its entirety without alterations.

---

1. E. Routley, *An English-Speaking Hymnal Guide* (Collegeville, MD, 1979), 42.

Music: Ithamar Conkey composed RATHBUN for use with this text in 1849 when he was organist for the Central Baptist Church of Norwich, CT. An ABA^1C tune, it was named for Conkey's soprano soloist, Mrs. Beria S. Rathbun. When first published in Henry Greatorex's *Collection of Psalm and Hymn Tunes* (New York, 1851), it was matched with Muhlenberg's "Savior, who thy flock art feeding." Robert McCutchan, in *Our Hymnody* (New York, 1937), quotes a fanciful story concerning this tune's origin. The first published appearance of this text and tune appeared in the United States in *Manual of Praise* (Oberlin, OH, 1880).

TAR/HE

442 *In the cross of Christ I glory*

Music: **TOMTER**

Although many texts and tunes have matchings of long standing, composers are often able to create new tunes for use with these words, thus adding a fresh perspective to their meaning. Such is the case with the association of this early nineteenth-century text with a tune written for it by a contemporary American composer, Bruce Neswick.

Words: See hymn 441.

Music: The tune TOMTER was written as a more lyrical alternative to the tune RATHBUN and was first sung during Lent 1983 at General Theological Seminary, New York, where the composer, Bruce Neswick, served as Acting Instructor in Music. One of the distinguishing attributes of the tune is the use of a three-note figure in a ♪♫ ♩ rhythmic pattern at the beginning and the end of each of the two balanced major phrases. There is also a striking modulation in the middle of the tune to the key of A. The second half of the tune opens with a chord of f#, echoing the beginning of the first phrase in F. The final cadence of the hymn is in A with A in the melody, thus facilitating the easy return to the original key of F, and the beginning of the tune on A. Another distinguishing characteristic of the tune is the primary harmonic movement of the setting on beats 1 and 2. This pattern is broken for one measure in the middle of each of the two phrases and at the final cadence. The tune is named for the Rev. Patrick Tomter, a priest of the Diocese of Olympia and a friend of the composer.

RG

443 *From God Christ's deity came forth*

Music: **SALEM HARBOR**

Some of the Rev. Dr. F. Bland Tucker's finest texts written for *H40* and continued in *H82* are his translations or paraphrases of passages from the scriptures or the writings of the early Church Fathers (see 164, 302/303, and 478). The gifts that produced these earlier works are here applied to the writings of a fourth-century Syrian writer, Ephrem of Edessa. This text, new to *H82*, is matched with a tune written for use with it by Dr. Ronald Arnatt.

Words: First in the collection of Easter Hymns by Ephrem of Edessa in Nisibis was one of twenty-two stanzas. Its pattern could be arranged as two lines expressing a parallel of the sort found in the Book of Proverbs, the next two a related parallel, and the fifth line a refrain of praise. In the original Syriac, these lines show metre, although less precise than that of English verse; some modifications are required to reflect this.

To show the scope of Christian hymnody in varied cultures, the compilers of *H82* sought to include representation of Syrian hymns. Little of the work of Ephrem of Edessa, the most prolific writer of Syrian hymns, was available in English. To help remedy this deficiency, Howard Rhys of the theological faculty of the University of the South in Sewanee, TN was asked to provide translations of some of Ephrem's hymns. He responded by offering literal renderings of some seventy stanzas from various hymn groups. Dr. F. Bland Tucker, a consultant to the Text Committee of the SCCM, whose translations of Greek hymns had graced *H40* and were retained for *H82*, selected five stanzas from Easter Hymn I. While Dr. Tucker made the modifications required for English rhythm, the sense of the stanzas was faithfully preserved.

The hymn is filled with scriptural references, ten from the Gospels, three from Paul, one each from Psalms and Hebrews. There are, however, no allusions to nature in these five stanzas.

Music: The tune SALEM HARBOR by composer, organist, conductor, and teacher Dr. Ronald Arnatt was commissioned by the SCCM for use with this text. The tune name honors the community in Massachusetts where the composer lived at the time of its composition. Of this, the composer writes "The tune was written on May 4, 1984 in the study of our house in Salem, which directly overlooks the harbor—a lovely spot for thinking and working."[1] After an initial statement, the unison tune that proceeds with three sequential phrases building to a climax is followed by a brief, bold refrain. Because of this, the tune moves with a very convincing sense of inner momentum and gives proper emphasis to the five-syllable declamatory phrase or refrain that ends each stanza of the text. Thus the form and structure of the entire tune skillfully support and illuminate both the form and the meaning of the text. Dr. Arnatt describes it in this way: "The form and metre of the hymn dictated the shape of the tune, especially in the feeling of climax that is achieved in the fourth line of every verse and in the thematic sequence suggested by lines 2, 3, 4 of verses 1 and 5." Harmonically, the tune centers in the key of g until the end of the fourth phrase, which ends with a cadence in F. The final cadence marks a return to G with a *Tierce de Picardie** on the final chord.

---

1. Arnatt to Glover, Church Hymnal Corporation Papers New York, NY.

JHR/RG

444 Blessed be the God of Israel

Music: **THORNBURY**

Soon after ordination in the Church of England, Michael Perry set his hand to rendering some of the traditional canticles from the BCP into metrical form, to enable ordinary congregations to sing them more easily than chant settings and to understand more of their meaning. Among these was the Benedictus or Song of Zechariah (Lk. 1:68-79).

Words: In Luke's narrative, the father of John the Baptist utters this Spirit-inspired prophecy when his son is born and named and his own speech is restored; in the British *Prayer Book* service of Morning Prayer it is called a "hymn" and follows the second (NT) lesson, appearing almost exactly in the 1611 King James Version translation "Blessed be the Lord God of Israel" with the Doxology.

Late in 1969, Michael Perry sent this and other paraphrases to Michael Baughen (then a Manchester vicar, later Bishop of Chester) who had just published some similar work in *Youth Praise 2* (London, 1969) and who then invited Perry to join a group of writers in producing a fuller collection that eventually became *Psalm Praise* (London, 1973). It was there that this text first appeared, in the form in which it was originally written at Bitterne, Southampton:

1. O praise the God of Israel,
   Within whose care are we:
   He visits and redeems us,
   He comes to set us free.

The prophets spoke of mercy,
Of freedom and release:
God shall fulfill His promise
And bring His people peace.

2. He, from the house of David,
A child of grace has given;
A Saviour comes among us
To raise us up to heaven.
Before Him goes His herald,
Forerunner in the way;
The prophet of salvation,
The harbinger of Day.

3. On prisoners of darkness
The sun begins to rise;
The dawning of forgiveness
Upon the sinner's eyes.
He guides the feet of pilgrims
Along the paths of peace
O praise our God and Saviour,
With songs that never cease!

Subsequent verbal changes were made in all three stanzas, notably in restoring the opening word "Blessed" which echoes more clearly the familiar original. The text was at first attached to an unnamed tune by Noel Tredinnick, but it has also been set to several other tunes.

Dean Frederic W. Farrar spoke of the Benedictus as "the last Prophecy of the Old Dispensation and the first of the New." More recently, E. Earle Ellis has written "The Magnificat describes a reversal of political and economic status in the coming age. The Benedictus speaks of the ethical transformation to be effected by the messianic redemption" (*The Gospel of Luke* [London, 1966]).

Music: THORNBURY was composed by Basil Harwood for the text "Thy hand, O God, has guided thy flock from age to age" and heard for the first time at the Annual Festival of the London Church Choir Association on November 17, 1898. Harmonically the tune, which places the B section in the key of the mediant, f#, gives the hymn an AABA feeling because of the strong return to the tonic (D) in the last phrase. The tune was printed in the composer's *Hymn Tunes, Original and Selected* (London, 1905-1906) and included in the 1916 *Supplement of Hymns Ancient and Modern*. It soon became very popular and is one of the most widely sung tunes in England. This is the first appearance of the tune in the *Hymnal*.

THORNBURY is a town in northwest Wiltshire, the area of England of which Harwood was a native. Most of his tunes are named for towns or villages in that part of the country.

MP/AW

445 Praise to the Holiest in the height

***Music:* GERONTIUS**

John Henry Newman, a major figure in English ecclesiastical history, is remembered for many things that reflect his incredible gifts as a theologian, reformer, and author. Among them is his poem *The Dream of Gerontius,* written in 1865. This text, taken from Newman's epic poem, appeared as a hymn soon after the publication of the full text and is here matched with a tune written for use with it.

Words: This hymn was extracted from the lengthy poem *The Dream of Gerontius* (1865) by John Henry Cardinal Newman, later made famous by the oratorio of Sir Edward Elgar.

Newman's poetry was primarily written during two periods of personal crisis and illness in which his life was threatened. The first, in 1833, during which he produced the poetry that was eventually published as *Lyra Apostolica* (London, 1836); the second, some thirty years later, gave birth to *The Dream of Gerontius*, a meditation on the progress of an individual soul through death.

Newman's verse in *The Dream of Gerontius* has a hymnic quality, and two hymns were later quarried from it: "Praise to the Holiest in the height" and "Firmly I believe and truly," which first appeared as a hymn in *EH*. At one point Newman seems to have had Faber's hymn "My God, how wonderful thou art" [643] at the back of his mind. The following lines echo sts. 1 and 5 of Faber's hymn, as well as anticipate his own "Praise to the Holiest," which would appear later in the poem:

O Lord, how wonderful in depth and height,
But most in man, how wonderful Thou art!
With what a love, what soft pervasive might
Victorious o'er the stubborn fleshly heart . . .

In the visionary poem, the journeying soul converses with an accompanying angel. Their discourse is repeatedly interrupted, first by concerted demons, then by five choirs of angels that sing in turn, always beginning with what is now known as the first stanza of the hymn. In the *Dream*, the stanzas that make up the hymn are sung by the "Fifth Choir of Angelicals," which led Percy Dearmer to remark "Very soon, thanks to the Dykes tune, it was being sung by most choirs of evangelicals also and appeared in many hymn books."[1] The repetition of the first stanza at the conclusion—which recalls the repetitions in the original *Dream*—was the work of the editors of *HA&M* when they introduced the text as a hymn in the *Appendix* of 1868 with Dykes's tune GERONTIUS (see below).[2]

For use in *H82*, st. 4:1 was altered from "and that a higher gift than grace" to "and that the highest gift of grace"; and sts. 5 and 6 were omitted:

5. O generous love! that He, Who smote
    In Man for man the foe,
The double agony in Man
    For Man should undergo;

6. And in the garden secretly,
    And on the Cross on high,
Should teach His brethren, and inspire
    To suffer and to die.

1. P. Dearmer, *Songs of Praise Discussed* (London, 1933), 331.
2. For an extended exposition of the hymn within the context of the original poem, see E. Routley, *Hymns and the Faith* (London, 1955), 283-92.

Music: The tune GERONTIUS was specifically composed by John Bacchus Dykes for Newman's "Praise to the Holiest in the height" and was first published in the 1868 *Appendix* to the first edition of *HA&M*. Dykes is known to have composed LUX BENIGNA for Newman's "Lead, kindly Light" in August 1865, a tune, in its revised form, that also appeared in the 1868 *Appendix*.[1] It therefore seems possible that GERONTIUS, composed for this other Newman text, may have originated during the same period. The remarkable opening first line, melodically shaped by the word-painting of "height" and "depths," appears to have grown out of another tune composed by Dykes. This is ALMSGIVING, a tune Dykes composed for inclusion in the musical edition of Christopher Wordsworth's *The Holy Year: or Hymns for Sundays and Holy Days* (London, 1865). The similarities between the first lines of the two tunes (see Example 1), and the fact that ALMSGIVING was published in 1865, perhaps underscore the possibility that GERONTIUS was composed in the same year.

Example 1

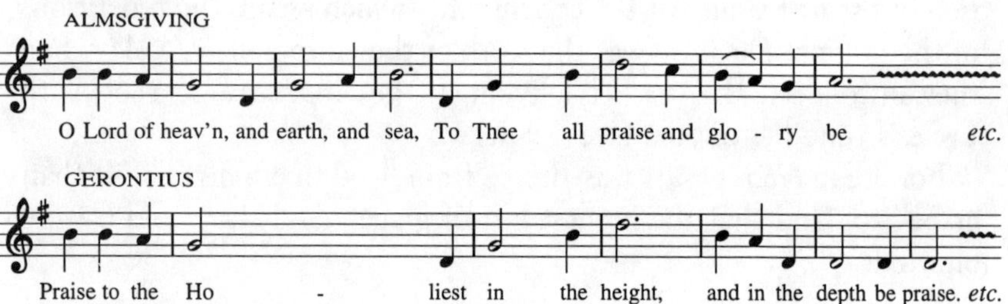
ALMSGIVING
O Lord of heav'n, and earth, and sea, To Thee all praise and glo - ry be etc.
GERONTIUS
Praise to the Ho - liest in the height, and in the depth be praise. etc.

Harmonically, the beginning of ALMSGIVING is built on a rising G chord (see Example 2).

Example 2

ALMSGIVING

By contrast, GERONTIUS begins with a tonic pedal-point, against which the tune expands both melodically and harmonically (Example 3a).

This opening tonic pedal-point is effectively matched by a second pedal-point—on the dominant, first in the alto and then in the soprano of measures 5 through 7 (see Example 3b)—reinforcing the imagery of "depths."

Example 3a

Example 3b

The creativity of Dykes's melodic and harmonic treatment of the opening line of Newman's text has rightly drawn praise from time to time.[2] The remainder of the tune, however, does not sustain the promising beginning. As Erik Routley observed, "If the rest of the tune does not really take the responsibilities that go with such a superb opening statement, that is where Dykes shows his limitations."[3]

---

1. See J. T. Fowler, ed., *Life and Letters of John Bacchus Dykes* (London, 1897), 103.
2. For example, A. Hutchings, *Church Music in the Nineteenth Century* (London, 1967), 155.
3. E. Routley, *The Music of Christian Hymns* (Chicago, 1981), 96.

RAL

446 Praise to the Holiest in the height

***Music:* NEWMAN**

The tune NEWMAN, which is strongly associated with this text in British Roman Catholic hymnals under the name BILLING, has gained acceptance and use with other texts in the hymnals of largely British

Protestant denominations. It first appeared in an Episcopal publication using the name NEWMAN in *H40*, matched with this text.

Words: See hymn 445.

Music: This tune was composed for Newman's text by Richard Runciman Terry, Director of Music at the Roman Catholic Westminster Cathedral, London. Called BILLING, it appeared first in the *Westminster Hymnal* (London, 1912), the source for its inclusion in *H40*. This latter edition is probably the source of the tune name NEWMAN. The tune has not found acceptance in other hymnals in the United States.

RG

447 The Christ who died but rose again

Music: **ST. MAGNUS**

One of the best-known and oft-quoted passages from the Epistle to the Romans is the basis of this paraphrase, the work of an Australian author. He in turn based his work on an earlier Scottish paraphrase. Matched with ST. MAGNUS, congregations are given added opportunity for the use of this magnificent eighteenth-century psalm tune.

Words: This four-stanza text comprises sts. 4 through 7 of a seven-stanza paraphrase of Rom. 8:34-39 prepared by the Rev. Granton Hay in consultation with the literary subcommittee of *The Australian Hymnbook* (Sydney, 1977). First appearing in that publication with a rubric that the hymn may begin at st. 4, the work is based on a dated and much wordier paraphrase of Romans from *Scottish Paraphrase* (Edinburgh, 1798). The first three stanzas are:

1. Let Christian faith and hope dispel
the fears from which we hide,
for who would dare oppose us now
that God is at our side?

2. We know he did not spare his Son
but gave him for us all:

how can we doubt that all his gifts
 will on us freely fall?

3. Who would accuse God's chosen ones
 and venture to condemn?
God safely takes them to himself;
 he has acquitted them.

Music: This invigorating tune, typical of the revival of interest in hymnody in Queen Anne's reign (1702-1714), can be confidently attributed to Jeremiah Clarke. It made its appearance in the second edition of Henry Playford's *Divine Companion* (London, 1707) in a two-voice setting with a version of Ps. 117, "Let all the nations of the world." A few pages back there is the statement "The three following Psalms sett by Mr. Jer. Clark." This is actually the fourth psalm following, as Leonard Ellinwood pointed out, so we do not have a positive attribution to Clarke here (*H40c*, 78). At page 16 in the same book, however, there is a version of the same tune in triple time, called A HYMN FOR CHRISTMAS DAY, and this one is attributed to "Jer. Clarke." It seems almost certain, therefore, that he was equally responsible for the duple-time version we know today, though it was not until 1762 that it was plainly attributed to him by William Riley in *Parochial Music Corrected* (London). It was Riley, too, who first called it ST. MAGNUS, after the splendid church of St. Magnus the Martyr, London Bridge, rebuilt by Sir Christopher Wren in 1690. Previously, the tune had been given a bewildering variety of names: BRANFORD, BRENTFORD, BUCKINGHAM, NEWBROUGH, NOTTINGHAM, ST. LEONARD'S; later eighteenth-century sources added BIRMINGHAM, BUXTON, GREENOCK, and ST. DUNSTAN. In the earliest American source, *The Essex Harmony, Part 2* (Salem, 1802), it is named BIRMINGHAM.

The harmonies in our version are from *EH*. Ralph Vaughan Williams, as musical editor, may have been partially influenced by John Pyke Hullah's setting in *The Psalter, a Collection of Psalm Tunes in Four Parts* (London, 1843), which is the basis of the *HA&M* harmonization.

RG/NT

448 O love, how deep, how broad, how high

Music: **DEUS TUORUM MILITUM**

One of the benefits of the Oxford and the Cambridge-Camden Movements was the rediscovery of the vast liturgical and musical resources of the early and medieval Church. Today, largely through the work of John Mason Neale and his colleagues, we enjoy a wealth of Greek and Latin hymnody from these periods, of which this text is a superb example (see the essay "British Hymnody in the Nineteenth Century," vol. 1, 417). The text matched with this tune appeared in *H40*.

Words: (The numbers in parentheses refer to the stanzas in *H82* derived from the Latin original.)

1. Apparuit benignitas
dei nec non humanitas
ex caritate nimia
ad nos atque gratuita.

2.(1) O amor quam exstaticus,
quam effluens, quam nimius,
qui deum, dei filium,
unum fecit mortalium!

3. Affectu superfervido,
quo nos tulit ab aeterno,
nequibat se comprimere,
qui venit nos invisere.

4. Non invisit nos angelo,
seu supremo seu infimo,
carnis assumens pallium
venit ad nos per se ipsum.

5. In se cum invisibilis
sit nostris lippis oculis,
tectus mortali tunica
huc processit ad publica.

6. Non solum se ostendere
voluit, sed convivere
deus homo hominibus
hic annis triginta tribus.

7. Nascitur nobis hodie
pauper, exsul [rex gloriae],
nobis vagit praesaepio
iunctus bovi et asino.

8. Post nobis circumciditur
nobis et Jesus dicitur,
pro nobis stellae visio,
nobis Jesu oblatio.

9.(2) Nobis baptisma suscipit,
nobis ieiunans esurit,
nobis et Satan hunc
temptat,
nobis temptantem superat.

10.(3) Nobis orat et praedicat,
pro nobis cuncta factitat,
verbis, signis et actibus
nos quaerens, non se penitus.

11.(4) Pro nobis comprehenditur,
flagellatur, conspuitur,
crucis perfert patibulum,
pro nobis tradit spiritum.

12.(5) Nobis surgit a mortuis,
nobis se transfert superis,
nobis suum dat spiritum
in robur, in solacium.

13. Vere talis dilectio
non audita a saeculo

de creatura aliqua
humana vel angelica.

14. Homo talem non habuit,
quia transgressor exstitit,
defuit hoc et angelo
fervore nimis tepido.

15. Dic, quis unquam spirituum
hic pro salute hominum
incarnari se pertulit,
non dico crucem subiit?

16. Hoc summus fecit dominus
sua bonitate tractus,
qui natus dedit pretium,
quo mortis solvit debitum.

17. Hinc ex plena laetitia
concinamus nunc gloria
sit deo in altissimis
una cum laetis angelis.

18. Hos si replet sic gaudio
nostri congratulatio,
nos, o, quantum gaudebimus,
[pro] quibus Christus est natus!

19. Delectemur in proprio
nobis nunc nato domino,
tot hunc mulcentes osculis,
quot eius membra corporis.

20. Transeamus in Bethlehem,
quo natus rex Jerusalem,
cernamus cum pastoribus
verbum, quod fecit dominus.

21. En, infans sapientia,
puer, qui ante omnia,
deus pannis involvitur,
in praesaepio ponitur.

22. Summa cum reverentia
adoremus hic singula,
dilectio hunc compulit,
quod hoc dominus pertulit.

23.(6) Deo patri sit gloria
per infinita saecula,
cuius amore nimio
salvi sumus in filio.

This hymn survives in only one source, a manuscript from the fifteenth century, where it appears as a nativity hymn, "Apparuit benignitas." Its extreme pietism (st. 2 begins "O ecstatic love, overflowing, beyond measure. . .") betrays the influence of St. Thomas à Kempis (1380-1471) (whose book *The Imitation of Christ* recently enjoyed a popular resurgence when it was revealed that Pope John Paul I had read from it shortly before he died), who is indirectly associated with the manuscript containing this hymn. Benjamin Webb selected eight stanzas from the original twenty-three for inclusion in the *Hymnal Noted*, Part 2 (London, 1854), and the current doxology, which is different from the one that appears in *HA&M* (London, 1861), refers back to the first translated stanza. Webb's translation has been used since *H40*, with slight alterations.

The late hymnologist Erik Routley preferred to sing sts. 1 through

4, and 6, to the tune at 449 (DEO GRACIAS), reserving DEUS TUORUM MILITUM [448] for st. 5 with its reference to the resurrection.

Music: See hymn 285.

JH

449 O love, how deep, how broad, how high

Music: **DEO GRACIAS**
This Latin fifteenth-century text is here matched with a strong English tune of the same century.

Words: See hymn 448.

Music: See hymn 218.

450 All hail the power of Jesus' Name!

Music: **CORONATION**
The text and tune of this hymn rank among the most popular with congregations of the Episcopal Church. Both text and tune are of eighteenth-century origin and have been matched from that time.

Words: The first stanza of this hymn was published anonymously in the November 1779 issue of *Gospel Magazine* with the tune by William Shrubsole that later became known as MILES LANE [451]. The April 1780 issue of that magazine contained the complete text of the hymn (*Julian*, 41):

All hail! the pow'r of Jesu's Name;
Let angels prostrate fall;
Bring forth the Royal Diadem,
To crown him Lord of all.

Let highborn seraphs tune the lyre,
And as they tune it, fall
Before His face who tunes their choir,
And crown Him Lord of all.

Crown Him ye morning stars of light,
Who fixed this floating ball;
Now hail the strength of Israel's might,
And crown Him Lord of all.

Crown Him, ye martyrs of your God,
Who from His altar call;
Extol the stem of Jesse's rod,
And crown Him Lord of all.

Ye seed of Israel's chosen race,
Ye ransom'd of the fall,
Hail Him Who saves you by his grace,
And crown Him Lord of all.

Hail Him, ye heirs of David's line,
Whom David Lord did call;
The God incarnate, man Divine,
And crown Him Lord of all.

Sinners! whose love can ne'er forget
The wormwood and the gall,
Go—spread your trophies at His feet,
And crown Him Lord of all.

Let every tribe and every tongue
That bound creation's call,
Now shout in universal song,
The crownèd Lord of all.

This text was attributed to Edward Perronet. A much altered form of the hymn appeared in John Rippon's *Selection of Hymns* (London, 1787), with the titles added to the stanzas and with alterations or additions (in italics) (*Julian*, 41-42):

The Spiritual Coronation, Cant. iii. 11
1. ANGELS.
All-hail, the power of Jesus' name!
Let angels prostrate fall:
Bring forth the royal diadem,
And crown Him Lord of all.

2. MARTYRS
[Crown Him, ye martyrs of *our* God,
  Who from His altar call;
Extol the Stem of Jesse's rod,
  And crown Him Lord of all.]

3. CONVERTED JEWS.
[*Ye chosen seed of Israel's race,*
  A remnant weak and small;
Hail Him, who saves you by His grace,
  And crown Him Lord of all.]

4. BELIEVING GENTILES
Ye Gentile sinners, ne'er forget
  The wormwood and the gall;
Go—spread your trophies at His feet,
  And crown Him Lord of all.

5. SINNERS OF EVERY AGE [SIC for capitalization]
[*Babes, men, and sires, who know His love*
  Who feel your sins and thrall,
Now joy with all the hosts above,
  And crown Him Lord of all.]

6. SINNERS OF EVERY NATION [SIC for capitalization]
Let every *kindred, every tribe,*
  On this terrestrial ball,
To Him all majesty ascribe,
  And crown Him Lord of all.

7. OURSELVES.
Oh that, with yonder sacred throng,
  We at His feet may fall;
We'll join the everlasting song,
  And crown Him Lord of all.

A version of this hymn was among the sixty-five added to the *Prayer Book Collection* (New York) in 1865. The first, second, and sixth stanzas of that version and the first line of st. 4 were Rippon's revision of the text (except for the substitution in st. 2 of "the altar" for "his altar"). The other stanzas were from Perronet's original version, except for the substitution of "Hail him, the Heir of David's line" for "Hail him, ye heirs of David's line" at the beginning of st. 3, and of "from the fall" for "of the fall" in st. 4. In the 1874 revision of the 1871 hymnal "his altar" and "of the fall" were restored. The 1874 version is the same as that in *H82*, except for the third line of st. 2, which in that book read "Extol the Stem of Jesse's rod." The line "Praise him whose way of pain ye trod" was substituted in *H40*. Scriptural allusions include Phil. 2:5-11, Is. 62:3, Heb. 2:5-9, Mt. 22:41-46, Mk. 12:35-37, and Lk. 20:41-44.

Music: CORONATION is unquestionably the most often printed and most frequently used of the eighteenth-century American hymn tunes. It was composed by Oliver Holden of Charlestown, MA and first published in his round-note *Union Harmony* (Boston, 1793), where it was printed with Edward Perronet's text "All hail the power of Jesus' name," mistakenly attributed there to the Rev. Mr. Medley (Example 1 on following page). It appeared in four parts with the melody in the tenor and with "choosing notes"* at the beginning of the second phrase in the bass and in the last phrase of the treble. Though not a true fuging tune, it contains elements reminiscent of the fuging tunes of the eighteenth century.

In the later editions of the *Worcester Collection of Sacred Harmony*, which was edited by Holden from 1797 on, there were corrections or changes in the counter part and the choosing note was dropped from the bass.

By the end of 1820 this four-part version, generally with the choosing notes in the treble but sometimes without, had appeared in round-note books published under more than thirty different titles. This version first appeared in a four-shape shape-note book in edition F of William Little and William Smith's *Easy Instructor* (Philadelphia, 1809) and was printed in many later shape-note books. In some books this version was printed with only two or three parts.

A new version of CORONATION was apparently published for the first time in Lowell Mason's *The Choir* (Boston, 1832) (Example 2). The tenor line remained unchanged, but the treble, counter, and bass parts were all rewritten.

Underneath the tune was a note that would be repeated in many later reprintings:

Example 1

Reproduced from *Union Harmony* (Boston, 1793) with permission of Moravian Music Foundation.

Example 2

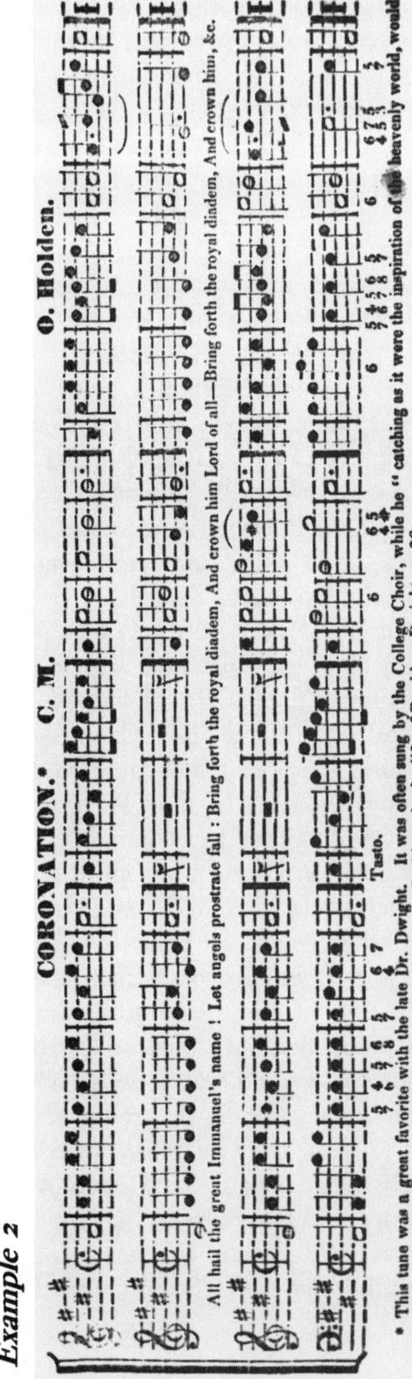

Reproduced from *The Choir* (Boston, 1832), with permission of Moravian Music Foundation.

> This tune was a great favorite with the late Dr. Dwight [author of hymn 524 in *H82*]. It was often sung by the College Choir, while he 'catching as it were the inspiration of the heavenly world, would join them, and lead them' with the most ardent devotion.—Incidents in the life of President Dwight, p. 26.

This version was printed in innumerable tunebooks, including denominational hymnals such as the *Methodist Harmonist* (New York, 1837), Thomas Hastings's *Presbyterian Psalmodist* (Philadelphia, 1852), the Southern Baptist Publication Society's *The Casket* (Charleston, 1855), *Hymns for the Use of the Methodist Episcopal Church* (New York, 1857), the Southern Methodist *The Wesleyan Hymn and Tune Book* (Everett, TN, 1859); W. D. Roedel's *Carmina Ecclesiae* (Baltimore, 1860), approved by the General Synod of the Evangelical Lutheran Church; George E. Thrall's *Episcopal Common Praise* (New York, 1867); the Northern Presbyterian *Hymnal of the Presbyterian Church* (Philadelphia, 1867); the Congregationalist *Book of Praise* (Hartford, 1868); *Baptist Hymn and Tune Book* (Philadelphia, 1871); editions of *Hymnal of the Protestant Episcopal Church with Music* (New York), edited by A. B. Goodrich and Walter B. Gilbert for both the 1871 and 1874 hymnals; the Southern Presbyterian *Book of Hymns and Tunes* (Richmond, 1874); and *The Hymnal of the Church . . . . With Music* (New York, 1897), edited by James H. Darlington for use with the 1892 Episcopal hymnal. In all of these books this tune was linked with "All hail the power of Jesus' name," as well as additional texts. In *Episcopal Common Praise* it was printed also with "While shepherds watched their flocks by night." Several books included three-part versions of this arrangement. In many books all four parts were filled out in the third phrase, which had originally been scored for treble and bass only. This version of the tune, printed on two staffs with the melody in the treble, is included in a book still used among Primitive Baptists, C. H. Cayce's *The Good Old Songs* (Thornton, AK, 1913). It is essentially this harmonization that is used in several other current hymnals, including the Reformed Church in America's *Rejoice in the Lord* (Grand Rapids, MI, 1985), *The United Methodist Hymnal* (Nashville, 1989) and *The Baptist Hymnal* (Nashville, 1991).

A distinctive version titled SOLEMN PRAISE was included in the third edition of Joseph Funk's *Genuine Church Music* (Winchester, VA,

1842) and its successors, *Harmonia Sacra* (Singers' Glen, VA, 1851) and *New Harmonia Sacra* (Singers' Glen, VA, 1867).

Another distinctive four-part version of CORONATION was printed in *The Plymouth Collection* (New York, 1855), edited by Henry Ward Beecher with the assistance of his brother Charles and his organist, John Zundel. This arrangement was reproduced in *The Baptist Hymn and Tune Book* (New York, 1858), Amos Sutton Hayden's *Christian Hymn and Tune Book* (Chicago, 1870), both the 1871 and 1878 editions of *The Service of Song for Baptist Churches* (Boston), *The Baptist Hymnal* (Philadelphia, 1883) and John R. and J. Harvey Daily's *Primitive Baptist Hymn and Tune Book* (Thornton, AK, 1902), which is still used among Primitive Baptists.

Lowell Mason's *The Asaph* (New York, 1861) contained an arrangement that was reproduced in *The Christian Hymnal* (Cincinnati, 1871) and in J. R. Graves's *Little Seraph*, the tunebook for his *The New Baptist Psalmist and Tune Book* (Memphis, 1874).

Another harmonization was apparently published for the first time in the Rev. J. H. Waterbury's *"Common Praise": A Tribute to Congregational Music* (New York, 1867), which had a preface dated "Epiphany 1866." This book was designed as a musical companion to the 1865 enlarged edition of the "Prayer Book Collection," a selection of psalms and hymns bound with the BCP. This harmonization was used in two of the tunebooks prepared for use with the 1871-1874 Episcopal *Hymnal*, Charles L. Hutchins's *The Church Hymnal* (Hartford, 1872) and J. Ireland Tucker's *Tunes Old and New Adapted to The Hymnal* (New York, 1871). This harmonization was also used in several of the tunebooks printed for use with the 1892 Episcopal *Hymnal*, including James Morris Helfenstein's *Grace Church Hymnal* (New York, 1909), Charles Hutchins's *The Church Hymnal* (Boston, 1894), Horatio Parker's *The Hymnal* (New York, 1903), and J. Ireland Tucker and William W. Rousseau's *The Hymnal . . . . With Tunes Old and New* (New York, 1894). This version was also used in all the tunebooks designed for use with the 1916 *Hymnal* and was used in *H40*. It has been retained in *H82* and is used, with modifications, in a number of other current hymnals.

A new harmonization by James Pearce was first printed in 1872 in his *Hymn Music* (New York), one of the tunebooks prepared for use with the 1871-1874 Episcopal *Hymnal*. This harmonization was also published in Harriett Reynolds Krauth's *Church Book, for Evangelical Lutheran Congregations . . . with Music* (Philadelphia, 1872).

Charles H. Hall and S. B. Whiteley's *Hymnal. . . . With Appropriate Tunes* (New York, 1872) did not include CORONATION, nor did A. H. Messiter's *The Hymnal . . . . With Music As used in Trinity Church, New York* (New York, 1893). It was not until the 1916 *Hymnal* that CORONATION was available in all the tunebooks designed to provide accompaniments for all of the hymns in the then current Episcopal *Hymnal*. *The Hymnal 1982* includes a descant by Michael E. Young.

MH

451 All hail the power of Jesus' Name!

Music: **MILES LANE**

This text and tune have been matched from the date of the first publication of the tune with the first stanza of the text in 1779. Because of the popularity of the American tune CORONATION, this tune of British origin is not sung in the United States as often as it deserves.

Words: See hymn 450.

Music: This tune was associated with Perronet's text from the start when it was published as a supplement to *The Gospel Magazine* in November 1779; at that time the composer, William Shrubsole, was only nineteen years old. The name MILES LANE is first found in the sixth edition of Stephen Addington's *A Collection of Psalm Tunes for Publick Worship* (London, 1786) and the attribution to Shrubsole in the eleventh edition of the same work (1792).

For many decades this tune was the exclusive preserve of dissenters and Methodists. The striking refrain, with threefold repetition of words, is characteristic of the fervent singing then practiced by those sects. The spectacular contrast between the prostration of the angels and the crowning of Jesus results in a range of a twelfth, and the climactic high note with fermata is apt to put a strain on most congregations.

All the early versions are in C, which produces a high G at the third "crown him." The earliest sources, however, did not require the bearer of the tune to sing this note. Originally (see Example 1) this G was not the last note of a rising triad, but the penultimate in a four-note rising arpeggio shared among the four voices: the real climax falls on the fourth and last "crown him"—sung on a C by the sopranos, who have been silent up to that moment. The Unitarian Ralph Harrison had the entire tune sung by the tenors but revised the melody, naming the tune SCARBOROUGH for his *Sacred Harmony* (London, 1784), with completely different third and fourth lines and no refrain; this version was especially popular in Scotland. The Independent Isaac Smith did it another way, with a simplified last line and again no refrain, in the fourth edition of *A Collection of Psalm Tunes* (London, 1784).

Example 1

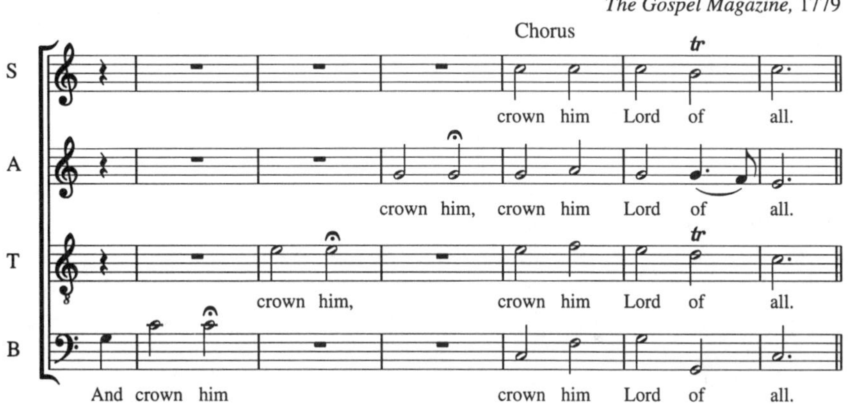

It was another Independent (or Congregationalist) who first took the tune itself to the high G (Example 2).

Example 2

Addington eliminated the sopranos, but allowed the altos to help out the tenors on the high note, and by adding dynamics he still delayed the climax until the last "crown him." Thomas Williams, in *Psalmodia Evangelica* (1789), renaming the tune HARBOROUGH, introduced a crescendo, ending with *forte* on the third "crown him" (Example 3).

Example 3

William Dixon, in *Psalmodia Christiana* (Guildford, 1789), avoided taking the tune to G, substituting D's on the third "crown him" with dominant harmony. The Baptist John Rippon's *A Selection of Psalm Tunes* (London, ca. 1792) follows Dixon's harmonic scheme (Example 4), but with the tune rising to G and marked *forte*. (The small notes in Exs. 3 and 4, and the bass G's in measure 3 of Example 4 are probably for the accompaniment only.)

Example 4

The tune reached the United States, with its original text, in Hans Gram, Samuel Holyoke, and Oliver Holden's *The Massachusetts Compiler* (Boston, 1795), under the new name MARLBOROUGH (Example 5); it looks as if Williams was the source.

Example 5

This remained the usual form in North America. The range remained a problem, especially when the tune reached the more sedate milieu of the Church of England. The editors of *HA&M* transposed down into B♭, but reduced the total range by changing the low tonic at the end of the second phrase into a mediant (in this case, D). It is in this form that MILES LANE is generally known in Britain today. In the *Hymnal*, a still lower key has been chosen, and the sopranos have been reinforced in the low-lying second phrase by tenors singing at the same pitch.

The name MILES LANE is sometimes found with an apostrophe and even an extra *s*, but in fact "Miles" is already a possessive form, being a centuries-old simplication of "Michaeles." Miles Lane, part of which still exists, was the road leading up to the parish church of St. Michael, Crooked Lane, near London Bridge. The medieval church was destroyed in the 1666 Great Fire, rebuilt by Sir Christopher Wren in 1684 to 1689 and demolished in 1831 to make way for a road-widening scheme. However, the reason for calling the tune after the street evidently had no connection with St. Michael's Church. Dr. Stephen Addington, in whose *Collection* (mentioned above) the name first appears, was minister of the Congregational Chapel in Miles Lane. (Compare SILVER STREET, no 548.) Very probably, the tune was first heard there. The tune, matched with this text, was included in J. Ireland Tucker's *The Hymnal With Tunes Old and New* (New York, 1874). The present harmonization with its unison voice parts in measures 3, 4, and 5 first appeared for Episcopalians in the music edition of the 1916 *Hymnal*. The source of this harmonization is not identified.

NT

452 Glorious the day when Christ was born

Music: **FROHLOCKT MIT FREUD**

Fred Pratt Green named this hymn "The Glorious Work of Christ" when he wrote it in 1976. The text appeared in *Hymns III*, where it was matched with this tune. Historic precedent allows performance in unison or in four parts.

Words: Several years prior to Fred Pratt Green's retirement from the active circuit ministry in 1969, he was appointed to a working party commissioned by the Methodist Conference in Great Britain to prepare a supplement to the *Methodist Hymn Book*. His first assignment by the committee was to write words for ILFRACOMBE, a tune by John Gardner that the committee wanted to include in the supplement. The melody called for three alleluias at the end of each line, which imposed peculiar restrictions on the writing: each line had to have some sort of grammatical completeness in itself and, of course, each line had to express a sentiment to which alleluia was an appropriate response.

This led to an attractive and bracing hymn that is rich, condensed, and filled with vivid images. The apocalyptic last stanza, which grows quite naturally out of the preceding stanzas, makes this hymn unusual among modern hymns. The author acknowledges a debt to Christopher Smart's *A Song to David* (London, 1763) for the repetitions of the word "glorious" at the beginning of every stanza, as well as some of the more vigorous and uncommon aspects of the hymn (see 386/387), which are derived from certain stanzas of Smart's poem, slightly modified.

Today the hymn is rarely sung to the intended music. *The Hymnal 1982* prints it with a tune that omits all the alleluias except the last set.

Music: The tune FROHLOCKT MIT FREUD is taken from the *Psalmen Davids, hiebevorn in Teutsche Reimen gebrachte, durch D.*

"Jesus came, the heavens adoring." The work of Gerald Near, composer and church musician, LOWRY is a tune of gentle warmth and harmonic richness. Written in ABA[1] form, the B phrase ascends by fourths, achieving a climax on the highest pitch of the tune. This sense of motion is enhanced by movement through chords as diverse as D, G, B, and E in contrast to the completely diatonic harmonies of the A sections. The repeat of the A phrase, sung to an alleluia refrain, gives quiet strength to these traditional cries of praise. The tune name honors friends of the composer.

CAD/RG

455 O Love of God, how strong and true

Music: **DUNEDIN**

This hymn on the Incarnational Love of God first appeared in a publication of the Episcopal church in *Hymns III*. It is continued in *H82* with two contemporary tunes.

Words: Horatius Bonar, a minister in the Free Church of Scotland, was a prolific hymn writer who included this text in his *Hymns of Faith and Hope*, 2nd series (London, 1861). The original hymn had ten stanzas. James Bonar, writing in the *Dictionary of Hymnology*, said of Dr. Bonar's hymns that they "satisfy the fastidious by their instinctive good taste; they mirror the life of Christ in the soul, . . . they win the heart by their tone of tender sympathy, they sing the truth of God in ringing notes" (*Julian*, 161). Certainly, this is the case in this hymn, which reflects the sentiments of Isaac Watts as found in "Nature with open volume stands" [434].

Music: See hymn 31.

MS

456 O Love of God, how strong and true

Music: **DE TAR**

This text appeared in *Hymns III* matched with this contemporary tune. The metrical structure of the text, four eight-syllable phrases each containing a separate thought, fits the form of the tune in which its four phrases are all satisfying musical lines each separated by rests.

Words: See hymn 455.

Music: Composed in 1970, the tune DE TAR brought to Calvin Hampton international recognition as a composer of hymn tunes. It was first included in manuscript form in a set of three tunes and made available to interested persons. Dr. Vernon de Tar, Organist/Choirmaster, Church of the Ascension, New York City, a close friend of the composer and a musician dedicated to the performance of new music, was the first to use the tune in a hymn festival at Ascension Church. Upon its acceptance for publication with ABREU and PAMBRUN in *Three Hymn Tunes* (St. Louis, 1973), Mr. Hampton named the tune DE TAR to honor his supportive colleague.

Originally intended for use with the Isaac Watts text "Before the Lord Jehovah's throne," it was included with other texts in the *Second Supplement to the Hymnal 1940* (New York, 1975) and *Hymns III*; the *Hymnal of the United Church of Christ* (Philadelphia, 1974); *Ecumenical Praise* (Carol Stream, IL, 1977); *Worship II* (Chicago, 1975), and *Worship*, 3rd ed. (Chicago, 1986); and *Hymns of the Saints* (Independence, MO, 1981). It is included with two texts in *H82*.

An LM tune in the style of a slow rock song, DE TAR is distinguished by a very linear, lyric melody. Its two carefully balanced phrases echo one another and provide formal unity and immediate accessibility. The accompaniment has three independent parts to which the composer has added an optional obbligato* fourth line. The organ pedal line opens with a very distinctive dotted rhythmic pattern ♩⁀♩. ♪ ♩⁀♩. ♪ that moves against the steady quarter and eighth note rhythm of the melody. In the second half, the pedal line moves briefly in half notes supporting the basically half note harmonic rhythm of the setting. The left-hand part throughout is chordal and moves in a steady, syncopated pattern of 𝄾 ♩ ♪. The melody, played by the right hand, is echoed at the interval of one measure by the obbligato part. Ever practical, the composer suggests that the obbligato in the right hand of the accompaniment may be played by an assistant, sung by sopranos, or played on a solo instrument. The composer further points out that this hymn works well with guitar and/or bass guitar.

Dr. Erik Routley writes of Mr. Hampton's scores as "usually complex and contrapuntal. An organ accompaniment independent of the melody line gives many of them an appearance of being strophic songs in the manner of the classic Lieder-writers. Each tune is composed with a clear eye to the text, and the number of styles he explores is as great as the number of tunes he has written . . . . It is fair to say that nobody so far has achieved as completely as Hampton a liberated hymn writing style while at the same time insisting on providing a truly congregational tune."[1] All these qualities are encapsulated in the tune DE TAR.

1. E. Routley, *The Music of Christian Hymns* (Chicago, 1981), 175.

RG

457 Thou art the Way, to thee alone

***Music:* ST. JAMES**

This hymn, which first appeared in an Episcopal hymnal in 1826, has the distinction of being one of the two hymns by American authors to appear in the first edition of *HA&M* (London, 1861). The tune ST. JAMES is also distinguished historically, being one of the tunes included in the *Proposed Book of Common Prayer* (Philadelphia, 1786) (see the essay "Psalmody in America to the Civil War," vol. 1, 393).

Words: "Thou art the Way, to thee alone" is one of the most highly regarded American hymn texts of the nineteenth century. It was introduced in Great Britain in Edward Bickersteth's *Christian Psalmody* (London, 1833). Its author, George Washington Doane, first published the hymn in his *Songs by the Way* (New York, 1824). Based on Jn. 14:6, each of the first three stanzas opens with one of Christ's self-descriptions as "the Way, the Truth, and the Life." Each attribute is then followed by material that builds on it. Stanza 4 combines all three statements and closes with a prayer that we may come to know that way. With very slight alterations, all stanzas are included in *H82*.

Music: There is no doubt of this tune's association with the fashionable church of St. James', Westminster (now known as St. James', Piccadilly), built by Sir Christopher Wren as a private chapel for Lord St. Albans in 1680 and made a parish church in 1685, for it was first printed in a booklet specially designed for that church, *Select Psalms and Hymns for the Use of the Parish-Church and Tabernacle of St. James' Westminster* (London, 1697). It is probable, though not certain, that the tune was composed by Raphael Courteville, Sr., organist there from 1691 to 1729. The only contemporary attribution to him is in Philip Hart's *Melodies Proper to be Sung to Any of the Versions of the Psalms of David* (London, 1716).

Another possible composer is William Croft. John Barker, a former pupil of Croft's who was in possession of some of his music in manuscript, attributed ST. JAMES to his old master in a book in which he also published some of Croft's charity hymns: *A Select Number of the Best Psalm Tunes* (Birmingham, ca. 1750).[1]

This was the only new tune introduced into John Playford's *Whole Book of Psalms in Three Parts* (London) between the first edition of 1677, and the nineteenth of 1738, and it was in more than 250 printed collections in the eighteenth century. The first American printing (out of 57 up to the year 1810) was in Thomas Walter's *Grounds and Rules of Music* (Boston, 1721). It was the first of the eighteen tunes attached to the *Proposed Book of Common Prayer* published in 1786.

Many texts have been used with this tune. According to Erik Routley, the first marriage with the current text was in *HA&M* (London, 1861).[2] The harmonization there was exactly as it is here apart from chords 6 and 7, where (oddly enough) the alto, tenor, and bass of chord 6 were exchanged with those of chord 7.

---

1. See *The Musical Times*, 119 (1978), 539-41. Compare hymn no. 680.
2. E. Routley, *The Music of Christian Hymnody* (Chicago, 1981), 93.

TAR/NT

458 My song is love unknown

***Music:* LOVE UNKNOWN**

This profound and beautiful poem on the true meaning of love as exemplified in the life of Jesus Christ is matched to a tune of equally sublime beauty. In this form, it is now found in many English-language hymnals around the world.

Words: Although *H40* was greatly enriched by numerous texts and tunes discovered in *Songs of Praise* (London, 1925), this hymn was one of its unfortunate omissions. It was included, however, in both *MHSS* and *Hymns III* and had gained considerable popularity among Episcopal congregations even before its first *Hymnal* appearance in the present collection.

A pattern of long neglect followed by great popularity has, in fact, characterized the history of this text. It originally appeared as one of nine poems in *The Young Man's Meditation, or some few Sacred Poems upon Select Subjects, and Scriptures. By Samuel Crossman, B.D.* (London, 1664). None of these was taken into eighteenth-century hymn collections. Though three other poems by Crossman found their way into various hymnals in the first half of the nineteenth century, "My song is love unknown" remained unused until the pioneering and largely self-taught hymnologist Daniel Sedgwick reprinted Crossman's small collection (London, 1863). Shortly thereafter it was included in the *Anglican Hymn Book* (London, 1868), set to Henry Lawes's PSALM 47. It then appeared in a succession of hymnals, eventually being set to the splendid tune John Ireland wrote for it, which has proved the perfect vehicle for the text.

Crossman's text is based primarily on Matthew's account of the Passion (especially chapter 27), with distinct overtones of Phil. 2:5-11 and Jn. 1:1-18. Additional allusions include: st. 1: Jn. 4:8-11; st. 3, Mt. 21:9 and Mk. 11:10; st. 4, Mt. 11:5; st. 6, Mt. 8:20, Lk. 9:58, and Lk. 23:50-53.

It is possible that the phrase "love unknown" in the opening line derives from George Herbert's allegorical poem by that title. The fourth line of st. 7 may also be an intentional echo of the refrain of Herbert's "The Sacrifice." Narrating Christ's Passion in the first person singular, the first sixty-two stanzas of that meditative poem end with the question "Was ever grief like mine?" and the final stanza concludes "Never was grief like mine."

Like Herbert and the other metaphysical poets, Crossman has adapted to devotional purposes the hyperbolic tone and intensifying techniques formerly associated with Renaissance love poetry. Indeed, the opening line of this hymn could equally well serve as the lament of a lovelorn suitor, and this would not be the first sacred text to be based on a now-forgotten secular original. It is unnecessary, however, to search for any particular model, because Crossman's poem incorporates conventions of countless Petrarchan poems in wordplay on a common root ("Love to the loveless shown, that they might lovely be"), oxymoron ("sweet injuries"), irony ("a murderer they save, the Prince of Life they slay"), claims of uniqueness (in the opening line and in the reiteration of "never"), and paradox ("he to suffering goes, that he his foes from thence might free"). Yet these standard devices here gain fresh luster and carry real conviction because they are for once applied to an event capable of sustaining all this heightened emotion: the suffering of Jesus Christ for the salvation of all humanity.

If all the stanzas are sung, this hymn is particularly powerful on Palm Sunday, either as a sequence hymn or during Communion. It can also provide an effective reflection on the mystery of the Incarnation on other occasions, however, if the starred stanzas are omitted.

For the present edition, a few alterations have been made in the text: in 3:1 "strew" was originally "strow" and in 5:5 "steadfast" was "cheerful."

Music: English public school hymnals of the twentieth century have been the source of many distinguished hymn tunes found in *H82* and its predecessor, *H40*. Among them are GONFALON ROYAL [86, 221, 234], MICHAEL [665], REPTON [653], WILDERNESS [39, 394], WOLVERCOTE [289], WOODLANDS [438], and LOVE UNKNOWN [458]. LOVE UNKNOWN, John Ireland's setting of the Crossman text, first appeared in the revision of the *Public School Hymnal* (London, 1919) and later in *Songs of Praise* (London, 1927). A most sympathetic setting of the Crossman text, it reflects the composer's fine skills as a song writer.

"A letter in the *Daily Telegraph*, April, 1950, says that the tune . . . was written in a quarter of an hour on a scrap of paper on the composer's receiving a request from Geoffrey Shaw for a setting of the words."[1] The composer sets his lyric melody in long lines combining the second 66. and two 44. metre phrases in sweeping lines of 12, 8, and 8. He thus makes possible the singing of long verbal lines in these places. The four-part harmonization is very straightforward. The second line, with its ascent to the dominant, is balanced with a startling but gracious descent to the subdominant in the first half of the final line, the overall harmonic pattern being a large I-V-IV-I, rather than the more typical I-IV-V-I.

---

1. W. Milgate, *Songs of the People of God* (London, 1982), 117.

CPD/RG

459 And have the bright immensities

***Music:* HALIFAX**

This text matched with this tune first appeared in *H40*, where it gained immediate attention because of its fresh poetic imagery and its charming tune. In succeeding years, with flights into outer space and landings on the moon, this hymn has gained even greater relevance and use because of its references to "the bright immensities," the constellations, "flaming suns," and "interstellar space."

Words: "And have the bright immensities," a striking text by Howard Chandler Robbins, was first printed in *The Living Church*, April 4, 1931, and later included in his *Way of Light* (New York, 1933). In addition to its inclusion in H. Augustine Smith's *New Church Hymnal* (New York, 1937), the text gained its greatest recognition through its inclusion in *H40*. Robbins served on the JCCM that prepared the texts of that edition. Although it is included among the hymns for "Jesus Christ our Lord," the text is also appropriate for use on the Feast of the Ascension.

Music: Over the years the oratorios and operas of George Frideric Handel have been fertile ground for hymnal editors in search of new hymn tunes. For example, in his work as musical editor of *H40*, Canon Winfred Douglas took an aria from Handel's late oratorio *Susanna*, "Ask if yon damask rose be sweet," as the basis of his tune HALIFAX. John Wilson writes that the popularity of this Handel tune was such that it appeared "in all sorts of versions and was given hymn tune status in the third edition of Butts's *Harmonia Sacra*[1] [see Example 1]. An American edition of this book was published at Andover, Massachusetts, in 1816."

Example 1

Reproduced from *The Southern Harmony & Companion* by William Walker. Edited by Glenn C. Wilcox. © 1987, 1993 by The University Press of Kentucky.

A comparison of the Butts and Douglas editions of HALIFAX reveals that Butts uses the complete Handel melody with occasional modifications in the bass line. Douglas uses the first three phrases of the Handel tune and, dropping the last ten measures, repeats the opening phrase as the final phrase of his arrangement. The end result is an AA^1BA tune of great appeal.

In their research into original sources, the Hymn Music Committee of the SCCM studied the score of Handel's aria and asked Dr. David Hurd, a member of the committee, to produce an arrangement that preserved as much of the original as was practical. The end result is an edition for keyboard and voice that preserves the form of the melody created by Canon Douglas, but includes, with some modifications, Handel's original introduction, coda, and accompaniment as scored for stringed instruments. In his report to the committee on his work, Dr. Hurd wrote "the instrumental scoring for the body of Handel's aria is more spare than would be desirable for hymn accompaniment and often is without a functional bass line. It was necessary, therefore, to devise a reasonable and stylistic bass line utilizing, where possible, Handel's own phrases." In writing of a performance practice for the tune, Dr. Hurd continued, " . . . it may be desirable to consider the body of the hymn tune as 'concertino' and play it on a secondary principal chorus or without mixture." In order to preserve the "concertato" flavor of the original music in the hymn setting, one might play the coda at the beginning of each stanza, beginning the next without introduction. Earlier in his report, Dr. Hurd also wrote of the performance practice for the introduction and coda, "these sections may be understood as intended for 'ripieno' and will be effective played on the principal chorus of a pipe organ."

---

1. *The Hymn*, vol. 37, no. 1, January 1986, 26.

TAR/RG

460 Alleluia! sing to Jesus!

Music: **HYFRYDOL**

This hymn of praise achieved a significant increase in popularity and use with its matching in *H40* with the Welsh tune HYFRYDOL. Because of the richness of its biblical allusions this hymn is appropriate for use on many liturgical occasions.

Words: William Chatterton Dix's text first appeared in his *Altar Songs, Verses on the Holy Eucharist* (London, 1867). The following year it was included in the Appendix to the first edition of *HA&M*. Rich in biblical imagery, it is based on several New Testament passages: Jn. 6:41-59, Heb. 9:11-14, and Rev. 5:9. Dix entitled it "Redemption by the Precious Blood." It is variously appropriate for Ascensiontide, the Eucharist, and General Use.

In his cryptic and not always kindly judgment, Percy Dearmer wrote of this text, "It makes up in heartiness what it lacks in beauty and intellectual power."[1] The hymn entered the *Hymnal* in 1892.

---

1. P. Dearmer, *Songs of Praise Discussed* (London, 1933), 152.

Music: This tune was composed by Rowland Hugh Prichard about 1830 when he was only twenty years old and was published in a three-part version in his *Cyfaill y Cantorion* (Llanidloes, 1844) (The Singer's Friend). It then appeared in *Halelwiah Drachefn* (Carmarthen, 1855) ("Hallelujah Again") edited by Griffith Harris. Its composition at that time is remarkable in that the reforms in hymn singing were barely beginning to stir (see the essay "The Welsh Hymn Tune," vol. 1, 310).

HYFRYDOL became widely popular after its inclusion in *Alexander's Hymns No. 3* (New York, 1915) and in *EH*. It has proved popular to both the texts to which it is set in this book and is useful with many others.

The present arrangement was made for *H40*: the pedal in the seventh line, as in the Geoffrey Shaw arrangement, *The Descant Hymn Tune Book* (London, n.d.), is added for *H82*.

The tune is unusual in two linked respects: first, that it is entirely within the compass of a fifth, except for the rise to the sixth degree of the scale in the last line; second, that having begun as if it were in the conventional AABA pattern, it surprises by having the last two lines as variants (a different sequence based on the same descending notes) on B, giving rise to the one high note in the last line. The tune name means "joyful."

The third in Vaughan Williams's *Three Preludes on Welsh Hymn Tunes for Organ* (1920), this tune receives a strong, dissonant treatment that must disturb many singers' understanding of the nature of what is, on one reading, a placid tune.

MS/AL

461 *Alleluia! sing to Jesus*

Music: **ALLELUIA**

The matching of this text and tune can be traced to the 1868 Supplement to *HA&M*. The first appearance of the text in an Episcopal collection was in the 1892 edition of the *Hymnal*, and it was matched with this tune in the Hutchins music edition of that book.

Words: See hymn 460.

Music: ALLELUIA was written by Samuel Sebastian Wesley for "Alleluia! sing to Jesus!" in the 1868 Supplement to *HA&M*. It is thus one of the tunes Wesley may have had opportunity to hear in use in his lifetime. The cadence on the mediant major in measures 11-12, together with the return via a secondary dominant, are noteworthy.

WTJ

462 *The Lord will come and not be slow*

Music: **YORK**

With the matching of this text and tune, we have one of those rare combinations in hymnody, the work of a father and son.

Words: This text is a cento* of verses from a group of psalm paraphrases by John Milton that appeared in his collected *Poems, &c upon Several Occasions* (London, 1673) with the following heading:

> April, 1648, J.M.
> Nine of the Psalms done into Metre, wherein all but what is in a different Character, are the very words of the Text, translated from the Original.

True to this promise, there then follow verse-by-verse CM paraphrases of Pss. 80 through 88, with all Milton's interpolated words in "a different character" (i.e., in italics) and marginal glosses to supply the Hebrew originals.

The cento printed here first appeared in the *New Congregational Hymn Book* (London, 1859), then in the *Primitive Methodist Hymnal* (London, 1889), W. Garrett Horder's *Worship Song* (London, 1905), and *EH*, from which it entered the *Hymnal* in *H40*. These stanzas are selected from paraphrases of the following verses:

1 Ps. 85:13
2 Ps. 85:11
3 Ps. 82:8
4 Ps. 86:9
5 Ps. 86:10

No changes have been made in the final three stanzas, but prior to its use as a hymn the first stanza appeared in this form:

Before him Righteousness shall go
His Royal Harbinger,
Then will he come, and not be slow,
His footsteps cannot err.

In st. 2 "show" was originally "then" and "on us below" was "on mortal men"; these changes for the sake of inclusive language (made for *H82*) do not violate Milton's literalism since the affected words were all italicized in his version.

Although portions of Milton's paraphrase of Ps. 84, "How lovely are thy dwellings fair," have met with some use (see 517), most of his very literal treatments of these nine psalms have proven too leaden to rise to the level of popular hymnody. The present text, however, can be very effectively used during Advent and on other occasions with an eschatological emphasis. Also, because it avoids Christianizing the psalms, it provides an appropriate text for interfaith worship.

Music: This tune, with its characteristic series of upward third leaps and its perfectly rounded sonatalike form, seems to be of Scottish origin. It first appeared in the 1615 Scottish psalm book *The CL. Psalmes of David, in Prose and Meeter* (Edinburgh, 1615) as one of "The XII Common Tunes, to the which all Psalmes of eight syllables in the first line, and sixe in the next may be sung." It was called THE STILT, perhaps in reference to its motion by long strides. Under that name it remained, with the other "common tunes," one of the twelve musical pillars of the Church of Scotland.

Thomas Ravenscroft, when rounding up the most popular tunes for his *Whole Booke of Psalmes . . . Composed into 4 Parts* (London,

1621), selected THE STILT and renamed it YORK, a choice that probably had no geographical significance, since Ravenscroft systematically used the names of cathedrals and choral foundations to designate the tunes in his book. The musical pitches of the tune were exactly as in the Scottish book, except that the thirteenth note (B) now lacked a sharp (in modern terms, a natural sign). There were some minor changes in rhythm.

Ravenscroft commissioned three different settings of the tune; one by Simon Stubbs for Pss. 100 and 115; another by John Milton, father of the poet, for Pss. 27 and 66; and a third, also by Milton, for Ps. 138 and "A Prayer to the Holy Ghost." The first Milton setting is the basis of the one in *EH* that was taken directly into the *Hymnal*. Milton's setting consisted of a somewhat crude, pretonal series of unrelated root-position triads, apart from the two cadences. His main chord choices were retained here, but with slightly smoother part-writing and, of course, with tenor and cantus parts exchanged. The rhythm returns to the Scottish original, apart from the rests between the phrases (*Frost*, 205). The Stubbs version has a high-ranging cantus part that makes an attractive descant.[1]

Example 1

The tune has always remained popular in Britain, and its history is like that of many other early psalm tunes. It was used many times over by John Playford, and an organ setting by Thomas Tomkins appeared in *Musica Deo Sacra* (London, 1668) (see Example 1).

The earliest treble-led, four-voice setting is in a 1698 tune supplement to Tate and Brady's *New Version of the Psalms* (London). Another originated in a parish church in the tune's name city, York; it was printed in Thomas Wanless's *The Metre Psalm-Tunes* (London, 1702). Sir John Hawkins, in his *History of Music* (London, 1776), writes, "This tune is so well known that within memory half the nurses of England were used to sing it by way of lullaby, and the chimes of many country churches have played it six or eight times in 24 hours from time immemorial"—presumably with a B^{b} rather than a B natural at the medial cadence.[2]

In the course of many decades of unaccompanied congregational singing, the many gaps in the melody tended to be filled in by stepwise passing notes. This can be seen in actual musical notation in a country psalmody collection: Robert Barber's *David's Harp Well Tuned*, 3rd ed. (London, 1753), gives a four-voice setting of Ps. 4, of which the tenor melody is as shown in Example 2.

Example 2

Psalm IV, called the Old Way of Singing.

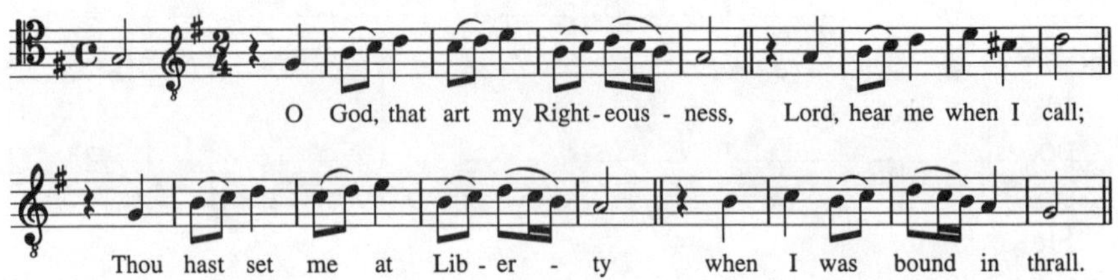
O God, that art my Right-eous - ness, Lord, hear me when I call;
Thou hast set me at Lib - er - ty when I was bound in thrall.

The same process could also take place in an urban setting where there was an organ. John Freckleton Burrowes, organist at St. James' Church, Westminster, published an equally ornate version of YORK for voice and bass in *A Collection of Old and New Psalm Tunes Containing Among Others Those Which are Sung at St. James Westminster* (London, 1819).

The tune was in the early American tune supplements from 1698 onwards, but never achieved in the United States the degree of popularity that it enjoyed in the British Isles. It is not known who first had the happy idea of uniting Milton's tune setting with his son's text; in the *Hymnal*, this match dates from 1940.

---

1. Given in M. Frost, *Historical Companion to Hymns Ancient and Modern* (London, 1962), 306, and *EH*, no. 472.

2. J. Hawkins, *A General History of the Science and Practice of Music* (London, 1853, repr. New York, 1963), 502.

CPD/NT

463 He is the Way

Music: **HALL**

Occasionally hymnal editors select from the works of major poets poems or portions of poems not written as hymns that show strong potential as congregational song. "He is the Way" from the Christmas oratorio *For the Time Being* by the modern poet W. H. Auden, is such a text. *For the Time Being*, a poem of major proportions, was written between 1941 and 1942 as a libretto for an extended work by Benjamin Britten, a work that the great British composer never completed. It is matched here with HALL, a tune written for use with it in *H82*.

Words: This brief poem, which makes a commanding hymn text, was originally a chorus appearing at the end of the W. H. Auden poem *For the Time Being* in the section "The Flight into Egypt." Each stanza of the text opens with a quotation from the Gospel of John 14:6: "He is the Way," " . . . the Truth," and " . . . the Life." Following each quote, the poet urges us to "follow him," "to seek him," and to "love him." Throughout the text, the author employs exceptional poetic language that evokes keenly imaginative faith responses. In st. 1, for example, Auden writes:

> Follow him through the Land of Unlikeness,
> you will see rare beasts and unique adventures.

What does he mean? Are these places where we live or perhaps the locale of our dreams? Are the "rare beasts" and "unique adventures" the people we encounter on the streets, at work, or in our dreams? Are these the unexpected events that occur both in and out of the conscious experience of life? The poet does not answer these questions, but he does give us the space and the freedom to fill in the gaps with our own answers, which may be different from those of the person singing the hymn with us and may change as we grow and experience more fully the living Lord as the "Way," the "Truth," and the "Life."

As a hymn text "He is the way" was first included in *The Cambridge Hymnal* (Cambridge, 1967) set to SANTA BARBARA by Arthur Bliss, a tune commissioned for use with it in that collection. In the United States it first appeared in the Presbyterian hymnal *The Worshipbook* (Philadelphia, 1972) and later in *Ecumenical Praise* (Carol Spring, IL, 1977). This is its first appearance in the *Hymnal* of the Episcopal Church. Dr. Richard Wetzel, a member of the *Worshipbook* committee, in a conversation with Dr. Glover, Editor of *H82c*, recalling the work of that group, assumed that inclusion of the Auden text in that hymnal came about as the result of a suggestion from the late Erik Routley, an enthusiastic supporter of the poem as a hymn text, who was interested in seeing its expanded use in contemporary collections.

Music: HALL by David Hurd, composer, concert organist, and teacher, is the first of the two tunes included for use with the Auden text "He is the way." Written for *H82* in 1984, the tune honors Dr. Barbara Hall, a teaching colleague of Mr. Hurd at General Theological Seminary in New York City at the time of the tune's composition, and now a retired Professor of New Testament at The Protestant Episcopal Theological Seminary in Virginia. HALL is a very lyrical setting, a spiritual song with a sensitive accompaniment in which the inner voices move at moments of repose in the melody line. The syncopated pattern of the bass sets up a wonderfully gentle rocking pulse. An expansive, sensuous line at the end of the tune creates a striking climax in a setting that effectively overcomes the obstacles of the irregular metre of the text.

RG

464 He is the Way

Music: **NEW DANCE**

An early appearance of this text as a congregational hymn was in the 1972 Presbyterian hymnal, *The Worshipbook*. In that appearance, it was matched with a tune written for use with it, NEW DANCE.

Words: See hymn 463.

Music: Richard Wetzel composed NEW DANCE in 1972 for use with "He is the Way" in *The Worshipbook* (Philadelphia, 1972). In this setting, the composer, a member of the committee that prepared this Presbyterian hymnal, uses an economy of means: simple harmonic progressions, moving inner voices and subtle rhythmic patterns, and a one-syllable, one-note melody that is diatonic in nature and limited to the first five notes of the scale of F, G, A♭, B♭, C. A downward octave leap at the end of the tune confidently supports the climax of the text. In this way, Richard Wetzel has skillfully fashioned a tune that beautifully fits the irregular metre of the text.

RG

465 Eternal light, shine in my heart

Music: **ACH BLEIB BEI UNS**

The great religious writings of the past have often provided the inspiration for the creation of new hymn texts. For example, one has only to look at the works of the priest-poet F. Bland Tucker, who was inspired by the writings of some of the early Church Fathers. "Father, we thank thee who hast planted" [302 and 303] is based on prayers from the *Didache*, while "From God, Christ's deity came forth" [443] is based on the writings of Ephrem of Edessa. The prayers of Alcuin, a medieval monastic scholar, were the motivation for the creation of this text by a contemporary British priest-poet, Christopher Idle. It is matched here with a sixteenth-century chorale tune.

Words: This text was written in 1977 at Limehouse Rectory in East London, England, where its author, Christopher Idle, then lived. It was suggested by the brief prayer of Alcuin included (in an English translation) in *Daily Prayer* (Oxford, 1941), a collection of prayers edited by Eric Milner-White and George Briggs. The compilers do not identify the source of Alcuin's words.

The poet often used this book as a source of prayers in leading public worship, and this particular prayer struck him as well suited to adaptation as a hymn. This text was drafted with the tune HERONGATE in mind; one of its first uses was to OMBERSLEY (at Ealing Parish Church in 1978 at the Institution of Michael Saward as Vicar). When first published in *Hymns for Today's Church* (London, 1982), two new tunes were provided as alternatives and in *H82* two further tunes are offered.

This metrical version enlarges slightly on Alcuin's prayer as translated, and puts more personally in the singular what he prayed for "our hearts" (etc.) in the plural. Most of the second stanza is an addition, although its series of requests (echoing themes in the opening part of Ephesians) are intended to continue the thought of st. 1. "Costly grace" is a phrase of Dietrich Bonhoeffer, expounded in *The Cost of Discipleship* (New York, 1949), contrasted not with "free grace" but with "cheap grace." Though the name of Jesus Christ is not mentioned, his title of Savior and the suggestion of costs to him (st. 3) should sufficiently point to his presence, crucified and now glorified.

Music: An embryonic form of this melody appeared in *Geistliche Lieder D. Martini Lutheri, und anderer frommen Christen* (Leipzig, 1589). Five years later a variant form (*Zahn* 439) appeared in Seth Calvisius's *Hymni sacri Latini et Germanici* (Leipzig, 1594), with the text "Danket dem Herrn heut und allzeit." The melodic form was further refined in Samuel Scheidt's *Tabulaturbuch hundert Geistlicher Gesänge* (Leipzig, 1650) and associated with the Melanchthon/Selnecker text "Ach bleib bei uns, Herr Jesu Christ." It is this latter form that is found in *H82*.

The harmonization is based on that of Calvisius, from his *Hymni sacri Latini et Germanici*, but with voice-part alterations following Laurentius Stiphel, *Odae Spirituales* (Jena, 1607). In the original Calvisius setting, the melody is given in the alto voice (see Example 1, which is slightly modified to follow the later form of the melody); Stiphel, with some minor modifications, rewrote the setting with the descant (soprano) voice in the tenor.

Example 1

ACH BLEIB BEI UNS. Setting by Calvisius (1594), melody in the alto

The immediate source for *H82* was the *Liedboek voor de Kerken* (The Hague, 1973).

By the eighteenth century the tune was sung in an isometric form. For example, Bach used it in the third movement of his Cantata 6, "Bleib bei uns, denn es will Abend werden," which he later rewrote as one of the Schübler chorales for organ (BWV 649).

CI/RAL

466 Eternal light, shine in my heart

***Music:* JACOB**

For the second appearance of this text in *H82*, a tune composed for use with it by a contemporary American composer was chosen.

Words: See hymn 465.

Music: The tune JACOB was composed for use with this text by the contemporary American composer Jane Marshall. It was commissioned by the parents of Sarah Jacob for use at her confirmation at First Methodist Church, Richardson, TX, thus the name JACOB. This richly harmonized tune in four balanced phrases fits within a very comfortable vocal range. The placement of a long note with important words enhances its singability, supports the verbal structure of the text and gives an added sense of momentum to the setting. JACOB is also used at 242 with the William Bright text for the Feast of St. Thomas, "How oft, O Lord, thy face hath shone."

RG

467 Sing, my soul, his wondrous love

Music: **ST. BEES**

This much-loved text has been included in the *Hymnal* of the Episcopal Church continuously since its first appearance in 1826. It appears matched with this Dykes tune, which has added to its popularity since matched with it in the Hutchins music edition of the 1892 *Hymnal*. Subsequent music editions have continued this relationship.

Words: This text's first known appearance was in *Hymns and Spiritual Songs* (Baltimore, 1801). Nothing is known of its author. The first stanza only appeared as an optional text with the Latin "O sanctissima, O purissima" for the tune SICILIAN MARINERS [344, 708] in Benjamin Carr's *Masses, Vespers, Litanies, Hymns . . .* (Philadelphia, 1805). The text, which has experienced very limited use in the hymnals of other denominations, has recently gained popularity and use through a setting for SATB chorus by Ned Rorem (New York, 1962).

Music: This tune is one of twenty-eight composed by John Bacchus Dykes that appeared in the second edition of Richard R. Chope's *The Congregational Hymn and Tune Book* (London, 1862). Under the date of 31 October 1862, Dykes wrote in his diary "Sent off the last batch of Tunes to Chope."[1] ST. BEES was presumably composed sometime before this date. It was originally associated with William Walsham How's "Jesus! Name of wondrous love!" [252], but was later more familiarly known in Britain as the tune for Cowper's "Hark, my soul, it is the Lord" after the editors of *HA&M* made the text/tune association in the new edition of 1875. The tune name recalls St. Bees College, founded in 1816 for the training of nonuniversity students.

---

1. See *Life and Letters of John Bacchus Dykes* (London, 1897), ed. J. T. Fowler, 80.

MBJ/RAL

468 *It was poor little Jesus*

Music: **IT WAS POOR LITTLE JESUS**

This spiritual, with its text appropriate for both Christmas and Easter, appears in the *Hymnal* for the first time. Written in a call and response style (see the essay "Cultural Diversity," vol. 1, 29), the hymn can be effectively sung in dialogue between a solo voice, a section of the choir, or the full choir (the call) and the congregation (the response).

Words:

Call: It was poor little Jesus,
Response: yes;
Call: He was born in a manger,
Response: Yes, yes;
Call: And laid in a manger;
Response: yes, yes;
Wasn't that a pity and a shame, Lord, Lord,
Wasn't that a pity and a shame.

This African Spiritual for Christmas and Easter covers both the birth and death of Christ and is sung by some congregations for both celebrations. While four stanzas are included in *H82*, another popular version not only includes seven stanzas, but replaces the internal refrain "yes, yes" with "Hail, Lord." *The Hymnal 1982* arrangement devotes the first two stanzas to the birth, st. 3 to his death, and st. 4 to the resurrection. In the other version, sts. 1 and 2 deal with the birth while sts. 3 through 7 describe his suffering, crucifixion, resurrection, and the Christians' hope for glory.

Po' li'l Jesus, Hail Lawd,
Child o'Mary, Hail Lawd,
Bawn in a stable, Hail Lawd,
Ain' dat a pity an' a shame?

Po' li'l Jesus, Hail Lawd,
Tuck 'im fum a manjuh, Hail Lawd,
Tuck 'im fum 'is mothuh, Hail Lawd,
Ain' dat a pity an' a shame?

Po' li'l Jesus, hail Lawd,
Dey gi'n 'im to de Hebrew, Hail Lawd,

Dey spit on 'is gahment, Hail Lawd,
Ain' dat a pity an' a shame?
Po' li'l Jesus, Hail Lawd,
Dey boun' 'im wid a haltuh, Hail Lawd,
Whupped 'im up de mountain, Hail Lawd,
Ain' dat a pity an' a shame?

Po' Li'l Jesus, Hail Lawd,
Dey nailed 'im to de cross, Hail Lawd,
Dey hung 'im wid de robbuh, Hail Lawd,
Ain' dat a pity an' a shame?

Po' li'l Jesus, Hail Lawd,
Risen fum de darkness, Hail Lawd,
'Scended into glory, Hail Lawd,
Ain' dat a pity and a shame?

Po' li'l Jesus, Hail Lawd,
Meet me in de kingdom, Hail Lawd,
Lead me to my Fathuh, Hail Lawd,
Ain' dat a pity an' a shame?

The text of this spiritual clearly illustrates the comparison of the life of Christ with that of the slaves, most notably in their reference to Christ as poor, and in the internal refrain "wasn't that a pity and a shame?" The sense of equality between "Poor Little Jesus" and the cruelly enslaved inspires no expressions of joy or happiness, only feelings of sorrow. The internal refrain, with its repetition of the word shame, is part of one of the "wandering couplets" found in spirituals. The complete couplet "wasn't that a pity and a (or awful) shame, He hung three hours in mortal pain" is included in "You Hear the Lambs A-Crying," while "wasn't that a pity and a shame" serves as one of the stanzas in "He Never Said A Mumblin' Word."

Music: The melody of this spiritual, set in the minor mode, employs only four of the seven tones in the diatonic scale: E, G, A, and B. While there are several spirituals with melodies based on fewer than five tones—the pentatonic scale so often used in spirituals—the reduced number of tones usually indicates a gradual melodic loss of what is considered superfluous tones. Despite the use of only four tones, the melody is spread over an eleven-note range  and is divided between leader and congregation, while the second part is assigned to both leader and congregation (see above).

The sorrowful nature of the song should in no way detract from a strong traditional rhythmic performance, emphasizing two pulses in each bar. Syncopation is a principal rhythmic feature of the melody, particularly on the word "wasn't," which should be pronounced as one syllable.

First published in *Songs and Games of American Children* (1844-1911), the melody, because its general mold is reminiscent of the Gregorian chant of the Roman Catholic Church, has often been associated with slaves in Creole Louisiana.

HCB

469 There's a wideness in God's mercy

Music: **ST. HELENA**

This text, an example of the sentimental poetry of much nineteenth-century hymnody, appears today in hymnals in a truncated and altered form. It entered the *Hymnal* in 1916 in the three-stanza form we maintain today. Matched with this tune of Calvin Hampton, which complements the altered Faber text, the hymn gains a particular charm missing in other settings.

Words: The Hymnal 1982 presents six of the thirteen quatrains* that Frederick Faber designed, to judge from their placement in his *Hymns* (London, 1861; a briefer version was published in *Oratory Hymns* [London, 1854]), for use during the parish missions that he conducted in both England and in Ireland, still reeling from "the great hunger." Centos* from Faber's work speedily entered the hymnals of many denominations, though hardly any two editors include the same selection or number of stanzas. This provides a most intriguing indication of how each editor viewed the priorities of his constituency. The present st. 1 combines Faber's 4 and 6; st. 2 combines 5 and 10; and st. 3 combines 8 and 13. The last is somewhat changed from the original:

> 13. If our love were but more simple,
> We should take him at his word,
> And our lives would be all sunshine
> In the sweetness of our Lord.

These changes were made by the Text Committee of the SCCM, who felt that Faber's appraisal of life in the original text was unacceptable to contemporary worshipers. Although hardly any editors include Faber's sts. 3 and 11:

> 3. It is God: his love looks mighty,
> But is mightier than it seems:
> 'Tis our Father: and his fondness
> Goes far out beyond our dreams.

> 11. 'Tis not all we owe to Jesus;
> It is something more than all;
> Greater good because of evil,
> Larger mercy through the fall.

His original opening finds favor with those who do not despise rhetorical questions:

> 1. Souls of men, why will ye scatter
> Like a crowd of frightened sheep?
> Foolish hearts, why will ye wander
> From a love so true and deep?

> 2. Was there ever kindest shepherd
> Half so gentle, half so sweet,
> As the Saviour who would have us
> Come and gather round his feet?

Hymns Ancient and Modern includes st. 12:

> 12. Pining souls! come nearer Jesus,
> And oh come not doubting thus,
> But with faith that trusts more bravely
> His huge tenderness for us.

Space exploration may yet bestow fresh relevance on st. 7:

7. There is grace enough for thousands
Of new worlds as great as this:
There is room for fresh creations
In that upper home of bliss.

Hardly anyone has dared include st. 9. The editor of the Canadian Anglican *Book of Common Praise* (Toronto, 1908) omitted it, but when he prepared the collection of 1938, it was included:

9. But we make his love too narrow
By false limits of our own;
And we magnify his strictness
With a zeal he will not own.

Music: The hymn tune ST. HELENA was written in 1978 for use with the Faber text "There's a wideness in God's mercy." It honors the Sisters of the Order of St. Helena who were resident for a number of years at Calvary Church, New York City, where the composer, Calvin Hampton, was Organist/Choirmaster. In this setting, Mr. Hampton has created a plaintive song in binary form. The first half of the A section is built around the reiterated pitch E, which is repeated a major third higher in the second half. The B section, which also consists of sequential sections, opens with a fragment of melody and the rhythm of the A section (Example 1).

Example 1

The tune is supported by a two-part, contrapuntal accompaniment in which the inner voice is a line of eighth notes in a pattern of four, four, and six: [i.] In the second half of the B section, the composer inserts two canonic episodes between the melody and the bass. A brief four-bar introduction is repeated as an interlude between stanzas and as a conclusion. Further interest is added by an instrumental descant for flute or violin, which is suggested for use with st. 3. The descant instrument may also play the top voice of the Interlude and Conclusion. The composer offers these suggestions:

This anthem has many performance possibilities. The accompaniment figure sounds well played by a stringed instrument—a good choir can sing the entire accompaniment under a soloist, on a "loo" syllable (transposing the lowest bass notes up an octave). The obbligato can be rendered on a vowel by a lyric soprano voice, or can be played by another person on the organ.[1]

---

1. C. Hampton, *The Calvin Hampton Hymnary* (Chicago, 1980), Foreword.

RG

470 There's a wideness in God's mercy

***Music:* BEECHER**

This text first appeared in *H16*, where it was matched with this tune, a relationship continued in subsequent editions of the *Hymnal*.

Words: See hymn 469.

Music: John Zundel composed this tune in 1870 (also called LOVE DIVINE, ZUNDEL) for "Love divine, all loves excelling." It was named for Henry Ward Beecher, the pastor of the Plymouth Congregational Church in Brooklyn where Zundel was organist for many years. Its first publication was in Zundel's *Christian Heart Songs, A Collection of Solos, Quartets and Choruses of All Metres* (New York, 1870). Zundel sought to indicate the correct length of time it took to sing each tune in this collection by indicating in the index the number of seconds required to sing a stanza. His time for BEECHER is sixty-five seconds. An early Episcopal use of BEECHER is in James H. Darlington's musical edition of the 1892 *Hymnal* where it is the setting for "Love divine, all loves excelling." The harmonization is altered in *H82* from Zundel's original, which is in B^b, the key it usually appears in in most hymnals.

HE

471 We sing the praise of him who died

Music: **BRESLAU**

This text, inspired by a quotation from the Epistle to the Galatians, entered the *Hymnal* in 1871 and until *H40* was found among the hymns for Lent and Holy Week. In its present position, this hymn gains greater flexibility in satisfying lectionary needs. It appeared matched with this tune in the Hutchins music edition of the 1892 *Hymnal*.

Words: This passion hymn by Thomas Kelly was first published in *Hymns by Thomas Kelly* (Dublin, 1815), under the heading "God forbid that I should glory save in the Cross: Gal. 4:14." In this early version, the final stanza concluded with:

'Tis all that sinners want below;
'Tis all that angels know above.

In the sixth edition of Kelly's *Hymns on Various Passages of Scriptures* (Dublin, 1826), the hymn was revised to provide the form that entered into common usage. It has been in the *Hymnal* since 1871. Speaking of this hymn and Kelly's "The head that once was crowned with thorns" [483], Erik Routley commented, "The two magnificent dogmatic utterances of Thomas Kelly are evangelical, in the sense of urging a total commitment to the mystery of the cross, and Calvinistic in their resurrection background."[1]

---

1. E. Routley, *A Panorama of Christian Hymnody* (Collegeville, MN, 1979), 44.

Music: See hymn 281.

RAL

472 Hope of the world, thou Christ

Music: **DONNE SECOURS**

In a world still torn by war and threats of war, this text speaks with great poignancy and urgency. Matched with a French psalm tune, it is a hymn that has strong ecumenical attributes.

Words: The hymn "Hope of the world, thou Christ" by the Rev. Dr. Georgia Harkness, an ordained Methodist minister, theologian, author, and teacher, was written for use at the Second Assembly of the World Council of Churches meeting in Evanston, IL, in the summer of 1952. The text, based on the assembly theme "Christ, the Hope of the World," was selected from the almost five hundred texts submitted in a search by the Hymn Society of America for ecumenical hymns.

Written in the years immediately following World War II, each stanza of the text opens by addressing Christ as "Hope of the World." Following this, a different descriptive phrase presents a particular quality of Christ's nature that leads to a particular petition. For example, st. 1 opens with "Hope of the world, thou Christ of great compassion" followed by the petition that we, who are spent "by our own false hopes," may be saved "from consuming passion." The succeeding two stanzas are for prayers for peace and guidance; the concluding stanzas are our responses of commitment and faithfulness to Christ as Lord "who dost forever reign!" This is the first appearance of this hymn in the *Hymnal* of the Episcopal Church.

Music: The tune for Marot's Ps. 12, "Donne secours, Seigneur il en est heure," in Calvin's *La forme des prieres et chantz ecclesiastiques* (Geneva, 1542) (*Pidoux* 12b) must have been considered to be inadequate, since it was replaced nine years later by another in *Pseaumes octante trois de David* (Geneva, 1551). This other tune (*Pidoux* 12e), the one that appears in *H82*, was a substantial recomposition of the 1542 tune: the first two lines are identical rhythmically and melodically share similar features, especially at the end of each line; the remaining lines were newly composed. A 10.10. 10.10 adaptation entered into restricted English use in Henry Ainsworth's *The Book of Psalmes Englished both in Prose and Metre* (Amsterdam, 1612) (*Frost*, 318).

The appearance of the 1551 form of the melody in *H82* reflects the contemporary rediscovery by the English-speaking world of the tune tradition of the French Calvinist psalters. The harmonization is based on that found in Claude Goudimel's *Les Pseaumes mis en rime françoise . . . mis en musique à quatre parties* (Geneva, 1565).

RG/RAL

473 Lift high the cross

Music: **CRUCIFER**

This hymn, long popular in the British Church, gained almost immediate acceptance with Episcopal congregations soon after its first appearance in an Episcopal hymnal in *Hymns III*. The text is rich in biblical and baptismal imagery.

Words: This text, considered by some as a possible twentieth-century replacement for "Onward Christian Soldiers," is a revision by Michael Robert Newbolt of a text written earlier by George William Kitchin. The thrust of the text recalls the words of the Emperor Constantine's vision as recorded in Eusebius's *Life of Constantine*, "In hoc signo vinces" ("in this sign thou shalt conquer"). The original form of the text was written by Kitchin for use at a Society for the Propagation of the Gospel Festival in Winchester Cathedral in 1887. The Newbolt revision, a text of twelve stanzas, the first being repeated as a refrain, first appeared in the 1916 Supplement of *HA&M* matched with this tune written for use with it. Newbolt's revision was:

1. Lift high the Cross, the love of Christ proclaim
   Till all the world adore his sacred name.

2. Come, brethren, follow where our Captain trod,
   Our King victorious, Christ the Son of God.
   Lift high the Cross, etc.

3. Led on their way by this triumphant sign,
   The hosts of God in conquering ranks combine.
   Lift high the Cross, etc.

4. Each new-born soldier of the Crucified
   bears on his brow the seal of him who died.
   Lift high the Cross, etc.

5. This is the sign which Satan's legions fear,
   The mystery which angel hosts revere.
   Lift high the Cross, etc.

6. Saved by this Cross whereon their Lord was slain,
   The sons of Adam their lost home regain.
   Lift high the Cross, etc.

7. From north and south, from east and west they raise
In growing unison their songs of praise.
Lift high the Cross, etc.

8. O Lord, once lifted on the glorious Tree,
As thou hast promised, draw men unto thee.
Lift high the Cross, etc.

9. Let every race and every language tell
Of him who saves our souls from death and hell.
Lift high the Cross, etc.

10. From farthest regions let them homage bring,
And on his Cross adore their Saviour King.
Lift high the Cross, etc.

11. Set up thy throne, that earth's despair may cease
Beneath the shadow of its healing peace.
Lift high the Cross, etc.

12. So shall our song of triumph ever be,
Praise to the Crucified for victory.
Lift high the Cross, etc.

A six-stanza form of the text with st. 1 as a refrain appeared in the *Catholic Book of Worship* (Ottawa, Canada, 1972). It uses sts. 1, 2, 3, 4, 8, and 12 of the Newbolt edition and is the source of the text as it first appeared for usage in the Episcopal Church in *Hymns III*. In order to employ more inclusive language, alterations were made in three stanzas. Their original forms were:

st. 2:1	Come, brethren, follow
4:1	Each new-born soldier
3	Bears on his brow
8:4	draw men unto thee.

(This six-stanza form with alterations also appears in the *LBW*.) For use in *H82*, st. 2 was omitted to remove militaristic imagery. The SCCM felt that the themes of this stanza were well covered in the refrain. All other alterations included in *Hymns III* are continued in *H82*.

Music: CRUCIFER was written by Sydney Hugo Nicholson for the Supplement to *HA&M* (London, 1916). Its very accessible, strong, and martial unison refrain has immediate appeal for a congregation. For the stanzas, the composer introduces a four-part setting, which in contrast is more lyric and contemplative than the refrain. In the last two measures there is an effective return to the mood of the refrain through the use of a dotted rhythm in the voice parts and a three-chord martial motif in the last measure of the accompaniment. The tune name CRUCIFER plays on the literal meaning of the word "cross-bearer" to suggest both the person who performs that function in a liturgical procession and each Christian who bears the cross as a baptismal sign (cf. st. 2).

RG

474 When I survey the wondrous cross

Music: **ROCKINGHAM**

This classic text by Isaac Watts is not only one of his finest works, but matched with the tune ROCKINGHAM is recognized as one of the most deeply loved hymns of English-speaking congregations around the world.

Words: Isaac Watts included this text, based on Gal. 6:14 in *Hymns and Spiritual Songs* (London, 1707). In the 1709 and later editions of this collection, Watts changed the second line of the hymn from "Where the young Prince of glory died" to "On which the Prince of glory died." *The Hymnal 1982* continues the form of the text established in *H40* and retains the more poignant original text.

Except for the omission of Watts's fourth stanza, the text appears unaltered. The fourth stanza was:

His dying crimson, like a robe
  spreads o'er his body on the Tree;
then am I dead to all the globe,
  and all the globe is dead to me.

Percy Dearmer writes of this hymn that Watts "in his moments of inspiration belongs to the great line of English poets."[1] "When I survey the wondrous cross" is not only the result of a "moment of inspiration" for Watts, but also has been a great source of inspiration for countless Christians both in life and in the hour of death. This text first appeared in an Episcopal hymnal in 1826.

---

1. P. Dearmer, *Songs of Praise Discussed* (London, 1933), 87.

Music: The present form of ROCKINGHAM is due to Edward Miller, who published it in his *Psalms of David* (London, 1790) with five different metrical psalm texts. It was scored for melody, vocal bass, and keyboard.

Miller stated that "part of the melody" was "taken from a hymn tune," and it is, indeed, very similar to an earlier tune TUNBRIDGE (5.5. 11.5. 5.11. anapaestic). This is found first in a rare collection entitled *Musica Sacra, being a Choice Collection of Psalm and Hymn Tunes, and Chants . . . as they are used in the Right Hon. The Countess of Huntingdon's Chapels, in Bath Bristol &c.* (Bath, ca. 1778) (see Example 1).

The three-part harmony is almost meaningless, yet the upper voice contains, at the end of the third phrase, the ending to that phrase that Miller selected.

TUNBRIDGE next appeared in the Second Supplement to Aaron Williams's *Psalmody in Miniature* (London, 1780). James T. Lightwood's copy of this work has a note below the tune, said to be in Miller's hand, that reads: "Would make good long M."[1] The name ROCKINGHAM, assigned by Miller, has endured; it is not known why he chose to call it after a small Northhamptonshire village. Leonard Ellinwood suggested it was named for the Marquis of Rockingham (1730-1782), sometime prime minister of Great Britain, but offers no evidence (*H40c*, 144).

This fine warm tune is one of the best of its period, with a characteristically complex origin. Its first printing in the United States was in *The Salem Collection of Classical Sacred Music* (Salem, 1805). It has been in Episcopal hymnals since the mid-nineteenth century. The

Example 1

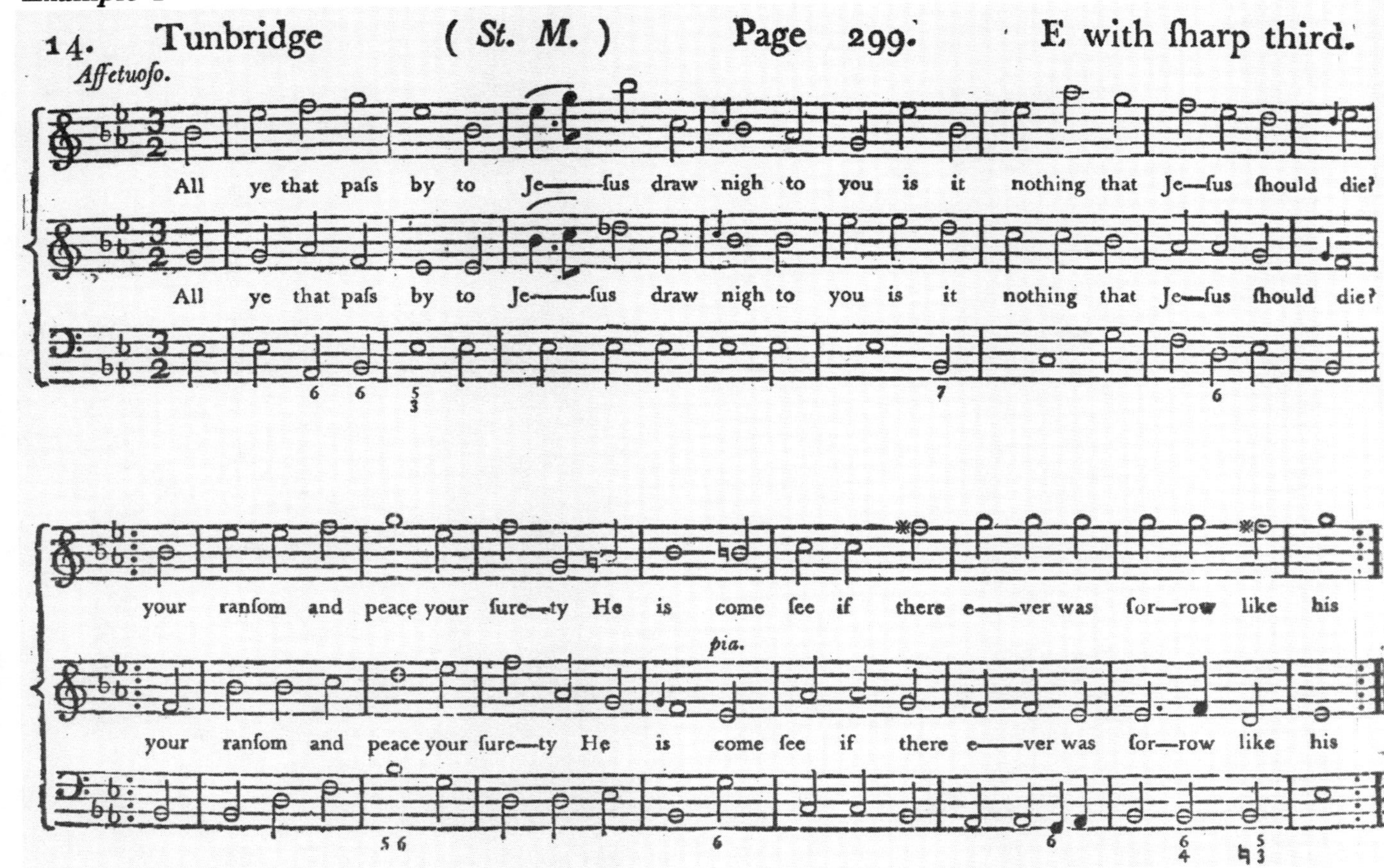

Courtesy of the Clifford E. Barboar Library, Pittsburgh Theological Seminary.

present harmonization is taken from *H40*; its original source is not known. Another harmonization may be found at no. 321.

---

1. This is reproduced in the *Musical Times*, 50 (1909), 314.

TAR/NT

475 God himself is with us

Music: **TYSK**

This text and tune, which entered the *Hymnal* in 1940, over the years have become an important part of the singing tradition of many congregations.

Words:

1. Gott ist gegenwärtig! Lasset uns anbäten
Und in Ehrfurcht vor Ihm tretten;
Gott ist in der Mitten! alles in uns schweige,
Und sich innigst vor Ihm beuge;
Wer Ihn kennt, wer Ihn nennt,
Schlägt die Augen nieder,
Kommt, erhebt euch wieder.

2. Gott ist gegenwärtig! dem die Cherubinen
Tag und Nacht gebücket dienen;
Heilig, Heilig, singen alle Engel-Chören,
Wann sie dieses Wesen ehren:
Herr, vernimm unsre Stimm,
Da auch wir Geringen
Uns're Opffer bringen.

3. Wir entsagen willig allen Eitelkeiten,
Aller Erden Lust und Freuden;
Da liegt unser Wille, Seele leib, und Leben,
Dir zum Eigenthum ergeben;
Du allein solt es seyn,
Unser Gott und Herre;
Dir gebührt die Ehre.

4. Mache mich einfältig, innig, abgeschieden,
Sanftte, und im stillen Frieden;
Mach mich reines Herzens, dass ich deine Klarheit
Schauen mag im Geist und Wahrheit;
Lass mein Herz überwärts
Wie ein Adler schweben,
Und in dir nur leben.

5. Majestätisch Wesen! möcht ich recht dich preisen,
Und im Geist dir Dienst erweisen!
Möcht ich, wie die Engel, immer vor dir stehen.
Und dich gegenwärtig sehen!
Lass mich dir für und für
Trachten zu gefallen,
Liebster Gott, in allen.

6. Luft, die alles füllet! drin wir immer schweben;
Aller Dingen Grund und Leben!
Meer ohn Grund und Ende! Wunder aller Wunder!
Ich senk mich in dich hinunter;
Ich in dir; du in mir;
Lass mich ganz verschwinden,
Dich nur sehn und finden.

7. Du durchdringest alles, lass dein schönstes Lichte
Herr, berühren mein Gesichte;
Wie die zarten Blumen willig ich entfalten,
Und der Sonnen stille halten;
Lass mich so, still und froh,
Deine Strahlen fassen
Und dich wirken lassen.

8. Herr, komm in mir wohnen, lass mein Geist auf Erden
Dir ein Heiligthun noch werden;
Komm, du nahes Wesen! dich in mir verkläre,
Dass ich dich stets lieb und ehre;
Wo ich geh sitz und steh
Lass mich dich erblicken,
Und vor dir mich bücken.

The text "Gott ist gegenwäertig" ("God himself is with us") was written by Gerhardt Tersteegen and first appeared in his *Geistliches Blumengaertlein* (Frankfurt am Main, 1729) as no. 11 in Book III of that volume, entitled "Remembrance of the glorious and delightful presence of God." Stanza 3 as it appears here in Henry Sloane Coffin's translation is from his *Hymns of the Kingdom of God* (New York, 1910). The remaining stanzas, with one minor alteration and a reordering of lines in st. 2 are from *H40*. They are a translation by the members of the Committee on Translations of the Joint Commission on the Revision of the *Hymnal*. In *H82* the stanzas are reordered, those appearing here as sts. 1 through 4 being sts. 1, 4, 2, 3 in *H40*. The alteration in st. 2:4 originally read "Gladly we surrender." The present "Help us to surrender" was felt to be a more honest appraisal of the human condition.

Music: TYSK (*Zahn* 7858) is the melody associated with the "Tysk" ("German") church in Stockholm, Sweden, and sung in the early eighteenth century by the congregation to Joachim Neander's text "Wunderbarer König." The melody, published in Johann Michael Müller's *Neu-aufgesetztes, vollständiges und nach der neu- und reinesten Composition eingerichtetes Psalm- und Choral-Buch* (Frankfurt, 1719), is usually attributed to Müller and was most likely sung by the congregation for some time before its publication. The harmonization is from *H40*.

CS

476 Can we by searching find out God

Music: **EPWORTH**

There is a certain affinity between the question that opens the text of this hymn and the question that God asks of Job, "Where were you when I laid the foundations of the earth?" As in Job's search for an understanding of God's actions in his life, the poet here probes the depths of the nature of God, particularly as she sees it revealed in Jesus Christ. As we sing this text, we gain a picture of the magnitude and mystery of the Creator and share with the poet in a broadened understanding of the meaning of God's actions in life.

Words: "Can we by searching find out God" is a reflective text that describes God's revelation in Christ in challenging and vividly described ways. It is the first published hymn of Elizabeth Cosnett, a member of the staff of St. Katharine's College, Liverpool, England.

Miss Cosnett writes of this text:

> "Can we by searching" was written during the early nineteen-seventies. On one level it arose because my friend and colleague, Ian Sharp, wanted words to set to music and thought that as I was writing a thesis on hymns at the time I could surely produce an actual hymn . . . There was however, another level to it, an eirenic one. I was at that time involved with a Bible study group at my own church in which the question of how to interpet the stories of the birth of Jesus loomed large and caused not merely intellectual debate but real distress to individuals. I badly wanted to put into words what I myself felt to be the meaning of the incarnation for me but in such a way that we could all sing them together without feeling that either our faith or our intellectual integrity was being undermined. As I was working on the words I could quite clearly in my mind see the faces of actual people in our congregation and their expressions of hurt or bewilderment as I had seen them in real life discussion . . . The first draft was revised several times over a period of some years. I once rashly asked my students to do a "practical criticism" exercise on it (without telling them who wrote it). Their response was so stringent that it very nearly ended up in the waste basket for good. I was also deeply indebted to some detailed correspondence with Canon (Cyril) Taylor and the editors of *Ancient and Modern*.[1]

The poet begins the hymn with a question and immediately confronts us with the realization that we, as finite human beings, can never gain by our own efforts a full understanding of the magnitude of God, infinite in every dimension. Elizabeth Cosnett reminds us that it is through Christ, the incarnate Son of God, that God is best comprehended. She also reminds us that it is only when we compare the actions of our lives to the example of the life of Jesus, born in very humble, ordinary surroundings and dying a criminal's death upon the cross, that our lives gain meaning and purpose. It is then that "God breaks in upon our search" and makes "his glory known."

In support of the SCCM's desire to use inclusive language, the first line of the text, which originally read "Can man by searching find out God?" was altered to its present reading. Also, the poet's original fourth stanza has been omitted:

We there may recognize his light,
may kindle in its rays,
find there the source of penitence,
the starting-point for praise.

The text first appeared in *More Hymns for Today*, the supplement to *HA&M* (London, 1980). It has also been included in *Hymns for Today's Church* (London, 1982), *Hymns and Psalms*, the English Methodist Hymnal (London, 1983) and *Rejoice in the Lord* (Grand Rapids, MI, 1985). This is its first appearance in the *Hymnal*.

---

1. Cosnett to Glover, 12 October 1988. Church Hymnal Corporation Papers, New York, NY.

Music: EPWORTH was composed by Charles Wesley, Jr. It appeared in his *Six hymns . . . composed by Charles Wesley, with a hymn by the later Dr. Boyce* (London, ca. 1795), where it was set to John Milton's version of Ps. 84. It was included in part two of Vincent Novello's *The Psalmist: A Collection of Psalm and Hymn Tunes* (London, 1835), where it was called LOUGHTON. In that collection, the ascription reads "Charles Wesley. Arr. by S. Wesley." The name EPWORTH can be traced to the *Free Church Hymn Book* (Paisley, 1882), where the tune was harmonized by Edward Hopkins.

Samuel Wesley once called his brother an "obstinant Handelian" and, indeed, Handelian elements are apparent in EPWORTH—leaps of a sixth and a fifth in the first phrase and in the sequences in measures 5 and 6. The harmonization in *H82* by Martin Shaw from *Songs of Praise* (London, 1931) enhances the tune's character. The tune name honors Epworth in Lincolnshire, the birthplace of John and Charles Wesley, respectively the uncle and father of the composer.

RG/WTJ

477 All praise to thee, for thou, O King divine

Music: **ENGELBERG**

The test of time and the verdict of critics of hymnology mark this text as one of the finest works of F. Bland Tucker. As a poet sensitive to the subtle nuances of music, the text reflects the sturdy, celebrative nature of Vaughan Williams's tune SINE NOMINE for which it is written. As in *H40*, the text appears here matched with the tune ENGELBERG, with SINE NOMINE as a suggested alternative.

Words: This text based on Phil. 2:5-11 was written in 1938 by the Rev. Dr. F. Bland Tucker for use in *H40*. As a member of the Committee preparing texts for that book, Dr. Tucker composed it with Ralph Vaughan Williams's tune SINE NOMINE [287] in mind, "having the same metre and style although more meditative than 'For all the saints' " (*H40c*, 237). Dr. Tucker later wrote: "Vaughan Williams' great tune SINE NOMINE [287] was written for the great words of 'For all the saints,' but since in the Episcopal Church those words are apt to be sung only around All Saints' Day, I ventured to write optional words for general use."[1] This text now appears in major English-language hymnals around the world.

---

1. F. B. Tucker, "Reflections of a Hymn Writer," *The Hymn*, 30 (April, 1979), 116.

Music: See hymn 296.

RG

478 Jesus, our mighty Lord

Music: **MONK'S GATE**

This translation by F. Bland Tucker of a very early Christian hymn first appeared in *H40*. In its present form, the poet gives us a fine example of the felicitous alteration of archaic language to contemporary forms more readily understood by the worshiper.

Words: At the conclusion of Clement of Alexandria's *Paedagogus*, in which Christ is represented as the universal Educator who reveals God's rationality, was the "Hymn to Christ the Saviour." This Dr. F. Bland Tucker translated and arranged as English verse. Four stanzas were adopted in *H40* as "Master of eager Youth" and matched with MONK'S GATE.

The Hymnal 1982 has omitted the first of these four stanzas and begins the hymn with st. 2. Other substantial revisions of the text were made by the poet to replace the archaic second person singular pronouns. In the final stanza "let word and life acclaim" has become "The God of peace acclaim." The imagery of the stanzas retained in *H82* may be seen as more congenial to modern thought than that of the first stanza, which has been omitted.

Dr. Tucker's original text is as follows:

1. Master of eager youth,
   Controlling, guiding,
   Lifting our hearts to truth,
   New power providing;
   Shepherd of innocence,
   Thou art our Confidence;
   To thee, our sure Defence,
   We bring our praises.

2. Thou art our mighty Lord,
   Our strength in sadness,
   The Father's conquering Word,
   True source of gladness;
   Thy Name we glorify,
   O Jesus, throned on high,
   Who gave'st thyself to die
   For man's salvation.

3. Good Shepherd of thy sheep,
   Thine own defending,
   In love thy children keep
   To life unending.
   Thou art thyself the Way:
   Lead us then day by day

In thine own steps, we pray,
   O Lord most holy.

4. Glorious their life who sing,
   With glad thanksgiving,
True hymns to Christ the King
   In all their living:
Ye who confess his Name,
Come then with hearts aflame;
Let word and life proclaim
   Our Lord and Saviour. Amen.

Bland Tucker was not the first translator of this hymn. H. M. Dexter in 1846 rendered Clement's first phrase Στόμιον πώ λων ἀδαῶν (Bridle for untamed colts) as "Shepherd of tender youth."

Music: The tune MONK'S GATE was adapted by Ralph Vaughan Williams for *EH* from a folk melody which he transcribed at Horsham, West Sussex, sung by a Mrs. Harriet Verral of the nearby village of Monk's Gate (see Example 1).

Example 1

This immensely successful hymn tune has become the popular choice in England for John Bunyan's "Pilgrim's Hymn" [565], despite the fact that the words, taken at a natural flow, demand a triple metre tune.

Vaughan Williams made the fundamental decision to change the phrase pattern of the tune from an ABBC to an AABC structure. Rhythmically, he gave weight to the first bar by extending the initial note, making it easier for a congregation to get started. Likewise, he extended the upbeats of lines 2 and 5—lines 3 and 4 are repetitions of 1 and 2—but broke the pattern from this point onward in a manner typical of his own tunes. He constructed line 6 by doubling the length of two notes and thus extending the melody over the bar line. Line 7 is as in the original, but Vaughan Williams omitted one note from the original measure of five beats; the melody pushes forward with no long note at the end of the line or at the beginning of line 8, an effect the composer much loved in his own tunes. The melodic changes are few: where the original melody in bar 3 drops to the lower sixth degree of the scale (B), Vaughan Williams takes it only to the seventh (C#), thus eliminating the distinctly modal sixth and intensifying the D tonality, and one note is omitted from the penultimate bar. The remainder of the tune is as in the original. These changes, though slight, lessened the melody's modal folk character, thus allowing for the "more modern" D harmonization.

In the debate between those who favor an "authentic original version" and those who favor a more free handling of hymn tunes, MONK'S GATE is a classic example. Neither the folk song version that Vaughan Williams notated nor other variants with a regular alternation between bars of four and five beats would have made the triumphantly successful hymn tune that we now have.

JHR/AL

479 Glory be to Jesus

Music: **WEM IN LEIDENSTAGEN**

This devotional text on the crucified Christ is thought to be eighteenth-century Italian in origin. It appears in the *Hymnal* in a much altered form, matched with a very accessible German nineteenth-century tune with which it has had a long association.

Words:

Viva! Viva! Gesù che per mio bene
Tutto il sangue verso dalle sue vene.

Il sangue di Gesù fu la mia vita;
Benedetta la sua bontà infinita.

Questo sangue in eterno sia lodato,
Che dall'inferno il mondo ha riscattato.

D'Abele il sangue gridava venedetta,
Quel di Gesù per noi perdono aspetta.

Se di tal sangue asperso è il nostro cuore,
Fugge il ministro del divin furore.

Se di Gesù si esalta il divin sangue,
Tripudia il ciel, trema l'abisso e langue.
Diciamo dunque insiem con energia
Al sangue di Gesù gloria si dia.

The author of this Italian text is unknown, despite an unfounded ascription to Siguori in the index of the *People's Hymnal* (London, 1867). It is thought to be of eighteenth-century origin. First published in *Raccolta di Orazioni e Pie Opere colle Indulgenze* (Rome, 1837), compiled by Fr. Telesforo Galli, it appeared in the collection as one of the "Aspirazioni Devote." The entire work was translated by J. H. Newman and Rev. Ambrose St. John and published as *The Raccolta: Collection of Indulgenced Prayers* (1880). The translation in the *Hymnal*, that of Edward Caswall, first appeared in a nine-stanza form in his *Hymns for the Use of the Birmingham Oratory* (1857). Stanzas 6 through 9 of Caswall's translation are as follows:

6. There the fainting spirit
   Drinks of life her fill;
There as in a fountain
   Laves herself at will.

7. Oh, the Blood of Christ!
   It soothes the Father's ire;
Opes the gate of Heaven;
   Quells eternal fire.

8. Abel's blood for vengeance
 Pleaded to the skies;
But the blood of Jesus
 For our pardon cries.

9. Oft as it is sprinkled
 On our guilty hearts,
Satan in confusion
 Terror-struck departs.

Stanza 4 originally concluded:

Hell with horror trembles,
 Heaven is filled with joy.[1]

This text first appeared in an Episcopal *Hymnal* in 1871.

---

1. For the complete original text see *EH*, 99.

Music: The tune WEM IN LEIDENSTAGEN (*Zahn* 1127) by Friedrich Filitz appeared in his *Vierstimmiges Choralbuch zu Kirchen und Hausgebrauch* (Hamburg, 1847), set to a funeral text by Heinrich Siegmund Osswald, "Wem in Leidenstagen." The *Vierstimmiges Choralbuch* was a book of four-part hymn settings for Bunsen's *Allgemeine Gesang- und Gebetbuch*, (Hamburg, 1846). The naive diatonic tune using, with one exception, only the first six notes of the scale of F, has been variously known as FILITZ (for the composer of the tune) and CASWALL (for its association with the Edward Caswall translation of this text). The harmonization given here is taken from *H40*.

MBJ/CS

480 When Jesus left his father's throne

Music: **KINGSFOLD**

This text first appeared in an Episcopal hymn collection in the 1826 edition of the *Hymnal* and was first matched with this tune based on an English folk tune melody in *H40*.

Words: This hymn by James Montgomery, published in Cotterill's *Selection of Psalms and Hymns* (London, 1819) was later published in an extended form in his *Christian Psalmist* (Glasgow and London, 1825). Julian found it preserved on a flyleaf among the Montgomery manuscripts with the note that it was written for the Hallam Sunday School, near Sheffield, and first sung there on October 26, 1816 (*Julian*, 1270-1271). The text originally had five stanzas of four lines each, while its extended form has eight four-line stanzas. The four-line stanzas have been combined to eight lines and the following are the omitted third and eighth stanzas:

3. Jesus passed by the rich and great,
 For men of low degree;
He sanctified our parents' state,
 for poor, like them, was he.

8. For we have learned to love his name;
 That name divinely sweet,
May every pulse through life proclaim,
 And our last breath repeat.

Music: See 292. This tune first appeared with this text in an Episcopal hymn collection in *H40*.

HLW

481 Rejoice, the Lord is King

Music: **GOPSAL**

The matching in *H82* and other current hymnals of this text of Charles Wesley and the tune GOPSAL, written for use with it by G. F. Handel, marks the restoration of the historic relationship neglected by earlier generations of hymnal editors.

Words: Charles Wesley's hymn "Rejoice, the Lord is King" was no. 8 in his anonymously published *Hymns for our Lord's Resurrection* (London, 1746) (*Poetical Works*, vol. IV, 140f.). It had first appeared in the third volume of the *Collection of Moral and Sacred Poems* (Bristol, 1744), published by his brother John, and was soon taken up by George Whitefield in his collection of *Hymns for Social Worship* (London, 1753), also by Martin Madan in his *Collection of Psalms and Hymns* (London, 1760) and A. M. Toplady in his *Psalms and Hymns for Public and Private Worship* (London, 1776). Omitted from the *Collection of Hymns for the Use of the People called Methodists* (London, 1780), the hymn was included in John Wesley's *Pocket Hymn Book* (London, 1785).

The following stanzas are retained as the fourth and fifth in British Methodist versions of the text:

He sits at God's right hand,
 Till all His foes submit,
And bow to His command,
 And fall beneath His feet:
Refrain: Lift up your heart, lift up your voice,
 Rejoice, again I say, rejoice.

He all His foes shall quell,
 Shall all our sins destroy,
And every bosom swell
 With pure seraphic joy:
Lift up your heart, lift up your voice,
 Rejoice, again I say, rejoice.

The former of those two stanzas was included in the hymn's first appearance in the *Hymnal* of 1892 and then again in 1916; these two versions, however, omitted the current third stanza, which was restored in 1940. The original and the British Methodists, as did the *Hymnal* in 1892 and 1916, also varied the refrain in the final stanza to:

We soon shall hear the archangel's voice,
The trump of God shall sound, Rejoice.

The removal of the name of Jesus from the first line of the second stanza ("Jesus the Saviour reigns"), from the fourth line of the third stanza ("Are to our Jesus given"), and the second line of the final stanza ("Jesus the Judge shall come") is first encountered in *H40*. An attempt to restore Jesus' name to the text was made by the Text Committee, but was rejected for musical reasons (the second, weak syllable of Jesus falls on an accented note in the tune).

The recurrent theme of rejoicing derives from Phil. 4:4 ("Rejoice in the Lord always; again I will say, Rejoice"). The second and third lines of the second stanza depend directly on Heb. 1:3b. The third stanza and the two omitted look to 1 Cor. 15:24f., with the third and fourth lines of the third stanza borrowing from Rev. 1:18 ("I have the keys of Death and Hades"). The final stanza relies on 1 Th. 4:16f. The link between Christ's ascension and his return is made at Acts 1:11, and between his resurrection and his final judgment of the world at Acts 17:31.

The text was set to a specially composed tune by John Frederic Lampe, no. 8 in the latter's *Hymns on the Great Festivals* (London, 1746).

The hymn figures in the *Consultation on Ecumenical Hymnody List* (see H82 a1, 712–713).

Music: In later life, Handel became associated with the Wesleys and their circle, and at some time after 1746 he set three of Charles Wesley's hymns to music as songs with instrumental bass; the exact circumstances of this collaboration are not known. Handel never published the songs, and they lay hidden until the one-page manuscript was discovered at the Fitzwilliam Museum, Cambridge, by Wesley's son Samuel, the composer and organist. As he put it when describing his find: "That the son of Charles, and the nephew of John Wesley, happened to be the first individual who discovered this manuscript after a lapse of seventy or eighty years, is certainly a circumstance of no common curiosity."[1] He published the three hymns in their original form in 1826 and in a four-part arrangement the following year.

Two of the hymns have long been current in English hymnals; the one, CANNONS, may be seen in *HA&M Revised* (1950) at no. 84. GOPSAL was considerably altered by nineteenth-century editors, beginning with William Henry Havergal in *Old Church Psalmody* (London, 1847), but it has generally retained its original form. In 1964 John Wilson made an edition faithful to the original melody, bass, and instrumental coda and published it in *Hymns for Church and School* (Henley-on-Thames, England, 1964) as no. 117. Wilson slightly revised his version in *Ecumenical Praise* (Carol Stream, IL, 1977), and it is this version that has been adopted in the *Hymnal*. According to Erik Routley, the tune has only been known to American hymnals since 1976.[2]

The name GOPSAL is taken from the small Leicestershire village that was the place of residence of Charles Jennens, compiler of the text of Handel's *Messiah*. Handel headed his setting "On the Resurrection." He marked both parts of the tune (lines 1 through 4 and 5 through 6) to be repeated.[3]

It seems that Handel, asked to compose English hymn tunes, consciously adopted the English style, which to him meant the late Restoration idiom of Purcell and Croft, in contrast to his normal Italianate manner. The forthright rhythms, melodic leaps, and cadences of the three tunes are all reminiscent of Purcell.

---

1. *The Methodist Magazine*, 49 (1826), 817.
2. E. Routley, *The Music of Christian Hymns* (Chicago, 1981), 76.
3. For a full account of the three tunes, see J. Wilson, "Handel and the Hymn Tune: I," *The Hymn*, 36 (October 1985), 18-23, with a facsimile of the autograph manuscript.

GW/NT

482 Lord of all hopefulness, Lord of all joy

Music: **SLANE**

This matching of text and tune first appeared in an Episcopal hymnal in *H40*, where, because of the direct appeal of the text and the accessibility and beauty of the tune, it gained immediate acceptance by congregations across the country. It continues in *H82* without alteration in either text or tune. A revised accompaniment for use in this edition was prepared by the Hymn Music Committee of the SCCM.

Words: Originally printed in the enlarged *Songs of Praise* (London, 1931), this text by Jan Struther is a prayer for God's presence at some of the daily activities of life, for example, waking, sleeping, laboring, and returning home. The almost naive imagery of the text suits the simple folk-song qualities of the melody SLANE with its gentle flowing metre. The text uses the classic collect form that includes an address describing an attribute of our Lord followed by a petition relating it, in this case, to our daily lives. To emphasize the structure of this hymn even more, it can be sung in alternation between a cantor or choir and congregation, the first group singing the address, and the congregation the refrainlike petition.

Music: Of Irish folk origin, the hymn tune SLANE seems to have been named for a hill about ten miles from Tara hill in County Meath. It is on Slane hill, according to the account in the *Confessions of St. Patrick*, that the Irish saint defied the command of the pagan king Loigaire[1] by lighting the Paschal fire on Easter eve. St. Patrick's act was done in defiance of the king's edict that no fire could be ignited before the royal fire was lit by the king's hand on Tara hill. The royal fire was kindled to celebrate the pagan Spring festival and symbolized the return of light and change of season following the darkness of winter.

The hymn tune known as SLANE is a slightly altered version of the Irish folk melody originally set to the ballad text "With my love on the road." Its first known publication is in Patrick W. Joyce's *Old Irish Folk Music and Songs: A Collection of 842 Irish Airs and Songs hitherto Unpublished* (London and New York, 1909). The folk melody was adapted and coupled with the text "Be thou My Vision" by Leopold McC. L. Dix for the Irish *Church Hymnal* (Dublin, 1919). The two versions of this hymn which appear in *H82* are derived from the adaptation and arrangement of the folk melody by David Evans published in *The Church Hymnary* (London, 1927). This form of the tune soon gained popularity and was included in many hymnals and hymn collections, including *Songs of Praise*, enl. ed. (London, 1931), with an arrangement by Martin Shaw; the British *Methodist Hymn Book* (London, 1933); the *BBC Hymn Book* (London, 1951), with melody and words recast; and *Congregational Praise* (London, 1951), with a setting by Erik Routley in four-part harmony. An early appearance of SLANE in an American hymn collection is in *The Hymnal* of the Presbyterian Church (Philadelphia, 1933/1937).

SLANE first appeared in a hymnal of the Episcopal Church in *H40* set to two texts. The melody has several characteristics usually associated with Irish folk tunes: a relatively wide range, a four-phrase structure with no repetition resulting in the formal design ABCD, and a singability and unique charm that gives the melody a broad popular appeal.

The original folk version of the melody is found here, while the adapted version appears with the text "Be thou my vision" [488]. The harmonization by the Hymn Music Committee of the SCCM is based on the setting found with this text in *H40*.

---

1. This name is also spelled Loegaire. His full name was Loegaire mac Neil. He reigned from 428-467 A.D.

TAR/JeW

483 The head that once was crowned with thorns

Music: **ST. MAGNUS**

This text, often associated with the Feast of the Ascension and rich with imagery of the Epistle to the Hebrews, is matched since the mid-nineteenth century with the classic eighteenth-century psalm tune ST. MAGNUS.

Words: "The head that once was crowned with thorns," based on Heb. 2:10, is the work of Thomas Kelly, who included it in the fifth edition of his *Hymns on Various Passages of Scriptures* (Dublin, 1820). The poet's inspiration was a poem of John Bunyan, "One Thing is Needful, or Serious Meditations upon the Four Last Things," which includes the lines:

> The head that once was crowned with thorns,
> Shall now with glory shine;
> That heart that broken was with scorns,
> Shall flow with life divine.

The text of Kelly's hymn provides the final words of Erik Routley's book *Hymns and Human Life* (London, 1955). It is prefaced by this sentence (page 315): "And lastly, here is what is perhaps the finest of all hymns; Thomas Kelly has here comprehended the whole Gospel, and he tells the Good News and of the mysterious mercy by which we may lay hold on it" (see also the citation given in the comment on no. 471).

911)

Music: See hymn 447 where the hymn appears transposed down one whole step.

RAL

484/485 Praise the Lord through every nation

Music: **WACHET AUF**

This text matched with this tune first entered the *Hymnal* in 1916. Although the tune is a famous chorale historically paired with the Advent text "Sleepers, wake!" [61/62], this second text affords opportunities for additional use.

Words:

1. Looft den Koning, alle volken!
Looft Hem, die boven lucht en wolken
Ten groon stijgt, Hem Gods eigen' Zoon!
Looft uw' Heiland, Christenscharen!
Zeit Hem voor u ten hemel varen,
U plaats bereiden voor Gods troon:
Verheft zijn majesteit
Met diep' eerbiedigheid,
Halleluja! Loof wereldrond!
Uit eenen mond,
Loof Jezus Christus, wereldrond.

2. Menschheid! tot Gods troon verheven.
Wie alle magt reeds is gegeven
In Jezus, waar God schepslen heest,
Menschheid juich, gevoel uw waarde,
Uw lot is niet bepaald aan d'aarde,
Eens leest g'omhoog, waar Jezus leest:
Hoe zalig is't verschiet,
Waar 't oog den Koning ziet
In zijn' luister.

Weg stof der aard, Een hart onwaard,
Dat eens tot God ten hemel vaart.

3. Jezus, Redder onzer zielen!
Zie ons aanbiddend nederknielen,
Gij werdt voor ons, voor ons gestagt:
Dank, aanbidding, eeuwig' eere,
Lof, dank, aanbidding, eewig' eere
Word' U. Verlosser! toegebragt.
Na lijden, hoon en spot
Wordt heerlijkheid ons lot.
Halleluja! Deugd triomfeert,
Want Gij regeert,
Ja, Halleluja! Gij regeert!

This Ascension Day hymn, "De Hemelvaart van Jezus," by Rhijnvis Feith, first appeared in the *Evangelische Gezangen . . . bij . . . Godsdienst in de Nederlandsche Hervormde Gemeeten* (Amsterdam, 1806).

The manuscript of James Montgomery's English paraphrase is dated January 10, 1828, but it was not published until the 1853 edition of his *Original Hymns* (London). The omitted second stanza reads:

God with God, dominion sharing,
And man with man, our image bearing,
Gentiles and Jews to him are given;
Praise your Saviour, ransomed sinners,
Of life, through him, immortal winners;
No longer heirs of earth but heaven:
O beatific sight,
To view his face in light!
Alleluia!
And while we see—transformed to be,
From bliss to bliss eternally.

The last line of st. 1 was altered for use in *H82* to support the SCCM's intent to use, whenever possible, inclusive language. The original read: Where're the race of man is found.

Music: See hymn 61.

RG

486 Hosanna to the living Lord!

Music: **HOSANNA**
This text, included in the 1865 edition of the *Hymnal*, was originally intended by its author, Reginald Heber, for use on the first Sunday of Advent. It is matched here with a tune written for use with it in 1865 by John Bacchus Dykes.

Words: This hymn by Reginald Heber was anonymously published in its first form in *The Christian Observer* of October 1811 accompanied with a letter signed D. R. The letter opened, "The following hymns are part of an intended series, appropriate to the Sundays and principal Holydays of the year; connected in some degree with their particular Collects and Gospels, and designed to be sung between the Nicene Creed and the Sermon." The version of the hymn that has been the source for all hymnals was published in Heber's *Hymns* (London, 1827). Among other changes, the most notable is the revision of the single word refrain "Hosanna" to "Hosanna Lord! Hosanna in the highest!"

Written for the first Sunday in Advent, "Hosanna to the living Lord" is based on Mt. 21, the first nine verses of which form the traditional Gospel for Advent Sunday. *The Hymnal 1982* uses all five stanzas of Heber's hymn with alterations in each:

1:3 Hosanna in the earth be said
And in the heaven which he hath made.
2:4 The dead and living
3. O Master! with parental care,
Return to this thine house of prayer;
Assembled in thy sacred Name
Where two or three thy promise claim.
4:1 But chiefest in our empty breast,
3 And cleanse our secret soul to be . . .
5:2 When heaven and earth have passed away
The rescued flock, and freed from sin,
Shall once again their song begin:
Hosanna!

Music: This tune was written by John Bacchus Dykes for inclusion in *Hymns for the Church of England* (London, 1865), edited by

Charles Steggall, who later became the music editor for the 1889 supplement and 1904 edition of *HA&M*. HOSANNA was specifically written for Heber's "Hosanna to the living Lord" and is not to be confused with other tunes with the same name, or with Dykes's HOSANNA WE SING. HOSANNA was included with the associated Heber text in the 1875 edition of *HA&M*. In the 1904 edition of *HA&M* it was replaced by the tune PRAISES by B. Luard Selby. Since the 1904 edition of *HA&M*, however, was itself ultimately replaced by the reissuing of the 1889 edition with the 1916 supplement, it was therefore made available again. It was included in *Tunes, Old and New: Adapted to the Hymnal* (Hartford, 1874), edited by John Ireland Tucker, and in subsequent *Hymnals*.

The refrain is an expansion of the second line. The tune has an upward drive beginning in the tenor and bass and continuing in the soprano that reaches an appropriate climax on "highest" in the penultimate measure.

TAR/RAL

487 Come, my Way, my Truth, my Life

Music: **THE CALL**

This short but profound text by the great English mystic, priest, and poet George Herbert achieved an added dimension of currency through its setting by Ralph Vaughan Williams in his *Five Mystical Songs*. More recently, through its arrangement as a congregational hymn, this piece has greatly enriched the singing tradition of the Church. Found in *H82* among the hymns honoring Jesus Christ our Lord, this hymn is also appropriate for a marriage service.

Words: This text by George Herbert appears here for the first time in an Episcopal hymnal, though it was previously introduced to many congregations through *MHSS* and *Hymns III*. In the posthumous collection of Herbert's poems, *The Temple* (Cambridge, 1633), it originally appeared with the title "The Call" (hence the name of the tune, discussed below).

Like much of Herbert's poetry, this text derives a considerable part of its energy from the strict structure into which its allusive phrases have been fitted. Like springs compressed into a box, paradoxes are packed into ordered lines that belie their complexity. The very opening line, for example, with its distinct allusion to Jn. 14:6, begins the pattern of straining at the limits of the 77. 77 stanza. The successive three lines of explication continue the process of intensification by reiterating the three elements of the opening line and by enlarging each one with a formulaic exegesis ("such a— as"). The potential for triteness and predictability in such a highly ordered form is very great, but Herbert avoids those pitfalls through images that are simultaneously accessible, engaging, and thought provoking.

In st. 1, for example, "a way as 'that' in Herbert's original gives us breath" is a path that leaves us not winded but refreshed, precisely the opposite of our experience with all earthly courses. In the second line, we invoke a truth that does not lead to quarrels but to harmony (there are possible allusions here to Jn. 8:32 and Gal. 4:15). The stanza climaxes in the affirmation of Christ's victory over death which is a constant theme throughout the New Testament (e.g., Rom. 6:9, 1 Cor. 15:54-56, 2 Tim. 1:10, Heb. 2:9-15, Rev. 21:4-5). The word "And" which appears at the beginning of this fourth line in the original edition of the poem has consistently been dropped by hymnal editors because it intrudes an extra syllable into the line. It is also notable that this line is the only place in this poem where Herbert employs an archaic and poetic third person singular verb ("killeth"), perhaps because it suits the scansion.

The second stanza is in many ways the least accessible. The three attributes of the opening line are perhaps gleaned from the sayings of Jesus to disciples in Jn. 8:12 and Jn. 6:35-58 and to the apostle Paul in 2 Cor. 12:9. The second line may recall Christ's saying about the proper place of lamps and candles (Mt. 5:15, Mk. 4:21, Lk. 8:16, 11:33). This natural function of light is contrasted with the supernatural banquet of the Eucharist; unlike meals of human preparation, the Lord's Supper does not cloy or surfeit but improves and heals in duration ("mends in length"). In terms of biblical precedent, it can be linked with the wedding feast of Cana, where the best wine came at the end of the feast (Jn. 2:10). The closing line of this stanza shows a profound capacity to perceive the connection of divine strength with both creativity and hospitality, and it manifests a characteristic metaphysical fascination with a God who forms the very creatures who then are offered the bounty of God's grace. For all its brevity, this line reveals a remarkable synthesis of the paradox of a Creator who is also Redeemer and Sanctifier.

The final stanza is the least allusive, though there may be some indebtedness here to 1 Cor. 13, particularly in the emphasis on the abiding ("none can [re]move") and indivisible ("none can part") qualities of love. The second line may also allude to Jn. 16:22. The stanza and the poem are brought to an especially satisfying close by Herbert's inclusion of all three epithets of the first line in the final line, a verbal contrivance made possible by transforming the noun "joy" into the verb "joys." Thus the threefold structure of the three stanzas, "a trinity of trinities," comes to a comprehensive and emphatic conclusion.

Music: The tune THE CALL is named after Herbert's poem and is derived from one of Ralph Vaughan Williams's *Five Mystical Songs* for baritone, chorus, and orchestra (1911), where it is no. 4. It is the only movement in which the chorus is not involved. In the full version, the melody is expanded and transposed upward for the third verse to give the setting a climax somewhat lacking when the original melody is simply repeated. The adaptation found in *H82* is from *Hymnal for Colleges and Schools*, edited by E. Harold Geer (New Haven, CT, 1956).

CPD/AL

488 Be thou my vision, O Lord of my heart

Music: **SLANE**

This text, long popular among the congregations of other denominations and included in the Ecumenical Hymn List, appears for the first time in an Episcopal hymnal in *H82*. The tune SLANE with which it is matched has been in the *Hymnal* since 1940.

Words:

1. Be thou my Vision, O Lord of my heart,
Naught is all else to me, save that Thou art.

2. Thou my best thought by day and by night,
Waking or sleeping, Thy presence my light.

3. Be thou my Wisdom, Thou my true Word;
   I ever with Thee, Thou with me, Lord.

4. Thou my great Father, I thy dear son,
   Thou in me dwelling, I with Thee one.

5. Be Thou my battle-shield, sword for the fight,
   Be Thou my dignity, Thou my delight.

6. Thou my soul's shelter, Thou my high tower,
   Raise Thou me heavenward, Power of my power.

7. Riches I heed not or man's empty praise,
   Thou mine inheritance now and always.

8. Thou, and Thou only, first in my heart,
   High King of Heaven, my treasure Thou art.

9. King of the seven heavens, grant me for dole,
   Thy love in my heart, Thy light in my soul.

10. Thy light from my soul, Thy love from my heart,
    King of the seven heavens,may they never depart.

11. With the High King of heaven, after victory won,
    May I reach heaven's joys, O heaven's Sun!

12. Heart of my own heart, whatever befall,
    Still be my Vision, O Ruler of all.

This prayer from the Irish monastic tradition, "Rop tú mo bhoile, a Comdi cride," may be as ancient as the year 700, although one scholar gives a convincing argument for placing it in the Early Middle Irish period, ca. 1000.[1] It is one of two examples in this hymnal of the Celtic lorica* or breastplate, almost a sort of incantation to be recited for protection, arming oneself for physical or spiritual battle. (The other lorica is "St. Patrick's Breastplate," hymn 370). A prose translation by Mary E. Byrne was published in 1905 in the journal *Ériu*; it was versified by Eleanor H. Hull and included in her *Poem-Book of the Gael* (London, 1912) in the form given above.

The metre comprises a fixed number of stressed syllables per line (four) but a varying number of unstressed syllables; most versions contain slight variations representing editorial attempts to regularize the metre. For this hymnal, additional alterations have been made to remove exclusively male imagery. Three (four-line) stanzas are omitted. In the first and second editions of *H82*, the second stanza contains a typographical error and should end "thou in me dwelling, and I one with thee."

Despite the phrase "thou my great Father," the final couplet in the Irish is addressed to Christ. The appellation "King of the seven heavens" (Ri secht nime) also occcurs three times in the original.

Echoes of the following scripture may be found: Col. 1:15-23; Col. 2:2-3; Pr. 9:1-6; Rev. 5:12; there is also a possible allusion to the antiphon in the service of Compline: "Guide us waking, O Lord, and guard us sleeping . . . "

---

1. The work of Monica Nevin is discussed by G. Murphy in *Early Irish Lyrics* (Clarendon, 1956), 190-191.

Music: See hymn 482. The arrangement by David Evans, also found in *H40*, has been associated with this text since they appeared together in the *Church Hymnary* (London, 1927).

MD

489 The great Creator of the worlds

Music: **TALLIS' ORDINAL**

This popular text by F. Bland Tucker was composed to save the tune TALLIS' ORDINAL when its continued use in *H40* was threatened. Although the tune appeared twice in *H16*, one text with which it was matched was dropped in the revision process and the other was matched with a different tune. In this form, it is a superb example of this poet's gifts in creating new texts for use with specific tunes (see also 477).

Words: This is a paraphrase made in 1939 by F. Bland Tucker from the Epistle to Diognetus. It paraphrases section VII, a strongly phrased passage that summarizes the Christian revelation.

The Epistle, formerly attributed to St. Justin Martyr, was probably written about A.D. 150 by an unknown author to one Diognetus, who may well have been the tutor of the Stoic emperor Marcus Aurelius. At the time it was written, Christians everywhere were being persecuted, without the opportunity to defend themselves or explain their positions. Thus, the main purpose of the Apologists was to compel their enemies to hear them before condemning them. Of all the Apologists, none presented a case for the defense with greater tact and judgment than this unknown author, who wrote in a style more to satisfy an inquirer than to conciliate an enemy.[1]

For use in *H82*, Dr. Tucker made several changes in his text in support of the SCCM's efforts to use, wherever possible, inclusive language. The original form of the text in these places is:

st. 1:4 To men on earth hath given.
st. 4 He sent him down as sending God;
As man he came to men;
As one with us he dwelt with us,
And dies and lives again.
st. 5:3 He came to win men by good will
st. 6:1 Not to oppress, but summon men

Since its introduction in *H40*, this text has found acceptance and use in English-language hymnals around the world.

---

1. See C. H. Blakeney's *Epistle to Diognetus* (New York, 1943). An English translation of the *Epistle* by Kirsopp Lake will be found in the Loeb Classical Library's *Apostolic Fathers*,(London, 1977), vol. II.

Music: See hymn 260.

RG

490 I want to walk as a child of the light

Music: **HOUSTON**

In contemporary American hymnody, there are many examples of composers who write their own texts. Such is the case with this hymn "I want to walk as a child of the light" by Kathleen Thomerson.

Words: A scriptural meditation and prayer, this hymn stands as a statement of its creator's personal faith. Its composition began in the summer of 1966, when a heat wave and an airline strike simultaneously hit the city of St. Louis. At the time, the composer's mother was visiting her there. To help her mother escape both the heat and being stranded, Mrs. Thomerson decided to drive her mother back to her home in Houston. For Kathleen Thomerson, the anticipation of returning to Houston, to family and to very close friends at the Church of the Redeemer, was a source of great joy and the inspiration for this hymn. Mrs. Thomerson writes of the experience:

> It was at that point that I started hearing the words and melody of this hymn. I remember walking around the house with paper and pencil in hand humming and writing while my mother said 'Kathleen, if we are leaving soon shouldn't you be packing?' We drove to Houston during which time I began to work out the harmonies in my head. I finished the harmonization in Houston at my parents' piano.[1]

The text, rich in biblically based images of light, was introduced in the summer of 1966 at the Church of the Redeemer and has since been published in several hymn collections and in an anthem setting. It first appeared in an Episcopal collection in *Songs for Celebration* (New York, 1980).

---

1. Thomerson to Glover, 10 November 1986, Church Hymnal Corporation Papers, New York, NY.

Music: HOUSTON, by Kathleen Armstrong Thomerson, is a very lyric part-song distinguished by long flowing lines in both the melody and the accompanying parts. A basic motif of D^b F G^b A^b, which appears several times at the beginning of phrases, both unifies the setting and enhances its accessibility for a congregation. The tune name honors the city of Houston, the home of Mrs. Thomerson's family and the location of the Church of the Redeemer, a parish with which the composer has deep emotional ties and where the hymn was first sung. It was first published in *Sound of Living Waters* (London, 1974).

RG

491 Where is this stupendous stranger?

Music: **KIT SMART**

When this text first appeared in *H40*, st. 1 was omitted! In *H82*, the opening stanza has been restored and the text appears with a tune that was composed for use with it. The tune's name, KIT SMART, honors the author of the text.

Words: These four stanzas are drawn from the nine that composed hymn XXXII for "The Nativity of Our Lord and Saviour Jesus Christ" in Christopher Smart's *Hymns and Spiritual Songs for the Fasts and Festivals of the Church of England*, printed as a portion of the volume beginning with his *Translation of the Psalms* (London, 1765). Smart's poem seems never to have been incorporated into a hymnal until it appeared in *H40*, for which F. Bland Tucker selected the three stanzas now numbered 2 through 4. Dr. Tucker was also involved in seeing that the first stanza was recovered for *Hymns III*, where the text first achieved its present form. Between the third and final stanzas of the eventual *Hymnal* version of the text stood five more stanzas in the original form:

4. If so young and thus eternal,
   Michael tune the shepherd's reed,
   Where the scenes are ever vernal,
   And the loves be love indeed!

5. See the God blasphem'd and doubted
   In the schools of Greece and Rome;
   See the pow'rs of darkness routed,
   Taken at their utmost gloom.

6. Nature's decorations glisten
   Far above their usual trim;

Birds on box and laurel listen,
As so near the cherubs hymn.

7. Boreas now no longer winters
On the desolated coast;
Oaks no more are riv'n in splinters
By the whirlwind and his host.

8. Spinks and ouzels sing sublimely,
'We too have a Saviour born,'
Whiter blossoms burst untimely
On the blest Mosaic thorn.

A few alterations have been made to achieve the present text: st. 1:2 originally read "Swains of Solyma advise," and for the sake of clarity the question mark was moved from the end of the fourth line to the end of the first line. In st. 2:3 "weak" has been substituted for "mean."

As a reflection on the mystery and paradox of the Incarnation, this hymn is particularly effective when used in conjunction with the Prologue to the Gospel of John (Jn. 1:1-18) or the hymn to Christ in Phil. 2:5-11. The emotional apex of the poem comes in st. 3, where almost every line consists of yoked opposites. By the judicious excision of the distracting allusive stanzas, the *Hymnal* version reveals with almost startling clarity how effectively Smart's meditation has countered the continuing appeals of a rationalistic and Deistic understanding of God.

Music: KIT SMART by Alec Wyton was written with its alternate accompaniment for this Christopher Smart text for inclusion in *Ecumenical Praise* (Carol Stream, IL, 1977). ("Kit" was the affectionate nickname by which Christopher Smart was known to his friends.) The composer has crafted a tune characterized by simplicity of range and movement in an effort to have the music "not get in the way at all" of what the poet was expressing in this moving text. The final chord is an unresolved discord, which is deliberate, expressing the wish that such poetry would go on forever. The tune first appeared in an Episcopal collection in *Hymns III*.

CPD/AW

492 Sing, ye faithful, sing with gladness

Music: **FINNIAN**
This text, which appeared in the 1892 edition of the *Hymnal*, was subsequently deleted until its restoration in *Hymns III*, felicitously matched with the tune FINNIAN.

Words: This Hymn of the Incarnation by John Ellerton was first published in *Select Hymns for Church and Home* (Edinburgh, 1871) compiled by Robert Brown-Borthwick. The first two stanzas of the original hymn were based on "Da puer plectrum," written by the Spanish author Aurelius Clemens Prudentius, and the seventh line refrain "Evermore and evermore," borrowed from the medieval cento* from the same hymn. The 1892 edition of the *Hymnal* omitted the second, third, and fourth stanzas and the refrain; the hymn was later dropped from the *Hymnal*, but was reinstated in *Hymns III* with one minor change (3:1, death for our sakes) and the additional omission of the last stanza. The missing stanzas read:

2. Offspring of the Father's wisdom,
   Ere the worlds began to be,
He, the Brightness of His glory,
   Image of His Person He,
Word of God, within His bosom
   Dwelt from all eternity
Evermore and evermore.

3. By that Word arose the creatures
   Fair and perfect in His sight;
Suns and stars in countless myriads
   Filled the dark[1] expanse of night,
God's Paternal love reflecting
   In the depth and in the height,
Evermore and evermore.

4. Yet a newer work of wonder
   All creating work surpassed;
When the Father loved so greatly
   one poor world by sin down-cast,
When He willed from death to save it,
   And upraise to life at last,
Evermore and evermore.

(last stanza)

Day of hoped-for[2] Restitution!
Fruit of all His sorrows past!
When the crown of His dominions[3]
He before the Throne shall cast,
And throughout the wide creation
God be all in all at last,
Evermore and evermore.

Other changes:

st. 2:1: Thus the Word came forth from heaven
st. 3:1: So, he tasted death for all men
st. 3:2: He, of all mankind the head
st. 3:5: So he wrought the full redemption

1. Altered by Ellerton to "void" in *Hymns Original and Translated* (London, 1888).
2. Altered by the author to "promised" in *Hymns Original and Translated*. The altered version was used in the 1892 *Hymnal*.
3. Altered by the author to "dominion" in *Hymns Original and Translated*.

Music: This strong processional-type tune was composed on December 18, 1966, the date of the birth of the youngest child of the composer, Christopher Dearnley. The tune name is derived from the name of a sixth-century Irish saint, whose name was one of the names given to Christopher Dearnley's child. It was intended for use with the Michael Hewlett text "Sing to him in whom creation," which appears in *H82* in an altered form, "Praise the Spirit in creation" [506]. It is AA[1]B in form.

BB/RG

493 O for a thousand tongues to sing

Music: **AZMON**

This important text by Charles Wesley has suffered at the hands of past Revision Committees of the *Hymnal*. It entered the *Hymnal* in 1871; was deleted in 1874; reentered in 1892, but was deleted in *H16*.

Restored in *H40*, the text is here matched with a tune associated with it in the hymnals of many other denominations.

Words: "O for a thousand tongues to sing" by Charles Wesley opened his brother John Wesley's definitive *A Collection of Hymns for the Use of the People called Methodists* (London, 1780) and has continued, with one exception (1935) as the opening hymn of every official American hymnal in the Methodist Episcopal tradition since that time. (The draft of 1778 had, in the second line, preferred the adjective "great," the form which then gained the day among Methodists from the American editions of *The Pocket Hymn Book* since 1811 and the official British Wesleyan edition of the *Collection* of 1831). The present version is made up of the seventh, eighth, ninth, eleventh, twelfth, and first stanzas from Charles Wesley's eighteen-stanza hymn "For the Anniversary Day of One's Conversion," first published in John and Charles Wesley's *Hymns and Sacred Poems* (London, 1740) (*Poetical Works*, vol. I, 299-301). The omitted tenth stanza has not posed problems for Methodist hymnals even to today (its intermittent appearances in the *Hymnal* illuminate a different attitude on the part of *its* revisers [see introductory paragraph]), since the Wesleyan and Methodist understanding of the *simul iustus et peccator* ("at once righteous and a sinner") is not the Lutheran one:

10. He breaks the power of cancelled sin,
He sets the prisoner free;
His blood can make the foulest clean,
His blood availed for me.

The fourth and fifth stanzas in the present ordering recall the messianic signs enumerated by Jesus in his reply to the people who came from John the Baptist (Mt. 11:5, Lk. 7:22; cf. Lk. 4:18f.). The first line of the present fifth stanza has up until now read "Hear Him, ye deaf; His praise, ye dumb" (see Mk. 7:32-37; cf. Isa. 35:5f.).

Apparently written on May 21, 1739, the first anniversary of Charles Wesley's evangelical conversion, the present opening line may recall Peter Böhler's remark to Wesley of a year earlier: "Had I a thousand tongues, I would praise Him (Christ) with them all," itself perhaps an echo of Johann Mentzer's otherwise quite different hymn of 1704, "O dass ich tausend Zungen hätte" (translated by

Catherine Winkworth in *Lyra Germanica*). The practice of starting a Wesleyan cento* from the present first line goes back to *Hymns and Spiritual Songs* (London, 1753), prepared by John Wesley as a general hymn book for the Methodist societies, where no. 44 consisted of sts. 7 through 13 and 15 through 18 of the original hymn. Wesley's original hymn text was:

1. Glory to God, and praise, and love
   Be ever, ever given,
   By saints below, and saints above,
   The church in earth and heaven.

2. On this glad day the glorious Sun
   Of Righteousness arose,
   On my benighted soul He shone,
   And fill'd it with repose.

3. Sudden expired the legal strife;
   'Twas then I ceased to grieve;
   My second, real, living life
   I then began to live.

4. Then with my *heart* I first believed,
   Believed with faith Divine;
   Power with the Holy Ghost received
   To call the Saviour *mine*.

5. I felt my Lord's atoning blood
   Close to *my* soul applied;
   Me, me He loved - the Son of God
   For *me*, for *me* He died!

6. I found, and own'd His promise true,
   Ascertain'd of *my* part;
   My pardon pass'd in heaven I *knew*,
   When written on my heart.

7. O for a thousand tongues to sing
   My dear Redeemer's praise!
   The glories of my God and King,
   The triumphs of His grace.

8. My gracious Master, and my God,
Assist me to proclaim,
To spread through all the earth abroad
The honours of Thy name.

9. Jesus, the name that charms our fears,
That bids our sorrows cease;
'Tis music in the sinner's ears,
'Tis life, and health, and peace!

10. He breaks the power of cancell'd sin,
He sets the prisoner free;
His blood can make the foulest clean,
His blood avail'd for me.

11. He speaks; and, listening to His voice,
New life the dead receive,
The mournful, broken hearts rejoice,
The humble poor *believe*.

12. Hear Him, ye deaf; His praise, ye dumb,
Your loosen'd tongues employ;
Ye blind, behold your Saviour come;
And leap, ye lame, for joy.

13. Look unto Him, ye nations; own
Your God, ye fallen race!
Look, and be saved through faith alone;
Be justified by grace!

14. See all your sins on Jesus laid;
the Lamb of God was slain,
His soul was once an offering made
For *every soul* of man.

15. Harlots, and publicans, and thieves
In holy triumph join;
Saved is the sinner that believes
From crimes as great as mine.

16. Murderers, and all ye hellish crew,
Ye sons of lust and pride,

Believe the Saviour died for you;
For me the Saviour died.

17. Awake from guilty nature's sleep,
And Christ shall give you light,
Cast all your sins into the deep,
And wash the Ethiop white.

18. With me, your chief, you then shall *know*,
Shall feel your sins forgiven;
Anticipate your heaven below,
And own that love is heaven.

Music: AZMON was written in 1828 by the German composer Carl Gotthilf Gläser. In the preface to Lowell Mason's tunebook, the *Modern Psalmist* (Boston, 1839), the compiler observed that

> during a recent tour in Europe, it was a leading object with him to obtain materials for a work like this. In the prosecution of the design he visited many of the most important cities, and obtained from distinguished composers of different nations much manuscript music; and also a great variety of recent musical publications, English, German, and French, which had not before reached this country. From these sources the selections of new music found in this volume, have been chiefly made.

A "List of European Authors, Specimens of Whose Works are Contained in This Volume" which appeared across from the Preface included the name "Glaser, J. M." with the notation that the composer was a German, born in 1780. One of the tunes noted as being "arranged, adapted, or composed for this work" was AZMON, which was printed in 4/4 metre and set to Isaac Watts's "Come, let us lift our joyful eyes." The source of the tune was given as "From Glaser." When combined with the naming of "J. M. Glaser" in the "List of European Authors," this somewhat ambiguous designation seems to indicate a misattribution on Mason's part. The crediting of the tune to "Glaser" continued to appear in most of Mason's subsequent collections that included this tune. In the *Sabbath Hymn and Tune Book* (New York, 1859), however, he correctly ascribed the tune to

"C. G." Mason is the one who named the tune AZMON. By 1845 Mason had altered the tune to its present triple-metre form.[1] For some reason, Mason later changed the name of the tune to DENFIELD, an alteration that occurred as early as *Cantica Laudis* (New York, 1850), compiled by Mason and George James Webb. This change of name was used in a few collections outside Mason's own, but the tune is generally known today under its initial title, AZMON. Mason often derived the titles of his tunes and arrangements from the Bible and AZMON is no exception, this being a place name mentioned in Num. 34:4-5 and Jos. 15:4. AZMON was first used in an Episcopal hymnal in *The Second Supplement* to *H40*.

---

1. See L. Mason, *Carmina Sacra: Or Boston Collection of Church Music* (Boston, 1845).

GW/DWM

494 Crown him with many crowns

***Music:* DIADEMATA**

This text is the work of two poets, although *H82* acknowledges only Matthew Bridges, the author of st. 1. Stanzas 2 through 5 are by Godfrey Thring. The tune DIADEMATA, written in 1868 for use with the text, has remained matched with it in every Episcopal hymnal since that time.

Words: The first stanza only of this hymn is from the second edition of Matthew Bridges's *Hymns of the Heart* (London, 1851). The remainder of Bridges's poem was:

2. Crown him the Virgin's Son!
   The God Incarnate born,—
Whose arm those crimson trophies won
   Which now his brow adorn
Fruit of the mystic Rose
   As of that Rose the Stem:
The Root, whence mercy ever flows,—
   The Babe of Bethlehem!

3. Crown him the Lord of love!
   Behold his hands and side,—
Rich wounds, yet visible above,
   In beauty glorified;
No angel in the sky
   Can fully bear that sight,
But downward bends his burning eye
   At mysteries so bright!

4. Crown him the Lord of peace!
   Whose power a sceptre sways,
From pole to pole,—that wars may cease,
   Absorbed in prayer and praise:
His reign shall know no end,
   And round his pierced feet
Fair flowers of paradise extend
   Their fragrance ever sweet.

5. Crown him the Lord of years!
   The Potentate of time,—
Creator of the rolling spheres,
   Ineffably sublime!
Glass'd in a sea of light,
   Where everlasting waves
Reflect his throne,—the Infinite!
   Who lives,—and loves,—and saves.

6. Crown him the Lord of heaven!
   One with the Father known,—
And the Blest Spirit, through him given
   From yonder triune throne!
All hail! Redeemer,—Hail!
   For thou hast died for me;
Thy praise shall never, never fail
   Throughout eternity!

The Bridges text was included in the 1871 edition of the *Hymnal*.

Stanzas 2 through 5 of this text were part of a poem by Godfrey Thring that appeared in his *Hymns and Sacred Lyrics* (London, 1874) and began:

Crown him with crowns of gold,
  All nations great and small,
Crown him, ye martyred saints of old,
  The lamb once slain for all;
The Lamb once slain for them
  Who bring their praises now,
As jewels for the diadem
  That girds his sacred brow.

The third stanza of this poem was omitted:

Crown him the Lord of light,
  Who o'er a darkened world
In robes of glory infinite
  His fiery flag unfurled,
And bore it raised on high,
  In heaven—in earth—beneath,
To all the sign of victory
  O'er Satan, sin, and death.

Thring appended the following note to the poem:

> The greater part of this hymn was originally written at the request of the Reverend H. W. Hutton, to supply the place of some of the stanzas in Matthew Bridges' well-known hymn, of which he and others did not approve; it was afterwards thought better to rewrite the whole, so that the two hymns might be kept *entirely distinct*.

The two hymns, however, were not kept distinct, as the present combined version appeared in the second edition of Thring's *Church of England Hymn Book* (London, 1882) and entered the *Hymnal* in 1892.

Music: Sir George J. Elvey composed this tune specifically for the text "Crown him with many crowns" for the 1868 Appendix to *HA&M*, and this stable marriage continues in English-speaking Christendom. The tune name is derived from the Greek word for crowns. In a number of hymnals this tune is also set to Charles Wesley's hymn "Soldiers of Christ, arise." The descant by Richard Proulx was composed in 1970 for a festival anthem setting based on this tune. It is equally effective when played by a trumpet, a solo reed on the organ, or sung.

MBJ/MS

495 Hail, thou once despised Jesus!

Music: **IN BABILONE**

This strong Christological text, often associated with the Feast of the Ascension, has been in the *Hymnal* since 1865. It appeared matched with this tune in *H16*, a relationship that has continued in all subsequent editions.

Words: The author of the original version of this hymn is usually given as John Bakewell, but the reasons for the attribution remain obscure since it was issued anonymously in two eight-line stanzas in *Hymns Addressed to the Holy, Holy, Holy, Triune God, in the Person of Jesus Christ, our Mediator and Advocate* (London, 1757). The first stanza of this original form appears as the first four lines of st. 1, and the original second stanza, divided in two, appears as the opening four lines of sts. 3 and 4.

An expanded version of the hymn, probably the work of Martin Madan, was included in the Lock Hospital hymnal *A Collection of Psalms and Hymns* (London, 1760), edited by Madan. The remainder of the hymn comes from this source, except that "love anointed" in st. 2:3 was a common substitution for Madan's "love appointed" in later eighteenth-century collections. Other versions of the hymn, including a substantial rewrite by Augustus Toplady, also circulated in the eighteenth century (see further, *Julian*, 479-480).

Music: See hymn 215. The accompaniment for this tune was composed by Roy Kehl for use in *H82*.

RAL

496/497 *How bright appears the Morning Star*

Music: **WIE SCHÖN LEUCHTET**

Philip Nicolai's combined gifts as poet and composer have greatly enriched Christian hymnody through this famous and much-loved chorale. This version of his text and tune entered the *Hymnal* in 1916. It is continued here with both the rhythmic and metric forms of the tune.

Words: The evolution of this English text is somewhat complex. Philip Nicolai wrote his sturdy chorale "Wie schön leuchtet der Morgenstern" toward the end of the sixteenth century. It was first published in the author's *Frewden Spiegel dess ewigen Lebens* (Frankfurt, 1599) with the following title: "A Spiritual Bridal Song of the Believing Soul Concerning Jesus Christ, her Heavenly Bridegroom: Based on the 45th Psalm of the Prophet David." John Christian Jacobi included a complete and fairly accurate translation of Nicolai's hymn in his *Psalmodia Germanica* (London, 1722). Its opening line was "How bright appears the Morning Star." A revised version appeared in the first part of the massive Moravian hymnal *A Collection of Hymns of the Children of God in All Ages* (London, 1754). Almost exactly one hundred years later *The Church Psalter and Hymn Book* (London, 1855), edited by William Mercer, included a composite four-stanza version, comprising five lines from Jacobi's original translation—including the opening line, assorted lines from the 1754 Moravian version, and newly written lines that make up about half the hymn. James Mearns stated that these "interjected lines are by Mercer, but bear very slight resemblance either to Nicolai's original text, or to any version of the German we have seen" (*Julian*, 807). In a later edition of *The Church Psalter* (London, 1859), Mercer offered another version of the hymn, of which only the opening first line from Jacobi was retained. It is this latter version that entered the *Hymnal* in 1916 and continues in *H82*, with the omission of st. 3:

Then will we to the world make known
The love thou hast to outcasts shone,
  In calling them before thee:

And seek each day to be more meet
To join the throng who at thy feet
  Unceasingly adore thee.
  Living, dying,
From thy praises, mighty Jesus!
  Shrink we never;
Sing we forth thy name for ever!

What began as a translation of Nicolai's famous hymn became, in Mercer's hands, an imitation of the German original that mirrored the opening first line, utilized the same metrical structure, but otherwise only approximated to the content of the original hymn. It would appear that Mercer's primary concern was to provide a suitable English text for Nicolai's magnificent German melody WIE SCHÖN LEUCHTET, which he designated FRANKFORT.

Music: The tune WIE SCHÖN LEUCHTET (*Zahn* 8359), commonly known as the "Queen of Chorales," is one of two great hymns (the other is WACHET AUF [61/62], the so-called "King of Chorales") written by Philip Nicolai included in his *Frewden Spiegel dess ewigen Lebens* (Frankfurt, 1599), a volume prompted by the devastation of the plague upon the citizens of Unna in Westphalia. The tune is thought by some to be a reconstruction of "Jauchzet dem Herren, alle lande," a version of Ps. 100 included in Wolff Koephel's *Psalter* (Strassburg, 1538), the opening line of which bears a striking resemblance to the first line of Nicolai's tune. The tune is given at 496 in its original rhythmic form in a harmonization by Johann Hermann Schein from *Liedboek voor de Kerken* (The Hague, 1973) and in its isorhythmic form at 497 in a harmonization by Johann Sebastian Bach. Bach used this tune in numerous cantatas (nos. 1, 36, 37, 49, 61, and 172) and also based an organ composition on it. Among the many other famous organ works based on this chorale is an extended work by D. Buxtehude[1].

---

1. See *HS7* (2 volumes) for additional organ works based on this chorale.

RAL/CS

498 Beneath the cross of Jesus

Music: **ST. CHRISTOPHER**
This text and tune entered the *Hymnal* in 1916. A popular text of personal piety, it is matched with ST. CHRISTOPHER, an expressive tune written for use with it and published in 1881.

Words: "Beneath the cross of Jesus" by Elizabeth Cecilia Clephane was first printed in *The Family Treasury* (1872), together with a few other hymns under the heading "Breathings on the Border." All of Miss Clephane's eight hymns were published in *The Treasury* through various volumes from 1872 to 1874. The present hymn has found wide usage in American hymnal service books and is particularly popular for the season of Lent. It is a deeply personal statement of the comfort and strength the poet, in her own unworthiness, received from the image of the cross. The text appeared for the first time in an Episcopal hymnal in 1916, but was not printed with ST. CHRISTOPHER until *H40*.

Music: Although there is strong compatibility between text and tune, there seems to be little affinity between the legend of St. Christopher and the sentiment expressed in the hymn "Beneath the cross of Jesus." Composed for this text by Frederick C. Maker, the tune first appeared in the supplement to *The Bristol Tune Book* (London, 1881). (The *Bristol Tune-Book* was first published in 1863, and a second series added in 1876. Both series went through a number of editions. These collections were edited by Alfred Stone, a musical colleague of Maker.)

In interpreting this hymn a strong sense of pulse is necessary, and careful attention to the dotted quarter and following eigth note is required to save the music from sounding trivial.

TAR/MS

499 Lord God, you now have set your servant free

Music: **SONG 1**
Since its publication in *H82*, this paraphrase by Rae E. Whitney of the Song of Simeon, "Nunc Dimittis," has also been included in *The*

Presbyterian Hymnal (Louisville, KY, 1990). It is matched here with a moving, reflective tune by Orlando Gibbons.

Words: This metrical version of the Canticle "Nunc Dimittis, The Song of Simeon" (Lk. 2:29-32) from the *BCP* appeared first in Book Two of *The Fig Tree Songs* (Scottsbluff, NE, 1981) by Rae E. Whitney. It is included there in a musical setting by the author with a metrical form of the Compline antiphon:

> O guide us waking, guard us sleeping, Lord,
> That we may live according to Your Word.

Writing about her text, the poet says:

> It is difficult to claim this text as "mine" since the text has travelled a long way! First it was Simeon's, then Luke's and then known and loved in a variety of translations. I was reading Compline from the 1976 Prayer Book with Clyde [the poet's husband, the Rev. Clyde Whitney] one night, and when we reached the Song of Simeon, this metrical hymn leapt out from the text for me to catch! My version is therefore very closely based on the new translation in the 1976 Prayer Book. (I caught a tiny glimpse of what Michelangelo went through when he "saw" David in a chunk of marble waiting to be released!)[1]

1. Whitney to Glover, April 1988, Church Hymnal Corporation Papers, New York, NY.

Music: See hymn 315.

RG

500 Creator Spirit, by whose aid

Music: **SURREY**

This translation of this Pentecost hymn "Veni Creator Spiritus" by the great British seventeenth-century poet John Dryden first appeared in an Episcopal collection in the "Proposed Prayer Book" of 1786 (see the essay "The Publication of the Hymnal of the Episcopal Church," vol.

1, 54-55). It is here matched with SURREY, an eighteenth-century tune of great charm and beauty.

Words: For the original Latin text, see hymn 503. These three stanzas are drawn from John Dryden's paraphrase of the ancient Latin hymn "Veni Creator Spiritus." Dryden's poem appeared with the works of other poets in a miscellaneous collection, compiled by the bookseller Jacob Tonson, called *Examen Poeticum: Being the Third Part of Miscellany Poems* (London, 1693). The thirty-nine lines of Dryden's version are grouped in seven stanzas ranging from four to seven lines long. The first two stanzas of the poem contain six lines each and are used in the hymn with only minor alterations (noted below). To reduce the remaining twenty-seven lines to six for a third stanza, the first two lines of the next stanza were joined to the four-line sixth stanza. The omitted lines were:

Thou strength of his Almighty Hand,
Whose Pow'r does Heav'n and Earth command:
Proceeding Spirit, our Defence,
Who do'st the Gift of Tongues dispence,
And crown'st thy Gift, with Eloquence!

Refine and purge our Earthy Parts;
But, oh, inflame and fire our Hearts!
Our Frailties help, our Vice controul;
Submit the Senses to the Soul;
And when Rebellious they are grown,
Then, lay thy hand, and hold 'em down.

Chace from our Minds th'Infernal Foe;
And Peace, the Fruit of Love, bestow:
And, lest our Feet shou'd step astray,
Protect, and guide us in the way.

Following the sixth stanza came a Trinitarian doxological conclusion:

Immortal Honour, endless Fame,
Attend th'Almighty Father's Name:
The Saviour Son, be glorify'd,
Who for lost Man's Redemption dy'd:

And equal Adoration be
Eternal *Paraclete*, to thee.

In 1688 Dryden had translated into English a French life of St. Francis Xavier by the Jesuit Dominique Bouhours (Paris, 1682), who had recorded that the "Veni Creator Spiritus" was the favorite hymn of that missionary saint. Whether this connection gave Dryden impetus towards attempting a translation can only be a matter of conjecture, though it is an appealing association. Nor can it be determined at this point whether Dryden was involved in the production of any of the other hymns published with his translation of the "Veni Creator Spiritus" in *The Primer, or, Office of the B. Virgin Mary, Revis'd: With a New and Approv'd Version of the Church-Hymns* (n.p., 1706). The matter is discussed at some length in Julian's articles on Dryden and on the Primers, but the sympathies implied there for Dryden's authorship of additional hymns are no longer seconded by literary scholars.

This text entered the *Hymnal* in 1786 and was included in the 1871 edition. Two long-standing alterations in the text are continued here: in st. 1:3 "humble" was originally "pious"; and in the first line of the third stanza, the phrase "come from on high" was "descend from high." It is worth noting that "humankind" in the fourth line of st. 1 is not a twentieth-century emendation for the sake of inclusive language; this is what Dryden wrote (albeit in two words rather than a compound) in the seventeenth century.

Like its Latin original, Dryden's hymn pulls together a wide range of biblical allusions about the work of the Holy Spirit. The first stanza appropriately begins with the work of the Spirit in creation (Gen. 1:2) and its final line recalls 1 Cor. 6:19. The term Paraclete mentioned in st. 2 is a characteristic Johannine expression (Jn. 14:16,26; 15:26; 16:7). The sevenfold gifts of the Spirit invoked in st. 3 are derived from Is. 11:2 and are traditionally identified as wisdom, understanding, counsel, fortitude, knowledge, piety, and fear of the Lord (based on the Septuagint and Vulgate texts that add piety). "Energy" is a reflection of the Greek word "dynamis," one of Luke's favorite attributes of the Spirit (e.g., Lk. 24:49; Acts 1:8). The ability of the Spirit to reveal the Father and the Son is another prominent Johannine theme (Jn. 16:13-14, 25).

Words: Henry Carey's tune for Joseph Addison's Ps. 23 ("The Lord my pasture shall prepare") was first printed in John Church's *An*

Introduction to Psalmody (London, 1723). Church was a trained musician, master of the choristers at Westminster Abbey, who intended by means of this book to provide professional guidance for the increasingly unruly practitioners of parish psalmody. Carey was a prominent theatre composer and poet who must have considered hymn tune writing a very minor aspect of his work. This tune, however, has far outstripped and long outlived the popularity of all his secular songs, even the once beloved ballad "Sally in our alley" (of which Carey wrote the *words*, not the tune).

With its expressive leaps, slowly lilting triple time, and strong binary structure (with repeat of the first half), Carey's tune has tended to proliferate in variants. Appoggiaturas and other ornaments are easily added. The original melody (Example 1) was plainer and did not distinguish between the second and fourth phrases: the elegant ornamental cadence to the fourth phrase was introduced later.

Example 1

A much more florid form, named CUMBERLAND (Example 2) was popular in America for some time after it first appeared in Aaron Williams's *The Universal Psalmodist* (London, 1763).

Example 2

Other adaptations turned the tune into long metre or 86. 86. 88.

The majority of the more than one hundred and fifty printings of the tune during its first century retained its original text, though eighteen others were used. There was no uniformity about the name, which varied among ADDISON'S, CAR(E)Y'S, MAGDALEN, MORETON, ST. MARTIN'S, SURREY, WOODBURN, and YARMOUTH. The present name, SURREY, was first used by Hugh Bond, lay-vicar of Exeter Cathedral, in *The Psalms of David in Metre* (London, ca. 1792), for reasons unknown. The tune was brought to the United States by the English-born John Cole in *Sacred Harmony, Part II* (New York, 1799) as CARY'S; when he reprinted it in *The Divine Harmonist* (of which the only surviving edition is the second [Baltimore, 1808]), he called it SURREY. The tune, in a form similar to that in *H82*, appeared in *A Tune Book* (New York, 1858). In *H40* the tune appears as at Example 1. The form of the tune and its harmonization found in *H82* is that of the 1875 second edition of *HA&M*.

CPD/NT

501 O Holy Spirit, by whose breath

Music: **KOMM, GOTT SCHÖPFER**

Since the mid-nineteenth century the hymnals of English-speaking congregations have been greatly enriched by the inclusion of translations of ancient hymns, primarily in Latin and German. This enrichment continues today in the work of a Canadian minister and scholar, John Webster Grant. In *H82*, his translation of the Latin Pentecost "Veni Creator Spiritus" joins those of other translators: John Dryden [500] and John Cosin [503/504]. (Three other translations by Dr. Grant are included in *H82* [161, 228, and 236].) This text is matched with a German chorale historically associated with a sixteenth-century German translation of the Latin root text. (For the Latin original, see entry 503.)

Words: This version of the "Veni Creator Spiritus" was written in 1968 and had its first public exposure in *The Hymn Book of the Anglican Church of Canada and the United Church of Canada* (Canada, 1971). It has since appeared in *The Australian Hymnbook* (London, 1979), the Canadian *Catholic Book of Worship* (Ottawa, 1971, 1980), *Worship*, 3rd ed. (Chicago, 1986), *Psalter Hymnal* of the

Christian Reformed Church, U.S. (Grand Rapids, MI, 1987), as well as in various local collections and manuals of devotion.

Cosin's 1627 translation of the "Veni Creator" has stood the test of time so well that proposing an alternative required considerable temerity. Its appeal today, however, is more that of a deservedly venerated antique than of a hymn expressing Christian faith in language natural to the twentieth century, and the intention of offering a new version was to make the old Latin words more immediately serviceable in contemporary worship. Since the piety of our time is not identical with that of the ninth century, some freedom in adaptation seemed justified. Within the limits imposed by rhyme and metre, however, an attempt has been made to preserve the language and ideas of the original.

The compilers have made two minor changes in the text. One of these, the substitution of "make" for "made" in st. 3, has transformed an acknowledgement of the Spirit's help into a petition for it. The other was required by the exigencies of the tunes selected. The original, which was designed for use with an arrangement of the Mechlin version of plainsong by the Canadian composer Dr. Healey Willan, contained only the first two lines of st. 6 as a coda to the hymn.

Music: The tune KOMM, GOTT SCHÖPFER first appeared in the *Erfurt Enchiridion* (Erfurt, 1524) (*Zahn* 294), with Luther's translation ("Komm Gott Schöpfer, heiliger Geist") of the Latin hymn "Veni Creator Spiritus" [502]. The form as given here is that found in

Example 1

Comparison of VENI CREATOR SPIRITUS and KOMM GOTT SCHÖPFER

Klug's *Geistliche Lieder* (Wittenberg, 1533) (*Zahn* 295). The melody is essentially that of the Gregorian plainsong tune, however, simplified by the elimination of melismas* and in a more regular syllabic style. It is an example of the manner in which Gregorian tunes were treated as they were carried over into the Reformation church (see Example 1 and the essay "German Church Song," vol. 1, 288). The harmonization is that of *The Lutheran Hymnal* (St. Louis, 1941).

JWG/CS

502 O Holy Spirit, by whose breath

Music: **VENI CREATOR SPIRITUS**

This contemporary translation of the Pentecost hymn "Veni Creator Spiritus" is matched with the chant melody with which it has been historically associated.

Words: See hymn 501. (For original Latin text, see 503.)

Music: Much disseminated but with little uniformity, VENI CREATOR SPIRITUS, writes Bruno Stäblein, appears in a Milanese source with the authentic Ambrosian text "Hic est dies verus dei" (*MMMA*, 507). The melodic traits of this tune, however—the drive toward the end of the first line, intensified in the second phrase, and the resumption of this melodic activity at the beginning of the third phrase—are not Ambrosian. Furthermore, VENI CREATOR SPIRITUS is, with only one exception, the only tune associated with the text "Veni Creator Spiritus," a fact that must be taken into consideration when addressing the still-open question of the origins of the melody.

VENI CREATOR SPIRITUS appears in *H82* in a Sarum form of the melody found in the *Antiphonale Sarisburensis* (London, 1966, vol. 2, 46), where it is associated with the hymn "Salvator mundi." The tune served as the plainsong model to the German hymn "Komm, Gott Schöpfer" (see the commentary on 501). The accompaniment is by Richard Proulx.

ME

503 Come, Holy Ghost, our souls inspire

Music: **COME HOLY GHOST**

This classic seventeenth-century translation of the "Veni Creator Spiritus," matched with a setting by a nineteenth-century American composer, is a form of the hymn often sung at ordinations.

Words:

1. Veni, creator spiritus:
mentes tuorum visita,
imple superna gratia
quae tu creasti pectora!

2. Qui paracletus diceris,
donum dei altissimi,
fons vivus, ignis, caritas
et spiritalis unctio:

3. tu septiformis munere,
dextrae dei tu digitus,
tu rite promissum patris
sermone ditans guttura:

4. accende lumen sensibus,
infunde amorem cordibus,
infirma nostri corporis
virtute firmans perpeti:

5. hostem repellas longius
pacemque dones protinus:
ductore sic te praevio
vitemus omne noxium:

6. per te sciamus da patrem
noscamus atque filium,
te utriusque spiritum
credamus omni tempore!

Of all Latin hymns, this has probably been the most familiar to Anglicans throughout the centuries. Most likely written during the ninth century, it has been in continuous use in English coronation rites since the accession of Edward II in 1307, and in the 1550 Ordinal it was included (in English translation) for use at ordinations as it is to this day. It was included in the proposed American Prayer Book of 1786. Its original use is unknown, but it has been sung at various Pentecost Offices at least since the tenth century and at ordination services at least since the eleventh. Current Roman use assigns it principally to Vespers of Pentecost.

The hymn is found in nine manuscripts of the tenth century, none of which contains an attribution. Two manuscripts, one from the fifteenth century, still extant, and one of unknown date, now lost, name Rabanus Maurus as author.[1] Heinrich Lausberg supports the ascription, citing identical words and phrases from the writer's other works, and suggests that the hymn was written for the Council of Aachen in 809, which enjoined all of Charlemagne's empire to include the filioque* in the Creed.[2] Lausberg bases his conclusion on the penultimate line of the hymn, which refers to the Spirit of "both" the Father and the Son. Lausberg's arguments are, however, untenable: the words and phrases he cites from other works were for the most part in common use throughout the Middle Ages, and the circumstances of composition are purely speculative. If the hymn was indeed written for the Council of Aachen, one would expect a greater emphasis on the doctrine under consideration; according to E. Gibson, writing in *Julian*, language similar to that in the hymn was used in the Church from early times (*Julian* 1208b). In summary, Rabanus Maurus is a possible author, but the evidence is far from convincing. A few other possibilities have been suggested (see *Julian* 1207-8), but none is even remotely credible.

The earliest surviving translation into English is found in an eleventh-century manuscript (Brit. Lib. Cotton Julius A.VI). The first stanza reads "Eala pu gast scyppend cum geneosa mod pinra pena gefyll breost pa oe pu gescope mid uplicra gifa."[3] The current translation by John Cosin was, according to *Julian*, included in his *Collection of Private Devotions in the Practice of the Ancient Church* (London, 1627) and in the 1662 edition of the Prayer Book (*Julian*, 1210). Some suggestion of this hymn's importance is indicated by the inclusion in the *Hymnal* of translations by Cosin, John Dryden, and John Webster Grant [500 to 504]. Of the three, the closest to the original is that of Grant, but none is more than a paraphrase; for this reason we provide a literal translation:

1. Come, creator Spirit, visit the souls of your people;
   fill with grace from above the hearts that you have
   created.

2. You who are called advocate, gift of the most high God,
   the living fountain, fire, love and balm of the spirit,

3. you bestow sevenfold [gifts]; you, the finger
   of God's right hand, you, the duly promised of the
   Father, providing tongues with speech,

4. kindle a light in [our] minds; pour love into
   [our]
   hearts, strengthening the weaknesses of our bodies with
   perpetual vigor.

5. Drive the enemy far away, and give peace forthwith, so
   that with you leading the way as our guide we may avoid
   all things harmful.

6. Grant that through you we may know the Father and also
   come to know the Son, and may we ever believe in you,
   the Spirit of both.

Despite the looseness of the *Hymnal* translations, the only serious misrepresentation of the original is the rendering of the beginning of st. 5 by Cosin and Grant. Cosin's translation begins "Keep far our foes, give peace at home," and Grant's begins "From inner strife grant us release; turn nations to the ways of peace"; the Latin on the other hand clearly refers to Satan as the foe in the first phrase and to an individual's inner peace in the second. Dryden does not translate the phrases in question.

---

1. See M. Bannister, *Analecta Hymnica* (New York and London, 1961), vol. 50, 194.
2. H. Lausberg, "Der Hymnus 'Veni creator spiritus,' " *Jahrbuch der Akademie der Wissenschaften in Göttingen* (1969), 46-47, 53-55.
3. H. Gneuss, *Hymnar und Hymnen im englischen Mittelalter* (Tübingen, 1968), 363.

Music: This chant melody to be sung in alternation between a bishop and the congregation or choir was composed by John Henry

Hopkins, Jr. and first sung by his father at the consecration of Robert Harper Clarkson, a missionary bishop of Nebraska and Dakota, on November 15, 1865, in Chicago. Its use soon became a tradition at ordinations.

In this work, Hopkins, a devotee and editor of plainchant, has retained some of the simplicity of the original chant tune associated with this venerable Latin text. It was composed with the expectation that any bishop should be able to manage the three notes required by the melody. The rubrics of Prayer Books prior to 1979 required the singing or recitation of the hymn be responsive, "the Bishop beginning, and the Priests, and others that are present, answering by verses." The present Prayer Book rubric, which also affords use of the "Veni Sancte Spiritus," states "The hymn, Veni Creator Spiritus, or the hymn, Veni Sancte Spiritus is sung." Performance suggestions in *H82* recommend that the hymn be sung in alternation between a cantor and "all." A new accompaniment for use with this tune in *H82* was composed by David Hurd. It adds a richer harmonic quality to the setting than was available with the original's constant and sterile repetition of the same chords. The tune was included in the J. Ireland Tucker music edition of the 1871 *Hymnal*.

JH/TAR and RG

504 Come, Holy Ghost, our souls inspire

***Music:* VENI CREATOR SPIRITUS**

This historically and liturgically important text is matched in *H82* with its proper classic Latin tune with accompaniment by Canon Charles Winfred Douglas as found in *H40*.

Words: See hymn 503.

Music: See hymn 503.

505 O Spirit of Life, O Spirit of God

***Music:* O HEILIGER GEIST**

This text, which first appeared in an Episcopal hymnal in *Hymns III*, comes from the German Lutheran tradition. It is matched here with a tune that is best known by many Americans because of its association with a text often used at Christmas, "O little one sweet, O little one mild."

Words:

O Heiliger Geist, o heiliger Gott!
Du Tröster wert in aller Not,
du bist gesandt vons Himmels Thron,
Von Gott, dem Vater und dem Sohn,
O heiliger Geist! o heiliger Gott!

The text "O heiliger Geist, o heiliger Gott" ("O Spirit of Life, O Spirit of God") first appeared in the third edition of the *Lutherischen Handbüchlein* (Altenburg, 1651), a collection of hymns and psalms organized and arranged by Johann Niedling, a teacher in Altenburg. While the text is not attributed to Niedling in that collection, it is generally assumed that he was the author. Wilhelm Nelle considers this hymn among the best and most powerful of the Pentecost hymns of its day.[1] Interestingly, the same collection contains an Easter song, apparently also by Niedling, "O heiliger Gott, allmächtiger Held," with the identical metrical pattern.

O heiliger Gott, allmächtiger Held,
Herr Jesu, Heiland aller Welt,
du hast uns durch dein teures Blut
erlöset von der Höllen Glut,
o heiliger Gott, allmächtiger Held.

The translation that appears here is by John Caspar Mattes and first appeared in the *Common Service Book of the Lutheran Church* (Philadelphia, 1917), the hymnal of the United Lutheran Church in America, to which Mattes contributed six translations. Of the six stanzas that appeared in the *Common Service Book*, four stanzas are given here in somewhat different order and with one slight alteration in the text.

The omitted stanzas are:

O Spirit of Life, O Spirit of God,
By Whom our souls to heaven are led,
Make us to fight so valiantly,
That we may reign eternally;
O Spirit of Life, O Spirit of God.

O Spirit of Life, O Spirit of God,
Forsake us not in death or need.
We'll sing Thy praise and honor Thee
With grateful hearts eternally;
O Spirit of Life, O Spirit of God.

Stanza 4:2 originally read: Enlighten us by Thy blest Word.

---

1. C. Mahrenholz and O. Söhngen, eds. *Handbuch zum Evangelischen Kirchengesangbuch* (Göttingen, 1970), vol. III/1, 403.

Music: This tune (*Zahn* 2016) first appeared in *Auserlesene Catholische Geistliche Kirchengesäng* (Cologne, 1623), where it was set to the text "Ist das der Lieb, Herr Jesu Christ." In Samuel Scheidt's *Tabulatur Buch* (Görlitz, 1650), it was set to the text "O Jesulein süss, O Jesulein mild," an association that has remained popular to the present day. (The tune is also widely known as O JESULEIN SÜSS, O JESULEIN MILD.) Johann Sebastian Bach included this tune in Georg Christian Schemelli's *Musikalisches Gesangbuch* (Leipzig, 1736), a volume for which Bach served as musical editor and which contained melodies "in part newly composed, and in part improved in the figured bass" by the Leipzig cantor. The harmonization given here is a simplification of Bach's figured bass made by Alastair Cassels-Brown for *Hymns III*.

CS

506 Praise the Spirit in creation

Music: **FINNIAN**

For many years the hymnody for Pentecost and the Holy Spirit was devoid of many of the dynamic images of the Holy Spirit as experienced at that first Pentecost and described in the book of Acts 2:1-11. This text, new to the *Hymnal*, helps fill this void. It is matched with a strong tune by a contemporary British composer.

Words: The Rev. Michael Hewlett wrote the hymn "Praise the Spirit in creation" to satisfy his perceived need for a processional hymn for Whitsunday. The text, with its vivid biblical allusions, adds a fresh, vibrant dimension to our hymnody for the Holy Spirit in its encompassing of the whole range of the Spirit's work. The first three stanzas call our attention to the work of the Spirit in creation, in our lives, and in history. In st. 3 the poet also includes the intriguing concept of the Holy Spirit acting in the world as "the truth behind the wisdoms which as yet know not our Lord." The power of the Spirit, manifested at Pentecost, is the theme of st. 4, while st. 5 is a prayer that the Spirit will enflame us to go out into the world to do God's will. The hymn closes with a doxology praising the Holy Trinity, through whose voice, speaking within us, we, God's creatures, know the Lord. Fr. Hewlett's original text, entitled "A Whitsun Procession," contained a sixth stanza that has been omitted. The Text Committee of the SCCM also made a number of other changes in consultation with the poet. The original form of the text is as follows:

1. Sing to Him in whose compulsion
   All things took their origin:
Spirit moving on the waters
   Troubled by the God within;
Source of breath to all things breathing,
   Life in whom all lives begin.

2. Sing to God, the close companion
   Of our inmost thoughts and ways:
Who, in showing us his wonders,
   Is Himself the power to gaze;
And the laws of thought and action
   By that still small Voice conveys.

3. Holy men, the priests and prophets,
   Caught his accents, spoke his word;
His the truth behind the Wisdoms
   Which as yet know not our Lord;
And in Christ the total manhood,
   Spirit-driven, is restored.

4. Tell of how the ascended Jesus
   Armed a people for his own:

How a hundred men and women
Turned the known world upside down,
To its dark and furthest corners
By the Wind of Whitsun blown.

5. Pray we then our Lord the Spirit,
On our lives descend in might;
Let the flame break out within us,
Fire our hearts and clear our sight;
Till, white-hot in thy possession,
We too set the world alight.

6. Reaching down the generations
Thou hast laid on us thy call:
Priest or parent, friend or teacher
Set thy mark upon us all.
Now on those whom Thou hast chosen
Let thy clear direction fall.

7. Praise to Thee, O Holy Spirit,
With the Father and the Word:
Source, and Truth, and Inspiration,
Trinity in deep accord.
Through thy Voice which speaks within us
We thy creatures own Thee Lord.

This is the first appearance of the text in the *Hymnal*.

Music: See hymn 492.

RG

507 Praise the Spirit in creation

Music: **JULION**

The suggestion for the matching of this text with JULION was made by the composer David Hurd. Dr. Hurd's descant to the tune as it appears at 268 may be played on a solo instrument.

Words: See hymn 506.

Music: See hymn 268.

508 Breathe on me, Breath of God

Music: **NOVA VITA**

This text and tune first appeared together in an Episcopal *Hymnal* in 1916 and have continued in this relationship in subsequent editions. It was not recommended for retention in the SCCM 1982 Report to General Convention, but was restored by action of the Convention.

Words: This hymn by Edwin Hatch, one of great popularity, was first published privately as an ordination hymn in his *Between Doubt and Prayer* (London, 1878). It was later included in Henry Allon's *The Congregational Psalmist Hymnal* (London, 1886) and in Hatch's *Towards Fields of Light: Sacred Poems* (London, 1890), published by his widow. The second line of st. 3 was originally "blend all my soul with thine." The word "blend" figures prominently with various nuances of meaning in much of Hatch's work regarding the influence of Greek ideas on Christian thought and organization. Scriptural references in this hymn include Jn. 3:3-8; Gen. 2:7; Job. 33-4; Jn. 20-22; 1 Jn. 2:17; 1 Cor. 3:15-16, and Mt. 3:11. John Telford said of Hatch's religious poems that they "are a beautiful supplement to his theology and reveal the depth of and tenderness of his religious life.'[1]

---

1. J. Telford, *The New Methodist Hymn-Book Illustrated* (London, 1934), 165.

Music: NOVA VITA was composed for this text by Lister R. Peace and published in the *The Church Hymnal for the Christian Year* (London, 1917), which he edited with Hugh Blair. Its relationship with this text is continued in the United States only in the Episcopal *Hymnal*.

MBJ/RG

509 Spirit divine, attend our prayers

Music: **NUN DANKET ALL UND BRINGET EHR**

This text entered the *Hymnal* in 1892, but was not matched with NUN DANKET ALL UND BRINGET EHR until *H40*. In that collection the tune was called GRÄFENBERG.

Words: Andrew Reed first published this hymn anonymously in the *Evangelical Magazine* of June 1829 under the heading "Hymn to the Spirit Sung on the late Day appointed for solemn Prayer and Humiliation in the Eastern District of the Metropolis." The "late Day" was Good Friday of that year. The day of prayer was to "promote, by the divine blessing, a revival of religion in the British Churches." The hymn was later published in the *Congregational Hymn Book* (London, 1836) and the eighth edition of Reed's own *Hymn Book Prepared from Dr. Watts's Psalms and Hymns and Other Authors, with Some Originals* (London, 1842).

The use of Reed's hymn with a repetition of the first stanza as the last stanza and the omission of the original fourth stanza was established by Samuel Longfellow (brother of the poet) in *Hymns of the Spirit* (Boston, 1864). The omitted fourth and fifth stanzas are:

Come as the dew, and sweetly bless
  This consecrated hour;
May barrenness rejoice to own
  Thy fertilizing power.

Come as the wind, with rushing sound
  And pentecostal grace;
That all of woman born may see
  the glory of thy face.

Each of the internal stanzas of the text are built around a metaphor for the Holy Spirit—light, fire, and dove.

Music: See hymn 374.

TAR

510 Come, Holy Spirit, heavenly Dove

Music: **SAINT AGNES**

Although this much-loved matching of text and tune has been in use since the Tucker music edition of the 1871 *Hymnal*, the text by Isaac Watts has the distinction of having appeared in every edition of the *Hymnal* since the first one in 1786.

Words: This text by Isaac Watts first appeared in his *Hymns and Spiritual Songs* (London, 1707, 1709 edition, Book II, no. 34), entitled "Breathing after the Holy Spirit; or, Fervency of Devotion Desired." The original reads:

1. Come, Holy Spirit, heavenly Dove
   With all Thy quick'ning powers,
Kindle a flame of sacred love,
   In these cold hearts of ours.

2. Look, how we grovel here below,
   Fond of these trifling toys:
Our souls can neither fly nor go
   To reach eternal joys.

3. In vain we tune our formal songs,
   In vain we strive to rise;
Hosannas languish on our tongues,
   And our devotion dies.

4. Dear Lord! and shall we ever lie,
   At this poor dying rate?
Our love so faint, so cold to Thee,
   And Thine to us so great?

5. Come, Holy Spirit, heavenly Dove,
   With all thy quick'ning pow'rs;
Come, shed abroad a Savior's love,
   And that shall kindle ours.

The numerous changes that have been made in this hymn text have dealt mainly with sts. 2 and 4. In his *A Collection of Psalms and Hymns* (London, 1743), John Wesley omitted st. 2 and altered st. 4, line 1 to read "And shall we then forever live." The hymn was published in the *Supplement to the Wesley Hymn Book* (London, 1830), the revised edition (London, 1875), and others, with the following reading of st. 2, line 3:

Our souls, how heavily they go

This form of st. 2 can also be found in the 1826 revision of the *Hymnal*, where the text is printed in four stanzas, omitting st. 4, with various minor changes. In spite of the textual differences that frequent American collections and those of Great Britain, the hymn has enjoyed almost three centuries of constant use.

Music: See commentary on no. 343. The harmonization here is the work of John Bacchus Dykes, the composer of the tune; a revision by Richard Proulx is given at no. 343.

TS and RAL

511 Holy Spirit, ever living

Music: **ABBOT'S LEIGH**

The first publication of this text and tune in an Episcopal collection occured in *Hymns III*. In this song of praise, matched with one of the fine hymn tunes of the mid-twentieth century, the ongoing activity of the Holy Spirit in the Church is vividly portrayed.

Words: This two-stanza text by Timothy Rees, Bishop of Llandaff, was first published in a four-stanza form in the *Mirfield Mission Hymn Book* (London, 1922). In 1946 it was published in a three-stanza much altered form in *Sermons and Hymns by Timothy Rees, Bishop of Llandaff* (London, 1946). That three-stanza form has become standard and is the structure in which the text appears in many British hymnals and in *Rejoice in the Lord* (Grand Rapids, MI, 1985). It attained its two-stanza form (sts. 2 and 3 of the original) in the *Church Hymnary, Third Edition* (London, 1973). It is in that form that it was introduced to congregations of the Episcopal Church.

The original st. 1 was:

> Holy Spirit, ever dwelling,
> In the holiest realms of light;
> Holy Spirit, ever brooding
> O'er a world of gloom and night;
> Holy Spirit, ever raising
> Sons of earth to thrones of high;
> Living, life-imparting Spirit,
> Thee we praise and magnify.

Music: ABBOT'S LEIGH, one of the most successful English tunes to appear since World War II, was composed on a Sunday morning in 1941 by Cyril Vincent Taylor. Canon Taylor, a priest of the Anglican Church, was then Assistant to the Head of Religious Broadcasting of the BBC in their wartime headquarters in Abbot's Leigh, a village across the Clifton suspension bridge from Bristol, England. Appearing first in a leaflet, it was later chosen by *HA&M, Revised* (London, 1950) for "Glorious things of thee are spoken" [523]. It then appeared in *The BBC Hymn Book* (London, 1951) and in the American Presbyterian *Worshipbook* (Philadelphia, 1972). It has subsequently been included in almost every major internationally used English-language hymnal. Erik Routley writes of the tune as:

> The archetypal example of a hymn tune taught to the whole of Britain through broadcasting. Its secret, which gives it a sort of timeless authority that makes one feel as soon as one has heard it that one knew it all one's life, comes from the fact that its composer remembered what it was like to be in a pew singing. It has exactly the kind of universal appeal that one attributes to Dykes' NICAEA, and for the same reason.[1]

Dr. Taylor, in a letter dated 21 March 1984, writes "to my great joy it has been sung at several great services, the last being that in Canterbury Cathedral (May 1983) in which the Archbishop and the Pope shared."[2]

The outline of the chord of D distinguishes the opening melody of the tune, which is repeated with a very small change in harmony as the second phrase and in an altered pattern as the opening of the last phrase (Example 1):

Example 1

Sudden movement to the chord of C marks the beginning of the third phrase, which moves through the keys of G and b. The tune at 523 appears transposed one step lower than its original key of D.

In its original form, measure 20 was

The tune has appeared in emended form since its inclusion in the 1950 edition of *HA&M*.

---

1. E. Routley, *The Music of Christian Hymns* (Chicago, 1987), 152.
2. Taylor to Glover, Church Hymnal Corporation Papers, New York, NY. March 21, 1984.

RG

512 Come gracious Spirit, heavenly Dove

Music: **MENDON**
This text, patterned after the Isaac Watts text "Come Holy Spirit, heavenly Dove" [510], first appeared in an Episcopal *Hymnal* in 1871 and appears matched with this tune in the Hutchins music edition of that book. That relationship has retained its popularity in music editions since that day.

Words: This hymn originally began with the same first line as Isaac Watts's "Come, Holy Spirit, Heav'nly Dove" [510]. Ellinwood's claim that "Simon Browne patterned this hymn on . . . Isaac Watts" is somewhat overstated (*H40c*, no. 378). Certainly both had the same first line and both were written in LM. But the rhyming schemes of the two hymns are different (Watts = ABAB; Browne = AABB); Browne does not follow Watts when the latter repeats the opening of his hymn at the beginning of the final stanza; and Watts's text was in the third person plural whereas Browne's was in the first person singular. Browne's text, therefore, is to be seen as complementary to Watts's hymn, rather than a reworking of it.

The original seven stanzas of the hymn were published in Browne's *Hymns and Spiritual Songs, in Three Books, Designed as a Supplement to Dr. Watts* (London, 1720) with the title "The Soul giving itself up to the Conduct and Influence of the Holy Spirit":

1. Come, Holy Spirit, heav'nly Dove,
My sinful maladies remove;
Be Thou my light, be Thou my guide,
O'er every thought and step preside.

2. The light of truth to me display,
That I may know and chuse my way;
Plant holy fear within mine heart,
That I from God may ne'er depart.

3. Conduct me safe, conduct me far
from every sin and hurtful snare;
Lead me to God, my final rest,
In His enjoyment to be blest.

4. Lead me to Christ, the living way,
Nor let me from his pastures stray;
Lead me to heav'n, the seat of bliss,
Where pleasure in perfection is.

5. Lead me to holiness, the road
That I must take to dwell with God;
Lead to Thy word, that rules must give,
And sure directions how to live.

6. Lead me to means of grace, where I
May own my wants, and seek supply;
Lead to Thyself, the spring from whence
To fetch all quick'ning influence.

7. Thus I, conducted still by Thee,
Of God a child beloved shall be;
Here to His family pertain,
Hereafter with Him forever reign.

The original form of the hymn did not, however, enter into common usage; instead it was treated to a bewildering variety of editorial emendations throughout the nineteenth century, leading John Julian to comment: "Few hymns in the English language have been subjected to so many alterations and changes as this" (*Julian*, 246). The Baptists John Ash and Caleb Evans made a number of significant alterations in their *Collection of Hymns Adapted to Public Worship* (Bristol, 1769). Two stanzas were omitted and the remainder were reordered in the following sequence: 1, 3, 2, 5, 4; the first person singular was exchanged for the third person plural; and various lines were rewritten, the most important being the second line of st. 1, becoming "With light and comfort from above," and st. 4 (now the final stanza) being addressed to God rather than to Christ (see further below).

In the second edition of Augustus Toplady's *Psalms and Hymns* (London, 1787) edited by Walter Row, the first line of st. 1 was altered to "Come, gracious Spirit, heavenly Dove."

The final stanza went through a number of different revisions until it reached the form given in *The Church Psalter and Hymn Book* (Oxford, 1864), edited by William Mercer, where the original "Lead me to Christ," later modified to "Lead us to God," became "Lead us to heaven . . . ," —as it now stands in *H82*. The "Lead us to Christ" stanza (4 of the original) was also restored to the hymn in a modified form (st. 3 in *H82*). The remaining stanzas in *H82* (1 and 2) retain somewhat more of the original first two stanzas. The four stanzas have been in the *Hymnal* since 1871.

Music: See hymn 419.

RAL

513 Like the murmur of the dove's song

Music: **BRIDEGROOM**

This text, written especially for use in *H82* with BRIDEGROOM, gained almost immediate acceptance and use after the text was published in the SCCM's 1982 Report to General Convention.

Words: During the preparation of the SCCM's report to the 1982 General Convention, many of the requests to the Text Committee for the inclusion of some particular text were discovered, upon careful examination, really to be based on attraction to a very fine tune rather than to the words associated with it. One such tune was BRIDEGROOM by Peter Cutts, which had been written for a text beginning "As the bridegroom to his chosen." The Committee found the original text, with such symbols as "King unto his realm" and "keep unto the castle" was not relevant to American congregations, but recognized the merit of the setting. They therefore asked one of their members, Carl P. Daw, Jr., to write a text to fit the tune.

While playing over the tune on various instruments in order to determine its intrinsic tone and message, the author became convinced that the final phrase of the music expressed a prayer for the coming of the Holy Spirit. With this in mind as a concluding refrain in every stanza, he was then able to use each stanza to consider different aspects of this prayer.

The first stanza portrays how the Spirit comes. It presents both the aural and visual aspects of the dove as a symbol of the Holy Spirit, as well as the two other traditional images of wind and fire. The opening phrase of the text derives from the author's recollection of a passage concerning the Holy Spirit in Louis Evely's book *A Religion for Our Time* (New York, 1968): " . . . the image of the dove was chosen not because of the shape of the bird, but because of the moan. The dove murmurs all the time. It is because the Holy Spirit moans all the time that he is represented under the form of a dove; it is a verbal and not a plastic image." Evely goes on to quote Rom. 8:26 and could have given further evidence by referring to Is. 38:14 or 59:11, which use the image of the moaning dove as metaphors for praying in distress.

The second stanza turns to the "where" aspect and affirms that the Spirit is a corporate gift to the whole Church. The images of body, vine, and assembly bring together, respectively, Pauline, Johannine, and Lucan understandings of the Church, all of which share a recognition of the Spirit as divine gift.

The third stanza concerns itself with the purpose for which the Spirit is given (the "why"): for reconciliation, prayer, divine power, and quiet confidence. Like the ancient hymn "Veni Sancte Spiritus," this new hymn pulls together diverse images of both the Holy Spirit and the people of God in an attempt to suggest the scope of divine power and the depth of human need.

Since its introduction in *H82*, this text has been translated into Spanish for inclusion in *Albricias* (New York, 1987), a collection of hymns published by the National Hispanic Office of the Episcopal Church. It has also been included in *The United Methodist Hymnal* (Nashville, 1989), *The Presbyterian Hymnal* (Louisville, KY, 1990), and has received several anthem settings.

Music: BRIDEGROOM, by the British composer, teacher, and now resident of the United States, Peter Cutts, matched with Carl Daw's text "Like the murmur of the dove's song" has proven to be one of the most accessible and durable new hymns in *H82*. The composer relates that the tune was composed at Erik Routley's grand piano in Newcastle-upon-Tyne for a projected Coventry Cathedral Hymnbook that never emerged, and was first published in *100 Hymns for Today* (London, 1969). Written for use with the text "As the bridegroom to his chosen," it appears in the United States with that text in *The Hymnal of the United Church of Christ* (Philadelphia, 1974) and the *Seventh-Day Adventist Hymnal* (Washington, DC, 1985). It appears with Dr. Daw's text in this collection, in the *United Methodist Hymnal* (Nashville, 1988), and *The Presbyterian Hymnal* (Louisville, KY, 1990), and with a Timothy Dudley-Smith text in *Worship*, 3rd ed., (Chicago, 1986).

The form of the original text with its two balanced lines and a short refrain determined the structure of the Cutts tune. That is seen through the use of two melodic lines, the second of which, with the exception of the last two notes, duplicates the first, one step higher. The upward thrust at the end of the second phrase leads directly into the brief refrain, the melody of which is distinguished by the use of syncopation, which gives important emphasis to the word "come." Erik Routley, in his *Music of Christian Hymns* (Chicago, 1981), speaks of this tune as having "a lightness of touch which exactly matched the lyric qualities of its text."

The antiphonal performance of the first two phrases of the tune, as suggested in the notes found under the hymn in *H82*, supports the structure of the text, gives it added emphasis and meaning, and adds a stimulating quality of variety.

CPD/RG

514 To thee, O Comforter divine

Music: **ST. BARTHOLOMEW'S**

This text, which first appeared in the 1982 edition of the Hymnal matched with the tune ST. BARTHOLOMEW'S, was restored in *Hymns III*.

Words: While Frances Ridley Havergal does not occupy a prominent place as a poet, through her distinct individuality she carved out a niche that only she could fill. Simply and sweetly, she sang the love of God and his way of salvation. "To Thee, O Comforter Divine" was written in 1872 with the subtitle "The Faithful Comforter" and was first published in *Under the Surface* (London, 1874). It was reprinted a few years later in *Life Mosaic* (London, 1879), two of seven collections that published Miss Havergal's hymns. Miss Havergal composed the tune TRYPHOSA for use with this hymn. *The Hymnal 1982* includes four of her original eight stanzas, with those omitted given below:

3. To Thee, whose faithful voice doth win
   The wandering from the ways of sin,
   Sing we Alleluia!

5. To Thee, whose faithful truth is shown,
   By every promise made our own,
   Sing we Alleluia!

6. To Thee, our Teacher and our Friend,
   Our faithful Leader to the end,
   Sing we Alleluia!

8. To Thee, who art with God the Son
   And God the Father ever One,
   Sing we Alleluia!

The text first appeared in the *Hymnal* in 1892 but was deleted in the 1916 and 1940 revisions. It was restored in *Hymns III*.

Music: ST. BARTHOLOMEW'S, a completely diatonic tune, exhibits skillful melodic development within its narrow melodic range. It was written by David McK. Williams in 1976 while the composer was living in a retirement home in Oakland, CA, and was commissioned by the SCCM for use in *Hymns III*. Dr. Williams was active in the Commission that produced *H40*. This, his last composition, is named for the New York City church that he served from 1920-1947.

TS/AW

515 Holy Ghost, dispel our sadness

Music: **GENEVA**

The hymnal supplement *Hymns III* was a successful effort by the SCCM to satisfy the Church's need for new hymnody in the years before *H82* was approved by General Convention and then published. Among the many hymns retained from that collection is this text for the Holy Spirit. The tune GENEVA with which it is matched was chosen after the text in *H40* for which it was written was not retained for use in the revised hymnal.

Words: The final form of this hymn text as it appears in *H82* is the product of a somewhat convoluted process of translation and editorial reworking. Its origin is to be found in the German hymn for Pentecost written by Paul Gerhardt "O du allersüsste Freude." This beautiful prayer for the gifts and graces of the Holy Spirit was written in ten eight-line stanzas, first published in Johann Crüger's *Praxis Pietatis Melica* (Berlin, 1648). The first three stanzas are as follows:

1. O du allersüsste Freude!
O du allerschönstes Licht!
Der du uns in Lieb und Leide
Unbesuchet lässest nicht,
Geist des Höchsten, höchster Fürst,
Der du hältst und halten wirst
Ohn Aufhören alle Dinge:
Höre, höre, was ich singe.

2. Du bist ja die beste Gabe,
Die ein Mensche nennen kann:
Wenn ich dich erwünsch und habe,
Geb ich alles Wünschen an.
Ach ergib dich: komm zu mir
In mein Herze, das du dir,
Da ich in die Welt geboren,
Sebst zum Tempel auserkoren!

3. Du wirst aus des Himmels Throne
Wie ein Regen ausgeschütt,
Bringst vom Vater und vom Sohne
Nichts als lauter Segen mit.
Laß doch, O du werther Gast,
Gottes Segen, den du hast
Und verwaltst nach deinem Willen,
Mich an Leib und Seele füllen!

John Christian Jacobi offered a complete translation of Gerhardt's hymn in his *Psalmodia Germanica* (London, 1725) and later revised it for his expanded edition of 1732. The first three stanzas of this revised version are as follows (note that Jacobi reverses the sequence of sts. 2 and 3):

1. O thou sweetest Source of Gladness!
Faith and Hope and Heav'nly Light,
Who, in Joy, as in our Sadness,
Dost convince us of thy Might!
Holy Spirit, God of Peace,
Great Distributor of Grace,
Life and Joy of the Creation,
Hear, Oh hear my Supplication.

2.(3) O thou best of all Donations
God can give, or we implore,
Having thy sweet Consolations,
We need wish for Nothing more.
Come, thou Lord of Love and Pow'r,
On my Heart thy Graces show'r:
Work in me a new Creation.
Make my Heart thy Habitation.

3.(2) From that Height that knows no Measure,
As a Show'r thou dost descend;
And bring'st down the richest Treasure
Man can wish, or God can send.
O! Thou Glory shining down
From the Father and the Son,
Grant me thy Communication,
Which makes All a new Creation.

Six stanzas of Jacobi's translation (sts. 1 through 4 and 9 through 10) were substantially rewritten by Augustus Toplady and appeared in print first in *The Gospel Magazine* (June 1776) and then in Toplady's *Psalms and Hymns for Public and Private Worship* (London, 1776). The first three stanzas in this Jacobi-Toplady version are as follows (notice that sts. 2 and 3 are restored to the original German sequence):

1. *Holy Ghost, dispel our sadness,*
Pierce the clouds of sinful night,
Come, thou source of sweetest gladness,
Breathe thy life, and spread thy light!
Loving Spirit, God of Peace,
Great distributor of grace,
Rest upon this congregation!
Hear, O hear our supplication.

2. *From that height which knows no measure,*
As a gracious show'r descend;
Bringing down the richest treasure
Man can wish, or God can send:
O thou Glory, shining down
From the Father and the Son,
Grant us thy Illumination!
Rest upon this congregation.

3. Come, thou best of all donations
God can give, or we implore;
Having thy sweet consolations,
We need wish for nothing more;
Come thou unction, and with pow'r,
On our souls thy graces show'r;
Author of the New Creation
Make our hearts thy habitation.

The hymn in this six-stanza Jacobi-Toplady form circulated widely in the hymnals of "Anglican" evangelicals, both within and without the Church of England, in the last quarter of the eighteenth century. For example, it stands as the first hymn in *A Select Collection of Hymns, to be universally sung in all the Countess of Huntingdon's Chapels* (London, 1780).

The two stanzas in *H82* are made up from various lines (italicized above) of the Jacobi-Toplady version. Stanza 1 comprises a slightly modified form of the first four lines of sts. 1 and 2 of the Jacobi-Toplady version. Stanza 2 is more complex: lines 1 through 4 are lines 5 through 8 of the Jacobi-Toplady version of st. 3, in the sequence 7, 5, 8, 6; and lines 5 through 8 are lines 5 through 8 of st. 1 of the Jacobi-Toplady version, but in the sequence 8, 5, 7, 6. The transposition of lines was made in order to retain a consistent alternating rhyming scheme throughout the hymn.

With one exception, the hymn appeared in this form in all American Methodist hymnals issued between 1849 and 1964. The 1964 *Methodist Hymnal* was the source from which it was taken into *Hymns III*, and then into *H82*.

Music: GENEVA was written in 1940 by George Henry Day for use in *H40* with the William Pierson Merrill text "Not alone for mighty empire." The tune honors Geneva, NY, where the composer served as organist/choirmaster of Trinity Church from 1935 until his death in 1967.

The Merrill text, not chosen for use with the tune in *H82*, consists of two carefully balanced but contrasting halves. To musically complement this structure, the composer wrote his tune with its two very similar but contrasting sections; the first is in the minor mode while the second is in the major. Measures 1 and 2 and 5 and 6 have a strong downward thrust that is intensified through the use of a descending interval of a fifth in measures 1 and 5, and a descending seventh in measures 2 and 6. In the second half, this movement is reversed through the use of an ascending melody line in the four comparable places. The only other alteration in the structure of the melody in the second half is the addition of a passing tone on the first full beat of measures 10 and 14.

The nobility of the tune is enhanced through a very strong accompaniment based on the primary triads of the key and utilizing passing tones in the bass line and inner voices.

RAL/RG

516 Come down, O Love divine

***Music:* DOWN AMPNEY**

The matching of this text with DOWN AMPNEY in *EH* is now the accepted norm in hymnals of English-speaking congregations around the world. The tune by Ralph Vaughan Williams, which in *EH* was attributed to an anonymous writer, is today deemed a masterpiece.

Words: This text comprises three of the four stanzas that R. F. Littledale included in *The People's Hymnal* (London, 1867), prepared for Anglicans who felt, as he did, that they might benefit from many Roman Catholic teachings and practices without quitting their own church. An omitted third stanza is:

Let holy charity
Mine outward vesture be,
And lowliness become mine inner clothing;
True lowliness of heart,
Which takes the humbler part,
And o'er its own shortcomings weeps with loathing.

The idealistic enthusiasm of groups like the Pre-Raphaelites, several of whom Littledale knew well, had, by the time of the publication of *The People's Hymnal*, persuaded many cultivated persons that the Middle Ages had been a halcyon era for Christianity. Therefore they responded to Bianco da Siena's raptures as disciplined by Littledale's rhetoric. The Italian original of the stanzas included here reads:

Discendi, amor santo
Visita la mie mente
Del tuo amore ardente,
Si che di te m'infiammi tutto quanto.

Vienne, consolatore,
Nel mio cuor veramente:
Del tuo ardente amore
Ardel veracemente:
Del tuo amor cocente
Si forte sie ferito;
Vada come smarrito
Dentro e di fuore ardendo tutto quanto.

Arda si fortemente
Che tutto mi consumi,
Si che veracemente
Lassi mondan costumi:
Li splendienti lumi
Lucenti, illuminanti
Mi stien sempre davanti,
Per il quali mi vesta il vero manto.

Si grande è quel disio
Ch'allor l'anima sente,
Che dir noi sapre' io,
a ciò non son potente:
Nulla umana mente
Entender noi potria,
Se noi gustasse pria
Per la vertù dello Spirito Santo
Deo gratias.

Littledale's penultimate line read "Till he become the place." His version will repay comparison with Charles Wesley's treatment of the same theme and imagery at hymn 704.

Music: The tune DOWN AMPNEY was composed to these words for *EH* and named after Vaughan Williams's birthplace. It has a very satisfying rhythmical structure typical of the composer, with the poise of the longer notes in the short lines and the sweep of melody in the long lines 3 and 6.

HMcK/AL

517 How lovely is thy dwelling place

Music: **BROTHER JAMES' AIR**

The introduction of this text matched with this much-loved psalm tune has given it an appeal and immediacy for congregations throughout the Church.

Words: From 1871 through 1940, Ps. 84 was represented in the *Hymnal* by Henry Francis Lyte's rather free paraphrase, "Pleasant are thy courts above." A more literal alternative was offered in *Hymns III*, which included four of the twelve stanzas of Milton's CM paraphrase beginning "How lovely are thy dwellings fair" (cf. the entry for hymn 462). In the course of preparing the texts for *H82*, it was felt that still another attempt needed to be made, and the Text Committee asked one of its consultant members, Carl P. Daw, Jr., to prepare a text based on a Scottish paraphrase, *The Psalmes of David in Meeter* (Edinburgh, 1650).

In that version, the first five verses of the psalm are paraphrased in three CMD stanzas, which became the basis for the first two stanzas of the present text. The remaining four Scottish paraphrase stanzas, covering the remainder of the psalm, were judged less successful and were replaced by a new version attempting to maintain the style of the first two stanzas. The first three original stanzas were:

1. How pleasant is thy dwelling place,
   O Lord of Hoasts to mee!
   The Tabernacles of thy grace
   how pleasant Lord they bee?
   My soul doth long full sore to go
   into thy courts abroad:
   Mine heart doth joy, my flesh also
   in thee the living God.

2. The sparrows find a roome to rest,
   and save themselves from wrong;
   And eke the swallow hath a nest
   wherein to keep her young.
   These birds full night thine Altar may
   have place to sit and sing:
   O Lord of Hoasts, thou art I say
   my God and eke my King.

3. Oh, they bee blessed that may dwell
   within thine house alwayes:
   For they all tymes thy facts do tell,
   and ever give thee praise.
   Yea happy sure likewise are they,
   whose stay and strength thou art:
   Who to thine house do mind the way,
   and seek it with their heart.

In order to tighten up the somewhat repetitive and rambling style of the seventeenth-century version, the stanza length was reduced from CMD to 86. 86. 86. Also, because it both allowed a bow to Milton's version and quoted verbatim the opening clause of the RSV translation, the adjective in the first line was changed from "pleasant" to "lovely." The subsequent changes necessitated by the reduced scope and revised rhyme scheme are numerous and can be traced by comparing the hymnal text with the Scottish paraphrase, the BCP version, and the translations of the King James Version and RSV Bibles.

The final two stanzas attempt to preserve the archaic idiom, though they are primarily structured after the translation of the current *BCP*. The concluding line of the fourth stanza is an intentional blending of the final line of "New every morning is the love" [10], and the last line of the first stanza of "Forgive our sins as we forgive" [674].

Since its introduction here, this version has also appeared in *The Baptist Hymnal* (Nashville, 1991).

Music: This much-loved tune originally set to a paraphrase of Ps. 23 is the work of James Leith Macbeth Bain, better known as Brother James. Called MAROSA by the composer, it is now commonly identified as BROTHER JAMES' AIR, the title under which it appears in the popular choral arrangement by Gordon Jacob (London, 1934). The following explanatory note by Bain precedes the original printing of the hymn in *The Great Peace Being . . .* (London, 1915) (see Example 1 on following page):

The *H82* version of BROTHER JAMES' AIR is an arrangement of the Gordon Jacob choral setting by Walter M. Gelton for use in the second edition of *A Hymnal for Friends* (Philadelphia, 1955). With a few slight alterations in voice leading, this arrangement was continued in the *LBW* and from there in *H82*.

CPD/JeW

Example 1

Marosa.
(This melody is so named after the seventh daughter of my friend Captain M'Laren, whom I christened some years ago. The words are a version, slightly modified by me to suit the melody, of the old, classic Shepherd-Psalm, than which I know of no more beautiful Hymn of Love. This hymn, sung slowly, will be found to be a potent requiem for the blessing of those dear men who have fallen in this war. For, the whole of the Christ-blessedness, and all the strength of the great Body of Christ, even the One Holy Catholic Church of Heaven and Earth, can be uttered, and has been uttered throughout the Ages in this Psalm of the Heart of God.)
Inscribed to
WILLIAM HENDRY.
Psalm xxiii.
The Lord's my shep - herd I'll not want, He
makes me down to lie In pas-tures green, He
lead-eth me The qui-et wa - ters by.
He lead-eth me, He lead-eth me, The
qui-et wa - ters by, In pas-tures green He
lead-eth me The qui-et wa - ters by.

518 Christ is made the sure foundation

***Music:* WESTMINSTER ABBEY**

A favorite hymn since it first entered the *Hymnal* in 1871, this text has gained an even greater measure of favor and use in the Episcopal Church since it was matched with the Purcell tune WESTMINSTER ABBEY in *Hymnal Supplement II* (New York, 1976). This text/tune relationship was first introduced to Americans through the broadcast of the marriage ceremony of Princess Margaret of England and Lord Snowden in 1960. It is now often used as a processional hymn at weddings in Episcopal churches.

Words:

1. Urbs beata Ierusalem, dicta pacis visio,
Quae construitur in caelis, vivis ex lapidibus,
Et angelis coronata ut sponsata comite,

2. Nova veniens e caelo, nuptiali thalamo
Praeparata, ut sponsata copuletur Domino;
Plateae et muri eius ex auro purissimo.

3. Portae nitent margaritis, adytis patentibus,
Et virtute meritorum illuc introducitur
Omnis qui pro Christi nomine hic in mundo premitur.

4. Tunsionibus, pressuris expoliti lapides,
Suisque aptantur locis per manum artificis;
Disponuntur permansuri sacris aedificiis.

5. Angularis fundamentum lapis Christus missus est
Qui conpage parietis in utroque necitur,
Quem Sion sancta suscepit, in quo credens permanet.

6. Omnis illa Deo sacra et dilecta civitas,
Plena modulis in laude et canore iubilo,
Trinum Deum unicumque cum favore praedicat.

7. Hoc in templo, summe Deus, exoratus adveni,
Et clementi bonitate precum vota suscipe;
Largam benedictionem hic unfunde iugiter.

8. Hic promereantur omnes petita adquirere,
Et adepta possidere cum sanctis perenniter,
Paradisum introire, translati in requiem.

9. Gloria et honor Deo usquequo altissimo,
Una Patri Filioque inclito Paraclito,
Cui laus est et potestas per aeterna saecula.

One of the oldest Latin hymn texts, "Christ is made the sure foundation" is found in manuscript collections of hymns from the ninth century, but perhaps dates back as early as the sixth century. The stanzas for this hymn, as well as 519 and 520, are actually part of one long hymn traditionally associated with the dedication of a church. The verses were usually divided into two parts, part I [519/520] being sung at the evening office and part II [518] reserved for morning prayer. Part II has been in the *Hymnal* since 1871, part I since 1892, both being used as general hymns. John Mason Neale's translation, published in *Mediæval Hymns and Sequences* (London, 1851) has been greatly altered over time. The four stanzas used in *H82* are sts. 5, 6, 7, and 8 of the Latin original. Hymn 519 uses sts. 1, 2, 3, and 4.

Music: The tune WESTMINSTER ABBEY is derived from an anthem by the great English composer Henry Purcell and was given its name by Sir Sidney Nicholson (organist of the Abbey from 1919 to 1928) for use in the *Shortened Music Edition* of *HA&M* (London, 1939). The name obviously reflects Purcell's various associations with the great London church. From 1674 to 1678 Purcell tuned the organ in Westminster Abbey and later succeeded John Blow (1649-1708) as the organist of the Abbey. On November 25, 1695 his funeral and burial were held there.

The tune as it appears in *H82* was adapted and arranged by the Music Committee of the SCCM from the concluding Alleluias in the anthem "O God, Thou art my God." The adaptation and arrangement as a separate melody was first made by Ernest Hawkins for Vincent Novello's publication of *The Psalmist* (London, 1842/1843). In this version, the melody is given the tune name BELLEVILLE. Another early appearance of this melody was in *A People's Tune Book*. Other tune names include LEXDEN and ST. ASAPH.

The first time this hymn tune appeared for use by congregations of the Episcopal Church was in *Hymnal Supplement II* (New York, 1976). The descant by James Gillespie is from *Hymns for Today's Church* (London, 1982) and was composed for the boys in the choir at the school where Gillespie was Director of Music.

LW/JeW

519 Blessed city, heavenly Salem

Music: **URBS BEATA JERUSALEM**

This text, part of a longer proper office hymn for the dedication of a church, first appeared in the 1892 edition of the *Hymnal*. It is matched here with the chant tune with which it has been historically associated.

Words: See hymn 518.

Music: See hymn 122. The accompaniment by Charles Winfred Douglas was composed for use with this tune in *H40*.

520 Blessed city, heavenly Salem

Music: **ORIEL**

A well-known metrical tune has been chosen for the second appearance of this medieval office hymn.

Words: See hymn 518.

Music: See hymn 248.

521 Put forth, O God, thy Spirit's might

Music: **CHELSEA SQUARE**

General Theological Seminary in the Chelsea neighborhood of New York City played an important part in the creation of this hymn as both the author/composer and harmonizer were faculty members there. This relationship and the Seminary itself are memorialized in the name of the tune that honors the location of the school.

Words: The text, a prayer for the Church, was written by Howard Chandler Robbins and published in H. Augustine Smith's *New Church Hymnal* (New York, 1937), of which the author was associate editor. Robbins, an Episcopal priest, was a member of the Joint Commission on the Revision of the Hymnal. The text first appeared in an Episcopal hymnal in *H40*.

Music: The tune CHELSEA SQUARE was hummed by the author of this text to Ray Francis Brown at the General Theological Seminary, Chelsea Square, New York City in 1941. With a harmonization by Mr. Brown the tune first appeared with the text in *H40*. A descant by Lois Fyfe from *The Christ Church Descant Book* (Nashville, 1974) has been added for optional use with st. 4.

***H40c* and RG**

522 Glorious things of thee are spoken

***Music:* AUSTRIA**

1889 marked the year of the first published matching of this text and tune in the *Primitive Methodist Hymnal* (London, 1889) and the Supplement (1889) to the 1875 edition of *HA&M*. Until the post-World War II years, that relationship seemed inviolate. The association of the tune, however, as the German national anthem and German oppression of the Jews during World War II have made the singing of AUSTRIA for many people difficult, if not impossible.

Words: For a substantial period of his life John Newton was accustomed to writing hymns, often at a rate of one each week, exploring the same biblical themes of his preaching. Presumably "Glorious things of thee are spoken" shares its origins with a sermon Newton preached on Is. 33:20-21 sometime before February 1779. The hymn is a fairly close paraphrase of the scriptural passage. It first appeared in print in Newton's *Olney Hymns* (London, 1779), Bk. 1, no. 60, in five stanzas. Newton's final stanza, which, like a good sermon contains the application of the text on which it is based, is omitted, possibly because of the oblique reference to the Calvinist doctrine of election in the first two lines:

Saviour, if of Zion's city
　I, thro' grace a member am;
Let the world deride or pity,
　I will glory in thy name:
Fading is the worldling's pleasure,
　All his boasted pomp and show;
Solid joys and lasting treasure,
　None but Zion's children know.

The only modification of Newton's text is in st. 2, where " . . . Ever will their thirst assuage?" replaces " . . . Ever flows their thirst t'assuage?" It first appeared in the musical edition of the 65 "Additional Hymns" in *Episcopal Common Praise* (New York, 1865).

The hymn is one of the best-loved in the English tradition, partially due to its connection with the tune AUSTRIA (see commentary below), an almost exclusive association that lasted until the beginning of the Second World War. Since then, although still sung to AUSTRIA, it has taken on new meaning with the tune specifically composed for it by Canon Cyril Taylor (see commentary on ABBOT'S LEIGH at no. 523).

Music: Haydn composed this tune as the Austrian national anthem. During his visits to London in 1791 to 1792 and 1794 to 1795 he had been much struck by the powerful hold that "God save the King" exercised over the emotions of the British people (see 716). Accordingly, the Imperial High Chancellor Count von Saarau commissioned for Austria a similar national song. The words "Gott erhalte Franz der Kaiser" were by Lorenz Leopold Haschka. Haydn composed his immortal melody in January 1797, and the song was first performed in the public theatres on the Emperor's birthday, February 12. After the establishment of the Austrian Republic in 1918 new words were written for the tune by Ottakar Kernstock, "Sei gesegnet ohne Ende."

In 1946 a new national anthem was substituted with music by Mozart. The German national song to Haydn's tune "Deutschland, Deutschland uber Alles" was written in the 1840s by Hoffmann von Fallersleben.

Example 1

The first phrase of the tune comes from a Croatian folk song, "Vjutro rano se ja vstanem" ("Just after dawn I rose and left").[1] However, the rest is original. Haydn made many attempts before he was satisfied.[2] Example 1 shows the form he finally decided on, written for voice and piano; he called it "Volck's Lied."

There was also an orchestral version, officially circulated for use in theatres and concerts.[3] Haydn became inordinately fond of the song, and he used it for a set of variations forming the slow movement of his string quartet in C, Op. 76, no. 3 (The "Emperor" Quartet), which he subsequently arranged for the piano. According to Carl Ferdinand Pohl it was the last thing he played on the piano on 26 May 1809, five days before his death.

Dr. Charles Burney published an arrangement for soloists and chorus in London about 1800, with his own translation of the text. The tune's potential as a hymn for use in worship was first recognized in Britain and America. Dr. Edward Miller adapted it to the text "Jesu, soft harmonious name" and printed it as No. 240 of his collection *Dr. Watts' Psalms and Hymns Set to New Music*, which was entered at Stationers Hall on 18 October 1800. The metre of this hymn was 7.7. 7.7. The first American adaptation was by John Cole to the text "Angels, roll the rock away," in the same metre with extended alleluias to take up the second half of the tune. That version was published in Cole's *Sacred Music* (Baltimore, 1803). In 1809 William Russell included it in his revised music book for the Foundling Hospital, London, where he had been organist since 1801; the text was "Praise the Lord, ye heavens, adore him" (see 373), which has been very frequently associated with the tune. In these early sources, it was often named GERMAN HYMN, HAYDN, or VIENNA; we do not know when AUSTRIA was first applied to it.

The exact form has varied from time to time. Haydn did not write a D appoggiatura to the C in measure 13, and his cadences at the ends of phrases 6 and 8 were slightly different from ours (see Example 1). He consistently marked the last phrase to be repeated, and this was observed in most of the earlier hymn tune forms. As may be seen in Example 1, he made use of rests in the first half of the tune; Cole was one of the few adapters who respected them. A harmony approximating Haydn's but in four parts throughout was used in early editions of *HA&M*. It was slightly touched up for *EH* and in this form is reproduced here. The descant is by Michael Young, from *55 Descants on Familiar Hymns* (Chicago, 1985).

---

1. For a detailed comparison, see H. Hadow, *Collected Essays* (1928), 97-101.
2. Ibid.
3. The full score is published in *The Harmonicon* (1825), 229, and also in H. C. Robbins Landon, *Haydn: Chronicle and Works, IV* (Bloomington, IN and London, 1977), 279-283.

RAL/NT

523 Glorious things of thee are spoken

Music: **ABBOT'S LEIGH**

The matching of this text with this tune, written as an alternative to AUSTRIA, is gaining a high degree of acceptance. The tune, which appears at two other places in *H82* [379 and 511], was one of the tunes most requested for inclusion in this revised edition of the *Hymnal*.

Words: See hymn 522.

Music: See also hymn 511. ABBOT'S LEIGH by Cyril Vincent Taylor first appeared in association with the John Newton text "Glorious things of thee are spoken" in *HA&M* (1950). It was written in 1941, while the composer was head of religious broadcasts at the wartime BBC headquarters in Bristol, a time when AUSTRIA, the tune hitherto associated with the text, was virtually unusable because of its association with the text of the German national anthem "Deutschland, Deutschland uber alles." The tune was widely known by the time it was published in 1950 through frequent use of the "Daily Services" and other BBC broadcasts.

RG

524 I love thy kingdom, Lord

Music: **ST. THOMAS (WILLIAMS)**

A Congregational minister and president of Yale University, Timothy Dwight, is the author of this text, which entered the *Hymnal* in 1826, twenty-five years after its first publication. One of the earliest of American hymn texts in common use, it was matched with this tune in the Hutchins edition of the 1871 *Hymnal*, a practice that is shared by Congregational and Reformed Church hymnals and which continues to the present.

Words: "I love thy kingdom, Lord" is the earliest American hymn text remaining in common use. It has been in the *Hymnal* since 1826. Timothy Dwight published the text in his edition of Isaac Watts's *The Psalms of David Imitated in the Language of the New Testament and Adapted to the Christian Use and Worship* (Hartford, CT, 1801). Although Dwight's text is listed as the "Third Part" of Ps. 137, it is only distantly related to verses 5 and 6: "If I forget thee, O Jerusalem, let my right hand forget her cunning. If I do not remember thee, let my tongue cleave to the roof of my mouth; if I prefer not Jerusalem above my chief joy." The title given to this hymn is "Love to the Church." Originally written in eight stanzas, the present hymn is a cento* consisting of sts. 1, 5, 6, 7, and 8. The original second, third, and fourth stanzas read:

2. I love thy church, O God!
   Her walls before thee stand,
Dear as the apple of thine eye,
   And graven on thy hand.

3. If e'er to bless thy sons
   My voice, or hands, deny,
These hands let useful skill forsake,
   This voice in silence die.

4. If e'er my heart forget
   Her welfare, or her woe,
Let every joy this heart forsake,
   And every grief o'erflow.

Music: This tune appeared anonymously in its original form as the second quarter of a long tune entitled HOLBORN in Aaron Williams's *The Universal Psalmist* (London, 1763), set to Charles Wesley's "Soldiers of Christ, arise." Because it is marked "never before printed" in that volume, it is generally attributed to Williams himself. HOLBORN was republished in *The American Harmony, or Universal Psalmodist* (Newburyport, MA, ca. 1774), thus becoming the earliest American tune for "Soldiers of Christ, arise." The shortened form of the tune appeared in Williams's *The New Universal Psalmodist* (London, 1770) as ST. THOMAS and was set to Ps. 48, beginning "Great is the Lord our God." ST. THOMAS also appeared in Isaac Smith's *A Collection of Psalm Tunes in Three Parts* (London, ca. 1780). Apparently, Williams himself shortened the original. The tune has appeared in various forms in many books.

HE/MBJ

525 The Church's one foundation

Music: **AURELIA**

This hymn, one of the most loved by people of many denominations, entered the *Hymnal* in 1871. The tune by Samuel Sebastian Wesley was matched with the text in the Appendix to *HA&M* (1868) and in the Hutchins and Ireland music editions of the 1871 *Hymnal*.

Words: This hymn has proved to have universal appeal. Although it has very specific Anglican origins, it has breached many denominational and linguistic barriers. The text was born out of a pastoral need. Samuel Stone, a curate in Windsor, was concerned that his parishioners should understand basic Christian doctrine. Thus, like Mrs. Alexander in her *Hymns for Children* (London, 1848) (see the essay "British Hymnody in the Nineteenth Century," vol. 1, 435-436), Stone chose to write hymns on the Creed. They were published as *Lyra Fidelium: Twelve Hymns on the Twelve Articles of the Apostles' Creed* (Oxford and London, 1866). The ninth hymn "The Church's one foundation," in seven stanzas, was headed: "Article XI. The Holy Catholic Church: the Communion of Saints. 'He is the Head of the Body, the Church' [Col. 1.8, etc.]." Two years later it appeared in the 1868 Appendix to *HA&M* (with AURELIA), slightly revised (by the author) and reduced to five stanzas, the form that subsequently had almost universal acceptance. A principal revision was in st. 2, which originally began "She is from every nation." Stone's st. 3 was omitted:

The Church shall never perish!
  Her dear Lord, to defend,
To guide, sustain, and cherish,
  Is with her to the end;
Though there be those who hate her,
  And false sons in her pale,
Against or foe or traitor
  She ever shall prevail.

The last stanza was a conflation of the last two of Stone's original seven:

6. Yet she on earth hath union
  With God, the Three in One,
So hath she sweet communion
  With those whose rest is won;
With all her sons and daughters
  Who, by the Master's hand
Led through the deathly waters,
  Repose in Eden-land.

7. O happy ones and holy!
  Lord, give us grace that we
Like them, the meek and lowly,
  On high may dwell with Thee;
There, past the border mountains,
  Where, in sweet vales, the Bride
With Thee, by living fountains,
For ever shall abide.

The subject matter of the hymn, especially the references "false sons" within the Church, which was being torn apart by "schisms" and "heresies," was Stone's reaction to the "Colenso Controversy." John William Colenso was the Anglican Bishop of Natal in South Africa who, from the early 1850s, became increasingly notorious on account of his nontraditional views and actions. To begin with, he appeared to condone polygamy when he did not insist on baptized black Africans divorcing all their wives except one. Then he published a commentary on Romans in which he denied the traditional understanding of eternal punishment and sacramental theology. It was Colenso's papers on *The Pentateuch and the Book of Joshua Critically Examined*, however, issued over a period of years beginning in 1862, that created the greatest storm. It was one of the early works of Higher Criticism in which Colenso challenged a whole range of traditional views of Scripture, primarily challenging its historical authenticity. Colenso, a former teacher of mathematics at Harrow, was charged with "doing sums on the Pentateuch" and undermining the foundations of the Christian faith. In 1863 Colenso was deposed from his see by the saintly Bishop Robert Gray of Cape Town. Colenso appealed to the Judicial Committee of the Privy Council in London and, although he won his case, Bishop Gray's worthy defense of the Catholic faith inspired many, including Stone, who was moved to write "The Church's one foundation."

Despite his legal victory, Colenso was excommunicated in 1866, but the controversy continued throughout the Anglican Communion. Canadian Anglicans called for a pan-Anglican conference to be set up so that the Church as a whole could resolve this and other controversies. The result was the first Lambeth Conference of 1867, when the implications of the Colenso case were high on the agenda.

In the remaining decades of the nineteenth century, Anglicanism was beset by other searing controversies, such as the challenges to traditional thinking posed by Darwinism and Liberalism and the unseemly ecclesiastical litigation that accompanied the rise of Anglo-Catholicism. Stone's hymn spoke to these times and became exceedingly popular.

The dean and chapter of Salisbury Cathedral wished to use "The Church's one foundation" as a processional hymn, thus, in 1885, Stone expanded his hymn to ten stanzas by the addition of three new stanzas to his original seven. These were inserted as a sequence following the first five and before the concluding two stanzas, which were renumbered 9 and 10:

6. So, Lord, she stands before Thee,
   For evermore Thine own;
No merit is her glory,
   Her boasting this alone:
That she who did not choose Thee
   Came, chosen, at Thy call,
Never to leave or lose Thee
   Or from Thy favour fall.

7. For Thy true word remaineth—
 No creature far or nigh,
No fiend of ill who reigneth
 In hell or haunted sky;
No doubting world's derision
 That holds her in despite,
Shall hide her from Thy vision,
 Shall lure her from Thy light.

8. Thine, Thine! in bliss or sorrow,
 As well in shade as shine;
Of old, to-day, to-morrow,
 To all the ages, Thine!
Thine in her great commission,
 Baptized into Thy name,
And to her last fruition
 Of all her hope and aim.

At the third Lambeth Conference in 1888, when the Lambeth Quadrilateral, the classic Anglican statement regarding the essence of the historic Christian faith, was adopted, this longer ten-stanza version was sung as the processional hymn at all the three great services at Canterbury Cathedral, Westminster Abbey, and St. Paul's Cathedral. Afterward, Bishop Nelson of New Zealand wrote the following lines, which were published in *Church Bells* November 1888:

Bard of the Church, in these divided days
For words of harmony to thee we praise:
Of love and oneness thou didst strike the chords,
The Church's one Foundation thou didst sing,
Beauty and Bands to Her thy numbers bring.
Through church and chancel, aisle, and transept deep,
In fullest melody thy watch-notes sweep;
Now in the desert, now upon the main,
In mine and forest, and on the citied plain;
From Lambeth's towers to far New Zealand coast,
Bard of the Church, thy blast inspires the host

(*Julian*, 1147).

Music: Samuel Sebastian Wesley composed this quintessentially Victorian tune for Charles Kemble's *Selection of Psalms and Hymns* (London, 1864), of which he was the musical editor. The book was in "Dutch door" format; that is, the top half containing the texts was detached from the bottom half containing the tunes, though they shared a common spine and covers. Thus, tunes and texts could be matched at will. This tune was no. 122 and was dated "S.S. Wesley, 1864" in the tune index; it was recommended for use with hymn texts 601, 602, and 603, which were the three parts of a John Mason Neale hymn, "Brief life is here our portion," "For thee O dear, dear country," and "Jerusalem the golden" (see no. 624).

According to Wesley's pupil John Kendrick Pyne, a group of friends were "discussing a dish of strawberries" in Wesley's drawing room in the Winchester Cathedral close "when Wesley came rushing up from below with a scrap of Ms. in his hand, a psalm-tune that instant finished. Placing it on the instrument he said: 'I think this will be popular.' My Mother was the first ever to sing it to the words, 'Jerusalem the Golden.' The company liked it, and Mrs. Wesley on the spot christened it 'Aurelia.' "[1] Although *aurelia* is not, in fact, the Latin word for "golden" that was doubtless the intention.

The name is the one that Wesley gave it; the harmonies are also his own, with the one minor exception that he wrote an E♭ rather than a G in the alto part of the seventeenth chord. In *The European Psalmist* (London, 1872) he altered this note to an F. The harsh chords in this and the following phrase are highly typical of Wesley; the overall melodic shape, with two high lines between two low ones, recalls a typical form of English folk songs. Nevertheless, Erik Routley thought this "one of his most commonplace and dreary tunes."[2]

The tune-text match dates from the 1868 Appendix to *HA&M*. Its popularity probably dates from 1872, when it was used in the thanksgiving service for the recovery of the Prince of Wales at St. Paul's Cathedral. For further information on the tune see *H40c*, page 253.

---

1. *English Church Music V/1* (London, 1935), 5-6.
2. *Bulletin* of the Hymn Society of Great Britain and Ireland, II/1 [January, 1948], 3.

RAL/NT

526 Let saints on earth in concert sing

Music: **DUNDEE**

Matched with a classic psalm tune, this text of Charles Wesley is a profound and beautiful poetic statement of the meaning of the Communion of Saints. It has added greatly to the enrichment of our hymnody and the spiritual lives of the faithful since it first entered the *Hymnal* in 1892. It is particularly appropriate at the Burial of the Dead.

Words: "Let saints on earth in concert sing" is drawn from the first hymn, in five eight-line stanzas, of Charles Wesley's anonymously published *Funeral Hymns: Second Series* (London, 1759) (*Poetical Works*, vol. VI, 215f). The original began with the powerful and unproblematic lines:

> Come let us join our friends above
> That have obtained the prize,
> And on the eagle wings of love
> To joy celestial rise—

a form that Methodists from John Wesley on have quoted and that has been much loved among them (it figured in Wesley's *Pocket Hymn Book* [London, 1785] and appeared in 1831 in the official British Wesleyan Supplement to the *Collection of Hymns for the use of the People called Methodists*).

Since the 1861 edition of *HA&M* (with a source in F. H. Murray's *Hymnal for Use in the English Church* [London, 1852]) and the *Hymnal* of 1892, Anglicans have known this hymn in a characteristic version that takes off from the original fifth and sixth lines:

> Let all the saints terrestrial sing
> With those to glory gone . . .

The original third stanza and the first half of the fourth have totally disappeared:

> Ten thousand to their endless home
> This solemn moment fly,
> And we are to the margin come,
> And we expect to die;
> His militant, embodied host,
> With wishful looks we stand,

And long to see that happy coast,
And reach that heavenly land.

Our old companions in distress
We haste again to see,
And eager long for our release
And full felicity . . .

The third line of the current fourth stanza (the seventh of the original fourth) originally read "the blood-besprinkled bands" (cf. Rev. 7:14). The present fifth stanza omits the first half and adapts the second half of the original fifth:

Our spirits too shall quickly join,
Like theirs, with glory crowned,
And shout to hear our Captain's sign,
To hear His trumpet sound:
O that we now might grasp our Guide!
O that the word were given!
Come, Lord of Hosts, the waves divide,
And land us all in heaven.

Music: For background to this tune, see hymn 126. The melody is given here in a harmonization based on Thomas Ravenscroft's four-part setting that appeared in his *Whole Booke of Psalms* (London, 1621). In Ravenscroft, the melody appears in the tenor. Another faux-bourdon setting is given at 709.

GW/RAL

527 Singing songs of expectation

Music: **TON-Y-BOTEL**

This text, which in prior editions of the *Hymnal* appeared with the opening line "Through the night of doubt and sorrow," is matched here with the popular Welsh hymn tune TON-Y-BOTEL.

Words: Written for the second Sunday in Advent, this Danish hymn has, through the translation of Sabine Baring-Gould, come into widespread use in the English-speaking Church. Written by Bernhard (or Bernhardt) Severin Ingemann in 1825, it first appeared in his

Hoimesse Psalmer (High-Mass Hymns) (Copenhagen, 1843). Baring-Gould's translation was published in *The People's Hymnal* (London, 1867) and in an altered form in the revised edition of *HA&M* (1875).

Hymns Ancient and Modern gives the hymn in its complete format, though its pairing with an 8 7. 8 7. tune results in a separation of the text at the midpoint of each stanza. The Text Committee of the SCCM has omitted the entire final stanza and has further altered the text, tranposing the first two couplets of st. 1. The Baring-Gould translation is as follows:

Through the night of doubt and sorrow
Onward goes the pilgrim band,
Singing songs of expectation,
Marching to the Promised Land.

A further alteration in support of the SCCM's intent to use inclusive language wherever possible, may be noted at st. 1, line 7, "Brother clasps the hand of brother . . . " Baring-Gould's translation of st. 4 is not found in *H82*:

Onward therefore, pilgrim brothers,
Onward with the Cross our aid!
Bear its shame, and fight its battle,
till we rest beneath its shade.
Soon shall come the great awaking,
Soon the rending of the tomb;
then the scattering of all shadows,
And the end of toil and gloom.

The text first appeared in an Episcopal collection in the 1892 edition of the *Hymnal*.

Music: See hymn 381.

TS

528 Lord, you give the great commission

Music: **ROWTHORN**

In its search for hymnody by contemporary poets for possible inclusion in *H82*, the SCCM was rewarded in its discovery of several poets whose works combine strengths in both biblical and liturgical imagery with poetical excellence. Such is this text by Jeffery Rowthorn that gained immediate acceptance and use soon after its approval by the 1982 General Convention.

Words: "Lord, you give the great commission" by the Right Rev. Jeffery Rowthorn is a strong text for mission based on sayings of our Lord from the gospels of Matthew and Luke. At the time of its creation, the poet (now Suffragan Bishop of the Diocese of Connecticut) was the Bishop Goddard Professor of Pastoral Theology, Berkeley Divinity School at Yale. Bishop Rowthorn also served as co-editor of the revision of the *Hymnal for Colleges and Schools* (New Haven, 1991) and as General Editor of *Laudamus* (New Haven, 1980), a hymnal supplement for use in daily worship at Yale Divinity School. It was written for use with the Cyril V. Taylor tune ABBOT'S LEIGH and first appeared in the 1980 supplement.

Each stanza of this text derives from a saying of our Lord, which the poet relates to a specific call to mission:

st. 1: Heal the sick and preach the word, Mt. 10:8
st. 2: In my name baptize and teach, Mt. 28:19
st. 3: This is my body, this my blood, Mt. 26:26-29
st. 4: Father, what they do forgive, Lk. 23:34
st. 5: I am with you to the end, Mt. 28:20

In st. 1, for example, the quotation from Mt. 10:8 "Heal the sick and preach the word" speaks directly to the call that we, as the body of Christ, the Church, witness to God's purpose "with renewed integrity." In succeeding stanzas we are called to mission, to a life of sharing, to forgiveness, and to servanthood. A refrain asking that the Holy Spirit "empower us for the work of ministry" closes each stanza.

Music: The tune ROWTHORN was written for use with the text "Lord, you give the great commission" by Alec Wyton. In its original manuscript form, it appeared with alternating three- and four-beat measures to reflect the movement of the text. After it had been sent out with many other tunes for trial use in parish churches across the country, it was suggested that the alternating pattern of beats could be confusing. Therefore, the tune was "straightened out" and for the most part, the three-beat measures were modified. The wonderful five-beat phrase climaxing on the highest pitch E$^{\flat}$ for the text "Spirit's gifts empower," however, was retained. This is an example of the care that the SCCM took in making the music of *H82* accessible to congregations. The composer and the poet, Jeffery Rowthorn, met while both were teaching at Union Theological Seminary in New York, and Dr. Wyton named the tune after his colleague and friend.

RG/AW

529 In Christ there is no East or West

Music: **MCKEE**

This text first appeared in an Episcopal hymnal in *H40* where it was matched with MCKEE, a tune that has the distinction of being one of the first works coming from the African-American culture to enter a hymnal of a major Protestant denomination (see the essay "Cultural Diversity," vol. 1, 29).

Words: "In Christ there is no East or West," John Oxenham's sole lyric to attain lasting use in worship, highlighted "The Pageant of Darkness and Light" that he mounted for the London Missionary Society in 1908 and restaged several times in Britain and the United States before including the verse in *Bees in Amber* (n.p., 1913) and the *Selected Poems of John Oxenham* (London, 1924). (John Oxenham is a pseudonym for William Arthur Dunkerley that he used when writing as a diversion. With the attainment of success he adopted both the name and the vocation.) The apprehensive publishers of the first collection limited the initial printing to two hundred copies, a number that proved to be less than 0.1% of the eventual sales!

In its efforts to use inclusive language whenever possible, changes were made in the text by the SCCM. In this particular instance work on textual alteration was begun prior to *H82* by the commission that produced the *LBW*, and has been continued more recently by editors of *The Psalter Hymnal* (Grand Rapids, MI, 1987), where a 1982 text by Michael A. Perry that employs the opening line of the Oxenham text was used; *The United Methodist Hymnal* (Nashville, 1989), and *The Presbyterian Hymnal* (Louisville, 1990). Regrettably, to date a common form of this important ecumenical text has not been found. In *H82* the original st. 2 has been deleted and two alterations have been made in st. 3. The middle two stanzas originally read:

In him shall true hearts everywhere
  Their high communion find;
His service is the golden cord
  Close binding all mankind.

Join hands, then, brothers of the faith,
  Whate'er your race may be!
Who serves my Father as a son
  Is surely kin to me.

Music: The tune MCKEE was adapted from the African-American spiritual "I know the angel's done changed my name," a song popularized in the latter part of the nineteenth century by the Jubilee Singers of Fisk University. Somewhat later, the melody was arranged for piano by Samuel Coleridge-Taylor in his *Twenty-Four Negro Melodies*, Op. 59 (Boston, 1905) under the title, "The Angels changed my name." Charles Villiers Stanford in a letter to Coleridge-Taylor states that the melody is an Irish tune taken by emigrants to the US and adapted by the negro. It is therefore doubtful if the tune is truly an "African-American Spiritual."[1] H. T. Burleigh adapted the spiritual for use with the above text, and named it MCKEE after the Rev. Elmer M. McKee, rector of St. George's Church in New York, where Burleigh sang for many years. The tune was published first in leaflet form and then made its hymnal debut in *H40*. It has now been published in many other hymnals in the United States and Britain, including *Hymns for Church and School* (London, 1964), the *Australian Hymnbook* (London, 1979), and *Hymns and Psalms: A Methodist and Ecumenical Hymn Book* (London, 1983).

1. See the *Bulletin* of the Hymn Society of Great Britain and Ireland, no. 133, p. 124.

RG and HMcK/RG

530 Spread, O spread, thou mighty word

***Music:* GOTT SEI DANK**

This text for mission, matched with this tune, first appeared in an Episcopal hymnal in *H40*. Alterations have been made in the text in response to the SCCM's intent to use inclusive language, and a new st. 4, retaining the former themes, has been written for this edition by F. Bland Tucker.

Words: This hymn bears witness to the transition that took place in early nineteenth-century thought and action in Germany. It represents a move away from individualistic pietism to a worldwide concern for education and mission. Jonathan Friedrich Bahnmaier, pastor of Kirchheim in Württemberg and a principal member of the editorial committee of the influential *Gesangbuch* (Württemberg, 1842), wrote the hymn sometime before 1827; after that year it was issued as a separate imprint. The first hymnal to include the seven four-line stanzas was the *Kern des deutschen Liederschatzes* (Nuremberg, 1828):

1. Walte, walte nah und fern,
Allgewaltig Wort des Herrn,
Wo nur seiner All-macht Ruf
Menschen für den Himmel schuf.

2. Wort vom Vater, der die Welt
Schuf und in den Armen hält
Und aus seinem Schoss herab
Seinen Sohn zum Heil ihr gab;

3. Wort von des Erlösers Huld,
Der der Erde schwere Schuld
Durch des Heil'gen Todes Tat
Ewig weggenommen hat;

4. Kräftig Wort von Gottes Geist,
Der den Weg zum Himmel weist
Und durch seine heil'ge Kraft
Wollen und Vollbringen schafft;

5. Wort des Lebens, stark und rein,
Aller Völker harren dein:
Walte fort, bis aus der Nacht
Alle Welt zum Tag erwacht!

6. Auf zur Ernt in alle Welt!
Weithin wogt das weisse Feld,
Klein ist noch der Schnitter Zahl,
Viel der Garben überall.

7. Herr der Ernte, gross und gut,
Wirk zum Werke Lust und Mut,
Lass die Völker allzumal
Schauen deines Lichtes Strahl.

Bahnmaier indicated that his hymn should be sung to NUN KOMM, DER HEIDEN HEILAND [54], an association that undergirds the advent themes that underlie the missionary concern of the text.

The hymn was also included in *Versuch eines allgemeinen evangelischen Gesang- und Gebet-buch* (Hamburg, 1833), edited by C. K. J. von Bunsen, the source used by Catherine Winkworth for her complete translation that appeared in *Lyra Germanica: Second Series* (London, 1858), beginning "Spread, oh spread, thou mighty Word." The hymn has justly earned its reputation as one of the finest among missionary hymns, although the first *Hymnal* to include it was *H40*. *The Hymnal 1940 Companion* comments: "The present translation comprises the first five stanzas of the original. It is basically a new rendering, made by two members of the Committee on Translations, JCRH, Arthur A. Farlander and Winfred Douglas, but using the incipit and occasional lines from the now traditional translation by Catherine Winkworth" (*H40c*, no. 253). For *H82*, st. 4 was replaced with newly written words by F. Bland Tucker.

Music: See hymn 47.

RAL

531 O Spirit of the living God

Music: **MELCOMBE**

The matching of this text and tune is one of long standing. It is found in both the Hutchins and Tucker editions of the 1871 *Hymnal*. The text, however, has been in the *Hymnal* since 1826.

Words: James Montgomery wrote "O Spirit of the living God," a text of six stanzas, to be sung at a public meeting of the Auxiliary Missionary Society of the West Riding of Yorkshire in Salem Chapel, Leeds, June 4, 1823. He revised it carefully for publication in his *Christian Psalmist* (Glasgow and London, 1825), where it appeared under the title "The Spirit Accompanying the Word of God." The following is omitted after the third stanza:

O Spirit of the Lord! prepare
  All the round earth her God to meet;
Breathe thou abroad like morning air,
  Till hearts of stone begin to beat.

The present fourth stanza began "Baptize the nations." It was followed by a concluding stanza:

God from eternity hath willed,
  All flesh shall his salvation see;
So be the Father's love fulfilled,
  The Saviour's sufferings crowned through thee.

Music: MELCOMBE was first attributed to Samuel Webbe in Ralph Harrison's *Sacred Harmony,* vol. 2 (London, 1791), where it received its present name. The tune's first appearance was as a hymn, "O Salutaris Hostia," in *An Essay on the Church Plain Chant* (London, 1782), probably compiled by Webbe. The tune also appears in the Webbe *Collection of Motetts and Antiphons* (London, 1792) with a notation that appears with every item in the collection, "Published by permission of Mr. Webbe."

HLW/WTJ

532 How wondrous and great thy works, God of praise

Music: **OLD 104TH**

This text is distinguished by having been written for inclusion in the *Hymnal* of 1826 and by appearing in every edition since that time. The matching of the text with this tune first occurred in an Episcopal publication in *H40*.

Words: This is one of nine hymns written by Henry Ustick Onderdonk for the *Hymnal* of 1826. It is a paraphrase of the Song of Moses and the Lamb, Rev. 15:3-4, Canticle 19, "The Song of the Redeemed." The Text Committee of the SCCM, in its effort to remove language that could be interpreted as either pejorative or discriminatory, altered line 1 of st. 2 that originally read "To nations long dark."

Music: This splendid tune first appeared, fully harmonized, in Thomas Ravenscroft's *Whole Booke of Psalmes . . . Composed into 4 Parts by Sundry Authors* (London, 1621), to the text of Ps. 104, Old Version, "My soul, praise the Lord." It is generally assumed to have been wholly of Ravenscroft's composition, though it is not possible to be certain of this, since Ravenscroft also attached his name to older tunes that he had merely harmonized. It was not really the "old" 104th tune, for in the Sternhold and Hopkins psalm books this text had been designed to go with a tune of twice the length, the French Ps. 104.[1] From 1622 onward, however, the older tune was displaced by that of Ravenscroft's in many editions of the psalm book.

The original rhythm of the last line was as in Example 1. (All examples are converted to the key and note values corresponding to the *Hymnal* version, with original clefs, signatures, and first notes preceding each example.) This was clearly an attempt to cater to the irregular word stress pattern at the end of the first verse: "Honour and majestie in thee shine most clear." However, it did not match the other verses of the psalm (see Example 1, verse 2), and it has caused constant trouble to subsequent editors.

Example 1

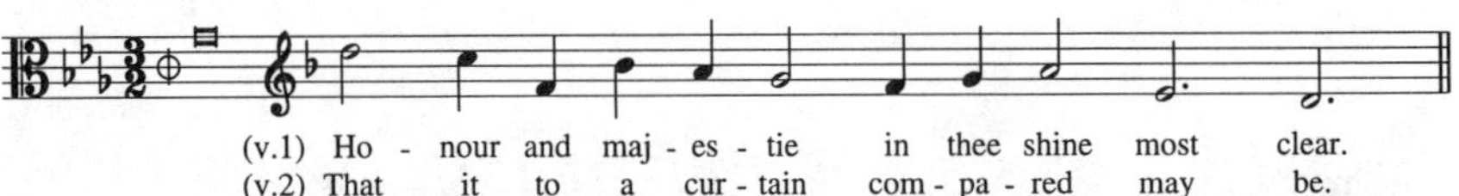

Tate and Brady's *Supplement to the New Version of the Psalms* (London, 1700) set the tune to their new alternate version of Ps. 67, "Our God bless us all with mercy and love." James Green, in *A Collection of Choice Psalm-Tunes*, 3rd ed. (Nottingham, 1715), gave his own rhythmic interpretation of the last line and brought it to rest in F (Example 2).[2]

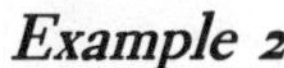

Example 2

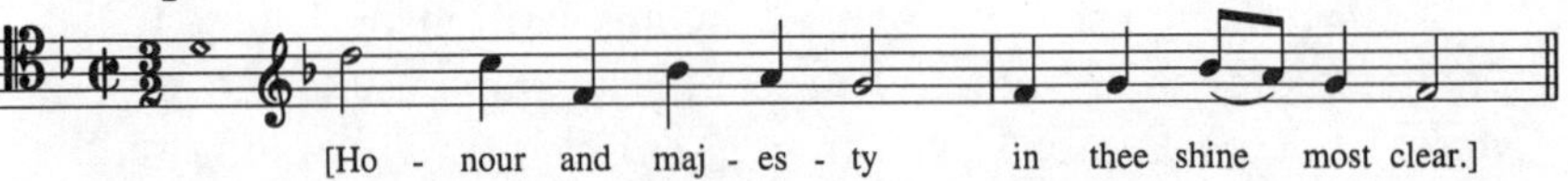

William Turner's 1728 edition of Ravenscroft's *Psalmes* completely reordered the tune rhythmically, in split common time (Example 3).

Example 3

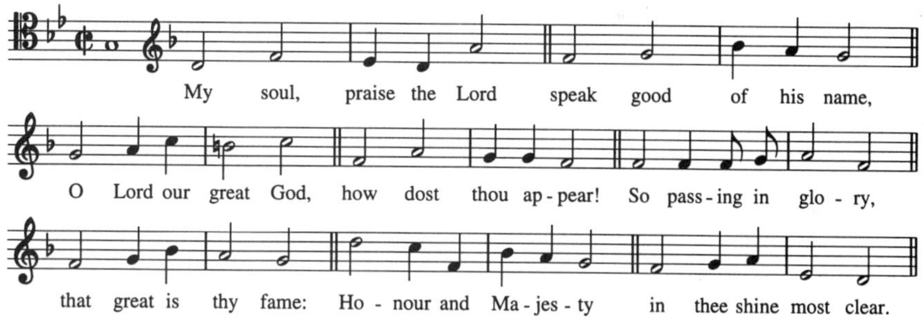

After 1750, OLD 104TH dropped out of use for a while, having been replaced for texts of this unusual metre by the popular HANOVER (see 388). It was revived for Baptist use in John Rippon's *Selection of Psalm and Hymn Tunes* (London, 1792), but it was slow to catch on. It is found in no American publication up to 1820. William Cross, in the preface to his *Collection of Psalm Tunes* (London, 1818), professed a desire to "revert to the genuine original tunes," yet he printed this tune in F, perhaps as a result of misreading the clef.

In *HA&M* (1861) the tune is set to "O worship the King" (see 388), Robert Grant's reworking of Ps. 104; Example 4 shows how the musical editor, William H. Monk, dealt with the rhythmic problem of the last line.

Example 4

In 1875 yet another solution was tried (Example 5), and this was retained until 1950.

Example 5

The Episcopal hymnals did not include the tune until 1940; then, as now, it followed *EH* in giving the last line the same rhythm as the third. Further discussion of the rhythm issue may be found in the *Bulletin* of the Hymn Society of Great Britain and Ireland, nos. 95 and 97.

The harmonization closely follows Ravenscroft's original,[3] with only such changes as are necessary when the tune is moved from the tenor to the soprano voice. The alto E in the third chord of line 3, however, faithfully copied from Ravenscroft, was almost certainly a misprint; F is a much more likely reading.

There is a particularly fine chorale prelude on OLD 104TH by Charles Hubert Hastings Parry, published in 1912; it is in 9/8 time and allots the tune to the pedals. Parry used the ending shown in Example 5.

---

1. See M. Frost, *English & Scottish Psalm & Hymn Tunes c. 1543-1677* (London, 1953), no. 118.
2. For the whole tune in this version see E. Routley, *The Music of Christian Hymns* (Chicago, 1981), Example 163.
3. See M. Frost, *A Historical Companion to Hymns Ancient and Modern* (London, 1962), 237.

RG/NT

533 How wondrous and great thy works, God of praise

Music: **LYONS**

The matching of this text and tune is one of long and persistent standing. It can be traced to *A Tune Book*, compiled by a committee of the House of Bishops and published in New York in 1859, and has been included in music editions of every edition of the *Hymnal* since that date.

Words: See hymn 532.

Music: The source of the tune LYONS has long been a matter of uncertainty. The tune appeared in the second volume of William Gardiner's *Sacred Melodies* (London, 1815), with the cryptic notation "Subject Haydn." Hymnologists have puzzled over whether this attribution referred to Franz Joseph Haydn or to his younger brother, Johann Michael Haydn. Various passages in the works of both men have been pointed out as possible germs for this familiar melody, but without any degree of certainty. In fact, the source of the tune appears to have been an English publication listed in Anthony van Hoboken's *Joseph Haydn: Thematisch-bibliographisches Werkverzeichnis* (Mainz, 1957, vol. 1, 728-729) as "A Sonatina with Twelve Variations for the Piano Forte, with Violin Accompaniments Composed by G. Haydn." This was issued by the London publishers Goulding, Phipps, D'Almaine & Co. sometime between 1804 and 1808. A comparison of the opening of LYONS with the theme of the "Tempo di Menuetto" from this publication reveals the relationship (Example 1):

Example 1

The G in "G. Haydn" refers to "Giovanni," the Italian equivalent of Joseph. Hoboken, quoting a communication from Pierre Pidona of Territet, also pointed out that the "Tempo di Menuetto" melody appeared with sacred text in two French/Swiss songbooks, one of which, *Recueil de Cantiques* (Vevey-Paris, 1810), antedated Gardiner's collection, and that the theme itself has also been attributed to Mozart.[1] Thus, the melody of the "Tempo di Menuetto" may not actually be by Haydn, and the whole "Sonatina with Twelve Variations" may very well be spurious. Be that as it may, the Goulding, Phipps, d'Almaine & Co. publication was almost certainly the source from which Gardiner drew both the tune and the attribution to Haydn. Since he named the tune for a French city, however, it is also possible that he was aware of the French connection. The first publication of the tune in America was in Oliver Shaw's *Sacred Melodies* (Providence, RI, 1818). LYONS appeared in the Episcopal *Tune Book* (New York, 1859).

---

1. See A. van Hoboken, *Joseph Haydn: Thematisch-bibliographisches Werkverzeichnis* (Mainz, 1978), vol. 3, 341.

DWM

534 God is working his purpose out

Music: **PURPOSE**

The rousing setting of this text first appeared in an Episcopal publication in *H40* and is an example of the influence of the enlarged *Songs of Praise* (London, 1931) upon that collection. To facilitate the singing of the canon it is written out in full with the canonic voice on a separate line.

Words: A distinguished Eton master and a man of wide accomplishments, Arthur Campbell Ainger wrote this hymn at Eton in 1894, with a dedication to Archbishop Benson. It was published that year in leaflet format and was later included in the *Church Missionary Hymn Book* (London, 1899). Its revised form, published in *HA&M* in 1904, is now the standard version. *The Hymnal 1982* has introduced a few changes. Stanza 2, line 1 originally read: "From utmost east to utmost west where'er man's foot hath trod." Furthermore, the hymn has been shortened, st. 3 being omitted:

3. What can we do to work God's work,
 to prosper and increase?
The brotherhood of all mankind,
 the reign of the Prince of Peace?
What can we do to hasten the time,
 the time that shall surely be,
When the earth shall be fill'd with the glory of God
 as the waters cover the sea?

Music: PURPOSE was composed by Martin Shaw for use with this text in the enlarged *Songs of Praise* (London, 1931). Its folklike tune with martial overtones moves in an almost constant pattern of quarter notes in canon at the octave with the bass. The simple plaintive melody moves for the most part in a smooth stepwise fashion and, with the exception of two eighth-note E naturals near the end, constantly avoids the raised leading tone. This produces an almost pentatonic quality found in many folk tunes. The structure of the tune, AA^1BC, carefully reflects the text structure where the contrasting C section is set to the refrain. A dramatic climax is reached in this refrain as the melody ascends from middle C to B and jumps to E on the word "God." The right hand accompaniment is a succession of three- and four-part chords usually in first inversion or root position. This pattern of solid chordal movement enhances the martial quality of the setting, echoing the words of st. 3 "March we forth in the strength of God."

TS/RG

535 Ye servants of God, your Master proclaim

Music: **PADERBORN**

Introduced together to Episcopalians in the supplement *Hymns III*, this is the first appearance of this text and tune in an Episcopal hymnal.

Words: This text by Charles Wesley was first published in John and Charles Wesley's *Hymns for Times of Trouble and Persecution* (London, 1744) (*Poetical Works*, vol. IV, 51f.). The Methodists were finding themselves attacked as Papists and Jacobites, with John Wesley even being taken as the Young Pretender in disguise. This peculiar origin did not prevent the hymn from being adopted into George Whitefield's *Hymns for Social Worship* (London, 1753), Martin Madan's *Collection of Psalms and Hymns* (London, 1760), and A. M. Toplady's *Psalms and Hymns for Public and Private Worship* (London, 1776).

The first among "Hymns to be sung in a tumult," the original contained second and third stanzas filled with maritime imagery, which Church of England and even Methodist hymnals have been willing to drop for the sake of a more general doxological use of the hymn:

> The waves of the sea Have lift up their voice,
> Sore troubled that we In Jesus rejoice;
> The floods they are roaring, But Jesus is here,
> While we are adoring He always is near.
>
> Men, devils engage, The billows arise,
> And horribly rage, And threaten the skies;
> Their fury shall never Our steadfastness shock,
> The weakest believer Is built on a Rock.

This is the text's first appearance in the *Hymnal*. Behind the retained verses stand the liturgical visions of the Book of Revelations, such as 4:9-11; 5:11-14; and 7:9-12.

Music: PADERBORN was a tune of great popularity in the eighteenth century. As a hymn tune, it appeared in *Catholisch-Paderbornisches Gesang-Buch* (Paderborn, 1765) with the text "Mein Hertz sey zufrieden" (see Example 1):

Example 1

The tune is a folk song and may have appeared in print as early as 1742; but the following form of the tune was published in 1807 in Buschnig and von der Hagen's collection of German folk songs (see Example 2):

Example 2

The tune appears in the *Hymnal* in a harmonization by Sir Sydney Nicholson, who first heard it in Paderborn Cathedral. The text and tune were first matched in the second Supplement to *HA&M* (1916).

GW/AW

536 *God has spoken to his people*

Music: **TORAH SONG** [Yisrael V'oraita]

The ethnic diversity of *H82* has been greatly enriched through the addition of texts and tunes that come from the Jewish tradition. This hymn, whose text is deeply rooted in the imagery of Hebrew scripture, is set to a traditional Hasidic folk melody arranged in a manner that honors its ethnic roots.

Words: "Open your ears, O faithful people," a stirring hymn by The Rev. Dr. Willard F. Jabusch, set to a very engaging Hasidic folk melody, TORAH SONG [Yisrael V'oraita], challenges God's people to action in response to the Creator's word. The text, which gained notice and use through its inclusion in *Songs for Celebration* (New York, 1980), a supplement to *H40*, was altered for use in *H82* to make its imagery totally consistent with Hebrew scripture and thus an even more authentic partner of the Hasidic melody to which it is sung. This text, written for St. Celestine Church in Chicago and placed among its hymns for the Church's Mission, is also useful for Advent, the Sundays immediately preceding Advent, and at liturgies centering on Holy Scriptures. The alteration in st. 2 supports the SCCM's desire to use inclusive language wherever possible.

The text as it appeared in *Songs of Celebration* is as follows:

Refrain: God has spoken to his people, hallelujah!
And his words are words of wisdom, hallelujah!

1. Open your ears, O Christian people,
Open your ears and hear good news.
Open your hearts, O royal priesthood,
God has come to you.
Refrain.

2. He who has ears to hear his message,
He who has ears, then let him hear.
He who would learn the way of wisdom,
Let him hear God's word.
Refrain.

3. Israel comes to greet the Savior,
Judah is glad to see his day.
From east and west the peoples travel,
He will show the way.
Refrain.

The need to fit the structure of the tune necessitated the repetition of st. 1 as the fourth stanza.

Music: The emphasis on joy, of which music is an essential component, is a characteristic feature of the Hasidic movement of Judaism, which was founded by Rabbi Israel Baal Shem Tov (1700-1760). This melody does not appear to be an authentic Hasidic melody, but one of a large number of melodies in "Hasidic style," a setting of which appeared in Harry Coopersmith's *Songs of Zion* (New York, 1942, 132). A similar rhythmic pattern to that found in the opening section of the setting here occurs in Samuel Zalmanoff's collection of melodies of the Chabad movement of Judaism, *Sefer Hanigunim*, (New York, 1957), vol. 1, no. 89. The mode is known as the Ahavah Rabbah, with the characteristic augmented second between the second and third degrees of the scale, which frequently modulates to a minor tetrachord on the fourth degree. This mode assumed a prominent place in the synagogue music of Eastern Europe, as well as in Jewish folk and Hasidic music.

RG/JGo

537 Christ for the world we sing!

Music: **MOSCOW**

This text with its strong ecumenical and missionary theme entered the *Hymnal* in 1892, but was not matched with this tune until the music edition of 1916.

Words: While pastor of Plymouth Congregational Church, Cleveland, Samuel Wolcott was a delegate to the annual convention of the Ohio State YMCA, held in Cleveland in 1869. Wolcott, having served as a missionary to Syria in his early ministry, was deeply impressed by the motto in evergreen branches over the convention platform: "Christ for the world, and the world for Christ." The text was formed in his mind as he walked home on February 2, 1869. In that year it appeared in print in two collections: J. W. Suffern, *Song Garland, or Singing for Jesus* (Cleveland, 1869) and Darius Jones, *Songs for the New Life* (Chicago, 1869).

Music: See hymn 365.

HE

538 God of mercy, God of grace

Music: **LUCERNA LAUDONIAE**

This text, which is more a hymn based on a Psalm than it is a paraphrase, appears in the *Hymnal* for the first time. In its three-stanza form it is common to most English hymnals, where it is most often matched with the Henry Smart tune HEATHLANDS. In *H82* it appears with LUCERNA LAUDONIAE, a tune that is also matched with "For the beauty of the earth" [416], the text for which it was composed.

Words: Based on Ps. 67, this text by Henry Francis Lyte first appeared in his *Spirit of the Psalms* (London, 1834), where it was comprised of three stanzas. In the present version, parts of sts. 2 and 3 have been combined. The original stanzas read:

2. Let the people praise Thee, Lord;
Let thy love on all be poured;
Let the nations shout and sing
Glory to their Savior King;
At Thy Feet their tribute pay,
And Thy holy Will obey.

3. Let the people praise Thee Lord;
Earth shall then her fruits afford;
God to man His blessing give,
Man to God devoted live;
All below, and all above,
One in joy, and light, and love.

Music: See hymn 416.

MS

539 O Zion, haste, thy mission high fulfilling

Music: **TIDINGS**

This popular mission hymn matched with this tune entered the *Hymnal* in 1892. For use in *H82*, the text was altered to allow for the use of inclusive language and to remove pejorative images of people who do not yet know the Lord.

Words: "O Zion, haste" is one of more than forty hymns written by Mary Ann Thomson. The greater portion of the hymn was written one evening in 1868 as she sat up with one of her children who was ill with typhoid fever. She states:

> I thought I should like to write a missionary hymn to the tune of 'Hark, hark my soul! Angelic songs are swelling,' as I was fond of that tune, but I could not then get a refrain I liked. I left the hymn unfinished and about three years later I finished it by writing the refrain which now forms a part of it. I do not think my hymn . . . is ever sung to the tune for which I wrote it . . . it is better for a hymn to have a tune of its own and I feel much indebted to the author of the tune TIDINGS for writing so inspired a tune to my words.[1]

The text has been in the *Hymnal* since 1892. It was paired with tunes by Henry Storer and J. Walch in *The Church Hymnal Revised and Enlarged* (Boston, 1894). Both *H40* and *H82* have included the hymn with its second and third stanzas omitted:

2. Behold how many thousands still are lying
   Bound in the darksome prison-house of sin,
With none to tell them of the Saviour's dying,
   Or of the life he died for them to win.

3. 'Tis thine to save from peril of perdition
   The souls for whom the Lord his life laid down.
Beware lest slothful to fulfill thy mission,
   Thou lose one jewel that should deck his crown.

Two slight alterations appear in *H82* in st. 3, which originally read:

3:1 Give of thy sons to bear the message glorious
3:4 And all thou spendest Jesus will repay.

---

1. W. B. Bodine, *Some Hymns and Hymn Writers* (Philadelphia, 1907), 223-224.

Music: Also known as ANGELIC VOICES and PROCLAMATION, TIDINGS was composed by James Walch in 1875 or 1876 for Frederick

Faber's hymn "Hark, hark, my soul! angelic songs are swelling." Mary Ann Thomson, author of "O Zion, haste," was of the mistaken opinion that the tune had been written for her text (see commentary on text).

Although Walch was British, his tune has a strong flavor of the American gospel hymn, complete with refrain. It is to be remembered that Sankey and Moody toured England in 1872, and about two years later the English publishers Morgan & Scott issued *Sacred Songs and Solos* by Sankey, which well may have influenced Walch, who served as a musician in nonconformist churches.

TS/MS

540 Awake, thou Spirit of the watchmen

***Music:* DIR, DIR, JEHOVAH**

The Hymnal 1940 enriched the singing tradition of Episcopalians through the introduction of many new texts, translations, and tunes, among them this text for mission matched with an early German chorale tune.

Words: A four-stanza form of this translation was made for use in *H40* by Canon C. Winfred Douglas and the Rev. Arthur W. Farlander using sts. 1, 2, 7, and 14 of the much longer text "Wach auf, du Geist der ersten Zeugen" by Karl Heinrich von Bogatzky. The original, reduced by various editors over a period of years to five stanzas and titled "For faithful labourers in the Harvest of the Lord, for the blessed spread of the Word to the world," was first published in 1750. The present translation uses the incipit of a translation of the Bogatzky text by Catherine Winkworth, "Awake, Thou Spirit Who of old," which appeared in her *Lyra Germanica*, 1st series (London, 1855).

Wach auf, du Geist der ersten Zeugen,
Die auf der Mauer als treue Wächter stehn,
Die Tag und Nächte nimmer schweigen,
Und die getrost dem Feind entgegen gehn;
Ja, deren Schall die ganze Welt durchdringt,
Und aller Völcker Schaaren zu dir bringt!

O dass dein Feur doch bald entbrennte!
O möcht' es doch in alle Lande gehn.
Ach Herr! gib doch in deine Ernte
Viel Knechte, die in treuer Arbeit stehn.
O Herr der Ern't! ach siehe doch darein!
Die Ernt' ist gross, da wenig Knechte seyn.

Ach, lass dein Wort recht schnelle laufen;
Es sey kein Ort ohn' dessen Glanz und Schein!
Ach führe bald dadurch mit Haufen
Der Heiden Füll' in allen Thoren ein.
Ja, wecke doch auch Israel bald auf,
Und also segne deines Wortes Lauf.

Du wirst wohl wissen recht zu richten,
Da du ja aller Welt ihr Richter bist;
Lass nur dein Wort den Streit hier schlichten,
Wenn deine Lieb in uns im Zweifel ist;
Und treib' uns ferner, dich nur anzuflehn,
Es wird doch indich noch viel mehr geschehn.

Stanzas 1, 2, and 4 of the Douglas/Farlander translation were retained for use in *H82*. The omitted third stanza is:

The prayer thy Son himself hath taught us
  We offer now to thee at his command;
Behold and hearken, Lord; thy children
  implore thee for the souls of ev'ry land:
With yearning hearts they make their ardent plea;
  O hear us, Lord, and say, "Thus shall it be."

Music: This melody first appeared in the metre 98. 98. 88. (*Zahn* 2781), associated with the Georg Neumark hymn "Wer nur den lieben Gott lässt walten" in *Musikalisch Hand-Buch der Geistlichen Melodien à Cant. et Bass* (Hamburg, 1690). It was then later expanded to 9 10. 9 10. 10 10. (*Zahn* 3067) for the hymn by Bärtholomaus Crasselius "Dir, dir, Jehovah, will ich singen" in Johann Anastasius Freylinghausen's *Geistreiches Gesangbuch* (Halle, 1704). The tune is also known, for example in *H40*, as CRASSELIUS, after the name of the author of the later text. The earlier and later melodic forms are compared in Example 1. The tune WINCHESTER NEW is a variant form of this melody (see commentary on no. 76). Johann Sebastian Bach composed an entirely different melody for Crasselius's hymn, which was entered in manuscript into Anna Magdalena Bach's *Notenbuch* in 1725 and appeared in print in Georg Christian Schemelli's *Musikalisches Gesangbuch* (Leipzig, 1736) (see *BWV* 452).

Example 1

RG/RAL

541 Come, labor on

***Music:* ORA LABORA**

The composition of the tune ORA LABORA for use with this text in *H16* assured its acceptance and immediate use. In his essay "Hymnody in the United States from the Civil War to World War I (1860-1916)," vol. 1, 447, Paul Westermeyer describes this text and tune as "heady with optimism," a quality that explains its ongoing popularity.

Words: Based on the Gospels of Jn. 4:35-37 and Mt. 9:37-38, this hymn for church workers by Jane Laurie Borthwick was first published in her *Thoughts for Thoughtful Hours* (London, 1859). The seven six-line stanzas were transformed into seven five-line stanzas in a later edition of 1863. Stanza 4 of the current version was the second in the 1863 version and was followed by:

Come, labor on.
The laborers are few, the field is wide,
New stations must be filled, and blanks supplied;
From voices distant far, or near at home,
  The call is, "Come."

The concluding stanza read:

Come, labor on.
The toil is pleasant, the reward is sure,
Blessed are those who to the end endure;
How full their joy, how deep their rest shall be,
  O Lord, with thee.

Music: ORA LABORA was composed by T. Tertius Noble when the Borthwick text "Come, labor on" entered the *Hymnal* in 1916 and was included in the music edition published as *The New Hymnal* (New York, 1918). In style and structure it reflects the grand English unison tunes of Dr. Noble's contemporaries Charles Villiers Stanford and C. Hubert H. Parry. Writing of Dr. Noble and this tune, Erik Routley states "His conservative style of composition did neither him nor American music any harm, because nothing so like the style of Parry and his best tune, ORA LABORA had been heard yet in the USA."[1] It is now more than seventy years since the composition of this tune—a tune that has reached the status of a classic for many.

Dr. Noble's melody moves with measured dignity. After the initial declamation "Come, labor on," the composer establishes a regular rhythmic pattern of 𝅗𝅥 ♩ ♩ 𝅗𝅥 𝅗𝅥 | ♩ ♩ ♩ ♩ 𝅝 for the three internal lines. The third of these moves upward by step to a climax on the highest pitch of the tune.

The breadth of the tune is sensitively supported by the accompaniment with its strong bass line and rich harmonies. The moving tenor line under the sustained D^b of the melody in the final cadence is most effective.

---

1. E. Routley, *The Music of Christian Hymns* (Chicago, 1981), 171.

MS/RG

542 Christ is the world's true Light

***Music:* ST. JOAN**

This text for mission first appeared in an Episcopal collection in *H40*, where it was matched with this tune written for use with it in 1941. The simple AA^1BA^2 song form of the tune enhances its accessibility for a congregation.

Words: This text is the work of George Wallace Briggs, a major British hymn writer of the second quarter of the twentieth century, whom Erik Routley describes as "one of the most sought-after of the writers of his time."[1] It was written for use with KOMMT SEELEN, a tune by J. S. Bach, in *Songs of Praise* (London, 1931). Conceived as an Advent text, its eschatological and ecumenical thrust makes it equally appropriate as a hymn for mission, a distinction observed in both *H40* and *H82*, where it is placed among the mission hymns. Minor alterations have been made in sts. 1 and 2 in support of the SCCM's desire to use inclusive language wherever possible. The original forms were:

st. 1:4	of every man and nation
st. 1:6	where'er men own his sway
st. 2:6	men shall forsake their fear

---

1. E. Routley, *A Panorama of Christian Hymnody* (Collegeville, MN, 1979), 176.

Music: The tune ST. JOAN was composed for use with this text in *H40* by Percy E. B. Coller. Submitted anonymously, the fanfarelike opening of its first, second, and fourth lines and the general confident thrust of the tune support the imagery and theme of the text in which Christ is described as "the world's true Light," "its Captain of salvation," "The Day-star clear and bright," and the "Prince of peace." The tune is named in honor of the composer's wife.

RG

543 O Zion, tune thy voice

***Music:* EASTVIEW**

The rubric in the BCP that states "metrical versions of the invitatory Psalms and the Canticles after the readings may be used" was the motivation for the inclusion in *H82* of many new metrical settings of canticle texts, of which this is one example. This marks the first appearance of this paraphrase of *The Third Song of Isaiah*, canticle 11, and the tune EASTVIEW in the *Hymnal*.

Words: The hymns of Philip Doddridge were published posthumously by John Orton in *Hymns founded on Various Texts in the Holy Scriptures by the late Reverend Philip Doddridge, D.D.* (Salop, 1755). This hymn in four stanzas is no. 118 in the collection, where it is given the title "The Glory of the Church in the latter Day." It is based on Is. 9. In st. 2, line 1, the original had "mourning" rather than "morning," and the phrase "nobler spheres", st. 4, line 6, is footnoted thus: "Orbs or Paths in which the Stars move."

Music: EASTVIEW by J. Vernon Lee was first published in *Congregational Praise* (London, 1951) matched with the George W. Briggs text "Now is eternal life." Its melody is quite extrovert, and the *H82* matching complements the text admirably. Written to celebrate the eightieth birthday of the composer's mother, the tune was originally designed as a setting for the Charles Wesley text "Rejoice, the Lord is King!"

RAL/AW

544 *Jesus shall reign where'er the sun*

Music: **DUKE STREET**

This text, one of the best-known of the works of Isaac Watts, matched with this eighteenth-century psalm tune ranks as one of the most-loved and extensively used hymns in the hearts and experience of English-speaking congregations around the world.

Words: Perhaps one of the most popular hymns by Isaac Watts, "Jesus Shall Reign Where'er the Sun" first appeared in his *Psalms of David* (London, 1719) as Part II of his version of Ps. 72. It appeared for the first time in an Episcopal collection in the 1826 *Hymnal*. One of the earliest editors to adopt this text for congregational use, outside of the foreign missions office, was Rowland Hill; his *Psalms and Hymns* (London, 1783) presents the hymn in six stanzas. The hymn went on to be presented by compilers in the Church of England, by the Wesleyans, the Baptists, and other denominations and is now found in every English hymnbook of any merit. In modern printings it most often appears in the four-stanza form established in *HA&M*.

The original second and third stanzas are generally omitted:

2. Behold the islands with their kings,
And Europe her best tribute brings;
From North to South the princes meet
To pay their homage at his feet.

3. There Persia, glorious to behold,
There India shines in Eastern gold;
And barbarous nations at his word
Submit, and bow, and own their Lord.

And before the final stanza:

Where he displays his healing power,
Death and the curse are known no more;
In him the tribes of Adam boast
More blessings than their father lost.

Music: This tune made its first appearance anonymously in *A Select Collection of Psalm and Hymn Tunes . . . By the late Henry Boyd, Teacher of Psalmody* (Glasgow, 1793) and was headed "Addison's 19th Psalm." The reference is to Joseph Addison's "The spacious firmament on high" [409]. At the beginning of the nineteenth century it was given the tune name DUKE STREET and attributed to John Hatton in *Euphonia, containing Sixty-Two Psalm and Hymn Tunes . . . Harmonized, Arranged and Composed . . . by William Dixon* (Liverpool, ca. 1805). It has also been known by the names WINDLE, ST. HELEN'S, and NEWRY. The last name occurs in *The Methodist Harmonist* (New York, 1822), the first official tunebook of American Methodism.

TS/RAL

545 Lo! what a cloud of witnesses

Music: **ST. FULBERT**

The 1826 edition of the *Hymnal* marked the introduction of this text into the singing tradition of Episcopalians. In prior music editions it had been matched with a variety of CM tunes, but this marks its first matching in the *Hymnal* with ST. FULBERT.

Words: This is a paraphrase of Heb. 12.1-3 that first appeared in the draft Scottish *Translations and Paraphrases* (Edinburgh, 1745), in twelve four-line stanzas, where it began "Behold what witnesses unseen." The original author is unknown. It was subsequently altered in the 1751 and 1781 editions of *Translations and Paraphrases*. Thereafter a variety of abbreviated and altered forms circulated on both sides of the Atlantic. It first appeared in its present form in the *Hymnal* of 1826.

Music: ST. LEOFRED was the name given this tune when it first appeared in the *Church Hymn and Tune Book* (London, 1852), edited by its composer, H. J. Gauntlett, and his associate W. H. Blew. It is there set to Blew's translation of the Latin hymn "Forti tegente brachio" by Charles Coffin. In the initial edition of *HA&M* (1861), however, it was matched to a translation of "Chorus novae Hierusalem" by St. Fulbert of Chartres; hence the name change to ST. FULBERT. Like many of Gauntlett's numerous hymn tunes, it harks back to the simplicity of psalm tunes rather than indulging in the popular harmonic excesses that were coming into vogue. Martin Shaw wrote a faburden arrangement of the melody especially for the enlarged *Songs of Praise* (London, 1931).

RAL/MS

546 Awake, my soul, stretch every nerve

Music: **SIROË**

The operas and oratorios of George Frideric Handel have been a favorite haunt for hymnal editors seeking melodies suitable for use as hymn tunes as this tune from his opera *Siroë* illustrates. Use of this text/tune association in an Episcopal collection can be found as early as *A Tune-Book* of 1859. There it is called CHRISTMAS because of an earlier association of the tune with the text "While shepherds watched their flocks by night."

Words: The hymns of Philip Doddridge were published posthumously by John Orton in *Hymns founded on Various Texts in the Holy*

Scriptures by the late Reverend Philip Doddridge, D.D. (Salop, 1755). This hymn, in five stanzas, is no. 296 in the collection, where it is given the title "Pressing on in the Christian Race." It is based on Phil. 3:12-14. *The Hymnal 1982* employs Doddridge's first three stanzas, to which is added a slightly modified form of st. 1. The last line of each stanza is repeated, made necessary by the use of SIROË, a five-line tune. The omitted stanzas are:

4. That Prize with peerless Glories bright,
   Which shall new Lustre boast,
When Victors' Wreaths and Monarchs' Gems
   Shall blend in common Dust.

5. Blest Saviour, introduc'd by thee
   Have I my Race begun;
And crown'd with Vict'ry at thy Feet
   I'll lay mine Honours down.

"Wreaths" in st. 4, line 3 is footnoted in the 1755 edition thus: "Crowns or Garlands given to Conquerors." The text has been in the *Hymnal* since 1826.

Music: This tune, based on a portion of the aria "Non vi piacque ingiusti Dei" from the Handel opera *Siroë* composed in 1728, has appeared in hymnals under many names, including SIROË, CHRISTMAS, LUNENBURG, and SANDFORD. As a hymn tune, this melody first appeared with a number of other arrangements from works of Handel in *The Psalms of David for the use of Parish Churches* (London, 1791) by Dr. Samuel Arnold and J. W. Callcott. Arnold at the time was editing the works of Handel, so it is easy to see how he came to find so many melodies of the great composer that were suitable as hymn tunes. John Wilson describes how Arnold created this particular setting:

> The arrangement is an ingenious one, calling for the last line of each stanza to be repeated, so there are five phrases. The first three come directly from the singer's opening phrases. To find the fourth, we have to jump for 16 measures, and then, for the fifth, we jump another three measures and end with the soloist's final phrase. Handel, therefore, is not to blame for those nine consecutive E's (D's in the transposed edition in *H82*) in the bass part; our big jump came in the middle of them. In any

case, passages on a pedal bass were not uncommon in hymn tunes of the period.[1]

The dotted rhythms of the melody line and occasionally in the inner parts of the accompaniment add a martial quality to the tune, which is well suited to the declamatory nature of the text.

---

1. J. Wilson, "Handel and the Hymn Tune: II," *The Hymn*, vol. 37, no. 1, 26.

RAL/RG

547 Awake, O sleeper, rise from death

Music: **MARSH CHAPEL**

Commissioned initially as an anthem text, "Awake, O sleeper" appears here matched with MARSH CHAPEL, the tune written for use with it. This new hymn makes an excellent addition to the pages of contemporary hymnals.

Words: The letter to the Ephesians is the inspiration for the hymn "Awake, O sleeper, rise from death" by Rev. Dr. F. Bland Tucker. In February 1980 the author wrote of this text, "The first two lines (Eph. 5:14) are a quotation from a very ancient Christian hymn, probably. There is no known copy of it in existence; so I filled it out with quotations from other verses in the same epistle."[1]

Taking chapters 3, 4, and 5 of the epistle as his source, Dr. Tucker encapsulates important themes from each to create a credal statement of God's redemptive acts in Christ combined with a charge to all people to follow the way of Christ. He frames the entire text with an antiphonlike device. Stanza 1 opens with the call,

Awake, O sleeper, rise from death,
and Christ shall give you light.

The original form of Dr. Tucker's text with his notes on sources from Ephesians is as follows:

Awake, O sleeper, rise from death, 5:14
And Christ shall give you light
So learn his love its breadth and
length 3:18, 19
its fullness, depth, and height.

For he descended here to bring 4:10
From sin and fears release.
To give the Spirit's unity 4:3
which is the bond of peace.

There is one Body and one Hope, 4:4b
One Spirit and one call,
One Lord, one faith, and one Baptism
One Father of us all.

Then walk in love as Christ has loved, 5:1, 2
Who died that he might save;
With kind and gentle hearts forgive 4:32
As God in Christ forgave.
For us Christ lived, for us he died 4:8-9
And conquered in the strife.
Awake, arise, go forth in faith, 3:17, 6:16
And Christ shall give you life. 4:24

The closing two lines of st. 4 are a repeat of the antiphon but, as if Dr. Tucker engaged in a subtle play on words, "rise from death" becomes "arise, go forth . . . " and "light" becomes "life".

Although found among the hymns for Christian Vocation and Pilgrimage, Dr. Tucker also felt this text was useful for Baptism.

This work first appeared in 1980 as the text of an anthem by David N. Johnson set for SATB chorus with organ and optional parts for trumpet, handbells, tympani, and congregation. This is its first appearance in the *Hymnal*. It has since been included in *Worship*, 3rd. ed. (Chicago, 1986) and *The Hymnal of the United Methodist Church* (Nashville, 1988).

---

1. Tucker to Glover, February 2, 1980, Church Hymnal Corporation Papers, New York, NY.

Music: MARSH CHAPEL was written in late 1983 by Max Miller for use with this text in *H82*. The melodic and rhythmic thrust of the first line establishes a pattern for the entire work. In the third phrase, the opening interval of a perfect fourth is used sequentially, the last time leaping directly to the climax on the highest note of the tune. The descending final phrase, which outlines the tonic chord of F, brings the tune to a graceful close.

The composer writes of the tune:

> Since I have been at the Chapel of Boston University so long and in all likelihood will finish my "time" there, I would like to call the tune, MARSH CHAPEL. The chapel lies at the heart of the University and has weekday as well as regular Sunday services, serving both the University community and the larger community as well, both live and through broadcasts of the Sunday morning service.[1]

---

1. Miller to Glover, 28 March 1984, Church Hymnal Corporation Papers, New York, NY.

RG

548 Soldiers of Christ, arise

Music: **SILVER STREET**

The trumpetlike call that highlights the opening measures of the tune SILVER STREET underlines the first words and the overall mood of the Charles Wesley text "Soldiers of Christ, arise." This text/tune matching has a long tradition in Episcopal hymnals; the relationship can be found as early as the Hutchins and Tucker music editions of the 1871 *Hymnal*.

Words: Under the heading "The whole armour of God," this hymn appeared practically simultaneously as a broadsheet and at the end of the first and second editions of John Wesley's *Character of a Methodist* (Bristol, 1742). It was no. 28 in the section "Hymns for Believers" contained in the two volumes of *Hymns and Sacred Poems* (Bristol, 1749) that were published in the name of Charles Wesley alone in 1739 (*Poetical Works*, vol. V, 40-44). The original had sixteen eight-line stanzas, which were largely taken up as three hymns (nos. 258 through 260) in John Wesley's *A Collection of Hymns for the Use of the People Called Methodists* (London, 1780). The sustained scriptural source is Eph. 6:10-18.

The Hymnal of 1826 included the present sts. 1 , 2, 3, and 5, which had constituted the first two stanzas of the original. The present st. 4—contained in *HA&M* since 1861 and the *Hymnal* since 1892—is the first half of the original sixteenth, which concluded:

Still let the Spirit cry
In all His soldiers, "Come,"
Till Christ the Lord descends from high,
And takes the conquerors home.

The last line of the present second stanza echoes Rom. 8:37 (*hypernikômen* — "we are more than conquerors").

Music: For many years this strenuous tune, typical of late-eighteenth-century revivalism, has been almost universally attributed to Isaac Smith. It is true that it was printed in Smith's *Collection of Psalm Tunes* (London, ca. 1780), but Smith makes no claim there to be the composer.

It appears in several books of similar or earlier date, but most of them are undated and it is difficult to be certain of the priority. The first was most probably James Kempson's *Collection of Psalm Tunes* (Birmingham, ca. 1772). There the tune was named FALCON STREET and had no text. It was in a four-part arrangement with the tune in the top voice. Next in probable date comes an anonymous book, *Select Hymns for the Voice and Harpsichord* (London, ca. 1775), with a two-voice setting (also suited to the keyboard) and with the text of Isaac Watts's Ps. 95, "Come sound his praise abroad." In this version there is a ten-measure coda to the words "Praise ye the Lord, Hallelujah." It is still called FALCON STREET.

Smith used the same text but called the tune SILVER STREET. In his three-voice setting the tune is given added bravura by the addition of dynamics and ornaments and the greater dramatization of the coda (shown in Example 1) by means of a fermata* and tempo change. This version with the alleluias was copied in many later books, often with attribution to Smith, and probably accounted for the great popularity of the tune in Dissenting circles and in the United States.

Example 1

There is, however, an independent line of descent to the version without alleluias, which Ralph Harrison (*Sacred Harmony*, [London, 1784]) called NEWTON, and Scottish books generally called INGLISTOWN or ENGLISHTOWN.

The end result of this tangle of evidence seems to be that the tune is best regarded as of unknown authorship. At all events, however, it is likely that it originated in London. There was a Congregational chapel in Silver Street in the City of London, and there was an adjoining street named Falcon Street; neither name is found on maps of Birmingham from this period. Moreover, someone has written the word "Londonwise" above the tune in the Birmingham Library copy of the Kempson collection mentioned above. This suggests that if Kempson's was indeed the first printing of the tune, it came to him from London, brought from there either in a manuscript copy or in the head of a visiting musician.

The key was C in all 178 pre-1821 sources found in the Hymn Tune Index at the University of Illinois. The first appearance of the tune with the current text is found in an obscure American source: Henry Little's *The Wesleyan Harmony, or a Compilation of Choice Tunes for Public Worship* (Hallowell, ME, 1820). The tune has never gained currency in the Church of England, but it entered the Protestant Episcopal Church of America at least as early as 1867, when it was included as hymn 23 in George E. Thrall's *Episcopal Common Praise* (New York, 1867). The origin of the *H82* harmonization is not known.

Early Methodist sources associate the text "Soldiers of Christ" with the tune JERICHO, an adaptation of a march from G. F. Handel's opera *Riccardo Primo*.

GW/NT

549 Jesus calls us; o'er the tumult

***Music:* ST. ANDREW**

Originally written for St. Andrew's Day and intended for use by children, this popular hymn, rich in scriptural references, now finds expanded use in liturgies where the theme is Christian Vocation and Pilgrimage.

Words: This text by Cecil Frances Alexander titled "Follow me/For St. Andrew's Day" first appeared in *Hymns for Public Worship* (London, 1852). The author had recently married William Alexander, a priest of the Church of Ireland, and was living in the remote parish of Trienamongan (or Termonamongan) in Co. Tyrone. The hymn was reprinted in *Narrative Hymns for Village Schools* (London, 1853) in the following year and in *Lyra Anglicana* (London, 1862). As a response to many unauthorized alterations, Mrs. Alexander rewrote the hymn in 1881; all modern hymnals prefer the original version, however.

The hymn has been in the *Hymnal* since 1892, where it contained two alterations from the 1852 text. *The Hymnal 1982* restores one of these changes, returning to "may we hear thy call" in st. 5 instead of the more restrictive "Make us hear thy call." "Clear voice" in st. 1 replaces "sweet voice."

Mrs. Alexander based her text on the Collect, Epistle, and Gospel for St. Andrew's Day, narrating Matthew's account of Andrew's call while emphasizing the aural aspect of every Christian's call to serve Christ (as found in Romans). Scriptural citations include Mk. 1:16, Rom. 10:17, Mt. 4:19, and Jn. 21:15.

Music: David Hurd's hymn tunes are often characterized by the use of a single thematic idea and are supported by rich and varied accompaniments (see especially ANDÚJAR [104]). Such is the case with the tune ST. ANDREW. Composed in 1980 for use with this text, it honors the saint who is therein mentioned. First appearing in *The David Hurd Hymnary* (Chicago, 1983) it is a simple folklike tune built around the tones of a pentatonic scale on F. The first melodic phrase, which corresponds to the first line of the text, is repeated exactly for the second, giving the tune accessibility and unity. A brief codalike phrase repeats the last five notes of the opening melody, ending on the tonic (F) rather than the second note of the key (G) as it does initially. Another unifying factor is found in the composer's use of a repeated note figure  or 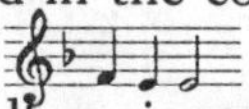 that appears in the first half of the melody line, in the alto voice at the cadences or phrases 1 and 2, and in the tenor voice at measures 9, 10, and 11. This is the first appearance of the tune in an Episcopal *Hymnal*.

MD/RG

550 Jesus calls us; o'er the tumult

Music: **RESTORATION**

A modal plaintive tune with origins in early nineteenth-century rural American hymnody reflects the introspective nature of this text.

Words: See hymn 549.

Music: This pentatonic tune was apparently first published in a three-part version with the name RESTORATION in the first edition of *The Southern Harmony* (New Haven, CT, 1835), compiled by William Walker (Example 1 on opposite page):

This version was reproduced in several later books.

In physician, Methodist minister, and planter William Hauser's *Hesperian Harp* (Philadelphia, 1848), a counter part was added. It was

Example 1

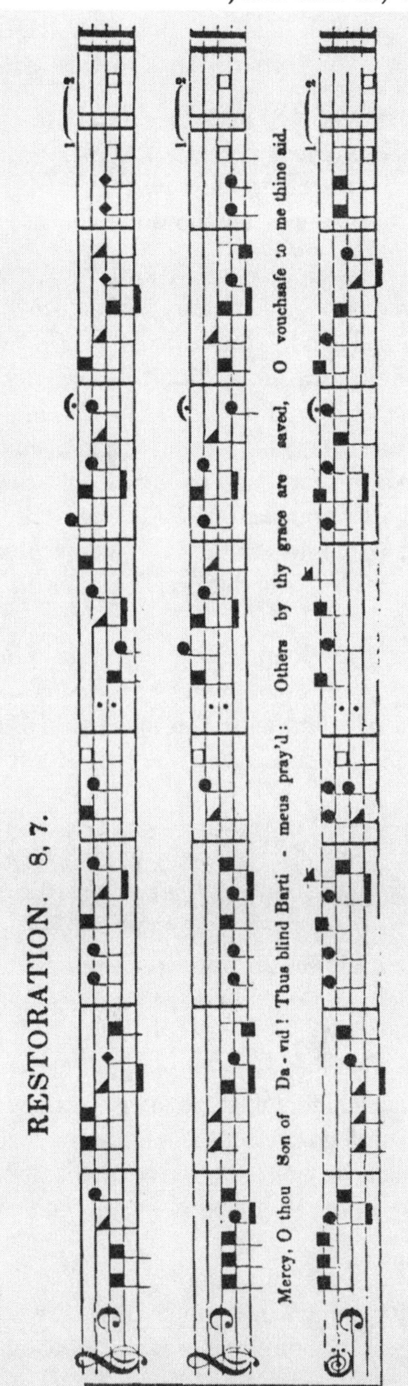

Reproduced from 1854 printing of *The Southern Harmony* (New Haven, CT, 1835), DuPont Library, University of the South.

printed with another tune on the page containing the text "Don't you see my Jesus coming." The second stanza of this hymn reads:

I'll arise and go and meet him,
He'll embrace me in his arms:
In the arms of my dear Jesus,
Oh, there are ten thousand charms!

In Lindsey Watson's numeral notation *Singer's Choice* (Louisville, 1854), Walker's three-part version was printed with Newton's text "Mercy, O, thou Son of David!," but under the title I WILL ARISE and with the above second stanza from "Don't you see my Jesus coming" (with "go to Jesus" substituted for "go and meet him") as a "Chorus" to be repeated after each stanza. The stanza had been taken out of an eschatological context and used as an invitation to discipleship.

Hauser's counter part was picked up in J. S. James's *Original Sacred Harp* (Cullman, AL, 1911), where the tune was printed with the text "Come, thou fount of e'ry [sic] blessing" and with the "Chorus" "I will arise and go to Jesus."

In C. H. Cayce's seven-shape shape-note *The Good Old Songs* (Thornton, AK, 1913), still used among Primitive Baptists, RESTORATION is printed on two staffs with the melody in the treble and a different alto part. It is associated with the text "Mercy, O Thou Son of David!"

A distinctive arrangement of the tune was published under the title RESTORATION in William Hauser's later book *Olive Leaf* (Wadley, GA, 1878). This harmonization is printed on two staffs with the melody in the treble in a book still used among Primitive Baptists, John R. and J. Harvey Daily's *Primitive Baptist Hymn and Tune Book* (Indianapolis, 1902). That book also contains a different arrangement by "J. H. H." under the title THE PRODIGAL SON.

Other variants of the tune have been published under the titles ATHENS, BEAUFORT, ARISE, and I WILL ARISE. Regardless of the text, the stanza "I will arise and go to Jesus" has often been printed as a "Chorus." George Pullen Jackson lists RESTORATION among the "Eighty Most Popular Tunes" in his *White Spirituals in the Southern Uplands* (Chapel Hill, NC, 1933).

This tune first entered an Episcopal hymn collection in *Songs IV*, in an arrangement by George Mims called ARISE. It was matched there with Joseph Hart's text "Come, ye sinners, poor and needy" and printed with the refrain "I will arise and go to Jesus." In *H82*, where it is associated with the text "Jesus calls us; o'er the tumult," two arrangements are provided. One is said to be "after *The Southern Harmony*" and is the harmonization found in C. H. Cayce's *The Good Old Songs*. The other is an alternative accompaniment written for use in *H82* by Margaret W. Mealy.

---

1. See H. L. Eskew, "The Life and Work of William Walker, 1809-1875," Unpublished M.S.M. thesis, New Orleans Baptist Theological Seminary, 1960.

MH

551 Rise up, ye saints of God!

Music: **FESTAL SONG**

Certain aspects of this popular text have been the cause of ongoing controversy since it was first published in 1911. For Episcopalians this text and tune first appeared in *H16*. The most persistent concern focused on the theology of the original third stanza and more recently on the strong sexist language of the opening phrase of the first stanza and the final line of the last stanza.

Words: This popular text was written by William Pierson Merrill on a steamer in Lake Michigan as he was returning to Chicago, where he served as pastor of Sixth Presbyterian Church. Reflecting on an article by Gerald Stanley Lee on "The Church of the Strong Men," Merrill was prompted to write the lines that came to him "almost without conscious thought or effort." The text was first published in the Presbyterian *Continent*, XLII, February 16, 1911.

The hymn has gained wide acceptance both in North America and Great Britain, but as early as the 1916 edition of the *Hymnal*, the third stanza garnered controversy on theological grounds; there it was omitted. In the University of Wales *A Student's Hymnal* (Aberystwyth and London, 1923), edited by Wolford Davies, it was altered to read:

> Her strength shall make your spirit strong,
> Her service make you great.

Preferring his original sentiment, Merrill responded, "How can the Church be made great without the service of men of God?" In the present version, the stanza has been deleted; it read thus:

Rise up, O men of God!
  The Church for you doth wait,
Her strength unequal to her task,
  Rise up, and make her great!

For reasons of inclusive language, certain changes have been made. In addition to the substitution of "ye saints" for "O men," the concluding stanza included the phrase "As brothers of the Son of Man." It now reads "and quickened by the Spirit's power."

Music: FESTAL SONG was composed by William H. Walter and first appeared in J. Ireland Tucker's *Hymnal Revised and Enlarged* (New York, 1894), where it was set to the Hammond text "Awake and sing the song." It became associated with the Merrill text in the *Pilgrim Hymnal* (Boston, 1912), a relationship that was continued in *H16* and in *H40*. Today this text/tune relationship is found in most main-line American hymnals, giving it a strong ecumenical thrust.

MS/RG

552 Fight the good fight with all thy might

Music: **PENTECOST**

The popular matching of this text and tune established by Arthur Sullivan in *Church Hymns with Tunes* (London, 1874) first appeared for use by Episcopalians in the Hutchins music edition of the 1892 *Hymnal*. Until *H40* it was printed as a hymn for Septuagesima, the third Sunday before Lent, when the Epistle reading, 1 Cor. 9:24, included references to running a race and to fighting.

Words: This hymn of John Samuel Bewley Monsell, based on 1 Tim. 6:12, was first published in his *Hymns of Love and Praise* (London, 1863) for the Nineteenth Sunday after Trinity; however, it has little application to the Epistle, Eph. 4:17-32 that deals with social virtues and renewed life in the spirit. Erik Routley suggests that this famous hymn was in fact inspired by an earlier hymn of James Montgomery written in 1834, which appeared in Montgomery's *Original Hymns* (London, 1853).[1] Stanzas 1 and 4 of Montgomery's "Valiant for Truth" are:

1. Fight the good fight: lay hold
   upon eternal life;
Keep but thy shield, be bold,
   stand through the bitterest strife;
invincible while in the field,
Thou canst not fail unless thou yield.

4. Trust in thy Savior's might;
   yea, till thy latest breath,
fight, and like him in fight,
   by dying conquer death;
and, all-victorious in the field,
then, with thy sword, thy spirit yield.

Stanzas 3 and 4 of Monsell's original text were altered for *H40*, following earlier changes found in *HA&M* (1868).

---

1. E. Routley, *An English-Speaking Hymnal Guide* (Collegeville, MN, 1979), 25.

Music: Unlike many hymn tunes, PENTECOST has a documented history. The London *Times*, on February 17, 1928, carried the following item:

> The name of the tune is PENTECOST because it was originally written for the words "Come, Holy Ghost, our souls inspire" at the request of Baring-Gould, who had organized a service for Yorkshire colliers at Whitsuntide.

The year of the composition was 1864, and it was first published in *Thirty-two Hymn Tunes composed by members of the University of Oxford* (Oxford, 1868). The name has another association. Boyd, in response to a request to reproduce the tune in facsimile for the *Musical Times*, wrote of his agreement and added, "And I will write the heading 'Pen-tecost,' because 'Pen" is the first syllable of my wife's name and she is very fond of the tune." Although the tune was conceived for another text, it is now wedded to Monsell's hymn "Fight the good fight." In the *Musical Times*, Boyd relates how the marriage came about:

> One day, as I was walking along Regent Street, I felt a slap on my back, and turning round I saw my dear old friend, Arthur Sullivan. "My dear Billy" he said, "I've seen a tune of yours which I must have." (He was then editing *Church Hymns*.) "All right," I said, "send me a cheque and I agree." No copy of the book, much less a proof was sent to me, and when I saw the tune I was horrified to find that Sullivan had assigned to it "Fight the good fight!" We had a regular fisticuffs about it, but judging from the favour with which the tune has been received, I feel that Sullivan was right in so mating words and music.[1]

This was not the only incident in which Boyd's rights were offended. In the same account, he continued,

> The tune was printed in the 1875 edition of *Hymns Ancient and Modern* without my permission. In their last edition they turned me out, also without my permission. Still they had to come back, I rejoice to say, for people said "the old was better." Since then it has found its way into most collections, Church of England and Nonconformist, and has gone all over the English-speaking world. There is hardly a week that I do not get a couple of letters, from far or near, asking me to allow its insertion in some new publication. And I do, in most cases, allow it, but with the proviso that the tune must be set to the words "Fight the good fight."

This tune to Monsell's text was sung at the funeral for Sir Winston Churchill at St. Paul's Cathedral, January 30, 1965.

---

1. *Musical Times*, 49 (1908), 786-788.

TS/MS

553 *Fight the good fight with all thy might*

Music: **RUSHFORD**

RUSHFORD, a tune that reflects its composer's sensitivity to the nuances of this text, is a strong alternative to the tune PENTECOST [552].

Words: See hymn 552.

Music: RUSHFORD was composed by the English composer Henry Ley (pronounced "Lee") for the text "Fight the good fight" by Monsell, in the *Clarendon Hymn Book* (London, 1936). It also appeared with this text in *H40*. A strong moving bass line undergirds a melody which, for the most part, moves in contrary motion to it. The melody reaches a telling climax just before the close.

AW

554 *'Tis the gift to be simple*

Music: **SIMPLE GIFTS**

This delightful text and tune from the tradition of the Shakers gained their place of affection in the hearts of music lovers across the nation through inclusion in the score for the ballet *Appalachian Spring* (1944) by the famous American composer Aaron Copland.

Words: This Shaker spiritual is described in Shaker communities as a "Gift Song from Mother's work." These songs were produced in "a period of renewed spiritual dedication that began in 1837 and lasted a full decade before tapering away. Its distinctive mark was that it was accomplished chiefly through spiritual phenomena."[1] In addition to the Alfred Ministry in Maine (see Music below), Daniel Patterson in *The Shaker Spiritual* (Princeton, NJ, 1979), lists the following sources as possible origins of this spiritual. "One written at Lebanon [New Hampshire] says that it was received from a Negro spirit at Canterbury [New Hampshire]." Patterson goes on to point out that "several manuscripts do record the song from the singing of Elder Joseph Brackett and a company from Alfred, who visited a number of societies in the summer of 1846." This latter citation is illuminated by his final two references: "In her youth at Hancock [Massachusetts] Mrs. Olive

H. Austin heard that it was Elder Joseph's own song. Eldress Caroline Helfrich there remembered seeing him sing it in a meeting room, turning about 'with his coat tails a-flying.' " In any event it is probably safe to say that although the identity of the author of this Shaker Gift Song is unclear; the author and the composer are the same person.

---

1. D. Patterson, *The Shaker Spiritual* (Princeton, NJ, 1979), 316.

Music: SIMPLE GIFTS is the Shaker melody generally associated with "Tis the gift to be simple." Labeled a "Quick Dance," the tune appeared in a number of Shaker manuscripts from the 1840s and later. According to one of these manuscripts, it was "composed by the Alfred Ministry [Maine] June 28, 1848,"[1] but other manuscripts contain conflicting attributions. The modern popularity of the tune is due primarily to the work of two men, Edward Andrews and Aaron Copland. Andrews made the tune known by publishing it in his collection of "Songs, Dances and Rituals of the American Shakers" and titling the book after the song (*The Gift to Be Simple*). Copland discovered the tune in Andrews's book and used it as a theme for variations in the seventh section of *Appalachian Spring*, a ballet depicting pioneer life in Pennsylvania. The ballet was first performed on October 30, 1944, and received both a Pulitzer Prize and the New York Music Critics' Award in 1945. Copland later observed that when he chose this tune for use in *Appalachian Spring* his research "evidently was not very thorough, since I did not realize that there never have been Shaker settlements in rural Pennsylvania!"[2] Nevertheless, Copland's use of the melody in *Appalachian Spring*—and subsequently in the first set of *Old American Songs* (1950)—brought the tune to the attention of a wider audience, a rare instance of a classical composer taking a nearly forgotten folk melody and reintroducing it to the people. In the late 1960s and early 1970s the tune began appearing in youth songbooks and a few hymnals, sometimes with the original text and at other times in association with Sydney Carter's "Lord of the Dance" (1964). For Episcopalians, the tune first appeared in *Hymns III* in a different form with an accompaniment by Dr. Alastair Cassels-Brown. The present arrangement was made by Margaret W. Mealy for *H82*. Roger L. Hall in *The Shaker Messenger* writes that this hymn should be sung "in a simple natural style." He adds, "But remember, it was written as a dance song—so sing it with gusto."[3]

---

1. E. D. Andrews, *The Gift to be Simple* (New York, 1940; repr. New York, 1962), 136.
2. A. Copland and V. Perlis, *Copland Since 1943* (New York, 1989), 33.
3. R. L. Hall, "Simple Gifts, Shaker simplicity in song," *The Shaker Messenger*, vol. 2, no. 2 (Winter, 1980), 13.

RG/DWM

555 Lead on, O King eternal

***Music:* LANCASHIRE**

An initial response to this hymn is that the martial mood of LANCASHIRE makes it a suitable matching for this text, which is rich in military imagery of marching, war, conquest, and battle. This attitude is to be questioned, however, for the mood of the hymn changes in st. 2 where the author expresses the sentiment that it is not in battle with sword and drum that the kingdom comes, but rather with "deeds of love and mercy." Here the positive harmonic and melodic structure of the tune makes a more lyric interpretation an appropriate understanding of the hymn.

Words: Ernest W. Shurtleff wrote this hymn for his 1888 graduation exercises from Andover Theological Seminary. Armin Haeussler, in *The Story of Our Hymns, the Handbook of the Evangelican and Reformed Church* (St. Louis, 1954), has shown that the year 1887, given in the 1915 edition of Julian's *Dictionary of Hymnology* and followed by most hymnal companions, is incorrect. Haeussler found that this text was not published in Shurtleff's publication *Hymns of Faith* (n.p., 1887) as previously thought, its first publication being for the Andover graduation in 1888. Presbyterians published Shurtleff's text in *The Hymnal* (Philadelphia, 1895). It entered the Episcopal *Hymnal* in 1916.

Music: LANCASHIRE was composed in 1836 to facilitate the singing of "From Greenland's icy mountains" at a missionary service in Blackburn, Lancashire, where Henry Smart was the young parish organist. It was not published nor perhaps named until 1867, when the composer returned to London, his birthplace, and contributed by invitation to the Presbyterian collection *Psalms and Hymns for Divine Worship* (London, 1867). This book commanded attention in North America, where Presbyterians were moving away from their previous exclusive use of metrical psalms. Editors of their new hymnals set Smart's tune to a variety of texts, thereby securing it wider usefulness than in Britain, where neither *HA&M* nor the Church of Scotland *Hymnary* has ever granted it space.

HE/HMcK

556 *Rejoice, ye pure in heart!*

***Music:* MARION**

The buoyant spirit of jubilant song permeates this text, written for use at an annual choir festival in Peterborough Cathedral in May 1865. MARION, composed for use with it in 1883, conveys a similar spirit, which has assured its continued use in music editions of the *Hymnal* to this day.

Words: This text was first published in the 1868 Appendix to *Hymns Ancient and Modern*. Line 3 originally read "Your orient banners wave on high." The omitted original third and fourth stanzas read:

Yes onward, onward still,
  With hymn, and chant, and song,
Through gate, and porch, and columned aisle,
  The hallowed pathways throng.

With ordered feet pass on;
  Bid thoughts of evil cease,
Ye may not bring the strife of tongues
  Within the Home of Peace.

The present third stanza was as follows:

With voice as full and strong
  As ocean's surging praise,
Send forth the hymns our fathers loved,
  The Psalms of ancient days.

The text first appeared in the 1892 edition of the *Hymnal* and continued in use in an eight-stanza form through *H82*. Because some of its imagery has become dated and limited, the original st. 2 was deleted for use in *H82*. It read:

Bright youth and snow-crowned age,
Strong men and maidens meek:
Raise high your free, exulting song!
God's wondrous praises speak!

Music: MARION by Arthur Henry Messiter was first published with this text in *Hymnal with Music* (New York, 1889), edited by the composer as the "preliminary report of the committee on the *Hymnal* appointed by the General Convention in 1886, modified with music used at Trinity Church New York." It was later included in Messiter's music edition of the 1892 *Hymnal*. The tune name honors the composer's mother.

RG

557 Rejoice, ye pure in heart!

Music: **VINEYARD HAVEN**

The installation of the Most Rev. John M. Allin as Presiding Bishop of the Episcopal Church in the Washington Cathedral on June 11, 1974, was the occasion for the commissioning and first performance with this text of the tune VINEYARD HAVEN.

Words: See hymn 556. For use with VINEYARD HAVEN, the original refrain "Rejoice, give thanks and sing" was replaced with "Hosanna, hosanna! Rejoice, give thanks and sing."

Music: VINEYARD HAVEN, a stirring tune, modal in nature and folklike in character, was composed by Dr. Richard Wayne Dirksen, Precentor, Organist, and Choirmaster of the Washington Cathedral. It was sung during a procession in the Cathedral in which the symbols of the Office of the Presiding Bishop were brought forward. Opening with a series of four gradually ascending phrases, the tune builds to a thrilling climax at "Hosanna," the first word of the refrain. The tune ends in a series of short descending phrases that reflect in their contours the accentual structure of the words "hosanna" and "rejoice." In each case the accented syllable gathers to itself two notes, of which one is the highest pitch in the phrase. The composer writes of his tune:

> The music reflects [the quality of rejoicing] most exactly at the two interpolated "Hosannas" . . . which rise like daily orisons, pointing the way and presaging the reward at the end . . . to raise such "Hosannas" forever in his presence and with the company of heaven in the life eternal.[1]

The nobility of the setting is further distinguished by a harmonically colorful accompaniment.

A festal setting for choir with a through-composed organ part by Dr. Dirksen is available in a separate edition. It is in this form that the tune was first performed.

The tune name honors the Very Rev. Francis D. Sayre, Jr., Dean of the Washington Cathedral from 1951 to 1978 and cherished friend of the composer. Dean Sayre now lives in retirement in the town of Vineyard Haven, Martha's Vineyard, MA.

---

1. Dirksen to Glover, January 5, 1981, Church Hymnal Corporation Papers, New York, NY.

RG

558 Faith of our fathers! living still

Music: **ST. CATHERINE**

This text has maintained a high level of use in many hymnals of American mainline Protestant denominations despite the fact that it reflected the Roman Catholic hopes of the author who, ordained as a Anglican priest in 1839, entered the Roman Catholic Church in 1845. The text entered the *Hymnal* in 1916, but has never been included in either of the major Church of England hymnals, *EH* and *HA&M*, nor does it appear in the contemporary American Roman Catholic hymnal, *Worship*.

Words: "Faith of our Fathers!" comes from *Jesus and Mary or Catholic Hymns* (London, 1849), the second step in the hymnal that author Frederick W. Faber had begun issuing the previous year and kept expanding until, by 1861, it had reached one hundred and fifty hymns in number. In every edition of this text printed under his supervision, "Fathers" is invariably capitalized, suggesting that he had primarily in mind the priests who went, under Queen Elizabeth I and for decades thereafter, in very real danger of "dungeon, fire and sword." At the same time, however, laymen who practiced Roman Catholicism surreptitiously were seldom molested unless they otherwise offended the government.

In his 1861 preface, Faber mentions that since "hymns are purely practical things" he had "in no instance refused either to Catholics or Protestants the free use of them," while asking the latter to omit, instead of amending, unpalatable stanzas, because "in many cases, the literary or metrical changes have not been such as met the Author's own judgment and taste." This *Hymnal* meets his wishes in part by omitting his original second stanza, which read:

> Our Fathers, chained in prisons dark,
> Were still in heart and conscience free;
> How sweet would be their children's fate
> If they, like them, could die for thee!

The fate he feared, however, has befallen his original third stanza:

> Faith of our Fathers! Mary's prayers
> Shall win our country back to thee;
> And through the truth that comes from God
> England shall then indeed be free.

Of this stanza, though, he had prudently printed an alternative version for use in Ireland, most of whose people had not only clung to Catholicism, but were already prone to reading political implications into "free":

> Faith of our Fathers! Mary's prayers
> Shall keep our country fast to thee;
> And through the truth that comes from God
> O we shall prosper and be free!

Stanza 3:4 replaces the original "words" with "deeds," which Faber presumably deemed part of "virtuous life."

Music: This tune is representative of the kind of congregational music that was generated by the Roman Catholic revival movement in mid-nineteenth-century Britain. The original tune appeared anonymously in *The Crown of Jesus* (London, 1864), edited by Henri F. Hemy, associated with a hymn with the title "St. Catherine, Virgin and Martyr" that began:

Sweet Saint Catherine, Maid most pure,
Teach us to meditate and pray.

The tune appeared in a substantially modified form in *Plainsong Music for the Holy Communion* (London, 1874), edited by James G. Walton. The first eight measures comprise the 1864 version; the remainder was newly composed, presumably by Walton. ST. CATHERINE, also known as PRINCE, ST. FINBAR, and TYNEMOUTH, proved popular and circulated in variant forms. The Walton form is found, for example, in *Tunes for the Family and the Congregation* (Bristol, 1877) and *The Bristol Tune Book* (Bristol, 1881). By the turn of the century it had found its way into a number of American hymnals and was included in the *Hymnal* of 1916.

HMcK/RAL

559 Lead us, heavenly Father, lead us

Music: **DULCE CARMEN**
This popular text appeared first in the 1871 edition of the *Hymnal* and was matched with this equally popular tune in the Tucker music edition of the 1871 *Hymnal*.

Words: "Lead us, heavenly Father, lead us" first appeared in James Edmeston's *Sacred Lyrics*, vol. 2 (London, 1821), with the title "Hymn, Written for the Children of the London Orphan Asylum." It was included in *Psalms and Hymns* (London, 1858), a collection published by the Baptist Church. In the 1867 edition of that publication, st. 2, lines 5 and 6 read as follows:

Lone and dreary, faint and weary,
through the desert thou didst go.

This popular hymn has been translated into many languages including Latin.

Music: This tune appeared in print, with no composer's name attached, in Samuel Webbe, the Elder's *An Essay on the Church Plain Chant* (London, 1782). It was given in quasi-plainsong notation and associated with the text "Tantum ergo sacramentum." It was also included in Samuel Webbe, the Elder, and Samuel Webbe, the Younger's *A Collection of Motetts or Antiphons* (London, 1792), but with modern notation. The tune has been known by a variety of other names, including ALLELUIA DULCE CARMEN, CORINTH, GLORIA PATRI, ST. WERBERGH'S, and LEBANON, and erroneously attributed to Johann Michael Haydn. The harmonization, by William Henry Monk for inclusion in the first edition of *HA&M* (1861), appeared in *Tunes, Old and New: Adapted to the Hymnal* (Hartford, 1874). In *H82* it is transposed down a step from A to G.

TS/RAL

560 Remember your servants, Lord

Music: **BEATITUDES**

This musical setting of the Beatitudes from the liturgy of the Russian Orthodox Church first became available for use in the Episcopal Church when it was included in a unison setting in *Hymns III*.

Words: The geneology of this setting of the Beatitudes as found in *H82* begins with *Ecumenical Praise* (Carol Stream, IL, 1977), the source of the text and tune, which first appeared in an Episcopal hymn collection in *Hymns III*. The translation there is by M. M. Gowan; the publisher, however, is unable to give any further information as to the identity of this person or the source of the translation. For use in *H82* the Text Committee of the SCCM altered the text to conform with the translation of Mt. 5:3-12 in the Revised Standard Version of the Bible. In the Divine Liturgy of St. John Chrysostom in the Russian Orthodox tradition, this text usually appears in lieu of the third antiphon and is sung after the Lesser Litany and before the Little Entrance.

Music: This setting in Tone 1 of the Russian Orthodox tradition appears in *H82* in a SATB arrangement composed for use in *H82* by Richard Proulx. Proper for All Saints' Day, the setting is also appropriate for use at the Burial Office. It could be used as the Song of Praise or during the communion of the people on All Saints' Day, or as a congregational hymn at the Burial Office. A responsorial performance, in which the antiphon is sung by the choir and congregation after a verse or group of verses sung by the choir, enhances its accessibility for a congregation. Peter Ilich Tchaikovsky makes use of the Tone 1 melody in his *1812 Overture*.

RG

561 *Stand up, stand up, for Jesus*

Music: **MORNING LIGHT**

The militant mood concerning the issue of slavery in the northern United States just prior to the American Civil War was a strong motivation for the extensive use of militaristic imagery that permeates this text. Upon publication, the popularity and use of the text were both immediate and international, for along with extensive currency in the United States it is found matched with this tune in many English hymnals.

Words: The author, George Duffield, Jr., has summarized the origin of this hymn in a letter dated May 29, 1883:

> "Stand Up for Jesus" was the dying message of the Rev. Dudley A. Tyng to the Young Men's Christian Association, and the ministers associated with them during the great revival of 1853, in the Noon-Day Prayer Meeting, usually known as "The Work of God in Philadelphia."
>
> A very dear personal friend, I know young Tyng as one of the noblest, bravest, manliest men I ever met . . . The Sabbath before his death he preached in the immense edifice known as Jaynes' Hall, one of the most successful sermons of modern times. Of the five thousand men there assembled, at least one thousand, it was

believed, were "the slain of the Lord." His text was Exodus 10:11, and hence the allusion in the third verse of the hymn.

The following Wednesday, leaving his study for a moment, he went to the barn floor, where a mule was at work on a horse-power, shelling corn. Patting him on the neck, the sleeve of his silk study gown caught in the cogs of the wheel, and his arm was torn out by the roots! His death occurred in a few hours . . .

The following Sunday the author of the hymn preached from Eph. 6:14, and the above verses were written simply as the concluding exhortation. The superintendent of the Sabbath school had a fly-leaf printed for the children—a stray copy found its way into a Baptist newspaper—and from that paper it has gone in English, and in German and Latin translations all over the world.[1]

The Rev. Dudley A. Tyng was rector of the Church of the Epiphany, Philadelphia. The *Companion to the Hymnal: A Handbook to the 1964 Methodist Hymnal* (Nashville, 1970), p. 381 mentions a conjecture "that since Tyng had been persecuted for his stand against slavery, he probably meant to say, 'Stand up for Jesus in the person of the downtrodden slave.' "

The hymn in six stanzas was first published as a broadside. It was then included in the Baptist hymnal *The Psalmist* (Boston, 1858), followed by the Presbyterian *Church Psalmist* (Philadelphia, 1859). It entered the Episcopal *Hymnal* in 1892. The four stanzas now commonly in use are sts. 1, 3, 4, and 6 of the original. In the original, the following appeared after the first stanza:

Stand up, stand up for Jesus,
  The solemn watchword hear;
If while ye sleep he suffers,
  Away with shame and fear.
Where'er ye meet with evil,
  Within you or without,
Charge for the God of battles,
  And put the foe to rout.

Stanza 2, line 5 was originally "Ye that are men now serve him." Inclusive language has also replaced the original closing lines of the last stanza:

To him that overcometh
  A crown of life shall be;
He with the King of glory,
  Shall reign eternally.

The fifth and sixth lines of st. 3 originally read:

Put on the gospel armor,
  Each piece put on with prayer.

The original stanza after st. 3 read:

Stand up, stand up for Jesus,
  Each soldier to his post;
Close up the broken column
  And shout through all the host!
Make good the loss so heavy
  In those that still remain,
And prove to all around you
  That death itself is gain.

---

1. A. Haeussler, *The Story of Our Hymns* (St. Louis, 1952), 324-325.

Music: MORNING LIGHT, also known as FRANCONIA, GOODWIN, MILLENIAL DAWN, NEW YORK, ROSY LIGHT, STAND UP, and WEBB, was first written by George James Webb in 1830 while aboard a ship bound for America. Composed for a secular song, "Tis dawn, the lark is singing," it was first published by Webb and Mason in *The Odeon: A Collection of Secular Melodies* (Boston, 1837). (The collection was named for the Odeon, an unused theater until Mason and Webb utilized it for their Boston Academy of Music.) The tune's first use as a hymn tune is apparently to Samuel F. Smith's "The morning light is breaking" in *The Wesleyan Psalmist* (Boston, 1842). This text was the source of the tune name. The earliest association of Webb's tune to "Stand up, stand up for Jesus" appears to have been in William B. Bradbury's Sunday school songbook *The Golden Chain* (New York, 1861). The earliest musical editions of *The Hymnal 1892* to use MORNING LIGHT with this text are Tucker and Rousseau's *The Hymnal Revised and Enlarged . . . Appointed by the General Convention of 1886 . . .* (New York,

1894) and Hutchins's *The Church Hymnal Revised and Enlarged . . . in the Year of Our Lord 1892 . . .* (Boston, 1894).

HE

562 Onward, Christian soldiers

Music: **ST. GERTRUDE**

There is probably no hymn in *H82* as controversial as this. Some critics decry its extensive use of military imagery, while others consider its setting to be trivial. Nonetheless the voices of people across the country are heard supporting its continued use despite the objections of hymnal editors and theologians working for world peace.

Words: Sabine Baring-Gould wrote this famous processional hymn for a children's Sunday school festival in 1865 at Horbury Bridge, near Wakefield, Yorkshire, England. It was first published with six stanzas in the *Church Times* during the same year. Stanza 4 is usually omitted, "certainly," says Julian, "to the advantage of the hymn" (*Julian*, 870):

4. What the saints established
   That I hold for true,
What the saints believed
   That believe I too.
Long as earth endureth
   Men and faith will hold,—
Kingdoms, nations, empires
   In destruction rolled . . .

The form of the text in *HA&M* (1868) that omits st. 4 is generally used in all English-speaking hymnals. In the 1904 edition of *HA&M*, however, st. 3 was altered to read "Though divisions harass" rather than "We are not divided." The change was soon reversed. *The Hymnal 1982* has reduced the amount of male imagery, substituting "Christians" for "brothers" (st. 3 and st. 4) and inserting "we with angels" rather than "men and angels" (st. 5). In *Songs of Praise Discussed* (London, 1933), Percy Dearmer tells the following anecdote:

It is indeed said that long ago a bishop, when a procession in one of his churches was about to start, pointed to the cross, and said, 'Leave that behind'; whereupon the choirmen conspired to end each chorus with the words '[. . . With the cross of Jesus,] left behind the door.'[1]

1. P. Dearmer, *Songs of Praise Discussed* (London, 1933), 217.

Music: Arthur Seymour Sullivan composed ST. GERTRUDE expressly for Baring-Gould's hymn and first published it in *The Musical Times* of December 1871 and then in *The Hymnary* (London, 1872). Though immensely popular, it did not reach *HA&M* until 1916, probably because of copyright difficulties; it was in Charles Hutchins's *Church Hymnal* (New York) by 1883. The harmony was the same as in *H82* except that the bass descended to F on the second beat of the penultimate measure and there was a touch of counterpoint in the tenor at measure 20 (see Example 1).

Example 1

Sullivan's tune has been thought "corny" and has been heavily parodied. Its sentiment may be outdated, and many commentators, including Erik Routley, have been unable to detach their minds from the fact that Sullivan was also a composer of light operas. It is time to recognize that ST. GERTRUDE is one of the greatest of all hymn tunes in its ability to arouse feeling and high spirit and is perfectly matched to its text in rhythm, structure, and sentiment. The notorious "table-leg bass" in the refrain, unvocal though it may be in conception, brilliantly suggests the determined tramp of a marching band. There are many other touches of fine musicianship, including the invertible counterpoint between treble and tenor in measures 1 through 2 and 5 through 6.

It is thought that the tune name may allude to Mrs. Gertrude Clay-Ker-Seymer, who was a friend of the composer's.[1]

---

1. See *The Musical Times* 43 (1902), 477. For Routley's discussion see the *Bulletin* of the Hymn Society of Great Britain and Ireland, 7 (July 1949), 105, and E. Routley, *The Music of Christian Hymns* (Chicago, 1981), 104.

TS/NT

563 Go forward, Christian soldier

Music: **LANCASHIRE**

Originally conceived and first published in 1861 as a hymn for confirmation, this text entered the *Hymnal* in 1892 and was immediately matched with this tune in the Hutchins music edition (Boston, 1894). This relationship remains unchallenged to this day.

Words: Written by Laurence Tuttiett, "Go forward, Christian Soldier" was first published in his *Counsels of a Godfather* (London, 1861). Designed for use at confirmation, it is based on Ex. 14:15, "Speak unto the children of Israel, that they go forward." It was originally composed as a text of eight stanzas of four lines. The characterization of the confirmand as a "Christian soldier" probably is derived from the signation prayer at baptism in former prayer books:

> We receive this Child (Person) into the congregation of Christ's flock, and do sign *him* with the sign of the Cross, in token that hereafter *he* shall not be ashamed to confess the faith of Christ crucified, and manfully to fight under his banner, against sin, the world and the devil; and to continue Christ's faithful soldier and servant unto *his* life's end. Amen (BCP, 1928 ed., 280).

Music: See hymn 555.

TS

564 *He who would valiant be*

Music: ST. DUNSTAN'S

The creative, imaginative, and daring genius of the two men who served as editors of *EH* brought this text from the pages of classic literature into the pages of contemporary hymnals of diverse denominations. The text first appeared in an Episcopal hymnal in *H16*, set to this tune, and was continued in *H40* and *H82*. It is with ST. DUNSTAN'S that the text gained popularity and use throughout the United States.

Words: This poem from John Bunyan's *Pilgrim's Progress* follows and reinforces Valiant-for-Truth's account of those who tried to discourage his being a pilgrim: his parents and friends. But he would not be discouraged. "I . . . fought all that set themselves against me, and by believing am come to this place." The poem was not in the first edition of *Pilgrim's Progress* (1678) but appeared in the 1684 edition, where it reads:

Who would true Valour see,
Let him come hither;
One here will Constant be,
Come Wind, come Weather.
There's no Discouragement,
Shall make him once Relent,
His first avow'd Intent,
To be a Pilgrim.

Who so beset him round'
With dismal Storys,
Do but themselves confound;
His strength the more is,
No Lyon can him fright,
He'll with a Gyant Fight,
But he will have a right,
To be a Pilgrim.

Hobgoblin, nor foul Fiend,
Can daunt his Spirit:
He knows, he at the end,

Shall Life Inherit.
Then Fancies fly away,
He'll fear not what men say,
He'll labor Night and Day,
To be a Pilgrim.

The Rev. Percy Dearmer writes:

> In 1904, we who were working at the *English Hymnal* felt that some cheerful and manly hymns must be added to the usual repertory; and this song sprang to mind. It was a daring thing to add the song to a hymnbook, and it had never been attempted before. To include the hobgoblins would have been to ensure disaster; to ask the congregation of St. Ignotus, Erewhon Park, to invite all to come and look at them, if they wished to see true valour would have been difficult. But when with the help of the marvellous folk-tune which Vaughan Williams had discovered, we had made a great hymn, it became easy for our imitators to complain that we had altered the words. We felt that we had done rightly; and that no one would have been more distressed than Bunyan himself to have people singing about hobgoblins in church. He had not written it for a hymn, and it was not suitable as a hymn without adaptation.[1]

Erik Routley remarks that, despite Dearmer's feelings about hobgoblins and foul fiends, most editors think that Bunyan's mind and work are "familiar enough to make it tolerable to sing his words, 'hobgoblins' and all, in public worship."[2]

1. P. Dearmer, *Songs of Praise Discussed* (London, 1933), 271.
2. E. Routley, *Hymns and Human Life* (London, 1952), 168.

Music: ST. DUNSTAN'S first appeared in *H16*, where it was the second of two new tunes composed for the text "He who would valiant be." (The other tune, EGBERT, was composed by Walter Henry Hall.)

Douglas's sturdy tune is the survivor of the two, appearing in *H40* and *H82* and in many other denominational hymnals.

Canon Douglas composed this tune on December 15, 1917 while on the train returning from New York City to his home on the grounds of the Community of St. Mary, Peekskill, NY, a stone house the Douglases had named "St. Dunstan's Cottage."

The unusual metre of poem and tune (6 5. 6 5. 6 6 6 5) caused Douglas to comment:

> Another characteristic [of modern hymn tunes] is a rhythmical freedom which gets away from uniform barring in threes or fours. Such freedom occurs in all of the older Chorales and Psalter tunes, when the proper pauses are made at the close of lines, as well as in Plainsong. It now reappears in modern composition, with stirring effect. Note, in our own Hymnal [i.e., 1916/18], the rhythms of ROSA MYSTICA, no. 82 and of EGBERT or ST. DUNSTAN'S, no. 117.[1]

1. W. Douglas, *Church Music in History and Practice: Studies in the Praise of God*, (New York, 1937), 260. The revised edition, edited by L. Ellinwood (New York, 1962, 222), gives as examples from *The Hymnal 1940*: TAYLOR HALL (no. 527), ST. DUNSTAN'S (No. 563), and THE KING'S MAJESTY (no. 64, first tune).

ALec and RG/DF

565 He who would valiant be

***Music:* MONK'S GATE**

The Hymnal 1982 includes this text with both ST. DUNSTAN'S and MONK'S GATE, the Sussex folk song arranged originally for use with it by Ralph Vaughan Williams. Of this matching Erik Routley notes:

> It has not been until the present century that the Pilgrim Song has become familiar, and it owes much of its popularity to the tune which Dr. Vaughan Williams arranged originally for Dearmer's hymn.[1]

It must however be pointed out that this has not been the experience in the United States.

---

1. E. Routley, *Hymns and Human Life*, (London, 1952), 168.

Words: See hymn 564.

Music: See hymn 478.

566 *From thee all skill and science flow*

Music: **THE CHURCH'S DESOLATION**

The opening in 1870 of a new wing of a children's hospital in Birmingham, England, was the occasion for the creation of this hymn in the praise of God, the source of all healing of body and mind, and a prayer for the coming of "that perfect day" when pain and death will be no more and the scars created by our defacing God's gifts in nature are removed. It is matched with an American folk hymn whose limited vocal range, reiterated rhythmic pattern, and repeated use of melodic material makes it both appropriate for use with this text and very accessible to a congregation.

Words: This hymn was written by Charles Kingsley and appears in his posthumous *Collected Poems* (London, 1889) dated "Eversley, 1870" with the note "sung by 1,000 School Children at the opening of the New Wing of the Children's Hospital, Birmingham." It made its first appearance in an Episcopal hymnal in *H40*. The hymn originally had six verses, the first two being:

1. Accept this building, gracious Lord,
   No temple though it be;
   We raised it for our suffering kin,
   And so, good Lord, for thee.

2. Accept our little gift, and give
   To all who here may dwell,
   The will and power to do their work,
   Or bear their sorrows well.

Stanzas 3 through 6 of the original hymn have become widely used as a standard hymn, appearing in *EH*, the *Anglican Hymn Book* (London, 1965), and *H40*. In *H40* the text appeared with the tune ALBANO. In *H82* the hymn was divided into two eight-line stanzas instead of the four-stanza version found in *H40*. The following sections were altered in *H82* from the *H40* version of the text:

st. 2:1	and part them
st. 4:3	And man's rude work
st. 4:4	the paradise of God

Although Charles Kingsley wrote much poetry, this is his only hymn to have come into common use. The hymn is appropriate for use in services with themes related to caring for the sick, civil and international peace, and respect for the environment.

Music: One of the first books in which folk songs from the American oral tradition were recorded was *The Christian Harmony or, Songster's Companion* (Exeter, NH, 1805), compiled by Jeremiah Ingalls, a cooper, farmer, tavern-keeper, and singing school teacher of Newbury, VT.[1] (A "songster" was a book of hymn texts without music.) In Ingalls's book a version of this tune was printed under the title MOURNING SOULS and linked with the text "Poor mourning souls in deep distress" (see Example 1 on following pages 1047–48):

This version was not reproduced in other books.

The third edition of Ananias Davisson's *A Supplement to the Kentucky Harmony* (Harrisonburg, VA, 1825) contained a related hexatonic LM tune, OVERTON (see Example 2 on page 1049):

This version was also not reprinted in other books.

The first time that this tune appeared under the name THE CHURCH'S DESOLATION and with the pentatonic melody line as it appears in *H82* was in the four-shape shape-note *Sacred Harp* (Philadelphia, 1844) compiled by Harris County, GA, newspaper editor and singing school teacher B. F. White and his associate E. J. King.[2] This tune, which was linked with the text "Well may thy servants mourn, my God," was attributed to J. T. White, a nephew of B. F. White (see Example 3 on page 1050):

An alto line was added in J. S. James's *Original Sacred Harp* (Cullman, AL, 1911). In C. H. Cayce's *The Good Old Songs* (Thornton,

Example 1

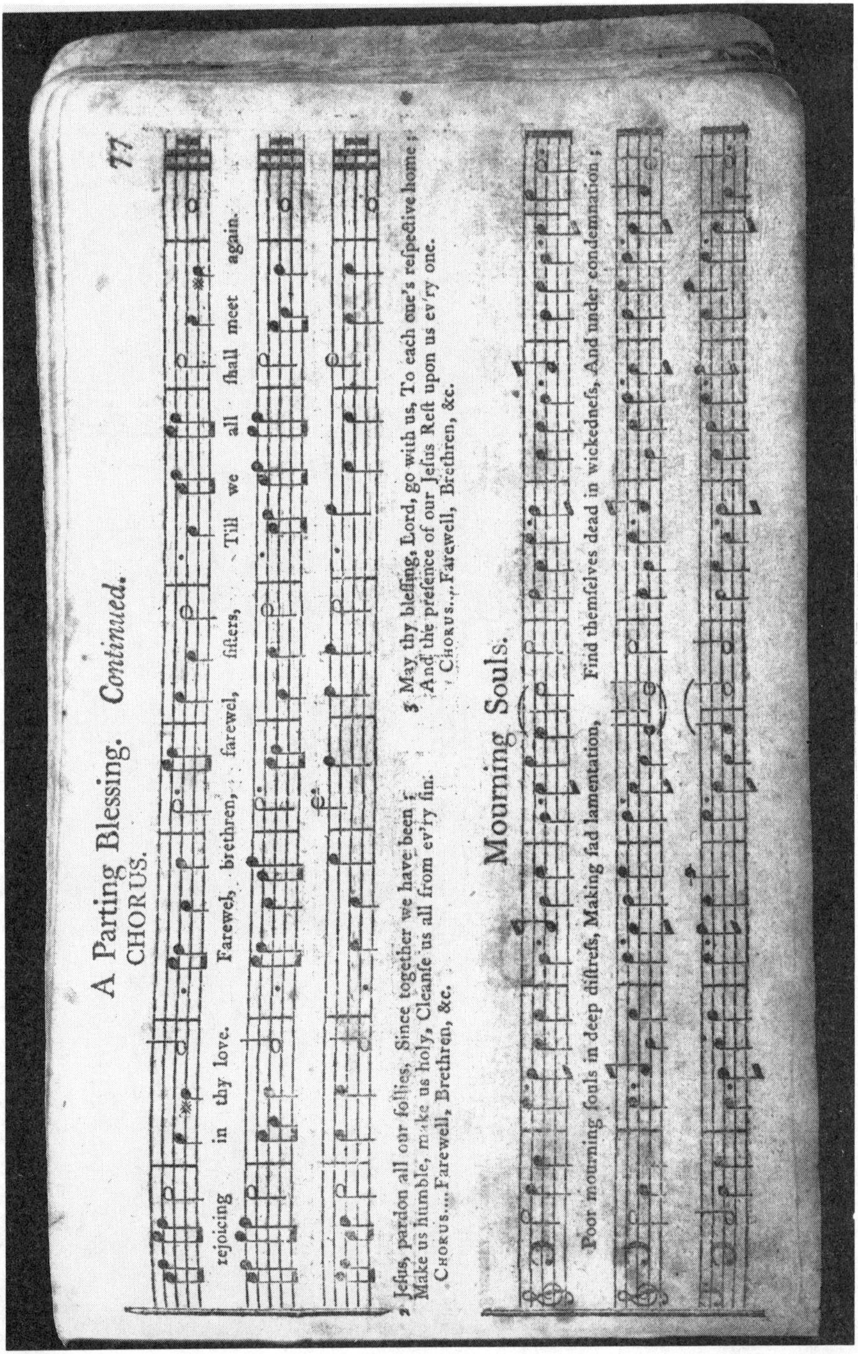

Reproduced from Ingalls's *Christian Harmony* (Exeter, NH, 1805), Brown University Library.

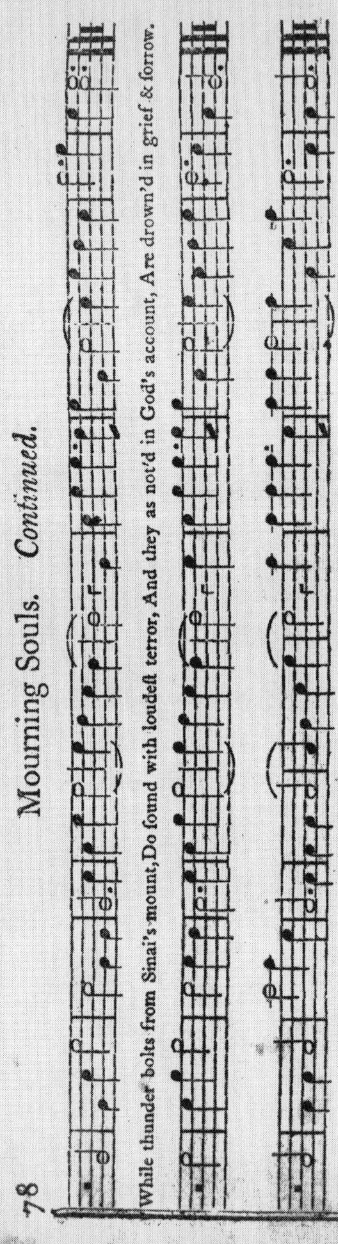

78 Mourning Souls. *Continued.*

While thunder bolts from Sinai's mount, Do ſound with loudeſt terror, And they as not'd in God's account, Are drown'd in grief & ſorrow.

2 Ah! woe is me that I was born, Or ever had beginning;
I would have had untimely birth, Or had no ſuture being;
Or elſe had dy'd when I was young, I might have been forgiven,
And might, like babes, with harmleſs tongues been praiſing God in heav'n.

3 But here I am in deep diſtreſs, Moſt worn away with trouble;
Day after day I ſeek for peace, But find my ſorrows double.
Saith ſatan, fatal is your ſtate, Times paſt you might repented,
But now you ſee it is too late, So make yourſelf contented.

4 How can I live, how can I breathe Under this ſore temptation,
Conclude my day of grace is o'er? Lord, hear my lamentation:
For I am weary of my life, Of pains and bitter crying;
My wants are great, my mind's in ſtrait, My ſpirit's almoſt dying.

5 But who is he that looketh forth, Sweet as the blooming morning,
Fair as the moon, clear as the ſun, 'Tis Jeſus Chriſt adorning.
Jeſus can clothe my naked ſoul; Jeſus for me hath died;
And now I can with pleaſure ſing, My wants are all ſupplied.

6 How can I ſtay, God calls await, And I muſt now be holy,
See Jeſus comes to cloſe my eyes, Soon I ſhall go to glory.
My Jeſus calls and I muſt go; Farewell to all things earthly,
I muſt be gone, God calls me home, To ſing to him more ſweetly.

7 Farewell, vain world, I bid adieu; My Jeſus is moſt holy;
Fain would I be with Chriſt above, Singing to him in glory.
My truſt is now in Jeſus' name, And in his arms is pleaſure;
Say, will you truſt in Jeſus' name, When he's the bleeding Saviour.

Example 2

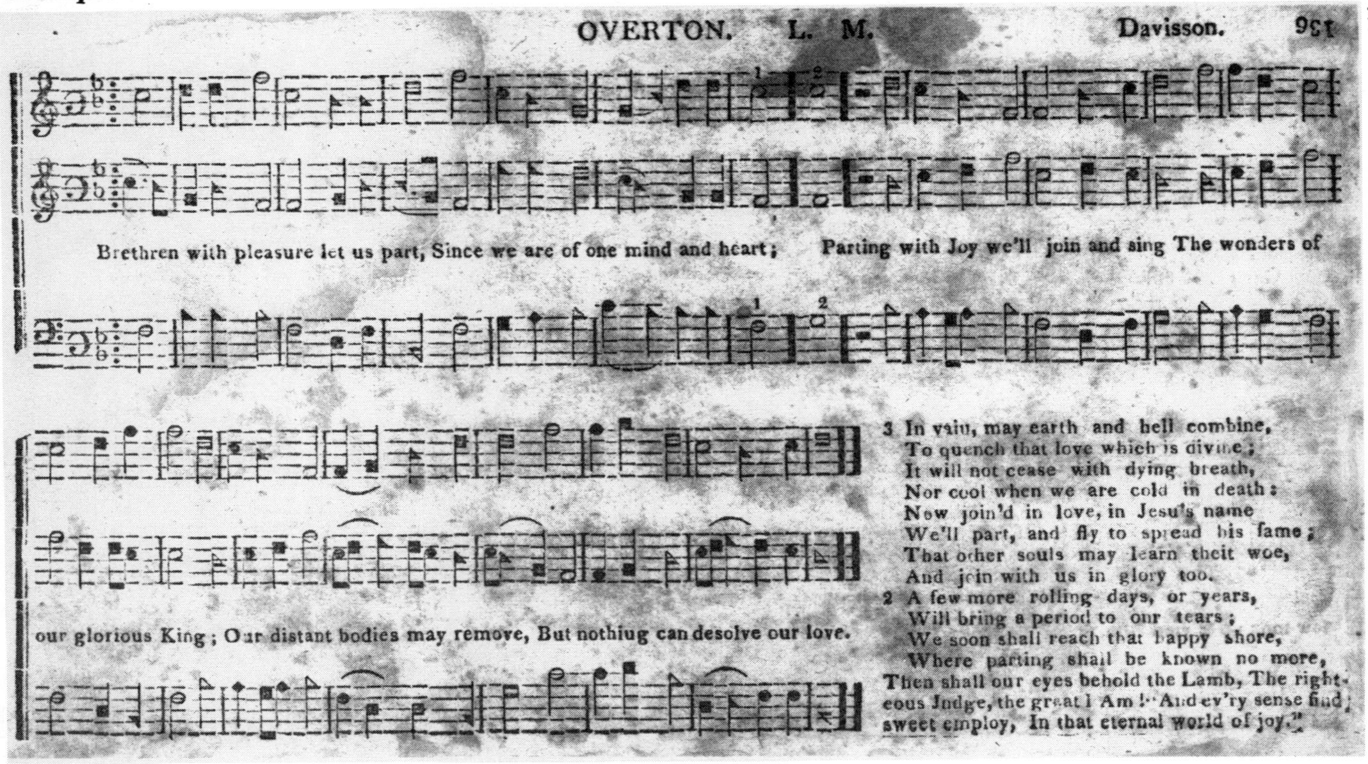

OVERTON. L. M. Davisson. 136

Brethren with pleasure let us part, Since we are of one mind and heart; Parting with Joy we'll join and sing The wonders of

our glorious King; Our distant bodies may remove, But nothiug can desolve our love.

3 In vain, may earth and hell combine,
To quench that love which is divine;
It will not cease with dying breath,
Nor cool when we are cold in death:
Now join'd in love, in Jesu's name
We'll part, and fly to spread his fame;
That other souls may learn their woe,
And join with us in glory too.
2 A few more rolling days, or years,
Will bring a period to our tears;
We soon shall reach that happy shore,
Where parting shall be known no more,
Then shall our eyes behold the Lamb, The righteous Judge, the great I Am!—And ev'ry sense find sweet employ, In that eternal world of joy."

Reproduced from the third edition of *A Supplement to the Kentucky Harmony* (Harrisonburg, VA, 1825), Special Collections, University of Tennessee Libraries.

Example 3

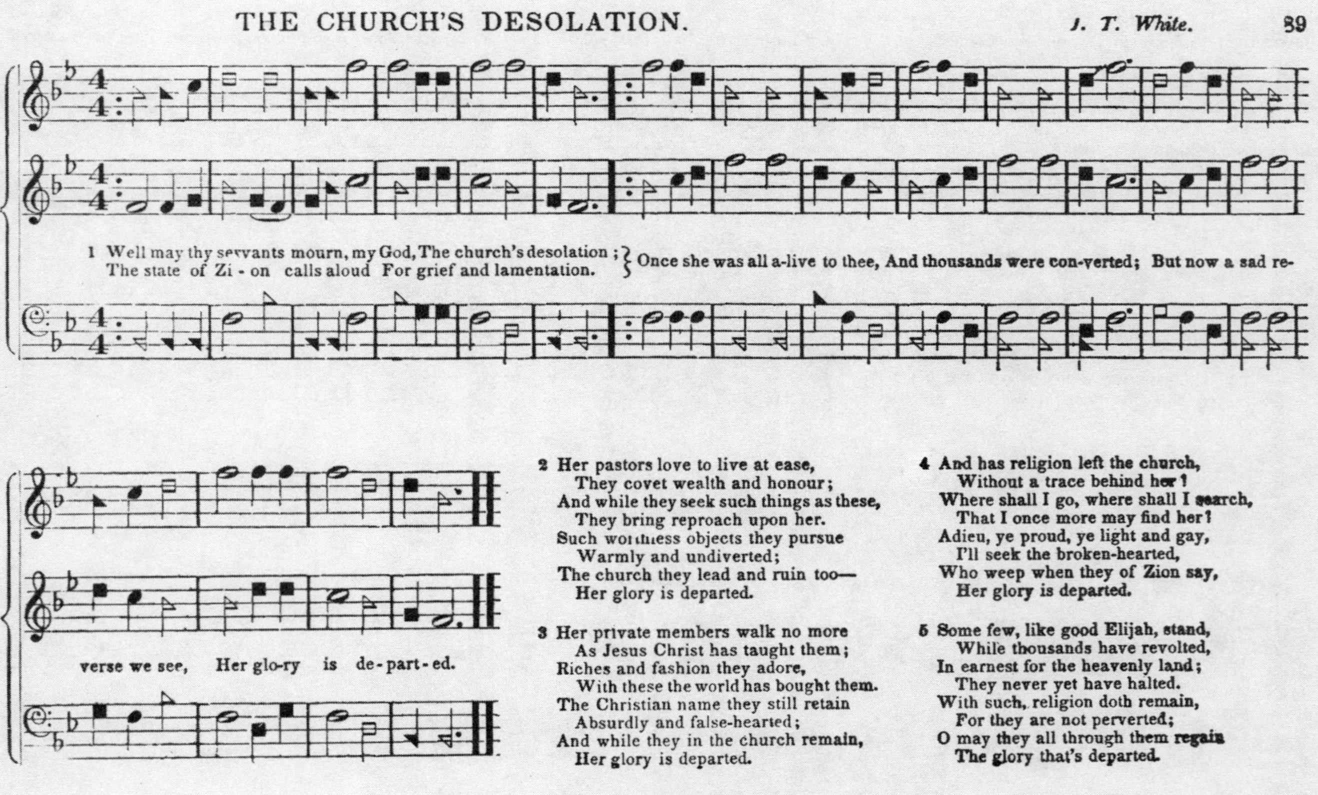

THE CHURCH'S DESOLATION.
J. T. White.
39
1 Well may thy servants mourn, my God, The church's desolation; Once she was all a-live to thee, And thousands were con-verted; But now a sad re-
The state of Zi - on calls aloud For grief and lamentation.
verse we see, Her glo-ry is de-part-ed.
2 Her pastors love to live at ease,
They covet wealth and honour;
And while they seek such things as these,
They bring reproach upon her.
Such worthless objects they pursue
Warmly and undiverted;
The church they lead and ruin too—
Her glory is departed.
3 Her private members walk no more
As Jesus Christ has taught them;
Riches and fashion they adore,
With these the world has bought them.
The Christian name they still retain
Absurdly and false-hearted;
And while they in the church remain,
Her glory is departed.
4 And has religion left the church,
Without a trace behind her!
Where shall I go, where shall I search,
That I once more may find her!
Adieu, ye proud, ye light and gay,
I'll seek the broken-hearted,
Who weep when they of Zion say,
Her glory is departed.
5 Some few, like good Elijah, stand,
While thousands have revolted,
In earnest for the heavenly land;
They never yet have halted.
With such, religion doth remain,
For they are not perverted;
O may they all through them regain
The glory that's departed.

Reproduced from *Sacred Harp* (Philadelphia, 1844), Library of Congress.

AK, 1913), which is still used among Primitive Baptists, the tune is printed on two staffs with the melody in the treble and a slightly altered alto part. Amos Sutton Hayden's *Sacred Melodeon* (Boston, 1849) contained an arrangement with the same name, melody line, and text, but with a different treble and bass, which was reproduced in Andrew W. Johnson's *Western Psalmodist* (Nashville, 1853) and Martin D. Wenger's *The Philharmonia* (Elkhart, IN, 1875). Just two years after the publication of *Sacred Harp*, William Walker, in *Southern and Western Pocket Harmonist* (Philadelphia, 1846), published a pentatonic tune entitled MOURNER'S LAMENTATION which he claimed as his own. The melody line was very close to THE CHURCH'S DESOLATION, although the treble and bass were quite different. It was linked with the text "Poor mourning soul! in deep distress," which was the text associated with MOURNING SOULS in Ingalls's *Christian Harmony* (see Example 4 on page 1052).

This version was printed (with a counter part added) in Walker's later *Christian Harmony* (New Haven, CT, 1867) and, on two staffs with the melody in the treble and an "Alto by C. H. C.," in C. H. Cayce's *The Good Old Songs* (Thornton, AK, 1913).

A variant form of the melody line only was published in Joseph Hillman's *The Revivalist* (Troy, NY, 1868), under the title HALLOWED SPOT, with the text "There is a spot to me more dear."

The melody line of A SACRED SPOT in John R. and J. Harvey Daily's *Primitive Baptist Hymn and Tune Book* (Indianapolis, 1902), still used among Primitive Baptists, is very close to that of THE CHURCH'S DESOLATION in *Sacred Harp*, except for the seventh phrase. It is linked with both "There is a spot to me more dear" and "Well may thy servants mourn, my God."

This tune is included in an Episcopal hymnal for the first time in *H82*. It is in the form that had appeared under the title THE CHURCH'S DESOLATION in Cayce's *The Good Old Songs*, except that it is printed in 3/2 rather than the incongruous 4/4 metre of earlier printings.

---

1. See J. Ingalls, *The Christian Harmony or Songster's Companion* with New Introduction by David Klocko (New York, 1981).

2. See B. E. Cobbs, Jr., *The Sacred Harp: A Tradition and Its Music* (Athens, GA, 1978).

MBJ/MH

Example 4

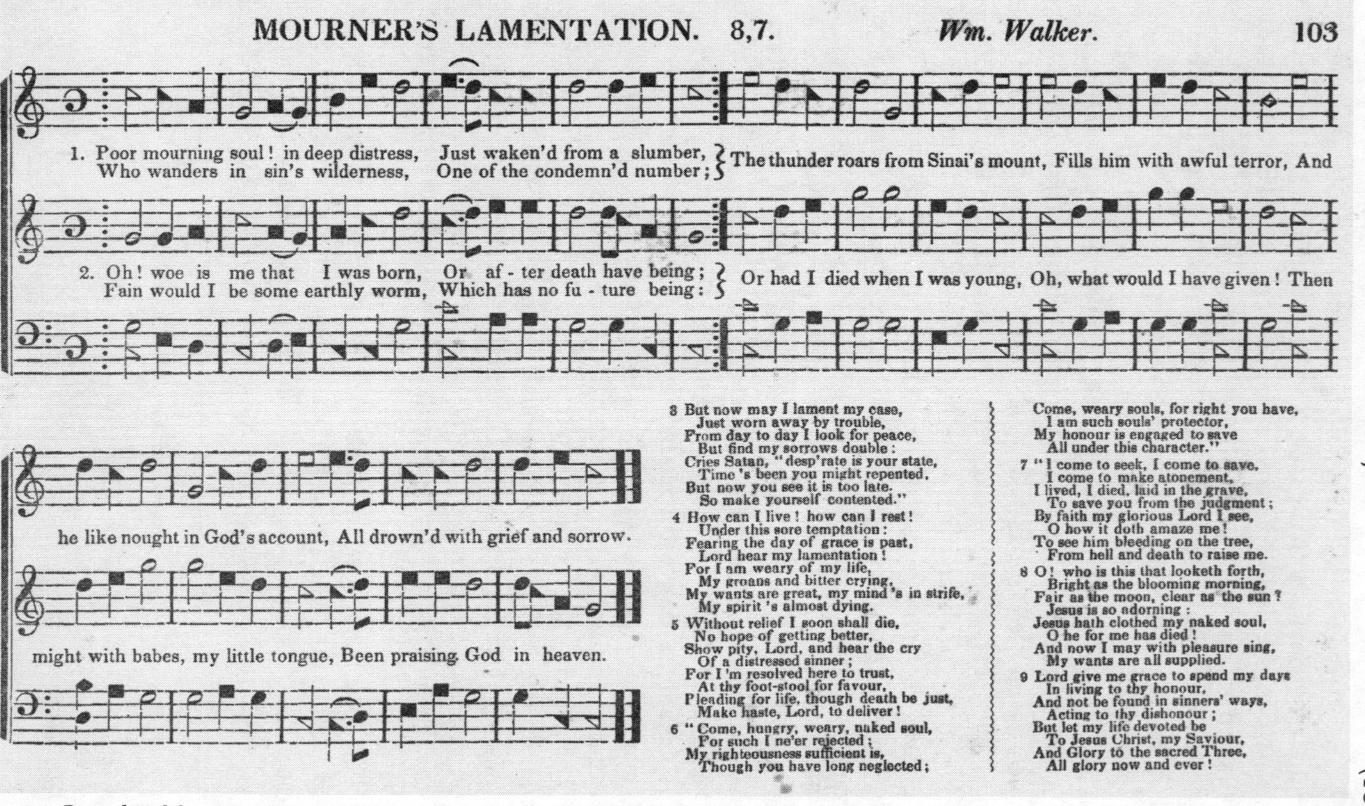

MOURNER'S LAMENTATION. 8,7. Wm. Walker. 103
1. Poor mourning soul! in deep distress, Just waken'd from a slumber,
Who wanders in sin's wilderness, One of the condemn'd number;
The thunder roars from Sinai's mount, Fills him with awful terror, And he like nought in God's account, All drown'd with grief and sorrow.
2. Oh! woe is me that I was born, Or af - ter death have being;
Fain would I be some earthly worm, Which has no fu - ture being:
Or had I died when I was young, Oh, what would I have given! Then might with babes, my little tongue, Been praising God in heaven.
3 But now may I lament my case,
Just worn away by trouble,
From day to day I look for peace,
But find my sorrows double:
Cries Satan, "desp'rate is your state,
Time 's been you might repented,
But now you see it is too late.
So make yourself contented."
4 How can I live! how can I rest!
Under this sore temptation:
Fearing the day of grace is past,
Lord hear my lamentation!
For I am weary of my life,
My groans and bitter crying,
My wants are great, my mind 's in strife,
My spirit 's almost dying.
5 Without relief I soon shall die,
No hope of getting better,
Show pity, Lord, and hear the cry
Of a distressed sinner;
For I'm resolved here to trust,
At thy foot-stool for favour,
Pleading for life, though death be just,
Make haste, Lord, to deliver!
6 "Come, hungry, weary, naked soul,
For such I ne'er rejected;
My righteousness sufficient is,
Though you have long neglected;
Come, weary souls, for right you have,
I am such souls' protector,
My honour is engaged to save
All under this character."
7 "I come to seek, I come to save,
I come to make atonement,
I lived, I died, laid in the grave,
To save you from the judgment;
By faith my glorious Lord I see,
O how it doth amaze me!
To see him bleeding on the tree,
From hell and death to raise me.
8 O! who is this that looketh forth,
Bright as the blooming morning,
Fair as the moon, clear as the sun?
Jesus is so adorning:
Jesus hath clothed my naked soul,
O he for me has died!
And now I may with pleasure sing,
My wants are all supplied.
9 Lord give me grace to spend my days
In living to thy honour,
And not be found in sinners' ways,
Acting to thy dishonour;
But let my life devoted be
To Jesus Christ, my Saviour,
And Glory to the sacred Three,
All glory now and ever!

Reproduced from *Southern and Western Pocket Harmonist* (Philadelphia, 1846), Special Collections, University of Tennessee Libraries.

567 *Thine arm, O Lord, in days of old*

Music: **ST. MATTHEW**

Readings of the healing miracles of our Lord as related in the Gospels appear with regularity in both the Eucharist and the Office and therefore call for hymnody that is contextual. This nineteenth-century text, rich in references to Christ's healing ministry, helps satisfy this need.

Words: This text was written by Edward Hayes Plumptre and published in leaflet form as *A Hymn used in the Chapel of King's College Hospital* (London, 1864). It was included in the *Appendix* to *HA&M* (1868), where it bore the caption "They brought unto him all that were diseased, and besought him that they might touch the hem of his garment, and as many as touched were made perfectly whole" (Mt. 14:35-36). The text that first appeared in the 1892 edition of the *Hymnal* was deleted from *H16* and restored in *H40*. For use in that edition and *H82*, an original third stanza was omitted. It read:

Though love and might no longer heal
  By touch, or word, or look;
Though they who do Thy work must read
  Thy laws in nature's book;
Yet come to heal the sick man's soul,
  Come, cleanse the leprous taint,
Give joy and peace, where all is strife,
  And strength, where all is faint.

For use in *H82*, language that the SCCM felt condoned a subtle contempt or discrimination against the sick and handicapped was altered. Original wordings were:

st. 1:5: The blind, the dumb
st. 1:7: the leper with his tainted life
st. 2:2: gave speech, and strength, and sight

Music: ST. MATTHEW has long been attributed to William Croft but, as with HANOVER [388] there is, in truth, no sound evidence of his authorship, and one can see how the attribution came to be made. The two cases are almost identical. The tunes were first printed in the sixth edition of *A Supplement to the New Version of Psalms* (London,

1708), whence they were copied in many other tunebooks—at first, almost exclusively in northern and central England. There was no mention of any composer until the tune was included in certain Birmingham publications printed by Michael Broome, one of which was John Barker's *A Select Number of the Best Psalm Tunes, Extant* (Birmingham, ca. 1750). Barker, a former pupil of Croft, evidently possessed a manuscript in his master's hand and assumed that the tunes were of Croft's composition, although some of them certainly were not. (For further details, see the commentary on the tune at 388).

There can be little doubt, however, that this sturdy tune was the product of a well-trained, up-to-date composer. The cadence is in the dominant, followed by a parallel one in the tonic; the excursion to related minor keys in the third quarter and the smooth return to the tonic to repeat the halfway cadence—these features of classical form point to a generation of composers, younger than Purcell, who were fully cognizant of the new tonal forms coming out of Italy. Croft is as likely a candidate as any other.

The tune was originally set to Tate & Brady's Ps. 33 ("Let all the just to God with joy/their cheerful voices raise"), but it is found with dozens of other texts during the next hundred years, none of which seemed to predominate. The original key was D, but C was equally common, and there are many different settings for two, three, and four voices, some full of appoggiaturas and passing notes, others relatively bare. Its first American printing was in James Lyon's *Urania* (Philadelphia, 1761), but it also appeared in a stripped-down form as one of the eighteen tunes printed with the *Proposed Book of Common Prayer* (1786). Since then it has held a secure place in Episcopal tradition.

No specific reason can be found for the tune's name. The unidentified editors of the 1708 *Supplement* seem to have chosen the names of major saints not already associated with psalm tunes and distributed them among the new tunes printed in that edition. In the case of ST. ANNE, there was an association with the parish church where Croft, its composer, was organist (see the commentary on 680), and ST. JAMES [457] is a similar case. No parallel clue, however, can suggest the identify of ST. MATTHEW's composer. The only London church dedicated to that Evangelist (St. Matthew, Friday Street) had no organ until 1735.

RG/NT

568 Father all loving, who rulest in majesty

***Music:* WAS LEBET**

The decade after World War II in England saw the creation of a movement to bring vitality into the Church through new hymnody. Out of this arose several authors and composers, some clergy, whose works were not only effective at the time of their creation and were influential in stimulating further creative change, but continue today as an enrichment of the Church's song (see the essay "British Hymnody Since 1950," vol. 1, 555). Several of the works created in the initial years of what later became known as the "Hymn Explosion" are found in *H82*, including this text by Patrick Appleford. Its matching with this eighteenth-century German tune first occurred in *100 Hymns for Today* (London, 1960).

Words: This text is part two of a seven-stanza hymn entitled "Alive for God" written about 1957 by the Rev. Patrick Appleford, then curate at All Saints', Poplar. Intended for use as an offertory hymn at a rally at Royal Albert Hall, London, sponsored by the Society for the Propagation of the Gospel, the text was first published in *Thirty 20th Century Hymn Tunes* (London, 1960), set to the tune CHESTNUT by the Rev. Geoffrey Beaumont. Chestnut is the location of Bishop's College where the poet was a lecturer in Church History and Worship. Both Fr. Appleford and the composer were cofounders of the 20th Century Light Music Group, an organization that sought through the use of "pop music" to attract young people to the Church (see the essay, "British Hymnody Since 1950," vol. 1, 555).

The original form of the text was three pairs of stanzas, each pair addressed to a member of the Holy Trinity, with an added seventh doxological stanza. The first of each pair describes the Person invoked, while the second is a prayer to that Person. For example, st. 1 is addressed to God as powerful king and judge, yet loving Father who gave his only Son to save his children. This is balanced in st. 2 by a prayer to the Father calling for his action in the lives of earthly leaders and people that they will be brought to "penitence and sorrow" for their sinful acts of vengeance. The text, a strong appeal for social action and peace in the world, would be useful at services focusing on the Holy Trinity and upon Christian responsibility. *The Hymnal 1982* uses sts. 2, 4, and 6 of the original. The omitted stanzas are:

1. Father all powerful, thine is the kingdom,
   thine is the power, the glory of love;
   Gently thou carest for each of thy children,
   lovingly sending thy Son from above.

3. Crucified Jesus, thou bearest our wickedness,
   now thou art risen that all men may live;
   Mighty Redeemer, despite our unworthiness,
   thou in thy mercy our sins dost forgive.

5. Comforter, Spirit, thou camest at Pentecost,
   pouring thy grace on thy Church here below;
   Still thou dost feed us by prayer and by sacrament,
   till all creation thy glory shall know.

Music: The tune WAS LEBET (*Zahn* 1454), as given here in a slightly altered form, appeared in the *Choral-Buch vor Johann Heinrich Reinhardt* (Üttingen, 1754). Its first appearance (*Zahn* 1455) was in the *Nürembergisches Gesangbuch* (Nuremberg, 1676) by H. S. Schwemmer, set to the text by the seventeenth-century hymnist and musician Matthaeus Appelles von Loewenstern (1594-1648) "Was lebet, was schwebet, was Odem nur hat." The harmonization given here is that of Ralph Vaughan Williams taken from *EH*.

RG/CS

569 God the Omnipotent! King who ordainest

***Music:* RUSSIA**

The pages of hymnological textbooks often cite instances where texts have been written to assure the use of particular tunes and this impulse continues to enrich our hymnody. F. Bland Tucker and F. Pratt Green are two contemporary poets who have written texts with this intent (see hymns 170 and 477). This text is a nineteenth-century example of the practice.

Words: This text is a conflation of portions of two texts by nineteenth-century poets. Stanzas 1 and 2 are taken from a four-stanza text written by Henry Fothergill Chorley in 1842 in an attempt to supply words to the tune RUSSIA. They were first published in John Hullah's *Part Music* (London, 1842) with the title "In the Time of War," beginning "God the All-terrible." On August 28, 1870, Ellerton wrote "God the Almighty One, wisely ordaining" for a country congregation during the Franco-German war, imitating the style of Chorley's "God the All-terrible! King who ordainest." Ellerton's four-stanza hymn was printed in Robert Brown-Borthwick's *Select Hymns for Church and Home* (London, 1871). At the same time, Ellerton and the co-editors of *Church Hymns* (London, 1871) printed three of Chorley's stanzas followed by the last three of Ellerton's text as a single hymn.

The text first appeared in the 1892 edition of the *Hymnal* with the credit RUSSIAN: Tr. H. F. Chorley. However, only Chorley's sts. 1 and 4 (3 and 4 of the original) are used. Stanzas 2 and 3 are the unaltered sts. 3 and 4 of John Ellerton's 1870 text. In *H16*, the six-stanza form was used. Here sts. 1, 2, and 6 are altered versions of Chorley's 1, 3, and 4. Stanzas 3, 4, and 5 are Ellerton's altered sts. 1, 3, and 4. *The Hymnal 1982* continues, with one small alteration, the form established in *H40*. Stanzas 1 and 2 are Chorley's altered sts. 1 and 3 and sts. 3 and 4 are Ellerton's altered 2 and 4. Chorley's omitted stanzas are:

2. God the omnipotent! mighty avenger,
   Watching invisible, judging unheard,
   Doom us not now in the day of our danger:
   Grant to us peace, O most merciful Lord.

3. So shall thy children in thankful devotion
   Praise him who saved them from peril and sword,
   Singing in chorus from ocean to ocean,
   'Peace to the nations, and praise to the Lord.'

Chorley's original form of sts. 1 and 3 are:

1. God the all-merciful! earth has forsaken
   Thy ways of blessedness, slighted thy word;
   Bid not thy wrath in its terrors awaken:
   Grant to us peace, O most merciful Lord.

3. God the all-terrible! King, who ordainest
   Great winds thy clarions, the lightnings thy sword,

Show forth thy pity on high where thou reignest:
Grant to us peace, O most merciful Lord.

The omitted sts. 1 and 3 of Ellerton's 1870 text are:

God the Almighty One, wisely ordaining[1]
Judgments unsearchable, famine or sword;
Over the tumult of war Thou art reigning;
Give to us peace in our time, O Lord!

God the All-pitiful! is it not crying,
Blood of the guiltless like water outpoured?
Look on the anguish, the sorrow, the sighing;
Give to us peace in our time, O Lord.

Other alterations are:

st. 3:1: God the All-righteous One! *man* has defied Thee;
st. 4:1: God, the All-*wise! by the fire of* Thy chast'ning

---

1. Amended by Ellerton in *Hymns Original and Translated* (London, 1888), to "God the *Almighty in wisdom* ordaining."

Music: See hymn 358.

RG and BB

570 All who love and serve your city

Music: **BIRABUS**

A close review of many contemporary English-language hymnals and their supplements will reveal the strong impact that the Rev. Dr. Erik Routley, author, composer, hymnal editor, and teacher has had upon their contents. This text, which was created at an important developmental period in Dr. Routley's life, is one of his best-known works (see the essay "British Hymnody Since 1950," vol. 1, 555). It was written for use with this tune.

Words: This was the first hymn text written by Erik Routley—born out of frustration at being unable to compose a hymn tune! The story is related from their differing viewpoints by both people concerned in its creation: Alan Luff and Erik Routley. Both were taking part in a consultation on hymnody at Dunblane Church House, Scotland, in October 1966.[1] Participants were given the task of writing a hymn expressing Christian social responsibility, and each went to their rooms to complete their task. Erik Routley was assigned a tune and Alan Luff a text. Luff, later Precentor of Westminster Abbey and an experienced singer, found that the only way he could write a text was by inventing a thread of melody on which he could string his words. In the process he hummed the melody again and again as he constructed his text. In the next room Routley was driven to distraction trying to write his own tune against this persistent humming that came through the intervening wall. Exasperated, he gave up the task and sat down and wrote a hymn text instead: "All who love and serve your city."

The text was specifically written for the Peter Cutts tune BIRABUS, which Erik Routley had included as Example 65 in his *Twentieth Century Church Music* (London, 1964), at that time a tune without a textual association. Although British in origin, the text has specific American associations. Routley had made several visits to America by this time; indeed, he had lectured in Princeton and Louisville earlier in that year, 1966. He was particularly affected by the American urban riots, which were then a summer feature, and by the grief and sorrow that surrounded them.

The text was first published with BIRABUS in the experimental and somewhat "home-grown" collection *Dunblane Praises No.2* (Dunblane, 1967) and later in *New Songs for the Church. Book 1* (London, 1969) and *Hymns and Songs* (London, 1969). Its first appearance in an American collection was in *Sing! Hymnal for Youth and Adults* (Philadelphia, 1970), edited by R.H. Terry. The association with the American tune CHARLESTOWN [571] was first made in *The Worshipbook* (Philadelphia, 1972), issued by the United Presbyterian Church.

---

1. See *Duty & Delight: Routley Remembered*, edited by R.A. Leaver, et. al. (Carol Stream, IL, 1985), 183; and E. Routley, *Companion to Westminster Praise*, (Chapel Hill, NC, 1977), no. 56.

Music: BIRABUS was composed by Peter Cutts in the fall of 1962 for use at a Student Christian Movement Congress where it was used with the text "In the cross of Christ I glory." The composer of the tune writes "the tune-title has significance purely within the S.C.M., being the nickname [of] the vehicle in which I and a number of others returned to Britain from an international conference in Austria, summer 1962." Its plaintive, folklike tune and harmonically rich accompaniment later provided the inspiration to Dr. Erik Routley for the composition of his text (see above). Dr. Routley describes the tune as having "a [Herbert] Howells-like richness and pathos."[1] This is noticeable in the gentle dissonance of the opening chord, the chromaticism and addition of a fifth voice to the texture of the third, fourth, and fifth measures, the use of the lowered leading tone at the end of the third phrase, the gentle return to e, and the final touch of color on the suspension over the final chord. It is intriguing to note the beginning of the tune, which opens with the ascending intervals of a minor third followed by a major second. The opening of the second phrase sees an expansion of these intervals through the use of two ascending thirds, the first minor, the second major. This pattern gives a particular sense of "lift" to the tune and leads to a point of climax at the third note of the third phrase. From this point on, the tune gently descends to its distinctive cadence in which the melody outlines the dominant minor chord F# D B and ends on the lower dominant, B below middle C. Thus, even at the conclusion, one is left with a sense of movement and perhaps of nostalgia.

---

1. E, Routley, *The Music of Christian Hymns* (Chicago, 1981), 165.

RAL/RG

571 All who love and serve your city

Music: **CHARLESTOWN**

This text first appeared in an Episcopal publication in the 1971 supplement *SLMHSS*, where it was matched with LYON 59 (DELIVRE DES

ADVERSAIRES). The matching here with CHARLESTOWN is found in many recent hymnals in the United States.

Words: See hymn 570.

Music: Amos Pilsbury, a precentor, singing teacher, and music copyist from Charleston, SC, was one of the first of the American compilers of tunebooks to record folk tunes. Several were included in his round-note *The United States' Sacred Harmony* (Charleston, SC, 1799)[1] including KEDRON [10 and 163]. Another was a hexatonic tune in an uncommon ABBC form that was named CHARLESTON and published in four parts with the text "Come, thou Fount of ev'ry blessing" (see Example 1 on following page):

A three-part version derived from Pilsbury's was published in several southern shape-note books under the title CHARLESTOWN and with the text "Mercy, O thou Son of David."

Variants of this tune were recorded by other compilers. Stephen Jenks and Elijah Griswold's *American Compiler of Sacred Harmony* (Northampton, MA, 1803) contains a version titled DETROIT and printed with "Come thou fount of ev'ry blessing." Joseph Funk, a Shenandoah Valley Mennonite printer, included the tune with a German text, "Seelen Weide, Meine Freude," in his *Die allgemein nützliche Choral-Music* (Harrisonburg, VA, 1816). Japheth Coombs Washburn, in the 1826 enlarged edition of his *Temple Harmony* (Hallowell, ME), included a version titled BALDWIN, linked with "Come, thou fount of ev'ry blessing."

Joshua Leavitt included a two-part version titled BARTIMEUS with John Newton's text "Mercy, O thou Son of David!" in his *Christian Lyre* (New York, 1831). Thomas Hastings, in the American Tract Society's *Sacred Songs for Family and Social Worship* (New York, 1842), added tenor and counter parts. This version was included in innumerable later books, including several denominational hymnals: for example, *Presbyterian Psalmodist* (Philadelphia, 1852); *Hymns for the Use of the Methodist Episcopal Church* (New York, 1857); W. R. Roedel's *Carmina Ecclesiae* (Baltimore, 1860), approved by the General Synod of the Evangelical Lutheran Church; the American Baptist *Devotional Hymn and Tune Book* (Philadelphia, 1864), edited by William B. Bradbury; the Presbyterian *Social Hymn and Tune Book: For*

Example 1

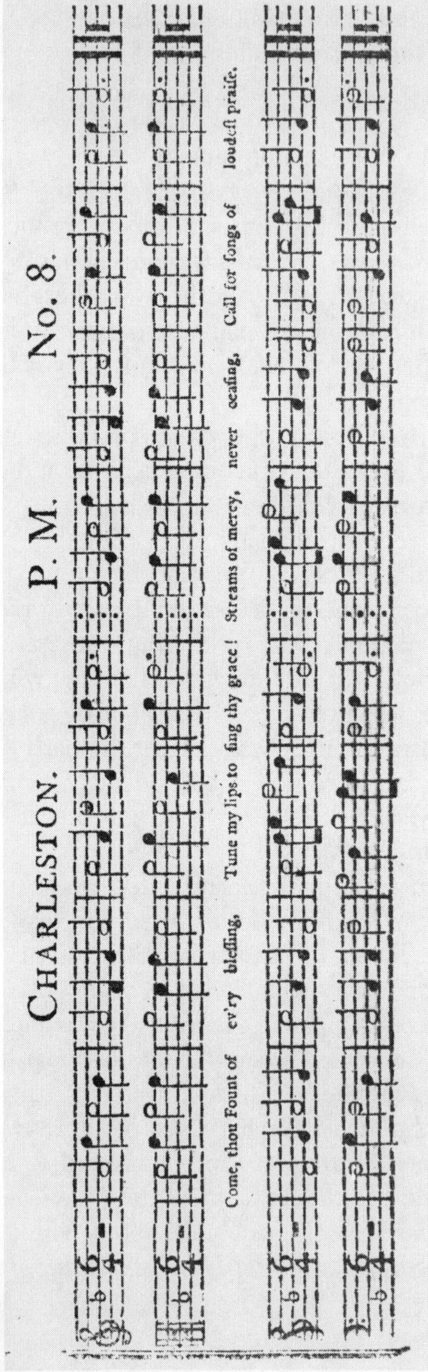

Reproduced from *The United States' Sacred Harmony* (Charleston, SC, 1799), Library of Congress.

the Lecture Room, Prayer Meeting, Family Circle, and Mission Church (Philadelphia, 1865); the Advent Christian *Jubilee Harp* (Boston, 1867); and *The Reformed Church Hymnal with Tunes* (Cleveland, 1878). This version is also included in two tunebooks still in use among Primitive Baptists, John R. and J. Harvey Daily's *Primitive Baptist Hymn and Tune Book* (Indianapolis, 1902) and C. H. Cayce's *The Good Old Songs* (Thornton, AK, 1913).

Other arrangements of this tune have been printed not only under the titles CHARLESTON and BARTIMEUS but also under the titles BELMONT, FREE GRACE, MERRITT, SWAINE, and DEAL GENTLY WITH THY SERVANTS, LORD.

A still different arrangement entitled BARTIMEUS was printed with three texts for use at burials in *The Congregational Hymn and Tune Book* (New Haven, CT, 1856).

An arrangement in 6/8 time, included in Lowell Mason's *The Asaph* (New York, 1861), was picked up in other books, including the Northern Presbyterian *Hymnal of the Presbyterian Church* (Philadelphia, 1867) and the Southern Presbyterian *Book of Hymns and Tunes* (Richmond, VA, 1874).

Still another version was printed with treble and counter parts only in J. R. Graves's *Little Seraph*, the tunebook bound with his *The New Baptist Psalmist and Tune Book* (Memphis, 1874).

During the nineteenth century this tune was printed in more denominational hymnals and in more books edited by reputable eastern seaboard musicians than almost any other early American folk tune.

This tune first entered an Episcopal hymnal in *Hymnal Supplement II* (New York, 1976), where two accompaniments by Alastair Cassels-Brown were printed with it. There it was linked with the text "In the cross of Christ I glory," with which it had been associated in some earlier tunebooks. One of these accompaniments has been retained in *H82*, where it is printed with Erik Routley's text "All who love and serve your city." CHARLESTOWN is also suggested as an alternative tune for "In the cross of Christ I glory" [441/442].

---

1. See K. Kroeger, "A Yankee Tunebook from the Old South: Amos Pilsbury's *The United States' Sacred Harmony*," *The Hymn* 32, (July, 1981), 154-162.

MH

572 *Weary of all trumpeting*

Music: **DISTLER**

This antiwar text, couched in strong prophetic rhetoric, matched with an equally strong tune punctuated by martial dotted rhythms, is in itself a paradox. It reflects the paradox of much of the Gospel, especially the paradox of the painful crucifixion and death of Christ upon the cross, which is seen by some as defeat, but by others as victory over sin and death.

Words: It was the tune DISTLER that inspired this text (see commentary below). The composer Jan Bender had long thought that the melody composed by his friend and mentor Hugo Distler deserved a hymnic text. Sometime after the publication of his *Variations for Organ on a Theme by Hugo Distler* (Wittenberg, OH, 1966), Bender asked Martin Franzmann to write a suitable text. This Franzmann did in 1971, producing this antitriumphalistic trumpeting of grace, a masterpiece that admirably matches Distler's music, as well as the conditions under which it was written.

The text first appeared in print with the tune DISTLER on a separate sheet issued by Chantry Press in 1972. The first hymnal to include it was *Worship* (Chicago, 1975).

Music: During 1965 the composer Jan Bender wrote *Variations for Organ on a Theme by Hugo Distler*, Opus 38 (Wittenberg, OH, 1966). In the Foreword, Bender wrote:

> The original manuscript of the theme by Hugo Distler is lost, 'gone with the wind,' so to speak. The composer of the variations, who was Distler's friend and first composition student, kept the theme in his mind for over thirty years until finally its inner force and spiritual power impelled him to 'get rid' of that which had developed around these tones.

Bender made the discovery that he had remembered the melody incorrectly when he came across a postcard of it with the original text, issued by Bärenreiter of Kassel in the mid-1930s.

The melody was written by Distler under duress. In 1934 the Third Reich was jubilant after its annexation of Austria and wished to celebrate this enforced unification. Distler was charged to compose a suitable melody for the official text "Deutschland und Deutschösterreich." Instead of being a triumphalist piece, Distler's melody has a sad strength about it.

The melody first appeared as a hymn tune with Franzmann's text on a single sheet issued by Chantry Press in 1972. It was given with a harmonization by Jan Bender. In *Worship II* (Chicago, 1975), it appeared with a harmonization by Richard Proulx, which was taken over into *H82*.

RAL

573 Father eternal, Ruler of creation

Music: **LANGHAM**

Written immediately after World War I, this text reflects truths that tragically remain relevant to our world after a second catastrophic World War and continuing regional engagements that scar our civilization. LANGHAM, a strong yet poignant tune, was written for use with this text.

Words: Written in 1919 for the Life and Liberty Movement by Laurence Housman at the request of H. R. L. Sheppard, Rector of St. Martin's-in-the-Fields, London, this text reflects the emotional climate of the English people at the end of World War I. Mirroring as it does the disillusionment of a nation in a war whose death toll included almost an entire generation of young men and whose ravages left a staggering level of loss and destruction in both city and countryside, the text voices a desire for international peace as exemplified in the ideals of the League of Nations. Paired with the tune LANGHAM, the text appeared in *Songs of Praise* (London, 1925) and later in *H40*.

In support of the SCCM's intent to use inclusive language wherever possible, the following portions of text were altered for use in *H82*:

st. 1:4:	man's blindness
st. 4:2:	sons of earth
st. 5:3	brother love

The alteration suggested for use in st. 5 was rejected by the 1982 General Convention's Joint Committee on the *Hymnal* and was replaced with: "Bind us in thine own love for better seeing." This change alters the focus from a prayer that love among nations may lead to a deeper understanding of the full ramifications of God's redemptive action in the birth of Jesus to a prayer that we may achieve this realization through oneness with God. Although this is a theologically defensible statement, this text has lost an important aspect of its original focus.

Music: LANGHAM was composed by Geoffrey Shaw for this text on the occasion of a meeting in Langham Place, Queen's Hall, London, of the Life and Liberty Movement. The first two measures of the tune are identical to the opening of JESU, MEINE FREUDE (see hymn 701), and as the tune proceeds it is interesting to compare the development of the work of Crüger [701] and Shaw [573]. Crüger's chromaticism and Shaw's diatonicism develop the initial phrase in characteristic styles and could be object lessons to students of composition.

The melody of the Shaw unison setting is solemn, dark, and poignant and moves over a solid four-part accompaniment. In the third section the composer begins to build to a stirring climax at the refrain, bringing the melody to its highest point of pitch and enriching the harmony through the addition of a fifth voice. The melody is brought to conclusion with a quick descent, ending on its lowest pitch, middle C.

RG/AW

574 Before thy throne, O God, we kneel

Music: **ST. PETERSBURG**

This text, which first appeared in an Episcopal *Hymnal* in *H40*, takes the form of a litany addressed to God the Divine Judge. In a series of petitions, the depth of human sinfulness is probed with vivid clarity. They conclude with a petition which implores that the petitioner, in the flames of the refining fire, may be assured of God's presence to rise "more pure, more true, more nobly wise." As in *H40*, the text is matched with an AA¹B tune from the repertoire of the Russian sacred song.

Words: This text is continued from its initial appearance in *H40* with one change: st. 2:2 was originally "wishful to give to all their due."

It is not found in general use in other English-language hymnals. The editors of *H40*, who were unable to ascertain the date of its composition, state that it was published in H. D. A. Major's *Life and Letters of William Boyd Carpenter* (London, 1925) (see *H40c*, 306).

Music: ST. PETERSBURG is attributed to Dimitri Bortniansky. It is said to be a setting of "O salutaris hostia" from an 1822 mass by the composer. The source of this information is I. H. Tscherlitsky's *Choralbuch* (Moscow, 1825), where the tune appears with a text by Gerhard Tersteegen, "Für dich sei ganz Herz," beginning with the fourth stanza "Ich bete an die Macht der Liebe" (*Zahn* 2964). The editors of *H40c* also identify it as "no. 116 in the edition of Dimitri Bortniansky's sacred works compiled by Peter Tschaikowsky, set to the Russian hymn Коль славенъ.[1] Wesley Milgate in *Songs of the People of God* remarks that "the melody was not ordinarily used in Russian churches, but was played on such semi-religious occasions as 'the blessing of the waters' on 6 January at St. Petersburg; it sounded on the bells of the church of St. Peter and St. Paul in that city."[2] Mr. Milgate then goes on to describe its use in maneuvers of the German army.[3] The tune first appeared in England in *Collection of Psalms and Hymns* (London, 1827) and in the 1875 Standard Edition of *HA&M*. The arrangement of the hymn in *H82* is as it appears in *H40* and is probably the work of Canon C. Winfred Douglas.

---

1. Joint Commission on the Revision of the *Hymnal*, *The Hymnal 1940 Companion* (New York, 1949, rev. 1951), 306.
2. W. Milgate, *Songs of the People of God* (London, 1982), 130.
3. Milgate, 131.

RG

575 Before thy throne, O God, we kneel

Music: **VATER UNSER IM HIMMELREICH**

A German chorale tune associated historically with a German paraphrase of the Lord's Prayer has been chosen for the second appearance of this text by William Boyd Carpenter.

Words: See hymn 574.

Music: Also known as OLD 112TH, this tune was first published in Valentin Schumann's *Geistliche Lieder auffs new gebessert und gemehrt zu Wittenberg* (Leipzig, 1539), set to Luther's version of the Lord's Prayer, "Vater unser im Himmelreich" (*Zahn* 2651). It was set to Richard Coxe's English version of the Lord's Prayer in the first edition of the *Anglo-Genevan Psalter* of 1558, but in the 1561 edition of that book, as well as the English and Scottish psalters, it is set to the 112th Psalm, thus the tune's name. Bach used the tune in his *St. John Passion* and Cantatas 90, 101, and 102, as well as in some of his organ preludes. It was a favorite tune of John Wesley's, and he included it as PLAYFORD'S TUNE in his *Foundery Collection* (London, 1742). Mendelssohn's *Sixth Organ Sonata* is also based upon this tune.

MBJ

576 God is love, and where true love is

Music: **MANDATUM**

In the past three decades congregational song has been enriched in a fresh and unprecedented way by Roman Catholic authors and composers, two of whom are represented in this hymn, Fr. James Quinn and Richard Proulx (see the essays "British Hymnody Since 1950," vol. 1, 555 and "Hymnody in the United States Since 1950," vol. 1, 600).

Words: "God is love, and where true love is," a paraphrase of the Latin text "Ubi Caritas" (see 581) by James Quinn from *New Hymns for All Seasons* (London, 1969), is appropriate to the theme of Christian Responsibility and to the ceremony of foot washing or the offertory at the Eucharist on Maundy Thursday. Father Quinn's translation preserves the original form of the text found in the Latin rite for the solemn evening Mass on Maundy Thursday, i.e., three four-line verses framed by an antiphon or refrain that introduces and follows each verse.

The theme, our love of Christ, the source and inspiration of our love for one another, is clearly shown in st. 1. In st. 2, the poet charges us to come to liturgy free of "anger, strife and every quarrel" and prays that Christ be present among us. A prayer to Christ, the "purest Light of all creation," with the petition that we may find the fulfillment of love in the presence of God and the blessed, brings the hymn to a close.

This text first appeared in an Episcopal publication in *Hymns III*.

Music: Richard Proulx wrote the tune MANDATUM in 1983 for use with this text. The tune, which flows gently in a stepwise manner, shows the composer's deep knowledge of plainsong. It hovers around B♭ and seldom moves below E♭ or above B♭ It thus lies comfortably within the range of the average singer in any congregation. Note should be made of the skillful way in which the composer varies the texture of the accompaniment. The opening refrain is largely in five voices. In contrast to this rich sound, Mr. Proulx starts the verse section with three-part writing, alternating four-part writing with imparting to the setting a feeling of dialogue of statement and response. Particular note should be made of the final cadence of the verse section with its half-close on the subdominant (A♭) and the moving alto voice, which adds the lowered leading tone of the key (D♭) and propels it back to the refrain in the tonic key. This setting lends itself to responsorial performance with the antiphon sung by congregation and choir and the stanzas by a cantor or the choir. An optional descant, available for use with the antiphon after sts. 2 and 3, imparts added richness to the setting.

RG

577 *God is love, and where true love is*

Music: **UBI CARITAS (MURRAY)**

A tune by a British priest and monastic, Dom Gregory Murray, has been matched with this contemporary translation of the text "Ubi caritas" by another monastic, Fr. James Quinn. Dom Gregory is a Roman Catholic composer and scholar who, like Fr. Quinn, has contributed greatly in these past decades to congregational song.

Words: See hymn 576.

Music: This setting, originally intended for use with Ronald Knox's translation of the Latin text "Ubi caritas," was composed in the key of D^{b} by Dom A. Gregory Murray in 1939 for inclusion in the *New Westminster Hymnal* (London, 1940). It was paired with a translation of the text by Anthony Petti in the *New Catholic Hymnal* (New York, 1971). It first appeared in an Episcopal publication in *Hymns III* with James Quinn's less archaic translation of the Latin. This text/tune combination, preferred by many hymnal editors, continues in *H82*.

Dom Gregory's unison responsorial setting honors the form and the name of the text for which it was written. Composed in a series of unbarred phrases that conform to the twelve-syllable structure of the four lines of the Latin text and the thirteen-syllable refrain, its chant-like diatonic melody is basically in a one-note-to-a-syllable style with the occasional use of two notes to a syllable at cadences. Harmonically, the setting remains firmly centered in the key of C with modulations to closely related keys G and a. Because of the gentle sensitivity of the setting with its uncomplicated melody, this tune is very accessible for congregational singing. Performance notes with the text in *H82 a2* suggest that the stanzas may be sung by a cantor or a choir.

RG

578 O God of love, O King of peace

***Music:* ELTHAM**

In the late 1850s and early 1860s, Europe and America were both dealing with ongoing or impending war. In Italy, the War of Liberation was being fought (1859-1861); in 1860 war seemed imminent between England and France; and in the United States 1861 marked the beginning of the devastating Civil War. It was under these world conditions that this text was written. It is matched with a tune harmonized by Samuel Sebastian Wesley that moves with wide strides of ascending intervals.

Words: In the original edition of *HA&M* (1861), there were four hymns included in the section marked "In Times of Trouble." This text by Sir Henry Williams Baker was among them; it bore the caption "The Lord shall give His people the blessing of peace" (Ps. 29:11). Since its inception, all too sadly, the text continues to have a poignancy that matches our deepest yearnings for a war-free society.

The following alterations have been made for the sake of inclusiveness:

st. 1:3 of sinful man now restrain
st. 2:2 our fathers told

A fourth stanza that has been omitted follows:

Where saints and angels dwell above,
All hearts are knit in holy love;
O bind in us that heavenly chain,
Give peace, O God, give peace again.

The text entered the *Hymnal* in 1871.

Music: See hymn 434.

MS

579 Almighty Father, strong to save

Music: **MELITA**

This text is based on the much loved "Eternal Father, strong to save" and is matched with the popular tune MELITA. With its close identification with all contemporary modes of transportation, it serves a very practical hymnological need.

Words: A compilation of texts by William Whiting and Robert Nelson Spencer, this hymn seeks to address the needs of travelers using various modes of transportation. The first and fourth stanzas, with slight alterations, are taken from Whiting's well-known hymn "Eternal Father, strong to save." (See hymn 608.) Spencer's contribution was first published in the *Missionary Service Book* (1937). In st. 2:4, the word "brethren" has been changed to "people." To adapt Whiting's text to the circumstances of the last quarter of the twentieth century, the last line of the hymn has been changed from "Glad praise from air and land and sea" to "Glad praise from space, air, land, and sea." The hymn entered the *Hymnal* in 1940.

Music: MELITA was written by John Bacchus Dykes, Precentor of Durham Cathedral, for the first edition of *HA&M* (1861). At the end of the previous year, Dykes had sent to the musical editor, William Henry Monk, a number of previously composed tunes. These presumably included NICAEA [362] and HOLLINGSIDE [707]. Dykes indicated that he had composed the submitted tunes some time before the end of 1860 for congregational use at Durham Cathedral. MELITA, however, could not have been among these tunes because it was specifically composed for a new text that made its first appearance in the first edition of *HA&M* (1861): William Whiting's hymn "Eternal Father, strong to save." One must therefore conclude that Dykes was commissioned to write it and that he composed it either toward the end of 1860 or during the early months of 1861. Its name, MELITA (Malta), recalls the safe haven St. Paul found after being shipwrecked off the island of Malta (Acts 28:1-2). MELITA is typical of Dykes's tunes at their best—well-crafted and balanced four-part writing of emotional intensity, created by a chromatic harmonic structure combined with a proclivity for word painting, such as the rising chromatic bass in the third line. Together with the Whiting text, this "Navy Hymn" is sung throughout the English-speaking world as *the* hymn for seafarers and is one of the most popular and best loved of all hymns in the English tradition. Benjamin Britten made impressive use of it in his *Noye's Fludde* Op. 59 (1957).

MS/RAL

580 God, who stretched the spangled heavens

Music: **HOLY MANNA**

This contemporary text probes deeply into concerns of the twentieth-century Christian about the scientific and technological advancements of our time, which seriously threaten the safety and stability of the world in which we live. It is matched here with an American folk hymn that, with its rugged forthright modal melody, sets forth the text in bold relief.

Words: This text is the work of Catherine Cameron, a poet and associate professor of social psychology at the University of La Verne,

La Verne, CA. In writing about her text, the poet says, "The hymn was written over a period of several months at a time when I was experiencing a new sense of direction, growth, and creativity in my life."[1] It was written for use with the tune AUSTRIA and was first published in *Contemporary Worship* (St. Louis, MO, 1969), the first in a series of booklets produced by the Inter-Lutheran Commission on Worship. It has since gained wide acceptance and is published in several major American hymnals. The hymn challenges us to question the full ramifications of our creative acts and to use our creative gifts to serve the good of others and to honor God.

---

1. M. K. Stulken, *Hymnal Companion to the Lutheran Book of Worship* (Philadelphia, 1981), 488.

Music: See hymn 238.

RG

581 Where charity and love prevail

Music: **CHESHIRE**

This metrical text based on the Latin hymn "Ubi caritas" first appeared in an Episcopal publication in *Hymns III* matched with this tune.

Words: This hymn, based on the Latin hymn "Ubi caritas" (see hymn 606 and hymns 576/77) was written by J. Clifford Evers, a pseudonym for Omer Westendorf, for the *Peoples Mass Book* (Cincinnati, 1961, 1962). The Latin model can be discerned in st. 1 and in st. 2:1-2, st. 3:3-4, st. 4:1-2 and st. 5:1-2. The following have been altered by the editors of *H82*:

2:3 mind and soul
6:1 nor race or creed can love exclude
6:3 our brotherhood

This is its first appearance in the *Hymnal*.

Music: This austere tune is first found in Thomas East's *Whole Booke of Psalmes* (London, 1592), in two settings—one to Ps. 146, "My soul, praise thou the Lord alway," set by John Farmer; the other to "A Prayer for the Queenes most Excellent Majesty," set by John Dowland. Both are in a; they are printed in Maurice Frost, *English and Scottish Psalm & Hymn Tunes c. 1543-1677* (London, 1953), nos. 192a and 192b. The tune appeared in some editions of the common psalm book from 1602.

Not used by Playford, the hymn's popularity gradually waned in the eighteenth century. It was revived in *HA&M* (1861), but did not appear in the *Hymnal* before the present edition. The harmonization is based on Farmer's version.

This was one of the few tunes named by East, who favored the names of English counties; whether they had any geographical significance for the origin of the tune is unknown.

JH/NT

582 *O holy city, seen of John*

Music: **SANCTA CIVITAS**

In 1910, Henry Sloane Coffin and Ambrose W. Vernon, editors of *Hymns of the Kingdom of God* (New York), wrote in their preface "We have been led to believe that, as the Kingdom was the burden of our Lord's message, it should be the burden of His Church's prayer and praise. This book is an attempt to furnish the Church with a hymnal in which the Christian communion with God is viewed as fellowship with the Father and the Son in the establishment of the Kingdom." "O holy city, seen of John," with its vision of the Kingdom of God as something that could be begun here on earth, certainly supports these goals. It is matched with a tune written for use with it by Herbert Howells, one of the finest of all twentieth-century British composers of church music.

Words: This song of the heavenly Jerusalem was written by Walter Russell Bowie for *Hymns of the Kingdom of God* (New York, 1910), edited by Henry Sloane Coffin and Ambrose White Vernon. It entered the *Hymnal* in 1940. Dr. Bowie has stated:

> It was written at the request of Dr. Henry S. Coffin who wanted some new hymns that would express the conviction that our hope of the Kingdom of God is not alone some far off eschatological possibility but in its beginnings, at least, may be prepared for here in our actual earth. It is in this sense that it would differ from the mood of "O mother dear, Jerusalem" [a popular text focusing on the traditional aspects of the heavenly Jerusalem] (*H40c*, 313).

Critics speak of this Bowie text as one of the finest of the twentieth century. It has gained acceptance and use in English-language hymnals around the world.

Textual alterations occur in st. 3:4 to support the mandate of the SCCM to use inclusive language wherever possible. The original was:

Whose ways are brotherhood.

An original second stanza was omitted in this edition:

Hark, how from men whose lives are held
  More cheap than merchandise;
From women struggling sore for bread,
  From little children's cries,
There swells the sobbing human plaint
  That bids thy walls arise!

Music: Considered to be one of the important tunes of our time, SANCTA CIVITAS was composed for this Walter Russell Bowie text by Herbert Howells by commission for inclusion in *Hymns for Church & School* (Henley-on-Thames, 1964). Soon thereafter it was included in *100 Hymns for Today* (London, 1969). The *Hymnal of the United Church of Christ* (Philadelphia, 1974) was the first hymnal in the United States to include it. (Prior to this, the tune was introduced in the Canadian *Hymn Book* [Canada, 1971].) To facilitate the use of the tune for congregational use, the Hymn Music Committee of the SCCM altered the beginning of the setting by removing a two-note introduction and using the melody line as the upper voice in the first measure of the accompaniment (see Example 1).

Another slight alteration was made at the end of the tune, where the penultimate measure was barred from a five- to four-beat measure. This may regularize the measures, but it denies the composer's sensitive setting of the text by placing the first and unaccented syllable for the word "again" on a strong downbeat (see Example 2).

Example 1

Example 2

An original descant published with the tune in the British and Canadian hymnals is not included in the American publications.

In SANCTA CIVITAS, Howells is able to create a sense of unity by using a common six-note figure for the beginning of each of its three phrases. In phrases 1 and 2 there is exact duplication, while in phrase 3 the figure is transposed up a fourth. Harmonically, the tune is enriched through the composer's use of suspensions, modulation, chromaticism, and the occasional use of five- and six-part chords in what is basically a four-part texture. Of particular interest is the dramatic use in the middle of the last phrase of the succession of the chords of F, e^{b}, and g in first inversion with a 2-1 suspension.

RG

583 *O holy city, seen of John*

Music: **MORNING SONG**

This text first entered the *Hymnal* in *H40* matched with this tune. At that time it marked an early use in mainline Protestant hymnals of tunes coming from early nineteenth-century folk hymn sources.

Words: See hymn 582.

Music: See hymn 9.

584 God, you have given us power to sound

Music: **CULROSS**

This powerful text, which challenges the human race to use wisely the power given us by God, appears for the first time in an Episcopal hymnal in *H82*. It is matched with a psalm tune whose solemn nature matches the profound content of the text.

Words: The late Canon Cyril Taylor, beloved and respected hymn writer and hymnal editor, writing about this text in *Hymns for Today Discussed* (Norwich, England, 1984, pg. 39), raises the question "This deals with another of those subjects of which, perhaps, we ask, is this something we really want to *sing* about?" The question relates to the profoundly serious nature of the text, whose subject is the reality of living in a world threatened by the prospect of nuclear disaster. In *A Commentary on New Hymns* (New York, 1987), the author of the commentary and General Editor of *H82* and *H82c* writes of this hymn:

> On January 10, 1954, the front page of the London *Sunday Times* contained, without comment, a three-stanza hymn entitled "The New Peril." The text, a meditation on the horrors of the atomic bomb, was by the Anglican priest and poet George Wallace Briggs. The revised form of the text with four stanzas, as in the *Hymnal 1982*, first appeared in *Hymns of the Faith* (pub. 1957) under the heading "science." "Science," possibly the poet's last hymn text . . . gives voice to the fervent prayer that humanity, though "given the power to sound depths hitherto unknown," will grow in wisdom. "Lest, maddened by the lust of power, we shall ourselves destroy."[1]

This text in a further altered form later appeared in several British hymnals. Its original opening line was "God who has given us power" and st. 2:1 was "Great are thy gifts." Stanza 4 was:

> So for thy glory and man's good
> May we thy gifts employ,
> Lest, maddened by the lust of power,
> Man shall himself destroy.

For use in *With One Voice* (London, 1979), pronouns were altered to a contemporary form. These alterations, with st. 4 revised to its present form, next appeared in *More Hymns for Today* (London, 1980). It is in this form that the text was included in *H82*.

---

1. R. F. Glover, *A Commentary on New Hymns* (New York, 1987), 104.

Music: This tune may well be the composition of Edward Millar (not Miller), the editor of the 1635 Scottish psalm book. It appears in a manuscript signed by him and dated April 2, 1626, forming 112 leaves bound with a copy of a 1615 edition now in private hands. According to William Cowan, these harmonies are almost identical to those found when the tune appeared in print in 1634.[1]

For the 1635 edition, however, Millar reharmonized the tune in five parts (see Example 1, where the note values are halved for comparison purposes). It may be noted that he did not shrink from the clash of simultaneous sharp and flat leading notes in the eleventh chord; the F in the contra cannot be emended to F# by *musica ficta**, for this would introduce a melodic interval of an augmented second.

As Erik Routley pointed out, the tune has the property that its first and third phrases harmonize each other in invertible counterpoint; Millar took advantage of this in both his settings. Oddly enough, Sullivan's ST. GERTRUDE [562] shares this unusual characteristic.

The next appearance of this tune in print was not until 1720, in the tune supplement to Simon Browne's *Hymns and Spiritual Songs* (London, 1720) (cf. no. 512), for singing with Browne's hymn "And now, my soul, the circling sun." Here it was in a three-voice setting and was named FAREHAM. In this form it was taken into a number of English books as well as American collections, beginning with a tune supplement printed by Thomas Johnston in Boston, ca. 1763, for binding up with Watts's or Tate and Brady's *Psalms*.

Culross, from which Millar took his name for the tune, is a small town on the north side of the Firth of Forth. This tune is new to the *Hymnal*, and the harmonization is taken from *Hymns III*.

Example 1

1. See W. Cowan, "A Bibliography of the Book of Common Order and Psalm Book of the Church of Scotland: 1556-1644," *Papers of the Edinburgh Bibliographical Society*, X (1913), 89, reproduced by M. Frost in *English and Scottish Psalm & Hymn Tunes c. 1543-1677* (London, 1953), no. 213.

RG/NT

585 *Morning glory, starlit sky*

Music: **BINGHAM**

This text, which opens with a gentle, almost naive, listing of images of natural phenomena, continues to develop as one of the most theologically substantial and poetically beautiful texts in the *Hymnal*, where it appears for the first time in an Episcopal publication. It is matched with a tune written for use with it in *H82*.

Words: "Morning glory, starlit sky" by Canon W. H. Vanstone of Chester, England, is a profoundly moving text on the true nature of Christian love. The text, which appears under the title "Hymn to the Creator" at the end of Canon Vanstone's book *Love's Endeavor, Love's Expense (The Risk of Love)* (New York, 1978), expresses the paradoxical nature of the love revealed on the cross.

The original form of Canon Vanstone's text is:

Morning glory, starlit sky,
  Leaves in springtime, swallow's flight,
Autumn gales, tremendous seas,
  Sound and scents of summer night.

Soaring music, tow'ring words,
  Art's perfection, scholar's truth,
Joy supreme of human love,
  Memory's treasure, grace of youth;

Open, Lord, are these, Thy gifts,
  Gifts of love to mind and sense;
Hidden is love's agony,
  Love's endeavor, love's expense.

Love that gives gives ever more,
  Gives with zeal, with eager hands,
Spares not, keeps not, all outpours,
  Ventures all, its all expends.

Drained is love in making full;
  Bound in setting other free;
Poor in making many rich;
  Weak in giving power to be.

Therefore He Who Thee reveals
  Hangs, O Father, on that tree
Helpless; and the nails and thorns
  Tell of what Thy love must be.

Thou art God; no monarch Thou
  Thron'd in easy state to reign;
Thou art God, Whose arms of love
  Aching, spent, the world sustain.

The text opens with a listing of some of God's gifts that are open to and easily grasped by our intellect and senses. Almost immediately thereafter the poet presents, in almost shocking starkness, the *hidden* nature of love—"love's agony, love's endeavor, love's expense." The paradoxical nature of love is spelled out with a sense of immediacy in succeeding stanzas, reaching a climax in the final two stanzas, which recount the ultimate act of love in which God gave his own Son "whose arms of love aching, spent, the world sustain."

The form of the text used in *H82* first appeared set to Gibbon's SONG 13 in *More Hymns For Today* (London, 1980), a second supplement to *HA&M*, and is continued in *HA&M*, New Standard Edition, (Beccles, Suffolk, 1983). This is the first appearance of this hymn in a hymnal in the United States.

Music: The tune BINGHAM by Dorothy Howell Sheets was written especially for this text in response to an appeal from the SCCM for tunes to new texts chosen for inclusion in *H82*. The tune name honors the late Seth Bingham (1882-1972), the composer's composition teacher. Mrs. Sheets has achieved an effective sense of unity through the skillful repetition of tune segments. In outline, the setting is ABB^1-A^1, and each of the four phrases opens on the pitch A^b. The melody of BINGHAM is very lyric and plaintive. Particular note should be given to the gentle melismata* added to the ends of the middle two phrases. Since the mood of the text changes dramatically in the last four stanzas, Mrs. Sheets, at the request of the Commission, wrote an alternative harmonization for use with these stanzas.

RG

586 *Jesus, thou divine Companion*

Music: **PLEADING SAVIOR**

This "Hymn of Labor" by Henry Van Dyke, a poet better known as the author of the text "Joyful, joyful, we adore thee" [376], is matched here with an early American folk hymn. In this form it first appeared in an Episcopal publication in *H40*.

Words: "Jesus, thou divine Companion" was written in 1909 by Henry Van Dyke for *Hymns for the Kingdom of God* (New York, 1910), edited by Henry Sloane Coffin and Ambrose Vernon White. The substance of the hymn is much older, however, for most of it may be found in Van Dyke's *Toiling of Felix* (New York, 1898), where it forms the conclusion of a narrative poem in which Christ addresses the penitent Felix. The hymn was published in H. Augustine Smith's *Hymns for the Living Age* (New York, 1923) and later found its way into *H40*, which altered the opening lines of st. 2 from the original:

> They who tread the path of labor
>   Follow where thy feet have trod;
> They who work without complaining
>   Do the holy will of God.

Music: New York Congegationalist clergyman, editor, and reformer Joshua Leavitt's *Christian Lyre* (New York, 1831) was apparently the first tunebook to include LIGHT [667] and the pentatonic tune PLEADING SAVIOR, which was set to "Now the Saviour stands a-pleading" by John Leland, a Massachusetts Baptist minister (see Example 1 on following page).[1]

The tune was published under the title THE SAVIOUR PLEADING in *Revival Hymns; Principally Selected by the Rev. R. H. Neale: Set to some of the most familiar and useful Revival Tunes . . . . Arranged and Newly Harmonized by H. W. Day, A. M. Editor of the Musical Visitor* (Boston, 1842), where a counter part was added and the bass altered. This version was printed in four parts with further alterations in the bass under the title PLEADING SAVIOUR in *The Plymouth Collection* (New York, 1855), a large collection of texts and tunes compiled by Henry Ward Beecher with the assistance of his brother Charles and his organist John Zundel (see Example 2, page 1084).

Example 1

Reproduced from *Christian Lyre* (New York, 1831) with permission of Moravian Music Foundation.

Example 2

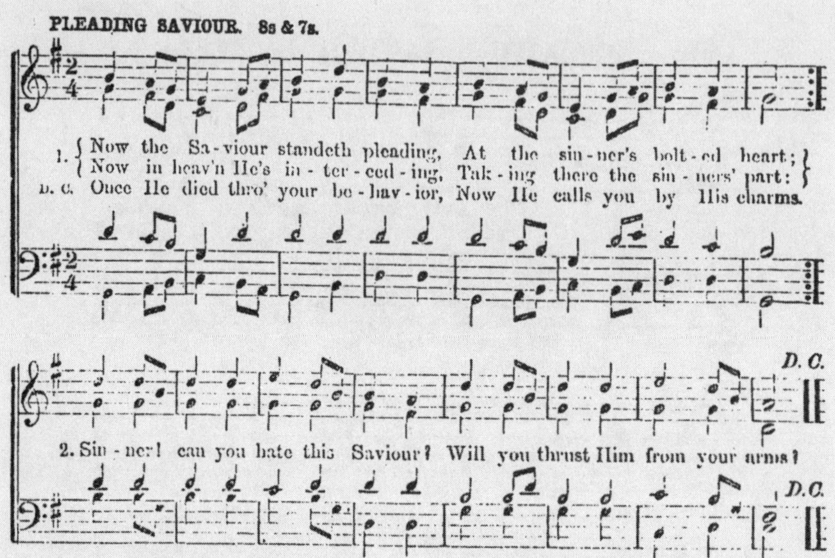

Reproduced from *Plymouth Collection* (New York, 1855), with permission of Moravian Music Foundation.

This version was also printed in *The Baptist Hymn and Tune Book* (New York, 1858), the Baptist *Songs of the Church* (New York, 1864), the enlarged edition of the American Tract Society's *Songs of Zion* (New York, 1864), the Presbyterian *Social Hymn and Tune Book: For the Lecture Room, Prayer Meeting, Family Circle and Mission Church* (Philadelphia, 1864), and *The Christian Hymnal* (Cincinnati, 1871). A variant form of this tune was printed in several books under the title SINNER, CAN YOU HATE THE SAVIOUR?

Another arrangement of PLEADING SAVIOR was included in William Walker's *Southern and Western Pocket Harmonist* (Philadelphia, 1846). In his *Christian Harmony* (Philadelphia, 1867) Walker added a counter part, and this version was reproduced in J. S. James's *Original Sacred Harp* (Cullman, AL, 1911). That version is also printed on two staffs with the melody in the treble and with slight editing of the alto in a book still in use among Primitive Baptists, C. H. Cayce's *The Good Old Songs* (Thornton, AK, 1913).

Another harmonization was included in the American Baptist Publication Society's *Devotional Hymn and Tune Book* (Philadelphia, 1864), edited by William B. Bradbury. This harmonization was printed in the 1872 "Harmonized and Revised" version of Joseph Hillman's *The Revivalist* (Troy, NY, 1868), but in 3/4 rather than 2/4 time.

Still another harmonization was printed in William Hauser's collection *Olive Leaf* (Wadley, GA, 1878).

One of the pioneering aspects of *EH*, for which Percy Dearmer served as editor of the words and Ralph Vaughan Williams as editor of the music, was the use of several dozen folk tunes as hymn tunes. Most of these were of English origin, but others were Scottish, Welsh, or Irish. Among the folk tunes included was PLEADING SAVIOR, which was traced back to *The Plymouth Collection* (see above). In *EH* a new harmonization was linked with a text for use "At Catechism," "Heavenly Father, send thy blessing." It has also been published in other English hymnals, sometimes under the name SALTASH.

PLEADING SAVIOR first entered an American Episcopal hymnal in *H40*, where the harmonization from *EH* was used with two texts, "Sing of Mary, pure and lowly" and "Jesus, thou divine Companion." In *H82*, the tune, with an accompaniment by Richard Proulx and with guitar chords, is used with "Jesus, thou divine Companion." This tune is suggested as an alternative tune for "Sing of Mary, pure and lowly" [277].

---

1. See further, J. C. Downey's "Joshua Leavitt's *The Christian Lyre* and the Beginning of the Popular Tradition in American Religious Song," *Latin American Music Review* 7 (Fall/Winter, 1986), 149-161; C. Stribling, "Joshua Leavitt's *The Christian Lyre*: An Historical Evaluation," M.A. thesis, William Carey College, 1976; H. H. Davis, "The Reform Career of Joshua Leavitt, 1794-1873," Ph.D. diss., Ohio State University, 1969.

TS/MH

587 Our Father, by whose Name

Music: **RHOSYMEDRE**

Written for use in *H40* with this Welsh tune, this text by F. Bland Tucker is one of the finest and most extensively used of the poet's works. It can now be found in English-language hymnals around the world.

Words: "Our Father, by whose Name" was written in 1939 by F. Bland Tucker on the theme of the Christian home. Of it, Dr. Tucker writes:

> On the [Joint Commission for the Revision of the *Hymnal*] we were all asked to make a topical index of all the hymns chosen. I wrote down among other topics, "Home and Family," but then discovered that there was no hymn on that topic among those chosen. I looked in other hymnals but could find none (this was 40 years ago), so I tried to write one. I chose the metre 6.6.6.6.8.8. because there seemed to be more good tunes than words in that metre. I started from Eph. 3:14-15 and then the Trinity suggested the home, parents, children, and the spirit of the family. When the tune RHOSYMEDRE was chosen for these words, the last line had to be repeated, so instead I inserted an extra line of text.[1]

The stanzas bring the Trinitarian formula into our personal lives with great immediacy. Stanza 2 is based on Lk. 2:52. Since its inclusion in *H40*, this text has gained acceptance and use in English-language hymnals around the world. Although its first line is often altered to support the use of inclusive language, the SCCM resisted that, preferring to retain the historical usage for the Trinity of Father, Son, and Holy Spirit.

---

1. F. Bland Tucker, "Reflections of a Hymn Writer," *The Hymn*, vol. 30, no. 2, April, 1979.

Music: This tune by the Rev. John David Edwards was published as LOVELY in *Y Drysorfa* (a periodical, "The Treasury," May, 1838), and in the following year in the composer's *Original Sacred Music*, vol. 1 (probably London, undated, probably 1839). It was widely used in Wales and was included under its original name in *EH*. In its original form, it serves the 66. 66. 88 metre with the last line repeated in the Welsh manner. The present words make skillful use of that repeat to fresh words.

As sung by the people of Wales, it is quite a stirring tune. Vaughan

Williams saw it quite differently, as can be seen from his pastoral setting of the tune (under its present name) as the second, and most popular, of *Three Preludes on Welsh Hymn Tunes for Organ* (1920).

The name of the tune is that of the parish in North Wales of which the composer was rector.

RG/AL

588 Almighty God, your word is cast

Music: **CALL STREET**

Although this text, in its original six-stanza form, was based on Mk. 4:3-9, in its present altered three-stanza form it relates more closely to the parable of the seeds in Lk. 8:11-15. CALL STREET was written for use with this text in *H82*.

Words: "Almighty God, thy word is cast" in its original six-stanza form was first published in Thomas Cotterill's *A Selection of Psalms and Hymns for Public and Private Use*, 8th edition (London, 1819), with the heading "After Sermon."

Over the years the text has been much altered. Two omitted stanzas after the present st. 2 are:

Oft as the precious seed is sown,
Thy quickening grace bestow;
That all whose souls the truth receive,
Its saving power may know.

Nor let thy word so kindly sent
To raise us to thy throne
Return to thee, and sadly tell
That we reject thy Son.

The final stanza was:

Great God, come down, and on thy word
Thy mighty power bestow,
That all who hear the joyful sound
Thy saving grace may know.

This text appears for the first time in an Episcopal hymnal in *H82*.

Music: CALL STREET was composed in late 1983 by Roy H. Johnson in response to an appeal by the SCCM for new tunes for possible use in *H82*. It follows the form of a classic strophic song in which the accompaniment has its own separate and distinctive character. Fortunately, however, the accompaniment skillfully supports the tune which, by its basically diatonic structure and chantlike nature, is very accessible. The setting is also notable because of its original harmonic treatment. This is immediately seen and heard through the alternation in the accompaniment between the chords of C and b♭ with an E♭ and D♭ suspension in the upper voice of the second chord. That pattern is repeated two measures later and leads to modulations to the keys of E♭ and A♭ and a very skillful return to C. The final cadence further illuminates the harmonic originality of the composer through his use of the minor forms of the subdominant and dominant seventh chords.

When introducing CALL STREET to a congregation, it would be advisable to have the choir sing it on one or two occasions as an anthem. For initial use with the congregation, it is helpful to accompany the hymn by playing the melody in octaves, adding the accompaniment on the third stanza or when the congregation is secure.

The tune name honors Call Street in Tallahassee, important to the composer because it connects the two places around which his professional life has centered during his more than twenty-five years at St. John's Church and Florida State University Music School. CALL STREET was named for the first territorial Governor of Florida, whose family has continued to be prominent in the community and in St. John's Parish.

RG

589 Almighty God, your word is cast

Music: **WALDEN**

The tune WALDEN, matched here with this text by John Cawood, appears in the *Hymnal* for the first time. It is the work of Jane Marshall, a respected American composer and teacher who has been very active in the production of recent supplements and the revision of the *Hymnal of the United Methodist Church*.

Words: See hymn 588.

Music: A melodic motif of a descending pattern of major and minor thirds, not unlike a peal of bells, distinguishes the tune WALDEN by Jane Manton Marshall. This motif is used sequentially twice at the beginning of the two major phrases of the unison tune. The composer continues her use of thirds in a slightly different sequential pattern in the second half of each of these lines. The tune name WALDEN honors the composer's mother, whose maiden name was WALDEN. Mrs. Marshall writes, "My mother, who is still living, (and playing hymns regularly in Presbyterian Village, her Dallas home now) continues to champion the cause of good hymns. Somehow [the] tune and the beautiful text that goes with it 'sounds' like her."[1]

---

1. Marshall to Glover, 31 January 1985, Church Hymnal Corporation Papers, New York, NY.

RG

590 O Jesus Christ, may grateful hymns be rising

Music: **CHARTERHOUSE**

One of the major purposes of the Hymn Society in the United States and Canada is to encourage the composition of new hymns. Several texts in *H82*, of which this is a fine example, come from "hymn searches" sponsored by the Society. The tune with which this text is matched appeared in *H40*.

Words: Bradford Gray Webster, a Methodist minister, wrote this text in response to an appeal by the Hymn Society of America for hymns on the city to be used at a Convocation on Urban Life in America called by the Council of Bishops of the Methodist Church. It was the first choice of the Society's committee and was included in *Five New Hymns for the City* published by the Society and sung at the Convocation in Columbus, OH, February 24-26, 1954 to the Barnby tune, PERFECT LOVE (SANDRINGHAM). Since that time it has been included in many hymnals in the United States and in a three-stanza form (sts. 2 and 5 omitted) in *The Australian Hymn Book* (London, 1979). *The Hymnal 1982* uses this three-stanza form of the text as found in the *LBW*. Here the archaic pronouns "thee" and "thy" have been altered to "you" and "your" and in st. 1:4 "brings men everywhere" has been altered to "rouses everywhere." The text was sung at a fiftieth anniversary celebration of the Hymn Society at St. Bartholomew's Church, New York City, to CITY OF GOD, a tune written for use with it in 1956 by Daniel Moe. The two omitted stanzas are:

2. Give us the strength to do Thy will eternal
   That summons men to leave their narrow strife;
   That leads the earthbound to the ways supernal,
   And brings to man the more abundant life.

5. Make strong our hope and grant Thine inspiration
   Till by Thy might the battle shall be won,
   Till love triumphant rules in every nation,
   And every city glorifies the Son.

Music: CHARTERHOUSE was composed by David Evans for use with the Frank Fletcher text "O Son of man, our hero strong and tender" in the *Church Hymnary* (London, 1927). It honors the English public school Charterhouse, where the composer was headmaster. It is a strong tune with fine development of the opening phrase, a sense of momentum, and a characteristic excursion to the flat side of the tonic in the third phrase.

RG/AW

591 O God of earth and altar

Music: **KING'S LYNN**

In this text G. K. Chesterton speaks with a strong prophetic voice of the ills of the world brought about through the pride of earthly leaders and the weakness of mankind. The text appeared with this tune in *EH* and *H40*.

Words: At the beginning of the twentieth century, England was a nation experiencing the end of the long reign of Queen Victoria, the beginning of the Edwardian era, and the Second Boer War. It was a time of national self-confidence and pride, of materialism and moral laxity. In response to this, the critic and writer G. K. Chesterton penned a strong and poignant plea to God for social and political justice. In vivid language, the poet indicts both rulers whose duplicity and "easy speeches" give comfort to "cruel men," and people who in blindness and lethargy succumb to corruption. Written in 1906 with the intensity of the Old Testament prophets, the poet in "O God of earth and altar" produced a text that spoke directly to the grim realities of his own time, but with equal intensity and relevance to our own. Chesterton, in st. 3, also "shows his characteristic enthusiasm for the Middle Ages, referring to the medieval idea of the 'three estates' of society—prince, priest, thrall."[1]

First printed in Canon Scott Holland's monthly magazine *The Commonwealth*, the text was given to Percy Dearmer, editor of *EH*, and was included in that collection with the tune KING'S LYNN. This pairing has been continued in *Songs of Praise* (London, 1926), *H40* and *H82*. Percy Dearmer in *Songs of Praise Discussed* (London, 1933) relates a conversation that he had in which Chesterton stated "that, not knowing one tune from another, he had written this with the idea that AURELIA [525] . . . was the typical tune for hymns, and therefore he had used that metre."[2]

---

1. W. Milgate, *Songs of the People of God* (London, 1982), 194.
2. P. Dearmer, *Songs of Praise Discussed* (London, 1933), 174.

Music: See hymn 231.

RG

592 *Teach me, my God and King*

Music: **CARLISLE**

Contemporary English-language hymnody is greatly enriched by texts derived from the poetry of the great mystic and seventeenth-century British poet George Herbert. Four are to be found in *H82*. This text, which first appeared in an Episcopal hymnal in *H40*, is matched here with a lyric tune by an eighteenth-century British composer.

Words: This text offers a rare opportunity to observe George Herbert's patterns of revision. When it appeared with his other poems in the posthumous collection *The Temple* (Cambridge, 1633), this poem was titled "The Elixir," and it comprised six SM stanzas, including the following two between the present first and third:

Not rudely, as a beast,
  To run into an action;
But still to make thee prepossest,
  And give it his perfection.

A man that looks on glasse,
  On it may stay his eye,
Or if he pleaseth, through it passe,
  And then the heav'n espie.

But this was not the original form of the poem. In fact, at first it was not even named "The Elixir" but "Perfection." It opened with this much less remarkable stanza:

Lord teach mee to referr
  All things I doe to thee
That I not onely may not erre
  But allso pleasing bee.

In addition, before the present second stanza another stanza originally followed the omitted two stanzas quoted earlier:

He that does ought for thee,
  Marketh y^{t} deed for thine.
And when the Divel shakes ye tree,
  Thou saist, this fruit is mine.

The most significant change in the shape of the poem came from the revision of the final stanza. Originally it had read:

But these are high perfections:
  Happy are they that dare
Lett in the light to all their actions
  And show them as they are.

In the process of revision, Herbert seems first to have rewritten the final stanza and to have deleted the "Divel" and "fruit" stanza. He did not retitle the poem, however, or replace the original first stanza with the present one until he recopied his early poems into the manuscript that ultimately yielded *The Temple*.

In many ways, the editing that resulted in the present hymn represents the continuation of Herbert's own revisions. The four-stanza form of the text increases its impact by paring it to the essential ideas. The retained stanzas share a matrix of images that are considerably less coherent in the longer form. In particular, the alchemical allusions of the present second and fourth stanzas form a kind of foil to set off the more mundane language of the first and third stanzas. For modern readers, some words may need glosses: in st. 2:2, mean = humble, inferior; in st. 2:3, tincture = an alchemical term for an immaterial substance or spiritual principle whose properties could be infused into material things; in st. 4:1, the famous stone = the so-called philosopher's stone capable of transforming baser metals into gold; in st. 4:3, touch = test with a touchstone in order to determine the purity of gold or silver; st. 4:3 own = acknowledge and claim as one's own.

What Herbert offers here is a sacramental understanding of human labor. Just as bread and wine, the common food of daily life, are consecrated to become the Body and Blood of Christ, so the ordinary tasks of human existence can be vehicles of God's presence and can be offered to God's glory. Behind Herbert's reflections also lie such passages as Jesus' parable of the Last Judgment (Mt. 25:31-46) and Peter's vision of the clean and unclean animals (Acts 10:9-15).

Music: See hymn 138.

CPD

593 Lord, make us servants of your peace

Music: **DICKINSON COLLEGE**

In these latter years of the twentieth-century, this prayer for peace attributed to St. Francis expresses with particular poignancy the desires of Christians all over the world for peace. It is matched with a tune that first appeared in the hymnal supplement *MHSS*.

Words: A prayer traditionally attributed to the medieval mystic St. Francis of Assisi is the source of the hymn "Lord, make us servants of your peace" by the noted Roman Catholic hymn writer and theologian Rev. James Quinn, S.J. The text, which appears in translation among the Prayers and Thanksgivings in the BCP (833, no. 62) and expresses the teachings of the revered founder of the Franciscan Order, cannot be dated any earlier than the present century. In the five stanzas of this hymn text, Fr. Quinn very clearly and precisely captures all the themes and images of the much-loved prayer.

Music: DICKINSON COLLEGE by Lee Hastings Bristol, Jr. was chosen by the SCCM for use with two texts in *H82*. It was adapted by the composer for use as a hymn tune from an anthem, "Lord of all being throned afar" (New York, 1960) and first appeared in *MHSS* with the Rosamond Herklots text "Lord God, by whose creative might." The opening phrase of the tune outlines the chord of D and establishes a melodic pattern for three succeeding phrases. After the second phrase and a modulation to the dominant, A, the tune modulates to the key of the relative minor, b, through a passage of four ascending diatonic pitches. The melody returns smoothly to the tonic key of D, in a form that duplicates exactly the second phrase. The tune name honors Dickinson College, PA, the composer's alma mater, as well as that of many of his forebears. Dickinson College is also one of many colleges and universities to recognize the composer with an honorary degree.

RG

594 God of grace and God of glory

Music: **CWM RHONDDA**

This text, one of the most popular hymns of the twentieth century in the United States, appeared in *H40* with the tune MANNHEIM. In response to massive popular appeal, it is matched with CWM RHONDDA, the Welsh tune with which it is ecumenically associated. The text with this tune first appeared in an Episcopal publication in *Hymnal Supplement II* (New York, 1975) and continues in *H82*.

Words: Written by Harry Emerson Fosdick at his summer home at Boothbay Harbor, Maine, this hymn was sung the following fall at the opening of the Riverside Church, New York, October 5,

1930. It was also sung at the dedication of the building, February 8, 1931. H. Augustine Smith included it in *Praise and Service* (New York, 1932), where changes had been made in the second stanza; which form has been in common use since that time. However, the Methodist Hymnals of 1935, 1964, and 1989 (Nashville) have printed the stanza as it was first sung (st. 2:3-4):

Fears and doubts too long have bound us;
Free our hearts to work and praise.

In the current version of st. 4 (originally st. 5), the words "gift of" have been substituted for "search for." The omitted fourth stanza read:

Set our feet on lofty places;
Gird our lives that they may be
Armored with all Christ-like graces
In the fight to set men free.
Grant us wisdom, grant us courage,
That we fail not man nor thee!

Fosdick, a preacher of international acclaim, conceived of the text being sung to the tune REGENT SQUARE, and it is reported that he was not happy about its being sung to other tunes. (This matching is found in *HA&M New Standard* [1983].) He wrote about "my hymn's divorce from REGENT SQUARE and remarriage to CWM RHONDDA. The Methodists did it! And both here and abroad they are being followed."[1]

The title of Dr. Fosdick's autobiography, *The Living of These Days* (New York, 1956), is derived from this text.

---

1. A. C. Ronander and E. K. Porter, *Guide to the Pilgrim Hymnal* (Philadelphia, 1966), 287.

Music: The tune CWM RHONDDA was composed by John Hughes for a Baptist *Cymanfa Ganu* (Singing Festival) in 1903, originally with the name RHONDDA. Though sung to many different texts in Welsh, it is most often linked in English with "Guide me, O thou great Jehovah" [690]. Its inclusion in most mainline hymn books was resisted for many decades and it therefore circulated in pamphlet form. Today, its increasing inclusion in such books is partly due to a wider view of what a good hymn tune is and to the inevitability of bowing to popular appeal. It is seen by many as the typical Welsh hymn tune in its fervor and strong rhetoric, though it does not possess the other characteristics often associated with Welsh tunes of being in a minor key and gloomy.

The value of the tune lies in its immense vigor and what can only be called its vulgar appeal (not necessarily a bad thing in a hymn). That being so, it is as well to use its full resource. The small notes in the present edition of the tune may be confusing. The small notes in the first repetition of the sixth line should be sung. Different, apparently authentic, versions of the tune have the descending figure in either the tenor or the soprano, but it should certainly be sung by one of them; there could be alternation. The small notes at the end of the line belong to the alto and bass parts and should likewise be sung to a repetition of the words (for example in 690, verse 1, "evermore"). This is essentially a tune to be sung in four parts, the bass being particularly important as it strides through the first four lines and mounts in line 5 to its strong and confident dominant seventh. The name of the tune means "Rhondda Valley."

MS/AL

595 God of grace and God of glory

Music: **MANNHEIM**

The matching of this text and tune first appeared in *H40*. It is a text/tune combination not found in any other mainline American Protestant hymnal.

Words: See hymn 594.

Music: The tune now called MANNHEIM first appeared under the title MANHEIM in *Congregational Church Music: A Book for the Service of Song in the House of the Lord. With a Preface by the Rev. T. Binney* (London, 1853). That book contained a number of tunes arranged by prominent English church musicians, including Goss, Turle, Hopkins, Horsley, Novello, Didbin, and one American, Lowell Mason. The attribution reads "Adapted from a Chorale, Harmonized by L. Mason" (see Example 1 on opposite page):

Mason spent 1852 through 1853 abroad, ending up with six months

Example 1

Reproduced from *Congregational Church Music* (London, 1853), Yale University Library.

in England lecturing on church music and the teaching of music. During this time he attended the church of which Binney was pastor and in his *Musical Letters from Abroad* spoke highly of its congregational music.[1] Mason does not seem to have included the tune in his later books published in the United States, but the tune did make its way into later hymnals published in England, generally with the text "Lead us, heavenly Father, lead us" [559]. In *H40* MANNHEIM, with slight alterations in passing tones in the bass and alto voices, was the only tune printed with the text "God of grace and God of glory." This harmonization, continued in *H82*, is that of *EH*. Its only appearance in American Episcopal hymnals prior to *H40* was in Charles H. Hall and S. B. Whiteley's short-lived *Hymnal with Tunes. Hymnal of the Protestant Episcopal Church with Music* (New York, 1872), one of the tunebooks designed for use with the 1871 *Hymnal*, in which it was linked with the text "Now, my soul, thy voice upraising" and in J. Ireland Tucker and William W. Rousseau's *The Hymnal . . . With Tunes Old and New* (New York, 1894), one of the musical editions of the 1892 hymnal, in which it was associated with the text "Jesus came, the heavens adoring" [454— now called "Jesus came adored by angels"]. For many of his hymn tunes Mason used pre-existing melodies (see, for example, ANTIOCH [100] and AZMON [493]). He apparently adapted the tune MANNHEIM from one in *Vierstimmiges Choralbuch herausgegeben von Dr. F. Filitz* (Berlin, 1847) that was associated with the Freylinghausen text "Auf! auf! weil der Tag erschienen" (see Example 2 on opposite page):

---

1. L. Mason, *Musical Letters from Abroad* (New York, 1854), 166-167.

MH

596 *Judge eternal, throned in splendor*

***Music:* KOMM, O KOMM, DU GEIST DES LEBENS**

Although first published almost one hundred years ago, this text is still one of the strongest hymns for social justice and national peace in the

Example 2

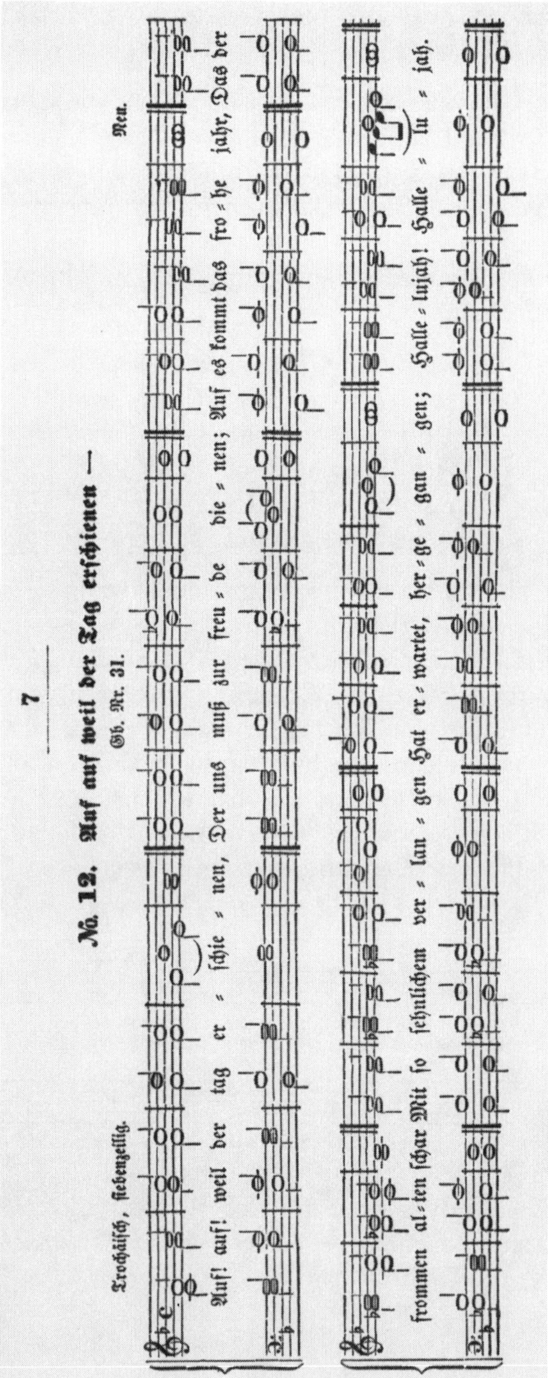

Reproduced from *Vierstimmiges Choralbuch* (Berlin, 1847), Yale University Library

Hymnal. Matched with this tune, it first appeared in an Episcopal hymnal in *H16*.

Words: A founder and strong supporter of the Christian Social Union, Henry Scott Holland was editor of *The Commonwealth*, the magazine of the Union, from its inception in 1896 to 1912. His only hymn, "Judge eternal, throned in splendor," first appeared in the July 1902 issue and four years later was included in *EH*. The hymn embodied the two chief interests of his fruitful life—social reform and missionary work. Originally, st. 3 read:

Crown, O God, thine own endeavor:
  Cleave our darkness with thy sword:
Feed the faint and hungry heathen
  With the richness of thy Word:
Cleanse the body of this empire
  Through the glory of the Lord.

Music: The tune KOMM, O KOMM, DU GEIST DES LEBENS (*Zahn* 3651) was included in the third edition of the *Neu-vermehrts und zu Übung Christliche Gottseligkeit eingerichtetes Meiningisches Gesangbuch* (Meiningen, 1693) (see Example 1), where it was set to J. C. Werner's funeral hymn "Ich begehr nicht mehr zu leben." Conrad Kocher's *Zionsharfe* dates this tune somewhat earlier, about 1680, and some have attributed the tune to Johann Christoph Bach. A mildly florid tune, it is representative of the melodies that found favor in the hymnody of Pietism. The harmonization is taken from *H40*.

Example 1

The tune gained its name through its association with the text "Komm, O komm, du Geist des Lebens" in the *Geistreiches Gesange Buch* (Halle, 1698).

TS/CS

597 O day of peace that dimly shines

Music: **JERUSALEM**

This text was created in response to two special requests received by the SCCM during the preparation of *H82*. The first, from General Convention's Joint Commission on Peace, urged that the revised hymnal contain a number of hymns on world peace. The second was an appeal from various sources to include the tune JERUSALEM by the British composer and teacher Sir Charles Hubert Hastings Parry. To satisfy these requests, the Commission asked Carl P. Daw, Jr. to write a text on peace that would fit the Parry tune.

Words: Following his usual practice for creating a text for a specific tune, the author played the tune over and over again on a variety of instruments for several days. After a series of abortive attempts at a text, he decided to set the project aside for a while in order to catch up on some neglected reading. As he began to read *Turning to Christ: A Theology of Renewal and Evangelization* (New York, 1981) by Urban T. Holmes III, he became aware that Is. 11:6-8 (quoted on page 25 of Holmes's book) held the heart of the hymn he was trying to write. This source of inspiration was especially meaningful to him because Dean Holmes (who had died suddenly only a few months before this) had been one of the great influences on him during his years as a seminarian at the School of Theology of the University of the South.

The writing of the text thus began with the second stanza, which is a paraphrase of Is. 11:6-9 adapted to the rhythmic and melodic patterns of the Parry tune. The first stanza then evolved as a prayer for the peaceful existence described in the second stanza. In conceptual terms, the first stanza approaches peace as *pax*, an understanding of peace based on the cessation of conflict. The second stanza offers a picture of a more dynamic view of peace as *shalom*, the condition of living abundantly in harmony and mutual goodwill. Although the text affirms that peace is always God's gift, it also recognizes the importance of human responsibility in preparing an environment in which peace can flourish.

Since its introduction in *H82*, this text has been included in several other hymnals, including the Roman Catholic hymnal *Worship III* (Chicago, 1986), the *David Hurd Hymnary Supplement* (Chicago, 1985), the *United Methodist Hymnal* (Nashville, 1989) and the *Presbyterian Hymnal* (Louisville, 1990).

Music: Charles H. H. Parry wrote the tune JERUSALEM for William Blake's poem "Jerusalem" in 1916. The text is one of almost fanatical zeal for all things English and the setting quickly became a second "national anthem"; it is still sung on many great public occasions in England. The music has a compelling drive and the figure ♪♫♩ ♩. is developed with growing intensity in the second half of the tune. Although the original setting was strophic, rhythmic differences occur in the tune in each stanza to better conform to the Blake text. The rhythm of the tune in the *H82* version has been regularized to be the same in each stanza.

The members of the SCCM were profoundly sorry that copyright restrictions prevented the use of Parry's original harmony in *H82*. The copyright at the time of publication forced the SCCM to use the Wyatt edition of the tune. It is recommended that, if possible, this music be played from an English hymnal.

CPD/AW

598 Lord Christ, when first thou cam'st to earth

Music: **MIT FREUDEN ZART**

Although Walter Russell Bowie is the author of only two published hymn texts, this text and "O holy city, seen of John" [582/583], both have been judged as among the finest by an American author written in the first half of this century. Both texts, though not written for Episcopal hymnals, appeared in *H40*.

Words: This profound text, which Erik Routley has described as a "masterpiece,"[1] was written by Walter Russell Bowie in 1928, and first published in *Songs of Praise* (London, 1931). It was composed at the request of Dean Dwelly of Liverpool Cathedral, one of the book's editors, who desired an Advent hymn in the "Dies irae" mood. Dr. Bowie wrote:

> It is an effort to express both the solemnity and inspiration of the thought of Christ coming into our modern world in judgment (*H40c*, 313).

The text is rich in scriptural references: Heb. 6:6; Zech. 12:10; Rev. 1:7; Mt. 24:2-3; Jn. 5:40, 14:27; 2 Cor. 5:17; Gal. 6:15; 1 Jn. 4:12, and Heb. 12:2. Pursuant to this hymnal's goal of using inclusive language whenever possible, the first line of the text has been altered from "Lord Christ, when first thou cam'st to men." Also mindful of a world-wide rise of anti-Semitism, the SCCM recommended the omission of the original second stanza. By action of the Joint Committee on the Hymnal of the 1982 General Convention of the Episcopal Church, this stanza was restored with two important changes. In st. 2:4 the word power was made plural to remove any consideration that Dr. Bowie could have even implied the Jewish nation. A congruent change was also made in line 6, where the original read: "A nation's pride." Today this text is found in English-language hymnals around the world.

---

1. E. Routley, *A Panorama of Christian Hymnody* (Collegeville, MN, 1979), 204.

Music: See hymn 408.

RG

599 Lift every voice and sing

Music: **LIFT EVERY VOICE**
The Johnson brothers, James Weldon and John Rosamond, collaborated many times on the composition of songs. By 1900, when they composed "Lift every voice and sing," they had written music for five Broadway musicals. Today, this song's forceful message of hope for freedom and its stirring musical setting speak with such a dynamic force that it is considered by many African Americans as their national anthem.

Words: In Jacksonville, Florida, on February 12, 1900, a chorus of schoolchildren at the all-black Stanton School sang a new song at a special assembly in honor of the birthday of Abraham Lincoln. The song, "Lift Every Voice and Sing," had been composed at the request of a group of young black men who sought to pay tribute to the President of the United States who had signed the Emancipation Proclamation. With words by James Weldon Johnson and music by his brother John Rosamond, the song became an immediate favorite of schoolchildren throughout the state of Florida, and by the late 1940s was being sung by black Americans throughout the United States as the Negro National Anthem.

The song became a national multiracial favorite after its use as a freedom song in the Civil Rights Movement of the 1960s and, like many songs that speak to freedom of the oppressed, it has been adopted by various groups of all races who seek liberation from oppression.

While the text is clearly addressed to freedom, it unfolds without anger or rage. With assurance that unity and respect among people of different cultures and races will prevail, the text admonishes both the Christian and the oppressed to "march on till victory is won."

Music: The tune LIFT EVERY VOICE, with its celebratory air, is associated with the African American jubilee spiritual, though it contains none of the characteristic melodic or rhythmic elements associated with that genre. Tradition has established the practice of singing in two rather than six pulses for each measure, incorporating the intensity of the recent gospel song. It is customary to observe the fermata* (at the sign) in each stanza.

HCB

600 O day of God, draw nigh

Music: **BELLWOODS**

For too long this text has not received the use it deserves. Matched with this tune, it appeared in *H40*. Hopefully, deeper understanding of the full meaning of the text and its expanded liturgical appropriateness will in time lead clergy and musicians to use it more fully. Serious consideration should be given to use of the text with the Southern shape-note tune LANDAFF, as found in *Hymnal Supplement II* (New York, 1975).

Words: R. B. Y. Scott composed and contributed this text, "O day of God, draw nigh," to a hymn sheet of the Fellowship for a Christian Social Order in 1937. In view of its expressed hope for peace and justice on the verge of a cataclysmic Second World War, it gained inclusion in *H40* as a General Hymn in section VIII, "Social Religion" under the subsection "War and peace." The original final stanza read:

O Day of God, bring nigh
  Thy bright and shining light,
To rise resplendent on the world
  And drive away the night.

By the time of its first hymnal appearance in *Hymns for Worship* (New York, 1939), Scott had substituted a last verse that became standard in all the many hymnals in which it has subsequently appeared. One further change in the last line of this early substituted verse occurs in most hymnal editions published after 1975, namely, emendation from "and set thy judgments *on* the earth" to "and set thy judgments *in* the earth." And from that alteration hangs a tale!

Even following World War II, the commentator of *H40c* exhausted his reflections on the hymn in one laconically hostile sentence, "[Scott's] concept of the 'Day of God' is in marked contrast to that of the Old Testament prophets as expressed in Zeph. 1:14-18" (p. 315). If in nothing else, then in view of Scott's status as a biblical scholar and his later international fame in Old Testament studies, the commentator's charge today appears ludicrous. The comment really depends, however, upon the failure to understand three things: 1) the distinction between apocalyptic and eschatological; 2) the conception of eternity (and thus of God's eternal judgments) as being nontemporal in mode (that is, "eternal" does not equal "time extended infinitely"); and, 3) that the outcome of history, the eschaton, by virtue of what happened through the death and resurrection of Jesus, is not exclusively relegated to the future, but is effectively present—now and yet still awaiting its fullest manifestation.

The first distinction is one more widely appreciated only in recent decades by virtue of developments in biblical scholarship. The second and third items, certainly, could easily have been appropriated by Anglicans from the theology of F. D. Maurice (1805-72), thus not indispensably requiring the tutelage of twentieth-century Reformed sources. The point is that Scott's theological achievement in this hymn has to do with the reading of the wrathful Old Testament "Day of God" as more than gratuitous destruction of a creation and humanity gone bad. It is to be seen, rather, as a judgment with a point. Such a view, in fact, exhibited in the Old Testament, is given especially high New Testament relief in the last chapter of the Apocalypse, where the vision following the cataclysm is one of "a new heaven and a new earth"—the peace and justice of God's reign as revealed and accomplished by the Christ of Judgment who says "Behold, I make all things new" (Rev. 21:5).

The text of the hymn, then, is at once a call for Christians to pray for this commencement as well as to live and work within the terms of that Reign of God that Jesus in his earthly ministry announced as "at hand." God's eternal judgments impinge upon the present. Thus, this hymn is theologically appropriable by its singers not simply as expressing aspirations for peace and justice, but as exhibiting in a most orthodox manner the principal focus of the Advent season as it is meant to affect the Church's life and mission now.

Yet that appropriation has taken a longer time, since confusion about this hymn was not limited to the commentator of *H40c* alone. There seems to have been a more general perplexity regarding what to say about or do with this text. The Topical Index to *H40* accorded the hymn two entries, one under "God, Purpose of" and the other under "Peace, International." Although the hymn is listed at the end of the Advent section of the Liturgical Index in that hymnal, it is, nonetheless, completely innocent of any approbation of "O day of God, draw nigh." This lacuna was sustained in the newer Liturgical Index prepared by the SCCM in 1960 for the *Supplement to the Hymnal 1940* (New York, 1961). Beyond the mentioned notices, it was commended elsewhere only once as a general hymn at the Holy Communion for Trinity IV (where, ironically, the Collect of the BCP 1928 talks of "passing through things temporal that we *finally* lose not the things eternal"). These instances exhaust the recommendations of the hymn.

Over four decades later, the situation is nearly reversed. Even a cursory glance at the liturgical indices of Marion Hatchett's *Hymnal Studies Five* (New York, 1986) reveals this hymn as one principally thematic for Advent as well as appropriate to the lectionaries of Daily Office and Holy Eucharist at the very inception of the season. As one would expect, it also is commended as a sequence or communion hymn under "Various Occasions," respectively no. 18 "For Peace" and no. 21 "For Social Justice."

This contemporary appreciation of the hymn has been occasioned by a number of factors, historical and theological. First, there has grown up an often tacit but nonetheless effective theological outlook among Anglicans that is consonant with its eschatological assumptions. Second, by the mid-1960s its further identification as an Advent hymn was advanced through the prominent place accorded to it in educational materials on the season prepared for the Episcopal Church by John and Mary Harrell (specifically, as sung to the tune LANDAFF, it was included as a principal exemplar of contemporary Advent hymnography on a recording "O come, O Come," featuring the Liturgical Choir at the Church Divinity School of the Pacific). Subsequently it enjoyed a broader exposure in the Episcopal Church as the text (still with the preposition "on" in the final line of the last stanza) provided a vehicle for the introduction of the tune LANDAFF in *Hymnal Supplement II* (New York, 1975). In *H82*, the preposition of the last stanza's final line achieved "in" status, and, though the text still appears within a section of General Hymns similar to that of *H40* (now entitled "Christian Responsibility"), responsible Christians—at least of the Anglican variety—have in fact appropriated it for Advent.

Finally, a note on the tunes associated with the text is in order. *The Hymnal 1982* features two, namely, BELLWOODS (composed by Scott's fellow Canadian James Hopkirk in 1938) and Louis Bourgeois's ST. MICHAEL. BELLWOODS was the single tune for *H40*. ST. MICHAEL was, however, associated with Scott's text from its initial publication in *Hymns for Worship*. In some other contemporary hymnals (for instance, *Rejoice in the Lord* [Grand Rapids, MI, 1985]), the text appears to the tune TYTHERTON. *The Hymnal 1982* features BELLWOODS and ST. MICHAEL. As excellent as these tunes are, however, none of these alternative tunes in conjunction with the text of "O day of God, draw nigh" achieves the strong inflections of LANDAFF as at once hauntingly urgent for and yearningly hopeful of a fully manifested parousia.

Music: BELLWOODS is named for the Toronto street that passes St. Matthias' Church, where the composer began and ended his career as an organist; his mother's baptism had begun the parish register. He wrote the tune for the Canadian Anglican *Book of Common Praise* (Toronto, 1938) for use with "Blest be the tie that binds." It was sung at the composer's requiem in St. Matthias' (January 3, 1973). *The*

Hymnal 1940 was the first to match the tune with Scott's lyric, an example that two Canadian hymnbooks have since followed without noticeable results. The tune is basically diatonic in structure with a flexible use of rhythm. This allows the use of two five-beat measures at the end of the tune while the others are all of four beats.

WHP/HMcK

601 *O day of God, draw nigh*

***Music:* ST. MICHAEL**

ST. MICHAEL was the tune initially associated with this text by a Canadian author, Robert B. Y. Scott, when it was first published in *Hymns for Worship* (New York, 1939). This is the first appearance of this text/tune relationship in the Episcopal *Hymnal.*

Words: See hymn 600.

Music: This tune underwent a number of transformations before it arrived at the form in *H82*. Its first appearance was as the tune for Ps. 101 (*Pidoux* 101c; A below) in *Pseaumes Octantetrois de David* (Geneva, 1551), for which the musical editor was Louis Bourgeois. It was remodeled into a SM English psalm tune (B in Example 1) (cf. *Frost*, 153a) in the fourth edition of the Anglo-Genevan psalter *Psalms* (Geneva, 1560). The third edition of the Anglo-Genevan psalter, which was probably issued in 1559, is no longer extant, and there is some justification for believing that the fourth edition was a simple reprint of the third. If so, the English form of the tune would date from 1559.

In the so-called Parson's part-book, *The whole Psalmes in foure partes* (London, 1563), line 3 was simplified (C in Example 1) (cf. *Frost*, 153b). It was subsequently adjusted rhythmically to conform to the common English psalm-tune style of a "gathering" note at the beginning and end of each line with a modified line 4 found, for example, in *The Whole Booke of Psalmes* (London, 1570) (D in Example 1) (cf. *Frost* 153c). By the time it appeared in William Crotch's *Psalm Tunes* (London, 1836) after a period of some neglect, the tune had substantially reached its familiar form and was given the name ST. MICHAEL. The harmonization by William Henry Monk (who gave the melody in equal half notes throughout) was made for the first edition of *HA&M* (1861).

Example 1

*e in 1562

RAL

602 *Jesu, Jesu, fill us with your love*

***Music:* CHEREPONI**

The cultural diversity of contemporary congregations of the Episcopal Church has led to the enrichment of the Church's hymnody through the addition of hymn texts and tunes from other cultures. Several represent the work of African and African-American poets and composers. This charming Ghanaian hymn is an addition that has gained almost immediate and extensive acceptance and use.

Words: During the twenty years that Thomas Stevenson Colvin served as a missionary in Malawi and Ghana, he encouraged the Christian natives to write their own hymn texts and sing them to some of the traditional African melodies. Colvin collected, translated from traditional Ghanaian dialect, arranged, and published several of these hymns in 1968 and 1976. A comprehensive collection of the poets' works are included in *Fill Us With Your Love* (Carol Stream, IL, 1981). This is one of the hymns from that collection. Called "Chereponi," this hymn is appropriate for any season of the church year, though it is particularly appropriate for the foot washing on Maundy Thursday. It first appeared in an Episcopal collection in the supplement *Hymns III*. It also appeared in *Lift Every Voice and Sing* (New York, 1981). Its inclusion in *H82* is its introduction to the wider Church.

Textual alterations occur in sts. 2 and 3 in support of the SCCM's desire to use inclusive language whenever possible. These alterations were first utilized in *Hymns III*. The original form of the text is:

2:1 Neighbors are rich men and poor
2 Neighbors are black men and white,
3:3 All men are neighbors to us and you.

A more recent revision by Mr. Colvin is:

Chorus: Jesu, Jesu, fill us with your love,
Show us how to serve the neighbors we have
from you.

Kneels at the feet of His friends,
Silently washes their feet,
Master who acts as a slave to them.

Neighbors are rich folk and poor,
Neighbors are black, brown and white,
Neighbors are nearby and far away.

These are the ones we should serve,
These are the ones we should love.
All are neighbors to us and you.

Loving puts us on our knees,
Serving us though we are slaves,
This is the way we should live with you.

Particular attention is called to the word "Jesu" which should be pronounced "Yay-soo."

Music: In the late nineteenth century pioneering Christians in Ghana were encouraged to write hymns to traditional tunes. Unfortunately, that custom of hymn writing was replaced in the 1930s by the practice of translating only the hymns that were popular in Europe. In 1951 Helen Taylor revived the old custom in Malawi, and Thomas Stevenson Colvin continued the practice in Malawi and Ghana. The revival was based on the belief that each group needed hymns appropriate to their situation, preferably to music from their own tradition. The tunes chosen by Colvin were among the most popular; they were melodies on which the words could ride with the greatest ease. "Jesu, Jesu, fill us with your love" has been set to such a tune. The 6/8 metre encourages the swaying of the body in time with the singing, a much-beloved custom in Africa. The tune was collected at Chereponi in Northern Ghana between 1959 and 1964. Its use implies a different style of singing and even a different approach to worship, for common in the African church is the spontaneous improvisation of harmonies, with treble and bass voices doubling at the octave and the use of percussion instruments for accompaniment.

HCB

603 When Christ was lifted from the earth

Music: **ST. BOTOLPH**

Brian Wren, one of the most prolific and influential hymn writers of these last decades of the twentieth century, is represented in *H82* by four texts (see the essay "British Hymnody Since 1950," vol. 1, 555). This 1970 text is matched with a tune by an English composer active earlier in the century.

Words: In the text "When Christ was lifted from the earth," the gifted contemporary British poet Brian Wren develops the admonition of St. Paul found in Rom. 15:7: "Welcome one another, therefore, as Christ has welcomed you, for the glory of God." Writing about this text, which he titled "Living Together," the poet explains that in "October 1970 the impulse to write this came from some now entirely forgotten controversy and tension in the congregation I ministered to, probably connected to the generation gap. Since hymns are for unified praise rather than polemic, I refrained from using it at the time, and cut down the original six stanzas to four which seemed more lasting."[1]

The poet paints an image of our Lord as the loving Savior who holds all people—people of differing ages, classes, and races—in his embrace. This is a Savior who accepts and loves us as we are—people often living in separation from others who are different. In contrast to human behavior, the poet depicts God's giving worth to every person. Therefore, as "Freely loved, though fully known," the poet leads us to pray that in Christ we may be "free to welcome and accept" others as we have been accepted by him.

The text appears here for the first time in the *Hymnal* of the Episcopal Church.

---

1. Brian Wren, *Faith Looking Forward* (Carol Stream, IL, 1983).

Music: See hymn 209.

RG

604 *When Christ was lifted from the earth*

Music: **SAN ROCCO**

This work of a contemporary poet, Brian Wren, is matched here with SAN ROCCO, a tune by a contemporary British composer, Derek Williams. The tune appears here transposed one step lower than its original key of D as found at no. 253.

Words: See hymn 603.

Music: See hymn 253.

605 *What does the Lord require*

Music: **SHARPTHORNE**

There are times in the editing of hymnals when the matching of a text and tune has an immediate quality of inevitability and maximum suitability. Such is the matching of this text by Albert Bayly with SHARPTHORNE, a tune written for use with it by Erik Routley and probably the composer's finest work.

Words: In our contemporary society, where Christians are challenged on every side by questions of profound moral complexity, the text "What does the Lord require" speaks with particular relevance and strength. Based on Mic. 6:6-8, this is one of a series of seventeen hymns by the British hymn writer and minister of the United Reformed Church, Albert F. Bayly, to interpret the message of each of the Hebrew prophets in the Old Testament. Written in January 1949, the text first appeared in 1951 in the author's collection *Rejoice O People* (Swanland, East Yorkshire, 1950).

Originally a five-stanza text, the form preferred by the author, st. 3 has been omitted in this hymnal. It is:

> Masters of wealth and trade,
>   all you for whom men toil,
> Think not to win God's aid,
>   if lies your commerce soil.
>   Do justly;
>   Love mercy;
> Walk humbly with your God.

The poet, in a letter to the SCCM dated December 18, 1981 wrote that "this verse seems to me to embody part of Micah's message still relevant today (see Mic. 6:10-11)."

Other textual changes include st. 2:2, originally "justice know" and st. 4:1, originally "our life." The first alteration appeared in *MHSS*, while the second was made for this edition.

Micah 6:8 provides the specific source for the first line and the refrain of the hymn; in a much broader sense, however, all the words of the prophet serve as inspiration to the poet, who relates questions about justice and mercy to contemporary situations and places them in the "light of the climax and fulfillment of Old Testament revelation in the coming of Christ,"[1] a goal of all the texts in the original series.

The hymn first appeared in an Episcopal publication in *MHSS*, in a three-stanza form (1, 2, and 5) with the tune SHARPTHORNE. This usage was continued in *Hymns III*. The original st. 4 was restored in *H82*.

---

1. Cyril Taylor, *Hymns for Today Discussed* (Norwich, 1984), 30.

Music: Erik Routley's SHARPTHORNE is one of the finest hymn tunes to have been written this century. It is truly prophetic in the way it gives appropriate musical form to the mighty words of Micah, mediated through the powerful poetry of Albert E. Bayly. It was not, however, Routley's first attempt to create a suitable melody for these words. His first effort was TYES CROSS, a tune that was issued with Bayly's text in the author's privately published *Rejoice O People: Hymns and Verse* (see Example 1):

Example 1

Nearly twenty years later Sir John Dykes Bower, for many years organist at St. Paul's Cathedral, London, was working with others on a supplement to *HA&M Revised*. Sometime during 1968 he wrote to Routley indicating that he was considering the tune for the supplement, but there was a problem: in the middle of the tune there was a section strongly reminiscent of John Ireland's LOVE UNKNOWN (no. 458 and "a" in Example 1). Dykes Bower suggested to Routley that he might consider the possibility of recomposing the offending section. Routley commented: "My immediate answer was to write a new tune, which will be seen to be a paraphrase of the old one in the minor mode. I think it was right to judge that E♭ is not the key for the prophet Micah."[1] SHARPTHORNE is a vastly superior tune when compared to its progenitor TYES CROSS (TYES CROSS and SHARPTHORNE are both place-names in Sussex, England). Particularly powerful is the falling octave—instead of fifth—at "mercy" and the steady rise to the dominant for the final cadence. The melody is cleverly constructed in an AA^1B form, with the final phrase echoing the opening phrase.

The new tune was first published in the supplement to *HA&M* entitled *100 Hymns for Today* (London, 1969). Its first United States appearance was in *MHSS*.

1. *Our Lives Be Praise: the texts, tunes and carols of Erik Routley* (Carol Stream, 1988-9), xxii.

RG/RAL

606 *Where true charity and love dwell*

***Music:* UBI CARITAS**

The introduction into the present BCP of the proper liturgy for Maundy Thursday, including the ceremony of the washing of feet, made very appropriate the inclusion of this text and tune, traditionally associated with this rite (see the essay "Proper Liturgies for Special Days," vol. 1, 111). This marks its first appearance in the *Hymnal*.

Words:

1. Ubi caritas et amor, Deus ibi est.
   Congregavit nos in unum Christi amor.
   Exsultemus, et in ipso iucundemur,
   timeamus, et amemus Deum vivum
   et ex corde diligamus nos sincero.

2. Ubi caritas et amor, Deus ibi est.
   Simul ergo cum in unum congregamur,
   ne nos mente dividamur caveamus.
   Cessent iurgia maligna, cessent lites
   et in medio nostri sit Christus deus.

3. Ubi caritas et amor, Deus ibi est.
   Simul quoque cum beatis videamus,
   glorianter vultum tuum, Christe Deus;

gaudium quod est immensum, atque probum,
saecula per infinita saeculorum.

This hymn exists in several forms; the above is the form used by the translator of the hymn in *H82*. The following version, edited by Karl Strecker and published in 1923, is as close to the original as we are likely to come, except that st. 12 does not appear in the two earliest manuscripts:

1. Congregavit nos in unum Christi amor,
exultemus et in ipso iucundemur,
timeamus et amemus Deum vivum
et ex corde diligamus nos sincero.
Ubi caritas est vera, Deus ibi est.

2. Qui non habet caritatem, nihil habet,
sed in tenebris et umbra mortis manet;
nos alterutrum amemus et in die,
sicut decet, ambulemus lucis fili!
Ubi caritas est vera, Deus ibi est.

3. Clamat dominus et dicit clara voce:
Ubi fuerint in unum congregati
meum propter nomen simul tres vel duo,
et in medio eorum ego ero.
Ubi caritas est vera, Deus ibi est.

4. Simul ergo cum in unum congregamur,
ne nos mente dividamus, caveamus.
Cessent iurgia maligna, cessent lites,
vere medium sic nostrum Christus erit.
Ubi caritas est vera, Deus ibi est.

5. Nam ut caritas coniungit et absentes,
sic discordia seiungit et praesentes.
Unum omnes indivise sentiamus,
ne et simul congregati dividamur.
Ubi caritas est vera, Deus ibi est.

6. Karitas est summum bonum, amplum donum,
in qua pendet totus ordo preceptorum,

per quam vetus atque nova lex impletur,
quae ad caeli celsa mittit se repletos.
Ubi caritas est vera, Deus ibi est.

7. Haec per coccum priscae legis figuratur,
qui colore rubro tingui bis iubetur,
quia caritas preceptis in duobus
constat, quibus deus amatur atque homo.
Ubi caritas est vera, Deus ibi est.

8. Tota ergo mente deum diligamus
et illius nil amori preponamus,
inde proximos in Deo ut nos ipsos
et amemus propter Christum inimicos.
Ubi caritas est vera, Deus ibi est.

9. Qui hoc geminum preceptum caritatis
mente humili contendit observare,
vere hic in Christo manet, et in illo
nocte sceleris expulsa manet Christus.
Ubi caritas est vera, Deus ibi est.

10. Ardua et arta via ducit sursum,
ampla est atque devexa quae deorsum;
sed perennem dat fraternus amor vitam,
et perpetuam maligna lis dat poenam.
Ubi caritas est vera, Deus ibi est.

11. Unanimiter excelsum imploremus,
ut det pacem clemens nostris in diebus,
iungat fidei speique opus bonum,
ut consortium captemus supernorum.
Ubi caritas est vera, Deus ibi est.

12. "Gloria aeterno regi" decantemus
et pro vita dominorum exoremus,
multos ut cum ipsis annos gaudeamus,
propter quorum his amorem congregamur.
Ubi caritas est vera, Deus ibi est.[1]

The history of research into this hymn's origins reads like a detective story. In 1924, the noted medievalist André Wilmart published an article suggesting from internal evidence that the hymn had originated in a Benedictine monastery and had been written for the weekly *mandatum* (foot washing) held on Saturday evenings. He traced its composition to the beginning of the ninth century, basing his conclusion on manuscript evidence and on a reference in the last stanza to the "lords" ("dominorum"), which he took to refer to Charlemagne and his sons.[2] The following decade he discovered a paraphrase of portions of the hymn in a monastic rule that he dated from the first half of the eighth century (although others have dated it as late as the tenth century),[3] and he revised his earlier findings to say that only the last stanza was written during the early ninth century, the rest having been written earlier.[4]

Wilmart's conclusion made a great deal of sense, especially since the hymn had quickly found its way into the *mandatum* for Maundy Thursday, its traditional place in the Roman liturgy. In 1950, however, Bernhard Bischoff, in a study of several hymns of the same genre, suggested that the hymn may have arisen not in connection with the foot-washing ceremony, but with the Benedictine Caritas (i.e., αγαπη) meal on Maundy Thursday, being transferred to the *mandatum* during the tenth and eleventh centuries.[5] In 1954, however, Dag Norberg disputed Wilmart's assertion that the hymn had originated in a Benedictine monastery, interpreting differently the internal evidence that Wilmart had cited as proof and proposing instead that the last stanza had been designed as a prayer for the benevolence of the sovereigns (Charlemagne and his son Pepin, King of Italy) under whose protection an ecclesiastical synod had assembled. The only likely candidate for such an event, Norberg found, was the provincial Synod of Cividale (also called the Synod of Forum Julii), held in 796 or 797. Presiding at that synod was Paulinus (ca. 750-802), Patriarch of Aquileia in Italy, who gave an opening address based upon Mt. 18:20: "For where two or three are gathered in my name, there am I in the midst of them."[6] This theme predominates in the hymn, and the passage itself is quoted in its entirety in the third stanza. Paulinus was also a writer of religious poetry, and Norberg found similarities, especially in metre, between poetry attributed to him and "Ubi caritas." Norberg therefore concluded that Paulinus of Aquileia wrote this hymn to support his address at the Synod of Forum Julii.[7] If he is correct, then Paulinus must have possessed great wisdom and insight, for this hymn effectively counteracts the tensions that must have arisen at the synod, which debated and eventually mandated within the region the use of the *filioque** (the words "and the Son") in the third article of the Creed.

Norberg's conclusions, though based on circumstantial evidence (there being no ascription to Paulinus or to anyone else in any of the manuscripts), represent the most likely origin of the hymn thus far proposed. The weakest part of Norberg's argument is the attribution to Paulinus: although the reasoning is insightful, it is nonetheless hampered by the absence of any surviving poetry unquestionably written by Paulinus, as opposed to poetry attributed to him in various manuscripts. But the possibility of the hymn's connection with the Synod of Cividale is too appealing to dismiss, and if there is indeed no decisive proof that Paulinus wrote the hymn, there is also no more likely candidate for its authorship.

Two other works on the hymn have appeared since the publication of Norberg's study. Thomas Schäfer's 1956 book on foot washing in monastic use and in the Latin liturgy treated the history of "Ubi caritas" in an appendix. Evidently unfamiliar with Norberg's work, he accepted Bischoff's arguments, concluding that "the hymn 'Congregavit' originated around the year 800 in the Reichenau [manuscript]."[8] The other study, E. Moeller's 1981 article, which is essentially a summary of previous work, reported favorably Norberg's conclusions but provided no new evidence for them.[9]

The translation of "Ubi caritas" by Joyce MacDonald Glover was prepared for the *Hymnal 1982*. The English version is in the rather unusual metre of the Latin original (with 8 + 4 syllables in each line, and 8 + 5 in the antiphon), and is a fairly literal rendering of it, the only significant departure from the Latin being the interpretation in stanza 1 of "timeamus" as "we hear" instead of "we fear." (The translator feels that this is a typographical error that appeared first in the SCN General Report [New York, 1982]).

For other versions of "Ubi caritas" see hymns 576, 577, and 581.

---

1. See E. Dümmler, L. Traube, P. von Winterfeld and K. Strecker, *Poetae latini aevi Carolini* (Berlin, 1923), vol. 4, 526-529.

2. See A. Wilmart, "L'Hymne de la charité pour le jeudi-saint," *La vie et les arts liturgiques* (April 1924), 253-55.

3. See T. Schäfer, *Die Fuβwaschung im monastischen Brauchtum und in der lateinischen Liturgie* (Beuron, 1956), 102.
4. See A. Wilmart, "Le Reglement ecclésiastique de Berne," *Revue bénédictine*, 51 (1939), 40.
5. See B. Bischoff, "Caritas-Lieder," *Liber Floridus: Mittellateinische Studien* (St. Ottilien, 1950), 171-72; see also Schäfer, *Die Fuβwaschung im monastischen Brauchtum*, 104.
6. For the acts of the synod, see *Sacrorum conciliorum nova et amplissima collectio* (Paris, 1901-27), vol. 13, cols. 827-56. This series, usually referred to by the name of the original editor, G. D. Mansi, was published in Italy and France over a long period of time. Volume 13 was originally published in Florence in 1767; the edition of this volume cited here is a facsimile reprint.
7. See D. Norberg, "Saint Paulin d'Aquilée et l'hymne 'Congregavit nos in unum,' " *La Poésie latine rythmique du haut moyen âge* (Stockholm, 1954), 90-91 and 93-97.
8. See Schäfer, *Die Fuβwaschung im monastischen Brauchtum*, 102.
9. See E. Moeller, "Paulin II d'Aquilée (756-802) et l'hymne 'Ubi caritas' du mandatum du jeudi saint," *Questions liturgiques*, 62 (1981), 106-112.

Music: An antiphon with verses used at the conclusion of the liturgy of the washing of the feet, Maundy Thursday, UBI CARITAS may have originated with the so-called Gallican rite—the liturgical tradition used in the Churches of Gaul before Gregorian (Roman) chant was imposed by Pepin (d. 768) and Charlemagne (d. 814). This category of antiphon, in which the antiphon is found alternating with verses (in the manner of a rondo: A V1 A V2 A V3 A), is characteristic of the Gallican rite.

UBI CARITAS appears in *H82* in a traditional form edited by the Benedictines of Solesmes (see *Liber Usualis*, 664). The accompaniment is by David Hurd. In the more recent choral literature the tune may be found as the theme of a motet *a cappella** by Maurice Duruflé, Op. 10, no. 1 (1960).

JH/ME

607 *O God of every nation*

Music: **LLANGLOFFAN**

This text reflecting the world we live in, a world divided by race and material wealth and devastated by the destruction and horror of wars, is balanced by the prayer that we never lose sight of the vision of God's will for his world, a world where love, peace, and justice will reign. The text is matched here with LLANGLOFFAN, a strong Welsh tune whose harmonization well suits the solemn mood of the text. This is the first appearance of the text in the *Hymnal*.

Words: The text "O God of every nation" was written by William W. Reid, Jr., for publication in *New World Order Hymns* (New York, 1958), published by the Hymn Society of America for the Fifth World Order Study Conference of 1958. Alterations were made in the text in *H82* to comply with the SCCM's desire to use inclusive language whenever possible: in st. 3:2, where the word "men" has been changed to "we" and in st. 4:7, where the word "brotherhood" is altered to "truth and justice." Other changes include st. 1:3-4 where "thy" is updated to "the" and "thine" to "your" and st. 3:6-8 where "thy" becomes "your."

Music: See hymn 68. This harmonization was composed by Ralph Vaughan Williams for use in *EH* and was introduced to Episcopalians in *Hymnal Supplement II* (New York, 1976).

MBJ

608 Eternal Father, strong to save

Music: **MELITA**

This hymn, matched with the tune MELITA, better known as the Navy Hymn, has, over the years, achieved international popularity among English-speaking peoples.

Words: Except for one change in st. 4:1 where "our brethren" has been altered to "thy children," this text is identical to that which appeared in the first edition of *HA&M* (1861). The compilers of that influential collection, however, made rather extensive revisions to the hymn, written by William Whiting the year before. The first stanza began:

> O Thou Who bidd'st the ocean deep,
> Its own appointed limits keep,
> Thou, Who didst bind the restless wave,
> Eternal Father, strong to save.
> O hear us when we cry to Thee
> For all in peril on the sea.

Stanza 2 began:

O Saviour, Whose almighty word
The wind and waves submissive heard.

There are other changes in the subsequent stanzas. The author continued revising the text in 1869 and again in 1874 and produced a version that very closely matched the changes made in *HA&M*. The hymn has been exceedingly popular not only with seafarers, but also, as Sir Evelyn Wood mused, "When the wind blows hard, by those on land." In this country it is known as the Navy Hymn and was sung at the funeral of Franklin D. Roosevelt, for whom it was a great favorite. It was also played at the funeral of John F. Kennedy on November 25, 1963. The text has been in the *Hymnal* since 1871.

Music: See hymn 579.

MS

609 Where cross the crowded ways of life

Music: **GARDINER**

This early twentieth-century hymn on the plight of the poor, especially in the ghettos of large American cities, still speaks with intensity to contemporary Americans living in places where the homeless wander the streets and living conditions for the poor continue to deteriorate. Matched with this tune, it has been in the *Hymnal* since 1916.

Words: One of the editors of the 1905 *Methodist Hymnal*, Caleb T. Winchester, suggested to Frank Mason North the need for a new missionary hymn. The author's long involvement in missions and his knowledge of the massive throngs of humanity in New York City came to compassionate expression in this hymn, based on Mt. 22:9: "Go ye therefore into the highways," and especially on the American Revised Version, "The partings of the highways," on which he had recently preached a sermon. This is the first of North's hymns to receive ecumenical acceptance. It was first published in *The Christian City*, XV, 4/1 (June 1903), 1, of which North was the editor. North's hymn entered *The Methodist Hymnal* in 1905 and the *Hymnal* in

1916. The beginning of st. 5 originally read: "Till sons of men shall learn thy love."

Music: William Gardiner, Leicester stocking manufacturer and amateur musician, was an enormously enthusiastic admirer of Beethoven and introduced the first of the master's works ever heard in England, the String Trio, Op. 3, which he played as early as 1794.

The first volume of Gardiner's most influential work, *Sacred Melodies, from Haydn, Mozart and Beethoven, Adapted to the Best English Poets, and appropriate to the Use of the British Church* (London) appeared in 1812. By this means Gardiner rather naively hoped to improve the quality of church music heard in English churches. The second volume (1815) included, at page 126, the present tune set to a mellifluous version of Ps. 23: "As a shepherd gently leads/Wand'ring flocks to verdant meads." Gardiner laid out the music for voice and string quartet and marked it "Subject Beethoven." The tune never caught on in England; but it was printed in Oliver Shaw's *Sacred Melodies* (Providence, 1818), and then in *The Boston Handel and Haydn Society Collection of Church Music* (Boston, 1822) with the name GERMANY and the text "Softly the shade of evening falls." Lowell Mason, the anonymous compiler of the latter book, was greatly influenced by Gardiner; his own influence in turn assured the tune's popularity in the United States.

All efforts to trace the "subject" to one of Beethoven's works have so far failed. Probably for this reason, the editors of the Episcopal *Hymnal* in 1916 changed the name of the tune from BEETHOVEN, by which it had been widely known, to GARDINER. Leonard Ellinwood suggested the *Allegretto* of Beethoven's Piano Trio, Op. 70, no. 2 (1808) as the source of the tune; but the only real resemblance is with the last phrase, which can hardly be called the "subject" (*H40c*, 306). The only theme from the Viennese classical masters that comes close to the opening phrase of the tune is the four-measure introduction to Sarastro's aria, "O Isis und Osiris," from *Die Zauberflöte*. Interestingly enough, that song itself was adapted by Gardiner to another hymn in the same volume.

HE/NT

610 *Lord, whose love through humble service*

Music: **BLAENHAFREN**

This text, rich in scriptural references to the life, ministry, and the suffering upon the cross of our Lord, closely relates the life and mission of Jesus to the lives and responsibilities of contemporary Christians. It appears here matched with the Welsh hymn tune BLAENHAFREN.

Words: "Lord, whose love through humble service" was written by Albert F. Bayly, a British Congregational minister, in response to a joint appeal by the Hymn Society of America and the Department of Social Welfare of the National Council of Churches of Christ in the United States. "These hymns were to express the interrelationship of worship and service of love as expressions of one deep, abiding faith in God."[1] Included in the booklet *Seven New Social Welfare Hymns* (New York, 1961) set to the tune HYFRYDOL, the hymn was chosen as the Conference Hymn for the Second National Conference of Churches and Social Welfare in Cleveland, OH, October 23-27, 1961. The text was later included, unaltered, in *The Methodist Hymnal* (Nashville, 1964) set to the tune BEECHER. An altered form in three stanzas was included in the *LBW* with the tune BEACH SPRING. Many of these alterations, made to bring the text closer to contemporary use of inclusive language and the replacement of "you" and "your" for "thee" and "thine," were continued in *H82*. The fourth stanza, omitted from the *LBW*, was also restored. This is the first appearance of this text in the *Hymnal*.

Textual alterations were made to the following sections of text ("L" indicates that the alterations first appeared in the *LBW*):

1:3 Who dids't on the cross forsaken, work thy mercy's perfect deed L
1:5 we, thy servants L
1:7 to thy purpose L
1:8 thou dids't impart L
2:1 Still the children L
2:4 men mourn their L
2:5 As, O Lord, thy
2:7 thy Spirit L

2:8	make men
3:2	Thy love's L
3:6	thy compassion L
3:8	Thine abundant L
4:1	Called from worship unto
4:2	in thy
4:7	thy children
4:8	thy mercy

The poet's deep immersion in classic hymnody is revealed in st. 4, line 2, where he uses the phrase "Forth in thy dear name we go" closely paralleling Charles Wesley's opening line "Forth in thy Name, O Lord, I go."

---

1. *Seven New Social Welfare Hymns*, The Hymn Society of America (New York, 1961), 2.

Music: BLAENHAFREN is seldom used as a hymn tune in Welsh hymn books. Among those currently in use, it appears only in the *Caniedydd* (Swansea, 1961), the Hymn-book of the Welsh Congregational Church. It is common, however, in the "Penillion" tradition as a harp melody against which a vocal line is sung. There is no indication in the published collections of its origin (see the essay "The Welsh Hymn Tune," vol. 1, 310).

RG/AL

611 Christ the worker

Music: **AFRICAN WORK SONG**

A native African melody and a text written for a Christian work camp in North Ghana are the sources for this hymn, which relate the life and labor of Christ to all, no matter what their race, who "labor and listen to his call."

Words: Among the many hymns collected, translated, and published by the minister and missionary of the United Reformed Church in Great Britain Thomas Stevenson Colvin during his many years in

Africa are two included in *H82*. First published in two collections in 1968 and 1976, "Christ the worker," like "Jesu, Jesu, fill us with your love" [602], resulted from a renewed emphasis among some Christian leaders in Africa on singing hymns composed by worshipers in their own language, reflecting their social and religious situation. This hymn is composed of few words, many of which are repeated, and is constructed so as to accompany and emphasize the physicality of group work. The special significance of the text is its concern with a Christian subject: the birth, childhood, youthful occupation of Christ, and their relationship to those who would follow after him.

While the hymn contains only seven stanzas, it is the type of song designed in such a way that its length and textual direction are determined by the leader who is free—and expected—to create each new line. The lines would not be composed extemporaneously, but would come from a well of stock couplets known to all members of the congregation. Since its first published appearance, the author/composer of the text has made one alteration to it. The first phrase of st. 5 was originally "You who labor, you who labor." A comprehensive collection of Tom Colvin's work is found in *Fill Us With Your Love* (Carol Stream, IL, 1983).

Music: As the text of this hymn came from the traditional poetry of African Christians, the tune AFRICAN WORK SONG was taken from a traditional work song in Southern Africa. Thomas Colvin, who encouraged the setting of hymn texts to traditional African melodies, transcribed and arranged the tune. A prime example of the type of work song that inspired the first work songs of black Americans, the duple metre setting of the hymn captures the rhythmic flow of the work to which it is sung.

Like the African-American spiritual THERE IS A BALM IN GILEAD, AFRICAN WORK SONG is based on a scale comprised of only five tones. Like the spiritual, the tones of this pentatonic scale are the first five tones of the standard musical scale. The construction of the tune has an inherent work rhythm, beginning with long rhythmic values moving to shorter rhythmic values as the work and song progress.

The hymn may be sung as a canon* or round by having a second group of singers begin the tune after the first group has sung the first measure. First published in *Free to Serve* (Glasgow, 1969), this hymn was first published in the United States in *Ecumenical Praise* (Carol Stream, IL, 1977). It first appeared in an Episcopal publication in *Songs for Celebration* (New York, 1980).

HCB

612 Gracious Spirit, Holy Ghost

Music: **TROEN**

There is often a fine line between what is a scriptural paraphrase and what is a hymn based on scripture. This text follows very closely the important themes of 1 Cor. 13. The text appears here with TROEN, a charming tune written especially for use with it in *H82*.

Words: Possibly Christopher Wordsworth's best-known hymn, "Gracious Spirit, Holy Ghost" is based on Paul's remarks on love, 1 Cor. 13. It is the hymn in Wordsworth's *The Holy Year* (London, 1862) for Quinquagesima, for which this chapter of 1 Cor. was the Epistle.

"Gracious Spirit, Holy Ghost" originally comprised eight stanzas. In *HA&M* (1868), 2 and 3 were omitted, and this six-stanza version became widely used. The eight-stanza original included the following, after st. 1:

Faith, that mountains could remove,
tongues of earth or heaven above,
knowledge—all things—empty prove
without heavenly love.

Though I as a martyr bleed,
give my goods the poor to feed,
all is vain, if love I need;
therefore give me love.

After the present st. 3:

Faith will vanish into sight,
hope be emptied in delight;
love in heaven will shine more bright,
therefore give us love.

and a final stanza:

From the overshadowing
of thy gold and silver wing,
shed on us, who to thee sing,
  holy, heavenly love.

The hymn's close following of scripture is typical of Wordsworth. What is not typical is the slip into the subjective in the original st. 3. Wordsworth was a strong advocate of objective hymns, as he himself explained in the preface to *The Holy Year*: "A hymn in public worship is the collective voice of the congregation speaking to God . . . "[1]

---

1. Quoted in E. E. Ryden, *The Story of Christian Hymnody* (Rock Island, IL, 1959), 373.

Music: TROEN, a unison hymn of naive charm, was written in late November 1983 by Daniel Moe in response to an appeal from the SCCM for new tunes for possible use with unset texts. The composer writes, "As I paged through this collection of texts late in the evening of November 28, the words of Christopher Wordsworth struck me with particular force. Within twenty minutes the tune in its final form was completed."[1] TROEN first appeared in *H82*.

The mood of the text—a positive affirmation of the primacy of God's gift of love—and its metrical form of three balanced rhyming lines and a final shorter nonrhyming line are sensitively supported by the tune. The first two lines, which are melodically the same, are cast in the form of a gentle curve. Line 3, which is almost circular in shape and uses a different rhythmic structure than the first two phrases, provides an effective contrast. The final phrase brings the tune to a conclusion with a half close. Ending as it does on the second step of the key (A) and supported by dominant harmony, there is a natural impulse for the setting to return to the beginning where the tune opens with a tonic chord (G). In its original form, the tune had a second ending for use after st. 4, which concluded with an ascending curve in the melody, ended on B, and was harmonized with the chord of E (see Example 1).

In general the Commission rejected second endings that varied melodically from the first as being confusing to a congregation.

Example 1

In writing on his choice of a tune name, Dr. Moe says, "The tune name TROEN was given for several personal and familiar reasons. TROEN is the name of my maternal grandparents who emigrated from Norway in the late nineteenth century. It is also the Norwegian word for 'faith.' And it will be, if I am ever so blessed, the name of my first daughter."[2]

---

1. Moe to Glover, 1 June 1985, Church Hymnal Corporation Papers, New York.
2. Ibid.

WTJ/RG

613 Thy kingdom come, O God!

***Music:* ST. CECILIA**

This hymn is rich with biblical references to the second coming and was originally intended for use during Advent. Since *H40*, it has gained greater use through its placement among the general hymns. It appeared matched with this tune in two music editions of the 1871 *Hymnal*, a relationship that continues to this day.

Words: This text by Lewis Hensley was first printed in *Hymns for Minor Sundays from Advent to Whitsuntide* (1867). A year later it appeared in the Appendix to *HA&M* (1868) and soon thereafter in other Anglican hymnals in England and North America. A quotation from the Lord's Prayer in Mt. 6:10 is the first of the many biblical references in the text. A reference to the "iron rod" of the heavenly warrior in Rev. 19:15 is the other reference in that stanza. The "reign of peace" in st. 2 is found in 2 Cor. 13:11 and the description of the qualities of the Heavenly Jerusalem are found in Rev. 21:4. Psalm 72:4 provides many of the references in st. 3 and Rev. 22:20 the prayer for the presence of God at the second coming. Rev. 22:16 gives us the reference to Christ as the "Morning Star" and Ex. 10:22 the image of the "thick darkness" that hung over ancient Egypt.

An omitted stanza following st. 4 is:

> Men scorn thy sacred name,
>   And wolves devour thy fold;
> By many deeds of shame
>   We learn that love grows cold.

The only other alteration, first made by the editors of the *BBC Hymn Book* (London, 1951), is:

st. 5:1 O'er heathen lands afar.

Music: ST. CECILIA, a serviceable melody from *The Merton Hymn Book* (Oxford, 1863), honors St. Cecilia, the patron saint of musicians. It appeared matched with this text in the Appendix to *HA&M* (1868), a practice that began in this country with the Hutchins and Tucker/Rousseau editions of the 1871 *Hymnal* and is continued to this day. The tune is typical of many psalm tunes in its regular quarter-note movement and modulation to the dominant at the end of the second phrase.

RG/HMcK

614 Christ is the King! O friends upraise

Music: **CHRISTUS REX**

A spirit of confident and positive joy permeates both the text and tune of this hymn honoring Christ the King who leads his children in their pursuit of the goal that "the whole Church, at last [may] be one." Both text and tune first appeared in an Episcopal Church publication in *H40*.

Words: This text was written by George Kennedy Allen Bell at the suggestion of Percy Dearmer, to be used with the Welsh tune

LLANGOEDMOR in the enlarged edition of *Songs of Praise* (London, 1931). The original began:

> Christ is the King! O friends rejoice;
> Brothers and sisters, with one voice
> Make all men know he is your choice.
> Ring out ye bells, give tongue, give tongue!
> Let your most merry peal be rung,
> While our exultant song is sung.
>
> O magnify the Lord, and raise
> Anthems of joy and holy praise . . .

It was designed for use on the Feast of St. Simon and St. Jude. Built on the theme of Christian unity, it was a favorite hymn in England in connection with the Religion and Life Movement.

First appearing in an Episcopal hymnal in *H40*, its use was continued in *H82* with one textual alteration in line 6 of the first stanza. The line, altered to make the usage more inclusive, originally read:

> Thousands of faithful men and true.

Music: CHRISTUS REX was composed in 1941 during David McK. Williams's tenure (1920-1947) as organist and choirmaster of St. Bartholomew's Church in New York City and was written for use in *H40* with the text "Christ is the King! O friends upraise." The music is strong and one might almost say "enthusiastic." The rising arpeggio in the first measure is balanced by a falling arpeggio in the last phrase and the intervening phrases are cumulative in their development.

RG/AW

615 "Thy kingdom come!" on bended knee

Music: **ST. FLAVIAN**

In the preparation of *H82*, the only change made in this text was to include the opening statement in quotation marks. It was the hope of the SCCM that this action would help congregations in securing a more meaningful performance of the text. The breath comes after the word "come" and the next part of the sentence is sung on one breath. The text entered the *Hymnal* in 1916 matched with this tune.

Words: Frederick L. Hosmer wrote this text for the commencement of Meadville Theological School, Meadville, PA on June 12, 1891. It was published in the second series of *The Thought of God in Hymns and Poems* (Boston, 1894), under the heading "The Day of God." It is based on the first petitions of the Lord's Prayer, a thematic device that Hosmer also used in his other hymn of 1891 (published in 1904), "Thy Kingdom come, O Lord."

A 1978 survey of clergy and church musicians to determine use of hymns in *H40* revealed that, of the five Hosmer texts included in that collection, only this text was consistently used. It was therefore retained without textual alteration. Although found in *H82* in the section "Kingdom of God," this text is appropriate for the Last Sunday of Pentecost, sometimes called "The Feast of Christ the King," as a means of ushering in the season of Advent.

Music: For the setting in its original rhythm see hymn 332; for this setting see hymn 142.

RG

616 Hail to the Lord's Anointed

Music: **ES FLOG EIN KLEINS WALDVÖGELEIN**

Although written initially as a Christmas Ode, this text, in its present shorter form, has gained broader use as a text under the heading "The Kingdom of God" or "The Kingdom of Christ." It is also appropriate for use on the Feast of the Epiphany. The first association with this tune occurred in *H40*.

Words: James Montgomery wrote this hymn based on Ps. 72 in 1821 to be used in a Christmas Ode at a Moravian settlement. A Moravian Ode is the leaflet for a special or festival service that is composed largely of hymns, hymn stanzas, and anthems. The Moravian settlement was probably Fulneck, near Leeds in Yorkshire, where Montgomery was a member, or Ockbrook, near Derby, where his younger brother Ignatius had been called that year as pastor. Part of the hymn was published in the *Evangelical Magazine* (London, May, 1822). The text has been in the *Hymnal* since 1826. Omitted lines following st. 2 are:

By such shall he be feared,
  While sun and moon endure,
Beloved, obeyed, revered;
  For he shall judge the poor
Through changing generations,
  With justice, mercy, truth,
While stars maintain their stations,
  Or moons renew their youth.

Originally following st. 3 were the colorful lines:

Arabia's desert-ranger,
  To him shall bow the knee;
The Ethiopian stranger
  His glory come to see;
With offerings of devotion
  Ships from the isles shall meet,
To pour the wealth of ocean
  In tribute at his feet.

Stanza 4 in the *Hymnal* is composed of the first four lines of the original st. 6 and the first four lines of the original st. 7. The omitted lines are:

For he shall have dominion
  O'er river, sea, and shore,
Far as the eagle's pinion,
  Or dove's light wing can soar.

The mountain-dews shall nourish
  A seed in weakness sown,
Whose fruit shall spread and flourish,
  And shake like Lebanon.

Music: See no. 48. The present harmonization was based on that of H. Walford Davies in *A Students' Hymnal* (London, 1923).

HLW

617 Eternal Ruler of the ceaseless round

Music: **SONG 1**

Although the work of an American poet, this text initially gained currency in England where it was introduced in hymnals toward the end of the nineteenth century. The major impetus for its use, however, came again in England with the publication of *EH*, where the text was matched with this tune. It is in this form that it is restored in *H82*.

Words: This hymn was written by John W. Chadwick for his graduation from Harvard Divinity School on June 19, 1864. Composed at a time when there was much anxiety concerning the outcome of America's Civil War, the hymn is a call for unity, clearly articulated in st. 2, which begins: "We would be one in hatred of all wrong." Chadwick's text was published in *Singers and Songs of the Liberal Church* (Boston, 1875). Its first use as a hymn text was in England where Garrett W. Horder included it in his *Congregational Hymns* (London, 1884). Its acceptance as a hymn text was assured after it was set to Gibbons's SONG 1 by Ralph Vaughan Williams in *EH*. The text entered the *Hymnal* in 1916 but was dropped from *H40*. It was restored in this *Hymnal* with the Gibbons tune.

Music: See hymn 315.

HE

618 Ye watchers and ye holy ones

Music: **LASST UNS ERFREUEN**

Contemporary hymnals, particularly *H40* and *H82*, owe an enormous debt of gratitude to the editors of *EH* for both their shape and content. The names of Percy Dearmer, General Editor of *EH*; Athelstan Riley, a member of the editorial committee and author of this text; and Ralph Vaughan Williams, Music Editor of the collection, are three of the important visionary people who provided the genius and leadership for the development of the seminal publication, the source of both the text and the arrangement of this tune.

Words: This text, which gained and continues to maintain a very high level of acceptance and use since its introduction to Episcopalians in *H16*, was written by Athelstan Riley for use with this tune in *EH*. An antiphonal song of praise, its imagery reflects the author's interest in the Eastern Church. Stanza 1 mentions the nine orders of angels codified by the pseudo-Dionysius. Stanza 2 is a direct paraphrase of the Theotokion, "Hymn to the Mother of God," sung at the end of each choir office of the early Greek Church. Stanza 3 calls upon the saints at rest, patriarchs, prophets, the apostles and martyrs to praise the Lord, while st. 4 is an invitation to the saints on earth to join this song of praise to the most Holy Trinity.

Music: See hymn 400. This arrangement of the tune by Ralph Vaughan Williams was composed for use in *EH*.

RG

619 Sing alleluia forth in duteous praise

Music: **MARTINS**

Over the centuries, curious liturgical rites have developed for the burial of alleluias on the Sunday before Ash Wednesday (see 122). Although none of these rites remain in use today, we have in our repertory hymns that refer to the giving up of the singing of alleluias during Lent. This text and "Alleluia, song of gladness" [122/123] are examples of these hymns.

Words: (The numbers in parentheses refer to the stanzas in *H82* derived from the Latin original.)

1.(1) Alleluia piis edite laudibus,
cives aetherei, psallite naviter
alleluia perenne.

2.(2) Hinc vos perpetui luminis accola
adsumet resonans hymniferis choris
alleluia perenne.

3.(3) Vos urbs eximia suscipiet dei,
quae laetis resonans cantibus excitat
alleluia perenne.

4. Felici reditu gaudia sumite,
reddentes domino glorificos melos
alleluia perenne.

5.(4) Almum sidereae iam patriae decus
victores capitis, quo canor est iugis
alleluia perenne.

6.(5) Illic regis honor vocibus inclitis
jocunda reboat carmina perpetim
alleluia perenne.

7.(6) Hoc fessis requies, hoc cibus et potus,
oblectans reduces haustibus affluis
alleluia perenne.

8. Nos te suavisonis conditor affatim
rerum carminibus laudeque pangimus
alleluia perenne.

9.(7) Te Christe celebrat gloria vocibus
nostris omnipotens, ac tibi dicimus
alleluia perenne.

This hymn is the liturgical version of Mardi Gras. Like "Alleluia, song of gladness" [122], it is a farewell to the alleluia. Assigned to the first Sunday in Lent in the Mozarabic (Spanish) breviary, it is the Christian's last chance before the Vigil of Easter to sing the word "Alleluia," which is not used during Lent. The words "an endless Alleluia" remind the singers that even though the word is not heard for several weeks it still governs their lives as they await Easter and Christ's resurrection.

The hymn is found in several tenth-century manuscripts, but its exact date and place of composition remain unknown. Franz Joseph Mone assigns it to the fifth century, citing the shortened form of the stanza and the hymn's inclusion in the Mozarabic breviary, which contains only hymns written before the eighth century. [1]

The translation is by the editorial committee of *H40* and is based on a translation by John Ellerton that was first published in *The Churchman's Family Magazine* in 1865 (see *Julian*, 49). Ellerton later revised it for the 1868 edition of *HA&M*. The hymn has been in the *Hymnal* since the 1871 edition.

---

1. See F. J. Mone, *Lateinische Hymnen des Mittelalters* (Freiburg im Breisgau, 1853-1855), vol. 1, 87.

Music: MARTINS, a tune by Dr. Percy C. Buck, Director of Music for twenty-six years at Harrow School, England, was originally written for this text and appeared in the composer's *Fourteen Hymn Tunes* (London, 1913). It moves forward with an irresistable momentum to a deeply satisfying final two measures on the words "an endless alleluia." The tune could almost be described as "seamless."

JH/AW

620 *Jerusalem, my happy home*

Music: **LAND OF REST**

It is to Ralph Vaughan Williams that we look with deep admiration for his matching of English folk tunes with texts in *EH*. A similar sense of gratitude is due Canon C. Winfred Douglas for his extensive use of American folk hymnody in *H40*, of which this matching of a classic text with a beautiful American folk hymn tune is an example and a stroke of sheer genius.

Words: The earliest form of this hymn is found in a manuscript in the British Library (British Library Additional MS 15225), to be dated ca. 1616.[1] It is, however, almost certainly somewhat older. First, some of the stanzas are very close to the "New Jerusalem" hymn in forty-four stanzas of CM found in W. Prid's *The glass of vaine-glorie* (London, 1585). Second, both of these hymns are based on a passage of Latin prose found in the medieval *Liber Meditationum*, frequently, but falsely, ascribed to St. Augustine.[2]

The poetic text in the British Library manuscript is in twenty-six stanzas of CM and headed: "A song mad[e] by F: B: P. To the tune of Diana.":[3]

1. Hierusalem my happie home
   When shall I come to thee
When shall my sorrowes haue an end
   Thy ioyes when shall I see

2. O happie harbour of the saints
   O sweete and pleasant soyle
In thee noe sorrow may be found
   Noe greefe, noe care, noe toyle

3. In thee noe sickness may be seene
   Noe hurt, noe ache, noe sore
There is noe death, nor uglie devill
   There is life for euermore

4. Noe dampishe mist is seene in thee
   Noe could, nor darksome night
There everie soule shines as the sunne
   There god himselfe gives light

5. There lust and lukar cannot dwell
   There envie beares no sway
There is noe hunger heate nor coulde
   But pleasure everie way

6. Hierusalem: Hierusalem
   God grant that I once may see
Thy endless ioyes and of the same
   Partaker aye to be

7. Thy wales are made of precious stones
   Thy bulwarkes Diamondes square
Thy gates are of right orient pearle
   Exceeding rich and rare

8. Thy terrettes and thy pinacles
   With carbuncles doe shine
Thy verie streetes are paued with gould
   Surpassinge clear and fine

9. Thy houses are of Ivorie
   Thy windoes cristale cleare

Thy tyles are mad of beaten gould
O god that I were there

10. Within thy gates nothinge doeth come
That is not passinge cleane
Noe spiders web, noe durt noe dust
Noe filthe may there be seene

11. Ah my sweete home Hierusalem
Would god I were in thee
Would god my woes were at an end
Thy ioyes that I might see

12. Thy saints are crownd with glorie great
They see god face to face
They triumph still, they still reioyse
Most happie is their case

13. Wee that are heere in banishment
Continualie doe mourne
We sighe and sobbe, we weepe and weale
Perpetually we groan

14. Our sweete is mist with bitter gaule
Our pleasure is but paine
Our ioyes scarce last the lookeing on
Our sorrowes still remaine

15. But there they liue in such delight
Such pleasure and such play
As that to them a thousand yeares
Doth seeme as yeaster day

16. Thy viniardes and thy orchardes are
Most beutifull and faire
Full furnished with trees and fruits
Most wonderful and rare

17. Thy gardens and thy gallant walkes
Continually are greene
There groes such sweete and pleasant flowers
As noe where eles are seene

18. There is nector and ambrosia made
    There is muske and civette sweete
There manie a faire and daintie drugge
    Are troden under feete

19. There cinomon there sugar groes
    There narde and balme abound
What tounge can tell or hart conceue
    The ioyes that there are found

20. Quyt through the streetes with siluer sound
    The flood of life doe flow
Upon whose bankes on everie syde
    The wood of life doth growe

21. There trees for euermore beare fruite
    And euermore doe springe
And euermore the Angels sit
    And euermore doe singe

22. There David standes with harpe in hand
    As maister of the Queere
Tenne thousand times that man were blest
    That might this musicke hear

23. Our Ladie singes magnificat
    With tune surpassing sweete
And all the virginns beare their parts
    Sitinge aboue her feet

24. Te Deum doth Sant Amrose singe
    Saint Augustine dothe the like
Ould Simeon and Zacharie
    Haue not more songes to seeke

25. There Magdelene hath left her mone
    And cheerefullie doth singe
With blessed Saints whose harmonie
    In everie streete doth ringe

26. Hierusalem my happie home
    Would god I were in thee
  Would god my woes were at an end
    Thy ioyes that I might see
      finis finis

Many attempts have been made to establish the identity of "F. B. P.," but all are speculative (see *Julian*, 583). The hymn exists in many variant forms on broadsides published in the seventeenth, eighteenth, and nineteenth centuries (see *Julian*, 581-583). *The Hymnal 1982* employs, respectively, stanzas 1, 12, 22, 23 combined with 25, and 6, slightly modified, of the "F. B. P." version. The text has been in the *Hymnal* since 1865.

---

1. See C. M. Simpson, *The British Broadside Ballad and Its Music* (New Brunswick, NJ, 1966), 535.
2. *Julian*, 580 cites from the Latin work, which was also the inspiration of Johann Hermann's "Herzliebster Jesu" [158].
3. On this tune, see Simpson, loc. cit.

Music: See hymn 304.

RAL

621 Light's abode, celestial Salem

Music: **RHUDDLAN**

For centuries, poets and artists have found rich resources for creativity in speculation about the heavenly Jerusalem. This Latin medieval text on this subject is matched in *H82* with a strong Welsh hymn tune.

Words:

1. Ierusalem luminosa,
    Verae pacis visio,
  Felix nimis ac formosa,
    Summi regis mansio,
  De te O quam gloriosa
    Dicta sunt a saeculo!

4. In te iugiter iocundum
Alleluia canitur,
Sollemne ac laetabundum
Semper festum agitur,
Totum sanctum, totum mundum,
In te quidquid cernitur.

5. In te numquam nubilata
Aëris temperies,
Sole solis illustrata
Semper est meridies;
In te non nox fessis grata,
Nec labor nec inquies.

15. O quam vere gloriosum
Eris, corpus fragile,
Cum fueris tam formosum,
Forte, sanum, agile,
Liberum, voluptuosum,
In aevum durabile.

16. Nunc libenter ac ferventer
Laborum fer onera,
Habeas ut condecenter
Dona tam magnfica,
Doterisque luculenter
Gloria perpetua.

17. Aeterne glorificata
Sit beata Trinitas,
A qua caelestis fundata
Ierusalem civitas,
In qua sibi frequentata
Sit laudis immensitas.

The stanzas of "Light's abode, celestial Salem" included in *H82* are from an original text of seventeen stanzas dating from the fifteenth century. Although the text has been attributed to Thomas à Kempis, there is no direct evidence as to the identity of the author. The earliest source for the hymn is a manuscript from Karlsruhe that was published in a collection of Latin hymns in 1853. The translation by John Mason Neale first appeared in the *Hymnal Noted*, Part II (London, 1854). It has been in the *Hymnal* since 1892.

Music: RHUDDLAN is a Welsh national melody from the harp tradition, where it is known as DOWCH I'R FRWDYR ("Come to battle"). It appeared in the second edition of Edward Jones's *Musical and Poetical Relicks of the Welsh Bards* (London, 1794). Although it was not in use in Welsh tunebooks until this century, it seems very likely that it was known by William Williams, of Pantycelyn. He wrote a hymn with exactly the same opening words, although of course as an invitation to the Christian to join in Christ's battle and victory. It appeared in Part 3 of *Ffarwel Weledig, Groesaw Anweledig Bethau* (Llandovery, 1769) ("Farewell Seen and Welcome Unseen Things"). In his hymn, the fifth line has only six syllables, making it necessary to slur the three notes at the end of the two short phrases that make up the line. It is probably the first appearance of the 87. 87. 67 metre that has been used effectively in Welsh but infrequently in English.

RHUDDLAN is one of the Welsh tunes introduced to English hymn singing in *EH*, from which this arrangement, probably by Vaughan Williams, is taken. In Welsh use, the opening notes are even, not dotted, and the fourth note is A.

The name is that of a town on the North Wales coast, the scene of many battles. The ruins of a Norman castle indicate its strategic importance.

LW/AL

622 Light's abode, celestial Salem

Music: **URBS BEATA JERUSALEM**

A twelfth-century form of a chant tune in proportional rhythm has been matched here with this possibly fifteenth-century Latin text.

Words: See hymn 621.

Music: "Light's abode, celestial Salem" is a binary rhythmicization of no. 140_1 in *MMMA* I, 82; it is from the twelfth-century *Nevers Hymnal* (Paris Bibliothèque Nationale, n.a. lat. 1235, ff. 152^r, 153^{rv}).

It is clear and unmistakable from the very nature of this melody that, in every two-note neume over a single syllable, each of the two notes should occupy a length that is one-half the length of a single note over a single syllable; that, in other words, the melody consists of "longs" and "shorts" in two-to-one proportion.

JB

623 O what their joy and their glory must be

Music: **O QUANTA QUALIA**

The matching of this translation and tune by the editors of the Appendix to *HA&M* (London, 1868) was a stroke of genius that assures this twelfth-century text an ongoing place in the singing tradition of the Church.

Words:

1. O quanta, qualia sunt illa sabbata
Quae semper celebrat superna curia!
Quae fessis requies, quae merces fortibus,
Cum erit omnia Deus in omnibus!

2. Vere Ierusalem est illa civitas,
Cuius pas iugis est, summa iucunditas,
Ubi non praevenit rem desiderium,
Nec desiderio minus est praemium.

3. Quis rex, quae curia, quale palatium,
Quae pax, quae requies, quod illud gaudium,
Huius participes exponant gloriam
Si, quantum sentiunt, possint exprimere.

4. Nostrum est interim mentem erigere
Et totis patriam votis appetere,
Et ad Ierusalem a Babylonia
Post longa regredi tandem exilia.

5. Illic molestiis finitis omnibus
Securi cantica Sion cantabimus,

Et iuges gratias de donis gratiae
Beata refret plebs tibi, Domine.

6. Illic ex sabbato succedet sabbatum,
Perpes laetitia sabbatizantium,
Nec ineffabiles cessabunt iubili,
Quos decantabimus et nos et angeli.

7. Perenni Domini perpes sit gloria,
Ex quo sunt, per quem sunt, in quo sunt omnia;
Ex quo sunt, Pater est; per quem sunt, Filius;
In quo sunt, Patris et Filii Spiritus.

This 12 12. 12 12 dactylic hymn for Vespers on Saturday by Peter Abelard appears in his *Hymnarius Paraclitensis*. The 10 10. 10 10. dactylic translation by John Mason Neale first appeared in his *Hymnal Noted*, Part II (London, 1854). In 1868 it appeared in *HA&M* with alterations and in this form entered the *Hymnal* in 1892. Stanzas 2 and 5 of the Neale original are omitted:

2. What are the Monarch, his court, and his throne?
What are the peace and the joy that they own?
O that the blest ones, who in it have share,
All that they feel could as fully declare!

5. There dawns no sabbath, no sabbath is o'er,
Those sabbath-keepers have one evermore;
One and unending is that triumph song
Which to the angels and us shall belong.

Music: See hymn 348. The harmony here was composed by John Bacchus Dykes.

LW and RG

624 Jerusalem the golden

Music: **EWING**

This is the only text retained in *H82* of four drawn from John Mason Neale's translation of excerpts from Bernard of Cluny's *De Contemptu Mundi* that appeared in *H40*. The deleted texts, "The world is very evil," "Brief life is here our portion," and "For thee, O dear, dear country," with their picture of the world filled with evil do not currently speak to Christians. This text, however, with its glowing description of the heavenly Jerusalem, still sustains the faithful. It has had a long association with the tune EWING.

Words: This text is one of four hymns translated by John Mason Neale from the long poem *De Contemptu Mundi* by Bernard of Cluny (ca. 1140). Neale translated parts of this lengthy text for the collection *Mediæval Hymns and Sequences* (London, 1851). Later, as a result of the popularity of these verses, Neale published a larger portion of Bernard's poem. It is written in a difficult metre, a succession of pure dactylic hexametres, each broken into three parts, and rhymed both at the end of each pair of lines and within each line at the end of the second and fourth feet.

Music: This may well be described as "the tune with many names." It has been designated as ARGYLE, BERNARD, JENNER, JERUSALEM, ST. BEDE'S, as well as EWING. BERNARD and JERUSALEM stem from the tune's association with portions of Bernard of Cluny's long poem *De Contemptu Mundi*; it was erroneously attributed to H. J. Jenner; ST. BEDE'S was the name given by its composer, Alexander Ewing; and one can surmise that ARGYLE came about because of Ewing's Scottish heritage.

Alexander Ewing was a member of the Aberdeen Harmonic Choir, which sang madrigals and anthems; it was after one of its rehearsals that he approached the director, William Carnie, with copies of a hymn tune he had composed, "For thee, O dear, dear country" suggesting that the group sing through it. This was the initial performance of EWING, which has had such wide popularity in English-speaking countries. Its first formal publication was in Rev. J. Grey's *Manual of Psalm and Hymn Tunes* (London, 1857), where it appeared in 3/2 metre, but it had been issued on a single sheet as early as 1853.

The common time form and its association with "Jerusalem the golden" date from the 1861 edition of *HA&M*, where the accommodations had been made by W. H. Monk. Because Ewing was out of the country, he was not consulted about the change in metre and later commented, "It now seems to me a good deal like a polka."

John Mason Neale said in 1861, "I have so often been asked to what tune the words of Bernard may be sung, that I may here mention that of Mr. Ewing, the earliest written, the best known, and with children the most popular; no small proof in my estimation of the goodness of church music."[1]

1. P. Dearmer, *Songs of Praise Discussed* (London, 1933), 126.

LW/MS

625 Ye holy angels bright

Music: **DARWALL'S 148TH**

This song of praise, in which the earthly chorus calls upon the assistance of the heavenly host and the saints above, first appeared in an Episcopal publication in *H16* matched with this tune. It appears here with a harmonization that was first used in *H40*.

Words: This text is derived from the first five stanzas of a hymn headed "A Psalm of Praise, to the Tune of Psalm 148" in Richard Baxter's *The Poor Man's Family Book* (London, 1672). The three hymns appended to the end of that collection form only a small part of its contents; most of it, as the title page announces, consists of "Forms of Prayer, Praise and Cathechism for the use of Ignorant Families that need them." This final hymn of the group contains sixteen stanzas organized into two parts of eight stanzas each. As indicated below, the first five stanzas bear marginal glosses identifying who is being addressed by each one:

1. Ye holy Angels bright, Angels.
Which stand before God's Throne,
And dwell in Glorious Light,
Praise ye the Lord each one!
You there so nigh,
Fitter than we
Dark sinners be,
For things so high.

2. You blessed Souls at Rest, The glorified Saints.
Who see your Saviour's face,
Whose Glory, even the Least,
Is far above our Grace,
God's praises sound
  As in his sight
  With sweet delight
  You do abound.

3. All Nations of the Earth The world.
Extoll the world's Great King!
With melodie and mirth
His glorious praises sing,
For He still Reigns,
  And will bring low
  The proudest foe
  That Him disdains.

4. Sing forth Jehovah's praise The Church.
Ye Saints that on him call!
Magnifie Him alwaies
His holy Churches all!
In him rejoyce,
  And there proclaime
  His holy name,
  With sounding voice.

5. My Soul bear thou thy part, My soul.
Triumph in God above!
With a well tuned heart,
Sing thou the songs of Love!
  Thou art his own,
  Whose precious blood
  Shed for thy good
  His Love made known.

The current form of the hymn is based on the revision made by John Hampden Gurney for his *Collection of Hymns for Public Worship* (Lutterworth, 1838). It reached its familiar present form in the 1889 Supplement to the 1875 edition of *HA&M*, except that st. 2:6 there reads "as in his light," a commonly repeated reading traceable to a misprint in the earliest editions that was later corrected to "as in his sight."

Biblical allusions in this hymn interweave Rev. 7:9-14, Heb. 12:1, and numerous portions of the Psalms (especially 103, 148, and 150).

Music: DARWALL'S 148TH is the work of the Rev. John Darwall, who composed tunes and basses for all 150 psalms in Tate and Brady's *New Version*. They are found in his autograph fair copy in British Library Additional MS 50891, dated 1783 (see *Frost*, 36).

The tunes, however, were doubtless tried out at Walsall Parish Church, Staffordshire, where Darwall was vicar from 1769. This tune was printed that year in Aaron Williams's *Psalmody in Miniature*, II, (London, 1769) without text; Williams reprinted it in *A New Universal Psalmody* (London, 1770) with the text "Ye boundless realms of joy." It was copied into other Nonconformist books and soon made its way across the Atlantic, where its first printing was in Andrew Law's *Select Number of Plain Tunes* (Cheshire?, 1781).

The tune is found in almost every Anglican and Episcopalian hymnbook of the last hundred years. The present harmonization seems to have evolved gradually; it is close to that in *EH*. The descant, by Sydney Nicholson, comes from *HA&M Revised* (London, 1950).

The characteristic metre of this hymn originated in the Old Version Ps. 148, first printed in 1561 with the tune OLD 148TH; the metre is not found in the French metrical psalter. Transferred to the New Version Ps. 148, it seems to owe its later popularity to Darwall's tune.

Darwall's manuscript version of the tune differs from all printed sources in beginning on the dominant (here, G) instead of the tonic.

CPD/NT

626 Lord, be thy word my rule

***Music:* QUAM DILECTA**

The Holy Year (London, 1862), a collection of hymns based on the liturgical year by Christopher Wordsworth, has been an ongoing source of hymn texts for Episcopal publications since they first started appearing in the 1871 edition of the *Hymnal*. This text, the latest addition to his work in an Episcopal collection, was included, matched with this tune, in *Hymns III*.

Words: This hymn appeared in the sixth edition of Christopher Wordsworth's *The Holy Year* (London, 1872) headed "at Confirmation." Though always and universally printed as two stanzas of 66. 66., formally it is really one stanza of 66. 66 D.

Routley calls it "one of the shortest hymns in common use, and one of the most perfect."[1] It is based on King Charles I's prayer "O Lord, make thy way plain before me. Let thy glory be my end, thy word my rule; and then, thy will be done."

---

1. E. Routley, *An English-Speaking Hymnal Guide* (Collegeville, MN, 1979), no. 410.

Music: The tune QUAM DILECTA was written by Henry Lascelles Jenner for William Bullock's hymn "We love the place, O God" for inclusion in the first edition of *HA&M* (1861). It is an uncomplicated tune that verges on the simplistic. The principal problem is with the metre—four short lines, each of just six syllables—which is too brief for elevated melodic treatment. Indeed, Percy Dearmer observed that it is a metre that "lends itself to parody," adding by way of example the following lines:

We love the Vicar's pram:
For there with tender care
the latest little lamb
is wheeled to Morning Prayer.[1]

Notwithstanding its weaknesses, the tune has proven to be durable, at least in Anglican hymnals. It has never been excluded from *HA&M* and has been associated with the *Hymnal* since 1892.

---

1. See P. Dearmer, *Songs of Praise Discussed* (London 1933), 366.

WTJ/RAL

627 Lamp of our feet, whereby we trace

Music: **NUN DANKET ALL UND BRINGET EHR**

This text on Holy Scripture, which has been in the *Hymnal* since 1892, appears here with the German tune with which it was matched in *H40*.

Words: This originally eleven-stanza text was written by Bernard Barton and first appeared in his publication *Reliquary* (London, 1836). Additional lines that followed the third stanza in the original version read:

Pole-star on life's tempestuous deep!
  Beacon! when doubts surround;
Compass! by which our course we keep;
  Our deep sea-lead, to sound!

Riches in poverty! our aid
  In every needful hour!
Unshaken rock! the pilgrim's shade;
  The soldier's fortress tower!

Our shield and buckler in the fight!
  Victory's triumphant palm!
Comfort in grief! in weakness, might!
  In sickness, Gilead's balm!

Childhood's preceptor! manhood's trust!
  Old age's firm ally!
Our hope—when we go down to dust,
  Of immortality!

Pure oracles of truth divine!
  Unlike each fabled dream
Given forth from Delphos' mystic shrine,
  Or groves of Academe!

Originally following the fourth stanza were the lines:

Yet to unfold thy hidden worth,
  Thy mysteries to reveal,
That Spirit which first gave thee forth
  Thy volume must unseal!

The final stanza originally read:

And we, if we aright would learn
The wisdom it imparts,
Must to its heavenly teaching turn
With simple, child-like hearts!

The text, continued unaltered in *H82* from *H40*, has never gained wide use in other English-language hymnals.

Music: See hymn 397.

MBJ

628 Help us, O Lord, to learn

Music: **ST. ETHELWALD**

This text on Holy Scripture by an American author appears for the first time in an Episcopal hymnal in *H82*. It is matched with a tune by William Henry Monk, the music editor of the first edition of *HA&M*, that also appears for the first time in an Episcopal hymnal.

Words: *The International Journal of Religious Education* celebrated its 35th anniversary in 1959. The journal collaborated with the Hymn Society of America, and hymn writers were invited to submit texts on themes connected with Christian education and the teaching role of the Church. Of the almost 400 texts received, fifteen, including this text by William Watkins Reid, were published by the Hymn Society in *Fifteen New Christian Education Hymns* (New York, 1959). This text subsequently appeared in a number of hymnals, including *100 Hymns for Today* (London, 1969), *The Australian Hymnbook/ With One Voice* (Sydney, 1977) and *Hymns and Psalms: A Methodist and Ecumenical Hymn Book* (London, 1983).

Music: See hymn 181.

RAL

629 *We limit not the truth of God*

Music: **HALIFAX**

This stimulating text on Holy Scripture is new to the *Hymnal* of the Episcopal Church. It is matched here with HALIFAX, a tune from an opera by George Frideric Handel. HALIFAX first appeared in an Episcopal hymnal in *H40* in an arrangement by Canon Douglas. The refreshing setting in *H82*, based more closely on the Handel original, is by David Hurd.

Words: The five stanzas of this text first appeared in *Psalms, Hymns, and Passages of Scripture for Christian Worship* (Leeds, 1853), otherwise known as the *Leeds Hymn Book*, the product of a group of Congregational ministers. One of the ministers was George Rawson, the author of this hymn, who headed it with an abbreviated extract of the valedictory address given by Pastor John Robinson (as recorded by Edward Winslow) to the Pilgrim Fathers before they left Leyden to sail to the New World on the *Mayflower* in 1620:

> He charged us before God, and His blessed angels, if God should reveal anything to us by any other instrument of His, to be as ready to receive it as any truth by his ministry; for he was very confident the Lord had more light and truth yet to break forth out of His holy world (*Julian*, 1243).

The hymn was included in Rawson's later hymn collections, *Hymns, Verses and Chants* (London, 1876) and *Songs of Spiritual Thought* (London, 1885), as well as in other British Congregational hymnals. It has achieved a wider circulation in the second half of this century, appearing in, for example, the *Baptist Hymnal* (London, 1962) and *The Australian Hymnal/With One Voice* (Sydney, 1977). This marks its first appearance in a hymnal of the Episcopal church.

Music: See hymn 459.

RAL

630 *Thanks to God whose Word was spoken*

Music: **WYLDE GREEN**

This text, which appears for the first time in an Episcopal hymnal in *H82*, conveys truths about the action of God in Holy Scripture, in the world, and in our lives. It is one of six new hymns on Holy Scripture to enter the *Hymnal*. The work of a contemporary British poet, it is matched with a tune by a contemporary British composer.

Words: This text was written by R. T. Brooks, an ordained minister of the United Reformed Church and a producer for BBC Television. Brooks wrote the text in 1954 for the 150th anniversary of the Bible Society of England. Each stanza of the hymn, except for the last, ends with the refrain "God has spoken: praise God for his open word." In support of the SCCM's desire to use inclusive language whenever possible the poet granted his permission for this alteration in the last line of each stanza. The original form was "God has spoken: praise him for his open word." In the last stanza, the poet creates a dramatic sense of immediacy by stating "God is speaking." The poet thus reinforces the Church's teaching that God was present at the beginning of creation and is active and present among us today. The hymn expresses thanksgiving to God for the Word spoken at Creation, for acting in the history of Israel, the Word Incarnate, the Word expressed in Holy Scriptures, and the Word experienced through the action of the Holy Spirit in our lives today.

Music: WYLDE GREEN, written by the British composer Peter Cutts in 1955-56, was sung at the 1960 conference in Cambridge of the Hymn Society of Great Britain and Ireland and in 1962 was included in a small booklet of hymns, *New Songs*, edited by Bernard Massey and published by the Congregational Church, Redhill, Surrey. Its first appearance in a hymnbook in the United States was in *The Methodist Hymnal* (Nashville, 1964).

In his setting, Mr. Cutts gives us a robust tune supported by rich harmonies. Of particular note is the setting of the refrain where the command "Praise God . . . " is thrust up to the highest pitch of the tune and sustained for three beats. The sense of climax is further enhanced by the chromatic harmonies and moving bass line of the accompaniment.

Wylde Green is the area in the English Midlands north of Birmingham where the composer lived and worshiped at the time the tune was composed.

RG

631 Book of books, our people's strength

Music: **LIEBSTER JESU**

Appearing first in *H40* matched with this tune, "Book of books, our people's strength" recognizes the place of the Bible in the lives of people throughout history, gives honor to its various authors, and praise to God the "author and giver of all good things" (BCP, 233).

Words: This text was composed by Percy Dearmer for use in the first edition of *Songs of Praise* (London, 1925) matched with this tune. The author conceived it as an expression of appreciation of the Bible in the contemporary world. It first entered the *Hymnal* in 1940 and continues unaltered in *H82*.

Music: See hymn 440.

ALeC

632 O Christ, the Word Incarnate

Music: **MUNICH**

Among the best-known of all the hymns for Holy Scripture, this text has been in the *Hymnal* since 1871. To clarify the misunderstanding of the use of "Word" as it appeared in the original first line of the text, "O Word of God Incarnate" meaning Christ, the Word Incarnate, the Text Committee of the SCCM made the alteration that now appears in *H82*. The text continues, matched with the tune with which it has been associated since the Hutchins music edition of the 1892 *Hymnal*.

Words: "O Word of God Incarnate" by William Walsham How appeared in the supplement to *Psalms and Hymns* (London, 1867) by How and Thomas Baker Morrell. It is based on Ps. 119:105,

"Thy word is a lantern unto my feet and a light unto my path." Textual alterations occur at st. 1:6, where the original read "That from the hallowed page." The present st. 2 is a conflation of the original sts. 2 and 3 that read:

2. The Church from her dear Master
   Received the gift divine,
And still that light she lifteth
   O'er all the earth to shine.
It is the golden casket
   Where gems of truth are stored,
It is the heaven-drawn picture
   Of Christ, the living Word.

3. It floateth like a banner
   Before God's host unfurled;
It shineth like a beacon
   Above the darkling world;
It is the chart and compass
   That o'er life's surging sea,
'Mid mists and rocks and quicksands,
   Still guides, O Christ, to thee.

Music: See hymn 255.

WTJ

633 Word of God, come down on earth

Music: **MT. ST. ALBAN NCA**

This is one of the texts for Holy Scripture that appear for the first time in an Episcopal hymnal in *H82*. The work of a contemporary Scottish priest who has been a major force in the writing of hymn texts for the Roman Catholic Church in Britain, it is matched with a tune written for use with it by Dr. Richard Wayne Dirksen.

Words: This is a text in which James Quinn, S.J., the noted Scottish poet and theologian, weaves with great dexterity a tapestry rich with theological images of the Word of God. For example, the divine

Creator is described as Word of God, Word almighty, Word eternal, Word that brought to life creation, Word of truth, and Word of life. For Christ he uses Word made flesh, Word that came from heaven to die, saving Word, Word that caused blind eyes to see, and Word that speaks your Father's love. While st. 1 ends in a declaration of praise, the remaining three end with petitions that the Word may speak to us, be with us as healer and forgiver, lead us to truth and feed us with one Bread. Written in an ABABCC rhyme scheme, the text first appeared in the poet's initial collection of hymns, *New Hymns For All Seasons* (London, 1969).

Music: MT. ST. ALBAN NCA is a very fluid unison hymn tune whose free rhythms—alternating patterns of three and two pulses—and phrase length barring show deep roots in plainsong. Although the structure of the individual phrases is free, there is a consistency within the whole. The rhythmic patterns set up in the first two phrases are repeated exactly in lines 3 and 4. These in turn are echoed, with slight variation, in the final two lines. Additional rhythmic stability is gained through a sensitive, flowing accompaniment in which the important harmonic changes occur on strong pulses. This ability to create free-flowing vocal lines that are easily sung reflects the composer's deep and lifelong involvement in the choral repertoire of the Church. The tune was written in early 1983 in response to an appeal by the SCCM for new tunes for possible inclusion in *H82*. MT. ST. ALBAN NCA not only honors the site in Washington, DC, of the Cathedral of Sts. Peter and Paul where the composer has served for many years as Organist/Choirmaster and until retirement in 1991 as Canon Precentor, but it also recognizes the National Cathedral Association whose fiftieth anniversary occurred at the time the tune was written.

RG

634 I call on thee, Lord Jesus Christ

Music: **ICH RUF ZU DIR**

This historically important German text, in a translation by Miles Coverdale, matched with its historically proper German chorale tune appears in an Episcopal *Hymnal* for the first time in *H82*.

Words: This single stanza is a translation of st. 1 (of five) of "Ich ruf zu dir, Herr Jesu Christ," written by Johann Agricola, which first appeared in print in broadsides issued around 1530. The earliest extant hymnal in which it is found is *Geistliche Lieder* (Wittenberg, 1533). The hymn was translated into English and appeared in the earliest-known published English hymnal: *Goostly psalmes and spiri-tuall songes drawen out of the holy Scripture, for the comforte and consolacyon of soch as loue to reioyse in God and his worde* (London, ca. 1535). The collection comprised forty-one items, virtually all translations from German, and was the work of Miles Coverdale, who later became Bishop of Exeter during the reign of Edward VI (see the essays "Plainchant Adaptation in England," vol. 1, 179; "English Metrical Psalmody," vol. 1, 324; and "The Tunes of Congregational Song in Britain from the Reformation to 1750," vol. 1, 349).

The German original is as follows:

Ich ruf zu dir, Herr Jesu Christ,
ich bitt, erhör mein Klagen;
verleih mir Gnad zu dieser Frist,
laß mich doch nicht verzagen.
Den rechten Glauben, Herr, ich mein,
den wollest du mir geben,
dir zu leben,
mein Nächsten Nütz zu sein,
dein Wort zu laten eben.

Since this is the earliest English hymn in *H82*, the complete text is given here. Stanzas 1 through 5 are translated from Agricola's hymn; st. 6 is Coverdale's own:

1. I call on the Lorde Jesu Christ,
I have none other helpe but the.
My herte is never set at rest
Tyll thy swete worde have conforted me.
A stedfast fayth graunt me therfore
To holde by thy worde evermore
Above all thynge,
Never resistynge
But to increase in fayth more and more.

2. Yet once agayne I call on the
Heare my request o mercyfull lorde
I wolde fayne hope on thy mercye
And can not be thereto restored
Excepte thou with thy grace oppresse
My blynde and naturall weaknesse
Cause me therefore
To hope evermore
On thy mercy and swete promises.

3. Lorde prynte into my harte and mynde
Thy holy spirite with ferventnesse
That I to the be not unkynde
But love the without faynednesse
Let nothynge drawe my mynde from the
But ever to love the earnestly
Let not my harte
Unthankfully departe
From the ryght love of thy mercye.

4. Geve me thy grace lorde I the praye
To love myne enemyes hartely
Howbeit they trouble me alwaye
And for thy cause do slaundre me
Yet in Jesu Christ for thy goodnesse
Fyll my harte with forgevenesse
That whyle I lyve
I maye them forgeve
That do offende me more or lesse.

5. I am compassed all round aboute
With sore and stronge tentacyon
Therefore good lorde, delyver me out
From all this wycked nacyon.
The devell the worlde my fleshe also
Folowe upon me where I go
Therefore wold I
Now fayne delyvered be
Thy helpe I seke lorde and no mo.

6. Now seist thou lorde what nede I have
I have none els to complayne to
Therefore thy holy goost I crave
To be my guyde wherever I go
That in all my adversite
I forget not the love of the
But as thou lorde
Hast geven me thy worde
Let me therein both lyve and dye.

After centuries of neglect Coverdale's hymn was included in *The Cambridge Hymnal* (Cambridge, 1961). In that publication Coverdale's first stanza is printed as two four-line stanzas. The text was subsequently adapted by *H82* as a one-stanza hymn.

Music: The tune ICH RUF ZU DIR (*Zahn* 7400) first appeared in the *Geistliche Lieder* (Wittenberg, 1533), where it was set to the text by Johannes Agricola, "Ich ruf zu dir, Herr Jesu Christ." The melody appears here in slightly altered form. The harmonization is from the *Evangelisches Gesangbuch* (Kassel, 1928).

RAL/CS

635 If thou but trust in God to guide thee

Music: **WER NUR DEN LIEBEN GOTT**

This particularly engaging hymn from the tradition of German religious song of the seventeenth century is an example of a work in which the author and composer are the same person. For use by congregations of the Episcopal Church, it first appeared in the hymnal supplement *MHSS*. In that book and in *Hymns III* the first line was "If thou but suffer God to guide thee."

Words: The German original of this hymn is often referred to as a classic example of the hymns of "German Pietism," but that is misleading, since it was written at least a generation before the Pietist movement was begun by Philipp Jakob Spener in the mid-1670s. It is rather a classic example of the intense and personal hymnody that developed and grew during and following the devastation of the Thirty Years War, the hymnody of such German poets as Paul Gerhardt, Johann Franck, and Martin Rinkart.

Both the text and melody of the hymn "Wer nur den lieben Gott lässt walten" were written by Georg Neumark in the winter of 1640-41, but not published until some years later in the *G. Neumarks . . . Fortgepflantzter Musikalisch-Poetischer Lustwald* (Jena, 1657). The seven stanzas appeared after the heading: "A Song of Comfort. That God, in his own time, will care for and preserve His own. After the verse: 'Cast thy burden on the Lord, and he shall sustain thee' [Ps. 55:22]."

Catherine Winkworth translated the hymn and published it in her *Lyra Germanica* (London, 1855), in a different metre than Neumark's original. The consequence was that the translation could not be sung to Neumark's beautiful melody. Thus for *The Chorale Book for England* (London, 1863), Miss Winkworth made a basically new translation, although some of the phrases were taken over from her earlier version.

The Hymnal 1982 employs, slightly revised, Miss Winkworth's translation of Neumark's first and last stanzas as they appear in *The Methodist Hymnal* (Nashville, 1964, 1966):

1. Wer nur den lieben Gott lässt walten
   und hoffet auf ihn allezeit,
den wird er wunderbar erhalten
   in aller Not und Traurigkeit.
Wer Gott, dem Allerhöchsten, traut,
   der hat auf keinen Sand gebaut.

7. Sing, bet und geh auf Gottes Wegen,
   verricht das Deine nur getreu
und trau des Himmels reichem Segen,
   so wird er bei dir werden neu.
Denn welcher seine Zuversicht
   auf Gott setzt, den verläßt er nicht.

The hymn, in the Winkworth translation, has had extensive use, especially in American Lutheranism from the last quarter of the nineteenth century.

Music: Both text and tune of WER NUR DEN LIEBEN GOTT (*Zahn* 2778) were written by Georg Neumark and were included in his *Fortgepflanzter Musikalisch-Poetischer Lustwald* (Jena, 1657) (see above). It is probably Neumark's finest hymn. The tune, also known as NEU-

MARK, is used by Johann Sebastian Bach in eight cantatas (21, 27, 84, 88, 93, 166, 179, and 197) and in several organ chorales. The harmonization from *MHSS* is that of the *Pilgrim Hymnal* (Boston, 1958), edited by Ethel and Hugh Porter. *The Pilgrim Hymnal* does not identify the source of the harmonization.

RAL/CS

636 How firm a foundation, ye saints of the Lord

Music: **FOUNDATION**

The matching of this text and this American folk hymn tune can be traced to their appearance in Joseph Funk's *Genuine Church Music* (Winchester, VA, 1832). For use with this text in a hymnal of the Episcopal Church, the tune was first included in *Hymnal Supplement II* (New York, 1976).

Words: This hymn made its first appearance in the second edition of *A Selection of Hymns from the Best Authors, Intended as an Appendix to Dr. Watts's Psalms and Hymns* (London, 1787), edited by John Rippon. Rippon's *Selection* was extremely popular on both sides of the Atlantic; early U.S. imprints include Elizabethtown (1792), New York (1792), Brooklyn (1803), and Baltimore (1804). The hymn entered the *Hymnal* of the Episcopal Church in 1826. In the 1787 London edition of *Selections* the hymn was in seven stanzas, carried the title "Exceeding great and precious Promises. 2 Pet.3:4," and was signed "K." Various suggestions have been made regarding the identity of the author (*Julian*, 537). The most likely appears to be Richard Keen, the precentor of the Baptist congregation in London where Rippon was minister.

The *Hymnal* version employs sts. 1, 3 through 5, and 7 of the original, with some slight modifications. The omitted stanzas are:

2. In every condition, in sickness, in health,
In poverty's vale, or abounding in wealth;
At home and abroad, on the land, on the sea,
As thy days may demand, shall thy strength ever be!

6. Even down to old age, all my people shall prove
My sovereign, eternal unchangeable love,
And when hoary hairs shall their temples adorn,
Like lambs they shall still in my bosom be borne.

Music: This pentatonic tune, "perhaps the most widely sung of any of the American folk-hymns,"[1] was apparently first printed in a four-shape shape-note tunebook, *Genuine Church Music* (Winchester, VA, 1832), compiled by Joseph Funk.[2] There it was titled PROTECTION and associated with the text "How firm a foundation, ye saints of the Lord" (see Example 1 on following page):

This version was reproduced in several other books, including the Mennonite *Brethren's Tune and Hymn Book* (Dade City, PA, 1872).

The next arrangement of this tune to appear seems to have been in Amos Sutton Hayden's *Introduction to Sacred Music* (Pittsburgh, 1835), where the tune was called HUGER and linked with "Behold how the prophets and martyrs of old, Were called to wander through tempest and cold!" This version also appeared in Hayden's later *Sacred Melodeon* (Boston, 1849) and in Martin D. Wenger's *The Philharmonia* (Elkhart, IN, 1875).

The next version was apparently that in William Caldwell's *Union Harmony* (Boston, 1837), where it is titled PROTECTION and printed with "Hom [sic] firm a foundation, ye saints of the Lord." This version, with or without the counter part, was printed in several other shape-note books under the title PROTECTION or the title THE CHRISTIAN'S FAREWELL. It is printed with the melody in the treble and an "Alto by C. H. C." in a book still used among Primitive Baptists, C. H. Cayce's *The Good Old Songs* (Thornton, AK, 1913).

An arrangement credited to Z. Chambless was published under the title BELLEVUE in several books, beginning with B. F. White and E. J. King's *Sacred Harp* (Philadelphia, 1844).

Still another version was apparently first printed in the Southern Methodist *The Wesleyan Hymn and Tune Book* (Nashville, 1859), which was edited by L. C. Everett. This arrangement was printed in several other books, including a book still in use among Primitive Baptists, John R. and J. Harvey Daily's *Primitive Baptist Hymn and Tune Book* (Indianapolis, 1902). It is this arrangement that is used in several other current hymnals, including the Roman Catholic *Hymnal for the Hours* (Chicago, 1989), *The United Methodist Hymnal* (Nash-

Example 1

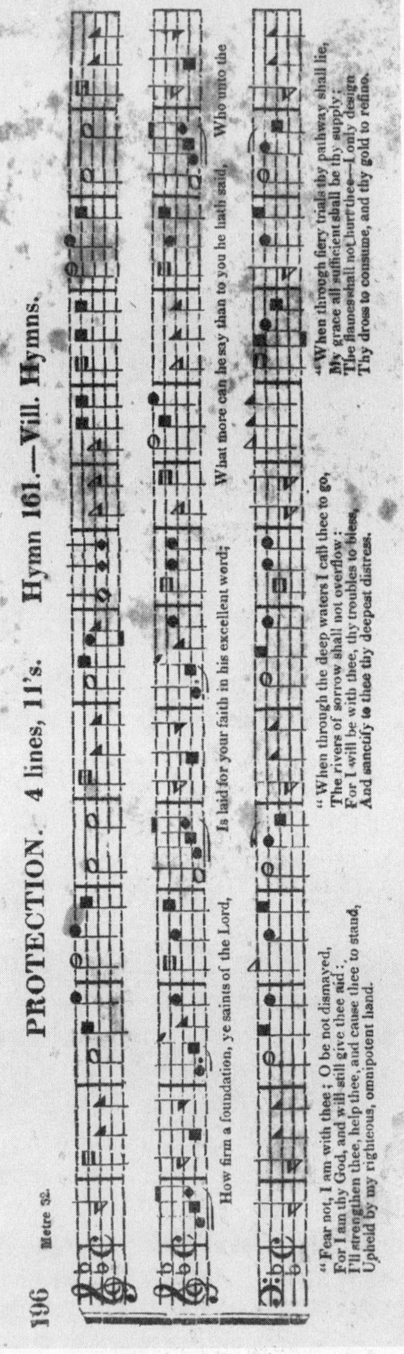

Reproduced from *Genuine Church Music* (Winchester, Va, 1832), Special Collections, University of Tennessee Libraries.

ville, 1989), *The Presbyterian Hymnal* (Louisville, KY, 1990) and *The Baptist Hymnal* (Nashville, 1991).

A version titled HOW FIRM A FOUNDATION was printed in *The Christian Hymnal* (Cincinnati, 1871), and another, titled PROTECTION, in the Southern Presbyterian *Book of Hymns and Tunes* (Richmond, VA, 1874).

Though the text normally associated with this tune has been in the hymnal since the enlargement of the "Prayer Book Collection" (New York) in 1826, this tune was first included in an Episcopal hymnal in *Hymnal Supplement II* (New York, 1976), with a harmonization by Alastair Cassels-Brown. In *H82* two accompaniments are included, one by Calvin Hampton and an alternative setting by Eugene W. Hancock, both composed for use in this collection. Guitar chords are provided.

---

1. See G. P. Jackson, *Down-East Spirituals and Others* (New York, 1939), 155.
2. See. J. W. Wayland, "Joseph Funk: Father of Song of Northern Virginia," *The Pennsylvania-German*, XII (October, 1911), 580-594.

RAL/MH

637 How firm a foundation, ye saints of the Lord

Music: **LYONS**

The editor of the *Hymnal 1940 Companion*, in writing about this setting, pointed out that this "is a hymn which has been a favorite for over a century and a half, and still lacks its own distinctive tune, having been sung to different tunes in each edition of the *Hymnal*." LYONS is the tune with which this text appeared in *H40*.

Words: See hymn 636.

Music: See hymn 533.

638 Come, O thou Traveler unknown

Music: **VERNON**

Two of the undisputed great writers of English hymns are Isaac Watts and Charles Wesley, and the increase in the number of their hymns in *H82* and other contemporary English-language hymnals reflects the restoration of the works of both of these men to their rightful place of honor. This text of Charles Wesley is recognized as among his finest verse.

Words: Charles Wesley's "Wrestling Jacob," based on Gen. 32:24-32, was published as 14 six-line stanzas in John and Charles Wesley's *Hymns and Sacred Poems* (Bristol, 1742) (*Poetical Works*, vol. II, 173-176). Apart from sts. 5 and 7, it figured as no. 136 in John Wesley's *Collection of Hymns for the Use of the People Called Methodists* (London, 1780).

Present in *HA&M* since 1904, "Wrestling Jacob" made its first appearance in the *Hymnal* in 1916, was dropped in 1940, and now returns. The present form consists of sts. 1, 2, 6, and 7 of the original, with the penultimate line borrowed from st. 11 to replace the now unacceptable "To me, to all, Thy bowels move."

Wesley's christological interpretation of the story is even clearer in several lines from the omitted stanzas:

3:3 Art Thou the Man that died for me?
11:1,2 I know Thee, Saviour, who Thou art,
Jesus, the feeble Sinner's Friend . . .

For the "name written on the hands," compare Is. 49:16; for "strength in weakness," 2 Cor. 12:10.

Among the occasions Charles Wesley's *Journal* record him as having preached on the scripture passage are May 24, 1741; July 16, 1741; October 6, 1743; June 12, 1744; February 7, March 7, May 20, 1748; January 29, 1749.

According to John Wesley's obituary tribute to his brother at the Methodist Conference of 1788, "Dr. Watts did not scruple to say that that single poem, 'Wrestling Jacob,' was worth all the verses he himself had written."

Music: One of the first books in which folk songs from the American oral tradition were recorded was *Christian Harmony; or, Songster's Companion* (Exeter, NH, 1805), compiled by Jeremiah Ingalls, a cooper, farmer, tavern-keeper, and singing and school teacher of Newbury, VT.[1] (A songster was a book of hymn texts without music.) Ingalls's book contained two tunes very similar to that which would later be known as VERNON. A four-part version titled FAREWELL HYMN was linked with the text "Give ear to me ye sons of men" (see Example 1 on following page):

The other, in three parts, was titled WISDOM and printed with the text "Now in a song of grateful praise" (see Example 2 on page 1169):

Neither was picked up by later books, but a variant titled VERNON and normally attributed to "Chapin" (probably Lucius Chapin [1760-1842])[2] was included in a great many books from as early as 1813. *Wyeth's Repository of Sacred Music: Part Second* (Harrisburg, PA, 1813) claimed to be the first to publish VERNON, but this hexatonic tune had come into print earlier the same year in a book compiled by Robert Patterson, *Patterson's Church Music* (Pittsburgh, 1813). The arrangement must have been in circulation in manuscript. In both books the tune was linked with the text "Lord, what a heav'n of saving grace." This version of the tune, with or without the counter part, was printed with this text in several books.

Charles Wesley's text "Come, O! thou traveller unknown" was first linked with this version of VERNON in the first edition of Samuel L. Metcalf's *Kentucky Harmonist* (Cincinnati, 1818) (see Example 3 on page 1170):[3]

The tune was printed with this text in well over a dozen later books. In Andrew W. Johnson's *Western Psalmodist* (Nashville, 1853) it was called TRAVELLER. This version of the tune, with the melody in the treble, is included in a book still used among Primitive Baptists, John R. and J. Harvey Daily's *Primitive Baptist Hymn and Tune Book* (Indianapolis, 1902), where it is attributed to Ingalls.

Other arrangements of the tune or variant forms of the melody line were included in other tunebooks. The tune became so closely associated with Wesley's text that in some books it is titled WRESTLING JACOB.

This tune, in a new arrangement by members of the Hymn Music

Example 1

Reproduced from Ingalls's *Christian Harmony* (Exeter, NH, 1805), Brown University Library.

Example 2

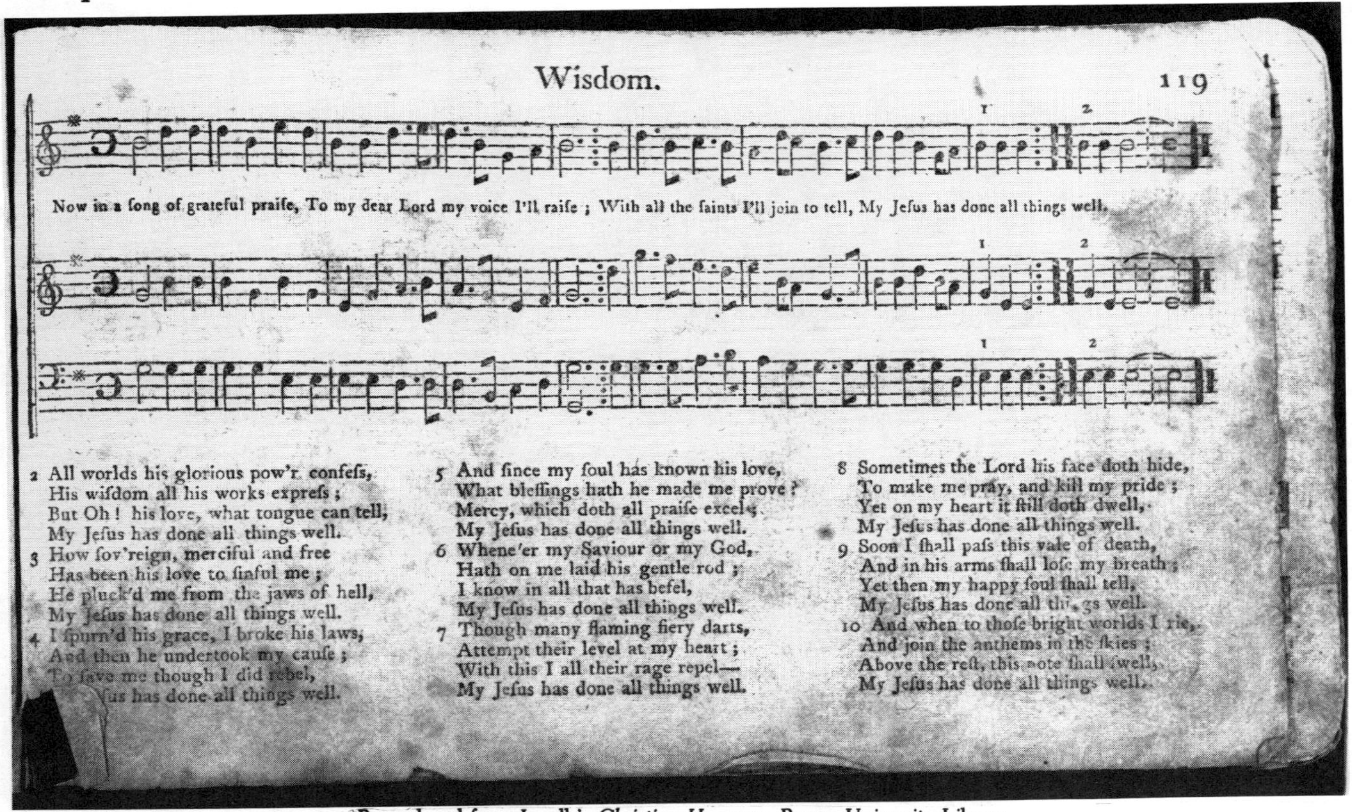

Wisdom.

119

Now in a ſong of grateful praiſe, To my dear Lord my voice I'll raiſe ; With all the ſaints I'll join to tell, My Jeſus has done all things well.

2 All worlds his glorious pow'r confeſs,
His wiſdom all his works expreſs ;
But Oh ! his love, what tongue can tell;
My Jeſus has done all things well.
3 How ſov'reign, merciful and free
Has been his love to ſinful me ;
He pluck'd me from the jaws of hell,
My Jeſus has done all things well.
4 I ſpurn'd his grace, I broke his laws,
And then he undertook my cauſe ;
To ſave me though I did rebel,
ſus has done all things well.

5 And ſince my ſoul has known his love,
What bleſſings hath he made me prove ?
Mercy, which doth all praiſe excel ;
My Jeſus has done all things well.
6 Whene'er my Saviour or my God,
Hath on me laid his gentle rod ;
I know in all that has befel,
My Jeſus has done all things well.
7 Though many flaming fiery darts,
Attempt their level at my heart ;
With this I all their rage repel—
My Jeſus has done all things well.

8 Sometimes the Lord his face doth hide,
To make me pray, and kill my pride ;
Yet on my heart it ſtill doth dwell,
My Jeſus has done all things well.
9 Soon I ſhall paſs this vale of death,
And in his arms ſhall loſe my breath ;
Yet then my happy ſoul ſhall tell,
My Jeſus has done all things well.
10 And when to thoſe bright worlds I riſe,
And join the anthems in the ſkies ;
Above the reſt, this note ſhall ſwell,
My Jeſus has done all things well.

Reproduced from Ingalls's *Christian Harmony*, Brown University Library.

Example 3

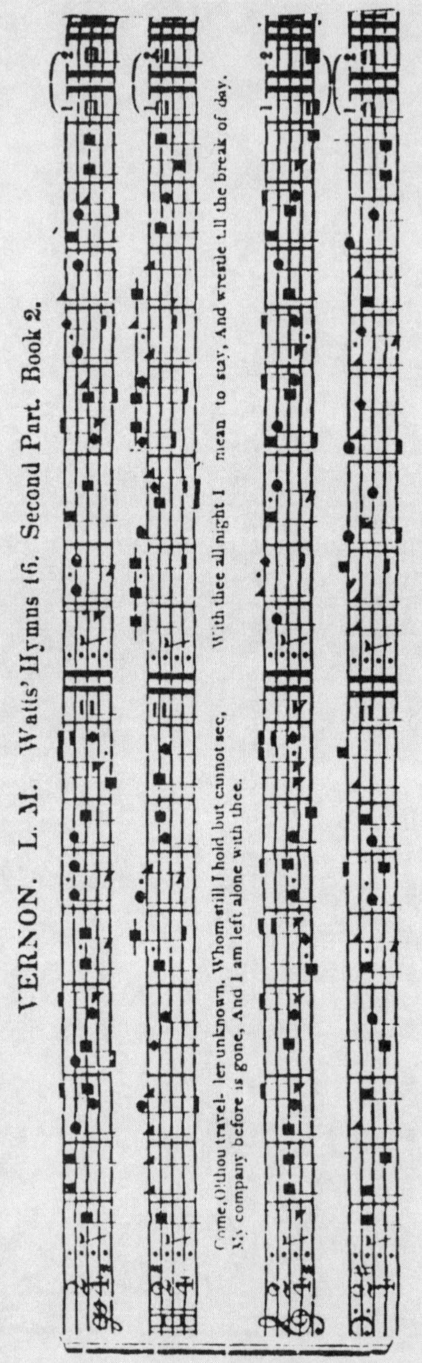
VERNON. L. M. Watts' Hymns 16. Second Part. Book 2.
Come, O thou travel- ler unknown, Whom still I hold but cannot see, With thee all night I mean to stay, And wrestle till the break of day.
My company before is gone, And I am left alone with thee.

Reproduced from *Kentucky Harmonist* (Cincinnati, 1818), Bowdoin College Library.

Committee of the SCCM, is included in an Episcopal hymnal for the first time in *H82*. Guitar chords are provided.

---

1. See J. Ingalls, *The Christian Harmony; or, Songster's Companion*, with new introduction by David Klocko (New York, 1981).

2. See "The Chapins: A Study of Men and Sacred Music West of the Alleghenies, 1795-1842," Unpublished Doctor of Ed. Diss., University of Michigan, 1972; C. Hamm, "The Chapins and Sacred Music in the South and West," *Journal of Research in Music Education* (Fall, 1960), 91-98.

3. See M. J. Hatchett, "Samuel L. Metcalf's *Kentucky Harmonist*," *The Hymn* 43 (April, 1992), 9-14.

GW/MH

639 Come, O thou Traveler unknown

***Music:* WOODBURY**

In several of his books, the composer of this tune, Erik Routley, has made eloquent and moving statements expressing his feelings about this Charles Wesley text. For example, in *A Panorama of Christian Hymnody* (Collegeville, MN, 1979), 25, he states, "[t]he majestic 'Come, O thou Traveller' is . . . a meditation on a mystery. In its full length it is moving though hardly singable; yet in its four-stanza form found in hymnals . . . it becomes an utterance of perfect clarity and trenchant communicativeness." It is only fitting that in *H82*, this text should be matched with WOODBURY, a tune that Dr. Routley wrote for use with it.

Words: See hymn 638.

Music: Erik Routley described this tune as one of his "American indiscretions," composed at a week-long conference of the Fellowship of Methodist Musicians, as it was then called, in Sioux City, Iowa, in the summer of 1969. He explained further: "I usually tell those who want to know about WOODBURY . . . that it was written at a time of deep personal suffering. This was associated with the damp heat, the lack of air-conditioning, and the stench of the meat-packing station which was wafted across the campus . . . "[1] Charles Wesley's magnificent "Wrestling Jacob" text had made a deep and lasting impression on Routley. In the immediate pre-World War II years of the late 1930s, when he began writing hymn tunes, Routley had made an attempt to compose an appropriate tune for the Wesley text. This earlier tune was never published and when planning the retrospective collection of his tunes, eventually published as *Our Lives Be Praise*, Routley felt that this earlier attempt could only be suppressed.

On the more direct background of this tune Routley wrote:

> I had always had the ambition to set the "Traveller" hymn [of Charles Wesley] . . . not that there are no tunes, or good ones, for this incomparable text, but that whoever sets it won't get all the juice out of it. Why—how many tunes do I know to it? Two by S. S. Wesley, DAVID'S HARP in the *English Hymnal* (beautiful), the original VATER UNSER [575], modern ones by Eric Thiman and Cyril Taylor and Francis Westbrook, and the one that first got me hooked on the hymn, Brent Smith's COTSWOLD (*Congregational Praise* no. 496). Well this one is unlike anything else I ever attempted—I don't usually give harmony so prominent a place as I do here.[2]

The tune appears in *H82* transposed down half a step to g. It comprises three melodic phrases, the first two being directly related, producing a basic AA^1B form.

WOODBURY was first published in Routley's collection of his own hymns, entitled *Eternal Light* (New York, 1971). Thereafter it appeared in the supplementary collections *Genesis Song Book* (Carol Stream, IL, 1973), and *Ecumenical Praise* (Carol Stream, IL, 1977). The first full-scale hymnal to include WOODBURY was *Rejoice in the Lord* (Grand Rapids, 1985), which was edited by Routley.

---

1. *Our Lives Be Praise: The Hymn Tunes, Carols and Texts of Erik Routley* (Carol Stream, 1990), xxiii.
2. Ibid.

RAL

640 Watchman, tell us of the night

Music: **ABERYSTWYTH**
This wedding of text and tune first appeared in *H40*. It has been so well accepted that it has been continued in the *Pilgrim Hymnal* (Boston, 1958), *The Hymnal of the United Church of Christ* (Philadelphia, 1974), the two most recent hymnals of the Presbyterian Church, *The Worshipbook* (Philadelphia, 1970) and *The Presbyterian Hymnal* (Louisville, KY, 1990), as well as *H82*.

Words: This text by John Bowring first appeared in his *Hymns* (London, 1825). The dialogue form of the hymn, reflective of the dialogue found in Is. 21: 11-12, captures a conversation between a traveler and watchman and is filled with imagery suggestive of the oriental cities with which its author was familiar. *The Hymnal 1940 Companion* suggests that the hymn "may be sung antiphonally to good effect." It has been in the *Hymnal* since 1871.

Music: See hymn 349.

TS

641 Lord Jesus, think on me

Music: **SOUTHWELL**
Interwoven in the score of Benjamin Britten's charming church opera *Noye's Fludde* are three hymns, of which this text by Synesius of Cyrene matched with SOUTHWELL is one. First paired in *EH* and given expanded currency in the Britten work, this matching is continued in *H82*.

Words: This is the tenth hymn of Synesius of Cyrene, written in the early years of the fifth century. It is an epilogue to his first nine hymns, asking, "Remember, Lord, your servant who composed these hymns." The translation, by Allen William Chatfield, which has been in the *Hymnal* since 1892, was first published in his *Songs and Hymns of Earliest Greek Christian Poets* (London, 1876). He described it as "a paraphrase or amplification rather than an exact translation of the original." Although in its first form there were five stanzas, Chatfield subsequently added four new ones, making nine stanzas in all. The four included in *H82* are the first four of the original, but 2, 3, 5, and 7 of the expanded version.

Music: This plaintive tune is unique among the early English psalm tune repertory in having a distinctive feature or motive—the repeated note—that pervades the whole melody. Its origin is unknown, but its earliest printed appearances are in two books of harmonized tunes intended for domestic use; as Ps. 45 in William Daman's *The Psalmes of David in English Metre* (London, 1579) and as Ps. 134 in John Cosyn's *Musike of Six, and Five Partes* (London, 1585). Daman's setting, with G as the final, has the tune in the tenor of a four-voice arrangement.[1] This strongly Dorian harmonization has been adapted here. Cosyn provided a six-voice setting (Example 1: melody in the tenor) much more modern in its effect, suggesting a modulation to the relative major and back.

Example 1

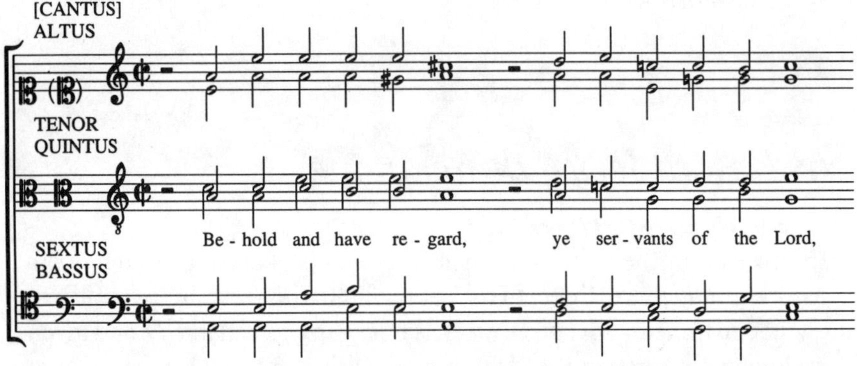
[CANTUS]
ALTUS
TENOR
QUINTUS
Be - hold and have re - gard, ye ser - vants of the Lord,
SEXTUS
BASSUS

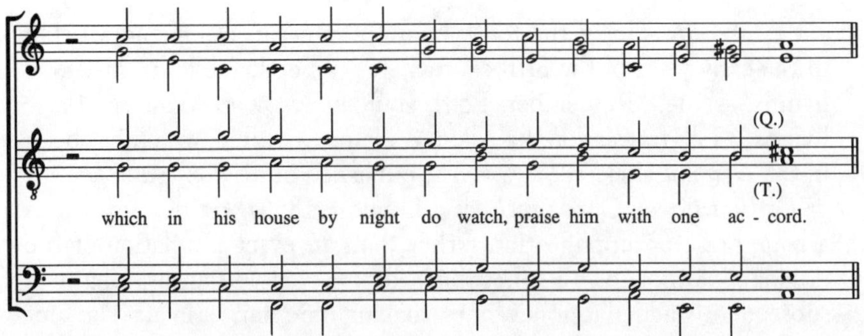
(Q.)
(T.)
which in his house by night do watch, praise him with one ac - cord.

Later, Thomas Ravenscroft printed a four-voice harmonization by Martin Peerson in *the Whole Booke of Psalmes . . . Composed into 4. Parts* (London, 1621), which, like Daman's, has a cadence on the subdominant major at the end of the third phrase. Maurice Frost, author of *English and Scottish Psalm & Hymn Tunes* (London, 1953) (see footnote 1), did not realize that the tune did appear in a few editions of the common psalm book, beginning in 1588. It never achieved, however, the same degree of popularity as many of its contemporaries.

The name was supplied by Ravenscroft, who comprehensively (but randomly, it would seem) spread the names of the endowed English choral foundations around the tunes in his books.[2] Thus it refers to Southwell Minster, the cathedral for the county of Nottinghamshire, and should, strictly speaking, be pronounced "suth-'ll," the first syllable as in "southern."

SOUTHWELL appeared in *HA&M* and other nineteenth-century hymnals with Wesley's hymn "Thou judge of quick and dead" in f, with the note-lengths evened out and with a harmonization that greatly emphasized the pathetic or penitential character of the tune. It was brought to the United States as PIERSON by George K. Jackson, organist of St. George's Episcopal Chapel, New York, in *David's Psalms* (New York, 1804). John Cole, who, like Jackson, was born and trained in England, called the tune ST. ALBAN'S in the second edition of *The Divine Harmonist* (Baltimore, 1808). The tune has enjoyed a checkered career in hymnals of the Episcopal Church. It appeared in J. Ireland Tucker's *The Hymnal With Tunes Old and New* (New York, 1874). A tune with the same name by Herbert S. Irons is included in *H16* and *H40*. The tune as in *H82* was included in the second supplement to *H40*.

---

1. For a transcription of the tune, see M. Frost, *English and Scottish Psalm & Hymn Tunes* (London, 1953), 65.

2. For further discussion of this point, see N. Temperley, *The Music of the English Parish Church* (Cambridge, 1979), 73.

JHR/NT

642 Jesus, the very thought of thee

Music: **WINDSOR**

This devotional and deeply personal hymn expressing the love of God in the person of his son, Jesus Christ, first entered the *Hymnal* in 1865. Matched with WINDSOR, a psalm tune of particular poignancy, it affords worshipers opportunity to give voice to their own deep personal experience and understanding of a loving, forgiving God.

Words: (The following Latin original is the source of the text at 642 and 649. The numbers in the left column indicate their usage.)

642:1 Dulcis Jesu memoria,
dans vera cordi gaudia,
sed super mel et omnia.
Eius dulcis præsentia.

642:2 Nil canitur suavius,
auditur nil jocundius,
nil cogitatur dulcius
quam Jesus dei filius.

642:3 Jesu spes penitentibus,
quam pius es petentibus,
quam bonus te querentibus
sed quid invenientibus?

649:1 Jesus, dulcedo cordium,
fons veri, lumen mentium,
excedit omne gaudium
et omne desiderium.

642:4 Nec lingua potest dicere
nec littera exprimere,
expertus novit tenere,
quid sit Jesum diligere.

649:4 mane nobiscum, domine,
mane novum cum lumine,
pulsa noctis caligine,
mundum replens dulcedine.

649:2 Qui te gustant esuriunt,
qui bibunt adhuc sitiunt;

desiderare nesciunt,
nisi Jesum quem sentiunt.

649:3 Quocumque loco fuero,
meum Jesum desidero,
quam lætus cum invenero,
quam felix cum tenuero.

The origin of "Dulcis Jesu memoria" is uncertain. Wilmart has disproved the traditional ascription to St. Bernard of Clairvaux (1091-1153), which was first made toward the end of the thirteenth century, by showing that the earliest manuscript containing the poem dates from the turn of the twelfth century, when Bernard was a small child.[1] The statement of Adey that the hymn is an excerpt from *De contemptu mundi* by Bernard of Cluny (also called Bernard of Morlas) is in error: it is not found in that work or in any of his extant works.[2] The earliest and best manuscripts are from England, indicating a probable English origin.

Most early manuscripts do not indicate a particular use for the poem, but one thirteenth-century Augustinian missal places it among the prayers of preparation for communion.[3] Several manuscripts label the poem a devotion on the name of Jesus, and indeed it eventually did become associated with the Feast of the Name of Jesus, which was first observed around 1500. Lausberg proposes a different use for the poem, suggesting that it was originally intended for use during the Easter season, especially on the Ascension, basing his supposition on the presence of stanzas dealing with those themes.[4] He attributes the lack of historical evidence to support his theory to a very early misunderstanding of the text, claiming that its correct use was known only to the poet and the earliest users.[5] Needless to say, Lausberg's theory is difficult to accept without external evidence, and the presence of a few references within the poem does not indicate an intended use, but merely a possible one. The real question is whether the poem was used as a private or a corporate devotion: all the evidence points strongly to the former, including headings in the manuscripts, the subjectivity of the text, its length, and the use of the first person throughout most of the poem.

There are a great number of variations of this text appearing in the manuscripts, including many with additional stanzas, many with the first two words reversed ("Jesu dulcis") and many centos*. Among the centos are three appearing in the traditional Roman breviary for the Name of Jesus: "Jesu dulcis memoria" (Vespers), "Jesu rex admirabilis" (Matins) and "Jesu decus angelicum" (Lauds); there is in addition a corrupted cento beginning "Lux alma Jesu mentium" (originally "Amor Jesu dulcissime") appointed for Lauds on the Transfiguration. In the current Roman use "Dulcis Jesu memoria" is appointed for that occasion.

Hymn 642 is a translation by Edward Caswall of the breviary cento "Jesu dulcis memoria." It first appeared in his *Lyra Catholica* (London, 1849) and has been slightly altered. The final stanza is a doxology added to the original; this doxology is associated in the manuscripts with more than one hymn. In the Roman breviary it reads:

Sis Jesu nostrum gaudium
qui es futurus praemium;
sit nostra in te gloria
per cuncta semper saecula.

For another cento from the same poem, see hymn 649.

---

1. See A. Wilmart, *Le "Jubilus" dit de Saint Bernard* (Rome, 1944), 50 and 60.
2. See L. Adey, *Hymns and the Christian "Myth"*, (Vancouver, BC, 1986), 71-72.
3. See Wilmart, *Le "Jubilus" dit de Saint Bernard*, 57.
4. See H. Lausberg, *Der Hymnus "Jesu dulcis memoria"* (Munich, 1967), 1, 40-42.
5. See Lausberg, *Der Hymnus "Jesu dulcis memoria"*, 41.

Music: WINDSOR is one of the short tunes which, in the early seventeenth century, rapidly supplanted the more stately eight-line tunes that had been printed in the Elizabethan psalm book. In later years it vied in popularity with OLD 100TH itself, appearing in more than seven hundred publications between 1591 and 1820.

It made its first appearance in the twin compilations that "W. Swayne Gent." issued in the year 1591, *The Former Booke of the Musicke of M. William Damon . . . in which Sett the Tenor Singeth the Church Tune* and *The Second Booke of the Musicke of M. William Damon.. in which Sett the Highest Part Singeth the Church Tune* (London, 1591). Each collection is in the form of four part books. Damon, one of the queen's musicians, had died before these books appeared, and there is some doubt as to whether he was really responsible for all the settings. He certainly did not write all the tunes, most of which were already in the English psalm books before he arrived in England in the 1560's. Thus, although WINDSOR was new in 1591, there is no good reason to suppose that Damon was the author of the melody.

It is one of those "minimalist" tunes forged from cells common to the music of the day, perhaps crafted by several hands, as anonymous as a table or a woven cloth. Many have pointed out its affinity with Christopher Tye's music for chapter 3 of *The Actes of the Apostles* (London, 1553). The Tye piece is scarcely a "tune," and the resemblance is one of general style and character, not of musical idea.[1] As a melody, WINDSOR bears quite as much resemblance to a secular song of the time, "How should I your true love know?" from William Chappell's *The Ballad Literature and Popular Music of the Olden Time* (London, 1855-59), pp. 56, 236, especially when considered in conjunction with COLESHILL (see Example 1).[2]

Example 1

Despite the contrasting title of the two Damon books, both contained the same setting of this tune, with the cantus part carrying the melody, and the lower parts providing points of imitation for each phrase. The last line differs from its modern form, and is extended by repetition of the last four syllables on the tonic.[3] The text is Ps. 116 in Thomas Norton's version, "I love the Lord, because my voice And prayer heard hath he."

The following year it appeared with the same text in Thomas East's *Whole Booke of Psalmes; With Their Wonted Tunes* (London, 1592), in a plain four-part setting by George Kirbye. This setting is exactly reproduced in the *Hymnal*, except for the halving of note-lengths, the inversion of the harmonies by trading tenor and cantus parts, the omission of a quarter rest before the second phrase, and the alteration of one note (the ninth tenor note, now B^{b}, was originally F).[4] From 1602 onward it began to be found in some editions of the common psalm books, still with Ps. 116. Henry Ainsworth used it with Ps. 15 in his *Book of Psalmes* (Amsterdam, 1612), which may have made its way to America with the Pilgrims. In 1615 it made its first appearance in the *Scottish Psalm Book*, as one of the twelve Common Tunes, that enshrined it in the Presbyterian canon for the next two centuries and more.

East called the tune SUFFOLK, while the Scottish name was DUNDIE. It was only when Thomas Ravenscroft used it for four texts in his *Psalmes* that it at last acquired the name WINDSOR or EATON. It was Ravenscroft who initiated the custom of naming tunes after choral foundations, and in this case he combined two that were scarcely a mile apart; the royal peculiar of St. George's Chapel, Windsor Castle, and the boy's school founded by Henry VI, Eton College, which also maintained daily choral services in its chapel. By the time John Playford printed the tune, its name had been shortened to WINDSOR alone.

It would be a monotonous task to record the subsequent history of this ubiquitous tune, but a few landmarks may be of interest. It is the only tune that survives in two seventeenth-century English organ settings; one of them, by Thomas Tomkins (from *Musica Deo Sacra*, 1668) is reproduced in Example 2.

Example 2

It duly appeared in the first American musical publication, the tune supplement to the ninth edition of the *Bay Psalm Book* (Boston, 1698). Meanwhile, it had given birth to an offshoot, the tune later known as

COLESHILL, which clearly had its origin as an improvised partial bass to WINDSOR.[5]

An excessively ornate version (Example 3) published by Michael Broome in *A Choice Collection of Sixteen Excellent Psalm Tunes* (Birmingham, 1733) is possibly the outcome of decades of modification by the "Old Way of Singing."[6] William Tans'ur seemed to claim the tune as his own in his publications from 1744 onward and, amazingly enough, some of the more gullible compilers accepted his claim, so that it began to appear quite frequently with an attribution to Tans'ur.

Example 3

In 1794, William Tattersall, in *Improved Psalmody*, produced a long-metre adaptation that hardly "improved" the tune.

The Protestant Episcopal Church of the United States was introduced to WINDSOR from the start, in the form of its offshoot, COLESHILL, which was one of the tunes annexed to the Proposed BCP. It is found in the *Hymnal* from 1916 onward.

---

1. The two settings may be compared in M. Frost, *English & Scottish Psalm & Hymn Tunes c. 1543-1677* (London, 1953), nos. 129 and 297; a different transcription of Tye's is in *Frost*, 320.
2. W. Chappell, *The Ballad Literature and Popular Music of the Olden Time* (London, 1855-1859), 56, 236.
3. *Frost*, 129.
4. For original form, see *Frost*, 320.
5. E. Routley, *The Music of Christian Hymns* (Chicago, 1981), Example 124. Routley did not know that they are also found together in a published seventeenth-century source: see *Journal of the American Musicological Society* 34 (1981), 531. For a general discussion of the phenomenon of "harmonic derivation" of hymn tunes, see N. Temperley, *The Music of the English Parish Church* (London, 1979), I, 73-5.
6. See N. Temperley, *The Music of the English Parish Church*, 70-73.

JH/NT

643 My God, how wonderful thou art

Music: **WINDSOR**

Quiet meditation on the nature of God and personal response of deep adoration and praise are the two themes of this text by a nineteenth-century poet. Matched with the psalm tune WINDSOR, it is a fitting companion to "Jesus, the very thought of thee" [642], a similar personal response of an anonymous poet to the love of God.

Words: "My God, how wonderful thou art" is the first five of the nine-stanza text entitled "Our Heavenly Father" that Frederick William Faber first published in *Jesus and Mary: Or Catholic Hymns* (London, 1849); in his *Hymns* (London, 1861), which he arranged by topics in the order he had found useful in teaching the Catholic faith to converts, it appears in the opening section. Faber felt bound to temper the zeal of persons who perceived that they had always to be *doing* something. He reminds them that their goal is simply to experience God and to "enjoy Him for ever." *The Hymnal 1940* is one of very few collections that end the hymn at the point at which the poet has a chance to explain how and why "my poor heart" is to be transformed:

O then this worse than worthless heart
  In pity deign to take,
And make it love thee, for thyself
  And for thy glory's sake.

No earthly father loves like thee,
  No mother half so mild
Bears and forbears, as thou hast done
  With me, thy sinful child.

Only to sit and think of God,
  O what a joy it is!
To think the thought, to breathe the name,
  Earth has no higher bliss!

Father of Jesus, love's reward!
  What rapture will it be
Prostrate before thy throne to lie,
  And gaze—and gaze on thee!

Music: See hymn 642.

HMcK

644 How sweet the Name of Jesus sounds

Music: **ST. PETER**

It is significant that in *H82* this text by a great late-eighteenth-century evangelical poet should be found alongside texts that are also deep personal expressions of love of God—one by an anonymous medieval poet and the other by a nineteenth-century Roman Catholic poet who had converted from Anglicanism. This text has been matched with the tune ST. PETER since the J. Ireland Tucker edition of the 1871 edition of the *Hymnal*.

Words: This well-loved hymn by John Newton has been in the mainstream of English hymnody for more than two hundred years. It first appeared in the first book of Newton's *Olney Hymns* (London, 1779) under the title: "The name of Jesus." In the first book of *Olney Hymns*, the hymns are arranged in a Biblical sequence. "How sweet the Name of Jesus sounds" appears as an exposition of Song of Solomon 1:3: "Thy name is as an ointment poured forth." When, in his hymn, Newton speaks of "Jesus! my Shepherd, *Husband*, Friend," it would appear that he followed St. Bernard in understanding the Bride in the Song of Solomon as the individual soul rather than as an image of the Church. Some have made another link between this hymn and the medieval mystic and observed that Newton's hymn in many ways echoes the Latin hymn "Jesu dulcis memoria" [642], a hymn frequently attributed to St. Bernard.

The line "Jesus! my Shepherd, *Husband*, Friend," which was used in the first appearance of the text in the 1871 *Hymnal*, has always created problems. One solution was to use "Surety" in place of "Husband"; another was "Brother," which has had some currency but now is too exclusive in an inclusive age. The solution, apparently first made in the *Leeds Hymn Book* (Leeds, 1853), of using "Guardian" was introduced into the 1892 edition of the *Hymnal* and continues in *H82*. Also, in the interests of inclusivity, "his" has been changed to "ours."

The Hymnal 1982 includes sts. 1 through 3 and 5 through 6 of the original. The omitted stanzas are:

4. By thee my pray'rs acceptance gain,
   Altho' with sin defil'd;
   Satan accuses me in vain
   And I am own'd a child.

7. 'Till then I would thy love proclaim
   With ev'ry fleeting breath;
   And may the music of thy name
   Refresh my soul in death.

Music: ST. PETER commemorates the Oxford church where the composer Alexander Reinagle played from 1822 to 1856. *Musical Times* (1906), 47, 542-543 reproduces the tune as it first appeared in *Psalm Tunes for Voice and Pianoforte* (Oxford, 1830). The tune appeared again under the name ST. PETER in *Collection of Psalm and Hymn tunes* (Oxford, 1840), and then appeared with the harmony adjusted in the original *HA&M*.

RAL/HMcK

645 The King of love my shepherd is

Music: **ST. COLUMBA**

Among the hymns that are common to the singing tradition of Anglicans around the world, this paraphrase of Ps. 23 is undoubtedly one of the most beloved. It is further distinguished in that it has attracted to itself two tunes that are equally well loved and international in their usage. ST. COLUMBA, an Irish melody of particular beauty, is used here.

Words: Sir Henry Williams Baker's paraphrase of Ps. 23 remains virtually unchanged, maintaining the form in which it first appeared in the Appendix to *HA&M* (1868), the monumental collection for which that author was the energizing force. Following the lead of Luther and Watts, Baker introduces New Testament Christianity into the psalm version: the cup becomes the eucharistic chalice, the cross takes its place with the rod and staff, and the pastoral caretaker assumes the role of the "Good Shepherd" in St. John's gospel (Jn. 10:11-18).

John Ellerton wrote in *Church Hymns* (London, 1874): "It may interest many to know that the third verse ['Perverse and foolish oft I strayed'] of this lovely hymn, perhaps the most beautiful of all the countless versions of Psalm xxiii, was the last audible sentence upon the dying lips of the lamented author. February 12, 1877." This hymn has been in the *Hymnal* since 1871.

Music: ST. COLUMBA is a traditional Irish melody, collected by George Petri around 1855. A starker (CM) form of the melody (A in Example 1, note values halved; note the similarity of the opening line to that of ALLEIN GOTT IN DER HÖH [421]) first appeared as a hymn tune in the *The Church Hymnal* of the Church of Ireland (Dublin, 1874), and was later included in the appendix of the *Scottish Hymnal* (Edinburgh, 1885).

Both the starker and more familiar forms of the tune can be found in *With One Voice* (London, 1978), where the earlier CM form appears with the alternative name ERIN.

Charles Villiers Stanford edited all the music of the Petri collection for the Irish Literary Society's *Complete Collection of Irish Music as noted by George Petri* (London, 1902-05). ST. COLUMBA appears as no. 1043 in a more elaborate form, with the elongation of the final notes of lines 2 and 4 (B in Example 1). In Stanford's edition, it was described as an "Irish hymn sung at the dedication of a chapel—County of Londonderry (Northern Ireland)." A more developed form of the tune appeared in the 1904 edition of *HA&M*. Two years later Ralph Vaughan Williams included ST. COLUMBA in *EH*, where it was associated with "The King of love" for the first time. Vaughan Williams's source was the Petri collection edition, from which he took Stanford's harmonization. There were two small but important changes made in the *EH* version of the melody: the ties at the end of lines 2 and 4 were removed to modify the melody from CM to 87. 87 to accommodate Baker's text, and the melodic figure in measure 6 was given as a triplet (see Example 2, which gives the evolution of measure 6, note values halved).

Example 1

It seems almost certain that these changes were the work of Ralph Vaughan Williams, the musical editor of *EH*.

The harmonization in *H82* is only marginally different from that of Stanford's as it appeared in *EH*. The melody can be sung as a two- or three-part canon, with subsequent voice-parts entering one measure after each other.

Example 2

MS/RAL

646 *The King of love my shepherd is*

Music: **DOMINUS REGIT ME**

The matching of DOMINUS REGIT ME, the tune composed for use with this text in its first appearance in the Appendix to *HA&M* (London, 1868), has been continued in the *Hymnal* since its first appearance in music editions of the 1871 edition.

Words: See hymn 645.

Music: Sir Henry Baker requested that John Bacchus Dykes write this tune for his version of Ps. 23, "The King of love my shepherd is." The name DOMINUS REGIT ME is derived from the incipit of the Latin Vulgate version of the psalm (which continues to be printed with the BCP psalter, page 612). The tune, with Baker's text, appeared for the first time in the Supplement to *HA&M* (1868). There are references in Dykes's diary to his visits to London in February, May, and July 1868 to work with Baker on the *HA&M* Supplement, but they apparently made no mention of the origins of this particular tune.[1] It was presumably a favorite of Dykes's, since the tune with Baker's text was the principal hymn sung at his funeral service on January 28, 1876.

Ralph Vaughan Williams thought sufficiently highly of the tune to wish to include it in *EH*, but was denied permission by the proprietors of *HA&M*, the copyright holders (see the essay "British Hymnody, 1900-1950," vol. 1, 484-485). Erik Routley characterized DOMINUS REGIT ME as exhibiting "gentle unaffectedness . . . which only in the lingering dominant sevenths of the final line makes any concession to sentimentality."[2] The descant was composed by Sir David Willcocks in 1985 for use with this tune in *H82*.

---

1. See J. T. Fowler, *The Life and Letters of John Bacchus Dykes* (London, 1897), 119-121.
2. E. Routley, *The Music of Christian Hymns* (Chicago, 1981), 97.

RAL

647 *I know not where the road will lead*

Music: **LARAMIE**

The text and tune of this hymn were new to congregations in the Episcopal Church when they were introduced in *H40*. Both have close connections to the Church. The author was the wife of an Episcopal priest and the composer who wrote the tune for use with this text was a priest of the Episcopal Church.

Words: "I know not where the road may lead" was written in 1922 by Evelyn Atwater Cummins. She has written:

> I was sick on Sunday and heard Dr. Samuel Parks Cadman preach a sermon called the *King's Highway* over the radio, a very early radio with earphones. The title sort of stuck in my head, and so I thought I would put down what the King's Highway meant to me. I sent it to Dr. Cadman and he read the poem several times over the radio (*H40c*, 269-270).

The text first appeared in an Episcopal hymnal in *H40*. It was not recommended by the SCCM in its report to the General Convention of 1982, but it was restored by the Convention, partly in recognition of its significance to the Diocese of El Camino Real. El Camino Real, which means "The King's Highway," is the name of the road built in Southern California by Spanish conquistadors, after which the Diocese is named.

Music: LARAMIE was composed for the text "I know not where the road will lead" by Arnold George Henry Bode in 1941, while the composer was on vacation in Newport Beach, CA. It is named after Laramie, Wyoming, where the composer served as Dean of St. Matthew's Cathedral from 1904 to 1912. It is a CMD tune in which the first, third, and fourth phrases share a common opening half. LARAMIE first appeared in an Episcopal hymnal in *H40* matched with this text.

TS/MBJ

648 When Israel was in Egypt's Land

Music: **GO DOWN, MOSES**

This spiritual was first included in an Episcopal publication in *Lift Every Voice and Sing* (New York, 1981), a hymnal supplement produced under the aegis of the Office of Black Ministries of the Episcopal Church. The commitment of that Office to publish a hymnal that would reflect the religious musical heritage of African-Americans is continued in *H82*, which contains several spirituals and hymns coming from the rich musical culture of African and African-American Christians.

Words: The words to this spiritual were copied from the singing of contrabands (refugee slaves residing within Union lines at Fortress Monroe and Hampton, Virginia) by the Rev. Lewis C. Lockwood. Lockwood, an employee of the New York Young Men's Christian Association, visited Fortress Monroe on behalf of the American Missionary Association and remained to serve as the Fort Chaplain. He sent the words to Harwood Vernon, secretary of the YMCA who, in turn, sent them to the *National Anti-Slavery Standard*, in which they were published on December 21, 1861. Lockwood did not attempt to preserve the dialect to which the words were more than likely sung, nor did he have a modern editor's respect for the integrity of the text, for he supplied a substantially different version of the twenty stanzas of the spiritual for the sheet music edition.

Recounting the story of the exodus of the Israelites from Egypt (Exodus), the spiritual also includes stanzas directly related to the hopes and aspirations of the slaves. Contained in the spiritual is not only the central idea of liberation from slavery, but the spiritual oppression. Throughout the stanzas, the internal refrain "Let my people go" interrupts the message, thereby serving as a unifying element.

Long regarded for its association with slavery, the spiritual has recently been adopted by other oppressed groups, whereby they replace the word "Pharaoh" with the name of the oppressor.

Music: The sheet music edition of this spiritual was published on December 14, 1861, becoming the first Negro Spiritual to be published with its music. The transcription and arrangement were done by Thomas Baker. Baker, believed to be an Englishman who came to America in 1853, was reputedly a capable violinist. His musical knowledge was little reflected in his arrangement, for he set the stanzas for solo voice and the refrain for mixed chorus, with piano accompaniment for the entire song. The spiritual was placed in 6/8 time, with a weak accent on the first syllable of "Pharaoh," not the quadruple time in which it is now sung, despite the descriptions of nineteenth-century performances which contain no mention of a dancelike metre.

The spiritual was not included in *Slave Songs of the United States* (New York, 1867), but an arrangement, harmonized in quadruple metre, was included in T. F. Seward's *Jubilee Songs as Sung by the Jubilee Singers of Fisk University* (New York and Chicago, 1872). It is the most beloved of the Sorrow Songs, a type of spiritual that is slow and performed with sustained tones and long phrases, in part because the line "Let my people go" is sung to the same haunting melodic fragment throughout the song. R. Nathaniel Dett used this melody in his cantata *The Ordering of Moses* (1937).

HCB

649 O Jesus, joy of loving hearts

Music: **DICKINSON COLLEGE**

This text, which Erik Routley describes "as one of the best known and finest of American hymns,"[1] is further distinguished as having been produced at a time in American history when the translation of ancient Latin hymns was not a common practice. Its author, Ray Palmer, a Congregational minister, is probably best known for his text "My faith looks up to thee." The text is matched here with a tune that appeared in *MHSS*.

---

1. *A Panorama of Christian Hymnody* (Collegeville, MN, 1972), 71.

Words: This hymn is a translation by Ray Palmer of the Roman breviary text "Jesu, rex admirabilis," which in turn is a cento* from the twelfth-century poem "Dulcis Jesu memoria." The translation first appeared in the *Sabbath Hymn Book* (New York, 1858) and has been substantially altered. The original first stanza reads:

Jesus, thou Joy of loving hearts!
  Thou Fount of Life! thou Light of men!
From the best bliss that earth imparts,
  we turn unfilled to thee again.

A second stanza, omitted in the *Hymnal*, reads:

Thy truth unchanged hath ever stood;
  thou savest those that on thee call;
to them that seek thee, thou art good,
  to them that find thee—All in All!

The translation first appeared in the *Hymnal* in 1892. For further information and the original Latin text of the hymn, see hymn 642.

Music: See hymn 593.

JH

650 O Jesus, joy of loving hearts

Music: **JESU DULCIS MEMORIA**

This text appears here with a traditional Latin tune in a form found in the *Liber Usualis*, where it is matched with the Latin text from which this translation is derived.

Words: See hymn 649.

Music: See hymn 18. The accompaniment was composed for use in *H82* by Gerald Farrell, OSB.

651 This is my Father's world

Music: **MERCER STREET**

To a world where ecological concerns are a priority matter, this text speaks with a particular appropriateness. Although usually sung to TERRA BEATA, it is here matched with MERCER STREET, a tune written for use with it by Malcolm Williamson.

Words: The first stanza of this text as it appears in *H82* is from the poem "My Father's World," first published in sixteen four-line stanzas in Maltbie Babcock's *Thoughts for Everyday Living* (New York, 1901) shortly after the author's death. It consists of sts. 2 and 3 of the original. The first hymnal to use this text appears to be Benjamin S. Winchester and Grace Wilbur Conart's *Worship and Song* (Boston, 1913). Although this hymn has been widely published in three eight-line stanzas from Babcock's poem, only the first was selected for *H82*. The two stanzas not included are:

This is my Father's world
  The birds their carols raise,
The morning light, the lily white,
  Declare their Maker's praise.
This is my Father's world:
  He shines in all that's fair;
In the rustling grass I hear him pass,
  He speaks to me everywhere.

This is my Father's world,
  O let me ne'er forget,
That though the wrong seems oft so strong,
  God is ruler yet.
This is my Father's world:
  The battle is not done;
Jesus who died shall be satisfied,
  And earth and heaven be one.

The second stanza used in *H82* was written in 1972 by a niece of Babcock, Mary Babcock Crawford, as an expression of ecological concern. Mrs. Crawford saw an article in her local newspaper concerning a search for new hymns on the environment by the Hymn Society of America. Instead of writing an entirely new hymn, she wrote a stanza to be appended to sts. 1 and 2 of her uncle's hymn. She reported that she wanted her stanza to say in effect, "Yes, this is our Father's world, but we'd jolly well better take care of it." Her stanza was first published in the October 1972 issue of *The Hymn*, the quarterly journal of the Hymn Society of America. The first use of her stanza in a hymnal with Babcock's sts. 1 and 2 was in the second edition of *MHSS* (1977) and in *Ecumenical Praise* (Carol Stream, IL, 1977), where it is matched with MERCER STREET.

Music: MERCER STREET was composed by Malcolm Williamson at the request of Dr. Lee Hastings Bristol for use in the second, expanded edition of *MHSS*, of which Dr. Bristol was the General Editor. Written for use with this text, the tune name MERCER STREET honors Dr. Bristol, whose home in Princeton, New Jersey, was on Mercer Street. The text/tune combination was continued in *Hymns III* and also appears in *Ecumenical Praise* (Carol Stream, 1977). In this setting, the composer combines his skills as a fine tunesmith and as an imaginative creator of harmonically rich accompaniments. The tune's basic melodic unit is the D major triad, but the underlying harmonies are the chords of b and F#, the tonic and dominant chords of the key. At the fourth beat of the measure one should note the wonderful dissonance that occurs between the A natural in the melody and the A# in the bass. In the second and third phrases the composer repeats this pattern expanding the third interval by one step—F# to B and F# to C#. All three phrases close with two descending seconds. The fourth phrase is an extension of this descending line. Melodically, this portion of the tune ends on the subdominant, but the G chord of the accompaniment, the subdominant of the key, immediately moves to a diminished seventh chord on A# leading directly to D. This is another example of the composer's use of a rich harmonic pallet. The second half of this SMD tune repeats the first two phrases of the melody, now harmonized in the key of the relative major (D). The first change appears at the end of the second phrase, which ascends to D. This marks a final resolution of the two repeated C# leading tones, found at the end of the first half of the tune and indicates a skillful, long-range development in this tune. The last two phrases, which include two presentations of the basic melodic unit introduced in the first measure, are a gradual descent to the final cadence with its original harmonization and lead to a harmonically colorful resolution on the chord of B. When sung at the slow tempo suggested by the composer, MERCER STREET offers very contemplative, sensitive support to this popular text.

HE/RG and CM

652 Dear Lord and Father of mankind

***Music:* REST**

In recent years, this text has been the source of great controversy for hymnal editors. Much of the poetry of John Greenleaf Whittier was written to be read, not sung as hymnody. In the late nineteenth century, however, W. Garrett Horder, a British hymnal editor, began to use selected stanzas of much longer poems, including works by Whittier, as sources for congregational hymnody. Today, because of the inappropriateness of much of his poetry as Christian hymnody, many of his texts have been deleted from hymnals of most denominations. This is one of the few of his texts that have been retained.

Words: This hymn is taken from John Greenleaf Whittier's seventeen-stanza poem "The Brewing of Soma," first published in the *Atlantic Monthly*, April 1872. The poem described the brewing by East Indian priests of a "drink of the gods" and its intoxicating effect on worshipers. Whittier, whose Quaker beliefs were opposed to form and ceremony as well as to emotional excess in religion, recalled in this poem how:

Age after age has striven
By music, incense, vigils drear,
And trance, to bring the skies more near,
Or lift man up to heaven.

And yet the past comes round again,
And new doth old fulfill;
In sensual transports wild as vain
We brew in many a Christian lane
The heathen Soma still!

He then concludes the poem with a six-stanza prayer for Christians beginning "Dear Lord and Father of mankind." Five of these six stanzas (12, and 14 through 17) were adapted as a prayer hymn by the English editor W. Garrett Horder in his *Worship Song* (London, 1884). The present selection consists of Whittier's sts. 12, 13, 14, 16, and 17. This hymn entered the *Hymnal* in 1916. Stanza 15, included in Horder's *Worship Song*, but omitted from all editions of the *Hymnal* is:

With that deep hush subduing all
  Our words and works that drown
The tender whisper of thy call,
As noiseless let thy blessing fall
  As fell thy manna down.

Recently hymnologists have questioned the appropriateness of Whittier's stanzas for use in Christian worship, as Erik Routley did in *A Panorama of Christian Hymnody* (Collegeville, MN, 1979), 143: "and if there is a case against 'Dear Lord and Father' . . . perhaps it is that there Whittier was writing a polemical piece, a poetic tract contrasting the serenity and sanity of the Christian faith with the vapourings of a kind of drug-addictive transcendental meditation associated with the drinking of 'Soma,' a potation designed to induce visions. The quietism of the hymn as we know it . . . takes on a very different tone when its context is made explicit."[1]

---

1. See also B. S. Massey, "Dear Lord and Father," *Bulletin 167*, 11, 6 (1986), Hymn Society of Great Britain and Ireland, 122-126. Thomas Strickland, Music Director and Precentor, the Cathedral Church of St. Paul, Burlington, VT, during the editorial preparation of this volume commented, "But even Routley misses Whittier's point—he is paralleling the pagan practice with the organized ritual of main-line religion of his and our days!"

Music: REST by Frederick C. Maker accompanied this text in one of its first British appearances, in the *Congregational Hymnal* (London, 1887). It scrupulously refrains from competing for worshipers' attention with the words, which require and amply repay more concentration than usual, since they were designed for silent reading rather than for singing; moreover, each stanza, instead of rising to a climax, builds down to one—an uncommon procedure that the tune faithfully complements, ending on the mediant as if to open a door to further reflection. It accepts a thoroughly ancillary role as willingly and graciously as did John the Baptist—"he must increase, but I must decrease."

In the April 1986 *Bulletin* of The Hymn Society of Great Britain and Ireland, the editor, Bernard S. Massey, sheds additional light on the source of this tune. He writes: ". . . it is clear from Barrett's preface [Congregational Church Hymnal of 1887] that the tune was composed much earlier, and in fact it comes from Maker's collection of 18 tunes *The New Tune Book for Special Hymns* (n.d.) in which it is set to 'There is an hour of peaceful rest,' a long-forgotten hymn by the American Congegationalist W. B. Tappen (1794-1849)" (see footnote 1 above).

HE/HMcK

653 Dear Lord and Father of mankind

***Music:* REPTON**

The matching of this text and tune occurred first at Repton School in Derbyshire, England, some years before it actually appeared in print. Matched as tune and text, it presents an unusual situation in that not only was the text not intended for singing as a hymn, but neither was the melody initially conceived as a hymn tune.

Words: See hymn 652.

Music: The tune name REPTON honors one of the older and more distinguished British public schools where the tune, matched with these words, was first introduced in *Repton School Hymns* (London, 1924), a supplement of about 70 hymns. The original source of the tune is the oratorio *Judith*, composed by Sir Hubert Parry for the Birmingham Festival of 1888 with a text by the composer derived from the book of Judith in the Apocrypha. In Act 1, Judith sings a ballad of four verses in which she retells for her children the story of ancient Israel's delivery from bondage in Egypt. Example 1 (on the opposite page) shows the vocal score of the first verse of the ballad from *Judith*, published by Novello & Co. in 1888, in which this tune appears.

Based on the reminiscences of an older graduate of the school, Sir Ashley Clarke, John Wilson tells us of REPTON's evolution as a hymn tune:

Example 1

Allegretto semplice.
Long since in E - gypt's plen - teous land, Our fa - thers were op -
Allegretto semplice. ♩ = about 112.
p
poco cres.
pressed; But God, whose cho - sen folk they were, Smote those who long en -
poco cres.
dim.
rit.
slaved them there, And all their woes re - dressed, and all their woes re -
dim.
rit.
G
a tempo.
dressed.
The Red Sea
a tempo.
dim.

> Hubert Parry and Gilbert Stocks (1877-1960, director of music of Repton School) had known each other very well in earlier years . . . Not long before his death, and probably in 1917, Parry broke a journey to spend a few days with Dr. and Mrs. Stocks at Repton, and as Dr. Stocks was already collecting and composing tunes for the future Repton supplement, the question of using the *Judith* tune may well have arisen. Sir Ashley remembers singing it in chapel as a boy, before ever seeing it in print. It is possible, therefore, that Parry gave the idea his blessing. If he was also party to calling the tune 'Repton,' that would have been a nice gesture to a friend and former pupil. In the Repton book, however, the tune is acknowledged not only to Novello & Co., as expected, but also to Parry's executors, suggesting the need for some special permission later.[1]

Despite this close association with the school, the tune with the Whittier text was first published in mid-June 1924 by Novello & Co. as a separate leaflet in their *Parish Choir Book* series. In July of that same year the "preface of the Repton book was signed by the headmaster, Geoffrey Fisher (later Archbishop of Canterbury), and publication of [*Repton School Hymns*] itself—by Oxford University Press—took place by late October, as a file copy shows."[2]

The *Repton School Hymns* form of the tune utilized a piano reduction of the orchestral score as seen in Example 1. This form was continued in *Songs of Praise* (London, 1931) and *EH* (1933) (see Example 2 on page 1199). The *H82* form of the tune is that of *The BBC Hymn Book* (London, 1951), which in turn is based on that of *HA&M Revised* (London, 1950).

---

1. For background on this tune we are deeply indebted to the article " 'Repton'—a Coming Centenary" by J. Wilson in the June 1987, Vol. 11, No. 11, *Bulletin of The Hymn Society of Great Britain and Ireland*, 241.
2. Ibid., 244.

RG

Example 2

From *Songs of Praise* (London, 1931).

654 Day by day

Music: **SUMNER**

This thirteenth-century text, which made its way into English-language hymnody early in this century and appeared in the *Hymnal* for the first time in *H40*, matched with this tune, has gained a place in popular culture through its inclusion in the musical "Godspell."

Words: "Day by Day," attributed at least partly to St. Richard, Bishop of Chichester, is found printed on a card published by Skeffington & Sons, Ltd. and dated as received March 18, 1915 by the British Museum. The text has appeared in many hymnals, including *Songs of Praise* (London, 1931), in the Irish *Church Hymnal* (Dublin, 1960), and *Hymns and Songs* (Peterborough, England, 1988).

Music: The tune SUMNER was composed in 1941 by Arthur H. Biggs for use with this text in *H40*. The name of the tune is derived from the avenue on which St. John's Cathedral, Spokane, is located and where Arthur Biggs served as organist and choirmaster for many years.

TS/MBJ

655 O Jesus, I have promised

Music: **NYLAND**

This text, which has been in the *Hymnal* since 1892, was written for the Confirmation of the author's children. It appears here matched with NYLAND, a Finnish folk melody that was introduced to congregations of the Episcopal Church through its inclusion in *H40*.

Words: This hymn was written by John Ernest Bode for the Confirmation of three of his children, two sons and a daughter, who were all confirmed on the same occasion. Originally printed in a leaflet for the Society for Promoting Christian Knowledge in 1868 as "Hymn for the Newly Confirmed," it was included in the Appendix to the Society's *Psalms and Hymns for Public Worship* (London, 1869). While *Hymns for Church and Home* (Boston, 1895) quotes st. 2 and st. 3 of the hymn as another hymn entitled "O let me feel Thee near me," the original six-stanza format can be found in *HA&M* (1904). Modern publications omit sts. 2, 4, and 6, given here:

2. O let me feel Thee near me:
 The world is ever near;
I see the sights that dazzle,
 The tempting sounds I hear;
My foes are ever near me,
 Around me and within;
But, Jesus, draw Thou nearer,
 And shield my soul from sin.

4. O let me see Thy features,
 The look that once could make
So many a true disciple
 Leave all things for Thy sake;
The look that beam'd on Peter
 When he Thy name denied;
The look that draws Thy loved ones
 Close to Thy pierced side.

6. O let me see Thy foot-marks,
 And in them plant mine own;
My hope to follow duly,
 Is in Thy strength alone;
O guide me, call me, draw me,
 Uphold me to the end;
And then in heav'n receive me,
 My Saviour and my friend.

Music: See hymn 232.

TS

656 Blest are the pure in heart

Music: **FRANCONIA**

The matching of this text and tune first occured in *HA&M* and continues to this day.

Words: Written on October 10, 1819, this text draws two verses from a long poem by John Keble for the Feast of the Purification of the Blessed Virgin Mary (February 2) and published with the inscription, "Blessed are the pure in heart: for they shall see God" (Mt. 5:8). It was published in Keble's *The Christian Year* (London, 1827). The present form of the text, which has been in the *Hymnal* since 1892, is that of *HA&M*, with minor alterations to remove archaisms and assure the use of inclusive language:

2:3	lowliness with men
4	Their pattern
3:2	Doth still himself
4	chooseth the pure
4:4	A temple meet

The original was a paraphrase of the Beatitudes (Mt. 5:1-11) and comprised some seventeen verses. The first and last verses of the poem survive as sts. 1 and 3 of this hymn. Stanzas 2 and 4 were added by W. J. Hall for *Psalms and Hymns*, also known as the *Mitre Hymn Book* (London, 1836).

Music: This tune is a shortened and slightly modified form of a six-line tune (*Zahn* 2207) found in Johann Balthasar König's *Harmonischer Lieder-Schatz, oder Allgemeines Evangelisches Choral-Buch* (Frankfurt, 1738), associated with the text "Was ist das mich betrübt?" by Georg Wolfgang Wedel (see Example 1). It was reworked into a four-line SM English tune by William H. Havergal, and published in the latter's *Old Church Psalmody* (London, 1847). Although Havergal's omissions and alterations appear simple, the result is a skillful reworking of the original. Lines 3 and 5 of the original tune are omitted; the penultimate note of line 2 is eliminated; the new line 3 is extended from seven to eight syllables by making the penultimate half-note into two quarters; and the final line was recreated from the opening falling fifth of the original last line (a in Example 1, opposite page) and the second half of the second line (b in Example 1). It is a well-balanced tune that has understandably become one of the best known SM tunes.

The editors of the first edition of *HA&M* included the tune with the text "Blest are the pure in heart," with which it has been invariably associated ever since.

1203)

Example 1

LW/RAL

657 Love divine, all loves excelling

Music: **HYFRYDOL**

This text, which, over the years, has achieved both international acceptance and use, gained additional favor for Episcopalians when it was first matched with the Welsh tune HYFRYDOL in *H40*.

Words: This text was no. 9 in Charles Wesley's anonymous *Hymns for Those that Seek and Those that Have Redemption in the Blood of Jesus Christ* (London, 1747) (*Poetical Works*, vol. IV, 219f). It was taken up into Martin Madan's *Collection of Psalms and Hymns* (London, 1760) and A. M. Toplady's *Psalms and Hymns for Public and Private Worship* (London, 1776). It was included as no. 374 in John Wesley's definitive *Collection of Hymns for the Use of the People called Methodists* (London, 1780) (reading "Let us all Thy *grace* receive," and "spotless" for the original "sinless" in the second line of the last stanza). The 1780 *Collection* omitted the original second stanza, to which John Fletcher of Madeley had already made theological objection:

Breath, O breathe Thy loving Spirit,
  Into every troubled breast,
Let us all in Thee inherit,
  Let us find that second rest:
Take away our power of sinning,
  Alpha and Omega be,
End of faith as its Beginning,
  Set our hearts at liberty.

Where the stanza has been restored, verbal suggestions have been taken from Fletcher to meet the difficulty he saw in "Take away the power of sinning": "Is not this expression too strong? Would it not be better to soften it, as Mr. Hill has done, by saying, 'Take away the love of' (or the bent to) 'sinning'? Can God take away from us our power of sinning without taking away our power of free obedience?"[1] The allusion in "that second rest" to Heb. 3 and 4 suggests that Wesley's prayer in this stanza, as indeed throughout the hymn, is strictly eschatological: in the finished "new creation" we shall find, as the Prayer Book collect puts it, our perfect freedom in the service of God, a moral *non posse peccare*.

The Hymnals of 1871 and 1874 contained the controversial stanza in modified form, but since 1892 the problem has been solved by its omission.

The hymn appears to be a spiritual parody of the "Song sung by Venus in honour of Britannia" in John Dryden's *King Arthur*:

Fairest Isle, all isles excelling,
Seat of pleasures and of loves;
Venus here will choose her dwelling
And forsake her Cyprian groves.

---

1. *The Last Check to Antinomianism* (London, 1775), § 19, 12.

Music: See hymn 460. The Henry Purcell tune for the song "Fairest Isle, all isles excelling" under the title WESTMINSTER, was provided for the Wesleyan words in *Select Hymns, with Tunes Annext, designed chiefly for the use of the people called Methodists* of 1761 (the tunebook itself being entitled *Sacred Melody*). WESTMINSTER, as it appears in the most recent edition of the British Methodist hymnal *Hymns and Psalms* (London, 1983), is as follows (Example 1, page 1205 et seq.):

GW/AL

Example 1

WESTMINSTER
(SACRED HARMONY) 8 7.8 7.D

Melody and bass from
John Wesley's *Sacred Harmony* (1780)
based on Purcell's song, *Fairest Isle*

1 LOVE divine, all loves excelling,
Fix in us thy humble dwelling,
Joy of heaven to earth come down,
All thy faithful mercies crown.
Jesu, thou art all compassion,
Pure, unbounded love thou art;

Vi - sit us with thy sal - va - tion,
En - ter ev - ery trem - bling heart.

658 As longs the deer for cooling streams

Music: **MARTYRDOM**
This psalm paraphrase, until the 1871 edition of the *Hymnal*, was included among the metrical psalms. In every succeeding edition since that time, it has been found among the general hymns in this form or in a version by George Gregory. It is matched here, as it was in *H40*, with a nineteenth-century Scottish psalm tune.

Words: Tate and Brady issued their *New Version of the Psalms of David* (London, 1696; 2nd rev. ed., 1698) as a more poetic alternative to the psalter of the "Old Version" of Sternhold and Hopkins (see the essay "English Metrical Psalmody," vol. 1, 333-37). The 1698 version of Ps. 42 is as follows:

1. As pants the hart for cooling Streams,
 when heated in the Chase,
 So longs my Soul, O God, for thee,
 and thy refreshing grace.

2. For thee, my God, the living God,
 my thirsty Soul doth pine;

O when shall I behold thy Face,
thou Majesty Divine!

3. Tears are my constant Food, while thus
insulting Foes upbraid,
"Deluded Wretch, where's now thy God?
and where his promis'd Aid?"

4. I sigh, when-e'er my musing Thought
those happy Days present,
When I with Troops of pious Friends
thy Temple did frequent.

5. When I advanc'd with Songs of Praise,
my solemn Vows to pay
And led the joyful sacred Throng
that kept the Festal day.

6. Why restless, why cast down my Soul?
trust God, who will employ
His Aid for thee; and change these Sighs
to thankful Hymns of Joy.

7. My Soul's cast down, O God, but thinks
on thee, and Sion still;
From Jordan's Bank, from Hermon's Heights,
and Missar's humbler Hill.

8. One Trouble calls another on,
and gath'ring o'er my Head,
Fall spouting down, till round my Soul
a roaring Sea is spread.

9. But when thy Presence, Lord of Life,
has once dispell'd this Storm,
To thee I'll midnight Anthems sing,
and all my Vows perform.

10. God of my Strength, how long shall I
like one forgotten mourn?
Forlorn, forsaken, and expos'd
to my Oppressor's Scorn.

11. My Heart is pierc'd, as with a Sword,
    whilst thus my Foes upbraid;
"Vain Boaster, where is now thy God?
    and where his promis'd Aid?"

12. Why restless, why cast down my Soul?
    hope still, and thou shalt sing
The Praise of him who is thy God,
    thy Health's Eternal Spring.

Familiar hymns enter deeply into the subconscious, and it is possible that the popularity of this metrical version of Ps. 42 influenced later hymn writers. Thus, Charles Coffin may have subconsciously taken over the phrase "Jordan's Bank" in st. 7 for his "On *Jordan's bank* the Baptist's cry" [76]; and William Cowper may have been inspired by "promised Aid" when writing the final stanza of "The saints should never be dismay'd":[1]

Wait for his seasonable *aid*,
    And tho' it tarry wait:
The *promise* may be long delay'd,
    But cannot come too late.

More direct use of this text by Tate and Brady was made by other authors of metrical versions of Ps. 42: for example, John Merrick's "As pants the hart for cooling springs" published in the author's *Psalms Translated or Paraphrased in English Verse* (Reading, England, 1765); George Gregory's "As pants the wearied hart for cooling streams" in Gregory's *Translation of Bishop Lowth's Lectures on the Poetry of the Hebrews* (London, 1787) (see further below); and the anonymous "As pants the hart for water-brooks" in *The Presbyterian Hymnal* (Philadelphia, 1874).

Robert Lowth, successively bishop of St. Davids, Oxford, and London—one of the few contemporary bishops of the Church of England who had a high regard for John Wesley—had also been Professor of Poetry at Oxford. His Latin lectures, later published as *De sacra poesi Hebraeorum* (Oxford, 1753), included a few Latin metrical psalms, among them Ps. 42, which Gregory translated into English verse, with the assistance of Tate and Brady. The Tate and Brady version of Ps. 42 was included in the selection of psalms issued with the American

Prayer Book of 1789, and thereafter was bound together with the hymns in the *Prayer Book* until 1871. In the *Tunebook* (New York, 1858) "As pants the hart for cooling streams" was listed among the Psalms; "As panting in the sultry beam" was listed among the hymns. In *Episcopal Common Praise* (New York, 1865), two versions appeared among the Psalms: "As pants the hart" and "As pants the wearied hart." "As panting in the sultry beams" appeared among the hymns. The 1871 *Hymnal* included two versions of the Psalm, that is Tate and Brady's and Gregory's; in the *Hymnals* of 1892 and 1916 only the Gregory version appeared; in *H40* the Gregory version was omitted and Tate and Brady's restored. *The Hymnal 1982* employs sts. 1, 2, 12, and the CM *Gloria Patri* found in the Appendix to the *New Version*.

---

1. *Olney Hymns* (London, 1779), Book 1, no. 6.

Music: This tune was originally in duple time and was named FENWICK, after the Ayrshire birthplace of its composer, the cobbler and sundial-maker Hugh Wilson. The exact date of its composition is unknown; according to James Love, it was "first published on single slips with the air and bass only, for the use of teachers in music classes"; Love's transcription of this source is the basis of Example 1:[1]

Example 1

The tune entered the general Scottish repertory after Wilson's death in 1824, through Robert A. Smith's *Sacred Music Sung at St. George's*

Church, Edinburgh (Edinburgh, 1825), where it was given its present form and name. According to Love, it was then published in its original form in John Robertson's *The Seraph*, which Love dates September 1827, and was there claimed as "the private property of Robertson."[2] There was at least one lawsuit concerning the ownership of this tune.

MARTYRDOM has a strong flavor of Scottish folk song, both in its predominantly pentatonic scale and in its archlike shape. This gives it a general similarity to American folk hymns like NEW BRITAIN [671]. Anne Gilchrist speculates that it is possibly derived from an actual ballad tune.[3]

---

1. See J. Love, *Scottish Church Music* (Edinburgh, 1891), 303.
2. Ibid., 333.
3. See A. G. Gilchrist, *The Choir* (London, 1934), no. 25, 155-156.

RAL/NT

659 O Master, let me walk with thee

***Music:* DE TAR**

This popular text is a prayer for Christ's presence as we pursue a life of service that will bring us closer to him. Matched with DE TAR, a tune by Calvin Hampton, a contemporary American composer, the text gains an added dimension of depth and introspection.

Words: Washington Gladden wrote this text in 1879 as a three-stanza, eight-line devotional poem for publication in the magazine *Sunday Afternoon*, for which he was editor. Gladden later wrote:

> Dr. Charles H. Richards found the poem . . . and made a hymn of it by omitting the second stanza, which was not suitable for devotional purposes. It had no liturgical purpose and no theological significance, but it was an honest cry of human need, of the need for divine companionship.[1]

The omitted stanza is:

> O Master, let me walk with thee
> Before the taunting Pharisee;
> Help me to bear the sting of spite,

The hate of men who hide Thy light,
The sore distrust of souls sincere
Who cannot read Thy judgments clear,
The dullness of the multitude,
Who dimly guess that Thou art good.

The text was published as a hymn in Richard's *Christian Praise* (New York, 1880; in later editions retitled *Songs of Christian Praise*). It entered the *Hymnal* in 1916.

---

1. A. Haeussler, *The Story of Our Hymns* (St. Louis, 1952), 249.

Music: See hymn 456.

HE

660 O Master, let me walk with thee

Music: **MARYTON**

The author of this text, Washington Gladden, chose MARYTON for his hymn, and it is reported that he gave permission for the text's use with the condition that it be sung to this tune. It entered the *Hymnal* matched with that tune in the 1916 edition.

Words: See hymn 659.

Music: The tune MARYTON was composed for John Keble's hymn "Sun of my soul" and first appeared with that text when it was published in *Church Hymns with Tunes* (London, 1874), edited by Sir Arthur Sullivan. Because of its association with Washington Gladden's text, the tune is more widely sung in the United States than in Great Britain.

Altered harmonies for the tune have been made by Eric Thiman and by Erik Routley.[1] Because the harmonic idiom of the Victorian hymn tune is endemic to its character, it is difficult if not impossible to separate the two components.

---

1. See the *LBW* and E. Routley, *Rejoice in the Lord* (Grand Rapids, MI, 1985), 428.

MS

661 *They cast their nets in Galilee*

***Music:* GEORGETOWN**

The miracle of the great catch at Galilee as related in Lk: 5:1 is the biblical basis for this text, which first appeared, matched with this tune, in *H40*.

Words: A poem, "His Peace" from *Enzio's Kingdom and Other Poems* (New Haven, 1924) by William Alexander Percy is the source of this text. It begins:

I love to think of them at dawn
  Beneath the frail pink sky,
Casting their nets in Galilee
  And fish-hawks circling by.

Casting their nets in Galilee
  Just off the hills of brown,

and continuing, with one alteration, as in the *Hymnal*. This one change, supportive of the SCCM's desire to use inclusive language whenever possible, occurs in st. 4:3, which in the original read "Yet, *brothers*, pray for but one thing." The text came under some criticism in the SCCM's review process due to the poet's freedom in st. 3, where he implies that the Fourth Gospel and the Book of Revelation were written by the same person.

Music: The tune GEORGETOWN was composed by David McK. Williams during his twenty-seven-year tenure as organist and choirmaster of St. Bartholomew's Church in New York City; it was written in 1941 for use in the music edition of *H40*, the same year he penned CHRISTUS REX [614]. The name GEORGETOWN derives from his friendship with Francis Bland Tucker, who was then the rector of St. John's Episcopal Church, Georgetown Parish, Washington, DC. The tune has a strong melodic outline and is completely diatonic. The measures are of unequal length and the resulting rhythmic freedom undergirds the text most effectively.

RG/AW

662 *Abide with me: fast falls the eventide*

Music: **EVENTIDE**

The combination of Henry Francis Lyte's text with the tune EVENTIDE to form the hymn "Abide with me" has produced without question one of the "classics" in the singing tradition of English-speaking congregations around the world.

Words: Two differing views have been held about the date of the composition of this text; one contends it was written as early as 1820, the other dates it at 1847. The earlier date was supported in a letter by T. H. Bindley published in the *Spectator*, CXXXV (October 1925), which claimed that Lyte wrote the hymn in 1820 after visiting a dying friend, William Augustus LeHunte, who repeatedly uttered the words "abide with me." As the story goes, Lyte then wrote the hymn and gave it to the invalid's brother.

This claim was refuted by Lyte's great-grandson, Walter Maxwell-Lyte, in an article published in *The Times* (November 1, 1947), in which he cited a letter dated August 25, 1847, written by the hymn-writer to "Julia," whom Maxwell-Lyte identified as Eleanor Julia Bolton, who married Lyte's youngest son in 1851. Included in that letter was a copy of a hymn which was referred to as "my latest effusion." This account is consonant with that given by Lyte's daughter, Anna Maria Maxwell Hogg, in the preface of his memoirs, *Remains* (London, 1850). She describes the last sermon that he preached and the last eucharist that he celebrated at Lower Brixham, September 14, 1847 and continues: "In the evening of the same day he placed in the hands of a near and dear relative the little hymn, 'Abide with me,' with an air of his own composing, adapted to the words."

The wide acceptance of this hymn more than fulfills the hopes of its author, who wrote:

Might verse of mine inspire
  One virtuous aim, one high resolve impart—
Light in one drooping soul a hallowed fire,
  Or bind one broken heart.

Death would be sweeter then,
  More calm my slumber 'neath the silent sod.
Might I thus live to bless my fellowmen.
  Or glorify my God.

In its original form the hymn had eight stanzas; the second through the fifth have been omitted and read:

2. Swift from my grasp ebbs out life's little day,
   Earth's joys grow dim, its glories pass away,
   Change and decay in all around I see;
   O thou who changest not, abide with me.

3. Not a brief glance I beg, a passing word;
   But, as thou dwell'st with thy disciples, Lord,
   Familiar, condescending, patient, free,
   Come not to sojourn, but abide with me.

4. Come not in terror as the King of kings,
   But kind and good, with healing in thy wings;
   Tears for all woes, a heart for every plea—
   Come, Friend of sinners, and thus 'bide with me.

5. Thou on my head in early youth didst smile;
   And, though rebellious and perverse meanwhile,
   Thou hast not left me, oft as I left thee;
   On to the close, O Lord, abide with me!

Minor alterations include the substitution of "deepens" for "thickens" in st. 1:2; the concluding line of st. 2 read, "O abide with me"; in st. 4:1 "Hold thou" read "Hold then," and in line 2 "speak" has been replaced by "shine."

The text, in a five-stanza form, first appeared in an Episcopal publication in *Additional Hymns* (New York, 1865). The text was set to VESPER, credited to Mendelssohn, and to a double Anglican chant credited to A. Loder (see Example 1) in *Episcopal Common Praise* (New York, 1867).

Music: Two different, but perhaps not unrelated stories surround the composition of this tune. One is that Henry Monk, the composer and musical editor of the first edition of *HA&M* (1861) and Sir Henry Baker, Chairman of the Editorial Committee, when leaving a committee meeting, realized that no tune had been selected for use with the Lyte text "Abide with me." Monk is said to have returned to his home where he composed the tune in ten minutes. The other story, based on a statement by Monk's widow, is that Monk wrote the tune at twilight after watching the setting of the sun, as was his custom, hand in hand with his wife. Wesley Milgate reconciles these stories in *Songs of the People of God*. He writes, "Baker often visited Monk's home, and the writing of the music might have been prompted by a discussion (as it were, at a 'committee meeting') during one of his visits."[1]

The tune, perhaps the composer's most characteristic, suffers ridicule more because of a slow, maudlin performance practice than from its qualities as a very simple, four-part hymn tune. A moving tempo (𝅗𝅥= 54) with a feeling of two beats in a measure is to be encouraged.

Example 1

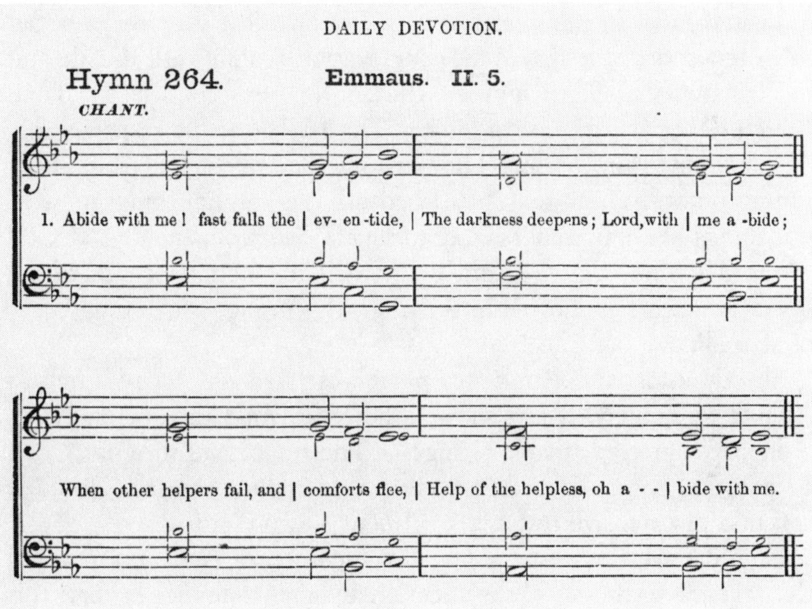
DAILY DEVOTION.
Hymn 264.
Emmaus. II. 5.
CHANT.
1. Abide with me! fast falls the | ev- en -tide, | The darkness deepens; Lord, with | me a -bide;
When other helpers fail, and | comforts flee, | Help of the helpless, oh a - - | bide with me.

1. W. Milgate, *Songs of the People of God* (London, 1982), 184.

MS/RG

663 The Lord my God my shepherd is

***Music:* CRIMOND**

The twenty-third Psalm is one of the most deeply loved of all the psalms and has probably provided more inspiration to poets, who have prepared countless paraphrases of it, than any other psalm. This most recent addition to the *Hymnal* of a paraphrase of the psalm is by the contemporary American hymn writer F. Bland Tucker. It joins in *H82* the paraphrases of the Psalm by Henry Baker and Isaac Watts.

Words: In early 1953 the late Rev. Dr. F. Bland Tucker, then Rector of Christ Church in Savannah, Georgia, was confronted with the necessity of major chest surgery for the removal of a large tumor in his left lung. In the brief rest period prior to the surgery, he began to write a series of letters to his congregation dealing with the life and death issues that faced him. At the end of his second letter, dated March 8, 1953, just prior to surgery, Dr. Tucker penned a paraphrase of the twenty-third Psalm "The Lord my God my shepherd is" as an expression of his faith that "neither death nor life, nor things present, nor things to come shall be able to separate us from the love of God which is in Christ Jesus" (Rom. 8:38-39). The emotional center of the poem was clearly indicated in the original printing, where the "here" of st. 3, line 3 was italicized.

Shortly after completing this paraphrase, Dr. Tucker returned to Atlanta for surgery; X-rays showed, however, what the doctors called "a dramatic and remarkable change."[1] The tumor had shrunk to such a significant degree that surgery was considered unnecessary, although a period of extensive rest and treatment was prescribed.

The SCCM, in preparing texts for inclusion in *H82*, has included this text as a testimony of the affection and gratitude they held for this great man who had served so unstintingly in the creation, revision, and selection of texts for the *Hymnal* and as a statement of faith for the use of ongoing generations of hymn singers.

---

1. F. Bland Tucker, *More than Conquerors* (Cincinnati, 1955), 1.

Music: This tune is named after the village of Crimond in northeastern Scotland, north of Aberdeen. The way in which this

Scottish psalm tune acquired its name depends upon which attribution one subscribes to, a source of controversy for historians researching the tune. There are two attributions: David Grant (1833-1893), an Aberdeen tobacconist with an interest in hymns and church singing, and Jessie Seymour Irvine (1836-1887), the daughter of the Rev. Dr. Alexandar Irvine, minister of the Crimond Parish Church from 1855 to 1884. The following is a chronological summary of the attributions of this tune.

From its first appearance in the *Northern Psalter* (1872), where it was set to "Thou art the Way, the Truth, the Life," until around 1950, CRIMOND was attributed to David Grant. In the preface to the *Northern Psalter*, the editor, William Carnie, mentions CRIMOND as being composed by Grant. In subsequent editions of the *Northern Psalter* up to 1900, Grant continues to be listed as CRIMOND's composer. In a speech dated 1897 and published in his *Reporting Reminiscences*, Carnie specifically referred to David Grant as the composer of two hymn tunes, RALEIGH and CRIMOND. Leaflet publications as late as 1948 again referred to Grant as the composer of the tune.

From about 1950 until recently, CRIMOND has been attributed to Jessie Seymour Irvine. The change in attribution seems to have been instigated by a brief article by the noted hymnologist Rev. Dr. Millar Patrick.[1] Undoubtedly, Dr. Patrick's reputation carried sufficient weight so that the attribution was not questioned. He based the attribution on a letter written by Ms. Irvine's older sister, Anna Barbara Irvine, addressed to the Rev. Robert T. Monteith, minister of the Crimond Parish Church during the second decade of this century, dated May 31, 1911:

> I shall . . . tell you all I know about the tune CRIMOND. It was composed by my late sister J. S. Irvine . . . I think it was William Carnie who got it harmonized by David Grant, as noted in [the Northern] Psalter . . . [2]

Later in the 1950s, James Fenton Wyness, an architect and historian from Aberdeen, became interested in the authorship issue involving CRIMOND. In his book *Let's Look around the Peterhead area* (Aberdeen, 1957), in a brief passage about the village of Crimond, he writes that ". . . the well-known psalm-tune was composed by an Aberdeen tobacconist, David Grant . . . the [tune] name was suggested by his friend Robert Cooper . . . " Mr. Wyness also refers to his belief that David Grant is the composer of CRIMOND in a booklet entitled *Crimond*, which presents his research on this topic, and in chapter 42 of *Spots from the Leopard* (Aberdeen, Scotland, 1971).[3]

If one subcribes to David Grant as the composer, the tune name appears to have been suggested by his friend Robert Cooper. If one subscribes it to Jessie Seymour Irving, it is assumed that the tune name is taken from the parish church and village where her father was minister.

When the tune was published in the *Scottish Psalter* (London, 1929) it was not associated with a particular psalm. Sir Hugh Roberton, the conductor of the Glasgow Orpheus Choir, made frequent broadcasts of a setting of CRIMOND with the text of Ps. 23 from the 1650 *Scottish Psalter*.[4] The post-Second World War popularity is undoubtedly due to its first usage in two royal services: the wedding of Princess Elizabeth in Westminster Abbey in 1947 and the silver wedding anniversary of King George VI and Queen Elizabeth in St. Paul's Cathedral. Sir John Colville, who was Private Secretary to Princess Elizabeth at the time of her marriage, records the following:

> One of Princess Elizabeth's ladies-in-waiting, Lady Margaret Egerton, endowed with a beautiful voice, had been wont to sing a metrical psalm, "The Lord's my Shepherd" (Crimond), in the heather at Balmoral and had taught the two princesses a little-known descant. Lady Margaret, tunefully accompanied by the two princesses, therefore sang it to the Organist [Sir William McKie] . . . of Westminster Abbey who took down the notes in musical shorthand and taught it to the Abbey Choir. On the wedding day nobody was more surprised than the composer of the descant [W. Baird Ross], who, far away in Stirling, listened to the service on his radio. Since then both the metrical psalm to the tune Crimond and the descant have been consistently popular in churches throughout the British Isles and the Commonwealth.[5]

This tune and text were first printed together in the *School Hymn Book of the Methodist Church* (London, 1950). Other early inclusions of this combination of text and tune are in the *BBC Hymn Book* (London, 1951) and *Congregational Praise* (London, 1951). The psalm tune matched with Ps. 23 appears to have surfaced in the United States in the mid-1950s. Some of the hymnals in which the text and tune have appeared include *The Hymnbook* (Richmond, et al., 1955); the *Pilgrim Hymnal* (Boston, 1958), and the *Service Book and Hymnal* (Minneapolis, et al., 1958). CRIMOND entered the Episcopal hymn repertoire in *Hymns III* and *Cantate Domino* (Chicago, 1979). The *H82* harmonization was prepared by members of the Hymn Music Committee of the SCCM.

Eric Routley calls CRIMOND " . . . musically unusual in being the only one in the repertory [Scottish psalmody] to make use of 'sequence'—which it does in its third line."[6]

---

1. See R. Johnson, "How far is it to Crimond?" the *Bulletin* 176 of the Hymn Society of Great Britain and Ireland, vol. XII, no. 3 (July, 1988), 39.
2. Ibid., 40.
3. Ibid., 41.
4. The Orpheus Choir first sang the metrical version of Ps. 23 to the tune CRIMOND at the Queen's Hall, London, on April 4, 1936.
5. J. Colville, *The Fringes of Power: 10 Downing Street Diaries 1939-1955* (London, 1985), 619-620.
6. See E. Routley, *The Music of Christian Hymns* (Chicago, 1981), 85.

RG/JeW and RAL

664 My Shepherd will supply my need

Music: **RESIGNATION**

This beautiful paraphrase of the twenty-third Psalm by Isaac Watts was introduced to congregations of the Episcopal Church in *Hymns III*, where it was matched with this American folk melody. This text/tune matching is one of long standing. One source is William Walker's *The Southern Harmony* (Philadelphia, 1854). In its original form, the text was in CM.

Words: Isaac Watts set three versions of Ps. 23. This, the second version, is found in his *Psalms of David* (London, 1719). Erik Routley suggests that while the psalm ends at st. 5, the addition of st.

6 to the setting is "perhaps the most inspired such addition ever made."[1]

> 6. There would I find a settled rest,
> (While others go and come)
> No more a stranger or a guest,
> But like a child at home.

---

1. E. Routley, *An English-Speaking Hymnal Guide* (Collegeville, MN, 1979), 58.

Music: Freeman Lewis, a Lewistown, PA, surveyor, included in the first edition of his four-shape shape-note *Beauties of Harmony* (Pittsburgh, 1814) the first printings of both BOURBON [147] and DUNLAP'S CREEK [276]. The tune now generally known as RESIGNATION was apparently first printed in the 1828 enlarged edition of *Beauties of Harmony* (Pittsburgh). There it was titled HOPEWELL and linked with the text "Come humble sinner in whose breast" (see Example 1).

Example 1

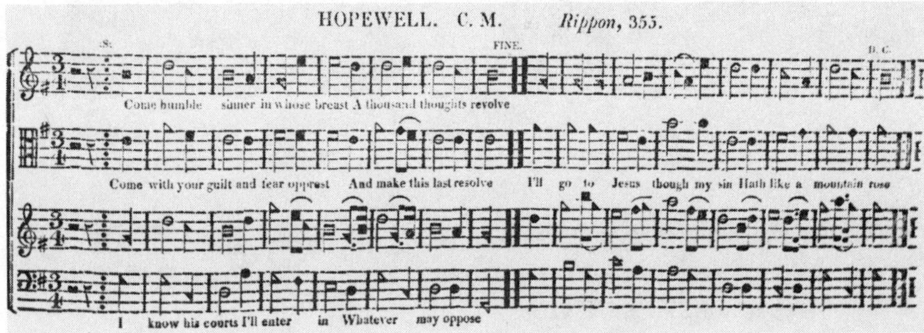

Reproduced from 1831 printing of the 1828 edition of *Beauties of Harmony* (Pittsburgh) with permission of Moravian Music Foundation.

Methodist clergyman Samuel Wakefield used this same title, text, and melody line for the version in his *American Repository of Sacred Music* (Pittsburgh, 1830). There, however, in his three-part arrangement, the melody is printed as the treble part and the other parts are quite different from those of Lewis.

The third appearance of this tune was a pentatonic version in three parts, titled RESIGNATION and linked with the text "And let this feeble body fail," which was published in Joseph Funk's *Genuine Church Music* (Winchester, VA, 1832). This setting was published in a number of books, including the Mennonite *Brethren's Tune and Hymn Book* (Dade City, PA, 1872). A counter part was added in the twelfth edition of *Harmonia Sacra* (Singers' Glen, VA, 1867), the successor to *Genuine Church Music*, and that version was also included in Martin D. Wenger's *The Philharmonia* (Elkhart, IN, 1875).

The three-part arrangement from Funk's *Genuine Church Music* was reproduced under the same title in another Shenandoah Valley book, the first edition of J. W. Steffey's *Valley Harmonist* (Winchester, VA, 1836). In this book the tune was first linked with the text "My Shepherd will supply my need" (see Example 2).

The tune with this text made its way from this book into other Southern shape-note books, including the 1854 edition of William Walker's *Southern Harmony* (New Haven, CT), one of the most popular of the four-shape shape-note books. Walker added a counter part in his later *Christian Harmony* (Philadelphia, 1867), and that version, with a largely rewritten alto, is printed on two staffs with the melody in the treble in a book still used among Primitive Baptists, C. H. Cayce's *The Good Old Songs* (Thornton, AK, 1913), where it is linked with the text "Let worldly minds the world pursue."

A variant three-part version was published under the title IRWINTON with the text "What poor, despised company of travelers are these" in *Sacred Harp* (Philadelphia, 1844), compiled by two Georgia residents, B. F. White and E. J. King. This tune was dropped at the time of the 1869 revision, but it was restored in the edition edited by J. S. James under the title *Original Sacred Harp* (Cullman, AL, 1911). The treble and bass were slightly edited, an alto attributed to S. M. Denson was added and it was renamed INVITATION.

A still different setting on two staffs with the melody in the treble is printed, under the name HOPEWELL, in John R. and J. Harvey Daily's *Primitive Baptist Hymn and Tune Book* (Indianapolis, 1902), which is still used among Primitive Baptists.

George Pullen Jackson lists RESIGNATION among the "Eighty Most Popular Tunes" in his *White Spirituals in the Southern Uplands* (Chapel Hill, NC, 1933). Only in recent years, however, has it made its way into mainline hymnals.

The first Episcopal hymnal to include the text "My shepherd will

Example 2

Reproduced from *Valley Harmonist* (Winchester, VA, 1836), University of Michigan Library.

supply my need" was *MHSS* where it was linked to a harmonization of RESIGNATION copyrighted 1917 from *Songs of All Times* and used by permission of the Society of Friends. The text and tune were retained in *Hymns III*, but with an accompaniment by David Hurd and a harmonization that goes back to Joseph Funk's *Genuine Church Music*, copied from William Walker's *Southern Harmony* and printed on two staffs with the melody in the tenor. David Hurd's version was retained in *H82*. Guitar chords are provided.

TS/MH

665 All my hope on God is founded

***Music:* MICHAEL**

This hymn was one of those for which the SCCM preparing *H82* received a significant number of requests for inclusion. Undoubtedly this is due to the popularity of the tune, which is one of Herbert Howells's most engaging. Through the matching of MICHAEL with the Bridges text, a work of singular beauty and strength, the worshiper is enabled to articulate faith in a very compelling way.

Words: "A free version of a hymn by Joachim Neander"—those are the descriptive words of Robert Bridges that reflect his approach to the German text "Meine Hoffnung stehet feste." In *Songs of Praise Discussed* (London, 1933), Percy Dearmer, writing about this hymn, states:

> It is important to remember that Bridges . . . does not really translate his German originals, but uses them merely for suggestion, not only paraphrasing freely, and omitting many verses, but also adding new verses of his own. Thus, although the individualistic note of the post-Luther German pietism is here retained in the opening stanzas, the hymn is on the whole on a wider and more modern note, and in line with [Bridges's] final mature thought in the *Testament of Beauty*.

"All my hope" first appeared in the *Yattendon Hymnal* (Oxford, 1899). Neander's hymn was included in his *Glaub- und Liebes-Übung: Auff-*

gemuntert Durch Einfältige Bundes-Lieder und Danck-Psalmen (Bremen, 1679). The five-stanza hymn was designated for "Grace after Meals." The first appearance of the hymn for use by congregations of the Episcopal Church was in the second edition of *MHSS*.

Several changes in st. 2 were made by the Text Committee of the SCCM to support their intent to use inclusive language whenever possible. The original was:

Pride of man and earthly glory,
Sword and crown betray his trust;
What with care and toil he buildeth,
Tower and temple, fall to dust.
But God's power,
Hour by hour,
Is my temple and my tower.

A minor alteration occurs in st. 3, line 1, where "aye" is replaced with "e'er."

Music: Dr. Herbert Howells wrote MICHAEL ca. 1930 for use with these words, at the request of Dr. Thomas Feilden, Director of Music of Charterhouse School. Dr. Howells recalls that on receiving the request, he wrote the entire tune while still at the breakfast table where he had been opening the mail. The tune is noteworthy for its profound lyric beauty and harmonic richness. It honors the composer's son, Michael, who died in childhood. The tune appeared with this text in *The Clarendon Hymn Book* (London, 1936). Slight alterations were made by the composer in the bass line at measures 8 and 9 for the appearance of the tune in *Hymns for Church and School* (Henley-On-Thames, England, 1964).

MS/RG

666 Out of the depths I call

***Music:* ST. BRIDE**

This tune was composed ca. 1760 for use with this text from Tate and Brady's *New Version*. The tune has been included in such Episcopal tunebooks as the *Collection* (Boston, 1851) of H. W. Greatorex and *A Tune-Book Proposed for the Use of Congregations of the*

Episcopal Church (New York, 1858) where it is suggested for use with this text.

Words: Tate and Brady issued their *New Version of the Psalms of David* (London, 1696; 2nd revised ed., 1698) as a more poetic alternative to the psalter of the "Old Version" of Sternhold and Hopkins (see the essay "English Metrical Psalmody," vol. 1, 333-337). The 1698 version of Ps. 130 is as follows:

1. From lowest Depths of Woe,
   To God I sent my Cry;
   Lord! hear my supplicating Voice,
   and graciously reply.

2. Shou'dst thou severely judge,
   who can the Tryal bear?
   But thou forgiv'st, lest we despond,
   and quite renounce thy Fear.

3. My Soul with patience waits
   for Thee the living Lord;
   My Hopes are on thy Promise built,
   thy never-failing Word.

4. My longing Eyes look out
   For thy enliv'ning Ray,
   More duly than the Morning-Watch
   to spy the dawning Day.

5. Let Isr'el trust in God;
   no Bounds his Mercy knows;
   The plenteous Source and Spring from whence
   Eternal Succour flows.

6. Whose friendly Streams to us
   Supplies in Want convey;
   A healing Spring, a Spring to cleanse,
   and wash our Guilt away.

The version in *H82* is based on sts. 1 and 3 through 5. Unlike "As longs the deer for cooling streams" [658], the appropriate *Gloria Patri* does not conclude the text.

Music: Samuel Howard, organist of St. Bride's Church, London, contributed this tune to William Riley's *Parochial Music Corrected* (London, 1762); it was named ST. BRIDGET in honor of the composer's church (Bride and Bridget are alternative forms of the name of a fifth-century Irish saint). It was set to Ps. 130 from Tate and Brady's *New Version*, "From lowest depths of woe," which is the basis of the present text. The barring and harmonization were somewhat different from the modern form.

Despite its Anglican origin, the tune gained its chief currency in books used by dissenters, such as Aaron William's *Psalmody in Miniature* (London, 1769), where it acquired the current form of its name, and Ralph Harrison's *Sacred Harmony* (London, ca. 1784), where it was named KERSALL. It very quickly entered American use in Josiah Flagg's *Collection of the Best Psalm Tunes* (Boston, 1766). An influential Anglican collection that included it was Edward Miller's *Psalms of David* (London, 1791) to the same words as in Riley's, but with yet another name, ALL SAINTS'. A fourth name, allocated by Thomas Hastings in 1815, was BRIDGEPORT. The tune reached the *Hymnal* at least as early as the J. Ireland Tucker music edition (1874), where it was used with three texts.

The mournful character of this tune, which lifts to the relative major only to fall sadly back to the minor tonic, is in a general way reminiscent of early psalm tunes like WINDSOR (see no. 642); it well suits the mood of Ps. 130. The *Hymnal* harmonization is in all essentials identical to that in *HA&M* and can probably be attributed to the musical editor of that hymnal, William H. Monk.

RAL/NT

667 Sometimes a light surprises

Music: **LIGHT**

This text by William Cowper from the important eighteenth-century collection *The Olney Hymns* (London, 1779) appeared matched with this American folk melody in *H40*. This is a matching that occurred in the United States early in the nineteenth century.

Its inclusion in the *Hymnal* of the Episcopal Church is another example of the knowledge of hymnody and wide vision of the music editor of both the 1916 and 1940 hymnals, C. Winfred Douglas, who was one of the first editors of an American mainline Protestant hymnal to introduce material from the wealth of early American folk sources.

Words: This remarkable hymn by William Cowper was written sometime between 1765 and 1773, his major period of hymn-writing.[1] It was first published in Book 3 of *Olney Hymns* (London, 1779), compiled by John Newton. It was entitled "Joy and Peace in believing," and appeared in the "Comfort" section. Cowper was a shy and sensitive man, given to periods of depression and despair, reflected, for example, in his hymn "O for a closer walk" [683/684]. Through the help and counsel of friends, however, especially Newton, the blackness of doubt was replaced by the light of faith, a theme not only explored in this hymn but also in "God moves in a mysterious way" [677]. What is remarkable in this hymn is Cowper's insightful perception that in the act of singing—and the singing of hymns is implied—the grace of God is sometimes experienced in a powerful way. Although in wide use throughout the nineteenth and twentieth centuries, its first *Hymnal* appearance was in *H40*. The text remains essentially faithful to Cowper's original. Minor changes are found in st. 2, line 7, where the original was "E'en let th'unknown to-morrow," and st. 4, line 1, misprinted in *Olney Hymns* as "The vine . . . " Scriptural references include st. 1, Mal. 4:2; st. 3, Mt. 6:25-33 and Lk. 12:22-31; and st. 4, Hab. 3:17-18.

---

1. See R. A. Leaver, "Olney Hymns 1779: 1. The Book and Its Origins," *Churchman* 93 (1979), esp. 328-330.

Music: This tune apparently first came into print in a two-part version in lawyer, clergyman, editor, and reformer Joshua Leavitt's *Christian Lyre* (New York, 1831), which also contained the first printing of PLEADING SAVIOR [586].[1] The heptatonic tune titled LIGHT was linked with William Cowper's text "Sometimes a light surprises" (see Example 1, next page).

Example 1

136 LIGHT. 7. 6.

Sometimes a light sur - pri - ses The
It is the Lord who ri - - ses, With
Christian while he sings·
heal - ing in his wings:
When comforts are de-
cli - ning, He grants the soul a - - gain A
season of clear shi - ning, To cheer it af - ter rain.

137

93. *Sometimes a light surprises.*

1 Sometimes a light surprises
The Christian while he sings;
It is the Lord who rises,
With healing on his wings:
When comforts are declining,
He grants the soul again
A season of clear shining,
To cheer it after rain.

2 In holy contemplation,
We sweetly then pursue
The theme of God's salvation,
And find it ever new:
Set free from present sorrow,
We cheerfully can say,
Let the unknown to morrow
Bring with it what it may.

3 It can bring with it nothing,
But he will bear us through;—
Who gives the lilies clothing,
Will clothe his people too:
Beneath the spreading heavens,
No creature but is fed;
And he who feeds the ravens,
Will give his children bread.

4 Though vine nor fig-tree neither,
Their wonted fruit shall bear,
Though all the fields should wither,
Nor flocks nor herds be there;
Yet God the same abiding,
His praise shall tune my voice;
For while in him confiding,
I cannot but rejoice.

Reproduced from *Christian Lyre* (New York, 1831), with permission of Moravian Music Foundation.

Henry Smith, that same year, included the tune in his *Church Harmony* (Chambersburg, PA, 1831), but printed the melody in the tenor and added a treble part.

The western Pennsylvania Methodist minister Samuel Wakefield printed a two-part version of the tune in his *The Christian's Harp*

(Pittsburgh, 1832). He attributed it to *Christian Lyre* but raised it one step, added a passing note in the first full measures of phrases 1, 3, and 7, and rewrote the bass. He associated the tune with Reginald Heber's text "From Greenland's icy mountains" and renamed it MISSIONARY.

The tune LIGHT, together with the text "Sometimes a light surprises" first appeared in an Episcopal hymnal in *H40*. The version in the Accompaniment Edition of *H82* is the same as that prepared for *H40* by Charles Winfred Douglas, except that in that book the first six phrases were set out for singing in harmony and only the last two phrases were marked "In unison."

1. See J. C. Downey, "Joshua Leavitt's *The Christian Lyre* and the Beginning of the Popular Tradition in American Religious Song," *Latin American Music Review* 7 (Fall/Winter, 1986), 149-161; C. Stribling, "Joshua Leavitt's *The Christian Lyre*: An Historical Evaluation," M.A. Thesis, William Carey College, 1976; H. H. Davis, "The Reform Career of Joshua Leavitt, 1794-1873," Ph.D. diss., Ohio State University, 1969.

RAL/MH

668 I to the hills will lift mine eyes

Music: **BURFORD**

This tune, which comes from the common treasury of psalm tunes, has appeared in prior editions of the *Hymnal*. This marks its first matching with this text, however.

Words: This is a revised version of the first three stanzas of the metrical paraphrase of Ps. 121 from the Scottish psalter, *The Psalms of David in Meeter* (Edinburgh, 1650). That psalter was largely a composite production, with more than half of its 8,620 lines being taken over from at least twelve previously published psalters, such as those of Sternhold and Hopkins, William Barton, Francis Rous, the Bay Psalm Book, and others.[1] Stanza 4 was newly written for *H82* by F. Bland Tucker to replace the final stanza of the 1650 version:

The Lord shall keep thy soul; he shall
Preserve thee from all ill.

Henceforth thy going out and in
God keep for ever will.

---

1. See M. Patrick, *Four Centuries of Scottish Psalmody* (London, 1949), 102.

Music: BURFORD appeared in two collections of 1718, the first edition of John Chetham's *Book of Psalmody* (London, 1718) and the fourth edition of James Green's *Collection of Choice Psalm Tunes* (London, 1718). Both emanated from the North Midlands, an area noted for the development of psalmody at that time, and we may safely assume that the tune came from that region, though its composer is not known.

Chetham's is probably the earlier of the two books; it was advertised for sale in the *Nottingham Weekly Courant* as early as 27 February 1717 (despite its 1718 imprint), while Green's was advertised there on 24 July 1718. Chetham set the tune to Ps. 42, Green to Ps. 30; the very strong four-part harmonization, with two augmented triads, is identical in both sources and is surely the work of a professional composer (see Example 1).

Example 1

The only difference in the tune was the dotted rhythm in the penultimate measure.

The tune appeared in well over 200 English collections during the next century under many names, including HEXHAM, NORWICH, and UXBRIDGE. The name BURFORD was first assigned in Nathaniel Gawthorn's *Harmonia Perfecta* (London, 1730) (see note on 434). Edward Miller, in *The Psalms of David* (London, 1791), attributed the tune to [Henry] Purcell for no apparent reason, and his prestige was enough to couple the great composer's name with the tune until recent times. It was even included in Anthony Lewis and Nigel Fortune's *The Works of Henry Purcell*, vol. 32 (London, 1962), 172; the editors cited a mid-eighteenth-century manuscript source, British Library Additional MS 28864, f. 56, which may possibly have been Miller's justification for the attribution. Franklin Zimmerman decided that the attribution was spurious, but ascribed the tune with even less reason to Henry Carey.[1] Another claimant is William Wheal (see 257), but no attribution to him earlier than 1777 has been found.

The first American printing appears to have been in Thomas Walters's *Grounds and Rules of Musick Explained* (Boston, 1759); it qualifies for Richard Crawford's *Core Repertory of Early American Psalmody* (Madison, WI, 1984), with forty-five printings up to the year 1810. Many nineteenth-century harmonizations, including that in *HA&M*, modulate to A^{b} major at the end of the second phrase. The one in *EH* does not modulate, and the *Hymnal* version appears to be based on that.

---

1. See F. Zimmerman, *Thematic Catalogue* (London, 1963), 430, no. S7.

RAL/NT

669 Commit thou all that grieves thee

Music: **HERZLICH TUT MICH VERLANGEN**

In this text the German poet Paul Gerhardt describes the creating and loving God, master of all things, who responds to the needs of all his creatures, "their anguish or delight." It first appeared in this translation in *H40*, where it was matched with this tune.

Words:

1. Befiehl du deine Wege,
   Und was dein Herze kränckt,
   Der allertreusten Pflege
   Dess, der den Himmel lenckt:
   Der Wolcken, Lufft und Winden,
   Giebt Wege, Lauf und Bahn,
   Der wird auch Wege finden,
   Da dein Fuss gehen kan.

2. Dem Herren must du trauen,
   Wann dirs sol wol ergehn;
   Auf sein Werck must du schauen,
   Wann dein Werck sol bestehn.
   Mit Sorgen und mit Grämen
   Und mit selbst eigner Pein
   Lässt Gott ihm gar nichts nehmen,
   Es muss erbäten seyn.

3. Dein' ewge Treu und Gnade,
   O Vater, weiss und sieht,
   Was gut sey oder schade
   Dem sterblichen Geblüt:
   Und was du denn erlesen
   Das treibst du, starcker Held,
   Und bringst zum Stand und Wesen,
   Was deinem Rath gefällt.

4. Weg, hast du allerwegen,
   An Mitteln fehlt dir's nicht;
   Dein, Thun ist lauter Segen,
   Dein Gang ist lauter Liecht:
   Dein Werck kan niemand hindern,
   Dein Arbeit darf nicht ruhn,
   Wann du, was deinem Kindern
   Erspriesslich ist, willst thun.

5. Und ob gleich alle Teufel
   Hier wolten wiederstehn,
So wird doch ohne Zweifel
   Gott nicht zurücke gehn:
Was Er ihm fürgenommen,
   Und was Er haben wil,
Dass muss doch endlich kommen
   Zu seinem Zweck und Ziel.

6. Hoff, O du arme Seele,
   Hoff' und sey unverzagt,
Gott wird dich aus der Höle,
   Da dich der Kummer plagt,
Mit grossen Gnaden rücken;
   Erwarte nur der Zeit
So wirst du schon erblicken,
   Die Sonn der schönsten Freud.

The text "Befiehl du deine Wege" ("Commit thou all that grieves thee") was written by Paul Gerhardt and was first published in Johann Crüger's *Praxis Pietatis Melica* (Frankfurt, 1656). The complete text of the original included twelve stanzas, the first word of each stanza forming an acrostic of Luther's German translation of Ps. 37:5. The text was most likely written during Gerhardt's ministry at Mittenwald. It has been called by Lauxmann "the most comforting of all the hymns that have resounded on Paul Gerhardt's golden lyre, sweeter to many souls than honey and the honeycomb."[1]

The most popular translation in English of Gerhardt's "Befiehl du deine Wege" is probably that of John Wesley, who, however, uses an SM scheme that makes impossible the use of the tune to which Gerhardt's text was long wedded. The most popular centos* are those beginning: "Commit thou all thy griefs" and "Give to the winds thy fears." Wesley's complete translation in sixteen SM stanzas may be found in the *Handbook to The Lutheran Hymnal* (St. Louis, 1942), together with an English translation of Gerhardt's original twelve stanzas in 76 76 D.

The four stanzas given here are joint translations of sts. 1, 2, 3, and 6 of the original by Arthur W. Farlander and Winfred Douglas, written in 1939. This translation appeared for the first time in *H40* and is reproduced here with only one slight alteration in st. 2:7 that originally read "God only sends his blessing."

---

1. E. Koch, *Geschichte des Kirchenlieds*, 8 vols., 3rd ed. (Stuttgart, 1866)—quoted in Polack's *The Handbook to The Lutheran Hymnal* (St. Louis, 1942).

Music: See hymn 168.

CS

670 Lord, for ever at thy side

Music: **SONG 13**

The rediscovery of the tunes of Orlando Gibbons has meant a great enrichment of the repertoire of congregational song. For this we are largely indebted to Ralph Vaughan Williams's work as music editor of *EH* and Charles Winfred Douglas as music editor of the 1916 and 1940 editions of the *Hymnal*. As evidence of increased interest in the tunes of this English renaissance composer, *H82* lists ten texts using Gibbons's tunes where *H16* and *H40* list four and seven, respectively. SONG 13 is matched here with a paraphrase of Ps. 131.

Words: This hymn by James Montgomery based on Ps. 131 was first published in Cotterill's *Selections of Psalms and Hymns* (London, 1819) and again in Montgomery's *Songs of Zion* (London, 1822). It was first included in the *Hymnal* in 1832. In *H82* the poet's sts. 2 and 3 have been replaced with new words by Charles P. Price. The omitted stanzas read:

2. Meekly may my soul receive
   All the Spirit hath reveal'd;
Thou hast spoken,—I believe,
   Though the prophecy were seal'd.

3. Quiet as a weaned child,
   Weaned from the mother's breast;
By no subtlety beguiled,
   On thy faithful word I rest.

1235)

In the original form of the text, the first two lines of st. 4 read:

Saints, rejoicing evermore,
  In the Lord Jehovah trust.

Music: SONG 13 was contributed by Orlando Gibbons to George Wither's *Hymnes and Songs of the Church* (London, 1623), for use with a paraphrase of The Song of Songs, ch. 4, vv. 1-15, the fifth "canticle" in a series of ten (see the essay "The Tunes of Congregational Song in Britain from the Reformation to 1750," vol. 1, 349). In that text, the lover begins to address his beloved as follows:

Oh my Love, how comely now,
  And how beautiful art thou!
Thou of dove-like eyes a paire
  Shining hast within thy haire,
And thy lockes like kidlings be,
  Which from Gilead hill we see.

Wither was here using, for the first time in English hymnody, the trochaic metre of seven syllables, already familiar in secular poems such as "Take, O take those lips away." Although he was eager to defend the inclusion of such an amorous text because it was scriptural, he can hardly have expected an ordinary congregation to sing it. Gibbons certainly did not. Since the words were those of a lover, he set them for what is evidently a tenor voice in the key of F. For lines 5 and 6 the music of lines 3 and 4 was repeated, and when using a four-line stanza we omit the repeat.

This gracious little melody has interesting features. Its "dip" at the end of the first phrase was fashionable in the new Italian vocal style of the day, and the little vocal flourish in the fourth phrase, which (in quarter-note units) was actually  clearly required a trained singer. Hymnal editors have understandably modified or omitted it.

The tune has appeared with various names, including CANTERBURY, SIMPLICITY, and NORWICH, and with differing degrees of simplification, as for example in *H40*. In performance, Gibbons's intention can be recalled if an occasional stanza is taken as a solo with continuo-style accompaniment.

In *H82*, the added alto and tenor parts differ considerably from those in *Songs of Praise* (London, 1931), especially in the second half of the tune.

HLW/JW

671 Amazing grace! how sweet the sound

***Music:* NEW BRITAIN**

This text and tune, which have been included in American hymn collections for more than one hundred and fifty years, appeared for the first time in an Episcopal hymnal supplement in *Lift Every Voice and Sing* (New York, 1981) and were continued in *H82*. The text by John Newton appeared first in the *Olney Hymns* (London, 1779), for which Newton was the major contributor (see the essay "British Hymnody from the Sixteenth Through the Eighteenth Centuries," vol. 1, 365).

Words: This is a truly remarkable hymn. It has been translated into many different languages and adapted into a multitude of different cultural styles. There is an incredible poignancy in the fact that the author, John Newton, was once a slave-ship captain and that this hymn continues to be sung with intensity by the descendants of those who were shipped as cargo in slave ships like Newton's, as well as by descendants of the ship's owners.

Newton wrote this hymn sometime before 1779, the year of its first appearance in print in his *Olney Hymns*, Bk. 1, no. 41. It is based on 1 Chr. 17:16-17, King David's questioning prayer: "Who am I, O Lord God, . . . that Thou hast brought me this far?" The six stanzas of the original are headed: "Faith's review and expectation." As with other hymns of Newton, "Amazing grace" is autobiographical, alluding to his conversion, and the change of lifestyle that it led to, together with a sense of thanksgiving for the guiding hand of God in his life.

Some people have difficulty in singing the second line of the first stanza: "That saved a *wretch* like me." It is to the credit of modern hymnal editors, who have not flinched to revise and rewrite other hymns, that they have left this "wretch" alone. When one understands something of the degrading way of life this man led as a sea captain involved in the slave trade, and recognizes that the hymn is to some degree autobiographical, it becomes clear that there were few other terms available for him to adequately describe his condition "before grace." It might be objected that this is just the point: how can modern worshipers sing about an experience they have never shared? That would be a valid argument if Newton were being only autobiographical. But the subtlety of his poetic genius was such that he used his own particular experience to enshrine the universal truth of the meaning of salvation.

Newton did not use "wretch" lightly. There are at least ten other hymns of Newton's in *Olney Hymns* that include the term, and in each one it is used to describe the human condition before the operation of the grace of God in Christ; it is part of the theological vocabulary of his hymns. Here are just three examples:

Lord, I am a wretch indeed!
I have sinned, but thou hast dy'd (Bk. 1, no. 79)

Fain would I hope that thou didst bleed
For such a wretch as I.
That blood which thou hast spilt,
That grace which is thine own,
Can cleanse the vilest sinner's guilt
And soften hearts of stone. (Bk. 3, no. 7)

Thy wond'ring saints rejoice to see
A wretch like me restor'd;
And point, and say, "how changed is he,
Who once defy'd the Lord!" (Bk. 3, no. 60)

These are all variations on the same theme that runs through this more famous hymn.

In *H82*, sts. 1 through 4 are, respectively, sts. 1, 2, 4, and 3 of Newton's original. The reversing of the order of sts. 3 and 4 was done to smooth the transition to st. 5. The omitted stanzas are:

5. Yes, when this flesh and heart shall fail,
   And mortal life shall cease;
I shall possess, within the veil,
   A life of joy and peace.

6. The earth shall soon dissolve like snow,
The sun forbear to shine;
But God, who call'd me here below,
Will be for ever mine.

The final stanza in *H82* was written neither by John Newton nor by John Rees. It is in fact an example of a "wandering" stanza in CM that appears at the end of a variety of hymns in nineteenth-century hymnals. This final stanza occurs, for example, at the end of "Hark! Hear the sound, on earth is found," in *The African Union Hymnal* (Wilmington, DE, 1822). The attribution to John P. Rees was made by William J. Reynolds after finding the name associated with the text in the 1859 edition of *The Sacred Harp*.[1] Subsequent research led Reynolds to discover that the attribution was erroneous.[2] The earliest occurrence of this anonymous stanza that so far has been discovered is attached to the end of the hymn "Jerusalem, my happy home" in *A Collection of Sacred Ballads* (Richmond, VA, 1790), compiled by Richard and Andrew Broaddus. It was around the end of the nineteenth century that it became the settled final stanza for "Amazing grace" in American hymnals. Although a widely popular hymn, it makes its first appearance in the *Hymnal* in *H82*.

---

1. In *Hymns of our Faith* (Nashville, 1964), 14.
2. See W. J. Reynolds, "Heavens No! Not John P. Rees," *The Hymn* 39, no. 3 (July 1988), 13-15.

Music: The pentatonic tune normally associated with the text "Amazing grace! how sweet the sound" apparently first appeared in print in two versions in Benjamin Shaw and Charles H. Spilman's four-shape shape-note *Columbian Harmony* (Cincinnati, 1829).[1] One, titled ST. MARY'S and printed with the text "Arise my soul, my joyful pow'rs," did not appear in any other book (see Example 1 on opposite page).

The other, titled GALLAHER, was printed with the text "Come let us join our friends above." This version of the tune, under this title, was later included in Robert Willis's *Lexington Cabinet* (Louisville, 1831),

Examples 1 & 2

Reproduced from *Columbian Harmony* (Cincinnati, 1829), Special Collections, University of Tennessee Libraries.

John B. Jackson's *Knoxville Harmony* (Madisonville, 1838), Silas W. Leonard and A. D. Fillmore's *Christian Psalmist* (Louisville, 1847), and Lindsey Watson's *Singer's Choice* (Louisville, 1854). In Willis's book it was printed with the same text, but in other books with one or more different texts. A counter part was added in Willis's book (see Example 2 on previous page).

This tune next appeared in print in David L. Clayton and James P. Carrell's *Virginia Harmony* (Winchester, VA, 1831). There it was titled HARMONY GROVE and linked with the text "There is a land of pure delight."

The next version in print was under the title HARMONY GROVE and with the text "When God revealed his gracious name" in Samuel Wakefield's *The Christian Harp* (Pittsburgh, 1832). This two-part version was copied into Henry Smith's *Church Harmony* (Chambersburg, PA) no later than the 1841 edition and into William R. Rhinehart's *American Church Harp* (Germantown, OH, 1848). In his *Western Harp* (Mount Pleasant, PA, 1843) Wakefield added a counter part.

The fifth version in print was SOLON, which appeared in Joseph Funk's *Genuine Church Music* (Winchester, VA, 1832) with the text "There is a fountain fill'd with blood." This version also appeared in several other books, including the Mennonite *Brethren's Tune and Hymn Book* (Dade City, PA, 1872).

The first book in which this tune was called NEW BRITAIN and linked with John Newton's text "Amazing grace! how sweet the sound" was in William Walker's *Southern Harmony* (New Haven, CT, 1835) (see Example 3 on following page).

This three-part version was copied into several other books. William Hauser added a counter part in his *Hesperian Harp* (Philadelphia, 1848), which was incorporated into Walker's own *Christian Harmony* (Philadelphia, 1867) and several other books, including some northern tunebooks that printed this four-part version under the title REDEMPTION. This version, with alterations in the alto, is included in a book still used among Primitive Baptists, C. H. Cayce's *The Good Old Songs* (Thornton, AK, 1913).

Another version called NEW BRITAIN, which first appeared in William

Example 3

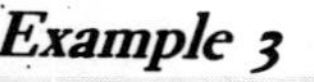

Reproduced from 1854 printing of *Southern Harmony*, Dupont Library, University of the South.

Hauser's *Olive Leaf* (Wadley GA, 1878), is printed twice with insignificant variations in another book still used among Primitive Baptists, John R. and J. Harvey Daily's *Primitive Baptist Hymn and Tune Book* (Indianapolis, 1902).

Other versions of the tune were published under the titles ANDERSON, CHALMERS, FRUGALITY, GALLAHER, HARMONY, HARMONY GROVE, MIDDLETON, SOLON, and SYMPHONY.

The first mainline denominational hymnal to include the tune (though not with Newton's text) was apparently the Southern Presbyterian *Book of Hymns and Tunes* (Richmond, VA, 1874), in which it was titled SOLON.

Edwin O. Excell, a composer and publisher of gospel songs, included an arrangement of this tune under the name AMAZING GRACE with Newton's text in his *Make His Praise Glorious* (Chicago, 1900). It was, however, his later *Coronation Hymns* (Chicago, 1910) that apparently contained the first printing of the arrangement of the tune that is found in a number of current hymnals, including *The Hymnal of the United Church of Christ* (Philadelphia, 1974), the Christian Reformed Church's *Psalter Hymnal* (Grand Rapids, MI, 1987), *The United Methodist Hymnal* (Nashville, 1989), *The Presbyterian Hymnal* (Louisville, KY, 1990), and the *Baptist Hymnal* (Nashville, 1991). This 1910 publication was also apparently the first book to print the final stanza "When we've been there ten thousand years" (see text commentary above).

George Pullen Jackson lists NEW BRITAIN among the "Eighty Most Popular Tunes" in his *White Spirituals in the Southern Uplands* (Chapel Hill, NC, 1933).

This tune first entered an Episcopal hymnal in *Hymnal Supplement II* (New York, 1976), with a harmonization by Alastair Cassels-Brown and with guitar chords. It was called AMAZING GRACE in that publication and printed with another text by John Newton, "How sweet the Name of Jesus sounds." An arrangement of this tune by Richard Smallwood was printed with the text "Amazing grace, how sweet the sound" in *Lift Every Voice and Sing: A Collection of African-American Spirituals and Other Songs* (New York, 1981), sponsored by the Office of Black Ministries, the first American Episcopal hymnal supplement to include this text. In *H82* the tune is called NEW BRITAIN and linked with the harmonization prepared by Austin Cole Lovelace (A. C. L.) for *The Methodist Hymnal* (Nashville, 1964).

---

1. See M. J. Hatchett, "Benjamin Shaw and Charles H. Spilman's *Columbian Harmony, or Pilgrim's Musical Companion*," *The Hymn* 42 (January, 1991), 20-23.

RAL/MH

672 O very God of very God

Music: **BANGOR**

It is of interest to note the inspiration that nineteenth-century hymn writers have derived from lines of the Nicene Creed. "All things bright and beautiful" [405], "Once in royal David's city" [102] by Cecil Francis Alexander, and this text by John Mason Neale are examples of such derivations. This text is matched with an eighteenth-century English psalm tune as it has been since the music edition of the 1916 *Hymnal*.

Words: This text, a meditation on lines from the Nicene Creed that begin the hymn, is from John Mason Neale's *Hymns for Children, Third Series* (London, 1846). It is assigned the date of December 21 and linked to the "O Antiphon" for that day, *O Oriens*. Thus it mirrors the Advent expectation for the coming of Christ to bring light to a darkened world. It entered the *Hymnal* in 1892. An omitted final Doxology was:

To God the Father power and might,
　Both now and ever be:
To him that is the Light of Light
　And, Holy Ghost, to thee.

Music: See hymn 164.

LW

673 The first one ever, oh, ever to know

Music: **BALLAD**

Appearing for the first time in an Episcopal hymnal in *H82*, "The first one ever, oh, ever to know" is notable for being a text and tune by a woman about women in the Gospels. Both the text and tune are the work of Linda Wilberger Egan.

Words: Three important events in Mrs. Egan's life coalesced to provide inspiration for this hymn. She writes that the work was composed

> after the first year of a three-year study of the Gospels . . . that year I was reading to discover Jesus' relationships with the women he encountered, and their function in his ministry. That year was also the first year of the Rev. Elaine Kebba's ministry at Trinity [Episcopal Church in Swarthmore, PA]. Because of their contact with her, many women there had begun to expand their views of their own ministries.

Mrs. Egan continues, "Later in that year I became musician for the Well Woman Project . . . among its purposes is a search for liturgical expression consistent with the spiritual experience of women as well as men . . ."[1]

Stanza 1 of the text focuses on Mary, the mother of our Lord, and st. 2 on the Samaritan woman whose meeting at the well with Jesus is related in the gospel of John. The three women, Mary, Joanna, and Mary Magdalene, the first to see the risen Lord, are central to st. 3. Mrs. Egan uses the form of a folk song with oft-repeated phrases to tell her story reminding "people what they already know about these three famous events in Jesus' life."[2]

To have a consistent use of verb tenses in all stanzas, in st. 1 "believed" has been altered to "believes." In st. 2, to remove an awkward accent, the order of the words "Jesus, Messiah" have been reversed. The change in st. 3, line 4, from "blessed is she" to "blessed are they" was made at the request of the SCCM so that all three Marys mentioned in this stanza would be included in the plural pronoun.

---

1. Egan to Glover, 21 March 1985, Church Hymnal Corporation Papers, New York, NY.
2. Ibid.

Music: BALLAD, the simple folklike tune composed by Linda Egan for use with her text, is, as her original manuscript indicates, to be sung emphatically like an "estampie," a medieval instrumental form that probably had its roots in dance. The tune, with its distinctive repeated rhythmic and melodic patterns, is basically diatonic, and, like many folk tunes, is modal. In presenting this tune to a congregation, careful distinction must be made between the dotted rhythms that appear throughout the setting, ♩. ♪ and ♪ ♩.. Although scored for performance with guitar, a simple keyboard accompaniment can be created by using the chords printed above the melody line. First appearing in *H82*, it has also been included in *The United Methodist Hymnal* (Nashville, 1989).

RG

674 "Forgive our sins as we forgive"

Music: **DETROIT**

This profound text on the theme of forgiveness opens with a paraphrase of words from the Lord's Prayer. It is deeply rooted in the life experience of the author, Rosamund Herklots. The text is matched here, as it is in *MHSS* and *Hymns III,* with DETROIT, an American folk hymn.

Words: The inspiration for the hymn "Forgive our sins as we forgive" came as Miss Rosamund Herklots, an English hymn writer, dug weeds in her nephew's garden. As she worked at the deep, tenacious roots, she saw a vivid parallel between the intrusive, smothering qualities of these weeds and the destructive ways in which deeply buried feelings of bitterness and resentment prevent us from growing as loving, concerned people. Framing her text with a line paraphrased from the Lord's Prayer, the poet reminds us of the smallness of others' debts to us when compared to our debt to our Lord who suffered and died on the cross for our sins. Miss Herklots closes her prayer with the petition that, through repentance and reconciliation with God and others, our lives will bear witness of God's peace.

The text, written in June 1966, one of the best known of her works, appeared first in the parish magazine of St. Mary's Church, Bromley,

Kent. It was published next in *100 Hymns for Today* (London), the 1969 supplement to *HA&M*. It gained immediate popularity and is now a part of many hymnals in England and North America. It first appeared in an Episcopal publication in *MHSS* and was subsequently included in *Hymns III* and *H82*.

Music: This hexatonic tune first appeared in print in a four-part arrangement under the name DETROYT in the first edition of the four-shape shape-note *A Supplement to the Kentucky Harmony* (Harrisonburg, VA, 1820), which was compiled by Ananias Davisson.[1] It was attributed to Bradshaw and linked with a text by the English Independent minister Philip Doddridge, "Do not I love thee, O my Lord?" (see Example 1 on opposite page).

In the third edition of Davisson's *Supplement* (Harrisonburg, VA, 1825), the name was spelled DETROIT. This version of the tune, with or without the counter part, was reprinted in more than two dozen books, including the Mennonite *Brethren's Tune and Hymn Book* (Dade City, PA, 1872). It is printed on two staffs with the melody in the treble in two books still being used among Primitive Baptists, John R. and J. Harvey Daily's *Primitive Baptist Hymn and Tune Book* (Indianapolis, 1902) and C. H. Cayce's *The Good Old Songs* (Thornton, AK, 1913).

In the 1867 edition of Joseph Funk and Sons' *Harmonia Sacra* (Singers' Glen, VA) a different counter part was added to the three-part version printed in earlier editions of that book, beginning with the 1857 edition. This version was reproduced in some later books.

B. F. White and E. J. King's *Sacred Harp* (Philadelphia, 1844) included a three-part version with alterations in the first phrase of the bass line and in the rhythm of the first and third phrases. This version was reproduced in John G. McCurry's *Social Harp* (St. Louis, 1854), and an alto slightly different from the original was added in J. S. James *Original Sacred Harp* (Cullman, AL, 1911). A hybrid version affected by that of *Sacred Harp* was printed in L. J. Jones's *Southern Minstrel* (Philadelphia, 1849).

Different harmonizations of the tune were printed in the Western Pennsylvania Methodist minister Samuel Wakefield's *Western Harp* (Mount Pleasant, 1843), the Philadelphian J. H. Biddle's *Harp of the Valley* (Philadelphia, 1853), and William Hauser's *Olive Leaf* (Wadley, GA, 1878).

Example 1

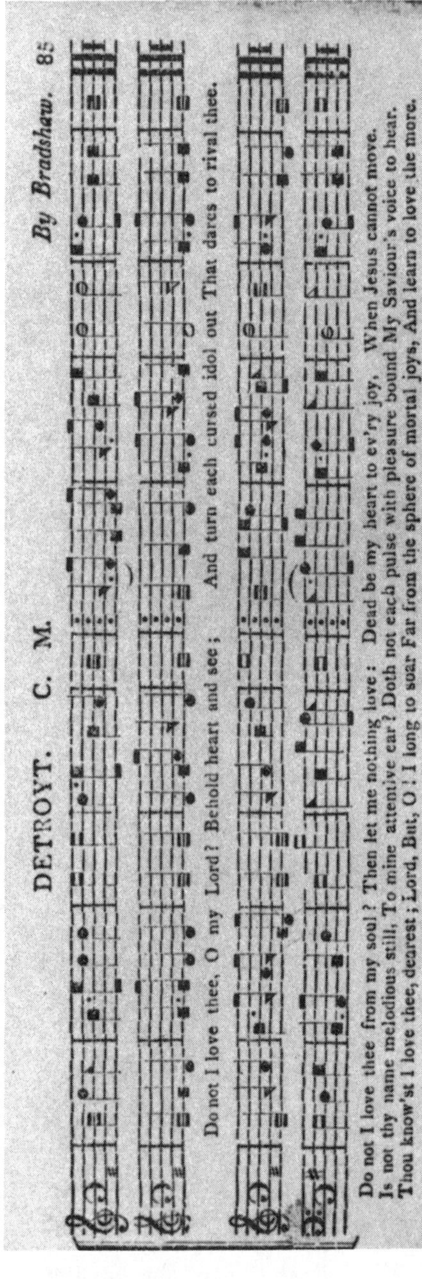

Reproduced from *A Supplement to the Kentucky Harmony* (Harrisonburg, VA, 1820), Union Theological Seminary Library, New York.

George Pullen Jackson lists DETROIT among the "Eighty Most Popular Tunes" in his *White Spirituals in the Southern Uplands* (Chapel Hill, NC, 1933). Only in recent years, however, has it been included in mainline hymnals. It is one of very few American folk tunes printed in hymnals published outside the United States.

The tune first entered an Episcopal hymnal under the name FORGIVE OUR SINS in *MHSS* with an accompaniment by Irving Lowens from *We Sing of Life* (Boston, 1955), edited by Vincent Silliman and Irving Lowens, with guitar chords. It was apparently in *MHSS* that this tune was first linked with the text "Forgive our sins as we forgive."

In *Hymns III*, where it was titled DETROIT, the tune was again linked with "Forgive our sins as we forgive." Two settings were provided, an accompaniment by Alastair Cassels-Brown commissioned for use in this collection and a three-part harmonization attributed to William Walker's *Southern Harmony* (New Haven, CT, 1835). Actually this was the version with changes in the bass line and the rhythm that had first appeared in B. F. White and E. J. King's *Sacred Harp*. The accompaniment for use in *H82* is by Margaret W. Mealy. Guitar chords are provided.

---

1. See R. A. B. Harley, "Ananias Davisson: Southern Tune-Book Compiler (1780-1857)," Ph.D. diss., University of Michigan, 1972.

RG/MH

675 Take up your cross, the Savior said

***Music:* BOURBON**

This text and tune appear for the first time in a hymnal of the Episcopal Church. BOURBON, the strong, angular, pentatonic American folk melody, enhances the strong evangelical thrust of the text, which calls us to take up our cross and to follow Christ.

Words: The original poem was written by the nineteen-year-old Charles William Everest, who later became an Episcopal rector in Connecticut. It was published in the author's *Vision of Death, and Other Poems* (Hartford, 1833):

1. Take up thy cross, the Saviour said,
   If thou wouldst my disciple be;

Take up thy cross with willing heart,
  And humbly follow after me.

2. Take up thy cross! let not its weight
  Fill thy weak soul with vain alarm:
His strength shall bear thy spirit up,
  And brace thy heart, and nerve thine arm.

3. Take up thy cross, nor heed the shame,
  Nor let thy foolish pride be still:
Thy Lord refused not e'en to die
  Upon the Cross, on Calvary's hill.

4. Take up thy cross then in his strength,
  And calmly sin's wild deluge brave;
'Twill guide thee to a better home,
  It points to glory o'er the grave.

5. Take up thy cross, and follow on,
  Nor think till death to lay it down;
For only he who bears the cross
  May hope to wear the glorious crown.

Percy Dearmer commented: "This is one of those hymns of poor quality which have to be always changed in order to make them possible for use."[1] Thus an altered form of the text appeared in the *Salisbury Hymn Book* (Salisbury, England, 1858), probably the work of the collection's editor, Horatio Nelson. This version was taken over in the first edition of *HA&M* (1861)—one of a number of American texts included in that influential British collection—and thereafter entered into common usage. The version in *H82* is reworked into a "you" form, and adjustments are made in the interests of inclusivity.

---

1. P. Dearmer, *Songs of Praise Discussed* (London 1933), 77.

Music: See hymn 147. The accompaniment was composed by John Leon Hooker for *H82*. Guitar chords are provided with this setting.

RAL

676 There is a balm in Gilead

***Music:* THERE IS A BALM IN GILEAD**

This spiritual which for many years has had a place in the repertoire of choral groups in the United States has more recently appeared in Protestant and Roman Catholic hymnals.

Words: This is one of many spirituals in which the chorus is based on a specific scriptural passage, while the verses may appear to be unrelated. The chorus of this spiritual responds to a question asked in Jer. 8:22 and answered by a command in Jer. 46:11. The singers represent those who have benefited from the balm (salvation) through having been made whole (finding the strength to endure slavery) and through having their sin-sick souls healed (accepting Christianity). Taken from the catalogue of stock "wandering couplets" usable in any number of spirituals, the verses speak to both the difficulty of bearing the chains of slavery (st. 1) and living a life acceptable to God and Christ (st. 2). The text with a different tune appeared in the 1989 edition of the Methodist Hymnal.

Music: The publication of Theodore Frelinghuysen Seward's *Jubilee Songs as Sung by the Jubilee Singers of Fisk University* (New York and Chicago, 1872) signaled the commencement of the publication of a series of collections containing Negro Spirituals arranged in four-part choral style. Unlike the single melody line spirituals contained in the first collection of songs of black America, *Slave Songs of the United States* (New York, 1867), collected by William Francis Allen, Lucy McKim Garrison, and Charles Pickard Ware, the Seward collection offered the standard soprano-alto-tenor-bass-arranged spirituals. It was not until the twentieth century, however, that spirituals collected and published by African-Americans became available. John Wesley Work II (1872-1925) and his brother, Frederick Jerome (1879-1942), published two collections, *New Jubilee Songs* (Nashville, TN, 1902) and *Folk Songs of the American Negro* (Nashville, TN, 1907). John Wesley published a lone effort, *The Folk Song of the American Negro* (Nashville, TN 1915). The 1907 collection of John and Frederick Work is significant for its introduction of "There is a Balm in Gilead" with its proper tune. For Episcopalians this Spiritual first appeared in *Lift Every Voice* (New York, 1981) in an arrangement by R. Nathaniel Dett.

The music for this spiritual is unusual in two respects from other well-known works of this genre. The most unusual feature is that the spiritual is based on a pentatonic (five-tone) scale, as found in such spirituals as "Swing Low, Sweet Chariot" and "Steal Away to Jesus," as well as "Amazing Grace." The first five tones of the scale are used as melody tones in this spiritual. The second unusual feature of the spiritual is that the verse is connected to the chorus by a tone that comes to rest one step above the beginning tone of the chorus, thereby obliging the singer to return to the chorus to complete the verse. Although this melodic construction is rare in Negro Spirituals, the verse of "Go Tell it On the Mountain" [99] is another example of this unifying element. The arrangement of this spiritual was composed by David Hurd for use in *H82*.

HCB

677 God moves in a mysterious way

Music: **LONDON NEW**

Although this text appeared in the *Hymnal* in 1826, its matching with this tune probably should be credited to *HA&M*. This setting gained an added impetus for congregational use through its inclusion in Benjamin Britten's cantata *Saint Nicolas* (1948).

Words: This hymn by William Cowper had already achieved popularity before it appeared in *Olney Hymns* (London, 1779). It was probably written before the end of the year 1772. The evidence comes from a manuscript collection of copies of letters of Cowper, Newton, and one or two others, compiled by various relatives of Cowper. The letters appear in a chronological sequence. The text of Cowper's hymn appears between copies of two letters written by John Newton, the first dated 4 November 1772, and the second, August 1773.[1] The implication is that a copy of the hymn was included with Newton's original letter of November 1772. Cowper therefore wrote it about a year before the onset of the intense period of depression that led to attempted suicide in October 1773, and brought his major hymn writing to an end. This early version was identical with the later printed form, with the exception of st. 5, line 4, which ran: "But wait to smell the flower."

In 1774 the hymn appeared in print three times: in *Twenty-Six Letters on Religious Subjects, to which are added Hymns, &c* (London, 1774), issued by Newton under the pseudonym "Omicron"; in the July issue of the journal *The Gospel Magazine* (over the initials "J. W."); and in the third edition of Richard Conyers's *Collection of Psalms and Hymns* (London, 1774). Two years later it appeared in Augustus Toplady's *Psalms and Hymns for Public and Private Worship* (London, 1776), and a year after that it was reprinted again in *The Gospel Magazine* (Dec. 1777), with an additional stanza by "Miss Uffington." In Book 3 of *Olney Hymns* the hymn appeared in its original six stanzas in the section on "Conflict" with the title "Light shining out of darkness" [see 667]. It has been in the *Hymnal* since 1826.

---

1. See J. E. B. Mayor, "Letters of William Cowper," *Notes and Queries*, Series X, Vol 2 (24 Sept. 1904), 244.

Music: See hymn 50.

RAL

678 Surely it is God who saves me

Music: **COLLEGE OF PREACHERS**

The provision in a revised *Hymnal* of metrical paraphrases for prayer book canticles was one of the special concerns of the Text Committee of the SCCM.[1] At the time he wrote this paraphrase, the author, the Rev. Dr. Carl P. Daw, Jr., was a consultant to the Text Committee.

---

1. See the list of these in *H82a1*, 680-681.

Words: This text is a metrical paraphrase of Is. 12:2-6, a passage presented for the first time as a canticle in the 1979 *BCP* (Canticle 9: The First Song of Isaiah, 86). The link between the prayer book and hymnal versions is most clearly evident in the opening line, which the paraphrase uses verbatim from the prayer book translation. The only other conscious echo in the text is the second line of the second stanza ("tell out his exalted Name"), a phrasing chosen to reflect Timothy Dudley-Smith's paraphrase of the Magnificat (see 437).

The hymnal version of this paraphrase represents the end result of several revisions. The original version was first used in the chapel of the School of Theology of the University of the South, where the author was a seminarian at the time.

Since its first publication in *H82*, this text has appeared in the Roman Catholic hymnal *Worship III* (Chicago, 1986) and in the Christian Reformed Church's *Psalter Hymnal* (Grand Rapids, MI, 1988).

Music: Two tunes were written especially for use with the text "Surely it is God who saves me" in *H82*. COLLEGE OF PREACHERS was composed by Arthur Rhea, a member of the SCCM, during the final meeting of that body in May 1985 at the College of Preachers at the National Cathedral in Washington, DC. At that time the Commission found itself unable, because of copyright complications, to use one of the tunes previously selected for pairing with this text.

Mr. Rhea's plaintive tune is basically diatonic in structure, using occasional leaps to underline important verbal stresses in the text; for example, in the third phrase of the tune at the words "the Lord" and "and shields." A more dramatic instance occurs in the beginning of the sixth phrase at the word "salvation" and at the same place in st. 2, "with you," where Mr. Rhea introduces an ascending major sixth. The climactic nature of the tune at this place is supported through the use of chromatic harmonies in the accompaniment. Here the composer starts in G and, passing through E and A, makes a quick return to D, the tonic of the key in which the tune is written. Harmonic richness is one of the telling qualities of this setting.

CPD/RG

679 Surely it is God who saves me

Music: **THOMAS MERTON**

A folklike tune by a contemporary American composer has been chosen for the second setting of this text.

Words: See hymn 678.

Music: THOMAS MERTON, honoring the late Roman Catholic Trappist monk and mystic, is the work of Ray W. Urwin, when Organist/Choirmaster of St. John's Cathedral, Wilmington, DE. It originated in 1980/81 as a setting of Canticle 9, "The First Song of Isaiah" and was composed as a wedding gift. The composer adapted the refrain and verses for this metrical setting in 1983 for use in *H82*. Basically, the melody lies comfortably within the range of a fifth, E to B, with an occasional drop to the lower dominant B and the use of the one C# above the upper B. In 6/8 metre, the rhythm of the tune reflects closely the natural rhythm of the words. At no place is this more effective than at the cadence, where the feminine (stressed-unstressed) cadences of the text are supported by the ♩ ♪ rhythm of the tune. In performance, this setting is equally effective when played on either a keyboard instrument or a guitar.

RG

680 O God, our help in ages past

Music: **ST. ANNE**

This text by Isaac Watts is probably not only his best-known work, but one of his finest. A masterful paraphrase of Ps. 90:1-5, it can be found in practically every English-language hymnal around the world. Its matching with this tune occurred early in the nineteenth century.

Words: "O God, our help in ages past" appeared as the first part of Isaac Watts's paraphrase of Ps. 90. It was published in his *Psalms of David* (London, 1719) and entitled "Man, Frail and God Eternal." The original hymn contained nine stanzas. In practice, however, the fourth, sixth, and eighth were and are regularly omitted. These omitted stanzas, as Julian says, "being unequal to the rest, impede the grandly sustained flow of thought; and in its commonly accepted form of six verses the hymn is seen to the fullest advantage" (*Julian*, 875).

John Wesley, who altered the opening from "Our God, our help" to "O God, our help," printed the complete text in his *Collection of Psalms and Hymns* (London, 1738). An arrangement in seven stanzas, sts. 4 and 8 having been omitted, was included in *A Collection of Hymns for the People Called Methodists* (London, 1780) and has been retained in all subsequent editions of that collection. Today it is considered to be one of the finest texts in the English hymn literature and is considered the finest hymn paraphrase written by Isaac Watts.

The text first appeared in an Episcopal hymnal in the *Hymnal* of 1871 with these stanzas omitted:

4. Thy word commands our flesh to dust,
 "Return ye sons of men":
All nations rose from earth at first,
 And turn to earth again.

5. The busy tribes of flesh and blood
 With all their lives and cares
Are carried downwards by thy flood,
 And lost in following years.

8. Like flowery fields the nations stand
 pleased with the morning light;
The flowers beneath the mower's hand
 Lie withering ere 'tis night.

Music: The authorship of this famous tune has long been disputed. Although it cannot be established with absolute certainty, there is now little room for doubt that it was composed by Dr. William Croft, organist of the Chapel Royal and Westminster Abbey and the leading composer of Queen Anne's reign.

There is no attribution in the earliest source, the 6th edition of Tate and Brady's *Supplement to the New Version of Psalms* (London, 1708), where the tune is named ST. ANNE's and is set to Ps. 42, New Version, "As pants the hart for cooling streams." Croft was, however, almost certainly organist of St. Anne's Church, Soho, from 1700 to 1711, so that name is circumstantial evidence of his authorship. Moreover, the tune is attributed to Croft by two contemporary editors who certainly knew him well, Philip Hart (in *Melodies Proper to be Sung to Any of the Versions of Ye Psalms of David, Figur'd for the Organ* [London, 1716]) and John Church (in *An Introduction to Psalmody* [London, 1723]), and also by his pupil John Barker, who possessed some of Croft's hymn tune settings in manuscript and published them in *A*

Select Number of the Best Psalm Tunes, Extant (Birmingham, ca. 1750).

Doubts have arisen on two counts. First, Abraham Barber printed a four-part version of the identical tune in the 7th edition of *A Book of Psalm Tunes* (York, 1715) with the name LEEDS and an attribution to the otherwise unknown "Mr. Denby"; some earlier commentators thought that a pre-1708 edition of Barber's book might be found to contain the tune, but this has not occurred, and it is not even in the 6th edition of 1711. Second, Croft's connection with St. Anne's Church has been doubted, because the vestry minutes actually record the appointment of Phillip Crofts rather than William Croft or Crofts to the organist post. It appears, however, that this was merely a clerical error. Watkins Shaw has pointed out that Croft described himself as "Organist of St. Ann's" in 1700.[1]

The tune, like many of the greatest, of course, is made up of phrases then in common use. The chance similarity of its first phrase to the theme of Bach's organ fugue in E^b has caused that work to be known in English-speaking countries as "St. Anne's Fugue." Handel's Chandos anthem "O praise the Lord" also begins in the same way. Major Crawford was inclined to trace the phrase back to a motet by Palestrina, while Routley thought the whole tune was made up of fragments of tunes by Henry Lawes. In reality the composer's achievement lay in making a powerful new synthesis of preexisting elements (compare no. 377). ST. ANNE, with its swinging "sawtooth" melodic line, is clearly modeled on some of the classic tunes of a century earlier, such as YORK [462], LONDON NEW [50], and ST. DAVID'S.[2]

ST. ANNE has enjoyed phenomenal and unbroken popularity since it was first introduced. It was printed in Ireland in 1749, Scotland in 1750, Holland in 1753, America in 1761 (in James Lyon's *Urania* [Philadelphia]), Canada in 1816 (as CHELSEA), and India in 1818. It is to be found in virtually every major Anglican or Episcopal hymnal of the nineteenth century.

Routley claimed that it was first joined to the present text in *HA&M* (1861), where it appeared in a four-part harmonization by William H. Monk, very similar to the one given here.[3] In fact, the earliest printing was in Theophania Cecil's collection, *The Psalm and Hymn Tunes used at St. John's Chapel, Bedford Row* (London, 1814). No doubt the text/tune match was made by her father, Richard Cecil, the Evangelical clergyman and amateur composer, who was minister at St. John's (an Anglican proprietary chapel) until his death in 1810.

The original (1708) version, whether it is Croft's or not, is for two voices only. Croft, however, did set it in four parts. We give, in Example 1, his four-part treble-led setting from John Barker's collection mentioned above.

Example 1

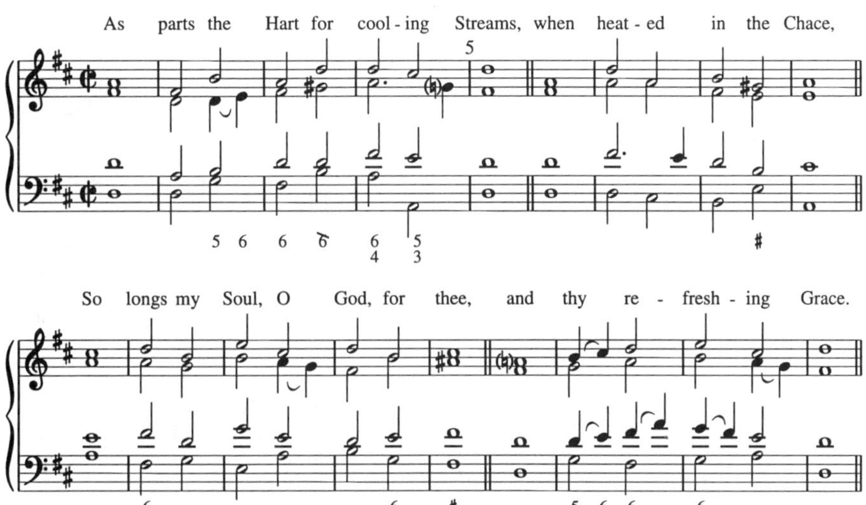

Because of Barker's relationship with Croft, it is more than likely that he was correct in calling this Croft's setting, but it has never been reprinted in modern times. It has a tenor part that is too high for modern practice, and is marred by parallelisms in measures 13 through 14 and 14 through 15. The latter is blatant, but one must recall that it was customary in 1750, as also in 1708, to play organ interludes between the phrases of a psalm tune.

Two other interesting settings may be mentioned. William Billings published one in *Music in Miniature* (Boston, 1779), which was probably his own, as Karl Kroeger has demonstrated.[4] Arthur Sullivan wrote a varied arrangement for choir and organ, to the text "The Son of God goes forth to war," for *Church Hymns with Tunes* (London, 1874).[5] The tune works almost perfectly in strict canon at the fifth below (Example 2, page 1258); if the original melisma is adopted in the last line, the only "cheats" are in the second line.

Example 2

© Copyright Nicholas Temperley 1987

---

1. The controversy may be traced in *Grove*, 1st ed., III (1883), at "Saint Anne's Tune" by Major G. A. Crawford; F. G. E[dwards], "Dr. William Croft," *The Musical Times* 41 (1900) 577-85; L. Ellinwood, *The Hymnal 1940 Companion*, 191; N. Temperley, "Croft and the Charity Hymn," *The Musical Times* 119 [1978], 539-41; W. Shaw, Letter to the Editor, *The Musical Times*, 119 [1978], 668; E. Routley, *The Music of Christian Hymns* (Chicago, 1981), 53, 56, and Exs. 141, 142.

2. Routley, *The Music of Christian Hymns*, 53.

3. M. Frost, *English & Scottish Psalm & Hymn Tunes c. 1543-1677* (London, 1953), no. 234.

4. It is reproduced in W. Billings, edited by K. Kroeger and H. Nathan, *Works*, III (Boston and Charlottesville, 1986), 356.

5. Reproduced in N. Temperley, *The Music of the English Parish Church* (Cambridge, 1979), II, Example 83.

TS/NT

681 Our God, to whom we turn

Music: **O GOTT, DU FROMMER GOTT**

This great German chorale matched with this text appears in *H82* with the restoration of its proper German name. The name was altered in *H40* because of the strong anti-German feelings present in the United States prior to World War II when the book was being prepared.

Words: This text from Edward Grubb's *Light of Life: Hymns of Faith and Consolation* (London, 1925) first appeared in *Songs of Praise* (Oxford, 1925) set to the tune O GOTT, DU FROMMER GOTT, called STEADFAST because of anti-German feelings prior to and between the two World Wars. This usage was continued unaltered in *H40*.

In support of the SCCM's statement on textual alteration to achieve theological orthodoxy and clarity of meaning through the deletion of archaic and obscure language and to "affirm the participation of all in the Body of Christ,"[1] several changes were made in the text. The original forms of altered lines are:

2:2 Though we who fain would find thee,
2:8 Our souls can find no rest.

3:4-8 The deep-toned organ blast
That rolls through arches dim
Hints of music vast
Of thy eternal hymn

4. Wherever goodness lurks
We catch thy tones appealing
Where man for justice works
Thou art thyself revealing;
The blood of man, for man
On friendship's altar spilt,
Betrays the mystic plan
On which thy house is built.

---

1. Appendix A, vol. 1, 639.

Music: The tune O GOTT, DU FROMMER GOTT (*Zahn* 5138) appeared in the *Neu ordentlich Gesangbuch* (Hanover, 1646), where it was set to Johann Hermann's text "Groß ist, o großer Gott." The harmonization is based on that of Johann Sebastian Bach from a set of organ variations. Taken from *H40*, it is slightly altered and the note values have been halved.

RG/CS

682 I love thee, Lord, but not because

Music: **ST. FULBERT**

This devotional text expressing the poet's questioning of his reasons for loving God entered the singing tradition of Episcopalians in the *Hymnal* of 1871. Its matching with ST. FULBERT, however, did not occur until *H40*.

Words:

1. No me mueue, mi Dios, para quererte
El cielo que me tienes prometido,
Ni me mueue el infierno tan temido
Par dexar por essor de ofenderte.

2. Tu me mueues, Señor, mueuenme el verte
Clauado en essa Cruz, y escarnecido;
Mueueme el ver tu cuerpo tan herido,
Mueuenme tus afrentas, y tu muerte.

3. Mueueme en fin tu amor, en tal manera,
Que auque no huuiera cielo, y te amara;
Yaunque no huuiera infierno, te temiera.

4. No me tienes que dar porque te quiera,
Porque aunque quanto espero no esperara,
Lo mismo que te quiero te quisiera.

Although tradition attributes this text to St. Francis Xavier, there is no evidence to support it. The editors of *H40c* trace the first-known source of the original text to *Epitome de la vida y muerte de San Ignacion de Loyola* (Ruromonda, Gaspar du Pres, 1662), where it appears anonymously. However, they further state that "the poem is older . . . for it had already been translated into Latin in 1657 by Joannes Nadasi in his *Pretiosae Occupationes Morientium*, beginning 'Non me movet Domine, ad amandum te.' " The translation of the text by Edward Caswall that first appeared in his *Lyra Catholica* (London, 1849) is based on a Latin form of the text found in the Cologne *Caeleste Palmetum* (1669) that begins:

O Deus ego amo te,
Nec amo te ut salves me.

The Caswall translation of the text first appeared in the 1871 edition of the *Hymnal*. The form of the text in that collection is:

1. My God, I love Thee—not because
I hope for heav'n thereby:
Nor yet because, if I love not,
I must forever die.

2. Thou, O my Jesus, Thou didst me
Upon the Cross embrace;
For me didst bear the nails and spear,
And manifold disgrace,

3. And griefs and torments numberless,
And sweat of agony,
Yea, death itself; and all for me
Who was Thine enemy.

4. Then why, O blessed Jesu Christ,
Should I not love Thee well?
Not for the hope of winning heaven,
Nor of escaping hell;

5. Not with the hope of gaining aught;
Nor seeking a reward;
But as Thyself hast loved me,
O everlasting Lord!

6. So would I love Thee, dearest Lord,
And in Thy praise will sing:
Solely because Thou art my God,
And my eternal King. Amen.

The *H82* form of the text is an altered version of the Caswall translation that first appeared in *Songs of Praise* (London, 1931) and later in *H40*. Percy Dearmer, in *Songs of Praise Discussed* (London, 1933), writes of the alterations, "We have endeavored to make the version a little more Christian by reducing its egoism; but otherwise Caswall remains."

Although the first line of the Caswall translation is strong poetically, it presents problems when set to music. To facilitate its singing, the

SCCM altered it to "I love thee, Lord, but not because." Other alterations in sts. 2 and 3, "mankind" to "the world" and "man" to "one," support the Commission's intent to use inclusive language whenever possible.

Music: See hymn 545.

ALeC/RG

683 O for a closer walk with God

Music: **BEATITUDO**

The *Olney Hymns* (London, 1779), an important Evangelical hymnal of the late eighteenth century, is the source of eight texts in *H82*, of which this much-loved work is one. Written by William Cowper, the text is autobiographical and expressive of the deep personal faith of the poet. Its matching with this tune can be traced to the Hutchins music edition of the 1892 *Hymnal*.

Words: This popular and well-loved hymn by William Cowper grew out of the anxiety of caring for a sick friend. It was begun on 9 December 1767 and completed the following day. The evidence comes from a letter he wrote to his aunt, dated 10 December 1767, in which he included the complete text:

> I began to compose them [these lines] yesterday morning before daybreak, but fell asleep at the end of the first two lines [stanzas?]: when I awaked again, the third and fourth were whispered to my heart in a way I have often experienced.[1]

The hymn comprised the six stanzas that became familiar through *Olney Hymns* (London, 1779), except for st. 2:4: "Of Jesus *in* His word?" It was first published in the second edition of Richard Conyers's hymn book *A Collection of Psalms and Hymns* (London, 1772), and then in Augustus Toplady's *Psalms and Hymns for Public and Private Worship* (London, 1776). In *Olney Hymns* it appeared in Bk. 1 with the title "Walking with God" and the reference Gen. 5:24. *The Hymnal 1940* omitted two stanzas; one is restored in *H82*. The omitted third stanza is:

What peaceful hours I once enjoy'd!
How sweet their mem'ry still!
But they have left an aching void,
The world can never fill.

The hymn has been in the *Hymnal* since 1826.

---

1. See J. E. B. Mayor, "Letters of William Cowper," *Notes and Queries*, Series X, Vol 2 (30 July 1904), 85.

Music: This tune was written specifically for the second edition of *HA&M* (1875) by John Bacchus Dykes, for the text "How bright those glorious spirits shine." There are references to his work on the 1875 edition of *HA&M* in Dykes's diary and correspondence from at least as early as 1872.[1] If the check for £100 Dykes received from Sir Henry Baker on 5 May 1874 represents the completion of his work of composition for the forthcoming new edition of *HA&M*,[2] then BEATITUDO must have been written sometime between 1872 and 1874.

---

1. See *Life and Letters of John Bacchus Dykes*, ed. J. T. Fowler (London, 1897).
2. Ibid., 191-92.

RAL

684 O for a closer walk with God

Music: **CAITHNESS**

The matching of this text by John Cowper with this Scottish psalm tune first appeared in an Episcopal hymnal in *H40*. Precedent for it was established by Ralph Vaughan Williams in *EH*.

Words: See hymn 683.

Music: See hymn 121.

685 Rock of ages, cleft for me

Music: **TOPLADY**

This classic hymn coming from the eighteenth-century Evangelical tradition is matched here with a tune by a nineteenth-century American composer. The name TOPLADY honors the author of the text.

Words: "Rock of Ages" has shared the fate of many popular hymns in that it has had "revisions" and "improvements" from many editors and authors for various publications. The original text was written by Augustus Montague Toplady.

In the October issue of the *Gospel Magazine* (1775), in an article entitled "Life a Journey," signed Minimus (one of Toplady's pseudonyms), the following appears:

> Yet, if you fall, be humbled; but do not despair. Pray afresh to God, who is able to raise you up, and to set you on your feet again. Look to the blood of the covenant and say to the Lord, from the depth of your heart,
>
> Rock of Ages, cleft for me,
> let me hide myself in Thee;
> Foul, I to the fountain fly,
> Wash me, Savior, or I die.
>
> Make these words of the apostle, your motto: 'Perplexed, but not in despair; cast down, but not destroyed' (*Julian*, 970).

In the *Gospel Magazine* dated March 1776, of which A. M. Toplady was then editor, there appeared a curious article entitled "A Remarkable Calculation: Introduced here, for the sake of the Spiritual Improvement subjoined. Questions and Answers, relative to the National Debt." This article is followed by another, a continuation entitled "Spiritual Improvement of the foregoing: By Another Hand."[1] The aim of this discussion was to calculate how many sins each member of the human race would be guilty of "supposing a person was to break the law (1) but once in every twenty four hours; (2) twice in the same time; (3) once in every hour; (4) once in every minute; (5) once in every second." Together, the two articles formed the basis of the metaphor drawn by Toplady in his comparison of England's National Debt and its inability to clear the debt with sin in the world and our inability to be freed from that sin, except through Jesus Christ. Toplady continues:

> 'Christ hath redeemed us from the curse of the Law; being made a curse for us'—Gal. iii.13—This, will not only counterbalance, but definitely over-balance ALL sins of the WHOLE believing world.

Questions and Answers follow, all of which support Toplady's Calvinistic creed. The last answer given states:

> We can only admire and bless the Father, for electing us in Christ, and for laying on Him the iniquities of us all: —the Son, for taking our nature and our debts upon Himself, and for that complete righteousness and sacrifice, where by He redeemed his mystical Israel from all their sins:—and the co-equal Spirit, for causing us (in conversion) to feel our need for Christ . . .

He ends the discussion with the complete hymn text with the heading "A Living and Dying Prayer for the Holiest Believer in the World":

1. Rock of Ages, cleft for me,
Let me hide myself in Thee!
Let the Water and the Blood,
From thy riven Side which flow'd,
Be of sin the double cure,
Cleanse me from its Guilt and Pow'r.

2. Not the labors of my hands
Can fulfill the Law's demands,
Could my zeal no respite know,
Could my tears forever flow,
All for sin could not atone:
Thou must save, and Thou alone!

3. Nothing in my Hand I bring;
Simply to the cross I cling;
Naked, come to Thee for dress;
Helpless, look to Thee for Grace;

Foul, I to the fountain fly:
Wash me, Savior, or I die!

4. Whilst I draw this fleeting breath
When my eye-strings break in death
When I soar through tracts unknown
See Thee on Thy Judgement Throne
Rock of Ages, cleft for me,
Let me hide myself in Thee.

In his *Psalms and Hymns* (London, 1776), Toplady repeats his text as "A Prayer, living and dying" with these slight alterations:

4:1 While I draw . . .
4:3 When I soar to worlds unknown.

As previously mentioned, the hymn has undergone numerous revisions, the most important being that of T. S. Cottterill in his *Selections of Psalms and Hymns* (London, 1815), a version that gained as great if not a greater following than the original:

1. Rock of Ages! cleft for me
Let me hide myself in Thee:
Let the water and the blood,
From Thy wounded side which flow'd,
Be of sin the double cure;
Save from wrath, and make me pure.

2. Should my tears forever flow,
Should my zeal no languor know,
This for sin could not atone;
Thou must save, and Thou alone
In my hand no price I bring,
Simply to Thy cross I cling.

3. When I draw this fleeting breath,
While mine eyelids close in death,
When I rise to worlds unknown,
And behold Thee on Thy throne,
Rock of Ages, cleft for me!
Let me hide myself in Thee.

This text, in a slightly altered form, was included for use by Episcopalians in the *Hymnal* of 1826 ("The Prayer-Book Collection"). In *Episcopal Common Praise* (New York, 1867) it was continued matched with two tunes: TOPLADY, in that publication called ROCK OF AGES, and INGRAHAM by George William Warren, a setting for soprano, tenor, bass, and organ marked "For the Choir." The text is continued in the four-stanza form found above in the 1871 edition of the *Hymnal* but in 1874 it was restored to the three-stanza form found in earlier editions. In the J. Ireland Tucker music edition, *The Hymnal With Tunes Old And New* (New York, 1874), it appears with three tunes, none of which is TOPLADY. In the 1892 edition of the *Hymnal* the three-stanza form of the text is continued. Further noteworthy versions of this text include Cotterill's additional revision for the 1819 edition of his *Selections* (London, 1819); that by the editors of the Supplement to the *Methodist Hymn Book* (London, 1830); and W. J. Hall's for his *Mitre Hymn Book* (London, 1836).

From 1776 to 1810 "Rock of Ages" was found only in a limited number of hymnbooks. After 1810 interest in the text grew rapidly and today the hymn is included in virtually all English-speaking hymnal publications. (The 1830 Cotterill/Wesley adaptation is the recognized Methodist version of the hymn used in most modern settings.) The hymn has been translated into many languages. The text has varied at the hands of the translators, some taking text from Toplady, some from Cotterill, and others from the *Methodist Hymn Book*.

Many of Toplady's hymns have been widely used, especially in the United States and in the Evangelical Hymnbooks of the Church of England. Year by year, however, the number of Toplady texts in use decreases. Julian calls him " . . . no poet or inspired singer . . . he has mere vanishing gleams of imaginative light . . . His greatness is the greatness of goodness" (*Julian*, 1183).

There is no evidence to support the popular story surrounding this hymn that it was written as an illustration of a providential deliverance from a thunderstorm.

---

1. Both are reprinted in full in E. Routley, *An English-Speaking Hymnal Guide* (Collegeville, MN, 1979), 113-114.

Music: In the United States this text is most commonly matched with TOPLADY, the well-known tune by Thomas Hastings. It was first published as a trio in *Spiritual Songs for Social Worship* (Utica, 1833), which Hastings edited with Lowell Mason. The tune is also known as DEVOTION.

TS/RG

686 Come, thou fount of every blessing

Music: **NETTLETON**

This text matched with this tune coming from the early nineteenth-century folk-hymn tradition of the American northeast, has gained wide acceptance and use in the hymnals of many Christian denominations across the United States. The text, in an altered form for use by Episcopalians, first appeared in the *Hymnal* of 1826 with the opening line "Saviour, source of every blessing." It was continued in this form through the 1916 edition of the *Hymnal*. Its first appearance with this tune was in *Episcopal Common Praise* (New York, 1867). That matching was restored in *The Mission Hymnal* (New York, 1913) and continued in *MHSS* and *Lift Every Voice and Sing* (New York, 1981).

Words: This hymn was written by Robert Robinson in 1758 for the festival of Whitsunday (Pentecost) and published in *A Collection of Hymns used by the Church of Christ in Angel-Alley, Bishopgate* (London, 1759). A fourth stanza beginning "O, that day when free from sinning" was omitted from Martin Madan's *Psalms and Hymns* (London, 1760), and the three-stanza pattern has been retained since then. The last two lines of st. 1 originally read "Praise the mount! I'm fixed upon it, mount of thy redeeming love." The first line of st. 2 originally read "Here I raise my Ebenezer," a reference to I Sam. 7:12. This hymn combining Christian experience with gratitude seems to reflect the author's spiritual pilgrimage during his youth.

This text first entered an American Episcopal hymnal in a very much altered four-stanza version in the enlarged "Prayer Book Collection" (New York, 1826):

1. Saviour, source of every blessing,
   Tune my heart to grateful lays;
Streams of mercy, never ceasing,
   Call for ceaseless songs of praise.

2. Teach me some melodious measure,
   Sung by raptured saints above;
Fill my soul with sacred pleasure,
   While I sing redeeming love.

3. Thou didst seek me when a stranger,
   Wandr'ing from the fold of God;
Thou to save my soul from danger,
   Didst redeem me with thy blood.

4. By thy hand restored, defended,
   Safe through life thus far I'm come;
Safe, O Lord, when, life is ended,
   Bring me to my heavenly home.

"I'm" in the second line of st. 4 was changed to "I've" in 1865. This version was retained through the 1916 edition of the *Hymnal*.

More authentic versions of the text appeared in *The Mission Hymnal as Adopted by the General Convention* (New York, 1913) and in *MHSS, Hymns III,* and *Lift Every Voice and Sing: A Collection of African-American Spirituals and Other Songs* (New York, 1981), sponsored by the Office of Black Ministries of the Episcopal Church.

Music: The tune now generally known as NETTLETON first appeared in print in a two-part version in 4/4 time in the four-shape shape-note *Wyeth's Repository of Sacred Music: Part Second* (Harrisburg, PA, 1813).[1] It was entitled HALLELUJAH and printed with the text "Come thou fount of ev'ry blessing" (see Example 1 on following page).

This version was included in several shape-note books. In one book it was titled SINNER'S CALL, in another GOOD SHEPHERD.

Joshua Leavitt's *Christian Lyre* (New York, 1831) contained a different version of the tune titled GOOD SHEPHERD and linked with the text "Let thy kingdom, blessed Savior." It was printed in 3/4 time and there were variations in the melody line, including the substitution of a one for a six at the end of the sixth phrase, a change that would show

Example 1

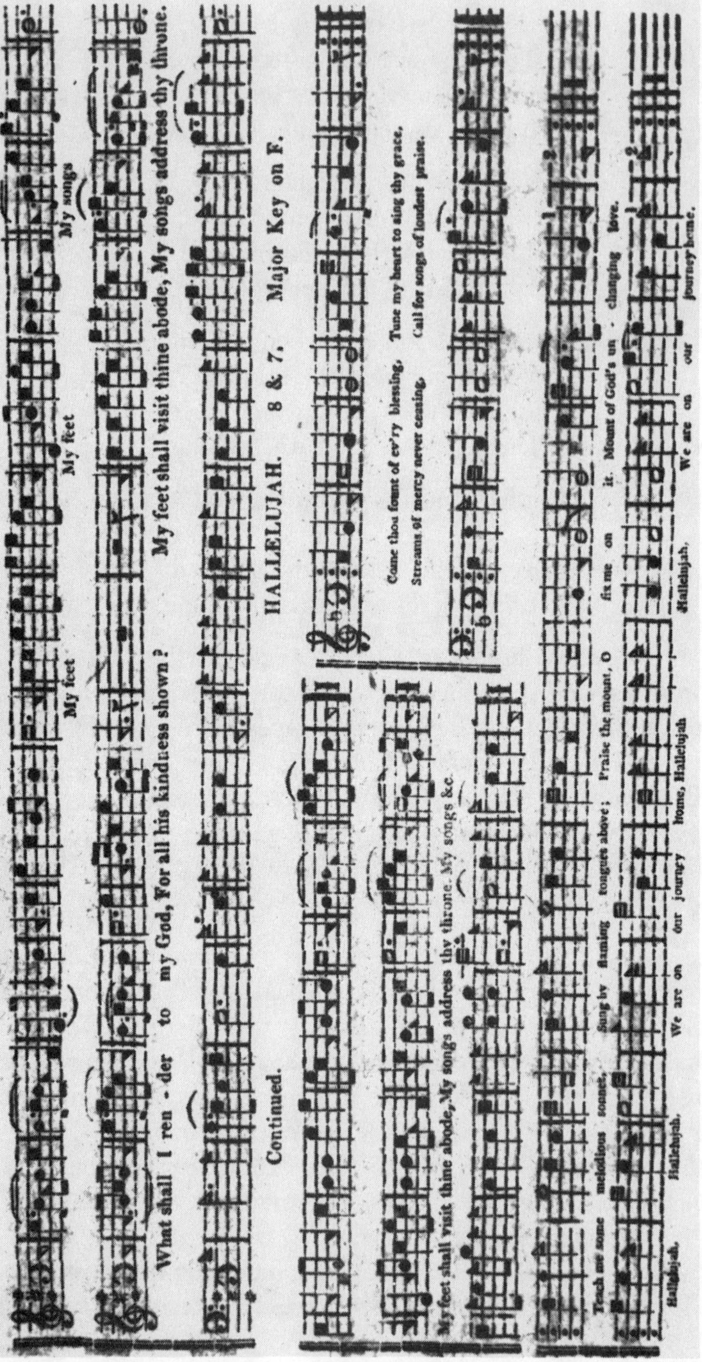

112 PROVIDENCE. C. M. Major Key on A. C. CURTIS.

My feet My feet My songs

What shall I ren - der to my God, For all his kindness shown? My feet shall visit thine abode, My songs address thy throne.

Continued.

My feet shall visit thine abode, My songs address thy throne. My songs &c.

HALLELUJAH. 8 & 7. Major Key on F.

Come thou fount of ev'ry blessing, Tune my heart to sing thy grace,
Streams of mercy never ceasing, Call for songs of loudest praise.

Teach me some melodious sonnet, Sung by flaming tongues above; Praise the mount, O fix me on it. Mount of God's un - changing love.

Hallelujah. Hallelujah. We are on our journey home, Hallelujah. Hallelujah. We are on our journey home.

Reproduced from 1920 printing of *Wyeth's Repository of Sacred Music: Part Second* (Harrisburg, PA, 1813), with permission of Moravian Music Foundation.

up in many but not all later printings. A variation titled GOOD SHEPHERD was printed in J. H. Hickok's *Sacred Harp* (Lewistown, PA, 1832), one titled FEMALE PILGRIM in the second edition of Joseph Funk's *Genuine Church Music* (Winchester, VA, 1835), and one titled NEWELL in the third edition of William C. Brown's *Wesleyan Harp* (Boston, 1841).

Moses Lewis Scudder's *Wesleyan Psalmist* (Boston, 1842) included a three-part version under the title GOOD SHEPHERD that was reproduced in Darius E. Jones's *Temple Melodies* (New York, 1852) with the text "Come, thou Fount of ev'ry blessing" under the title NETTLETON (see Example 2).

Example 2

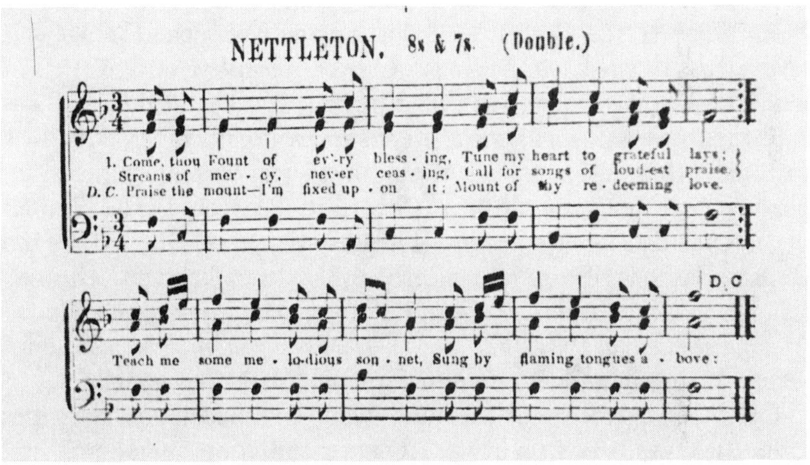

Reproduced from 1863 printing of *Temple Melodies* (New York), Union Theological Seminary Library, New York.

This is apparently the first time this title was used. It was possibly to honor Asahel Nettleton, a well-known evangelist who compiled a collection of texts, *Village Hymns for Social Worship* (New York, 1824) which included "Come, thou Fount of every blessing." The tunebook designed to accompany that volume, *Zion's Harp* (New Haven, CT, 1824), compiled by N. and S. S. Jocelyn, did not contain the tune. It remains a mystery how Nettleton's name became attached to this tune at this point in its history.

The three-part version from *Wesleyan Harp* was reproduced in several later books. A fourth part was apparently first added in the American Tract Society's *Songs of Zion* (New York, 1851). That version, with minor variations, was printed in innumerable later books, including several denominational hymnals: for example, Thomas Hastings's *Presbyterian Psalmodist* (Philadelphia, 1852); *Hymns for the Use of the Methodist Episcopal Church* (New York, 1857); W. D. Roedel's *Carmina Ecclesiae* (Baltimore, 1860), approved for use by the General Synod of the Evangelical Lutheran Church; the American Baptist Publication Society's *Devotional Hymn and Tune Book* (Philadelphia, 1864); the Presbyterian *Social Hymn and Tune Book* (Philadelphia, 1865); *Baptist Hymn and Tune Book* (Philadelphia, 1871); *The Christian Hymnal* (Cincinnati, 1871); the Mennonite *Brethren's Tune and Hymn Book* (Dade City, PA, 1879); and the Episcopal *The Mission Hymnal as Adopted by the General Convention* (New York, 1913). In many books this version was called NETTLETON, but in others it was called FOUNT, STANHOPE, GOOD SHEPHERD, or COME, YE SINNERS. It is essentially this version that is printed in several current hymnals, including *The Mennonite Hymnal* (Scottdale, PA, 1969), *The Hymnal of the United Church of Christ* (Philadelphia, 1974), the *LBW*, the Roman Catholic *Worship* (Chicago, 1986), the Christian Reformed Church's *Psalter Hymnal* (Grand Rapids, MI, 1987), *The United Methodist Hymnal* (Nashville, 1989), *The Presbyterian Hymnal* (Louisville, KY, 1990), and *The Baptist Hymnal* (Nashville, 1991).

Other arrangements of the tune were published under the titles LIVING WATERS, PARISH, FOUNT, MULLINS, and GOOD SHEPHERD.

A distinctive version titled BARTIMEUS was printed in *The Plymouth Collection* (New York, 1855), which was edited by Henry Ward Beecher with the assistance of his brother Charles and his organist, John Zundel. That version, with slight changes, was included in several later books, including *The Congregational Hymn and Tune Book* (New Haven, CT, 1856); *The Baptist Hymn and Tune Book* (New York, 1858); *The Baptist Hymnal* (Philadelphia, 1883); John R. and J. Harvey Daily's *Primitive Baptist Hymn and Tune Book* (Indianapolis, 1902), which is still in use among Primitive Baptists; and *Lift Every Voice and Sing: A Collection of African-American Spirituals and Other Songs* (New York, 1981), sponsored by the Office of Black Ministries of the Episcopal Church.

George E. Thrall's *Episcopal Common Praise* (New York, 1867), designed for use with the 1865 enlarged "Prayer Book Collection" of psalms and hymns, printed a version of NETTLETON with the altered version of Robinson's text that began "Saviour, source of every blessing."

Still another version, titled FOUNT, was printed in both the Northern Presbyterian *Hymnal of the Presbyterian Church* (Philadelphia, 1867) and the Southern Presbyterian *Book of Hymns and Tunes* (Richmond, VA, 1874).

George Pullen Jackson lists NETTLETON among the "Eighty Most Popular Tunes" in his *White Spirituals in the Southern Uplands* (Chapel Hill, NC, 1933). It has been included in more denominational hymnals than most other folk tunes.

An altered version of Robinson's text had entered the Episcopal *Hymnal* in 1826 and was retained through the 1916 edition, but it was linked with this tune only in the short-lived *Episcopal Common Praise*. This tune was printed with more authentic versions of the text in *The Mission Hymnal* (New York, 1913), *MHSS*, and *Lift Every Voice and Sing*. NETTLETON was printed twice in James H. Darlington's *The Hymnal of the Church . . . with Music* (New York, 1897), one of the several editions of the 1892 *Hymnal*. It is linked there with the text "Guide me, O thou great Jehovah" [690] and with a hymn for children, "Heavenly Father, send thy blessing."

This text and tune, with guitar chords, were included in both *MHSS* and *Hymns III*. The tune appears in *MHSS* with an accompaniment by Gerre Hancock and in *Hymns III* with an accompaniment by Alastair Cassels-Brown. *The Hymnal 1982* retains the accompaniment by Gerre Hancock. Slight variations were made in the guitar chords in *H82*.

---

1. See "John Wyeth's *Repository of Sacred Music, Part Second* (1813): A Northern Precursor of Southern Folk-Hymnody" in I. Lowens, *Music and Musicians in Early America* (New York, 1964), 138-155; I. Lowens, "Introduction," Da Capo edition of *Wyeth's Repository of Sacred Music: Part Second* (New York, 1964), v-xvi.

HE/MH

687 A mighty fortress is our God

***Music:* EIN FESTE BURG**

This text and tune are among the most important of all Christian hymns. As a psalm paraphrase, it ranks as one of the earliest examples of the genre; the text was spoken of by the poet Heine as "the *Marseillaise* of the Reformation." Today it is a standard hymn for Christians of all denominations. At 687, the rhythmic form of the tune in a harmonization by Hans Leo Hassler has been used. At 688 the isorhythmic harmonization of J. S. Bach continues a usage established in music editions of the *Hymnal* of the Episcopal Church for more than one hundred years.

Example 1

Words: This famous hymn by Martin Luther has attracted an ever-growing bibliography of studies in which every aspect of its text and melody has been scrutinized and investigated.[1] Notwithstanding this library of literature, many aspects of the hymn remain unknown or enigmatic. To begin, there is uncertainty concerning exactly when it was written and when it was first published. The older literature includes some stirring but conjectural accounts of its being written at the time of either the Diet of Worms (1521), the Diet of Speyer (1529), or the Diet of Augsburg (1530).[2] The first appearance of the complete hymn in print (both text and melody) was probably in the first edition of Luther's congregational hymn book, *Geistliche Lieder* (Wittenberg, 1529), of which no copy has survived. The earliest extant edition of the Wittenberg hymnal is the single copy of the second edition, issued in 1533, now in the Lutherhalle in Wittenberg (see Example 1).[3]

Markus Jenny[4] has advanced the hypothesis, based on internal evidence and comparison with other hymns by Luther, that the original hymn comprised sts. 1 through 3, written sometime after 1524, and that the remaining stanza was added either in 1527 or 1528. That the hymn was written in two stages, separated by a period of some four years, is highly debatable, and the hypothesis has not been generally accepted. The consensus of contemporary scholarship inclines to the view that the complete hymn was written sometime around 1527-1528 (see further below). It is almost certain that the four stanzas were first issued as a Wittenberg broadsheet sometime before 1529. There is an extant Augsburg broadsheet of 1529 that, considering the practice of the time, was probably a reprint of an earlier Wittenberg broadsheet. The Augsburg broadsheet contains the complete text (but not the melody) of "Ein feste Burg":

1. Ein feste Burg ist unser Gott,
ein gute Wehr und Waffen.
Er hilft uns frei aus aller Not,
die uns jetzt hat betroffen.
Der alt böse Feind
mit Ernst ers jetzt meint;
groß Macht und viel List
sein grausam Rüstung ist,
auf Erd ist nicht seinsgleichen.

2. Mit unsrer Macht ist nicht getan,
wir sind gar bald verloren,
es streit' für uns der rechte Mann,
den Gott hat selbst erkoren.
Fragts du, wer der ist?
Er heißt Jesus Christ,
der Herr Zebaoth,

und ist kein andrer Gott,
das Feld muß er behalten.

3. Und wenn die Welt voll Teufel wär
und wollt uns gar verschlingen,
so fürchten wir uns nicht so sehr,
es soll uns doch gelingen.
Der Fürst dieser Welt,
wie saur er sich stellt,
tut er uns doch nicht;
das macht, er ist gericht.
Ein Wörtlein kann ihn fällen.

4. Das Wort sie sollen lassen stahn
und kein' Dank dazu haben;
er ist bei uns wohl auf dem Plan
mit seinem Geist und Gaben.
Nehmen sie den Leib,
Gut, Ehr, Kind und Weib:
laß fahren dahin,
sie habens kein' Gewinn,
das Reich muß uns doch bleiben.

The title on the Augsburg broadsheet is revealing: "A Hymn of Comfort." The accepted view of this hymn, however, is somewhat different. It has been referred to by a whole range of Protestant triumphalistic epithets, including "The Marseillaise of the Reformation" (Heine), "God Almighty's Grenadier March" (Leopold of Anhalt-Dessau/Carlisle), and "The Battle Hymn of the Reformation," (various). This later interpretation was created largely by a combination of a concentration on Luther's prophetic role in the Reformation, especially his defiance in the whole Indulgence debate, 1517-1521, and the stirring nature of the later "four-square" version of the tune (see commentary on 688). It was an interpretation that was given musical reinforcement by such composers as Mendelssohn (in movement 5 of his *Reformation Symphony*, 1830), Meyerbeer (in his opera *Les Hugenotten*, 1836), and Wagner (in his *Kaisersmarsch*, 1871). But this later interpretation is out of character with Luther's understanding of his own hymn. He saw it as expressing the grounds on which Christians can take comfort and hope in times of trial and conflict, and not as a vehicle of belligerent and provocative Protestantism.

Luther is known to have sought and found comfort in Ps. 46, on which his hymn is based. In his summaries of the Psalms of 1531-1533, Luther gave a brief outline of Ps. 46 that parallels his hymnic form of the psalm:

> This is a psalm of thanksgiving which the people of Israel sang at that time in response to the miracles of God, who had defended and sustained the city of Jerusalem, where they lived, against the rantings and ravings of all kings and nations, and preserved it in peace against all war and conflict. Then, speaking after the manner of scripture, the essence of the city is portrayed as a little spring, a small rivulet, that will not run dry, in contrast to the great rivers and oceans of the nations (that is, the great kingdoms, principalities and estates) that will dry up and disappear.
>
> But we sing in praise to God because he is with us—God who miraculously preserves his Word and Christendom against the gates of hell, against the ravings of all devils, fanatical spirits, the world, the flesh, sin, death, etc., so that our little spring remains a living fountain, while foul and stinking drains, puddles and cisterns will run dry.[5]

Luther did not draw a strong line of distinction between the external pressures of life and the internal struggles of the soul. Therefore, if one examines Luther's life around 1527, a number of factors combine to suggest a possible context for his writing of this hymn that deals with the spiritual aspects of conflict and anxiety. In the fall of 1527, Wittenberg was experiencing an outbreak of the plague, which did not leave Luther's household untouched; around the same time a report had been received in Wittenberg that one Leonard Kaiser had been martyred for confessing the evangelical faith; the tenth anniversary of the posting of the *95 Theses* occurred at the end of October 1527; and this was also the period of the second confinement of Luther's wife. Thus, sometime between the end of 1527 and the beginning of 1528 would seem to be a likely period when Luther wrote this hymn of comfort.

"Ein feste Burg" is one of Luther's psalm hymns, but unlike the others (including his version of Ps. 130, "Aus tiefer Not schrei ich zu dir" [151]) this example does not confine itself to the Old Testament text on which it is based, but interprets the content of Ps. 46 in strongly Christological terms,[6] thus anticipating Isaac Watts by almost two hundred years (see the essay "English Metrical Psalmody," vol. 1, 337-342).

In many respects "Ein feste Burg" shares the same basic imagery of Luther's earlier (1524) Easter hymn "Christ lag in Todesbanden" [185], especially the second stanza:

> It was a strange and dreadful strife
> when life and death contended;
> the victory remained with life,
> the reign of death was ended;
> stripped of power, no more he reigns,
> an empty form alone remains;
> his sting is lost for ever!
> Alleluia!

Here in "Ein feste Burg" the strife between life and death is personified as the struggle between Christ and the devil. Martin Brecht argues against Markus Jenny's hypothesis of a two-stage process of composition (see above) by establishing the essential unity of all four stanzas: "The Devil's stanzas 1 and 3 are contrasted by 2 and 4, the Christ stanzas."[7] This is clearly seen in the final lines of each of the four stanzas:

st. 1: "auf Erd ist nicht seinsgleichen"
(On earth the devil has no equal)
st. 2: "das Feld muß er behalten"
(Christ will not lose the battle)
st. 3: "Ein Wörtlein kann ihn fällen."
(A little word will fell the devil)
st. 4: "das Reich muß uns doch bleiben"
(The kingdom of God will remain for us in Christ)

The key to the whole hymn is perhaps to be found in the final line of the last stanza with its emphatic statement about the permanence of the kingdom of God. Toward the end of 1528 Luther was working on his catechetical exposition of the Lord's Prayer, which would be published the following year within his *Large Catechism*. On the second petition, "Thy kingdom come," he wrote:

> What is the kingdom of God? Answer: Simply what we learned in the Creed, namely, that God sent his Son, Christ our Lord, into the world to redeem and deliver us from the power of the devil and to bring us to himself and rule as a king of righteousness, life, and salvation against sin, death, and an evil conscience. To this end he also gave his Holy Spirit to teach us this through his holy Word and to enlighten and strengthen us in faith by his power. We pray here at the outset that all this may be realized in us and that God's name may be praised through his holy Word and our Christian lives. This we ask, both in order that we who have accepted it may remain faithful and grow daily in it and in order that it may gain recognition and followers among other people and advance with power throughout the world. So we pray that, led by the Holy Spirit, many may come into the kingdom of grace and become partakers of salvation, so that we may all remain together eternally in this kingdom which has now made its appearance among us.[8]

Thus, if "Ein feste Burg" is to be fully understood, it should be interpreted primarily from within Luther's own understanding of theology, rather than from an attempt to link its creation to one of the many dramatic events in his struggle with the papacy.[9]

Luther's hymn was, and remains, extraordinarily popular. Within Luther's own lifetime it was translated into many European languages, including the somewhat free English version by Miles Coverdale in *Goostly psalmes and spirituall songes* (London, ca. 1535):

1. Oure God is a defense and towre
A good armoure and good weapen
He hath ben ever oure helpe and sucoure
In all the troubles that we have ben in.
Therfore wyll we never drede
For any wonderous dede
By water or by londe
In hilles or the sea sonde
Our god hath them al in his hond.

In Germany the hymn has remained part of the primary corpus of hymnody, although it was subjected to various textual emendations, especially between 1770 and the 1860s, when a Rationalist revision, beginning "Ein starker Schutz ist unser Gott," was current. Luther's original version was substantially restored to the hymnals as part of the Lutheran liturgical and confessional renewal movement of the mid-nineteenth century.[10]

After some 450 years, the hymn is sung in at least 200 different languages, and there must be approaching 100 different English translations (*Julian*, 324-325). The principal reason for this high number of translations is that Luther's rugged poetry is difficult to render into appropriate English verse.[11] The primary translator of German hymns into English, Catherine Winkworth, had particular difficulty with this hymn. Her translation appeared in the first edition of *Lyra Germanica* (London, 1855), but she was clearly unhappy with it since, in the second edition issued a little later, the translation by her mentor, William Gaskell, was substituted for her own. By and large, although there are others, two English translations have predominated: Thomas Carlisle's "A safe stronghold our God is still," which the author included in his essay on "Luther's Psalm" in *Fraser's Magazine* (1831)—the translation employed in most British hymnals—and Frederick H. Hedge's "A mighty fortress is our God," which first appeared in W.H. Furness's *Gems of German Verse* (Philadelphia 1852)—found predominantly in North American hymnals. The *Hymnal* of 1871 included the translation of Bishop W. R. Whittingham, "A mountain fortress is our God" (1860), which was in turn replaced by H.J. Buckoll's "A tower of strength our God doth stand" (1850). *The Hymnal 1982* employs the Hedge translation, which has been in the *Hymnal* since 1916.

---

1. In addition to the titles cited in the notes below, the following include the more recent and substantial treatments of the hymn, both text and melody, and also supply additional bibliography: G. Hahn, *Evangelium als literarische Anweisung: Zu Luthers Stellung in der Geschichte des deutschen kirchlichen Liedes* (Munich, 1981), 267-83; M. Jenny, *Luthers geistliche Lieder und Kirchengesänge* [Archiv zur Weimarer Ausgabe der Werke Martin Luthers, 4] (Cologne, 1985), esp.100-01, 247-49; J. Stalmann ed. *Liederkunde Zweiter Teil: Lied 176-394* [*Handbuch zum Evangelischen Kirchengesangbuch* 3/2] (Göttingen, 1990), 58-69.

2. See, for example, *Julian* 323; and W. G. Polack, *The Handbook to the Lutheran Hymnal*, 3rd ed. (St. Louis, 1958), 192-3.

3. See K. Ameln, "Die älteste Überlieferung der Weise 'Ein feste Burg ist unser Gott,'" *Jahrbuch für Liturgik und Hymnologie* 1 (1955), 110-12.

4. Jenny, "Neue Hypothesen zur Entstehung und Bedeutung von 'Ein feste Burg,'" *Jahrbuch für Liturgik und Hymnologie* 9 (1964), 143-52.

5. *Martin Luthers Werke: Kritische Gesamtausgabe* (Weimar, 1883-), Vol. 38, 35 (translation: R.A.L.).

6. See M. Brecht, "Zum Verständnis von Luthers Lied 'Ein feste Burg,'" *Archiv für Reformationsgeschichte* 70 (1979), 106-22.

7. Brecht, op. cit., 118; see also I. Mager, "Martin Luthers Lied 'Ein feste Burg ist unser Gott' und Psalm 46," *Jahrbuch für Liturgik und Hymnologie* 30 (1986), 87-96, who also argues, against Jenny, for the hymn as an integrated whole.

8. *The Book of Concord: The Confessions of the Evangelical Lutheran Church*, ed. T. G. Tappert (Philadelphia, 1959), 426-27.

9. See H. Thomke, "'Das Wort sie sollen lassen stahn!': Überlegungen zur Sprache und zur poetischen Form von Luthers Liedern am Beispiel des Reformationsliedes 'Ein feste Burg,'" *Jahrbuch für Liturgik und Hymnologie* 29 (1985), 79-89; R. Uitti, "The Imagery Behind Luther's 'Ein feste Burg,'" *Church Music* 75.1 (1975), 41-45; J. Wit, "'Und kein Dank dazu haben': Versuch einer Interpretation aus dem Kontext," *Jahrbuch für Liturgik und Hymnologie* 19 (1975), 209-13.

10. See J. Sólyom, "'Das Reich muß uns doch bleiben': Zur letzten Zeile des Liedes 'Ein feste Burg,'" *Jahrbuch für Liturgik und Hymnologie* 20 (1976), 166-71.

11. See J. Vajda, "Translations of 'Ein feste Burg,'" *The Hymn* 34 (1983), 134-40; cp. L. C. Green, "The Chorales of Martin Luther: How Have They Fared in the *Lutheran Book of Worship*?," *Church Music* 79 (1979), 65.

Music: Luther wrote this now famous tune for his version of Ps. 46 probably sometime between the end of 1527 and the beginning of 1528 (see commentary on the text above). The first appearance of the tune was almost certainly in the first edition of Luther's congregational hymn book, *Geistliche Lieder* (Wittenberg, 1529), of which no copy has survived, although there is just one extant copy of the second edition of 1533 (*Zahn* 7377a; see Example 1 in text commentary). The form of the melody in this second edition is probably the same as in the first edition of 1529, since it is found reprinted without alteration in *Geistliche lieder auffs new gebessert zu Wittenberg* (Erfurt, 1531). Confirmation of the basic form of the melody is found in a manuscript tenor part-book compiled by the composer Johann Walter (the so-called "Luthercodex"), with a title page written by Luther himself.[1] The date on the title page, 1530, presumably represents the year by which the manuscript was completed. EIN FESTE BURG, therefore, must have been entered into it not long after its composition (see Example 1 on following page).

With the exception of a small rhythmic variation in the 5th line, it is identical with the form found in the Wittenberg *Geistliche Lieder* of (1529) 1533 (cp. Example 1 with Example 1 of text commentary on page 1274). It is an open question as to which represents the earliest form of the melody.

Example 1

A 1523 Luther
Ein neu - es Lied wir heb - ben an, etc.
B 1524 Walter (Bass - transposed)
Ge - lo - bet seist du, Je-sus Christ,etc.
C (1529) 1533 Luther
Ein fe - ste Burg ist un - ser Gott, etc.
D 1539 Luther
Von Him-mel hoch, da komm ich her, etc.
E 1541 Walter
Von Him-mel hoch da kommich her, etc.

There has been much discussion about whether the melody is to be considered an original composition or an adaptation of earlier material by Luther. Wilhelm Bäumker's view that the melody was constructed from various melodic fragments of Gregorian chant is unconvincing,[2] as is the suggestion that it is in some way derived from the late twelfth-century French chanson, "Quant hom honratz torna."[3] In Johann Walter's part-books of 1524, the so-called *Chorgesangbuch*, the bass voice part of his setting "Gelobet seist du, Jesu Christ" (no. XXII) shows some affinity with Luther's later hymn melody, but the correspondence is surely coincidental (see melody B in Example 2).[4]

A more important correlation is found in the tune assigned to Ps. 77 in the complete Dutch psalter *Souterliedekens* (Antwerp, 1540), which shares many features with Luther's more familiar melody (see the comparison in Example 3a, page 1284).[5]

Since the *Souterliedekens* (1540) appeared in print more than a decade after Luther's melody was composed (1529), it is tempting simply to conclude that the Dutch tune was modeled on Luther's. But the issue is not that clear-cut. A majority of the melodies in the *Souterliedekens* are secular folk tunes of the fifteenth century or even earlier, and the implication is that the tune assigned to Ps. 77—the heading reads: "Nae die wise (to the tune:) Die wissel drijft die en is gheen narre"—is of an earlier secular origin. But an earlier existence of the Dutch Ps. 77 melody has not been established. Although many of the other *Souterliedekens* melodies have been identified in earlier manuscript and printed sources, no prior concordances of the melody "Die wissel drijft die en is gheen narre" can be dated before 1540. This increases the possibility that the Dutch tune "Die wissel drijft die en is gheen narre" was influenced by Luther's EIN FESTE BURG, which had already been circulating in the Netherlands for some years. For example, Dutch Anabaptists are known to have sung a variant form of the melody in 1535-1536.[6] The debate concerning which is the dependent tune is by no means fully settled, and there is the further possibility that the similarities between the two melodies are coincidental.[7]

Example 2

A 1523 Luther
Ein neu - es Lied wir heb - ben an, etc.
B 1524 Walter (Bass-transposed)
Ge - lo - bet seist du, Je - sus Christ, etc.
C (1529) 1533 Luther
Ein fe - ste Burg ist un - ser Gott, etc.
D 1539 Luther
Vom Him - mel hoch, da komm ich her, etc.
E 1541 Walter
Vom Him - mel hoch da komm ich her, etc.

Example 3a

Unless further research produces evidence to resolve the debate, the latter conclusion is probably correct: that EIN FESTE BURG was freely written by Luther, and that correspondences between it and possible sources are to be explained more by the common use of the Ionian mode and contemporary compositional techniques, rather than by conscious adaptation. With its range of an octave and final on c, the Ionian mode favors certain melodic and cadential patterns. Similarly, the contemporary *Hofwiese* (Court-song, related to the *Meistergesang*—see further below), with its bar-form and proclivity for anacrusis* beginnings, inevitably promoted analogous melodic forms. This can be clearly seen when various melodies composed by Martin Luther and Johann Walter between 1523 and 1541 are compared (see Example 2).

The similarity between the final lines of Luther's EIN FESTE BURG and VOM HIMMEL HOCH [80] is particularly marked (see Example 3b).

Example 3b

Building on the research of earlier writers, Walter Blankenburg[8] has argued that the general characteristics and the foundational structure of EIN FESTE BURG were developed from the "Silberweise" (Silver tune), composed in 1513 by Hans Sachs, who later wrote for it a Christocentric expansion of the *Salve Regina* (see Example 4, page 1286).[9]

Although the exact correlation between the established Meistergesang tradition and the newly emerging Lutheran chorale melodies has not been clearly delineated, there are notable and obvious links, such as this between Sachs's "Silberweise" and Luther's EIN FESTE BURG. But the similarities are to be seen primarily in terms of the basic, bar-form structure, rather than in the use of common melodic material. The principal difference between the two melodies is that Luther's is much more concise than Sachs's. This is to be explained by the difference in function: Luther, unlike Sachs, was not writing for solo performance but rather for congregational participation.[10] Thus his melody, while sharing the same basic structure as Sachs's "Silberweise," is more succinct and appropriate for corporate song. As Luther brilliantly demonstrated again and again in his theological and liturgical thinking, he could be both conservative and radical at the same time—conservative in taking over something traditional, such as the soloistic style of the Meistergesang tradition, and radical in its application, as in the creation of this magnificent example of congregational song.

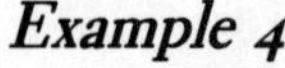
Example 4
Sal - ve ich grus dich scho - ne, Rex Chri - ste in dem
All - er barm - her - tzi - kei - te, Am hei - land man dich
thro - ne, der du tre - gest die kro - ne, Mi - se - ri - cor - di - e,
sei - te, an un - sern letz - ten zei - te, uns hilf - lich bei - ge - ste.
vi - ta dul - ce - do bist fur - war, des le - bens u - re - sprung, Et spes no - stra wan an
dir gar, leit all un - ser hoff - nung, Sal - ve Chri - ste wir gru - ssen dich,
Ein herr him - mel und erd - te - reich, gar hoch in Hie - rar chei - e.
Ad te Chri - ste gar frei - e, Cla - ma - mus wir stets schrei - e,
Hilff uns auss al - lem we - e.

Until quite recently, the English-speaking world as a whole had universally sung the isometric form of EIN FESTE BURG [688]. It is only in the last five to ten years that North American Christians, other than Lutherans, have begun to sing a rhythmic version closer to the original form of the melody. A major influence has been the Lutheran Church-Missouri Synod, whose congregations have been consistently singing rhythmic forms of this and other German hymn melodies for more than a century.[11] It was the participation of Missouri Synod Lutherans in the editorial process of the *LBW* that led to the inclusion of the rhythmic versions of sixteenth-century tunes such as EIN FESTE BURG. This wider Lutheran usage has taken on ecumenical dimensions. Thus, in addition to *H82*, a rhythmic version of the tune can be found in such hymnals as the Roman Catholic *Worship III* (Chicago, 1986) and *The Presbyterian Hymnal* (Louisville, 1990).

The rhythmic version in *H82* is a compromise between the original (1529) 1533 form of the melody and the later isometric form (see commentary on 688). The original melody had an irregular tactus*, which was later evened out by an additional note—and therefore an additional beat—in each of the three lines 5 through 7, altering their metrical structure from five to six syllables (see Example 5).

Example 5

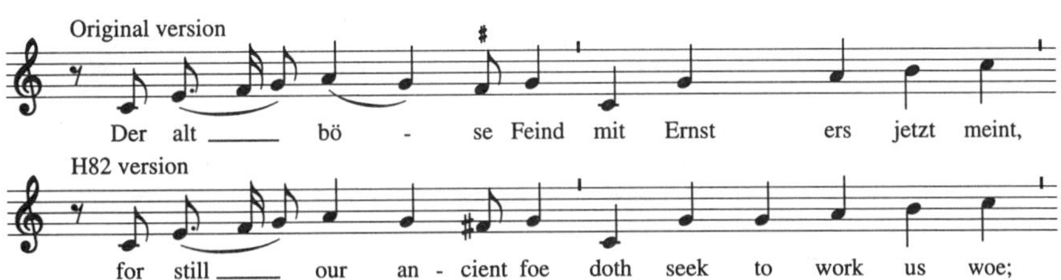

The original harmonization of Hans Leo Hassler is found in his *Kirchengesäng: Psalmen und geistliche Lieder, auf die gemeinen Melodeyen mit vier Stimmen simpliciter gesetzt* (Nuremberg, 1608). The immediate source was the Dutch *Liedboek voor de Kerken* (The Hague, 1973) that the editors adapted to produce the *H82* form.

---

1. *Martin Luthers Werke: Kritische Gesamtausgabe* (Weimar, 1883-), Vol. 35, 85.

2. W. Bäumker, *Das katholische deutsche Kirchenlied in seinen Singweisen* Vol. 1 (Freiburg, 1886), 29-30.

3. U. Aarburg, "Zu den Lutherliedern im jonisch Oktavraum," *Jahrbuch für Liturgik und Hymnologie* 5 (1960), 125-31.

4. In the same bass part-book there is another melodic correspondence with the opening of EIN FESTE BURG, the second part of the Latin motet "Deus misereatur nostri" (no. XLI):

5. There is a possible "Dutch" connection with Luther's Ps. 46 melody: his earlier tune, "Ein neues lied," which is related to EIN FESTE BURG (A in Example 2), is associated with a text narrating the death of two evangelical Augustinian monks in "Brussel in dem Niederland" [Brussels in the Netherlands].

6. A number of martyr songs were written to celebrate the deaths of notable Anabaptists between 1529 and 1536. They were later collected together by David Joris and published as *Een Geestelijck Liedt-Boecxken* (n.p. [between 1576-1582]). Many of the songs carry specific dates. "Die Heere is Coninck in Israel," with the EIN FESTE BURG variant (which is unnamed), appears with the date: "In Iulio. Anno 1535" (see facsimile ed. I. B. Horst [Amsterdam, (1971)]. fol. 58[v]-62[r]). Another, with the date "In Decemb. Anno 1536," is headed "Op die wijse [to the tune:] Een vasten Burch is onser Godt/ &c, Of [or] Die Heere is Coninck in Israel/ &c" (op. cit. fol. 71[r]). Significantly the 5th line of this variant follows the Luthercodex of 1530.

7. See further the debate between K. Hlawiczka and K. Ameln, "Ein niederländische Psalm-Weise, Vorlage oder Nachbildung der Melodie von 'Ein feste Burg'?" *Jahrbuch für Liturgik und Hymnologie* 18 (1973-74), 189-95.

8. W. Blankenburg, *Geschichte der Melodien des Evangelischen Kirchengesangbuchs* [*Handbuch zum Evangelischen Kirchengesangbuch* 2/2] (Göttingen, 1957), 60-61.

9. A number of variant forms of the melody exist, including one in triple time; see Blankenburg, op. cit., 61.

10. See further, K. Ameln, "Die 'Silberweise' von Hans Sachs - Vorlage evangelischer Kirchenlieder?" *Jahrbuch für Liturgik und Hymnologie* 21 (1977), 132-37.

11. See C. Schalk, *The Roots of Hymnody in The Lutheran Church-Missouri Synod* (St. Louis, 1965).

RAL

688 A mighty fortress is our God

Music: **EIN FESTE BURG**
Words: See hymn 687.

Music: The background of the origin of this famous tune by Martin Luther is given in the commentary on no. 687. Here the melody is found in its later, more familiar, isometric form.

Throughout the sixteenth century and well into the seventeenth century, the original form of the melody was in widespread use in Germany. For example, in *Ausserlesene Geistliche Lieder* (Schleswig, 1676), EIN FESTE BURG appears almost exactly in its original form. But even before the end of the sixteenth century various adjustments were made to its melodic and rhythmic structure (A-E in Example 1).[1] By the eighteenth century, largely due to a slowing of the tempo of congregational singing, the metrical structure was slightly expanded by the addition of one syllable to lines 5 through 7 and the elimination of syncopations; by the early nineteenth century the melody had become a regular 4/4 tune with equal note values throughout (F-H in Example 1).[2]

Example 1

When the hymn began to be sung in English in England around the middle of the nineteenth century, it was in this later isometric and simplified form. For example, the tunebook prepared for the English-language hymnal for the London German Hospital, *Choral-Melodies: Adapted to the Collection of Hymns for Public Worship and Private Devotion* (London, 1848), included a form of EIN FESTE BURG almost identical with H in Example 1.[3] *The Chorale Book for England* (London, 1863) included a less angular version with some passing notes, similar to G in Example 1. Sometime after this appearance of the tune in the *Chorale Book for England* it was adapted into an Anglican chant, which became the standard chant for Ps. 46 in Anglican worship; indeed, it is still to be found in *The Anglican Chant Psalter*, edited by A. Wyton (New York, 1987) (see Example 2).

Example 2

With the Bach revival of the later nineteenth century and the discovery of the "Bach Chorale," hymnal editors tended to follow the melodic form that Bach used at the end of Cantata 80, "Ein feste Burg," with a harmonic setting based on Bach. Thus the isometric form of the melody in *H82* follows this "Bach" version with a harmonization in the Bach style that first appeared in *H16*—probably the work of Canon Douglas.

---

1. A = *Geistliche Lieder* (Wittenberg, (1529) 1533); B = J. Walter, *Bicinia Gallica, Latina, Germanica Tomus Primus* (Wittenberg, 1545); C = S. Calvisius, *Harmonia Cantionum Ecclesiasticarum* (Leipzig, 1597); D = H. L. Hassler, *Kirchengesäng: Psalmen und geistliche Lieder* ((Nuremberg, 1608); E = J. Crüger, *Newes vollkömliches Gesangbuch, Augspurgischer Confession* (Berlin, 1640); see further, K. Ameln, "Kirchenliedmelodien der Reformation im Gemeindegesang des 16. und 17. Jahrhunderds," *Das protestantische Lirchenlied im 16. und 17. Jahrhundert*, ed. A. Dürr and W. Killy [Wolfenbütteler Forschungen Herausgegeben von der Herzog August Bibiothek 31] (Wiesbaden, 1986), 61-71.

2. F = D. Vetter, *Musicalische Kirch- und Hauß-Ergötzichkeit* [Pt. I] (Leipzig, 1709); G = G. P. Telemann, *Fast allgemeines Evangelisch-Musikalisches Lieder-Buch* (Hamburg, 1730); H=C. H. Rinck, *Neues Choralbuch für das Grossherzogthum Hessen* (Darmstadt, 1814); see also the comparison in vol. 1, 304-05.

3. Although the German Hospital tunebook generally included isometric forms of the tunes, it did include a rhythmic version of NUN DANKET ALLE GOTT [396].

RAL

689 *I sought the Lord, and afterward I knew*

Music: **FAITH**

Christian hymnody throughout the ages has been enriched by the work of poets and composers whose names are known only to God. Such is the case with this text. Published first in the late nineteenth century, it is matched here with a folklike tune by a contemporary American composer, Harold Moyer.

Words: Although subjective in content, this text has a quaint but beautiful archaic charm that enhances its strength as a statement of faith in God's unfailing love for his children. The middle stanza suggests that the hymn may have been written as a meditation on Peter's attempt to walk to Jesus on the water (Mt. 14:22-33). With its overtones reminiscent of passages in Augustine, this text is an effective expression of the doctrine of prevenient grace.

The text was included in *Holy Songs, Carols and Sacred Ballads* (Boston, 1880), published by Robert Brothers. Other hymnals give an earlier date without documentation. It later appeared in the *Pilgrim Hymnal* (Boston, 1904) and continued in the 1958 edition. This text is also found in *The Methodist Hymnal* (Nashville, 1932, 1964, and 1988) and *The Mennonite Hymnal* (Scottdale, PA, 1969). The text first appeared in an Episcopal publication in the *Hymnal* of 1916 and was continued in *H40*. It first appeared for use by Episcopalians matched with this tune in *Songs For Celebration* (New York, 1980).

Music: Written in an unusual metre, the text "I sought the Lord" has appeared in publications wedded to several different tunes. With the tune FAITH, however, the text has found a sensitive, complimentary mate. This tune, which first appeared in the *Mennonite Hymnal* (Scottdale, PA, 1969), came into being in 1965 as the result of an invitation to Harold Moyer, the compiler of the hymnal, to compose a new tune for use with this text. Dr. Moyer, who had worked on the compilation of this hymnal from its beginning, was honored at the invitation but viewed it with some apprehension. "To write a new tune seemed to him more difficult than writing a symphony—a project he had recently completed for his doctorate in composition from the University of Iowa."[1]

Mary Oyer in *Exploring the Mennonite Hymnal: Essays* writes further about Dr. Moyer's work:

> He commented on his concern to write in an idiom that genuinely interested him and at the same time to provide music which Mennonites could honestly enjoy singing. The four-part, unaccompanied style of many Mennonite congregations presented severe limitations, but he agreed to try a setting. In the tune, FAITH, he worked imaginatively within the limitations. He used the natural minor scale, rejecting the chromatic effects of the Romantic period found in a tune like REST, "Dear Lord and Father of Mankind," [652] for example. In the Moyer tune there is variety in texture and rhythmic patterns. The tune wears well.[2]

The composer writes:

> In the mid-twentieth century composers found some difficulty in choosing an authentic style for writing hymn tunes. The choices seemed to be an older nineteenth-century idiom, or a newer type of melody and harmony which would be difficult for congregational use. In this tune I have tried to combine freshness with practicality. It was written in 1965 during meetings of the joint Hymnal Committee at Goshen.[3]

---

1. M. Oyer, *Exploring the Mennonite Hymnal: Essays* (Newton, KS and Scottdale, PA, 1983), 72.
2. Ibid., 72.
3. Ibid., 72.

RG

690 Guide me, O thou great Jehovah

Music: **CWM RHONDDA**

This text, which first appeared in the *Hymnal* in 1826, is one of the truly great Welsh hymns to come into use in English. It is universally popular and has been further translated into some seventy-five languages. It is matched here with the vigorous and widely used Welsh tune CWM RHONDDA.

Words: This hymn appeared first in Welsh in William Williams's first mature collection of hymns *Caniadau y rhai sydd ar y Mor o Wydr* (Aberhonddu, 1773) ("The Songs of Those upon the Sea of Glass") with the title "A Prayer for Strength to go through the Wilderness of the World." It had six stanzas. In Episcopal hymnals (beginning in 1826) usually only the first four lines of each stanza were given. However, a six-line version, as in *H82*, appeared in the 1871 and 1874 editions of the *Hymnal*, but subsequent editions, until *Hymns III*, returned to the four-line version. In *Hymns III* and *H82* it is given in its full six-line form, with the distinctive repetitions of the words in lines 5 and 6.

The first English version was made by Peter Williams in *Hymns on Various Subjects* (Carmarthen, 1771), and it is this version that supplies st. 1 of the present hymn with the last line altered from "feed me 'till I want no more." William Williams (or possibly his son John) preserved this stanza, which is, in fact, a free rendering of themes from sts. 1 and 2 in the original, and added two others for *The Collection of Hymns sung in the Countess of Huntingdon's Chapels in Sussex* (Edinburgh, ca. 1774); a fourth stanza, which has no counterpart in the Welsh, appeared in later collections of the Countess of Huntingdon:

Musing on my habitation,
  Musing on my heavenly home,
Fills my soul with holy longing:
  Come, my Jesus, quickly come:
  Vanity is all I see:
Lord, I long to be with Thee.

Of the present stanzas, the second is a combination of themes from the original Welsh sts. 3 and 4, and the third is a combination from the original sts. 5 and 6. The translation gives a good impression of the original except in one respect: many hymn books have "Redeemer" in the first line in place of "Jehovah." Williams himself used "Jehovah" in his translation to represent what is simply "Lord" in his original. "Redeemer" does, however, give a better interpretation of the whole hymn, which in the original is explicitly Christ-centered. This is most clear in Williams's st. 5, with its strong imagery recalling themes of baptism and resurrection:

Pan b'wy'n myned trwy'r Iorddonen,
  Angeu creulon yn ei rym,
Ti est trywddi gynt dy Hunan,
  Pam yr ofnaf bellach ddim?
  Buddugoliaeth, etc.
Gwna i mi waeddi yn y llif.

(When I pass through the Jordan, cruel death in full force, You Yourself went through it first, why should I fear any more? Victory! make me to shout it aloud in the flood.)

The only other change from Williams's version is in st. 3:3, where he has "death of deaths."

Life as a pilgrimage was one of William Williams's chief themes, and he often wrote as though the geography of ancient Palestine could be superimposed upon his contemporary Wales. Here he has reinterpreted the archetypal biblical imagery of Exodus in the kind of Christian sense that St. Paul seems to take for granted in I Cor. 10:4: "For they drank from the supernatural Rock which followed them, and the Rock was Christ." There may also be some recollection here of Jesus' discussion of the manna in the wilderness and himself as the Bread of Life (Jn. 6:30-35).

Music: See hymn 594.

AL

691 My faith looks up to thee

Music: **OLIVET**

Written when the poet Ray Palmer was only twenty-one, this text, matched with this tune, after almost one hundred and fifty years of usage, has gained a secure place in the singing traditions of congregations of many denominations. This reality is ironic in the sense that, because of the deeply personal nature of the text, the author neither intended to show it to others nor ever to have it used as a hymn.

Words: This is Ray Palmer's first and best-known hymn, written in New York City in 1830 shortly after his graduation from Yale. The poet left a detailed account of its creation in his *Poetical Works* (New York, 1876). He had moved to New York to teach for a year "in a select school for young ladies," residing with the family of the woman who directed the school. It was there that the hymn was created. Because it was written as a personal expression of faith, Palmer had no idea of its being used as a hymn for worship. Although described by the author as a work of six stanzas, it seems that only four have ever appeared in print. A year or so after the composition of the text, when Palmer met Lowell Mason on a street in Boston, Mason requested hymn texts for the new hymn and tunebook he and Thomas Hastings were compiling. Palmer then and there made a copy of "My faith looks up to thee" for Mason, who set it to music and published it in *Spiritual Songs for Spiritual Worship* (Utica, NY, and Boston, 1831/1832), edited by Mason and Hastings. This text has been in the *Hymnal* since 1865.

Music: Lowell Mason's OLIVET was composed for Ray Palmer's words. The tune was first published in Mason and Thomas Hastings's *Spiritual Songs for Social Worship* (Boston), which is variously dated in hymnological sources as 1831 or 1832. The reason for this discrepancy is that the book was registered for copyright in 1831, but the date given on the title page is 1832. In Mason and George James Webb's *The Psaltery* (Boston, 1845), the tune OLIVET carried the attribution "Music by L. Mason, 1832." Thus the actual date of publication of *Spiritual Songs* was almost certainly 1832. In its early printings, the second phrase of OLIVET began on the fifth degree of the scale, rather than the second degree as commonly found today. The alteration to the current form was made by the time of Mason's *Modern Psalmist* (Boston, 1839). Subsequent publications contained still other changes that must have been authorized by Mason, since he had a hand in preparing the books in which they appeared (e.g., *The Psaltery*). These later alterations, however, have been little used in recent hymnals. The word "Olivet" is a variant form of "Mount of Olives" (see Acts 1:12). Mason's tune appeared with Palmer's text in *Episcopal Common Praise* (New York, 1867).

HE/DWM

692 I heard the voice of Jesus say

Music: **THE THIRD TUNE**

The matching of this text and tune in *H40* not only introduced to Episcopalians the magnificent Tallis tune THE THIRD TUNE, but assured the continued use of the Bonar text that entered the *Hymnal* in 1874.

Words: First published in the author's *Hymns Original and Selected* (London, 1846), this text by Horatius Bonar was included in *Hymns of Faith and Hope* (London, 1857), where it was titled "The Voice from Galilee." It is based on Jn. 1:16, "And from his fullness have we all received, grace upon grace." Various alterations have been made through the years. Lines 3 and 4 of st. 1 read:

Lay down, thou weary one, lay down
Thy head upon my breast:

Another alteration in st. 1 occurs in line 6, which originally read: "Weary and worn and sad"; st. 2:3 read: "The living water *freely take*"; and changes occur in three lines of the third stanza:

3:3-4 Look unto Me, thy day shall *break*,
And all thy *path* be bright.
3:8 Till travelling days are done.

The hymn entered the *Hymnal* in 1874.

Music: See hymn 170.

MS

693 Just as I am, without one plea

Music: **WOODWORTH**

This deeply personal text is the statement of the profound faith of its author, an invalid woman who lived a very secluded life. It is matched with a tune with which it has been popularly associated in hymnals produced in the United States for close to one hundred and fifty years.

Words: Some of the most popular hymns of the Victorian era were "invalid hymns," such as "Lead, Kindly Light," "Abide with me," and many of those written by the patient and heroic Charlotte Elliott, who wrote "Just as I am" for her *Invalid's Hymn Book* (Dublin, 1836), with the heading "Him that cometh Unto Me, I will in no wise cast out." (There is no evidence that a printed version of this hymn was in existence for the 1834 publication of this book.) Her hymnal was a great success, containing no less than 112 hymns that she contributed throughout the various editions, the result of "more than half a century of patient suffering."[1] The original st. 2 was deleted in *H40*:

Just as I am, and waiting not
To rid my soul of one dark blot,
To thee whose blood can cleanse each spot,
O Lamb of God, I come.

Stanza 6 in *H82* is a slightly altered additional verse included with this text in Miss Elliott's *Hours of Sorrow Cheered and Comforted* (London, 1836). The original verse began "Just as I am, of that free love."

This hymn has been transferred to almost every hymnal published in English-speaking countries and has been translated into many European languages.

Charlotte Elliott's brother, the Rev. V. H. Elliott, who edited *Psalms and Hymns* (1835), says concerning this hymn, "In the course of a long ministry, I hope I have been permitted to see some fruit of my labors; but I feel far more has been done by a single hymn of my sister's."[2]

The text of "Just as I am" is usually given in full without alteration, as it appears in *Church Hymns* (London, 1871). The hymn ranks among the most beautiful and popular hymns of the English language and has given rise to many imitations, the best of which is R. S. Cook's "Just as Thou art, without one trace." Percy Dearmer relates the following concerning Edward Quillian, son-in-law of William Wordsworth, who sent a message to Miss Elliott in July of 1847 to thank her for her beautiful hymn. He stated that it proved to be of great comfort to his wife while she lay on her death bed. He added, "I do not think Mr. Wordsworth could bear to have it repeated in his presence, but he is not the less sensible of the solace it gave his one and matchless daughter."[3]

The text first appeared in an Episcopal collection of sixty five *Additional Hymns* (New York, 1865), authorized by General Convention.

---

1. P. Dearmer, *Songs of Praise Discussed* (London, 1933), 149.
2. J. Dahle, *Library of Christian Hymns* (Minneapolis, 1975), 642.
3. *Songs of Praise Discussed*, 149.

Music: WOODWORTH was composed by William B. Bradbury and first published in Bradbury and Thomas Hastings's *Mendelssohn Collection or . . . Third Book of Psalmody* (New York, 1849), set to Elizabeth Scott's hymn "The God of love will sure indulge." The earliest-known association of the tune with Charlotte Elliott's text was in Bradbury's *Eclectic Tune Book* (Philadelphia, 1860). The tune first appeared for Episcopalians in *Episcopal Common Praise* (New York, 1867), where it was titled MANASSEH.

TS/DWM

694 God be in my head

Music: **LYTLINGTON**

Although this sixteenth-century prayer first appeared as a hymn text in England early in this century, it is probably safe to say that its introduction to Episcopalians came through its use in a popular short anthem setting by Sir Walford Davies. As a hymn text matched with this tune, it first appeared in *H40*.

Words: The text of this beloved prayer first appeared in a Sarum Primer, *Hore beate marie/virginis ad usum in/signis ac preclare ec/clesie Sarum* (London, 1541) by Richard Pynson. Of obvious popularity in its day, the text also appeared as the first of the preparatory prayers in Archbishop Cosin's *Collection of Private Devotions* (London, 1627) and abroad, in French, in similar collections of prayers. For most Anglicans, the text is best known in the short anthem setting by Sir Walford Davies. As a hymn text, it first appeared in *The Oxford Hymn Book* (Oxford, 1908), where it is also used as the motto to the collection. It was later included in the enlarged *Songs of Praise* (London, 1931) and *H40*. It appears unaltered in *H82*. Percy Dearmer, in

Songs of Praise Discussed (London, 1933), describes the metre of the text as "Irregular, practically in rhythmical prose."

Music: This tune was composed by Sir Sydney Nicholson for use with the text, "God be in my head" in *The Winchester Hymn Supplement* (1928). It was later used with this text in *H40*, and this relationship continues in *H82*. Melodically, the setting follows a very simple ABABA form that fixes the tune quickly in the singer's memory. The use of longer notes on principal words in that text makes for a most effective setting. A similar harmonic simplicity, in which the harmonic structure of the first two phrases is repeated for the last three phrases, subtly reinforces the simple directness of the text. The tune name, LYTLINGTON, honors the house where the composer lived when he was organist of Westminster Abbey. The house is so named because it is purported to be the home of a former Abbot of Westminster called Lytlington.

RG/AW and RG

695 By gracious powers so wonderfully sheltered

Music: **INTERCESSOR**

This text stands as one of the most moving expressions of faith to come out of the horrors of World War II. It is based on the personal expression of faith found in the writings of one of the martyrs of that war, Dietrich Bonhoeffer. This testimony was given shape as a hymn text by F. Pratt Green, probably one of the finest British hymn writers of this last quarter of the twentieth century. It is matched with a tune that appeared in *H40* with the Whittier text "O brother man."

Words: "Von guten Mächten," in seven stanzas, was the last poem written by Dietrich Bonhoeffer while in a Gestapo prison in Berlin. It is found in a letter dated 28 December 1944, addressed to his mother, who was to celebrate her seventieth birthday two days later. It is a poem that combines reflections on the turning of the years and on the end of one's life. Bonhoeffer lived with the fear of death; indeed, within a few months of penning this poem he was executed.[1]

After his death the poem was published along with his other prison writings in *Widerstand und Ergebung. Briefe und Aufzeichnungen aus der Haft* (Munich, 1951), edited by E. Bethge.[2] In the late 1950s the young people's group of a Berlin church used the final (first in *H82*) stanza of Bonhoeffer's poem for their evening prayers. This inspired the composer Otto Abel to write a melody so that these young people could sing the whole poem as a hymn. The text and tune were later included in a youth hymnal: *Die singende Schar. Ein Liederbuch für junge Christen, III* (Berlin, 1959), edited by T. Rothenberg. At a later date, as the hymn was picked up by other hymnals, sts. 1 and 5 were omitted, and st. 7 became the new st. 1. It appeared in this form in the hymnal *Cantate Domino* (Kassel, 1974). For this multilanguage international hymnal, published by the World Council of Churches, Fred Pratt Green was commissioned to provide a translation of the modified form of the text. The *H82* version is taken from this source.

The 60th anniversary convocation of the Hymn Society of America was held in Atlanta in 1982. Fred Pratt Green, whose collected hymns, *The Hymns and Ballads of Fred Pratt Green* (Carol Stream, 1982), edited by Bernard Braley, had just been published, was the honored guest on that occasion. During the convocation, the present author discussed with Green his translation of the Bonhoeffer text. Since it was incomplete, I urged him to translate the two missing stanzas. This he did and the complete text first appeared in *News of Hymnody*, No. 4, October, 1982.

To understand this moving text, it is important to read it in the original sequence that Bonhoeffer created:

1. Von guten Mächten treu und stillumgeben,	By gracious powers so faithfully protected,
behütet und getröstet wunderbar,	so quietly, so wonderfully near,
so will ich diese Tage mit euch leben	I'll live each day in hope, with you beside me,
und mit euch gehen in ein neues Jahr.	and go with you into the coming year.
2. Noch will das alte unsre Herzen quälen,	Yet is this heart by its old foe tormented
noch drückt uns böser Tage schwere Last,	still evil days bring burdens hard to bear;

ach, Herr, gib unsern aufgescheuchten Seelen das Heil, für das Du uns bereitet hast.	O give our frightened souls the sure salvation, for which, O Lord, you taught us to prepare.
3. Und reichst Du uns den schweren Kelch den bittern des Leids, gefüllt bis an den höchsten Rand, so nehmen wir ihn dankbar ohen Zittern aus Deiner guten und geliebten Hand.	And when this cup you give is filled to brimming with bitter sorrow, hard to understand, we take it thankfully and without trembling out of so good and so beloved a hand.
4. Doch willst Du uns noch einmal Freude schenken an dieser Welt und ihrer Sonne Glanz dann wolln wir des Vergangenen gedenken, und dann gehört Dir unser Leben ganz.	Yet when again in this same world you give us the joy we had, the brightness of your sun, we shall remember all the days we lived through and our whole life shall then be yours alone.
5. Lass warm und still die Kerzen heute flammen, die Du in unsre Dunkelheit gebracht, führ, wenn es sein kann, wider uns zusammen. Wir wissen es, Dein Licht scheint in der nacht.	Today they burn, the warm and silent candles you brought us in the darkness of the night; when it is possible, again unite us. We know that in our darkness shines your light.
6. Wenn sich die Stille nun tief um uns breitet, so lass uns hören jenen vollen Klang der Welt, die unsichtbar sich um uns weitet, all Deiner Kinder hohen Lobgesang.	Now as your silence deeply spreads around us, O let us hear all your creation says— that world of sound which soundlessly invades us, and all your children's highest hymns of praise.
7. Von guten Mächten wunderbar geborgen erwarten wir getrost, was kommen mag.	By gracious powers so wonderfully sheltered, and confidently waiting come what may,

Gott ist mit uns am Abend und am Morgen	we know that God is with us night and morning,
und ganz gewiss an jedem neuen Tag.[1]	and never fails to greet us each new day.
© Christian Kaiser Verlag, Munich	© 1974 Hope Publishing Company, All rights reserved. Used by permission.

1. See further, J. Henkys, *Dietrich Bonhoeffers Gefangnisgedichte: Beitrage zu ihrer Interpretation* (Berlin, 1986).
2. English translation, *Letters & Papers from Prison* (London & New York, 1953).

Music: This tune was composed by Sir Hubert Parry for use with Ada R. Greenway's text "O word of pity" in the 1904 edition of *HA&M*. The expressive opening with the melody and bass moving from tonic to dominant in contrasting motion, is developed into a diatonic, almost modal, tune of great intensity. The alto, tenor, and bass parts move with an almost "contrapuntal" feeling. The matching of INTERCESSOR with the Bonhoeffer text is becoming the standard in many recent hymnals produced in the United States. This wedding first occurred in the hymnal supplement *Songs of Thanks and Praise* (Chapel Hill, NC, 1980) edited by Dr. Russell Schulz-Widmar who later served as Chair of the Hymn Music Committee of the SCCM.

RAL/AW and RG

696 By gracious powers so wonderfully sheltered

Music: **LE CÉNACLE**

It was for this Bonhoeffer text that the tune LE CÉNACLE was composed in 1971 and with which it was first published in 1974. In the United States, this matching appeared first in *Ecumenical Praise* (Carol Stream, IL, 1977).

Words: See hymn 695.

Music: LE CÉNACLE was composed in 1971 by Joseph Gelineau and first appeared in the ecumenical hymnal *Cantate Domino* (Kassel, 1974). Father Gelineau, the noted priest, best known for his translations and musical settings of the Psalms, writes about the origin of the tune:

> The World Council of Churches in Geneva had convened an international committee of experts to revise the publication, *Cantate Domino*. During a session which was held at "Le Cénacle," a house in Geneva, we examined works of all different backgrounds and came upon a hymn by Dietrich Bonhoeffer, "Von gute Mächten."
>
> We unanimously decided that we must have this splendid text in *Cantate Domino*, but we only had a mediocre piece of music. While the group's work continued, I took paper in hand and wrote, on the spot, the melody and accompaniment for the German text. I gave the composition to Erik Routley, President of the group, and it was immediately adopted. Later, F. Pratt Green created an English version of the text.[1]

LE CÉNACLE falls into that genre of contemporary hymnody that can be compared to the art song. The four-note figure of the opening of the first phrase gives unity to the long lyric line of the melody (see Example 1).

Example 1

This figure is repeated one measure later and is used in an abbreviated form two other times in the first half of the tune. The second long phrase, which begins a fifth lower, repeats the pattern of the first. Its final appearance, repeating the pitches of the beginning, occurs at the very end of the tune. As an accompaniment for his very haunting melody, Fr. Gelineau uses a progression of open fifths that move in a regular pattern of half notes. To this he adds a third voice or alto melody, which provides moving counterpoint to the tune. This setting is equally effective played on the piano or organ.

---

1. Gelineau to Glover, April 1985, Church Hymnal Corporation Papers, New York, NY.

RG

697 My God, accept my heart this day

Music: SONG 67

This text was included in 1865 in the collection of sixty-five *Additional Hymns* authorized by the 1865 General Convention. Its matching with SONG 67 for use by Episcopalians was made by the editors of the music edition of *H40*.

Words: Matthew Bridges included this text in his *Hymns of the Heart* (London, 1848), where it was called "Confirmation." It was published and possibly written the same year (1848) that Bridges converted to Roman Catholicism. It first appeared in an Episcopal *Hymnal* in 1865. Line 4 of st. 2 read "Let Christ . . . " and line 2 of st. 3 originally read "Adopt me for thine own." The following was omitted after st. 3:

May the dear blood, once shed for me,
My blest atonement prove,—
That I from first to last may be
The purchase of thy love.

Music: The melody (only) of this tune first appeared anonymously in the *Llyfr y Psalmau* (London, 1621) of Archdeacon Edmwnd Prys, and its exact form there is retained in *H82*, apart from altering one note that seems to have been misprinted in Prys. It next appeared, slightly modified in rhythm, set to the 67th song, a metrical version of Acts 1 with its description of the calling of Matthias in Wither's *Hymnes and Songs of the Church* (London, 1623), with a bass-line that may have been by Orlando Gibbons, who provided most of the other tunes in the book (see the essay "British Hymnody from the Sixteenth Through the Eighteenth Centuries", vol. 1, 365). The CMD for St. Matthias' Day begins:

When one among the Twelve there was,
That did thy Grace abuse;
Thou left'st him, Lord, and in his place
Did'st just Matthias chuse.

Our present version adopts the bass-line from Wither's book and adds the editorial alto and tenor parts from *H40*—mostly taken from *The Yattendon Hymnal* (Oxford, 1899). The tune has also been known as PALATINE and ST. MATTHIAS (see *Frost*, nos. 332, 332a, and 332b).

MBJ/JW

698 Eternal Spirit of the living Christ

Music: **FLENTGE**

This hymn is a fine example of the hymn text and hymn tune writing of contemporary American poets and composers. Both appear for the first time in an Episcopal hymnal in *H82*.

Words: This text by the Presbyterian minister and poet Frank von Christierson was written around 1975 and appeared in the *LBW* to the tune ADORO TE. Gilbert E. Doan, Jr. says of the text, "it is written in the first person singular . . . . Constructed chiefly of verbs and nouns, and with only an occasional adjective, it is unvarnished, simple (mostly monosyllabic) and direct, not to say intimate. It petitions without groveling and aspires without presuming. And it moves—from private need to a vision of cosmic redemption in Christ—and then comes to a conclusion that ties up all the loose ends." Doan further writes that he considers this text "the best of all von Christierson's texts."[1] Stanza 3 was slightly altered for use in *H82*. The original text was:

Come with the strength I lack, the vision clear
Of neighbor's need, of all humanity;
Fulfillment of my life in love outpoured:
My life in You, O Christ; Your love in me.

The text is also included in von Christierson's book *Make a Joyful Noise* (Fort Bragg, CA, 1987).

---

1. See G. E. Doan, "Hymn Writers of Today: Frank von Christierson," *American Organist*, 1983.

Music: The tune FLENTGE by Carl Schalk was written in 1979 at the request of Dr. Russell Schulz-Widmar for inclusion with this text in *Songs of Thanks and Praise: A Hymnal Supplement* (Chapel Hill, NC, 1980). It is a basically diatonic tune with a strong accompaniment that fits comfortably within the key of D. Its gently arching phrases complement each other in a very natural way. All these qualities, plus the immediate accessibility of the tune for a congregation, reflect the skills of the composer who, as a master of his art, is able to use the simplest of means to create a work of freshness and interest.

The tune name, FLENTGE, is that of the composer's mother, Elsie Flentge Schalk (1892-1966).

MBJ/RG

699 *Jesus, Lover of my soul*

Music: **ABERYSTWYTH**

This text, written shortly after Charles Wesley's conversion, is not only expressive of his deep personal faith in the saving grace of his savior, Jesus Christ, but is also illustrative of his profound skills as a poet. It is matched here with a strong Welsh tune.

Words: Headed "In Temptation," "Jesu, Lover of my soul" appeared as a poem of five eight-line stanzas in John and Charles Wesley's *Hymns and Sacred Poems* (London, 1740)(*Poetical Works*, vol. I, 259f). It was taken into Martin Madan's *Collection of Psalms and Hymns* (London, 1760) and A. M. Toplady's *Psalms and Hymns for Public and Private Worship* (London, 1776). John Wesley, however, disliked a tendency to the "amatory" in some of his brother's hymns (see his sermon of 1789/90 "On Knowing Christ after the Flesh"), and he excluded this hymn from the definitive *Collection of Hymns for the Use of the People called Methodists* (London, 1780). By 1785 it was back in the *Pocket Hymn Book* (London) that John Wesley issued, and it was inserted into the 1797 London Publishing House edition of the *Collection* and the official Conference revision of 1831; it has since never lost its place in Methodism.

In various versions it has figured in the *Hymnal* since 1826, usually without the original third (which even the Methodists have normally omitted since *Hymns and Spiritual Songs* [London, 1753]) and fourth stanzas:

3. Wilt Thou not regard my call?
Wilt Thou not accept my prayer?
Lo! I sink, I faint, I fall—
Lo! on Thee I cast my care:
Reach me out Thy gracious hand!

While I of Thy strength receive,
Hoping against hope I stand
Dying, and behold, I live!

4. Thou, O Christ, art all I want,
More than all in Thee I find:
Raise the fallen, cheer the faint,
Heal the sick, and lead the blind.
Just and holy is Thy name,
I am all unrighteousness;
False and full of sin I am,
Thou art full of truth and grace.

The Lord is called "Lover of souls" in the Wisdom of Solomon 11:26 (cf. collect no. 5, BCP, 395). Nevertheless, the *Hymnals* of 1826, 1865, and one 1874 version read "Jesus, Saviour of my soul." This and other changes fall within the innumerable attempts to "improve" the first four lines in particular.[1] *The Hymnal 1982* has retained the original form of the chosen stanzas, except for changing the vocative from "Jesu" and retaining the alteration that has been in the *Hymnal* since 1892, "Grace to cleanse from every sin" in place of "Grace to cover all my sin."

---

1. See *Proceedings of the Wesley Historical Society*, vol. 2/1 (Burnley, England, 1899), 15-17.

Music: See hymn 349. The composer of ABERYSTWYTH used this tune with this text in his cantata, *Ceridwen*. Probably the earliest matching of the text and tune in a hymnal was in the British *Baptist Church Hymnal* (London, 1900). Its matching in the *Hymnal* of the Episcopal Church occurred in the music edition of *H40*. Earlier matchings in the United States can be found in *The Methodist Hymnal* (Nashville, 1932) and *The Hymnal* (Philadelphia, 1938) of the Presbyterian Church. Today, this is the standard matching of the text and tune in English-language hymnals around the world.

GW/RG

700 O love that casts out fear

Music: **MOSELEY**

The work of Horatius Bonar, a prolific Scottish hymn writer and minister of the Free Church of Scotland, this text first entered the *Hymnal* in 1892. It was matched with this tune in the music edition of the 1916 *Hymnal*.

Words: Based on I Jn. 4:18, this hymn by Horatius Bonar was first published in his *Hymns of Faith and Hope*, Second Series (London, 1861). Alterations have been made in st. 2, where the singular pronouns have been made plural. Originally the hymn, which is no longer in common use by other denominations, concluded with the following doxology:

Praise to the Father give,
The Spirit and the Son;
Praise for the mighty love
Of the great Three-in-one.

Music: MOSELEY by Henry Smart is named for a village that has since been swallowed up by the growth of the city of Birmingham, England. Perhaps privately printed during the composer's lifetime, it attracted attention in *The Children's Hymn Book* (London, 1881) compiled by Carey Brock. Brock gave permission for the tune's inclusion in the 1889 supplement to *HA&M* and the 1890 edition of the *Hymnal Companion* (London, 1890). The Church of Scotland's *Church Hymnary: Third Edition* (London, 1973) attaches the name to a tune by Birmingham University music professor John Joubert.

MS/HMcK

701 Jesus, all my gladness

Music: **JESU, MEINE FREUDE**

This famous text and tune, first matched in 1656, unite as a profound and deeply personal expression of the yearning for spiritual union between the worshiper and Jesus Christ.

Words:

1. Jesu meine Freude
Meines Hertzens Weyde
  Jesu meine Zier.
Ach wie lang, ach lange
Ist dem Hartzen bange
  Und verlangt nach dir!
Gottes Lamm, mein Bräutigam
Ausser dir sol mir auff Erden
Nichts sonst liebers werden.

2. Unter deinem Schirmen
Bin ich für dem Sturmen
  Aller Feinde frey.
Lass den Satan wittern
Lass den Feind erbittern
  Mir steht Jesus bey.
Ob es jetzt gleich kracht und blizt
Ob gleich Sund und Hölle schrecken
Jesus wil mich decken.

3. Trotz dem alten Drachen
Trotz dem Todtestrachen
  Trotz der Furcht darzu!
Tobe Welt und springe:
Ich steh hier und singe
  In gar sicher Ruh.
Gottes macht hält mich in acht
Erd und Abgrund muss verstummen
Ob sie noch so brummen.

4. Weg mit allen Schätzen
Du bist mein Ergötzen
  Jesu meine Lust:
Weg ihr eitlen Ehren
Ich mag euch nicht hören
  Bleibt mir unbewust
Elend, Noth, Creuz, Schmach und Tod

Sol mich ob ich viel muss leiden
Nicht von Jesu scheiden.

5. Gute Nacht, O Wesen
Das die Welt erlesen
  Mir gefällst du nicht.
Gute Nacht ihr Sunden
Bleibet weit dahinden
  Kommt nicht mehr ansliecht.
Gute Nacht, du Stolz und Pracht
Dir sey ganz, du Lasterleben
Gute Nacht gegäben.

6. Weicht ihr Trauergeister
Denn mein Freudenmeister
  Jesus, trit herein.
Denen die Gott lieben
Muss auch ihr Betrüben
  Lauter Zucker seyn.
Duld ich schon hie Spott und Hohn:
Dennoch bleibst du, auch im Leide
Jesu meine Freude.

The text "Jesu, meine Freude" ("Jesus, all my gladness") was written by Johann Franck and first appeared in Johann Crüger's *Praxis Pietatis Melica* (Berlin, 1653) with Crüger's tune. The text, originally six stanzas, was apparently modeled on the love song "Flora, meine Freude, Meiner Seele Weide" from Heinrich Alberti's *Arien* (Koenigsberg, 1641):

Flora meine Freude,
Meiner Seelen Weide,
Meine ganze Ruh;
Was mir so verzuecket
Und den Geist bestricket,
Flora, das bist du.
Deine Pracht glaenzt Tag und Nacht
Mir vor Augen und im Herzen
Zwischen Trost und Schmerzen.

Jesu meine Freude,
Meines Herzens Weide,
Jesu meine Zier!
Ach wie lang, ach lange
Ist dem Herzen bange
Und verlangt nach dir.
Gottes Lamm, mein Brautigam!
Auszer dir soll mir auf Erden
Nichts sonst liebers werden.

The first translation of this text into English was by Catherine Winkworth for the *Chorale Book for England* (London, 1863). The text as it appears in *H82* is a translation of sts. 1, 4, and 6 of the original and is a slightly altered version of the translation by Arthur Wellesley Wotherspoon that appeared in the *Scottish Mission Hymnbook* (1912). The text entered the *Hymnal* in *H40*.

Music: The tune JESU, MEINE FREUDE (*Zahn* 8032) by Johann Crüger first appeared in his *Praxis Pietatis Melica* (Berlin, 1653), where it was set to Johann Franck's text of the same title. Johann Sebastian Bach based his great five-part motet on this text and tune and also utilized the tune in cantatas 12, 64, 81, and 87 and as the basis for several organ works. It is considered one of the finest of post-Reformation tunes and texts. The harmonization in *H82* is from *The Lutheran Hymnal* (St. Louis, 1941), slightly altered.

CS

702 Lord, thou hast searched me and dost know

Music: **TENDER THOUGHT**

This paraphrase of Ps. 139:1-11 comes from the tradition of Christian Reformed Churches in North America and is matched here with an early nineteenth-century American folk hymn melody. Both appear in the *Hymnal* for the first time.

Words: "Lord, Thou hast searched me," a modern paraphrase of Ps. 139:1-11, has been taken from the *Psalter Hymnal* (Pittsburgh, 1927), a hymnal of the United Presbyterian Church. The author of the text is unknown. This hymn was first paired with the tune TENDER THOUGHT in the *Hymnal for Colleges and Schools* (New Haven, CT, 1956).

Music: The tune SALVATION [243] was apparently first printed in the four-shape shape-note *Kentucky Harmony* (Harrisonburg, VA, 1816), edited by Ananias Davisson.[1] The hexatonic tune TENDER

THOUGHT also apparently first appeared in print, in a four-part version with the melody in the tenor, in this book, in which Davisson claimed the arrangement as his own. It was linked with a text by Philip Doddridge, an English Independent minister, "Arise, my tender thoughts, arise" (see Example 1 on opposite page).

This version was reproduced, sometimes without the counter part, and sometimes with a different counter part, in a number of shape-note books. In William Walker's *Southern and Western Pocket Harmonist* (Philadelphia, 1846) it is called THE LORD'S SUPPER, and in his *Christian Harmony* (Philadelphia, 1867) it is called THE LORD'S SUPPER (or, TENDER THOUGHT). In both it is linked with the text "Twas on that dark and doleful night." It is printed in Thomas Hastings's round-note *Presbyterian Psalmodist* (Philadelphia, 1852) in an appendix introduced with a note:

> A few tunes embraced in the Assembly's list were found so imperfect in their structure, that any efforts towards appropriate correction would have destroyed their identity. These tunes the editor has thought fit to throw together at the close of the volume, without the slightest revision.

After its first publication in *Kentucky Harmony* the next book to print this tune under the title TENDER THOUGHT was James M. Boyd's *Virginia Sacred Musical Repository* (Winchester, VA, 1818). Though Boyd's three-part version was obviously dependent on that of Davisson, passing notes were added in the tenor and the treble and bass largely rewritten.

Another version was published on two staffs with the melody in the treble in *The Lute of Zion: A Collection of Sacred Music Designed for the Use of The Methodist Episcopal Church* (New York, 1853), which was edited by I. B. Woodbury, with the assistance of the Rev. H. Mattison, pastor of the John Street Methodist Church, New York City. This harmonization was reproduced on four staffs with the melody in the tenor in Martin D. Wenger's *The Philharmonia* (Elkhart, IN, 1875).

Kentuckian Samuel L. Metcalf's four-shape shape-note *Kentucky Harmonist* (Cincinnati, 1818), which was registered for copyright November 1, 1817, the year after the publication of *Kentucky Harmony*,

Example 1

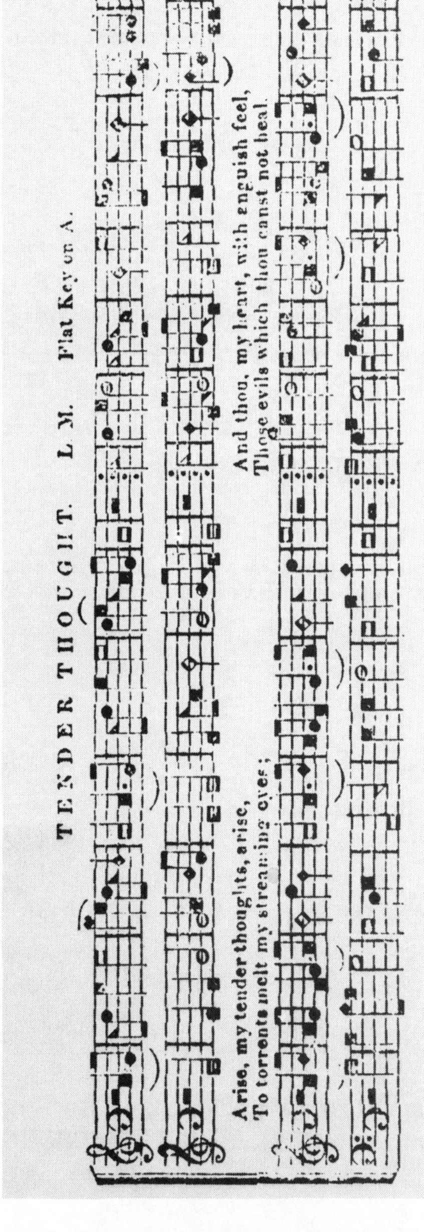
17
TENDER THOUGHT. L. M. Flat Key on A.
Arise, my tender thoughts, arise,
To torrents melt my streaming eyes;
And thou, my heart, with anguish feel,
Those evils which thou canst not heal.

Reproduced from *Kentucky Harmony* (Harrisonburg, VA, 1816), University of Michigan.

contained a variant titled CHESTER NEW and linked with the text "He dies, the friend of sinners dies." Another variant was published by Methodist minister Samuel Wakefield in his *Sacred Choral* (Pittsburgh, 1854) under the title INVITATION and with the text "Come, sinners, to the gospel feast."

George Pullen Jackson lists TENDER THOUGHT among the "Eighty Most Popular Tunes" in his *White Spirituals in the Southern Uplands* (Chapel Hill, NC, 1933).

The tune first entered an Episcopal hymnal in *Hymns III*, linked with the text "Lord, thou hast searched me and dost know" with an accompaniment by Alastair Cassels-Brown.

The harmonization in *H82* is from the *Hymnal for Colleges and Schools* (New Haven, CT, 1956), where it was used with this same text. It was also reproduced in this form in the *Pilgrim Hymnal* (Boston, 1958) and *The Mennonite Hymnal* (Scottdale, PA, 1969). The tune, though with a different text and with slight modifications of the harmonization and a different barring, was included in the *LBW*. In *H82* the barring is as in *Kentucky Harmony*.

---

1. See the Facsimile Edition with introduction by Irving Lowens (Minneapolis, 1976); R. A. B. Harley, "Ananias Davisson: Southern Tune-Book Compiler (1780-1857)," Ph.D. Diss., University of Michigan, 1972.

TS/MH

703 Lead us, O Father, in the paths of peace

Music: **SONG 22**

This hymn for peace is the work of William Burleigh, a very active mid-nineteenth-century social reformer, whose concerns focused on the areas of temperance and slavery. This is the only one of his many hymns that remains in general use today. *The Hymnal 1982* continues the text/tune matching established in *H40*.

Words: Burleigh's text was published in Elias Nason's *The New Congregational Hymn-Book* (Boston, 1859). Entitled "A Prayer for

Guidance," it reflects the troubled state of America as the Civil War was approaching. It became widely known in England through Charles D. Cleveland's *Lyra Sacra Americana* (New York, 1868). This hymn entered the *Hymnal* in 1892 and continued unaltered until the present revision, in which the following third stanza has been omitted:

Lead us, O Father, in the paths of right;
Blindly we stumble when we walk alone,
Involved in shadows of a darksome night;
Only with thee we journey safely on.

In this omitted stanza "darksome" originally read "moral."

Music: SONG 22 was contributed by Orlando Gibbons to George Wither's *Hymnes and Songs of the Church* (London, 1623), where it is associated with two of the scriptural paraphrases (see the essay "British Hymnody from the Sixteenth Through the Eighteenth Centuries," vol. 1, 365). It is printed with Song 22 ("The Prayer of Hezekiah"), beginning "O Lord of Hosts, and God of Israel"; and it is also specified for Song 29 ("The Prayer of Daniel"), beginning "Lord God Almightie, great, and full of feare." From the punctuation of these openings and the placing of the caesura in the tune, it seems likely that Gibbons originally had the Daniel text in mind.

This is a fine tune, vigorous and concise, with the rhythmic activity of the first two lines balanced by the steadier flow of the third and fourth. The character of the bass in line 2 is a reminder that the Gibbons basses were essentially for continuo rather than for voice. The tune was originally in G and was the only Gibbons hymn tune in what we should call a "sharp" key.

In some hymnals—even as late as *H40*—the tune appeared with its rhythms regularized. The original form had, however, been restored by Robert Bridges in *The Yattendon Hymnal* (Oxford, 1899) for his own made-to-measure text "Love of the Father, love of God the Son." This passed into *EH* and thence into other English books. In *H82*, the alto and tenor parts are taken from the *EH* version (*Frost*, 359).

HE/JW

704 O thou who camest from above

Music: **HEREFORD**

The Wesley name stands in bold letters in pages of English ecclesiastical and musical history of the eighteenth and nineteenth centuries. In this instance we have a text by the great eighteenth-century hymn writer Charles Wesley matched with a tune by his grandson, the nineteenth-century composer and church musician, Samuel Sebastian Wesley.

Words: This text comes from Charles Wesley's *Short Hymns on Select Passages of the Holy Scriptures* (Bristol, 1769) (*Poetical Works*, vol. IX, 58f). The biblical pretext is Lev. 6:13: "The fire shall ever be burning upon the altar; it shall never go out."

The hymn figured as no. 318 in the definitive *Collection of Hymns for the Use of the People called Methodists* (London, 1780), where John Wesley introduced "*the* sacrifice" for "my" and thus lost the antithesis with "*thy* endless mercies."

The hymn first appeared in an Episcopal hymnal in *H40*, following the English *HA&M* (1904) in varying the second line from "The pure celestial fire t' impart." Further, in *H82* the fourth line was independently changed from "On the mean altar of my heart." Notwithstanding Anglican doubts that date at least from E. H. Bickersteth's *The Hymnal Companion to the Book of Common Prayer* (London, 1872), Methodists find no difficulty in syllabifying the original second line of the second stanza, "With *inextinguishable* blaze"; moreover, the meaning of the offending word is clear to any who have ever engaged in a fire drill.

Hildebrandt and Beckerlegge choose this text for inclusion among their "heavily documented samples" of the closely scriptural texture of the Wesleyan hymns.[1] Thus:

O thou who camest from above	Jn. 3:31
The pure celestial fire t'impart	1 Kg. 18:38; Lk. 12:49
Kindle a flame of sacred love	1 Chr. 21:26
On the mean altar of my heart!	Lev. 9:24
There let it for thy glory burn	2 Cor. 4:15
With inextinguishable blaze,	Lev. 6:13
And trembling to its source return	Job. 5:7
In humble prayer, and fervent praise	Jas. 4:6, 10

Jesus, confirm my heart's desire — Acts. 14:22; Rom 10:1
To work, and speak, and think for thee; — Col. 3:17
Still let me guard the holy fire, — Lev. 6:13; 1 Th. 5:19
And still stir up thy gift in me; — 2 Tim 1:6

Ready for all thy perfect will, — Rom. 12:2
My acts of faith and love repeat — 1 Th. 1:3
Till death thy endless mercies seal, — Eph. 4:30
And make my sacrifice complete. — Rom. 12:1; Phil. 2:17; 2 Tim. 4:6; Heb. 13:15

---

1. F. Hildebrandt and O. A. Beckerlegge, eds., *A Collection of Hymns for the Use of the People called Methodists*, vol. 7 of *The Works of John Wesley* (Oxford, 1983), 733 (adapted).

Music: HEREFORD first appeared in Samuel Sebastian Wesley's *The European Psalmist* (London, 1872). It is an instance of Wesley using a simple harmonic scheme in order to pursue melodic interests. The tune was included in *HA&M* (1904) and is repeated in *H40* and *H82* transposed down a whole step with the note values halved. The tune was written for the Three Choirs Festival at Hereford, and derived its name from that event.

GW/WTJ

705 As those of old their first fruits brought

Music: **FOREST GREEN**

This text by a contemporary American Presbyterian minister and poet appears for the first time in an Episcopal hymnal in *Hymns III* matched with FOREST GREEN, the English folk melody too long limited in use to the Christmas text "O little town of Bethlehem."

Words: This text was written for use with the tunes FOREST GREEN and ELLACOMBE [210] by the Rev. Frank von Christierson, a Presbyterian pastor and poet, and first appeared in *Ten New Stewardship Hymns* (New York, 1961), a collection obtained and published by the Hymn Society of America in cooperation with the Department of

Stewardship and Benevolence of the National Council of Churches of Christ in the U.S.A. for the observance of the Fortieth Anniversary of the Department. Reverend von Christierson's original text was:

1. As saints of old their first fruits brought
   Of orchard, flock, and field
   To God the Giver of all good,
   The Source of bounteous yield;
   So we today first fruits would bring—
   The wealth of this good land,
   Of farm and market, shop and home,
   Of mind, and heart, and hand.

2. A world in need now summons us
   To labor, love and give;
   To make our life an offering
   To God, that man may live;
   The Church of Christ is calling us
   To make the dream come true:
   A world redeemed by Christ-like love;
   All life in Christ made new.

3. In gratitude and humble trust
   We bring our best to thee
   To serve thy cause and share thy love
   With all humanity.
   O Thou who gavest us thyself
   In Jesus Christ thy Son,
   Teach us to give ourselves each day
   Until life's work is done.

The text, matched with this tune, appears in *The Presbyterian Hymnal* (Louisville, KY, 1990) and is included in an anthology of the author's texts, *Make a Joyful Noise* (Fort Bragg, CA, 1987).

Music: See hymn 78.

MBJ

706 In your mercy, Lord, you called me

Music: **HALTON HOLGATE**

This text by Josiah Conder, a nineteenth-century author, publisher, and editor, appears for the first time in an Episcopal hymnal in *H82*. It is set to a tune by William Boyce, an eighteenth-century composer, that is also new to the *Hymnal*.

Words: The text of this hymn by Josiah Conder has had a checkered history. Its first-known appearance was in John Leifchild's collection entitled *Original Hymns, Adapted to General Worship And Special Occasions, By Various Authors* (London, 1843, 2nd. ed. 1856). It was included in the *Sabbath Hymn Book* (New York, 1858), edited by Lowell Mason, Edwards Park, and Austin Phelps, and its companion volume *The Sabbath Hymn and Tune Book* (New York, 1859). In these sources it is in 76. 76. D metre with the first line " 'Tis not I that did choose thee." The *Original Hymns* version consisted of three stanzas, whereas the *The Sabbath Hymn Book* had only two.

A generation later the text found a place in *The Church's Praise Book* (New York and Chicago, 1881), edited by M. Woolsey Stryker and Hubert P. Main. Here the two-stanza *Sabbath Hymn Book* version was adapted to 85. 85. D metre, and its first line to "Lord! 'tis not I that did choose thee." The hymn had little currency thereafter until the two-stanza form appeared in *The Lutheran Hymnal* (St. Louis, 1941), this time in 87. 87. D metre. The version prepared for *H82* is based on this Lutheran text.

The hymn is a meditation on Jn. 15:16, "You did not choose me, but I chose you." In fact, this text appeared at the head of the hymn in Leifchild's collection. The final two lines of the hymn echo I Jn. 4:19, "We love, because he first loved us."

This hymn has had limited use until the present. It is not found in nineteenth- and early twentieth-century hymnals of major Protestant denominations. Although it did appear in *The Lutheran Hymnal* of 1941, it did not find a place in either the 1978 *LBW* or *Lutheran Worship* (St. Louis, 1982), or in any edition of *HA&M* or of *EH*; in addition, no previous hymnal of the Episcopal Church in the United States has included it. More recently another modernization in *Hymns For Today's Church* (London, 1982) has appeared and *The Baptist Hymnal* (Nashville, 1991) has a version closer to its original form in 76. 76. D.

Music: See hymn 280.

CP

707 *Take my life, and let it be*

Music: **HOLLINGSIDE**

The matching of this text with HOLLINGSIDE first appeared in *H40*. That relationship continues in *H82* with ABERYSTWYTH as an alternative tune.

Words: Written on February 4, 1874, "Take my life, and let it be" originated in December 1873 when Frances Ridley Havergal was visiting Areley House in Worcestershire, England. She later wrote:

> There were ten persons in the house, some unconverted and long prayed for, some converted but not rejoicing Christians. He gave me the prayer, 'Lord, give me all this house.' And He just did. Before I left the house everyone had got a blessing . . . The last night of my visit I was too happy to sleep, and passed most of the night in praise and renewal of my own consecration, and these little couplets formed themselves and chimed in heart, one after another, till they finished, 'ever, only, all for Thee'(*Julian*, 1114).

The hymn was first published in the Appendix of Charles Snepp's *Songs of Grace and Glory* (1874), followed by publications in Miss Havergal's *Loyal Responses* (London, 1878) and in *Life Chords* (London, 1880). It has also been published as a leaflet in various forms for Confirmation and self-consecration. *Julian* states " . . . it has been translated in French, German, Swedish, Russian, and other European languages, and into several of those of Africa and Asia" (*Julian*, 1114).

Called a "consecration hymn," the following quotation precedes the hymn in *Loyal Responses*:

> Here we offer and present unto Thee, O Lord, ourselves, our souls and bodies, to be a reasonable, holy, and lively sacrifice unto Thee (cf. BCP, 1979 ed., 336).

Music: HOLLINGSIDE is one of a group of tunes written by the Precentor of Durham Cathedral, John Bacchus Dykes, that the composer sent—on his own initiative rather than by invitation—to William Henry Monk, musical editor of the forthcoming *HA&M*. In the covering letter, dated 12 October 1860 (cited in the commentary to hymn 362), Dykes indicated that he had composed these tunes sometime before the end of 1860 for congregational use at Durham Cathedral because no other "suitable music" was available for the associated texts. The first edition of *HA&M*, published in 1861, contained seven tunes by Dykes, including HOLLINGSIDE, NICAEA [362] and MELITA [579]. HOLLINGSIDE was originally composed specifically for Charles Wesley's hymn "Jesus, lover of my soul" [699], with which it appeared in the first edition of *HA&M* in 1861, and in subsequent Episcopal hymnals.

TS/RAL

708 Savior, like a shepherd lead us

Music: **SICILIAN MARINERS**

This popular text first appeared in the *Hymnal* in 1871 and was matched with this equally popular tune in the music edition of *H16*. This relationship has continued in every edition of the *Hymnal* since that date.

Words: The authorship of this hymn cannot be established, although both Dorothy Ann Thrupp and H. F. Lyte have been suggested as possible authors. It first appeared, anonymously, in Miss Thrupp's *Hymns for the Young* (London, ca. 1830), and has been in the *Hymnal* since 1871.

Music: See hymn 344. The harmonization here, transposed down a half-step, is found in *H16*. The dotted rhythms at measures 1 and 4, beat 4 in the soprano and tenor parts, and at measures 2 and 5 in the tenor part were added by the Hymn Committee of the SCCM in the hope of encouraging a slower performance practice.

***H40*ced/RG**

709 O God of Bethel, by whose hand

***Music:* DUNDEE**

This text of Philip Doddridge first appeared in the 1871 edition of the *Hymnal*, was dropped from the 1874 edition and restored in the 1892 version. It was matched with this psalm tune in the Hutchins music edition of the 1892 *Hymnal* and the relationship has continued in every music edition of the *Hymnal* since that time.

Words: In the original manuscript, the five stanzas of Philip Doddridge's hymn are headed "Jacob's Vow. From Gen. xxviii. 20, 22," and dated Jan. 16, 173^{6}_{7} (see *Julian*, 831):

1. O God of Bethel, by whose Hand
Thine Israel still is fed
Who thro' this weary Pilgrimage
Hast all our Fathers led:

2. To thee our humble Vows we raise,
To thee address our Prayer,
And in thy kind and faithful Breast
Deposite [sic] all our Care

3. If thou thro' each perplexing Path
Wilt be our constant Guide;
If thou wilt daily Bread supply,
And Raiment wilt provide

4. If thou wilt spread thy Shield around
Till these our Wand'rings cease
And at our Father's lov'd Abode
Our Souls arrive in Peace

5. To thee, as to our Covenant-God
We'll our whole selves resign
And count that not our Tenth alone
But all we have is thine.

The hymn appeared in this form in *Scottish Translations and Paraphrases* (Edinburgh, 1745). In John Orton's collection, *Hymns founded on Various Texts in the Holy Scriptures by the late Reverend Philip Doddridge, D.D.* (Salop, 1755), the hymn appears in substantially the same form, the only change being the alteration of the first line to "O God of *Jacob*, by whose hand."

The poet John Logan rewrote the hymn and included it in *Poems. By the Rev. Mr. Logan, One of the Ministers of Leith* (n.p. 1781). Logan's alterations and additions are shown here in italic:

1. O God of *Abraham*, by Whose hand
   Thy people still are fed
Who through this weary Pilgrimage
   Hast all our Fathers led:

2. *Our vows, our prayers, we now present*
   Before Thy throne of grace
God of our fathers! be the God
   Of their succeeding race.

3. Through each perplexing path *of life*
   Our wandering footsteps guide;
Give us each day our daily bread,
   And raiment *fit* provide

4. *O* spread thy *cov'ring wings* around,
   Till *all* our wand'rings cease;
And at our Father's lov'd Abode
   Our Souls arrive in peace!

5. *Now with the humble voice of prayer,*
   Thy mercy we implore;
Then with the grateful voice of praise,
   Thy goodness we'll adore.

Logan's version was further revised for the *Scottish Translations and Paraphrases* (Edinburgh, 1781). "Abraham" in the first line was restored to "Bethel," and st. 5 was completely rewritten (only the word "implore" at the end of line 2 was retained).

In *H82* the basic version of the *Scottish Translations and Paraphrases* is followed, but with some significant alterations. In st. 1, line 3, "weary" is changed to "earthly"; in st. 2, "God of our fathers" becomes "O God of Israel" (which picks up the thought in st. 2, line 1 of Doddridge's original); in st. 4, line 1, "cov'ring" becomes "sheltering"; and in st. 5, line 3, "chosen God" becomes "covenant

God," which Doddridge originally used in the first line of his final stanza.

Music: Commentary on this tune is found at no. 126. This faux-bourdon setting, with the melody in the tenor, first appeared in the great Scottish psalter *The Psalmes of David in Prose and Meeter. With their whole Tunes in foure or more parts . . .* (Edinburgh, 1635).

RAL

710 Make a joyful noise unto the Lord (Singt dem Herren!)

Music: **SINGT DEM HERREN**

A section of Rounds and Canons is a new feature in the *Hymnal* of the Episcopal Church. This accessible form of music, widely practiced in churches in Germany, provides congregations with satisfying and varied opportunities for liturgical participation. These settings, once learned by a congregation, can be sung from memory. This makes many appropriate for use during the Communion of the People at Eucharist.

Words: The German text of this canon is not original to the setting but was added by Fritz Jöde for use with the melody in his *Der Kanon* Vol. 1 (Berlin, 1929). The English text is a free adaptation of the German by Anne and Lawrence Gilman in their hymnal supplement *Song and Spirit* (New Haven, 1979). A literal translation is:

> Sing to the Lord! Sing to him and praise him altogether in this morning hour; come hither and thank him.

Music: The present form of this setting in the Ionian mode was edited from a work of Michael Praetorius and appeared in a group of Praetorius canons in Fritz Jöde's *Der Kanon* (Berlin, 1929) (see Example 1). The source of the melody is not identified in the collected works of Praetorius. Jöde's method was to extract canonic material from various compositions, which could be instrumental rather than vocal, without identifying the immediate sources. Some of the originals of this canonic material in Jöde's collection have been located, but not this particular canon.

Example 1

RG

711 Seek ye first the kingdom of God

***Music:* SEEK YE FIRST**

The inspiration for this simple song of faith can be traced to the "spirit" of the 1960s, an era when the author felt challenged to live what she believed and, as a consequence, left her job as an entertainer to pursue full-time Christian service.

Words: In the midst of a personal financial crisis in 1971, Karen Lafferty attended a Bible study at her home church; the teaching that night was based on Mt. 6:33, "seek ye first . . . " She returned home, her bills still unpaid, but her faith strengthened. She picked up her guitar and set the words to music in a song that has since become known internationally, has launched the composer into a full-time ministry and (appropriately enough) now provides, through royalty income, more than half of the support needed to finance her missionary work. The song was first published in *Rejoice in Jesus Always* (Laguna Hills, CA, 1973). No information is available about the background of st. 2. Based on Mt. 7:7, it was probably spontaneously created during worship and has been passed down in the pattern of traditional folk music. Its first appearance in an Episcopal publication occurred in *Songs for Celebration* (New York, 1980).

Music: This simple two-part song provides even small congregations an opportunity for part-singing. When sung in the manner of a round, the soaring "Alleluia" section counterbalances the lower-lying first theme and adds a dimension of praise. It is helpful for congregations to sing through parts 1 and 2 separately before combining them as a round. Originally composed with guitar in hand, the song demands some rhythmic strength (if not available through the guitar itself) in its accompaniment. A folk ensemble, such as guitar, bass guitar, and piano or organ, provides the ideal accompaniment. Solo instruments may be added to reinforce the melodies. To achieve the antiphonal beauty inherent in the melody, a broad tempo is necessary, allowing the "Alleluias" to soar.

BP

712 Dona nobis pacem

Music: **DONA NOBIS PACEM**

This traditional and well-known canon has an immediate accessibility for congregations because of the extensive use of the setting in schools and camps. The Latin text is the last phrase of the Agnus Dei (see S 157). This is the first appearance of this text and tune in an Episcopal hymnal.

Words: The Latin phrase "Dona nobis pacem" ("grant us peace") is the concluding petition of the Agnus Dei from the Mass. In its original form, the Agnus Dei consisted only of the words "Agnus Dei, qui tollis peccata mundi, miserere nobis" ("Lamb of God, who takes away the sins of the world, have mercy on us"). As early as the ninth century these words were being sung three times. By the eleventh century, the third statement of "miserere nobis" began to be replaced by the phrase "dona nobis pacem," an alteration that ultimately became the standard.

Music: The origin of the music for the round DONA NOBIS PACEM is not known. In most collections it is simply labeled "traditional." Estimates of its date range from the fifteenth to the seventeenth centuries.[1] Its musical style, however, would seem to indicate an origin no earlier than the eighteenth or nineteenth century.

---

1. See, for example, W. E. Studwell, *Christmas Carols: A Reference Guide* (New York, 1985), 63.

DWM

713 Christ is arisen (Christ ist erstanden)

***Music:* CHRIST IS ARISEN**

The text and tune of the great German Easter Chorale CHRIST IST ERSTANDEN is the basis for both the text and tune of this canon.

Words: This text, the traditional Christian greeting during the Easter season, is a translation of the first three words of the chorale "Christ ist erstanden," upon whose melody this canon is based (see no. 184).

Music: The composer, Richard Rudolf Klein, uses the first six notes of the chorale tune as the first phrase of his five-part canon. The remainder of the canon is freely composed. In it, four-note motives are used in pairs. The first is an exact repetition, the second repeats the pitches but varies the rhythm, and the third is done in a sequence with the second appearance starting a third lower and ending on the tonic. It was included in the ecumenical hymnal *Cantate Domino* (Geneva, 1980) and is dated 1964. This is its first appearance in an Episcopal hymnal.

RG

714 Shalom, my friends (Shalom chaverim)

***Music:* SHALOM CHAVERIM**

This text and tune from Israeli sources has gained extensive use in contemporary ecumenical settings. Its plaintive, modal melody gives it great appeal for congregational use.

Example 1

Sha - lom ha-ve-rim, sha - lom ha-ve-rim, sha - lom, sha - lom. Le -
hit - ra - 'ot be - e - rets yis - ra - 'el.

Words and Music: The precise origins of this song are uncertain. It would appear that it arose out of Zionist youth movements in the Diaspora in the 1920s or 1930s. Partial evidence for this is the text of a German Zionist version that is "Goodbye friends, *Aufwiedersehn*, in the Land of Israel."[1]

This setting is one measure shorter than the melody sung today as in *H82*, an American notation of which is given by Harry Coopersmith in *Songs of My People* (New York, 1937) (see Example 1, page 1327):[2]

In Palestine the tune was used as a school children's song, in which greetings were exchanged between teachers and pupils (see Example 2):[3]

Example 2

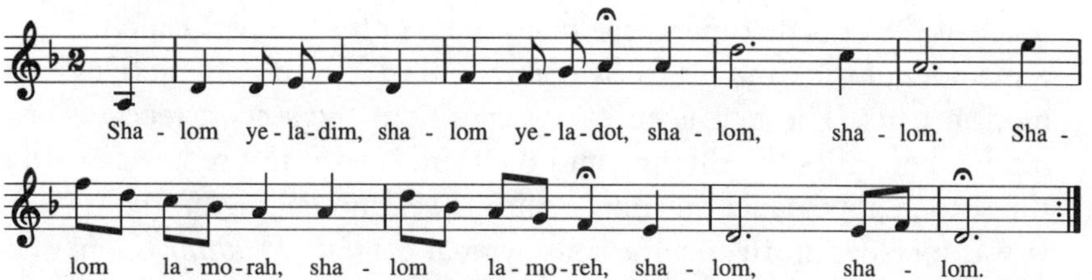
Sha - lom ye - la-dim, sha - lom ye - la - dot, sha - lom, sha - lom. Sha -
lom la - mo - rah, sha - lom la - mo - reh, sha - lom, sha - lom.

Rendered as a round, its lack of the distinctive musical features of the "Folk Song Style" of Palestine-Israel (such as a narrow range, the avoidance of a tonic-dominant axis, the presence of a plagal area of musical activity) perhaps betray its Diaspora origins. If the g minor guitar chord suggested here for measure 4 is changed to b minor, it would emphasize the major-minor structure of the Magein 'Avot synagogue mode to which the tune is somewhat related.

1. J. Schongerg, ed. *Shirei Erets Yisrael* (Berlin, 1935), 29, Example 1.
2. See H. Coopersmith, *Songs of My People* (New York, 1937), 29.
3. See *Shiryon le-Shalom Aleph* (Jerusalem, 196?), 3, Example 2.

RG/JGo

715 When Jesus wept, the falling tear

***Music:* WHEN JESUS WEPT**

This canon is by William Billings, the first American composer to achieve and retain over the centuries a position of acceptance and respect (see the essay, "Psalmody in America to the Civil War," vol. 1, 393). Both the text and music first appeared in his *The New England Psalm Singer* (Boston, 1770).

Words: This text was apparently first printed in William Billings's *The New England Psalm Singer* (Boston, 1770). In Billings's *The Singing Master's Assistant* (Boston, 1778), where this text is printed with the tune EMMAUS, it is attributed to P. M. The *Boston Musical Gazette* of April 17, 1892, page 204 identifies P. M. as Perez Morton, a member of the Harvard Class of 1771. A copy of the 1778 edition of *The Singing Master's Assistant*, in the William L. Clements Library at the University of Michigan, has an attribution of the text to "P. Morton" in what appears to be a contemporaneous hand. The Scriptural allusion is to Jn. 11:35.

Music: This four-part canon was composed by one of the most creative and prolific of the early American composers, William Billings, who published six collections of music.[1] The tune was included in the first of these, *The New England Psalm-Singer* (Boston, 1770), which consisted entirely of original compositions (see Example 1).

Example 1

Reproduced from *The New England Psalm-Singer* (Boston, 1770), John Carter Brown Library, Providence, Rhode Island.

The frontispiece of *The New England Psalm-Singer* was engraved by Paul Revere. This canon was included in *MHSS*, which was probably its first appearance in a denominational hymnal.

---

1. See *The Complete Works of William Billings*, 4 vols. (Boston, 1977).

MH

716 God bless our native land

Music: **AMERICA**

There is something ironic in the fact that three of the most important national hymns of the United States of America should use tunes that are rooted in the culture of England, the country with which this nation fought to gain independence.

Words: These stanzas are a free version of a German patriotic hymn written in 1815 by Siegfried Augustus Mahlmann and published in the same year in G. W. Fink's *Zeitung für die elegante Welt*. This German hymn inspired Samuel Francis Smith to write "My country, 'tis of thee" (see no. 717). The German original read:

1. Gott segne Sachsenland,
Wo fest die Treue stand
  In Sturm und Nacht!
Ew'ge Gerechtigkeit,
Hoch über'm Meer der Zeit,
Die jedem Sturm gebuet,
  Schütz uns mit Macht!

2. Blühe, du Rautenkranz,
In schönrer Tage Glanz
  Freudig empor!
Heil, Friedrich August, Dir!
Heil, guter König, Dir!
Dich, Vater, preisen wir
  Liebend im Chor!

3. Was treue Herzen flehn,
Steigt zu des Himmels Höh'n
Aus Nacht zum Licht!
Der unsre Liebe sah,
Der unsre Thränen sah,
Er ist uns hülfreich nah,
Verlasst uns nicht!

Mahlmann's hymn was first sung on November 13, 1815, in the presence of the King of Saxony. It has been given a number of English and American translations (*Julian*, 1566). Various versions have appeared in the *Hymnal* since 1871.

This translation is a composite. Charles T. Brooks wrote the first five lines of the first stanza, with the final two lines and st. 2 being written by John S. Dwight. Brooks was at that time a student at Harvard Divinity School, while Dwight was a Boston music critic. The translation by Brooks and Dwight was published in Mason & Webb's *The Psaltery* (Boston, 1845).

Music: Perhaps the most famous tune in the world, it has been played as "God Save the King (or Queen)" for more than 200 years on ceremonial occasions throughout the British Empire and Commonwealth; has been admired and used by Continental composers including Beethoven, Weber, Brahms, and Debussy; has been taken up as a national song in the United States, Germany, and many other countries; and has been the model for national anthems throughout the world, including Haydn's AUSTRIA [522]. In view of this glorious history, it is a little surprising to discover that its composer cannot be identified.

Percy A. Scholes investigated the prehistory of the anthem.[1] It may well have been a Jacobite song originating in the 1680s, but its first documented appearance was in a collection called *Harmonia Anglicana* (London ca. 1744) (see Example 1 on following page).[2]

In this early form, the second, third, and last phrases were strikingly different from what they are today, but the second had already taken its modern form by the second edition of *Harmonia Anglicana* entitled *Thesaurus Musicus* (London, 1745). The nationwide popularity of the song dates from its performance, in a version by Thomas Arne, in London theatres at the height of the second Jacobite rebellion of 1745.

Whether it was Jacobite in origin, it now served to focus the loyalty of the British majority behind King George II. It was this rallying power that was so much coveted by foreign rulers.

Example 1

God save our Lord the King, Long live our no - ble King,
God save our Lord the King, Long live our no - ble King,

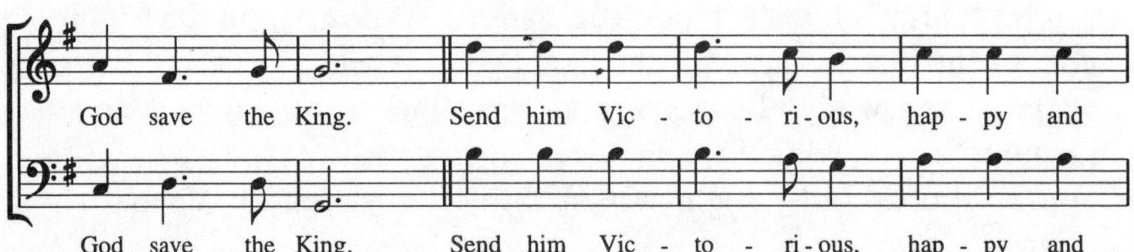
God save the King. Send him Vic - to - ri - ous, hap - py and
God save the King. Send him Vic - to - ri - ous, hap - py and

Glo - ri - ous, Long to reign o - ver us, God save the King.
Glo - ri - ous, Long to reign o - ver us, God save the King.

Scholes lists some twenty song books of the later eighteenth century that included "God Save the King," but he also cites contemporary comments denying that it was church music. The use of the tune as a worship song originated with the Methodists. Following their deliberate policy of taking over and sanctifying whatever was best and most effective in secular music of the day, they introduced a pointed religious parody, "Come, thou almighty king," calling on the king of heaven, rather than any earthly monarch, to "arise, Scatter our enemies, And make them fall." Its author is unknown; it was first printed on a leaf inserted in George Whitefield's *Hymns for Social Worship* (London) from about 1757 and was fully incorporated into editions of that book from 1761. In the latter year it was printed, for the first time, with the tune in James Lyon's *Urania* (Philadelphia), where it is named WHITE-

FIELD's; clearly Whitefield had used this version on his recent visit to Philadelphia. It is found with the same text in a British Methodist collection, Thomas Knibb's *The Psalm Singers Help* (London, ca. 1765). Its distinctive metre was imitated in such tunes as Giardini's MOSCOW [365] and Lowell Mason's OLIVET [691] and DORT.

It is as a national song, however, that this tune appears in the *Hymnal*; it is not known who first called it AMERICA, but so far as the Episcopal Church is concerned it dates back at least to 1874, when it appeared with that name in Charles Hutchins's *Church Hymnal* (New York). Of the two harmonizations, this one is almost identical to the "official" British setting used on royal occasions and found in British hymnbooks.

---

1. P. Scholes, *God Save the Queen! The History and Romance of the World's First National Anthem* (London, 1954).
2. Full bibliographical details may be found in a note by D. W. Krummel in *The Musical Times* 103 (1962), 159.

HE/NT

717 My country, 'tis of thee

***Music:* AMERICA**

This text, although not the National Anthem of the nation, is probably the best known and most often used of all our national songs.

Words: The Baptist minister Francis Smith wrote this patriotic hymn during his first year of study at Andover (MA) Theological Seminary. Lowell Mason had received a large number of German chorale books brought by his friend William C. Woodbridge upon his return from Germany. Mason, unable to read German, brought the books to Smith, requesting translations that could be used in his music collections. Smith was attracted to a German patriotic text, Mahlmann's "Gott segne Sachsenland" (God bless Saxony) [716]. As recounted by Smith, "I instantly felt the impulse to write a patriotic hymn of my own, adapted to the tune. Picking up a scrap of paper which lay near me, I wrote at once, probably within half an hour, the hymn 'America' as it is now known."

Smith's text, written in 1831, to be sung to the tune now known as "America," was recommended by his friend the Rev. William Jenks to the Rev. Dr. Wisner, pastor of Boston's Park Street (Congregational) Church, for use at the church on July 4, 1831, at an Independence Day celebration by the Boston Sabbath School Union. It was first sung in public on that date by the Juvenile Choir directed by Lowell Mason. Two extant copies of the program for this service, one in the Chapin Collection at Williams College and the other at the American Antiquarian Society, give five stanzas of "My country, 'tis of thee." The original third stanza, which expressed strong views concerning the treatment of the American colonies by England, seems to have been omitted from all later printings.

3. No more shall tyrants here
With haughty steps appear,
And soldier bands;
No more shall tyrants tread
Above the patriot dead—
No more our blood be shed
By alien hands.

After its publication in the Independence Day program, Mason published Smith's hymn in his *Choir, or Union Collection of Church Music* (Boston, 1832). The first appearance of this hymn in an Episcopal hymnal was limited to only one of Smith's stanzas. In the 1892 *Hymnal*, the final stanza of "America" beginning "Our fathers' God, to thee" formed the first stanza of no. 196, attached to two stanzas of Mahlmann's "God bless our native land" (*H40*, no. 146). The four-stanza "My country, 'tis of thee" first appeared in *H16*.

Music: See 716. This setting is taken from *H40*, but beyond that its source is unknown.

HE

718 God of our fathers, whose almighty hand

Music: **NATIONAL HYMN**

This hymn, which gained widespread popularity within the first decade of its publication in the Tucker/Rousseau music edition of the 1892 *Hymnal*, now enjoys ecumenical acceptance and still ranks high in the esteem of congregations. In response to popular request, *H82* restores the trumpet fanfares that were deleted in *H40*.

Words: This national hymn was written for the centennial Fourth of July in 1876 by Daniel Crane Roberts, then rector of St. Thomas', Brandon, Vermont. It is interesting that this American centennial hymn was first sung to the tune RUSSIAN HYMN. Roberts sent his text, without his name as author, to the commission revising the Episcopal *Hymnal*. The text was accepted, appearing in the *Hymnal* of 1892. Although American in origin, this hymn of praise and prayer for peace does not refer to a specific nation; it can be sung by any freedom-loving people.

Music: Although "God of our fathers, whose almighty hand" had been written for the centennial of the Declaration of Independence in 1876, it was selected in 1892 to be used as the hymn for the centennial of the adoption of the United States Constitution. For that latter occasion, George W. Warren composed his majestic tune, used in the Columbia celebration on October 8, 1892, at New York City's St. Thomas' Church, where he was organist. The tune was first published in Arthur H. Messiter's *The Hymnal Revised and Enlarged* (New York, 1892), where it is named AMERICA. This early publication of the tune appears to be designed for choral rather than congregational use, for it is in the key of F and above the first line of the hymn is the direction "Voices alone." This is the only hymn of ecumenical acceptance that features an accompaniment with trumpet fanfares in the organ. The tune name NATIONAL HYMN is given to the tune in J. Ireland Tucker and William W. Rousseau's *The Hymnal Revised and Enlarged* (New York, 1894). A third early name is COLUMBIA, found in James H. Darlington's *The Hymnal of the Church* (New York, 1897).

HE

719 O beautiful for spacious skies

Music: **MATERNA**

This text, which was altered three times by the poet in response to criticism, was revised again for inclusion in *H82* to make it more responsive to contemporary attitudes of justice.

Words: The original version of this text was written in the summer of 1892. Following a summer school at Colorado Springs, Katherine Bates and other instructors celebrated with a trip to the top of Pike's Peak. Due to the uneasiness caused by the high altitude, the group stayed on the peak just long enough for "an ecstatic gaze." As Miss Bates recounted in 1918, "it was then and there, as I was looking out over the sea-like expanse of fertile country spreading away so far under those ample skies, that the opening lines of the hymn floated into my mind. When we left Colorado Springs, the four stanzas were penciled in my notebook." The poem was not published until two years later, in the July 4, 1895, issue of the *Congregationalist*. The original four stanzas read:

1. O beautiful for halcyon skies,
   For amber waves of grain,
   For purple mountains majesties
   Above the enameled plain!
   America! America!
   God shed his grace on thee,
   Till souls wax fair as earth and air
   And music-hearted sea!

2. O beautiful for pilgrim feet,
   Whose stern, impassioned stress
   A thoroughfare for freedom beat
   Across the wilderness!
   America! America!
   God mend thine every flaw,
   Till paths be wrought through wilds of thought
   By pilgrims foot and knee!

3. O beautiful for glory-tale,
   In liberating strife,

When once and twice, for man's avail,
Men lavished precious life!
America! America!
May God thy gold refine,
Till selfish gain no longer stain
The banner of the free.

4. O beautiful for patriot dream
That sees beyond the years
Thine alabaster cities gleam,
Undimmed by human tears!
America! America!
God shed his grace on thee,
Till nobler we keep one again
Thy whiter jubilee!

The images of the fourth stanza, "alabaster cities" and "whiter jubilee" were inspired by the "White City" of the Chicago Columbian World Exposition which Miss Bates visited on the way west.

In 1904 Miss Bates revised her poem, and it was first published in this form in the Boston *Evening Transcript*, November 19, 1904. In that version, sts. 1, 2, and 4 are identical to those found in most hymnals today. While the latter half of st. 3 was revised to its usual form, the first four lines in 1904 read:

O beautiful for glory tale
Of liberating strife
When valiantly for man's avail,
Men lavished precious life!

Later, as related by Miss Bates, "after the lapse of a few years, during which the hymn had run the gauntlet of criticism, I changed the wording of the opening quatrain of the third stanza." That final change by thc author dates at least from 1918, the year in which Miss Bates wrote a history of this hymn for Boston's Athenaeum library.

The four-stanza hymn has been reduced to three stanzas in *H82* by combining the first half of st. 3 with the second half of st. 2 to create st. 2 of the three-stanza version. These revisions reflect the SCCM's concern with the references in st. 2 ("A thoroughfare for freedom beat/Across the wilderness!") that glorify the settlement of America at the expense of Native Americans, and in st. 4 ("May God thy gold refine,/Till all success be nobleness,/And every gain divine.") as being preoccupied with wealth and success.

Music: MATERNA ("mother") was composed for "O mother dear, Jerusalem" by Samuel A. Ward. There are two conflicting accounts of its composition. One story holds that Ward composed the tune, jotting it down on his cuff, while crossing New York Harbor. An employee of Ward's music store reported the tune's year of composition as 1882, and that it was first performed by a choir of 200 men and boys at Grace Episcopal Church, Newark, where Ward was organist. The other account, given by Ward's son-in-law, the Rev. Henry W. Armstrong, stated that the tune was composed in memory of Ward's eldest daughter, Clara, who died in 1885.

MATERNA was first published in *The Parish Choir* (July 12, 1888). Its first inclusion in the *Hymnal* was in Charles L. Hutchins's music edition of 1894 as the first tune for "O mother dear, Jerusalem." This text and tune union continued in Episcopal hymnals through *H40*.

In 1912 the president of Massachusetts Agricultural College asked the composer's widow for permission to use the tune with Miss Bates's text. Set to MATERNA, this patriotic hymn became widely popular during World War I, and the matching has become inseparable ever since.

HE

720 O say can you see, by the dawn's early light

Music: **NATIONAL ANTHEM**

A popular eighteenth-century British song is the source of the melody to which Francis Scott Key set his patriotic text written during the bombing of Fort McHenry by vessels of the British fleet in September 1814. On March 3, 1931, by Act of Congress, this patriotic song became the "official" National Anthem of the United States of America.

Words: Late in August 1814, the British made a sortie from their fleet in Chesapeake Bay into Washington, D.C., where they set fire to the Capitol, the White House, and other public buildings. On their way back a Dr. Beanes of Upper Marlborough, Maryland, was arrested. Because of his political influence, Francis Scott Key was persuaded by friends to undertake Dr. Beanes's release. Key left Washington for Baltimore on September 3, and together with Col. John S. Skinner, the U. S. cartel agent, set sail down Chesapeake Bay on an unidentified sloop, reaching the British fleet off the mouth of the Potomac River on September 7. The prisoner's release was agreed to, but the party was detained lest they give warning of the proposed attack on Baltimore. The whole fleet sailed north on September 8 and was sighted off Baltimore on Sunday morning, September 11. During the night, troops were landed on North Point for a flank attack, and the next day the smaller bombers and rocket ships worked up the mouth of the Patapsco River for frontal attack on Fort McHenry. The Americans were returned to their sloop under guard. During the day and evening of September 13, the British lobbed some 1800 bombs into and around the fort. When the firing ceased around 1 A.M. on September 14, tension on the sloop was high for they had no way of telling whether or not the fort had fallen; only when they saw through the mist and drizzle of the morning that the oversized flag was still flying could they relax. Actually the British had no desire to risk a serious engagement, since their orders from London were to attack New Orleans rather than the eastern seaboard; consequently when they saw how well Baltimore was defended they started reembarking their troops during the night.

When Key saw that the attack was over, he started sketching this text on the back of a letter. The sloop was allowed to proceed into Baltimore that evening, and in his hotel Key wrote out a clean copy. It is probably this manuscript that is now preserved in the Walters Art Gallery, Baltimore. The next morning, September 15, Col. Skinner persuaded the author to go to the offices of the Baltimore *American*, where the poem was set up in handbill form. In less than a week, it had been reprinted in two Baltimore papers, and not much more than a month later a sheet music edition was published by Joseph Carr. Other newspapers around the country printed it, and before the year was out it appeared in three songsters.

Key's words were soon recognized as the best embodiment of the

American ideals of patriotism that had been produced in song form. The text was consistently published in songsters beside the popular airs of succeeding decades, so that its final elevation to the position of national anthem was by popular usage long before it was so declared by Act of Congress on March 31, 1931. The tune and Key's first and fourth stanzas entered the *Hymnal* in 1916 when the section for "National Days" was first introduced. This usage has continued in *H40* and *H82*. The omitted second and third stanzas are:

2. On the shore dimly seen through the mists of the deep,
Where the foe's haughty host in dread silence reposes,
What is that which the breeze, o'er the towering steep,
As it fitfully blows, half conceals, half discloses;
Now it catches the gleam of the morning's first beam,
In full glory reflected now shines in the stream.
'Tis the star spangled banner, O long may it wave
O'er the land of the free, and the home of the brave.

3. And where is that band who so vauntingly swore
That the havoc of war and the battle's confusion
A home and a country shall leave us no more.
Their blood has washed out their foul footsteps' pollution.
No refuge could save the hireling and slave,
From the terror of flight or the gloom of the grave.
And the star spangled banner in triumph doth wave
O'er the land of the free, and the home of the brave.

Music: The musical setting of the national anthem of the United States of America is called both STAR SPANGLED BANNER and NATIONAL ANTHEM. One must be cautious, however, in using the latter name because in Great Britain it is the name of the tune for "God save our gracious queen." This same tune is known as AMERICA in the United States (see 716).

Through the years, controversy about this National Song has arisen around four issues: 1. The origin of the tune and the identity of its composer; 2. the attempts in Congress during the 1950s and 1960s to name an "offical" version (i.e., exact words and tune); 3. efforts to determine the most "accurate," "authentic," "original," and "well-known" version of the melody; and 4. the arguments supporting its replacement as national anthem with some other patriotic song.

For many years this tune was usually cited as being of unknown origin and dating from the late eigtheenth century. For some time, however, it has been acknowledged that the tune was originally associated with the text "To Anacreon in Heaven" written by Ralph Tomlinson and first published in *The Vocal Magazine* (London, 1778). It is presumed that both text and tune originated between 1775 and 1777 since the first-known publication of the tune was a sheet music version issued ca. 1777-1781.[1]. The Anacreontic Song is also found in John Stafford Smith's *Fifth Book of Canzonets, Canons and Glees* (London, 1799). As a result of this later publication, Smith's name has been associated with the tune as arranger and composer for almost two centuries. One can be fairly secure in this attribution since John Stafford Smith (1750-1836) is known to be the composer of all the other works in the collection. Additionally, on page 33 of Smith's collection, where "The Anacreontick Song" is found in a three-part arrangement, the following statement appears: "harmonized by the Author." The highly respected American musicologist and first Chief of the Music Division of the Library of Congress, Oscar G. T. Sonneck, wrote in his book *The Star-Spangled Banner*:

> Available evidence . . . compel(s) me to believe that the music of Ralph Tomlinson's poem, 'To Anacreon in Heaven' was indeed composed by John Stafford Smith. Words and music of this song, later on popularly known as "The Anacreontic Song" probably originated about the year 1775.[2]

More recently, William Lichtenwanger, former Head of Music Reference at the Library of Congress, wrote extensively about the national anthem in his article "The Music of the 'The Star-Spangled Banner'; From Ludgate Hill to Capitol Hill."[3] Mr. Lichtenwanger begins by quoting from Oscar Sonneck's 1914 study:

> One may indeed express surprise that John Stafford Smith waited until 1799 before he publicly claimed the music of "To Anacreon in Heaven" as his own. But are we really certain that he did not

> claim it years before? May there not be hidden away somewhere in 'the wreck of time' . . . directed evidence of Smith's authorship if not his own manuscript then perhaps some reference in contemporary letters of the like?[4]

He continues with the discovery of the historical material "hidden away in the 'wreck of time' ":

> . . . in 1961 . . . Charles Cudworth, Librarian of the Pendlebury Music Library at Cambridge University, acquired just such a reference, one lone sentence buried in ten volumes of manuscript 'Recollections and Diaries' written by Richard John Samuel Stevens (1757-1837) . . . . He returns in 'Recollections' to the Anacreontic Society, still writing (in 1808) under the general heading of 1777:[5]
>
> > . . . The President was Ralph Tomlinson Esq . . . . He wrote the Poetry of the Anacreontic Song; which Stafford Smith set to music:[6]
>
> We have seen, at last, a matter-of-fact and unequivocal statement that it was indeed Stafford Smith who set Ralph Tomlinson's poetry to music, a statement by someone who participated in music making at the society when Ralph Tomlinson was president and "The Anacreontic Song" was in its early years.[7]

Although not yet universally recognized or accepted, William Lichtenwanger appears to have proven that John Stafford Smith was the composer of the tune we know as the STAR-SPANGLED BANNER.

The tune apparently became known in the United States around 1790. By the mid-1790s it began to appear in various American collections, sometimes set to Tomlinson's text, but more frequently set to other patriotic poetry or parodies. In this last group may be found an example by Francis Scott Key himself. Key composed a set of words to the tune, which he performed in honor of Stephen Decatur on November 30, 1805.[8] In this parody Key employed both rhymes and phrases later to be found in his poetry for the National Anthem.

Following its publication in the *American Musical Miscellany* (n.p., 1798), the tune became widely popular. It was coupled there with the patriotic text "Adams and Liberty" written in commemoration of the fourth anniversary of the Massachusetts Charitable Fire Assocation of Boston.[9]

The second controversy centers on the question of establishing the "official" version. The *Star-Spangled Banner* was authorized as the National Anthem of the United States by an act of Congress on March 3, 1931. Before then it shared the honor with *My Country, 'Tis of Thee* (see 717). Since 1931 further proposals, primarily those by Congressman Joel Broyhill of Virginia during the 1950s and 1960s, have been presented to Congress for an "official version" (i.e., exact words and tune).[10]

The third controversy is similar to the second and deals with which version of the melody (and words) is most "accurate," "authentic," "original," and "well-known." According to William Lichtenwanger, ". . . there are at least five copies of the work in Key's autograph in which other melodic and textual differences are clearly evident."[11] There have also been other versions from James Hewitt's of 1819 to a mid-nineteenth-century version for "social orchestra" to an orchestral arrangement by Igor Stravinsky (1941).[12] An arrangement published by the Defense Department in April 1955 and authorized for use by United States military bands is at present the closest to an "offical version" in existence.

The fourth controversy centers around the contention that *The Star-Spangled Banner* should be replaced by another patriotic song. Arguments to support its replacement include: the tune is unsingable (it has a range that makes it inaccessible for most people); the tune did not originate in the United States (it is of British origin); and its text is primarily about war (see text entry). Arguments for its retention include: it is part of our national tradition; it is well known by most Americans; it embraces the American patriotic spirit; and it is a long-standing symbol of the nation.

Of the numerous arrangements of the *National Anthem*, two are by Stravinsky. Of interest is Puccini's use of the tune as a motto theme for the American character Lieutenant Pinkerton in his famous opera *Madama Butterfly*.[13]

The musical setting found in *H82* is drawn from *H40* with slight modifications by Roy Kehl, a member of the Hymn Music Committee of the SCCM. These alterations are based on his study of military band versions of the tune from various periods as found in the holdings of the Library of Congress.

---

1. A facsimile of this sheet music version may be found in W. Lichtenwanger's "The Music of 'The Star-Spangled Banner': From Ludgate Hill to Capitol Hill," *Quarterly Journal of the Library of Congress*, July, 1977 (repr. 1977 in booklet format), 3.

2. O. G. T. Sonneck, *The Star-Spangled Banner* (Washington, 1914), 56.

3. Lichtenwanger, "Music of the Star-Spangled Banner," 3.

4. Sonneck, *Star-Spangled Banner*, 56; Lichtenwanger, 12.

5. Lichtenwanger, 12-13.

6. R. J. S. Stevens, "Recollections," Pendlebury Music Library, Cambridge University, MS, vol. I, 68 and 70-73, as quoted in Lichtenwanger, 13.

7. Lichtenwanger, 15.

8. Key's parody text "When the Warrior returns from the battle afar" was sung by Key at a dinner in Georgetown, District of Columbia. The dinner was given in honor of naval commander Stephen Decatur. The text was first published in the Boston *Independent Chronicle*, December 30, 1805.

9. Various phases of the history of the *Star-Spangled Banner* are presented in detail in: P. W. Filby and E. G. Howard's *Star-Spangled Books* (Baltimore, 1972); G. J. Svejda, *History of the Star-Spangled Banner from 1814 to the Present* (Washington, 1969); and in R. S. Hill's "The Melody of 'The Star-Spangled Banner' in the United States before 1829," in *Essays Honoring Lawrence C. Wroth*, ed. F. R. Goff (Portland, ME, 1951), 151-193.

10. This issue is discussed in the article "A Proposed Official Version of THE STAR SPANGLED BANNER" in *Notes*, XV, 1 (December, 1957), 33-42.

11. Letter from David T. Albee of the Library of Congress to Roy Kehl of Evanston, IL, September 1, 1983.

12. An excellent source about early versions of the tune is J. Muller's *The Star-Spangled Banner, Words and Music, Issued between 1814-1864: An Annotated Bibliographical List with Notices of the Different Versions, Texts, Variants, Musical Arrangements, and Notes on Music Publishers in the United States* (New York, 1973), Supplement by L. S. Leby and J. J. Fuld. Further information about the Stravinsky arrangements of the *National Anthem* may be found in E. W. White's *Stravinsky: The Composer and His Works* (London, 1979), 2nd. ed., 547.

13. *The New Grove Dictionary of Music and Musicians*, vol. XIII, 73.

H40c alt/JeW

Hymnal 1982 Companion, Vol. 3 Glossary

Alternatum canticle setting—a fully written out chant-like setting of a canticle text with alternating vocal textures and appropriate changes of key; for English parish choirs.

Anacrusis—an unstressed syllable at the beginning of a line of poetry or an unstressed note or group of notes at the beginning of a phrase of music; an upbeat.

Calends—the first day of the ancient Roman month from which days were counted backwards to the ides.

Canon—the prescribed rule or authorized standard. The multiple meanings of this word begin from this basic definition: 1. contrapuntal works in which there are strict rules of imitation determining both the interval of time and pitch between the entry of each voice of the composition. A simple type of canon is the round (see hymns 25, and 710–715); 2. canon of scripture: the authorized list of books accepted as authoritative; 3. canon of the mass: the prescribed rule or form for the Great Thanksgiving of the Roman rite; 4. canon of nine odes: the set of nine canticles from the Old and New Testaments used in the Byzantine morning office; also the set of troparia or refrains used for these canticles; 5. canon of psalmody: prescribed set of psalms used in worship by Eastern monks.

Cantus firmus—see vol. 1, 677.

Cantus Fractus—Latin, a melody in metrical rhythm that resulted from a note of long value being divided into smaller parts.

Cento—see vol. 1, 677.

Choosing Notes—alternative notes printed on the same staff as the main tune that were either higher or lower than the average person might be comfortable singing and were therefore printed as options for those who were capable of reaching them.

Common Practice Era—the period of major/minor tonality beginning around 1600 and extending to about 1900 in traditional music and extending into the 20th century in various types of tonal music: hymnody, popular music, very late romantic and commercial music.

Compline—the last service of the day in the daily services observed by monastic orders, recited immediately before retiring.

Ferias—weekdays in the Church calendar on which no feast is celebrated. It is the opposite of festal, which refers to feasts on weekdays or Sundays.

Fermata—a symbol[I] [i] indicating a pause.

Filioque—Latin, a phrase added by Western churches to the description of the Holy Spirit in the Nicene Creed. The Creed adopted by the ecumenical councils of Nicea and Constantinople cited John 15:26, "who proceeds from the Father," to describe the Spirit. Western churches unilaterally added to this the phrase *"filioque,"* "and from the Son." The Western alteration of a text promulgated by an ecumenical council caused dissension and ultimately schism between the Greek-speaking East and the Latin-speaking West.

Hemiola—a rhythmic device in which note values are in the relation of 3:2. In modern terms this refers to the use of three half-notes in place of two dotted half-notes in 6/4 time or the rhythmic pattern in which two measures in 3/4 become one measure of 3/2. The latter device is often found at cadence points in music up to and during the Baroque period and in compositions of Brahms.

Homophonic—a term used to describe music in which one voice, usually the upper, called the melody, predominates and is supported by an accompaniment in a chordal style. It is also used to describe part-music in which all the voices move in the same rhythm. The structure of a hymn tune, such as ST. ANNE [680], illustrates both aspects of this definition.

Labarum—Latin, a military standard, taken on by the Emperor Constantine after his conversion, with the Greek monogram for Christ X P substituted for the original pagan emblems. It was taken up by the Eastern Empire as well in 324. The term is thought to be a corruption of the Latin word *laureum*, commonly used by soldiers for a standard (*vexillum*).

Lauds—the principal morning office in the Western tradition, named for the last three psalms used in the service. Psalms 148/149/150, which begin, *Laudate* ("Praise . . .").

Lorica—a Celtic poetic form expressing protective invocation or prayer. Although St. Patrick's breastplate, "I bind unto myself today/the strong name of the Trinity" [370] is its most famous example, the lorica as a form predates Christianity in the Celtic world.

Macaronic—see vol. 1, 679.

Matins (or Mattins)—1. in medieval texts, this sometimes means the "morning" vigil, occasionally (as in Benedict) the 'morning' office after the vigil later known as lauds, and in other instances the series of services recited together in the morning (the vigil, lauds and sometimes prime). 2. In the BCP, the service of Morning Prayer constructed out of elements of the vigil, lauds, and prime.

Melisma (pl. Melismata)—a vocal line in which many notes are sung to one syllable; for example, in the refrain of the carol "Angels we have heard on high" [96] in which the first syllable of the word "Gloria" in the melody is sung to a passage of sixteenth notes.

Metz Notation—a form of neumatic notation for chant developed at the German Monastery of Metz in the ninth through the tenth centuries which gives the general outline of the melody, but not of actual intervals.

Musica Ficta—Latin, false notes, or in the modal music of the tenth through the sixteenth centuries, chromatic tones used to avoid certain awkward intervals. An oral rather than notated tradition.

None(s)—the service in the monastic sequence of hours in the daily office which is appointed for the ninth hour (*"hora nona"* or 3:00 P.M.).

Obbligato—an independent vocal or instrumental line played or sung with an established melody. It is an essential part of the musical structure and not to be treated "ad libitum."

Patibulum—Latin, the horizontal beam of the cross which the condemned were often required to carry to their execution.

Pifferari—Italian country people in the eighteenth century who, in imitation of the biblical shepherds, went to Rome on Christmas morning to play their wind instruments.

Prime—the service in the monastic sequence of hours of the daily office which is appointed for the first hour *(prima hora)* of the day. It ordinarily follows lauds, the principal morning office, which is appointed for dawn. It was an early addition to the monastic sequence of services.

Punctum—Latin, in plainsong notation a neume □ indicating a single pitch. It is also a term indicating forms of cadences in the lesson and gospel tones given in *The Holy Eucharist, Altar Edition* (New York, 1977).

Quatrain—a unit or group of four lines of verse.

Sapphic Metre—see vol. 1, 680.

Sarum—Latin, the local variant of the liturgical and musical tradition of the Roman rite in the diocese of Salisbury.

Septuagint—the Greek version of the Old Testament originating in Alexandria in the third century B.C.E. As the Bible of Greek-speaking Jews at the time of Christ, it was adopted by Greek-speaking Christians in the early Church.

Sext—the service in the monastic sequence of hours in the daily office which is appointed for the sixth hour (*"hora sexta"* or 12:00 noon).

Tactus—the fifteenth and sixteenth century term for beat.

Terce—the service in the monastic sequence of hours in the daily office which is appointed for the third hour (*"hora tertia"* or 9:00 A.M.).

Tierce de Picardie—the raised third or major third found in the final chord of a composition in a minor key. The practice arose around 1500 when the third, for the first time, was admitted in the final chord of a piece. No explanation can be given for the name Tierce de Picardy which occurs for the first time in J. J. Rousseau's *Dictionnaire de musique* (Paris, 1764).

Vespers—the evening service in the daily office in Western traditions. The ordinary English translation was Evensong.

Vox Principalis—Latin, in the ninth through eleventh centuries the term used for the main melody, or cantus firmus, over which the added part, or **vox-organalis** was added in parallel organum.

Authors, Translators, and Sources

Abelard, Peter (1079–1142) 164, 623
Addison, Joseph (1672–1719) 409, 415
Afro-American spiritual 99, 172, 325, 468, 648, 676
Afro-American spiritual, 19th cent. 99
Ainger, Arthur Campbell (1841–1919) 534
Alcuin (735–804) 465, 466
Alexander, Cecil Frances (1818–1895) 102, 167, 180, 276, 370, 405, 549, 550
Alexander, James Waddell (1804–1859) 168, 169
Alford, Henry (1810–1871) 209, 290
Alington, Cyril A. (1872–1955) 205
Ambrose of Milan (340–397) 5, 14, 15, 19, 20, 21, 22, 54, 55, 233, 234
American folk hymn 385
American folk hymn, ca. 1835 439
Anonymous 213, 229, 267, 365, 373, 425, 433, 467, 689
Antiphoner and Grail, The, 1880 183
Appleford, Patrick Robert Norman (b. 1925) 568
Arthur, John W. (1922–1980) 299, 417, 418
Auber, Harriet (1773–1862) 393
Auden, W. H. (1907–1973) 463, 464

Babcock, Maltbie D. (1858–1901) 651
Bahnmaier, Jonathan Friedrich (1774–1841) 530
Baker, Henry Williams (1821–1877) 47, 82, 432, 578, 645, 646
Baker, Theodore (1851–1934) 81, 433
Bakewell, John (1721–1819) 495
Bangor Antiphoner, ca. 690 327, 328
Barbauld, Anna Laetitia (1743–1825) 288
Baring-Gould, Sabine (1834–1924) 42, 265, 527, 562
Barton, Bernard (1784–1849) 627
Basque carol 265
Bates, Katherine Lee (1859–1929) 719
Baxter, Richard (1615–1691) 625
Bayly, Albert F. (1901–1984) 222, 605, 610
Beadon, Hyde W. (1812–1891) 138
Bede, The Venerable (673–735) 217, 218, 271, 272
Bell, George Kennedy Allen (1883–1958) 614
Bell, Maurice F. (1862–1947) 143
Bennett, John (b. 1920) 196, 197
Benson, Edward White (1829–1896) 292
Benson, Louis F. (1855–1930) 340, 341
Bernard of Clairvaux (1091–1135) 649, 650
Bernard of Cluny (12th cent.) 624
Bianco da Siena (d. 1434?) 516
Blacker, Maxwell Julius (1822–1888) 360, 361
Bode, John Ernest (1816–1874) 655
Bonar, Horatius (1808–1889) 316, 317, 318, 455, 456, 692, 700
Bonhoeffer, Dietrich (1906–1945) 695, 696
Book of Common Prayer, The, 1979 153, 354, 355
Borthwick, Jane Laurie (1813–1897) 541
Bourne, George Hugh (1840–1925) 307
Bowers, John E. (b. 1923) 51
Bowie, Walter Russell (1882–1969) 582, 583, 598
Bowring, John (1792–1872) 441, 442, 640
Brackett, Joseph, Jr. (1797–1882) 554
Brady, Nicholas, (1659–1726), 94, 95, 364, 658, 666
Brenner, Scott Francis (1903–1991) 297
Bridges, Matthew (1800–1894) 494, 697
Bridges, Robert Seymour (1844–1930) 5, 36, 46, 158, 168, 169, 427, 665
Briggs, George Wallace (1875–1959) 289, 305, 306, 542, 584
Bright, William (1824–1901) 242, 281, 337
Brokering, Herbert F. (b. 1926) 412
Brooks, Charles Timothy (1813–1883) 716
Brooks, Phillips (1835–1893) 78, 79
Brooks, R. T. (1918–1985) 630
Browne, Simon (1680–1732) 512
Brownlie, John (1859–1925) 73, 313
Bunyan, John (1628–1688) 564, 565

Burleigh, William Henry (1812–1871) 703
Byrne, Mary Elizabeth (1880–1931) 488
Byrom, John (1692–1763) 106

Cain, Thomas H. (b. 1931) 149
Caird, George B. (1917–1984) 422
Cameron, Catherine (b. 1927) 580
Campbell, Jane Montgomery (1817–1878) 291
Campbell, Robert (1814–1868) 174, 223, 224, 244
Carpenter, William Boyd (1841–1918) 574, 575
Casanate, Hieronimo (d. 1700) 261, 262
Caswall, Edward (1814–1878) 257, 310, 311, 479, 642, 682
Cawood, John (1775–1852) 588, 589
Chadwick, James (1813–1882) 96
Chadwick, John White (1840–1904) 617
Chandler, John (1806–1876) 3, 4, 29, 30, 76, 124
Charles, Elizabeth Rundle (1828–1896) 97, 190, 217, 218
Chatfield, Allen William (1808–1896) 641
Chesterton, Gilbert Keith (1874–1936) 591
Chorley, Henry Fothergill (1808–1872) 569
Christian Hymnbook, 1865 116
Claudius, Matthias (1740–1815) 291
Clausnitzer, Tobias (1619–1684) 440
Clement of Alexandria (170?–220?) 163, 478
Clephane, Elizabeth Cecilia (1830–1869) 498
Coffin, Charles (1676–1749) 3, 4, 29, 30, 76, 124
Coffin, Henry Sloane (1877–1954) 475
Coles, Vincent Stucky Stratton (1845–1929) 268, 269
Colvin, Thomas Stevenson (b. 1925) 602, 611
Conder, Josiah (1789–1855) 323, 706
Cosin, John (1594–1672) 503, 504
Cosnett, Elizabeth (b. 1936) 476
Coventry carol, 15th cent. 247
Coverdale, Miles (1487–1568) 634
Cowper, William (1731–1800) 667, 677, 683, 684
Cox, Frances Elizabeth (1812–1897) 194, 195, 286, 408
Crawford, Mary Babcock (b. 1909) 651
Crossman, Samuel (1624–1683) 458
Crum, John Macleod Campbell (1872–1958) 204
Cummins, Evelyn Atwater (1891–1971) 647

Daw, Carl P., Jr. (b. 1944) 18, 61, 62, 266, 358, 359, 513, 517, 597, 678, 679
Dearmer, Percy (1867–1936) 1, 2, 98, 145, 211, 312, 564, 565, 631, 682
Decius, Nikolaus (1490?–1541) 421
de Santeüil, Jean Baptiste (1630–1697) 257
Dix, William Chatterton (1837–1898) 115, 119, 460, 461
Doan, Gilbert E. (b. 1930) 85, 86
Doane, George Washington (1799–1859) 457
Doane, William Croswell (1832–1913) 363
Doddridge, Philip (1702–1751) 71, 72, 284, 321, 543, 546, 709
Donne, John (1573–1631) 140, 141, 322
Douglas, Charles Winfred (1867–1944) 76, 173, 375, 530, 540, 669
Drake, Carol Christopher (b. 1933) 69
Draper, William H. (1855–1933) 400
Dryden, John (1631–1700) 500
Dudley-Smith, Timothy (b. 1926) 431, 437, 438
Duffield, George, Jr. (1818–1888) 561
Dwight, John Sullivan (1812–1893) 716
Dwight, Timothy (1725–1817) 524

Eastern Orthodox Memorial Service 355
Eddis, Edward W. (1825–1905) 37
Edmeston, James (1791–1867) 559
Egan, Linda Wilberger (b. 1943) 673
Ellerton, John (1826–1893) 24, 77, 179, 255, 259, 280, 345, 492, 569
Elliott, Charlotte (1789–1871) 693
English carol, 18th cent. 109
English carol, ca. 18th cent. 453
English Hymnal, The, 1906 175, 216, 225
English Praise, 1975 347
Ephrem of Edessa (4th cent.) 443
Epistle to Diognetus, ca. 150 489
Evans, Mark (b. 1916) 295
Everest, Charles William (1814–1877) 675
Evers, J. Clifford (b. 1916) 581
Exodus 15:1–2 425

Faber, Frederick William (1814–1863) 469, 470, 558, 643
Farjeon, Eleanor (1881–1965) 8

Farlander, Arthur William (1898–1952) 375, 530, 540, 669
Fawcett, John (1739/40–1817) 344
F.B.P. (ca. 16th cent.) 620
Feith, Rhijnvis (1753–1824) 484, 485
Findlater, Sarah B. (1823–1907) 68
First Song of Isaiah, The 678, 679
Fishel, Donald (b. 1950) 178
Fortunatus, Venantius Honorius (540?–600?) 161, 162, 165, 166, 175, 179, 216, 225
Fosdick, Harry Emerson (1878–1969) 594, 595
Foundling Hospital Psalms and Hymns, 1797 373
Francis of Assisi (1182–1226) 400, 406, 407, 593
Franck, Johann (1618–1677) 399, 701
Franz, Ignaz (1719–1790) 366
Franzen, Frans Mikael (1772–1847) 65
Franzmann, Martin H. (1907–1976) 381, 572
Frazier, Philip (1892–1964) 385
French carol 96

Gaunt, Howard Charles Adie (1902–1983) 334
Gellert, Christian Furchtegott (1715–1769) 194, 195
Gerhardt, Paul (1607–1676) 46, 168, 169, 515, 669
German 319, 383, 384, 710
German, 15th cent. 81
German, ca. 1529 713
German, ca. 1800 427
Geyer, John Brownlow (b. 1932) 296
Ghanaian 602, 611
Gilman, Ann M. (b. 1932) 710
Gilman, Lawrence (b. 1930) 710
Gladden, Washington (1836–1918) 659, 660
Gloria in excelsis 421
Glover, Joyce MacDonald (b. 1923) 606
Grant, John Webster (b. 1919) 161, 228, 236, 501, 502
Grant, Robert (1779–1838) 388
Greek 73
Greek, ca. 110 302, 303
Greek, 3rd cent. 25, 26, 36, 37
Green, F. Pratt (b. 1903) 74, 170, 348, 420, 424, 452, 695, 696
Gregory the Great (540–604) 146, 147, 152
Grieve, J. Nichol (1868–1954) 404
Grindal, Gracia (b. 1943) 256
Griswold, Alexander Viets (1766–1843) 368
Grubb, Edward (1854–1939) 681
Gurney, John Hampden (1802–1862) 625

Hall, William John (1793–1861) 656
Hammond, William (1719–1783) 181
Harkness, Georgia (1891–1974) 472
Hatch, Edwin (1835–1889) 508
Havergal, Frances Ridley (1836–1879) 514, 707
Hay, Granton Douglas (b. 1943) 447
Heber, Reginald (1783–1826) 117, 118, 258, 301, 362, 486
Hebrews 12:1–3 545
Hedge, Frederic Henry (1805–1890) 687, 688
Heermann, Johann (1585–1647) 158
Hensley, Lewis (1824–1905) 613
Herbert, George (1593–1633) 382, 402, 403, 487, 592
Herklots, Rosamond E. (1905–1987) 246, 674
Hermann, Nikolaus (1480?–1561) 201
Hernaman, Claudia Frances (1838–1898) 142
Hewlett, Michael (b. 1916) 506, 507
Hilary of Poitiers (4th cent.) 223, 224
Hispanic folk song 113
Holland, Henry Scott (1847–1918) 596
Holmes, Oliver Wendell (1809–1894) 419
Hopkins, John Henry, Jr. (1820–1891) 128, 336
Hosmer, Frederick Lucian (1840–1929) 615
Housman, Laurence (1865–1959) 133, 134, 573
How, William Walsham (1823–1897) 52, 252, 254, 287, 632
Hughes, Donald W. (1911–1967) 148
Hull, Eleanor H. (1860–1935) 488
Hume, Ruth Fox (1922–1980) 103
Humphreys, Charles William (1840–1921) 312, 326
Hunterian MS. 83, 15th cent. 266
Hymnal 1940 56, 60, 81, 152, 193, 233, 234, 282, 283, 314, 320, 329, 330, 331, 390, 475, 619
Hymnal 1982 16, 17, 19, 20, 38, 39, 40, 41, 44, 45, 48, 63, 64, 91, 159, 162, 165, 166, 176, 177, 231, 232, 261, 262, 314, 320, 364

Hymn Book of the Anglican Church of Canada and the United church of Canada, The, 1971 131, 132
Hymns Ancient and Modern, 1861 59, 124, 127, 136, 137, 244, 248, 249, 263, 264, 518, 519, 520, 624
Hymns for the Festivals and Saints' Days of the Church of England, 1846 267
Hymns for the Young, ca. 1830 708

Idle, Christopher (b. 1938) 465, 466
Ingemann, Bernard Severin (1789–1862) 527
Irish, ca. 700 488
Isaiah 9:2–7 125, 126
Israeli round 714
Italian, 18th cent. 479

Jabusch, Willard F. (b. 1930) 536
Jacobi, John Christian (1670–1750) 515
Janzow, F. Samuel (b. 1913) 245
Jenkins, William Vaughan (1868–1920) 350
Jervois, William Henry Hammond (1852–1905) 338
Jewish liturgy, Medieval 372
John of Damascus (8th cent.) 198, 199, 200, 210
John 6 335
Johnson, James Weldon (1871–1938) 599
Joseph, Jane M. (1894–1929) 92
Joseph the Hymnographer (9th cent.) 237

K. 636, 637
Keble, John (1792–1866) 10, 656
Kelly, Thomas (1769–1855) 471, 483
Ken, Thomas (1637–1711) 11, 43, 380
Kethe, William (d. 1608?) 377, 378
Key, Francis Scott (1779–1843) 720
Kingo, Thomas Hansen (1634–1703) 298
Kingsley, Charles (1819–1875) 566
Kitchin, George William (1827–1912) 473
Knox, Ronald A. (1888–1957) 187

Lafferty, Karen (20th cent.) 711
Landsberg, Max (1845–1928) 372
Latin 16, 17, 31, 32, 47, 144, 190, 236, 273, 274, 354, 356, 576, 577, 581, 606
Latin, Traditional 712
Latin, 5th cent. 193
Latin, 5th–8th cent. 619
Latin, 6th cent. 3, 4, 27, 28, 29, 30, 40, 41, 44, 45, 143
Latin, ca. 6th cent. 59, 85, 86
Latin, ca. 7th cent. 63, 64, 518, 519, 520
Latin, 7th–8th cent. 202, 263, 264
Latin, Medieval 220, 221
Latin, 9th cent. 60, 503, 504
Latin, ca. 9th cent. 56, 360, 361
Latin, 10th cent. 1, 2, 38, 39, 133, 134
Latin, 11th cent. 122, 123
Latin, 12th cent. 226, 227, 228, 235, 238, 239, 244, 642
Latin, 13th cent. 159
Latin, 14 cent. 103, 207
Latin, 15th cent. 98, 136, 137, 248, 249, 448, 449, 621, 622, 642
Latin, 1632 174
Latin, 1661 308, 309
Latin, 1695 208
Laurenti, Laurentius (1660–1772) 68
Layritz, Friedrich (1808–1859) 81
LeCroy, Anne K. (b. 1930) 16, 17, 27, 28, 31, 32, 33, 34, 35, 38, 39, 144, 263, 264, 273, 274
Lew, Timothy T'ing Fang (1892–1947) 342
Littledale, Richard Frederick (1833–1890) 516
Liturgy of St. Basil 346
Liturgy of St. James 324, 326
London carol, 18th cent. 105
Luther, Martin (1483–1546) 54, 80, 139, 151, 185, 186, 319, 687, 688
Lutheran Book of Worship, 1978 80
Lyra Davidica, 1708 207
Lyte, Henry Francis (1793–1847) 410, 538, 662

Maclagan, William Dalrymple (1826–1910) 285, 349
Madan, Martin (1726–1790) 495
Mahlmann, Siegfried August (1771–1826) 716
Mann, Newton M. (1836–1926) 372
Mant, Richard (1776–1848) 279, 367, 414
Marier, Theodore (b. 1912) 354
Marriott, John (1780–1825) 371
Mason, Jackson (1833–1889) 235
Massie, Richard (1800–1887) 185, 186
Mattes, John Caspar (1876–1948) 505
Matthew 5:3–12 560
Matthew 6:33 711
Matthew 7:7 711
Mauburn, Jean (1460–1503) 97
Maurus, Rabanus (776–856) 282, 283, 501, 502

McCrady, James Waring (b. 1938) 14, 15, 19, 20, 21, 22, 44, 45, 54, 102, 173
McDougall, Alan G. (1875–1964) 33, 34, 35
Mealy, Norman (1923–1987) 205
Mercer, William (1811–1873) 496, 497
Merrill, William Pierson (1867–1954) 551
Micklem, Caryl (b. 1925) 369
Middleton, Jesse Edgar (1872–1960) 114
Milligan, James Lewis (1876–1961) 75
Milman, Henry Hart (1791–1868) 156
Milton, John (1608–1674) 389, 462
Mohr, Joseph (1792–1848) 111
Monastic Breviary, A, 1976 176, 177
Monsell, John Samuel Bewley (1811–1875) 552, 553
Montgomery, James (1771–1854) 93, 171, 343, 411, 426, 480, 484, 485, 616, 670
Morison, John (1749–1798) 125, 126
Moultrie, Gerard (1829–1885) 324
Mozarabic, 10th cent. 33, 34, 35

Neale, John Mason (1818–1866) 3, 4, 14, 15, 21, 22, 29, 30, 82, 107, 122, 123, 131, 132, 136, 137, 154, 155, 165, 166, 198, 199, 200, 202, 203, 206, 210, 237, 238, 239, 263, 264, 270, 271, 272, 327, 328, 518, 519, 520, 621, 622, 623, 624, 672
Neander, Joachim (1650–1680) 390, 665
Nelson, Horatio Bolton (1823–1913) 231, 232
Neumark, Georg (1621–1681) 635
New England Psalm Singer, The, 1770 715
New Version of the Psalms of David, 1696 658
Newbolt, Michael Robert (1874–1956) 473
Newman, John Henry (1801–1890) 445, 446
Newton, John (1725–1807) 351, 522, 523, 644, 671
New York, 1850 383, 384
Nicolai, Philipp (1556–1608) 61, 62, 496, 497
Niedling, Johann (1602–1668) 505
Noel, Caroline Maria (1817–1877) 435
North, Frank Mason (1850–1935) 609

Oakeley, Frederick (1802–1880) 83
Olearius, Johann G. (1611–1684) 67
Olivers, Thomas (1725–1799) 401
Onderdonk, Henry Ustick (1759–1858) 532, 533
Osler, Edward (1798–1863) 332
Oxenham, John (1852–1941) 529

Pagura, Frederico J. (b. 1923) 74
Palmer, Edmund Stuart (1856–1931) 357
Palmer, Ray (1808–1887) 649, 650, 691
Palmer, Roland Ford (1891–1985) 277
Paraphrases, 1781 447
Patrick (372–466) 370
Peacey, John Raphael (1896–1971) 347
Percy, William Alexander (1885–1942) 661
Perronet, Edward (1726–1792) 450, 451
Perry, Michael A. (b. 1942) 444
Piae Cantiones, 1582 92, 270
Pierpoint, Folliot Sandford (1835–1917) 416
Pilgrim Hymnal, 1904 689
Plumptre, Edward Hayes (1821–1891) 556, 557, 567
Pocknee, Cyril E. (1906–1980) 346
Pott, Francis (1832–1909) 208
Praise the Lord, 1972 146, 147
Price, Charles P. (b. 1920) 12, 13, 18, 23, 40, 41, 48, 55, 65, 226, 227, 284, 336, 352, 670, 706
Price, Frank W. (1895–1974) 342
Prudentius, Marcus Aurelius Clemens (348–410?) 82, 127
Psalm 19 431
Psalm 19:1–6 409
Psalm 23 645, 646, 663, 664
Psalm 42:1–7 658
Psalm 46 687, 688
Psalm 72 616
Psalm 84 517
Psalm 90:1–5 680
Psalm 95 (Venite) 399
Psalm 98 413
Psalm 100 377, 378, 391
Psalm 103:1–5 411
Psalm 117 380
Psalm 118:19–29 157
Psalm 121 668
Psalm 130 151, 666
Psalm 136 389
Psalm 139:1–11 702
Psalm 145 404
Psalm 145:1–12 414
Psalm 146 429
Psalm 148 373, 432
Psalm 150 432

Psalms, Hymns and Anthems, 1774 229
Psalms of David in Meeter, The, 1650 517, 668
Psalter Hymnal, The, 1927 702

Quinn, James (b. 1919) 399, 576, 577, 593, 633

Rawson, George (1807–1889) 629
Reed, Andrew (1787–1862) 509
Rees, John (19th cent.) 671
Rees, Timothy (1874–1939) 379, 511
Reid, William Watkins, Jr. (1923–1983) 607, 628
Revelation 5:12–13 417, 418
Reynolds, William M. (1812–1876) 54
Rhys, John Howard Winslow (b. 1917) 443
Richard of Chichester (1197–1253) 654
Riley, John Athelstan Laurie (1858–1945) 308, 309, 618
Rinckart, Martin (1586–1649) 396, 397
Rist, Johann (1607–1667) 91, 173
Robb, John Donald (1892–1989) 113
Robbins, Howard Chandler (1876–1952) 108, 163, 406, 407, 459, 521
Roberts, Daniel Crane (1841–1907) 718
Robinson, Robert (1735–1790) 686
Roh, Jan (1485?–1547) 53
Romans 8:34–39 447
Rossetti, Christina (1830–1894) 84, 112
Routley, Erik (1917–1982) 413, 570, 571
Rowthorn, Jeffery (b. 1934) 394, 395, 528
Russell, Arthur T. (1806–1874) 219
Russian Orthodox liturgy 560
Rygh, George Alfred Taylor (1860–1942) 298

Sarum Primer, 1514 694
Saward, Michael (b. 1932) 294
Scagnelli, Peter (b. 1949) 3, 4
Schenck, Theobald Heinrich (1656–1727) 286
Schulz-Widmar, Russell (b. 1944) 319, 353
Schütz, Johann Jacob (1640–1690) 375, 408
Scott, Lesbia (b. 1898) 293
Scott, Robert Balgarnie Young (b. 1899–1987) 600, 601
Sears, Edmund H. (1810–1876) 89, 90
Sedulius, Caelius (5th cent.) 77, 131, 132
Selection, 1787 636, 637
Shurtleff, Ernest Warburton (1862–1917) 555
Slovak, 17th cent. 250
Smart, Christopher (1722–1771) 212, 240, 241, 386, 387, 491
Smith, Horace (1836–1922) 251
Smith, Samuel Francis (1808–1895) 717
Smith, Walter Chalmers (1824–1908) 423
Smyttan, George Hunt (1822–1870) 150
Song of Creation, A 428
Song of Mary, The 437, 438
Song of Simeon, The 499
Song of the Redeemed, The 532, 533
Song of Zechariah, The 444
Song to the Lamb, A 374
Source unknown, 19th cent. 110
Southern Harmony, 1835 213
Spaeth, Harriet Reynolds Krauth (1845–1925) 81
Spanish, 17th cent. 682
Sparrow-Simpson, William J. (1860–1952) 160
Spencer, Robert Nelson (1877–1961) 579
Stone, Samuel John (1839–1900) 525
Struther, Jan (1901–1953) 243, 482
Studdert-Kennedy, Geoffrey Anketel (1883–1929) 9
Supplement to the New Version of the Psalms of David, A, 1698 364, 666
Synesius of Cyrene (375?–414?) 641
Syriac Liturgy of Malabar 312

Tate, Nahum (1625–1715) 94, 95
Te Deum 364, 366
Terry, Charles Sanford (1864–1936) 201
Tersteegen, Gerhardt (1697–1769) 475
Theodulph of Orleans (d. 821) 154, 155
Third Song of Isaiah, The 543
Thomas Aquinas (1225?–1274) 310, 311, 314, 320, 329, 330, 331
Thomerson, Kathleen (b. 1934) 490
Thomson, Mary Ann (1834–1923) 539
Thring, Godfrey (1823–1903) 454
Timms, George B. (b. 1910) 120, 230, 278
Tisserand, Jean (15th cent.) 203, 206
Toolan, Suzanne (b. 1927) 335
Toplady, Augustus Montague (1740–1778) 685
Traditional carol 101
Translations and Paraphrases, 1745 545
Tucker, F. Bland (1895–1984) 25, 26, 121, 135, 139, 164, 220, 221, 268, 269, 302, 303, 322, 356, 366, 421, 428, 443, 477, 478, 489, 530, 547, 587, 663, 668

Turton, William Harry (1856–1938) 315
Tuttiett, Laurence (1825–1895) 563

Vajda, Jaroslav J. (b. 1919) 250, 333
Van Dyke, Henry (1852–1933) 376, 586
Vanstone, W. H. (b. 1923) 585
Veni Creator Spiritus 500, 501, 502, 503, 504
Veni Sancte Spiritus 226, 227
von Bogatzky, Karl Heinrich (1690–1774) 540
von Christierson, Frank (b. 1900) 698, 705
von Spee, Friedrich (1591–1635) 173, 211

Wade, John Francis (1711–1786) 83
Walworth, Clarence Augustus (1820–1900) 366
Waters, Moir A. J. (1906–1980) 70
Watts, Isaac (1674–1748) 50, 100, 253, 321, 369, 374, 380, 391, 392, 398, 429, 434, 474, 510, 544, 664, 680
Webb, Benjamin (1819–1885) 217, 218, 220, 221, 448, 449
Webster, Bradford Gray (1898–1991) 590
Weisse, Michael (1480–1534) 184
Weissel, Georg (1590–1635) 436
Wesley, Charles (1707–1788) 6, 7, 49, 57, 58, 66, 87, 188, 189, 207, 213, 214, 300, 352, 481, 493, 526, 535, 548, 638, 639, 657, 699, 704
Wesley, John (1703–1791) 429
Whiting, William (1825–1878) 579, 608
Whitney, Rae E. (b. 1927) 499
Whittier, John Greenleaf (1807–1892) 652, 653
Wigbert [Wipo of Burgundy] (d. 1050?) 183
Wilbur, Richard (b. 1921) 104
Williams, George W. (b. 1922) 260
Williams, Peter (1722–1796) 690
Williams, William (1717–1791) 690
Winkworth, Catherine (1827–1878) 53, 67, 151, 184, 339, 396, 397, 436, 440, 635
Wither, George (1588–1667) 430
Wolcott, Samuel (1813–1886) 537
Woodward, George R. (1848–1934) 192
Wordsworth, Christopher (1807–1885) 48, 88, 135, 191, 215, 275, 612, 626
Work, John W. (1901–1967) 99
Wortman, Denis (1835–1922) 359
Wotherspoon, Arthur Wellesley (1853–1936) 701
Wren, Brian A. (b. 1936) 129, 130, 182, 304, 603, 604

Young, John Freeman (1820–1885) 111

Composers, Arrangers, and Sources for Hymns

African work song 611
Afro-American spiritual 172, 325, 468, 529, 648, 676
Afro-American spiritual, 19th cent. 99
Ahle, Johann Rudolph (1625–1673) 440, 631
Airs sur les hymnes sacrez, odes et noëls, 1623 203, 206
Albright, William (b. 1944) 196, 227, 303
Allison, Richard (16th cent.) 259
Alte Catholische Geistliche Kirchengesäng, 1599 81
American folk melody 304, 620, 664
Antes, John (1740–1811) 389
Antiphonale Sarisburiense, Vol. II 15, 44
Antiphoner, 1681 1, 348, 623
Antiphoner, 1728 282
Antiphoner, 1753 285, 448
Arnatt, Ronald (b. 1930) 74, 443
Arne, Augustine (1710–1778) 57
Auserlesene Catholische Geistliche Kirchengeseng, 1623 400, 618

Bach, Johann Sebastian (1685–1750) 46, 61, 91, 108, 135, 141, 168, 174, 186, 244, 297, 309, 310, 334, 336, 484, 497, 505, 669, 681, 688
Bain, J. L. Macbeth (1840?–1925) 517
Bancroft, Henry Hugh (1904–1988) 75
Barnby, Joseph (1838–1896) 42, 427
Barnes, Edward Shippen (1887–1958) 96
Barthélémon, François Hippolyte (1741–1808) 11
Basque carol 265
Beebe, Hank (b. 1926) 177, 262
Beethoven, Ludwig van (1770–1872) 376
Bender, Jan O. (b. 1909) 224, 430
Benedictine Processional, 14th cent. 103
Biggs, Arthur Henry (1906–1954) 654
Billings, William (1746–1800) 715
Bode, Arnold George Henry (1866–1952) 647
Bohemian Brethren, Kirchengeseng, 1566 224, 430
Book of Psalmody, A, 1718 668
Booke of Musicke, 1591 643
Bortniansky, Dimitri S. (1751–1825) 574
Bourgeois, Louis (1510?–1561?) 36, 301, 302, 377, 380, 413, 601
Boyce, William (1711–1779) 280, 351, 706
Boyd, William (1847–1928) 552
Boyer, Horace Clarence (b. 1935) 99, 648
Brackett, Joseph, Jr. (1797–1882) 554
Bradbury, William Batchelder (1816–1868) 693
Bridges, Mary Monica Waterhouse (1863–1949) 697
Bristol, Lee Hastings, Jr. (1923–1979) 593, 649
Brown, Ray Francis (1897–1964) 521
Buchanan, Annabel Morris (1889–1983) 304, 620
Buck, Percy Carter (1817–1947) 86, 221, 234, 348, 619
Burleigh, Harry T. (1866–1949) 529
Burnam, Jack W. (b. 1946) 53, 97, 213, 266, 468
Burney, Charles (1726–1814) 239
Butts, Thomas (?) 188

Calvisius, Seth (1556–1615) 465
Caniadau y Cyssegr, 1839 423
Cantate, 1851 366
Cantica Spiritualia, 1847 23
Cantionale Germanicum, 1628 3, 310
Carey, Henry (1690?–1743) 500
Cassels-Brown, Alastair (b. 1927) 187, 505, 571
Catolisch-Paderbornisches Gesang-Buch, 1765 535
Cayce, C. H. (19th–20th cent.) 566
Chansons populaires des provinces de France, 1860 324
Chants ordinaires de l'Office Divin, 1881 249, 331

Chapin, Lucius (1760–1842) 638
Chávez-Melo, Skinner (1944–1991) 277
Childs, David Thompson (b. 1938) 240
Choral-Buch vor Johann Heinrich Reinhardt, 1754 568
Chorale Book for England, The, 1863 313, 390
"Christ ist erstanden" 713
Christian Hymns, 1977 307
Christian Lyre, The, 1830 586, 667
Christmas Carols New and Old, 1871 115
Church Hymnal for the Church Year, The, 1917 11
Church Hymnary, The, 1927 482, 488
CL Psalmes of David, The, 1615 126, 462, 526, 709
Clarke, Jeremiah (1670–1707) 148
Cobb, Gerard Francis (1838–1904) 275
Collection of Motetts or Antiphons, ca. 1840 559
Coller, Percy E. B. (b. 1895) 542
Colvin, Thomas Stevenson (b. 1925) 602, 611
Compleat Melody or Harmony of Zion, A, 1734 164, 672
Compleat Psalmodist, The, 1749 207
Conkey, Ithamar (1815–1867) 441
Copes, Vicar Earle (b. 1921) 429
Courteville, Raphael (d. 1735) 457
Cowley Carol Book, 1902 124
Croft, William (1678–1727) 284, 388, 680
Cruger, Johann (1598–1662) 158, 313, 338, 339, 374, 396, 397, 509, 627, 701
Cummings, William H. (1831–1915) 87
Cutts, Peter (b. 1937) 130, 197, 513, 570, 630

Dahl, David (b. 1937) 27
Daman's Psalter, 1579 641
Daman, William (1540?–1591?) 642, 643
Dancing Master, The, 1686 405
Danta De: Hymns To God, Ancient and Modern 69
Dare, Elkanah Kelsay (1782–1826) 9, 10, 163, 583
Darke, Harold (1888–1976) 144
Darwall, John (1731–1789) 625
Das ander Theil des andern newen Operis Geistlicher Deutscher Lieder, 1605 198
Das grosse Cantional oder Kirchen-Gesangbuch, 1687 440, 631
Davies, Henry Walford (1869–1941) 616
Day's Psalter, 1562 142, 332, 615
Day, George Henry (1883–1966) 515
de Giardini, Felice (1716–1796) 365, 371, 537
Dearnley, Christopher (b. 1930) 492, 506
Decius, Nikolaus (1490?–1541) 421
Dirksen, Richard Wayne (b. 1921) 34, 51, 211, 254, 392, 557, 633
Distler, Hugo (1908–1942) 572
Divine Companion, 1707 447, 483
Doran, Carol (b. 1936) 77, 131
Douglas, Charles Winfred (1867–1944) 9, 105, 107, 110, 149, 172, 215, 314, 359, 366, 404, 504, 564, 667, 697
Dowland, John (1563–1626) 378
Dublin Troper, ca. 1360 226
Dulcimer, or New York Collection of Sacred Music, 1850 409
Dupré, Marcel (1886–1971) 204
Dutch melody 230
Dykes, John Bacchus (1823–1876) 343, 362, 445, 467, 486, 510, 579, 608, 623, 646, 683, 707

Edwards, John (1806–1885) 587
Egan, Linda Wilberger (b. 1946) 673
Einsiedeln MS., 10th cent. 155
Einsiedeln MS., 12th cent. 55
Einsiedeln MS., 13th cent. 13
Elvey, George Job (1816–1893) 290, 494
Engels, Adriaan (b. 1906) 226
English ballad melody 218, 449
English carol, 17th cent. 109
English Hymnal, The, 1906 21, 72, 83, 119, 121, 212, 264, 285, 288, 323, 328, 339, 346, 352, 384, 423, 428, 448, 607, 684
English melody 12, 78, 88, 90, 115, 116, 231, 245, 272, 292, 398, 453, 480, 591, 705
Erfurt Enchiridia, 1524 54
Erickson, John F. (1938) 193
Erneuerten Gesangbuch, 1665 390
Essay on the Church Plain Chant, An, 1782 228, 559
Este, Thomas (1540?–1608?) 642
Ett, Caspar (1788–1847) 248, 520
European Magazine and London Review, The, 1792 344, 708
Evans, David (1874–1948) 232, 416, 538, 590, 655
Ewing, Alexander (1830–1895) 624
Excell, Edwin Othello (1851–1921) 671
Eyn Enchiridion, 1524 501

Farmer, John (c. 1570–?) 581
Farrell, Gerald (b. 1919) 15, 19, 44, 223, 650
Fedak, Alfred V. (b. 1953) 250

Ferguson, William Harold (1874–1950) 289
Filitz, Friedrich (1804–1860) 479
Finnish folk melody 232, 655
Fischel, Donald (b. 1950) 178
Fleur des noëls, 1535 152
Foster, Thomas (b. 1938) 118, 136, 147, 190, 261, 583
Freiburg MS., 14th cent. 33
French carol 96, 145
French carol, 17th cent. 324
French church melody, Mode 5 314, 357
French folk melody, 16th cent. 114
Freylinghausen, 1704 389
Freylinghausen, Johann Anastasius (1670–1739) 375
Fritsch, Ahasuerus (1629–1701) 108
Fyfe, Lois (b. 1927) 521, 637

Gaelic melody 8
Galley, Howard E. (1929–1993) 157
Gallican chant 157
Gardiner, William (1770–1853) 609
Gauntlet, Henry John (1805–1876) 102, 194, 267, 279, 545, 682
Gawthorn, Nathaniel (18th cent.) 434, 578
Geist und Lehr-reiches Kirchen und Haus Buch, 1694 141
Geistliche Gesangbüchlein, 1524 319
Geistliche Kirchengesang, 1623 505
Geistliche lieder auffs new gebessert und gemehrt, 1539 80, 575
Geistliche Lieder, 1533 184, 634
Geistliche Lieder, 1543 132, 143, 297
Geistreiches Gesang-buch, 1698 286
Geistreiches Gesangbuch, 1704 47, 530
Gelineau, Joseph (b. 1920) 696
George, Graham (b. 1912) 156
German carol, 14th cent. 107
German folk song 48, 616
Gerovitch, Eliezer (1844–1914) 425
Gesangbuch . . . der Herzogl. Wirtembergischen katholischen Hofkapelle 1784 210
Geystliche gesangk Buchleyn, 1524 7, 139, 185, 186
Ghanaian folk song 602
Gibbons, Orlando (1583–1625) 21, 264, 315, 328, 346, 499, 617, 670, 697, 703
Gillespie, James (b. 1929) 518
Gläser, Carl Gotthilf (1784–1829) 493
Goss, John (1800–1880) 410
Goudimel, Claude (1514–1572) 36, 67, 258, 301, 472
Graduale, 1685 17, 120
Graduale Romanum, 1974 354
Gray, Alan (1855–1935) 59
Greatorex, Walter (1877–1949) 438
Griffiths, Vernon (1894–1985) 31, 455
Gross Catolisch Gesangbuch, 1631 341
Gruber, Franz Xaver (1787–1863) 111

Hallock, Peter R. (b. 1923) 418
Hamburger Musikalisches handbuch, 1690 540
Hampton, Calvin (1938–1984) 403, 407, 456, 469, 636, 659
Hancock, Eugene (b. 1929) 243, 636
Hancock, Gerre (b. 1934) 350, 636
Handel, George Frideric (1685–1759) 100, 459, 481, 546, 629
Harding, James Proctor (1850–1911) 117
Harmonia Sacra, ca. 1760 188, 257
Harwood, Basil (1859–1949) 285, 444, 448
Hasidic melody 536
Hassler, Hans Leo (1564–1612) 80, 132, 168, 169, 184, 185, 298, 575, 669, 687
Hastings, Thomas (1784–1872) 685
Hatton, John (d. 1793) 544
Havergal, William Henry (1793–1870) 7, 47, 66, 127, 414, 530, 656
Haweis, Thomas (1734–1820) 72, 212
Haydn, Franz Joseph (1732–1809) 28, 29, 409, 522
Haydn, Johann Michael (1737–1809) 533, 637
Hayes, William (1706–1777) 387
Hayne, Leighton George (1836–1883) 613
Hebrew melody 372, 393, 401, 714
Heinlein, Paul (1626–1686) 323
Held, Wilbur (b. 1914) 246
Helmore, Thomas (1811–1890) 56
Hemy, Henri Frédéric (1818–1888) 558
Herbst, Martin (1654–1681) 150
Hermann, Nikolaus (1480?–1561) 201
Hill, Jackson (b. 1941) 122, 123, 329
Hillert, Richard (b. 1923) 417
Hilton, John (1599–1657) 140
Himlischer Lieder, 1641 173
Hintze, Jakob (1622–1702) 135, 174
Hispanic folk melody 113
Hodges, Edward (1796–1867) 376
Holden, Oliver (1765–1844) 450
Holst, Gustav Theodore (1874–1934) 92, 112
Hooker, John Leon (b. 1944) 675
Hopkins, Edward John (1818–1901) 345
Hopkins, John Henry (1861–1945) 293
Hopkins, John Henry, Jr. (1820–1891) 128, 503

Hopkirk, James (1908–1972) 600
Horsley, William (1774–1858) 167
Howard, Samuel (1710–1782) 666
Howells, Herbert (1892–1983) 582, 665
Hughes, John (1873–1932) 594, 690
Hullah, John Pyke (19th cent.) 447, 483
Hundert Arien, 1694 187, 269
Hunterian MS., 15th cent. 266
Hurd, David (b. 1950) 16, 35, 41, 55, 103, 104, 161, 233, 268, 273, 283, 319, 320, 322, 325, 354, 361, 395, 459, 463, 503, 507, 549, 606, 629, 664, 676
Hutchings, Arthur, (b. 1906) 17, 120
Hymnal 1940 299, 330, 697
Hymnal 1982 10, 25, 43, 67, 173, 203, 364, 532, 550, 641, 663
Hymnau a Thonau er Gwasanaeth yr Eglwys yng Nghymru, 1865 68, 607
Hymns Ancient and Modern, 1875 20, 137, 353, 365, 371, 372, 401, 537
Hymns Ancient and Modern, 1916 228
Hymns Ancient and Modern, 1922 94
Hymns Ancient and Modern, Historical Edition, 1909 348
Hymns Ancient and Modern, Revised, 1950 72, 193, 207, 284, 449
Hymns and Sacred Poems, 1749 428
Hymns for Church and School, 1964 315, 414, 499, 617
Hymns III, 1979 581

Ireland, John (1879–1962) 458
Irish ballad melody 482, 488
Irish melody 69, 370, 645
Irvine, Jesse Seymour (1836–1887) 663
Isaac, Heinrich (1450?–1517) 46, 309

Jackish, Frederick, (b. 1922) 114
Jackson, Francis (b. 1917) 424
Jacob, Gordon (b. 1895) 517
Jenner, Henry Lascelles (1820–1898) 626
Johnson, David N. (1922–1987) 373, 412
Johnson, J. Rosamond (1873–1954) 599
Johnson, Robert Sherlaw (b. 1932) 189
Johnson, Roy Henry (b. 1933) 588
Jones, W. Thomas (b. 1956) 49
Jones, William (1726–1800) 73

Katholisches Gesangbuch, 1686 366
Katholisches Gesangbuch, 1863 210
Kehl, Roy (b. 1935) 2, 22, 32, 136, 140, 146, 202, 204, 311, 495
Keiser, Marilyn J. (b. 1941) 213
Kempton MS., circa 11 cent. 32
Kentucky Harmony, 1816 243, 702
Kievan chant 355
King, Charles John (1859–1934) 426
Kirchengeseng darinnen die Heubtartickel des Christlichen Glaubens gefasset, 1566 408, 598
Kirkpatrick, William James (1838–1921) 101
Klein, Richard Rudolf (b. 1921) 713
Klosterneuburger Hymnar, 1336 22
Knapp, William (1698–1768) 20, 137, 353
Kocher, Conrad (1786–1872) 119, 269, 288, 366
König, Johann Balthasar (1691–1758) 244, 334, 656
Koralbok for Svenska Kyrkan, 1939 65
Kremser, Eduard (1838–1914) 433

Lafferty, Karen (20th cent.) 711
Lang, Craig Sellar (1891–1971) 72, 94, 290, 326, 368, 390, 410
Laudi Spirituali, 14th cent. 239
Layriz, Friedrich (1808–1859) 338
Lee, J. V. (1892–1959) 543
Les cent cinquante Pseaumes de David, 1564 252, 308
Lewis, Freeman (1780–1859) 147, 276, 675
Ley, Henry G. (1887–1962) 52, 553
Little Book of Christmas Carols, ca. 1850 105
Llyfr Tonau Cynnulleidfaol, 1859 299
Llyfr y Psalmau, 1621 697
Lochamer Gesangbuch, 1450? 281, 471
Lockhart, Charles (1745–1815) 138, 592
Loh, I-to (b. 1936) 340, 342
Löhner, Johann (1645–1705) 244, 334
Lovelace, Austin Cole (b. 1919) 671
Luther, Martin (1483–1546) 151, 575, 687, 688
Lutheran Hymnal, The, 1941 501
Lvov, Alexis (1799–1870) 358, 569
Lyra Davidica, 1708 207

Mailander Hymnen, 15th cent. 40, 217, 263
Maintzisch Gesangbuch, 1661 159
Maker, Frederick Charles (1844–1927) 498, 652
Mallory, Charles (b. 1950) 178
Mann, Arthur Henry (1850–1929) 102
Marshall, Jane Manton (b. 1924) 242, 466, 589
Mason, Lowell (1792–1872) 100, 182, 365, 371, 411, 419, 436, 493, 512, 524, 537, 595, 691

McGregor, James (b. 1930) 40, 45, 134
Mealy, Margaret W. (b. 1922) 238, 276, 550, 554, 674
Mealy, Norman (1923–1987) 69
Medieval French carol 204
Medieval [German or] Bohemian Carol Melody, 1544 200, 237
Mehrtens, Frederik August (b. 1922) 274
Melodia Sacra, 1815 546
Mendelssohn, Felix (1809–1847) 87, 255, 281, 397, 471, 632
Messiter, Arthur Henry (1834–1916) 556
Methodist Harmonist, 1821 419, 512
Miller, Edward (c. 1605–?) 584
Miller, Edward (1731–1807) 321, 474
Miller, Max (b. 1927) 547
Miltenberger Processionale, 15th cent. 319
Milton, John, Sr. (1563?–1647) 462
Mims, George (b. 1938) 178, 204
Moe, Daniel (b. 1926) 612
Moissac MS., 12th cent. 123, 273
Monk, William Henry (1823–1889) 59, 76, 119, 150, 154, 181, 208, 210, 286, 288, 337, 391, 397, 447, 483, 559, 601, 625, 628, 662, 680
More Hymns for Today, 1980 284, 670
Moyer, J. Harold (b. 1927) 689
Münster Gesangbuch, 1677 384
Murray, A. Gregory (1905–1992) 202, 233, 577
Musicalishes Hand-Buch, 1690 76, 391

Native American Melody 385
Neander, Joachim (1650–1680) 180
Near, Gerald (b. 1942) 37, 454
Nederlandtsch Gedenckclank, 1626 433
Neswick, Bruce (b. 1956) 26, 60, 82, 85, 217, 263, 442
Neu ordentlich Gesangbuch, 1646 681
Neu-vermehrtes und zu Ubung Christl Gottseligkeit eingerichtetes Meiningisches Gesangbuch, 1693 255, 596, 632
Neumark, Georg (1621–1681) 635
Nevers MS., 13th cent. 2, 4, 16, 63, 311, 519, 622
New Hymnal, The, 1916 365, 371, 537
Nicholson, Sydney Hugo (1875–1947) 137, 473, 535, 625, 694
Nicolai, Philipp (1556–1608) 61, 62, 484, 485, 496, 497
Noble, Thomas Tertius (1867–1953) 383, 541
Novello, Vincent Francis (1781–1861) 58

Orgelbuch Zum Gesangbuch Der Evangelisch-Reformierten Kirchen Der Deutschsprachigen Schweiz, 1926 14, 64
Osiander, Lucas (1534–1604) 139
Oude en Nieuwe Hollantse Boerenlities en Contradanseu, 1710 215, 495
Owen, William (1813–1893) 307

Pageant of the Shearmen and Tailors, 15th cent. 247
Palestrina, Giovanni Pierluigi da (1525–1594) 208
Palmer, George Herbert (1846–1926) 440, 631
Paris MS., 12th cent. 202
Parker, Horatio (1864–1919) 222
Parratt, Walter (1841–1924) 355
Parry, Charles Hubert Hastings (1848–1918) 278, 367, 432, 597, 653, 695
Parry, Joseph (1841–1903) 349, 640, 699
Peace, Lister R. (1885–1969) 508
Pelz, Walter (b. 1926) 49
Petrie Collection of Irish Melodies, Part II, 1902 84
Pettman, Edgar (1865–1943) 265
Piae Cantiones, 1582 82, 92, 97, 98, 270
Pilgrim Hymnal, 1958 610
Plainsong, Mode 1 5, 22, 32, 55, 56, 85, 103, 136, 155, 161, 162, 165, 183, 217, 220, 223, 226, 261, 283, 361
Plainsong, Mode 2 4, 18, 40, 63, 122, 123, 134, 146, 263, 271, 311, 519, 622, 650
Plainsong, Mode 3 2, 166, 329
Plainsong, Mode 4 26, 60, 273
Plainsong, Mode 5 16, 19, 330
Plainsong, Mode 6 606
Plainsong, Mode 7 33, 354
Plainsong, Mode 7, 12th cent. 320
Plainsong, Mode 8 13, 15, 27, 30, 38, 44, 45, 202, 233, 236, 354, 502, 504
Playford, John (1623–1686) 50, 251, 677
Poston, Elizabeth (1905–1987) 140
Powell, Robert (b. 1932) 70
Praetorius, Hieronymous (1560?–1629) 421
Praetorius, Jakob (1586–1651) 62, 485
Praetorius, Michael (1571–1621) 81, 124, 193, 219, 235, 710
Prichard, Rowland Hugh (1811–1887) 460, 657
Processionale, 15th cent. 56
Processionale, 1697 314, 357
Proulx, Richard (b. 1937) 5, 33, 56, 123, 155, 162, 183, 206, 218, 271, 343,

399, 405, 431, 473, 477, 494, 502, 536, 560, 576, 586
Psalm and Choralbuch, 1719 475
Psalmen, 1685 192
Psalmes of David in Prose and Meeter, The, 1635 50, 121, 251, 352, 584, 677, 684, 709
Psalmodia Evangelica, Part II, 1789 182, 436
Psalmodia Sacra, oder Andächtige und Schöne Gesange, 1715 66, 127, 414
Pseumes cinquante de David, 1547 408, 598
Pseumes octante trois de David, 1551 149, 359, 377, 378, 380, 404
Pulkingham, Betty (b. 1928) 178, 335
Purcell, Henry (1659–1695) 518

Ratcliff, Cary (b. 1953) 133
Ravenscroft, Thomas (1592?–1635?) 126, 259, 364, 415, 526
Redhead, Richard (1820–1901) 142, 171, 241, 615
Redner, Lewis H. (1831–1908) 79
Reimann, Heinrich (19th cent.) 408, 598
Reinagle, Alexander Robert (1799–1877) 644
Reinecke, Carl H. (1824–1910) 111
Repository of Sacred Music, A, Part II, 1813 437, 686
Rhea, Arthur (b. 1919) 678
Rheinfelsisches Deutsches Catholisches Gesangbuch, 1666 14, 64
Robb, John Donald (1892–1989) 113
Robbins, Howard Chandler (1876–1952) 521
Roberts, John (1822–1877) 423
Robinson, McNeil, II (b. 1943) 18, 95
Rockstro, William Smith (1823–1895) 341
Rome MS., 12th cent. 161, 162
Roth, Robert (b. 1928) 176
Routley, Erik (1917–1982) 347, 402, 413, 605, 639
Russian Orthodox hymn 560

Sachs, Hans (1494–1576) 61, 62, 484, 485
Sacred Harp, The, 1844 636
Sacred Melodies, 1815 609
Sanctus trope, 11th cent. 82
Sarum Melody 166
Schalk, Carl Flentge (b. 1929) 333, 698
Scheidt, Samuel (1587–1654) 465
Schein, Johann Hermann (1586–1630) 151, 198, 496
Schlesische Volkslieder, 1842 383
Schola Antiqua, 1983 2, 32, 123, 155, 161, 165, 261, 283, 361, 622
Scholefield, Clement Cottevill (1839–1904) 24
Schop, Johann (d. 1665?) 91, 336
Schulz, Johann Abraham Peter (1747–1800) 291
Schütz, Heinrich (1585–1672) 452
Second Supplement to Psalmody in Miniature, ca. 1780 321, 474
Shaw, Geoffrey Turton (1879–1943) 88, 98, 573
Shaw, Martin Fallas (1875–1958) 145, 247, 405, 476, 534
Sheets, Dorothy Howell (b. 1915) 585
Shrubsole, William (1760–1806) 451
Shuler, David (b. 1954) 22
Sicilian melody 344, 708
Simmons, Morgan F. (b. 1929) 146, 236
Slater, Gordon (1896–1979) 209, 603
Small, Howard Don (b. 1932) 4, 63, 236
Smart, Henry Thomas (1813–1879) 93, 368, 555, 563, 700
Smith, Alfred Morton (1879–1971) 306, 406
Smith, Henry Percy (1825–1898) 660
Smith, Isaac (1734?–1805) 548
Smith, K. D. (b. 1928) 127
Smith, Robert (1780–1829) 658
Sohren, Peter (1630?–1692?) 375
Solly, Richard P. (b. 1952) 13, 38, 220
Solesmes, 271
Songs and Games of American Children, 1884–1911 468
Songs for liturgy and More Hymns and Spirtual Songs, 1971 148, 243
Songs of Praise, 1925 249, 331, 437
Songs of Praise, 1931 670
Songs of Syon, 1904 200, 237
Source Unknown 77, 131
Source Unknown, ca. 18th cent. 720
Southern Harmony, The, 1835 10, 118, 213, 238, 439, 550, 571, 580
Sowerby, Leo (1895–1968) 110, 125, 305
St. Gall MS., 10th cent. 155, 165
Stainer, John (1840–1901) 109, 160
Stanford, Charles Villiers (1852–1924) 84, 296, 370, 420, 477
Strassburger Kirchenamt, 1525 429
Student's Hymnal, A, 1923 616
Suitor, M. Lee (b. 1942) 229, 256
Sullivan, Arthur Seymour (1842–1900) 90, 179, 191, 199, 245, 562
Supplement to Kentucky Harmony, 1820 674
Supplement to the New Version of Psalms by Dr. Brady and Mr. Tate, 1708 567
Sussex melody 478, 565

Swenska Psalmboken, Then, 1697 65
Swenson, Warren (b. 1937) 318

Tallis, Thomas (1505?–1585) 25, 43, 170, 260, 489, 692
Taylor, Cyril Vincent (1907–1991) 129, 195, 379, 511, 523
Terry, Richard Runciman (1865–1938) 270, 446
Teschner, Melchior (1584–1635) 74, 154
Thatcher, Reginald Sparshatt (1888–1957) 39, 394
Theorelikerquellen, MS. 12 cent., 271
Thesaurus Musicus, 1745 716, 717
Thomerson, Kathleen (b. 1934) 490
Thuringer Evangelisches Gesangbuch, 1928 634
Toolan, Suzanne (b. 1927) 335
Traditional canon 712
Traditional melody 566, 638
Trente quatre pseumes de David, 1551 472
Trier MS., 15th cent. 124, 193
Trinity College MS., 15th cent. 218, 449
Turle, James (1802–1882) 20, 137, 353

"Une pastourelle gentille," 1529 408, 598
Urwin, Ray W. (b. 1950) 679

Vaughan Williams, Ralph (1872–1958) 1, 12, 57, 78, 101, 116, 175, 216, 225, 231, 259, 272, 287, 292, 370, 398, 400, 435, 478, 480, 487, 499, 516, 565, 568, 591, 598, 617, 618, 705
Verona MS., 11th cent, 27
Verona MS., 12th cent. 146
Vesperale, 1746 360
Vierstimmiges Choralbuch, 1847 595
Virginia Harmony, 1831 671
Vulpius, Melchior (1560?–1616) 54, 205, 295, 356

Wade, John Francis (1711–1786) 58, 83
Wainwright, John (1723–1768) 106
Walch, James (1837–1901) 539
Walker, David Charles (b. 1938) 294, 382
Walter, William H. (1825–1893) 551
Walton, James G. (1821–1905) 558
Ward, Samuel Augustus (1848–1903) 719
Warren, George William (1828–1902) 718
Watson, Sydney (1903–1991) 317
Webb, George James (1803–1887) 561
Webbe, Samuel (1740–1816) 228, 531
Webbe, Samuel, Jr. (1770–1843) 72, 212, 321
Weisse, Michael (d. 1534) 53
Welsh hymn 423
Welsh melody 610, 621
Werner, Eric (1901–1988) 393
Wesley, Charles (1757–1834) 476
Wesley, Samuel Sebastian (1810–1876) 386, 422, 434, 461, 525, 578, 704
Westbrook, Francis B. (1903–1975) 300
Wetzel, Richard (b. 1935) 464
White, David Ashley (b. 1944) 327
White, J. T. (19th cent.) 566
White, Jack Noble (b. 1938) 453
Whitlock, Percy William (1903–1946) 241
Whole Booke of Psalmes, The, 1570 259
Whole Booke of Psalmes, The, 1592 94, 581
Whole Booke of Psalmes, The, 1621 71, 462, 532
Wigbert [Wipo of Burgundy] (d. 1050?) 183
Wilkes, John Bernard (1785–1869) 389
Willan, Healey (1880–1968) 109, 114, 360
Willcocks, David (b. 1919) 646
Williams, Aaron (1731–1776) 411, 524
Williams, David McKinley (1887–1978) 312, 316, 514, 614, 661
Williams, Derek (b. 1945) 253, 604
Williams, Robert (1781–1821) 214
Williams, Thomas John (1869–1944) 381, 527
Williamson, Malcolm (b. 1931) 6, 651
Willis, Richard Storrs (1819–1900) 89
Wilson, Hugh (1764–1824) 658
Wilson, John (1905–1991) 170, 414, 481, 692
Winn, Cyril (1884–1973) 210
Wood, Charles (1866–1926) 192
Woodward, George Ratcliffe (1848–1934) 48, 235
Worcester MS., 13th cent. 5, 38, 233, 236, 261, 283, 361
Wyatt, Janet (b. 1934) 597
Wyton, Alec (b. 1921) 8, 30, 163, 230, 363, 369, 491, 528, 622

Yin-Lan, Su (20th cent.) 342
Young, Carlton, R (b. 1926) 439
Young, Michael E. (b. 1939) 450, 522

Zisterzienser Hymnar, 14th cent. 136, 166, 220, 223, 329, 330
Zundel, John (1815–1882) 470

Index of Tune Names

A la ru 113
A la venue de Noël 152
Abbot's Leigh 379, 511, 523
Aberystwyth 349, 640, 699
Ach bleib bei uns 465
Ach Gott, vom Himmelreiche 235
Ach Herr, du allerhöchster Gott 219
Ad cenam Agni providi 202
Adeste fideles 83
Adon Olam 425
Adoro devote 314, 357
Adoro te supplex, *see:*
Adoro devote
Aeterne Rex altissime 136, 220
African Work Song 611
Agincourt Hymn, *see:*
Deo gracias
Albright 303
Aldine 431
All Saints, *see:*
Zeuch mich, zeuch mich
Alle Menschen müssen sterben, *see:*
Salzburg
Allein Gott in der Höh 421
Alleluia 461
Alleluia No. 1 178
Alles ist an Gottes Segen 244, 334
Alta Trinità beata 239
Amazing Grace, *see:*
New Britain
America 716, 717
Andújar 104
Angel's Song, *see:*
Song 34
Angelus, *see:*
Du meiner Seelen
Angelus emittitur 270
Antioch 100
Arbor Street 227
Ascension 75
Assisi 406
Augustine 402
Aurelia 525
Aus der Tiefe rufe ich 150
Aus tiefer Not 151
Austria 522
Ave caeli janua 273
Ave Maria klare, *see:*
Ellacombe
Azmon 493

Ballad 673
Balm in Gilead 676
Bangor 164, 672
Beata nobis gaudia 223
Beatitudes 560
Beatitudo 683
Bedford, *see:*
Edmonton
Beecher 470
Bellwoods 600
Beng-Li 340
Benifold 300
Bereden väg för Herran 65
Bickford 177, 262
Bingham 585
Birabus 570
Birmingham 437
Blaenhafren 610
Bohemian Brethren, *see:*
Mit Freuden zart
Bourbon 147, 675
Bourgeois, *see:*
Psalm 42
Breslau 281, 471
Bridegroom 513
Bristol 71
Bromley 28, 29
Brother James' Air 517
Bryn Calfaria 307
Bunessan 8
Burford 668

Caelites plaudant 282
Caelitum Joseph 261, 283, 361
Caithness 121, 352, 684
Call Street 588
Camano 399
Canticum refectionis 316
Carey, *see:*
Surrey
Carlisle 138, 592

Carol 89
Caswall, *see:*
Wem in Leidenstagen
Charlestown 571
Charterhouse 590
Chelsea Square 521
Chereponi [Jesu, Jesu] 602
Cheshire 581
Christ is arisen 713
Christ is my Life, *see:*
Christus der ist mein Leben
Christ ist erstanden 184
Christ lag in Todesbanden (isometric) 186
Christ lag in Todesbanden (rhythmic) 185
Christ unser Herr zum Jordan kam 139
Christ Whose Glory 6
Christe, Lux mundi 33
Christe, qui Lux es et dies 40
Christe, Redemptor omnium 85
Christe sanctorum 1
Christmas, *see:*
Siroë
Christus, der ist mein Leben 295, 356
Christus Rex 614
Claudius, *see:*
Wir pflügen
Coburn 363
College of Preachers 678
Come Holy Ghost 503
Compline 41
Conditor alme siderum 26, 60
Consolation, *see:*
Morning Song
Cornhill 1446
Cornish 229, 256
Cornwall 386, 422
Coronation 450
Coventry Carol 247
Cradle Song 101
Cranham 112
Crasselius, *see:*
Dir, dir, Jehovah
Creation 409
Crimond 663
Croft's 136th 284
Cross of Jesus 160
Crucifer 473
Culross 584
Cwm Rhondda 594, 690

Dakota Indian Chant [Lacquiparle] 385
Danby 12
Daniel's Tune 373
Darmstadt, *see:*
Was frag ich nach der Welt
Darwall's 148th 625
De eersten zijn de laatsten 274
de Tar 456, 659
Decatur Place 51
Deirdre, *see:*
St. Patrick's Breastplate
Den des Vaters Sinn geboren 269
Deo gracias 218, 449
Detroit 674
Deus tuorum militum 285, 448
Diademata 494
Dicamus laudes Domino 16
Dickinson College 593, 649
Dies est laetitiae 97
Dir, dir, Jehovah 540
Distler 572
Divinum mysterium 82
Dix 119, 288
Dominus regit me 646
Dona nobis pacem 712
Donne 140
Donne secours 472
Down Ampney 516
Du Lebensbrot, Herr Jesu Christ 375
Du meiner Seelen 23
Duke Street 544
Dulce carmen 559
Dundee 126, 526, 709
Dunedin 31, 455
Dunlap's Creek 276
Durham 415

Earth and All Stars 412
East Acklam 424
Easter Hymn 207
Eastview 543
Ebenezer, *see:*
Ton-y-Botel
Edmonton 257
Ein feste Burg (isometric) 688
Ein feste Burg (rhythmic) 687
Eisenach, *see:*
Mach's mit mir, Gott
Elbing, *see:*
Du Lebensbrot, Herr Jesu Christ
Ellacombe 210
Ellers 345
Elmhurst 133
Eltham 434, 578
Ely, *see:*
Manchester
Engelberg 296, 420, 477

England's Lane 88
Epworth 476
Erhalt uns, Herr (isometric) 143, 297
Erhalt uns, Herr (rhythmic) 132
Ermuntre dich 91
Erschienen ist der herrlich Tag 201
Es flog ein kleins Waldvögelein 48, 616
Es ist das Heil 298
Es ist ein Ros 81
Evening Hymn 37
Eventide 662
Ewing 624
Ex more docti mystico 146

Faciem ejus videtis 240
Fairest Lord Jesus, *see:*
  Schönster Herr Jesu
Faith 689
Festal Song 551
Festival Canticle 417
Finnian 492, 506
Fisk of Gloucester 190
Flentge 698
Forest Green 78, 398, 705
Fortunatus 179
Foundation 636
Franconia 656
Frankfort, *see:*
  Wie schön leuchtet (isometric)
Frohlockt mit Freud 452
From heaven high, *see:*
  Vom Himmel hoch

Gabriel's Message 265
Gardiner 609
Gartan 84
Gaudeamus pariter 200, 237
Gelobt sei Gott 205
General Seminary 382
Geneva 515
Georgetown 661
Gerontius 445
Gloria 96
Gloria, laus, et honor 155
Go Down, Moses 648
Go Tell It on the Moutain 99
God Rest You Merry 105
Gonfalon Royal 86, 221, 234
Gopsal 481
Got sei Dank 47, 530
Gott sei gelobet 319
Gottes Sohn ist kommen 53
Gräfenberg, *see:*
  Nun danket all und bringet Ehr

Grafton 249, 331
Grand Isle 293
Grand Prairie 197
Greensleeves 115
Grosser Gott 366

Halifax 459, 629
Hall 463
Halton Holgate 280, 351, 706
Hampton 95
Hanover 388
Heinlein, *see:*
  Aus der Tiefe rufe ich
Helmsley 57
Herald, Sound 70
Hereford 704
Herr Jesu Christ (isometric) 310
Herr Jesu Christ (rhythmic) 3
Herr Jesu Christ, meins Lebens Licht, *see:*
  Breslau
Herzlich tut mich verlangen (rhythmic) 169
Herzlich tut mich verlangen [Passion Chorale] (isometric) 168, 669
Herzliebster Jesu 158
Hilariter 211
Hollingside 707
Holy Manna 238, 580
Holy Name, *see:*
  Louez Dieu
Horsley 167
Hosanna 486
Houston 490
Hyfrydol 460, 657
Hymn to Joy 376

I Am the Bread of Life 335
Ich ruf zu dir 634
Immense caeli Conditor 32
In Babilone 215, 495
In Bethlehem 246
In dulci jubilo 107
In paradisum 354
Innisfree Farm 34
Innsbruck, *see:*
  O Welt, ich muss dich lassen
Intercessor 695
Irby 102
Irish 428

Jacob 242, 466
Jacob's Ladder 453
Jam lucis orto sidere 217
Jerusalem 597

Jesu dulcis memoria 18, 134, 650
Jesu, Jesu, du mein Hirt 323
Jesu, Joy, *see:*
  Werde munter
Jesu, meine Freude 701
Jesu, nostra redemptio (equalist rhythm) 38, 236
Jesu, nostra redemptio (syllabic rhythm) 233
Jesus, all my gladness, *see:*
  Jesu, meine Freude
Jesus, meine Zuversicht 313
Julion 268, 507

Kedron 10, 163
King 395
King's Lynn 231, 591
King's Weston 435
Kingsfold 292, 480
Kit Smart 491
Komm, Gott Schöpfer 501
Komm, o komm, du Geist des Lebens 596
Kontakion [Kievan Chant] 355
Kremser 433

Lacquiparle, *see:*
  Dakota Indian Chant [Lacquiparle]
Lancashire 555, 563
Land of Rest 304, 620
Langham 573
Laramie 647
Lasst uns erfreuen 400, 618
Lauda anima 410
Lauda Sion Salvatorem 320
Laudate Dominum 432
Laudes Domini 427
Laus Deo 241
Le Cantique de Siméon 36
Le Cénacle 696
Leoni 372, 401
Let Us Break Bread 325
Liebster Jesu 440, 631
Lift Every Voice 599
Light 667
Litton 347
Llanfair 214
Llangloffan 68, 607
Lledrod 299
Lobe den Herren 390
Lobet den Herren 338
London New 50, 251, 677
Louez Dieu 252
Love Unknown 458
Lowry 454
Lübeck, *see:*
  Gott sei Dank
Lucerna Laudoniae 416, 538
Lucis Creator optime 27
Luise, *see:*
  Jesus, meine Zuversicht
Lukkason 407
Lux eoi 191
Lyons 533, 637
Lytlington 694

MacDougall 403
Mach's mit mir, Gott 198
Magdalen College 387
Mainz, *see:*
  Stabat Mater dolorosa
Malabar 312
Manchester 364
Mandatum 576
Mannheim 595
Maoz Zur 393
Marion 556
Marsh Chapel 547
Martins 619
Martyrdom 658
Maryton 660
Materna 719
McKee 529
Meadville 49
Melcombe 531
Melita 579, 608
Mendelssohn 87
Mendon 419, 512
Mercer Street 651
Merrial 42
Merton 59
Messiah, *see:*
  Bereden väg för Herran
Michael 665
Middlebury 213
Mighty Savior 35
Miles Lane 451
Mit Freuden zart 408, 598
Mon Dieu, prête-moi l'oreille, *see:*
  Psalm 86
Monk's Gate 478, 565
Monkland 389
Morestead 317
Morning Hymn 11
Morning Light 561
Morning Song 9, 583
Morning Star 117
Moscow 365, 371, 537

Moseley 700
Moultrie 275
Mowsley 129, 195
Mt. St. Alban NCA 633
Munich 255, 632

National Anthem 720
National Hymn 718
Neander, *see:*
Unser Herrscher
Nettleton 686
New Britain 671
New Dance 464
Newman 446
Nicaea 362
Nocte surgentes 2
Noel 90, 245
Noël nouvelet 204
Northampton 426
Nova, nova 266
Nova Vita 508
Now 333
Nun danket all und bringet Ehr 374, 509, 627
Nun danket alle Gott (isometric) 397
Nun danket alle Gott (rhythmic) 396
Nun komm, der Heiden Heiland 54
Nunc Sancte nobis Spiritus 19
Nunc dimittis, *see:*
Le Cantique de Siméon
Nyack 318
Nyland 232, 655

O Esca viatorum, *see:*
Psalm 6
O filii et filiae (carol) 203
O filii et filiae (chant) 206
O Gott, du frommer Gott 681
O Heiland, reiss 14, 64
O heiliger Geist 505
O lux beata Trinitas 30
O quanta qualia 348, 623
O Traurigkeit 173
O Welt, ich muss dich lassen 46, 309
Oblation, *see:*
Lobet den Herren
Old 100th 377, 378, 380
Old 104th 532
Old 112th, *see:*
Vater unser im Himmelreich
Old 113th 429
Old 120th 259
Old 124th 149, 404
Olivet 691
Omni die 341
Ora Labora 541
Oriel 248, 520

Paderborn 535
Palmer Church 327
Pange lingua (Mode 1) 165
Pange lingua (Mode 3) 166, 329
Parker 222
Passion Chorale, *see:*
Herzlich tut mich verlangen (isometric)
Pentecost 552
Perry 125
Personent hodie 92
Petra 171
Petrus 196
Picardy 324
Pleading Savior 586
Point Loma 294
Poor Little Jesus 468
Praetorius, *see:*
Ach Gott, vom Himmelreiche
Praise to the Lord, *see:*
Lobe den Herren
Psalm 6 308
Psalm 42 67
Psalm 47, *see:*
Frohlockt mit Freud
Psalm 86 258
Puer natus in Bethlehem 103
Puer nobis 124, 193
Puer nobis nascitur 98
Purpose 534

Quam dilecta 626
Quem terra, pontus, aethera 263
Quittez, Pasteurs 145

Raquel 277
Rathbun 441
Ratisbon 7
Raymond 418
Rector potens, verax Deus 22
Regent Square 93, 368
Rendez à Dieu 301, 302, 413
Repton 653
Resignation 664
Rest 652
Restoration 550
Resurrexit 189
Rhosymedre 587
Rhuddlan 621
Richmond 72, 212
Rockingham 321, 474

Rosa mystica, *see:*
Es ist ein Ros
Rosedale 305
Rouen 360
Rowthorn 528
Royal Oak 405
Rushford 52, 553
Russia 358, 569
Rustington 278, 367

St. Agnes 343, 510
St. Albinus 194
St. Andrew 549
St. Anne 680
St. Bartholomew's 514
St. Bees 467
St. Botolph 209, 603
St. Bride 666
St. Catherine 558
St. Cecilia 613
St. Christopher 498
St. Clement 24
St. Columba 645
St. Denio 423
St. Dunstan's 564
St. Elizabeth 383
St. Ethelwald 181, 628
St. Flavian 142, 615
St. Flavian (original rhythm) 332
St. Fulbert 545, 682
St. George 267, 279
St. George's, Windsor 290
St. Gertrude 562
St. Helena 469
St. James 457
St. Joan 542
St. Keverne 326
St. Kevin 199
St. Leonard, *see:*
Komm, o komm, du Geist des Lebens
St. Louis 79
St. Magnus 447, 483
St. Mark's, Berkeley 69
St. Mary Magdalene 350
St. Matthew 567
St. Michael 601
St. Patrick's Breastplate 370
St. Peter 644
St. Petersburg 574
St. Stephen 73
St. Theodulph, *see:*
Valet will ich dir geben
St. Thomas 58
St. Thomas (Williams) 411, 524

Salem Harbor 443
Salvation 243
Salve festa dies 175, 216, 225
Salzburg 135, 174
San Rocco 253, 604
Sancta Civitas 582
Savannah 188
Schmücke dich 339
Schönster Herr Jesu 384
Schop, *see:*
Ermuntre dich
Seek Ye First 711
Shalom chaverim 714
Sharpthorne 605
Sheng En 342
Shillingford 130
Shorney 369
Sicilian Mariners 344, 708
Silver Street 548
Simple Gifts 554
Sine Nomine 287
Singt dem Herren 710
Siroë 546
Sixth Night 250
Slane 482, 488
Sleepers, Wake, *see:*
Wachet auf (isometric)
So giebst du nun 141
Solemnis haec festivitas 17, 120
Sollt es gleich bisweilen scheinen, *see:*
Stuttgart
Song 1 315, 499, 617
Song 4 346
Song 13 670
Song 22 703
Song 34 21, 264
Song 46 328
Song 67 697
Song of the Holy Spirit 230
Sonne der Gerechtigkeit 224, 430
Southwell 641
Spires, *see:*
Erhalt uns, Herr (isometric)
Splendor paternae gloriae 5
Stabat Mater dolorosa 159
Star in the East 118
Steadfast, *see:*
O Gott, du frommer Gott
Stille Nacht 111
Straf mich nicht 187
Stuttgart 66, 127, 414
Sumner 654
Surrey 500
Sursum Corda 306

Tallis' Canon, *see:*
The Eighth Tune
Tallis' Ordinal 260, 489
Tantum ergo Sacramentum 330
Te Deum, *see:*
Grosser Gott
Te lucis ante terminum (Sarum) 15, 44
Te lucis ante terminum (Sarum ferial) 45
Tender Thought 702
The Call 487
The Church's Desolation 566
The Eighth Tune 25, 43
The First Nowell 109
The King's Majesty 156
The Third Tune 170, 692
The Truth From Above 272
Third Mode Melody, *see:*
The Third Tune
This Endris Nyght 116
Thomas Merton 679
Thornbury 444
Three Kings of Orient 128
Tibi, Christe, splendor Patris 123
Tidings 539
Tomter 442
Ton-y-Botel 381, 527
Toplady 685
Torah Song [Yisrael V'oraita] 536
Toulon 359
Troen 612
Truro 182, 436
Tucker 322
Tysk 475

Ubi caritas 606
Ubi caritas (Murray) 577
Uffingham 148
Unde et memores 337
Une jeune pucelle 114
Unser Herrscher 180
Urbs beata Jerusalem (equalist rhythm) 122, 519
Urbs beata Jerusalem (syllabic rhythm) 622
Ut queant laxis 271

Valet will ich dir geben 74, 154
Vater unser im Himmelreich 575
Veni Creator Spiritus 502, 504
Veni Redemptor gentium 55
Veni Sancte Spiritus 226
Veni, veni, Emmanuel 56
Venite adoremus 110
Verbum supernum prodiens (Einsiedeln) 13
Verbum supernum prodiens (Nevers) 4, 63, 311
Vernon 638
Vexilla Regis prodeunt (equalist rhythm) 162
Vexilla Regis prodeunt (syllabic rhythm) 161
Victimae Paschali laudes 183
Victory 208
Vigiles et sancti, *see:*
Lasst uns erfreuen
Vineyard Haven 392, 557
Vom Himmel hoch 80
Vom Himmel kam der Engel Schar 77, 131
Vruechten 192

Wachet auf (isometric) 61, 484
Wachet auf (rhythmic) 62, 485
Walden 589
Wareham 20, 137, 353
Was frag' ich nach der Welt 108
Was lebet 568
Webb, *see:*
Morning Light
Webbe 228
Wem in Leidenstagen 479
Wer nur den lieben Gott 635
Werde munter 336
Were You There 172
West Park 176
Westminster Abbey 518
When Jesus Wept 715
Wie schön leuchtet (isometric) 497
Wie schön leuchtet (rhythmic) 496
Wilderness 39, 394
Winchester New 76, 391
Winchester Old 94
Windsor (isometric) 643
Windsor (rhythmic) 642
Wir pflügen 291
Wolvercote 289
Wondrous Love 439
Woodbird, *see:*
Es flog ein kleins Waldvögelein
Woodbury 639
Woodlands 438
Woodworth 693
Wylde Green 630
Wyngate Canon 254

York 462
Yorkshire 106

Zeuch mich, zeuch mich 286

Index of First Lines

A child is born in Bethlehem, Alleluia! 103
A hymn of glory let us sing 217, 218
A light from heaven shone around 256
A mighty fortress is our God 687, 688
A mighty sound from heaven 230
A stable lamp is lighted 104
Abide with me: fast falls the eventide 662
Ah, holy Jesus, how hast thou offended 158
All creatures of our God and King 400
All glory be to God on high 421
All glory, laud, and honor 154, 155
All hail the power of Jesus' Name! 450, 451
All my hope on God is founded 665
All people that on earth do dwell 377, 378
All praise to thee, for thou, O King divine 477
All praise to thee, my God, this night 43
All praise to you, O Lord 138
All things bright and beautiful 405
All who believe and are baptized 298
All who love and serve your city 570, 571
Alleluia, alleluia, alleluia!
O sons and daughters *Easter* 203
O sons and daughters *Second Sunday of Easter and St. Thomas' Day* 206
Alleluia, alleluia, alleluia! The strife is o'er 208
Alleluia, alleluia! Give thanks to the risen Lord 178
Alleluia, alleluia! Hearts and voices heavenward raise 191
Alleluia! sing to Jesus! 460, 461
Alleluia, song of gladness 122, 123
Almighty Father, strong to save 579
Almighty God, your word is cast 588, 589
Alone thou goest forth, O Lord 164
Amazing grace! how sweet the sound 671
Ancient of Days, who sittest throned in glory 363
And have the bright immensities 459
And now, O Father, mindful of the love 337
Angels, from the realms of glory 93
Angels we have heard on high 96
As Jacob with travel was weary one day 453
As longs the deer for cooling streams 658
As now the sun shines down at noon 18
As those of old their first fruits brought 705
As with gladness men of old 119
At the cross her vigil keeping 159
At the Lamb's high feast we sing 174
At the Name of Jesus 435
Awake and sing the song 181
Awake, arise, lift up your voice 212
Awake, my soul, and with the sun 11
Awake, my soul, stretch every nerve 546
Awake, O sleeper, rise from death 547
Awake, thou Spirit of the watchmen 540
Away in a manger, no crib for his bed 101

Baptized in water 294
Be thou my vision, O Lord of my heart 488
Before the Lord's eternal throne 391
Before thy throne, O God, we kneel 574, 575
Beneath the cross of Jesus 498
Blessed be the God of Israel 444
Blessèd city, heavenly Salem 519, 520
Blessèd feasts of blessèd martyrs 238, 239
Blessed is the King who comes 153
Blessèd Jesus, at thy word 440
Blest are the pure in heart 656
Blest be the King whose coming 74
Book of books, our people's strength 631
Bread of heaven, on thee we feed 323
Bread of the world, in mercy broken 301
Break forth, O beauteous heavenly light 91
Breathe on me, Breath of God 508
Brightest and best of the stars of the morning 117, 118
By all your saints still striving 231, 232
By gracious powers so wonderfully sheltered 695, 696
By the Creator, Joseph was appointed 261, 262

Can we by searching find out God 476
Christ for the world we sing! 537

Christ is alive! Let Christians sing 182
Christ is arisen (Christ ist erstanden) 713
Christ is made the sure foundation 518
Christ is the King! O friends upraise 614
Christ is the world's true Light 542
Christ ist erstanden (Christ is arisen) 713
Christ Jesus lay in death's strong bands 185, 186
Christ, mighty Savior, Light of all creation 33, 34, 35
Christ, the fair glory of the holy angels 282, 283
Christ the Lord is risen again! 184
Christ the Victorious, give to your servants 358
Christ the worker 611
Christ upon the mountain peak 129, 130
Christ, when for us you were baptized 121
Christ, whose glory fills the skies 6, 7
Christians, awake, salute the happy morn 106
Christians, to the Paschal victim 183
Come away to the skies 213
Come down, O Love divine 516
Come, gracious Spirit, heavenly Dove 512
Come, Holy Ghost, our souls inspire 503, 504
Come, Holy Spirit, heavenly Dove 510
Come, labor on 541
Come, let us join our cheerful songs 374
Come, let us with our Lord arise 49
Come, my Way, my Truth, my Life 487
Come now, and praise the humble saint 260
Come, O come, our voices raise 430
Come, O thou Traveler unknown 638, 639
Come, pure hearts, in joyful measure 244
Come, risen Lord, and deign to be our guest 305, 306
Come sing, ye choirs exultant 235
Come, thou almighty King 365
Come, thou fount of every blessing 686
Come, thou Holy Spirit bright 226, 227
Come, thou long-expected Jesus 66
Come, we that love the Lord 392
Come with us, O blessèd Jesus 336
Come, ye faithful, raise the strain 199, 200
Come, ye thankful people, come 290
Comfort, comfort ye my people 67
Commit thou all that grieves thee 669
Completed, Lord, the Holy Mysteries 346
Creating God, your fingers trace 394, 395
Creator of the earth and skies 148
Creator of the stars of night 60
Creator Spirit, by whose aid 500
Cross of Jesus, cross of sorrow 160
Crown him with many crowns 494

Day by day 654
Dear Lord and Father of mankind 652, 653
Deck thyself, my soul, with gladness 339
Descend, O Spirit, purging flame 297
Dona nobis pacem 712
Dost thou in a manger lie 97
Draw nigh and take the Body of the Lord 327, 328
Duérmete, Niño lindo (Oh, sleep now, holy baby) 113

Earth and all stars 412
Earth has many a noble city 127
Eternal Father, strong to save 608
Eternal light, shine in my heart 465, 466
Eternal Lord of love, behold your Church 149
Eternal Ruler of the ceaseless round 617
Eternal Spirit of the living Christ 698

Fairest Lord Jesus 383, 384
Faith of our fathers! living still 558
Father all loving, who rulest in majesty 568
Father eternal, Ruler of creation 573
Father, we praise thee, now the night is over 1, 2
Father, we thank thee who hast planted 302, 303
Fight the good fight with all thy might 552, 553
For all the saints, who from their labors rest 287
For the beauty of the earth 416
For the bread which you have broken 340, 341
For the fruit of all creation 424
For thy blest saints, a noble throng 276
For thy dear saints, O Lord 279
"Forgive our sins as we forgive" 674
Forty days and forty nights 150
From all that dwell below the skies 380
From deepest woe I cry to thee 151
From east to west, from shore to shore 77
From glory to glory advancing, we praise thee, O Lord 326
From God Christ's deity came forth 443
From heaven above to earth I come 80
From thee all skill and science flow 566

Gabriel's message does away 270
Give praise and glory unto God 375
Give rest, O Christ 355
Give us the wings of faith to rise 253
Glorious the day when Christ was born 452
Glorious things of thee are spoken 522, 523
Glory be to Jesus 479
Glory, love, and praise, and honor 300
Go forth for God; go to the world in peace 347
Go forward, Christian soldier 563
Go tell it on the mountain 99
Go to dark Gethsemane 171
God be in my head 694
God bless our native land 716
God has spoken to his people 536
God himself is with us 475
God is Love, and where true love is 576, 577
God is Love, let heaven adore him 379
God is working his purpose out 534
God moves in a mysterious way 677
God, my King, thy might confessing 414
God of grace and God of glory 594, 595
God of mercy, God of grace 538
God of our fathers, whose almighty hand 718
God of saints, to whom the number 280
God of the prophets, bless the prophets' heirs 359
God rest you merry, gentlemen 105
God the Omnipotent! King, who ordainest 569
God, who stretched the spangled heavens 580
God, you have given us power to sound 584
Good Christian friends, rejoice 107
Good Christians all, rejoice and sing! 205
Gracious Spirit, Holy Ghost 612
Guide me, O thou great Jehovah 690

Hail the day that sees him rise, Alleluia! 214
Hail thee, festival day! *Ascension* 216
Hail thee, festival day! *Easter* 175
Hail thee, festival day! *Pentecost* 225
Hail this joyful day's return 223, 224
Hail, thou once despisèd Jesus! 495
Hail to the Lord who comes 259
Hail to the Lord's Anointed 616
Hark! a thrilling voice is sounding 59
Hark! the glad sound! the Savior comes 71, 72
Hark! the herald angels sing 87
Hark! the sound of holy voices 275
He is risen, he is risen! 180
He is the Way 463, 464
He sat to watch o'er customs paid 281
He who would valiant be 564, 565
Hearken to the anthem glorious 240, 241
Help us, O Lord, to learn 628
Herald, sound the note of judgment 70
Here, O my Lord, I see thee face to face 318
Holy Father, greast Creator 368
Holy Ghost, dispel our sadness 515
Holy God, we praise thy Name 366
Holy, holy, holy! Lord God Almighty! 362
Holy Spirit, ever living 511
Holy Spirit, font of light 228
Holy Spirit, Lord of love 349
Hope of the world, thou Christ 472
Hosanna in the highest 157
Hosanna to the living Lord! 486
How bright appears the Morning Star 496, 497
How firm a foundation, ye saints of the Lord 636, 637
How lovely is thy dwelling-place 517
How oft, O Lord, thy face hath shone 242
How sweet the Name of Jesus sounds 644
How wondrous and great thy works, God of praise 532, 533
How wondrous great, how glorious bright 369
Humbly I adore thee, Verity unseen 314

I am the bread of life 335
I bind unto myself today 370
I call on thee, Lord Jesus Christ 634
"I come," the great Redeemer cries 116
I come with joy to meet my Lord 304
I heard the voice of Jesus say 692
I know not where the road will lead 647
I love thee, Lord, but not because 682
I love thy kingdom, Lord 524
I sing a song of the saints of God 293
I sing the almighty power of God 398
I sought the Lord, and afterward I knew 689
I to the hills will lift mine eyes 668
I want to walk as a child of the light 490
If thou but trust in God to guide thee 635
I'll praise my Maker while I've breath 429
Immortal, invisible, God only wise 423

In Bethlehem a newborn boy 246
In Christ there is no East or West 529
In the bleak midwinter 112
In the cross of Christ I glory 441, 442
In your mercy, Lord, you called me 706
Into paradise may the angels lead you 354
It came upon the midnight clear 89, 90
It was poor little Jesus 468

Jerusalem, my happy home 620
Jerusalem the golden 624
Jesu, Jesu, fill us with your love 602
Jesus, all my gladness 701
Jesus calls us; o'er the tumult 549, 550
Jesus came, adored by angels 454
Jesus Christ is risen today, Alleluia! 207
Jesus lives! thy terrors now 194, 195
Jesus, Lover of my soul 699
Jesus! Name of wondrous love! 252
Jesus, our mighty Lord 478
Jesus, Redeemer of the world 38, 39
Jesus shall reign where'er the sun 544
Jesus, Son of Mary 357
Jesus, the very thought of thee 642
Jesus, thou divine Companion 586
Joy to the world! the Lord is come 100
Joyful, joyful, we adore thee 376
Judge eternal, throned in splendor 596
Just as I am, without one plea 693

Kind Maker of the world, O hear 152
King of glory, King of peace 382
King of the martyrs' noble band 236

Lamp of our feet, whereby we trace 627
Lead on, O King eternal 555
Lead us, heavenly Father, lead us 559
Lead us, O Father, in the paths of peace 703
Let all mortal flesh keep silence 324
Let all the world in every corner sing 402, 403
Let saints on earth in concert sing 526
Let thy Blood in mercy poured 313
Let us break bread together on our knees 325
Let us now our voices raise 237
Let us, with a gladsome mind 389
Lift every voice and sing 599
Lift high the cross 473
Lift up your heads, ye mighty gates 436
Lift your voice rejoicing, Mary 190
Light's abode, celestial Salem 621, 622
Like the murmur of the dove's song 513
Lo! he comes, with clouds descending 57, 58
Lo, how a Rose e'er blooming 81
Lo! what a cloud of witnesses 545
Look there! the Christ, our Brother, comes 196, 197
Lord, be thy word my rule 626
Lord Christ, when first thou cam'st to earth 598
Lord, dismiss us with thy blessing 344
Lord, enthroned in heavenly splendor 307
Lord, for ever at thy side 670
Lord God, you now have set your servant free 499
Lord Jesus, Sun of Righteousness 144
Lord Jesus, think on me 641
Lord, make us servants of your peace 593
Lord of all being, throned afar 419
Lord of all hopefulness, Lord of all joy 482
Lord, thou hast searched me and dost know 702
Lord, we have come at your own invitation 348
Lord, who throughout these forty days 142
Lord, whose love through humble service 610
Lord, you give the great commission 528
Love came down at Christmas 84
Love divine, all loves excelling 657
Love's redeeming work is done 188, 189
Lully, lullay, thou little tiny child 247

Make a joyful noise unto the Lord (Singt dem Herren!) 710
Many and great, O God, are thy works 385
May choirs of angels lead you 356
May the grace of Christ our Savior 351
Morning glory, starlit sky 585
Morning has broken 8
Most High, omnipotent, good Lord 406, 407
Most Holy God, the Lord of heaven 31, 32
My country, 'tis of thee 717
My faith looks up to thee 691
My God, accept my heart this day 697
My God, how wonderful thou art 643
My God, thy table now is spread 321
My Shepherd will supply my need 664
My song is love unknown 458

Nature with open volume stands 434
New every morning is the love 10
New songs of celebration render 413

Not far beyond the sea, nor high 422
Not here for high and holy things 9
Nova, nova 266
Now greet the swiftly changing year 250
Now Holy Spirit, ever One 19, 20
Now let us all with one accord 146, 147
Now let us sing our praise to God 16, 17
Now, my tongue, the mystery telling 329, 330, 331
Now quit your care 145
Now thank we all our God 396, 397
Now that the daylight fills the sky 3, 4
Now the day is over 42
Now the green blade riseth from the buried grain 204
Now the silence 333
Now yield we thanks and praise 108

O all ye works of God, now come 428
O beautiful for spacious skies 719
O bless the Lord, my soul! 411
O blest Creator, source of light 27, 28
O Bread of life, for sinners broken 342
O brightness of the immortal Father's face 37
O Christ, the Word Incarnate 632
O Christ, you are both light and day 40, 41
O come, all ye faithful 83
O come, O come, Emmanuel 56
O day of God, draw nigh 600, 601
O day of peace that dimly shines 597
O day of radiant gladness 48
O Food to pilgrims given 308, 309
O for a closer walk with God 683, 684
O for a thousand tongues to sing 493
O gladsome Light, O grace 36
O God, creation's secret force 14, 15
O God of Bethel, by whose hand 709
O God of earth and altar 591
O God of every nation 607
O God of love, O King of peace 578
O God of love, to thee we bow 350
O God of truth, O Lord of might 21, 22
O God, our help in ages past 680
O God, to those who here profess 352
O God, unseen yet ever near 332
O God, we praise thee, and confess 364
O God, whom neither time nor space 251
O gracious Light, Lord Jesus Christ 25, 26
O heavenly Word, eternal Light 63, 64
O holy city, seen of John 582, 583
O Holy Spirit, by whose breath 501, 502
O Jesus Christ, may grateful hymns be rising 590
O Jesus, crowned with all renown 292
O Jesus, I have promised 655
O Jesus, joy of loving hearts 649, 650
O Light of Light, Love given birth 133, 134
O little town of Bethlehem 78, 79
O Lord Most High, eternal King 220, 221
O love, how deep, how broad, how high 448, 449
O Love of God, how strong and true 455, 456
O love that casts out fear 700
O Master, let me walk with thee 659, 660
O praise ye the Lord! Praise him in the height 432
O sacred head, sore wounded 168, 169
O saving Victim, opening wide 310, 311
O Savior of our fallen race 85, 86
O say can you see, by the dawn's early light 720
O sorrow deep! 173
O Spirit of Life, O Spirit of God 505
O Spirit of the living God 531
O splendor of God's glory bright 5
O thou who camest from above 704
O Trinity of blessèd light 29, 30
O very God of very God 672
O what their joy and their glory must be 623
O wondrous type! O vision fair 136, 137
O worship the King, all glorious above! 388
O ye immortal throng 284
O Zion, haste, thy mission high fulfilling 539
O Zion, open wide thy gates 257
O Zion, tune thy voice 543
Of the Father's love begotten 82
Oh, sleep now, holy baby (Duérmete, Niño lindo) 113
On earth has dawned this day of days 201
On Jordan's bank the Baptist's cry 76
On this day earth shall ring 92
On this day, the first of days 47
Once he came in blessing 53
Once in royal David's city 102
Only begotten, Word of God eternal 360, 361
Onward, Christian soldiers 562
Our Father, by whose Name 587
Our Father, by whose servants 289
Our God, to whom we turn 681

Out of the depths I call 666
Over the chaos of the empty waters 176, 177

Praise God for John, evangelist 245
Praise, my soul, the King of heaven 410
Praise our great and gracious Lord 393
Praise the Lord, rise up rejoicing 334
Praise the Lord through every nation 484, 485
Praise the Lord! ye heavens adore him 373
Praise the Spirit in creation 506, 507
Praise to God, immortal praise 288
Praise to the Holiest in the height 445, 446
Praise to the living God! 372
Praise to the Lord, the Almighty 390
Praise we the Lord this day 267
Prepare the way, O Zion 65
Put forth, O God, thy Spirit's might 521

Redeemer of the nations, come 55
Rejoice! rejoice, believers 68
Rejoice, the Lord is King 481
Rejoice, the Lord of life ascends 222
Rejoice, ye pure in heart! 556, 557
Remember your servants, Lord 560
Ride on! ride on in majesty! 156
Rise up, ye saints of God! 551
Rock of ages, cleft for me 685
Round the Lord in glory seated 367

Savior, again to thy dear Name we raise 345
Savior, like a shepherd lead us 708
Savior of the nations, come! 54
See the Conqueror mounts in triumph 215
Seek ye first the kingdom of God 711
Shalom chaverim (Shalom, my friends) 714
Shalom, my friends (Shalom chaverim) 714
Shepherd of souls, refresh and bless 343
Silent night, holy night 111
Sing alleluia forth in duteous praise 619
Sing, my soul, his wondrous love 467
Sing, my tongue, the glorious battle 165, 166
Sing now with joy unto the Lord 425
Sing, O sing, this blessèd morn 88
Sing of Mary, pure and lowly 277
Sing praise to God who reigns above 408
Sing praise to our Creator 295
Sing we of the blessèd Mother 278
Sing, ye faithful, sing with gladness 492
Singing songs of expectation 527
Singt dem Herren! (Make a joyful noise unto the Lord) 710
"Sleepers, wake!" A voice astounds us 61, 62
Soldiers of Christ, arise 548
Sometimes a light surprises 667
Songs of praise the angels sang 426
Songs of thankfulness and praise 135
Spirit divine, attend our prayers 509
Spirit of God, unleashed on earth 299
Spirit of mercy, truth, and love 229
Spread, O spread, thou mighty word 530
Stand up, stand up, for Jesus 561
Strengthen for service, Lord 312
Sunset to sunrise changes now 163
Surely it is God who saves me 678, 679

Take my life, and let it be 707
Take up your cross, the Savior said 675
Teach me, my God and King 592
Tell out, my soul, the greatness of the Lord! 437, 438
Thanks to God whose Word was spoken 630
That Easter day with joy was bright 193
The angel Gabriel from heaven came 265
The Christ who died but rose again 447
The Church's one foundation 525
The day of resurrection! 210
The day thou gavest, Lord, is ended 24
The duteous day now closeth 46
The eternal gifts of Christ the King 233, 234
The first Nowell the angel did say 109
The first one ever, oh, ever to know 673
The flaming banners of our King 161
The fleeting day is nearly gone 23
The glory of these forty days 143
The God of Abraham praise 401
The golden sun lights up the sky 12, 13
The great Creator of the worlds 489
The great forerunner of the morn 271, 272
The head that once was crowned with thorns 483
The King of love my shepherd is 645, 646
The King shall come when morning dawns 73
The Lamb's high banquet called to share 202
The Lord ascendeth up on high 219
The Lord my God my shepherd is 663
The Lord will come and not be slow 462

The people who in darkness walked 125, 126
The royal banners forward go 162
The sinless one to Jordan came 120
The snow lay on the ground 110
The spacious firmament on high 409
The stars declare his glory 431
The whole bright world rejoices now 211
The Word whom earth and sea and sky 263, 264
There is a balm in Gilead 676
There is a green hill far away 167
Therefore we, before him bending 330
There's a voice in the wilderness crying 75
There's a wideness in God's mercy 469, 470
They cast their nets in Galilee 661
Thine arm, O Lord, in days of old 567
This day at thy creating word 52
This is my Father's world 651
This is the day the Lord hath made 50
This is the feast of victory for our God 417, 418
This is the hour of banquet and of song 316, 317
This joyful Eastertide 192
Thou art the Way, to thee alone 457
Thou hallowed chosen morn of praise 198
Thou, who at thy first Eucharist didst pray 315
Thou, whose almighty word 371
Through the Red Sea brought at last, Alleluia! 187
Thy kingdom come, O God! 613
"Thy Kingdom come!" on bended knee 615
Thy strong word did cleave the darkness 381
'Tis the gift to be simple 554
To God with gladness sing 399
To mock your reign, O dearest Lord 170
To the Name of our salvation 248, 249
To thee, O Comforter divine 514
To you before the close of day 44, 45
'Twas in the moon of wintertime 114
Two stalwart trees both rooted 273, 274

Unto us a boy is born! 98

Virgin-born, we bow before thee 258

Watchman, tell us of the night 640
We gather together to ask the Lord's blessing 433
We know that Christ is raised and dies no more 296
We limit not the truth of God 629
We plow the fields, and scatter 291
We sing of God, the mighty source 386, 387
We sing the glorious conquest 255
We sing the praise of him who died 471
We the Lord's people, heart and voice uniting 51
We three kings of Orient are 128
We walk by faith, and not by sight 209
We will extol you, ever-blessèd Lord 404
Weary of all trumpeting 572
"Welcome, happy morning!" age to age shall say 179
Were you there when they crucified my Lord? 172
What child is this, who, laid to rest 115
What does the Lord require 605
What is the crying at Jordan? 69
What star is this, with beams so bright 124
What thanks and praise to thee we owe 285
What wondrous love is this 439
When all thy mercies, O my God 415
When Christ was lifted from the earth 603, 604
When Christ's appearing was made known 131, 132
When I survey the wondrous cross 474
When in our music God is glorified 420
When Israel was in Egypt's land 648
When Jesus died to save us 322
When Jesus left his Father's throne 480
When Jesus went to Jordan's stream 139
When Jesus wept, the falling tear 715
When morning gilds the skies 427
When Stephen, full of power and grace 243
Where charity and love prevail 581
Where cross the crowded ways of life 609
Where is this stupendous stranger? 491
Where true charity and love dwell 606
Wherefore, O Father, we thy humble servants 338
While shepherds watched their flocks by night 94, 95
Who are these like stars appearing 286
Wilt thou forgive that sin, where I begun 140, 141
Word of God, come down on earth 633

Ye holy angels bright 625
Ye servants of God, your Master proclaim 535
Ye watchers and ye holy ones 618
Ye who claim the faith of Jesus 268, 269
You are the Christ, O Lord 254
You, Lord, we praise in songs of celebration 319
Your love, O God, has called us here 353

Zion, praise thy Savior, singing 320

Metrical Index With Incipits

The earliest index of tunes to include musical incipits is found in an early edition of William Barton's metrical psalter: *The Book of Psalms in Metre, Lately Translated . . .* (London, 1645). It also has the distinction of being the earliest printed thematic catalogue. Barton's index appears on a single page and includes the incipits of 22 psalm tunes. Some later tune books issued in the 17th and 18th centuries included a tune index with musical incipits but it was not a widespread practice. The first hymnal in recent times to included such an index is *The Anglican Hymn Book* (London, 1965).

Chelsea Square 521
Cheshire 581
Cornhill 144
Crimond 663
Culross 584
Detroit 674
Dundee 126, 526, 709
Dunlap's Creek 276
Durham 415
Edmonton 257
Epworth 476
Georgetown 661
Gerontius 445
Hampton 95
Horsley 167
Irish 428
Land of Rest 304, 620
London New 50, 251, 677
Manchester 364
Marsh Chapel 547
Martyrdom 658
McKee 529
New Britain
Newman 446
Nun danket all und bringet Ehr 374, 509, 627
Perry 125
Richmond 72, 212
St. Agnus 343, 510
St. Anne 680
St. Botolph 209, 603
St. Flavian 142, 615
St. Flavian (original rhythm) 332
St. Fulbert 545, 682
St. James 457
St. Mangus 447, 483
St. Peter 644
St. Stephen 73
San Rocco 253, 604
Shorney 369
Song 67, 697
Tallis' Ordinal 260, 489
This Endris Night 116
Walden 589
Winchester Old 94
Windsor (isometric) 643
Windsor Rhythmic 642

York 462
CM with Repeat 86. 86 with Repeat
Common Meter with Repeat
Antioch 100
CMD 86. 86. D
Common Meter Double
Carol 89
Forest Green 78, 398, 705
Halifax 459, 629
Kingsfold 292, 480
Laramie 647
Materna 719
Noel 90, 245
Resignation 664
St. Louis 79
St. Matthew 567
Salvation 243
The Church's Desolation 566
The Third Tune 170, 692
LM 88.88
Long Meter
A la venue de Noël 152
Ach bleib bei uns 465
Ad cenam Agni providi 202
Adon Olam 425
Aeterne Rex altissime 136, 220
Bourbon 147, 675
Breslau 281, 471
Bromley 28, 29
Christe, qui Lux es et dies 40
Christe, Redemptor omnium 85
Compline 41
Conditor alme siderum 26, 60
Cornish 229, 256
Danby 12
de Tar 456, 659
Deo gracias 218, 449
Deus tuorum militum 285, 448
Dicamus laudes Domino 16
Dickinson College 593, 649
Du meiner Seelen 23
Duke Street
Dunedin 31, 455
Elmhurst 133
Eltham 434, 578
Ethalt uns, Herr (isometric) 143, 297
Erhalt uns, Herr (rhythmic) 132
Ex more docti mystico 146
Gardiner 609
Gonfalon Royal 86, 221, 234

Hereford 704
Herr Jesu Christ (isometric) 310
Herr Jesu Christ (rhythmic) 3
Immense caeli Conditor 32
In Bethlehem 246
Jacob 242, 466
Jam lucis orto sidere 217
Jesu dulcis memoria 18, 134, 650
Jesu, nostra redemptio (equalist rhythm) 38, 236
Jesu, nostra redemptio (syllabic rhythm) 233
Kedron 10, 163
King 395
Komm, Gott Schöpfer 501
Lledrod 299
Lucis Creator optiome 27
Maryton 660
Melcombe 531
Mendon 419, 512
Morning Hymn 11
Nunc Sancte nobis Spiritus 19
O Hieland, reiss 14, 64
O lux beata Trinitas 30
Old 100th 377, 378, 380
Parker 222
Pentecost 552
Puer nobis 124, 193
Quem terra, pontus, aethera 263
Rector potens, verax Deus 22
Rockingham 321, 474
Rushford 52, 553
Solemnis haec festivitas 17, 120
Song 34 21, 264
Splendor paternae gloriae 5
Te lucis ante terminum (Sarum) 15, 44
Te lucis ante terminum (Sarum ferial) 45
Tender Thought 702
The Eighth Tune 25, 43
The King's Majesty 156
The Truth from Above 272
Truro 182, 436
Uffingham 148
Ut queant laxis 271
Veni Creator Spiritus 502, 504
Veni Redemptor genitum 55
Verbum supernum prodiens (Einsiedeln) 13
Verbum supernum prodiens (Nevers) 4. 63, 311

Vexilla Regis prodeunt (equalist rhythm) 162
Vexilla Regis prodeunt (Syllabic rhythm) 161
Von Himmel hoch 80
Vam Himmel kam der Engel Schar 77, 131
Wareham 20, 137, 353
When Jesus Wept 715
Wilderness 39, 394
Winchester New 76, 391
Woodworth 693
LM with Alleluia 88. 88 with Alleluia
Long metre with Alleluia
Erschienen ist der herrich Tag 201
LM with Alleluias 88. 88 with Alleluias
Long metre with Alleluias
Deo gracias 218
Frolockt mit Freud 452
LM with Refrain 88. 88 with Refrain
Long Metre with Refrain
Grand Prairie 197
Hosanna 486
Petrus 196
Veni, veni Emmanuel 56
LMD 88. 88 D
Long Metre Double
Creation 409
Jerusalem 597
St. Patrick's Breastplate 370
Schmücke dich 339
44. 6. D with refrain
Coventry Carol 247
445. 9
African Work Song 611
447. 76
O Traurigkeit 173
45. 7. D with Refrain
Earth and All Stars 412
4. 10. 10. 10. 4
Ora labora 541
55. 54. D
Bunessan 8
558. 558
Point Loma 294
568. 558
St. Elizabeth 383
Schönster Herr Jesu 384
65. 65
Merrial 42
Wem in Leidenstagen 479
65. 65. D
King's Weston 435
65. 65. D with refrain
St. Gertrude 562
65. 65. 6665
St. Dunstan's 564
664. 6664
America 716, 717
Moscow 365, 371, 537
Olivet 691
665. 665. 786
Jesu, meine Freude 701

66. 66
Moseley 700
Quam dilecta 626
St. Cecilia 613

66. 66 with Refrain
Augustine 402
Gopsal 481
MacDougall 403

66. 66. 33. 6
Sharpthorne 605

66. 66. 44. 44
Camano 399
Croft's 136th 284
Darwall's 148th 625
Love Unknown 458

666. 66 with Refrain
Personent hodie 92

666. 666
Laudes Domini 427

66. 66. 66
Gottes Sohn ist kommen 53
Old 120th 259

66. 66. 88
Eastview 543
Wyngate Canon 254

66. 66. 888
Rhosymedre 587

667. 667
Le Cantique de Siméon 36

66. 77. 78. 55
In dulci jubilo 107

66. 84. D
Leoni 372, 401

668. 668. 666
Tysk 475

669. 669
Middlebury 213

66. 11. D
Down Ampney 516

67. 67
Gartan 84

67. 67 with Refrain
Vruechtnen 192

67. 67. 66. 66
Nun danket alle Gott (isometric) 397
Nun danket alle Gott (rhythmic) 396
O Gott, du frommer Gott 681
St. Joan 542
Was frag' ich nach der Welt 108

74. 74. D
General Seminary 382

76. 76
Ave caeli janua 273
Christus, der is mein Leben 295, 356
De Eersten zijn de laatsten 274

76. 76 with Refrain
Gloria, laus, et honor 155
Go Tell It on the Mountain 99

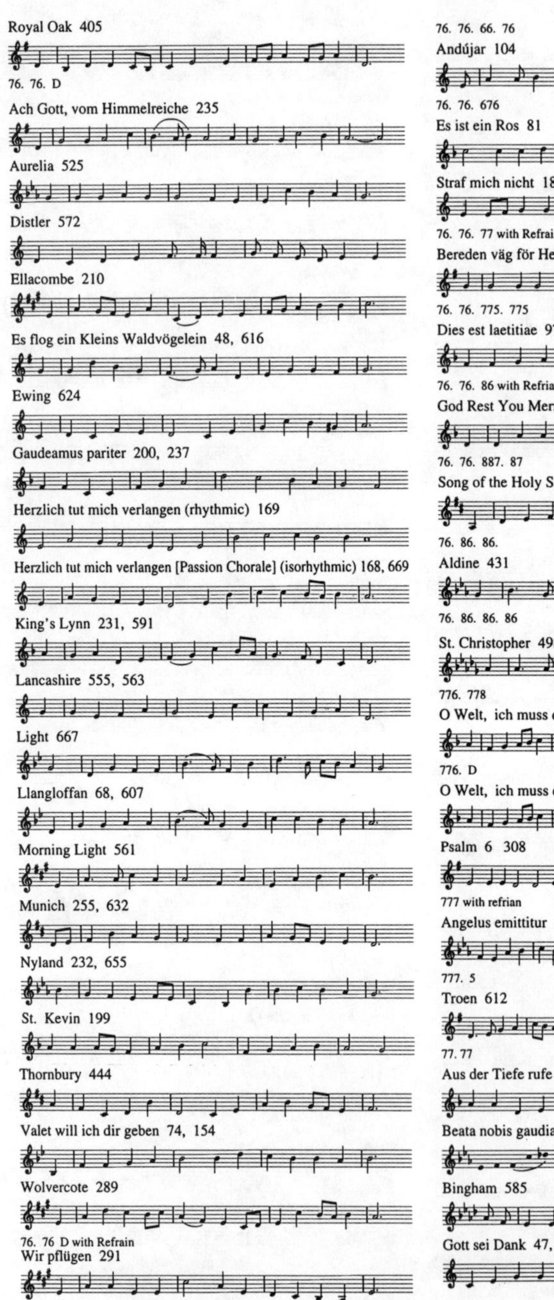

Royal Oak 405

76. 76. D

Ach Gott, vom Himmelreiche 235

Aurelia 525

Distler 572

Ellacombe 210

Es flog ein Kleins Waldvögelein 48, 616

Ewing 624

Gaudeamus pariter 200, 237

Herzlich tut mich verlangen (rhythmic) 169

Herzlich tut mich verlangen [Passion Chorale] (isorhythmic) 168, 669

King's Lynn 231, 591

Lancashire 555, 563

Light 667

Llangloffan 68, 607

Morning Light 561

Munich 255, 632

Nyland 232, 655

St. Kevin 199

Thornbury 444

Valet will ich dir geben 74, 154

Wolvercote 289

76. 76 D with Refrain

Wir pflügen 291

76. 76. 66. 76

Andújar 104

76. 76. 676

Es ist ein Ros 81

Straf mich nicht 187

76. 76. 77 with Refrain

Bereden väg för Herran 65

76. 76. 775. 775

Dies est laetitiae 97

76. 76. 86 with Refrian

God Rest You Merry 105

76. 76. 887. 87

Song of the Holy Spirit 230

76. 86. 86.

Aldine 431

76. 86. 86. 86

St. Christopher 498

776. 778

O Welt, ich muss dich lassen 46

776. D

O Welt, ich muss dich lassen 309

Psalm 6 308

777 with refrian

Angelus emittitur 270

777. 5

Troen 612

77. 77

Aus der Tiefe rufe ich 150

Beata nobis gaudia 223

Bingham 585

Gott sei Dank 47, 530

Louez Dieu 252
Monkland 389
Northampton 426
Nun komm der Heiden Heiland 54
Puer nobis nascitur 98
St. Bees 467
Savannah 188
Song 13 670
The Call 487
Tucker 322
77. 77 with Alleluia
Sonne der Gerechtigkeit 224, 430
77. 77 with Alleluias
Easter hymn 207
Llanfair 214
Resurrexit 189
77. 77 with Refrain
Gloria 96
77. 77. D
Aberystwyth 349, 640, 699
Hollingside 707
St. George's, Windsor 290
Salzburg 135, 174
77. 77. D with refrain
Mendelssohn 87
77. 77. 4 with Refrain
Christ ist erstanden 184
77. 77. 67. 67
Maoz Zur 393
77. 77. 77
Christ Whose Glory 6
Dix 119, 288
England's Lane 88
Jesu, Jesu, du mein Hirt 323
Lucerna Laudoniae 538, 416
Petra 171
Ratisbon 7
Toplady 685
777. 777
Arbor Street 227
Veni Sancte Spiritus 226
Webbe 228
78. 78 with Alleluia
Mowsley 129, 195
St. Albinus 194
Shillingford 130
78. 78. 77
Grosser Gott 366
Jesus, meine Zuversicht 313
78. 78. 88
Liebster Jesu 440, 631
Mt. St. Alban NCA 633
8. 33. 6. D
Benifold 300

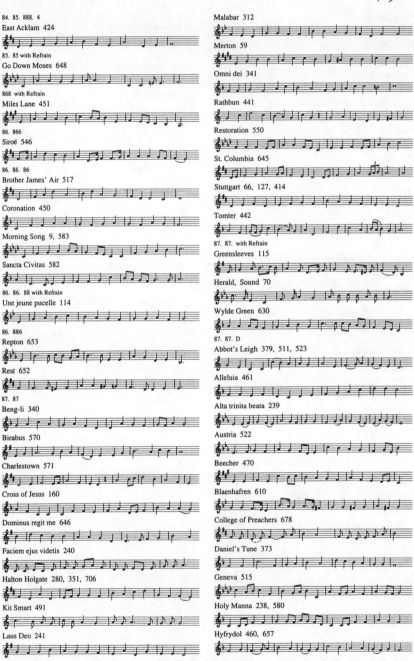

84. 85. 888. 4

East Acklam 424

85. 85 with Refrain

Go Down Moses 648

868 with Refrain

Miles Lane 451

86. 866

Siroë 546

86. 86. 86

Brother James' Air 517

Coronation 450

Morning Song 9, 583

Sancta Civitas 582

86. 86. 88 with Refrain

Une jeune pucelle 114

86. 886

Repton 653

Rest 652

87. 87

Beng-li 340

Birabus 570

Charlestown 571

Cross of Jesus 160

Dominus regit me 646

Faciem ejus videtis 240

Halton Holgate 280, 351, 706

Kit Smart 491

Laus Deo 241

Malabar 312

Merton 59

Omni dei 341

Rathbun 441

Restoration 550

St. Columbia 645

Stuttgart 66, 127, 414

Tomter 442

87. 87. with Refrain

Greensleeves 115

Herald, Sound 70

Wylde Green 630

87. 87. D

Abbot's Leigh 379, 511, 523

Alleluia 461

Alta trinita beata 239

Austria 522

Beecher 470

Blaenhafren 610

College of Preachers 678

Daniel's Tune 373

Geneva 515

Holy Manna 238, 580

Hyfrydol 460, 657

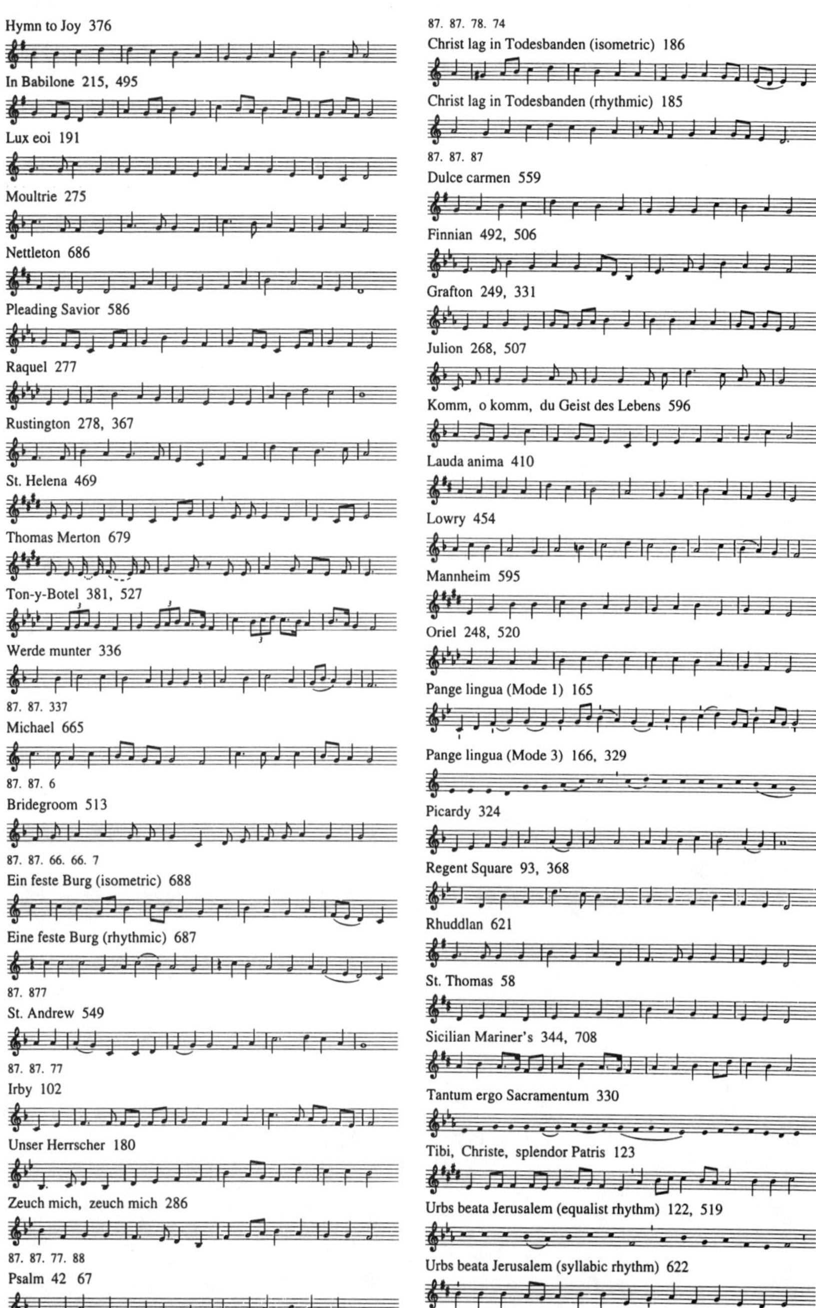
Hymn to Joy 376
In Babilone 215, 495
Lux eoi 191
Moultrie 275
Nettleton 686
Pleading Savior 586
Raquel 277
Rustington 278, 367
St. Helena 469
Thomas Merton 679
Ton-y-Botel 381, 527
Werde munter 336
87. 87. 337
Michael 665
87. 87. 6
Bridegroom 513
87. 87. 66. 66. 7
Ein feste Burg (isometric) 688
Eine feste Burg (rhythmic) 687
87. 877
St. Andrew 549
87. 87. 77
Irby 102
Unser Herrscher 180
Zeuch mich, zeuch mich 286
87. 87. 77. 88
Psalm 42 67
87. 87. 78. 74
Christ lag in Todesbanden (isometric) 186
Christ lag in Todesbanden (rhythmic) 185
87. 87. 87
Dulce carmen 559
Finnian 492, 506
Grafton 249, 331
Julion 268, 507
Komm, o komm, du Geist des Lebens 596
Lauda anima 410
Lowry 454
Mannheim 595
Oriel 248, 520
Pange lingua (Mode 1) 165
Pange lingua (Mode 3) 166, 329
Picardy 324
Regent Square 93, 368
Rhuddlan 621
St. Thomas 58
Sicilian Mariner's 344, 708
Tantum ergo Sacramentum 330
Tibi, Christe, splendor Patris 123
Urbs beata Jerusalem (equalist rhythm) 122, 519
Urbs beata Jerusalem (syllabic rhythm) 622

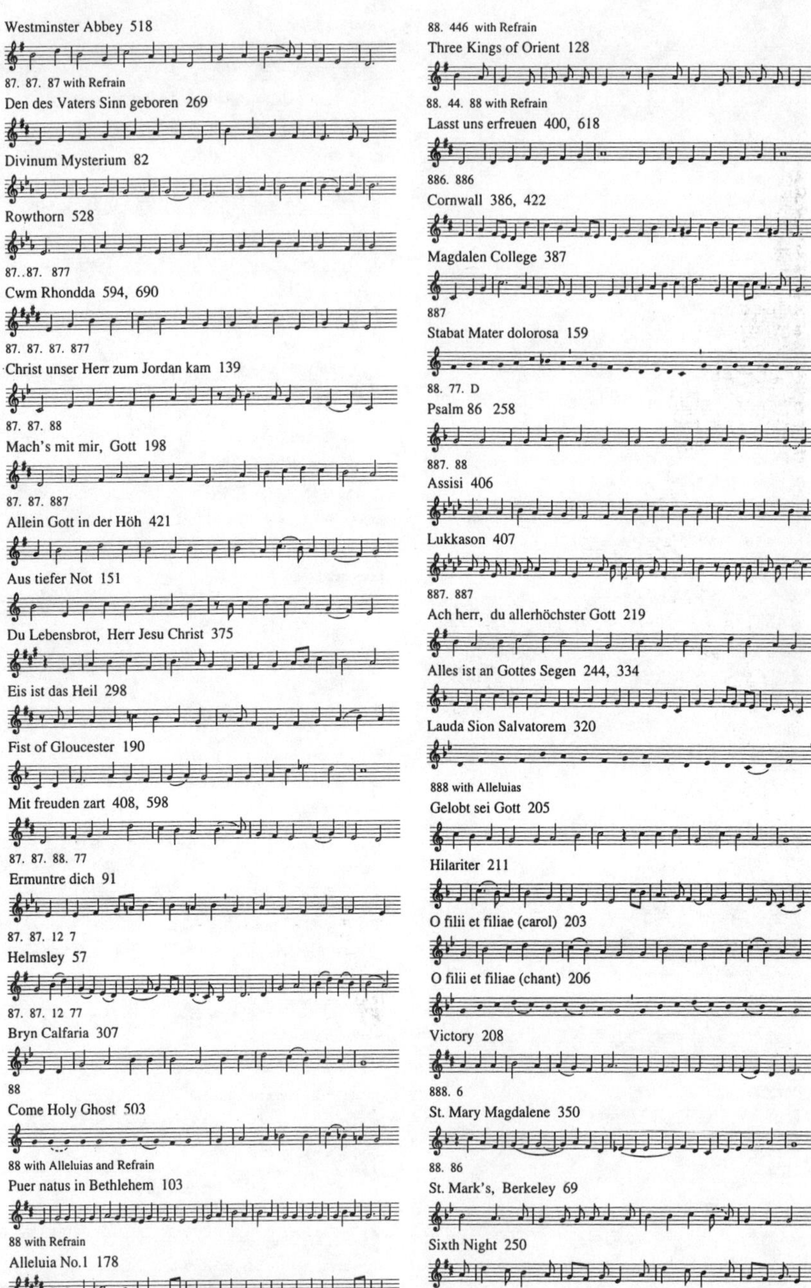

Westminster Abbey 518

87. 87. 87 with Refrain

Den des Vaters Sinn geboren 269

Divinum Mysterium 82

Rowthorn 528

87..87. 877

Cwm Rhondda 594, 690

87. 87. 87. 877

Christ unser Herr zum Jordan kam 139

87. 87. 88

Mach's mit mir, Gott 198

87. 87. 887

Allein Gott in der Höh 421

Aus tiefer Not 151

Du Lebensbrot, Herr Jesu Christ 375

Eis ist das Heil 298

Fist of Gloucester 190

Mit freuden zart 408, 598

87. 87. 88. 77

Ermuntre dich 91

87. 87. 12 7

Helmsley 57

87. 87. 12 77

Bryn Calfaria 307

88

Come Holy Ghost 503

88 with Alleluias and Refrain

Puer natus in Bethlehem 103

88 with Refrain

Alleluia No.1 178

88. 446 with Refrain

Three Kings of Orient 128

88. 44. 88 with Refrain

Lasst uns erfreuen 400, 618

886. 886

Cornwall 386, 422

Magdalen College 387

887

Stabat Mater dolorosa 159

88. 77. D

Psalm 86 258

887. 88

Assisi 406

Lukkason 407

887. 887

Ach herr, du allerhöchster Gott 219

Alles ist an Gottes Segen 244, 334

Lauda Sion Salvatorem 320

888 with Alleluias

Gelobt sei Gott 205

Hilariter 211

O filii et filiae (carol) 203

O filii et filiae (chant) 206

Victory 208

888. 6

St. Mary Magdalene 350

88. 86

St. Mark's, Berkeley 69

Sixth Night 250

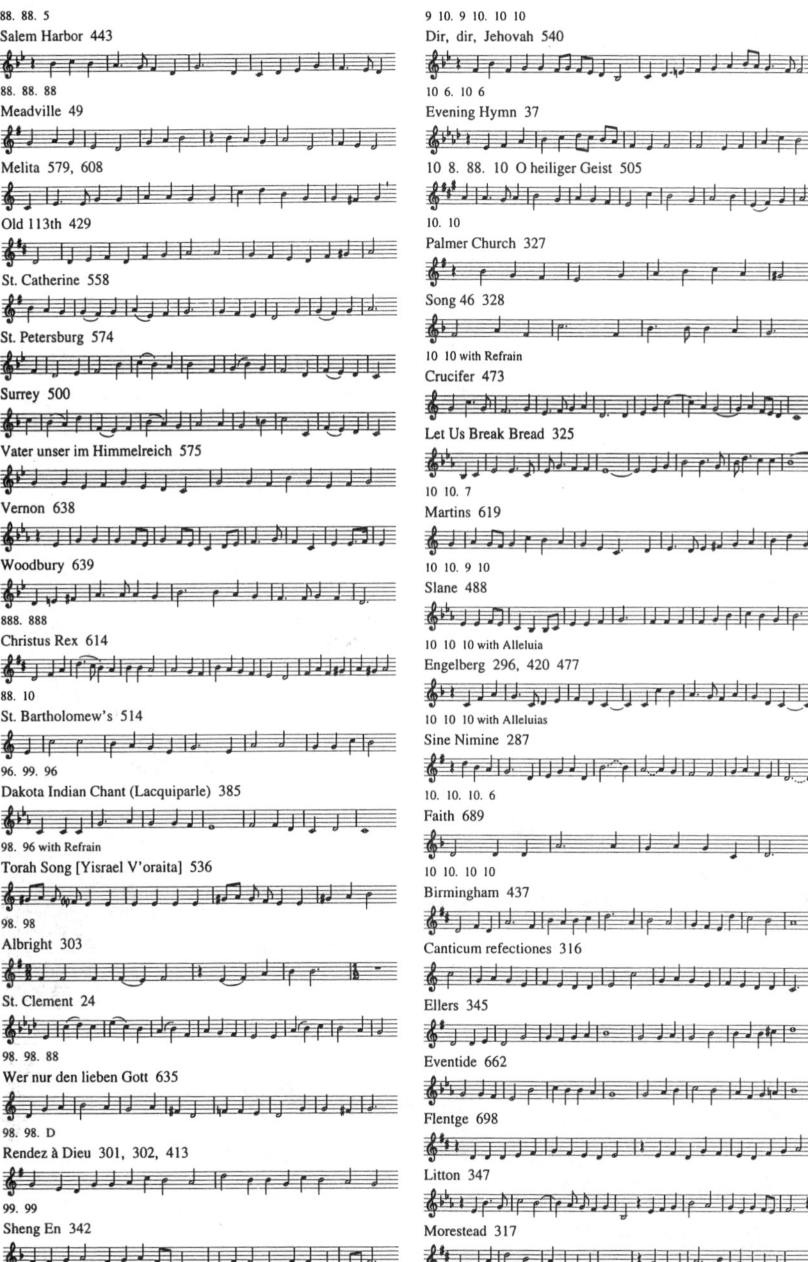
88. 88. 5
Salem Harbor 443
88. 88. 88
Meadville 49
Melita 579, 608
Old 113th 429
St. Catherine 558
St. Petersburg 574
Surrey 500
Vater unser im Himmelreich 575
Vernon 638
Woodbury 639
888. 888
Christus Rex 614
88. 10
St. Bartholomew's 514
96. 99. 96
Dakota Indian Chant (Lacquiparle) 385
98. 96 with Refrain
Torah Song [Yisrael V'oraita] 536
98. 98
Albright 303
St. Clement 24
98. 98. 88
Wer nur den lieben Gott 635
98. 98. D
Rendez à Dieu 301, 302, 413
99. 99
Sheng En 342
9 10. 9 10. 10 10
Dir, dir, Jehovah 540
10 6. 10 6
Evening Hymn 37
10 8. 88. 10 O heiliger Geist 505
10. 10
Palmer Church 327
Song 46 328
10 10 with Refrain
Crucifer 473
Let Us Break Bread 325
10 10. 7
Martins 619
10 10. 9 10
Slane 488
10 10 10 with Alleluia
Engelberg 296, 420 477
10 10 10 with Alleluias
Sine Nomine 287
10. 10. 10. 6
Faith 689
10 10. 10 10
Birmingham 437
Canticum refectiones 316
Ellers 345
Eventide 662
Flentge 698
Litton 347
Morestead 317

Metrical Index

National Hymn 718

Nyack 318

O quanta qualia 348, 623

Rosedale 305

Song 4 346

Song 22 703

Sursum corda 306

Toulon 359

Woodlands 438

10 10. 10 10. 84

Donne 140

So giebst dun nun 141

10 10. 10 10 10

Old 124th 149, 404

10 10. 10 10. 10 10

Song 1 315, 499, 617

Unde et memores 337

Yorkshire 106

10 10. 11 11

Hanover 388

Laudate Dominum 432

Lyons 533

Old 104th 532

Paderborn 535

10 10. 12 10

Gabriel's Message 265

10 11. 11 12

Slane 482

11 10. 10 11

Noël nouvelet 204

11 10. 11 9

Russia 358, 569

11 10. 11 10

Charterhouse 590

Coburn 363

Donne secours 472

Intercessor 695

Le Cénacle 696

Morning Star 117

11 10. 11 10 with Refrain

Star in the East 118

Tidings 539

11 10. 11 10. 10

Langham 573

11 11. 11 5

Bickford 177, 262

Caelites plaudant 282

Caelitum Joseph 261, 283, 361

Christe sanctorum 1

Herzliebster Jesu 158

Lobet den Herren 338

Nocte surgentes 2

Rouen 360

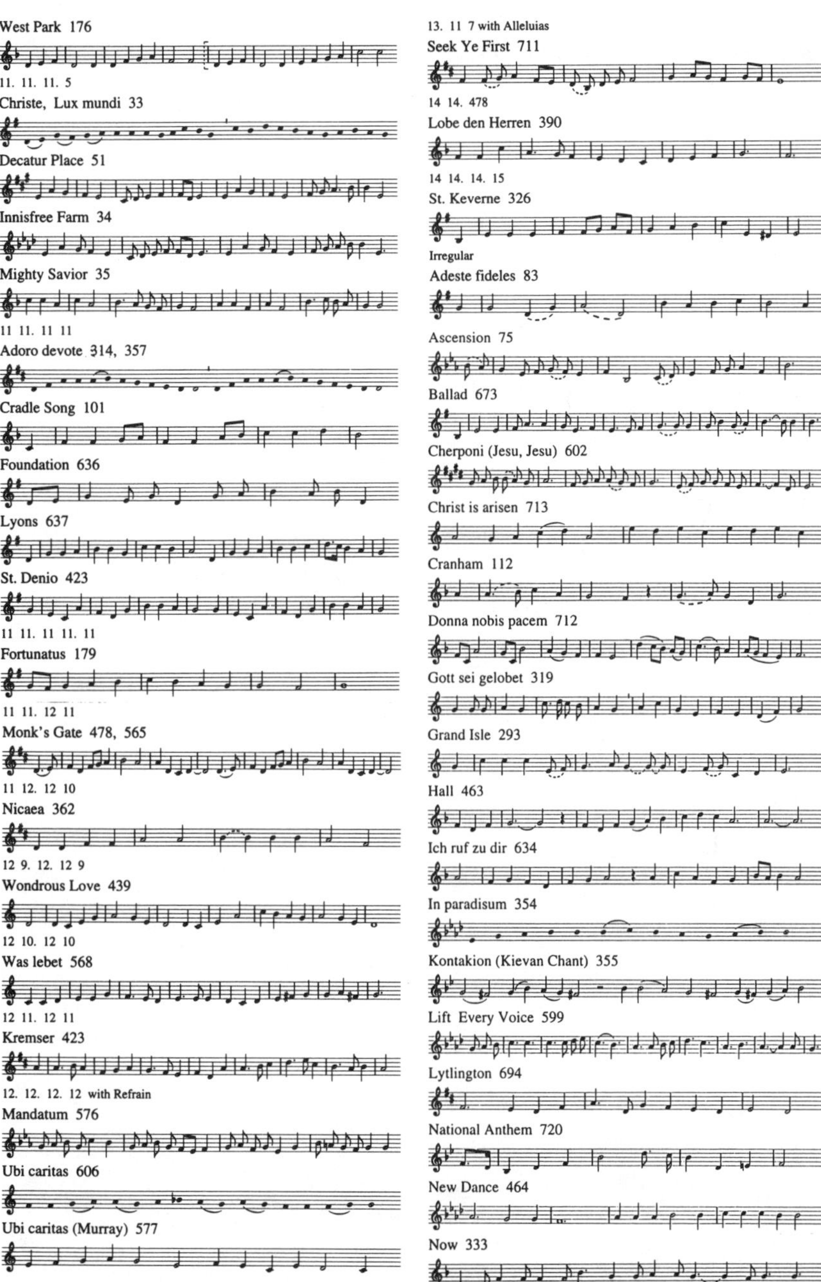
West Park 176
11. 11. 11. 5
Christe, Lux mundi 33
Decatur Place 51
Innisfree Farm 34
Mighty Savior 35
11 11. 11 11
Adoro devote 314, 357
Cradle Song 101
Foundation 636
Lyons 637
St. Denio 423
11 11. 11 11. 11
Fortunatus 179
11 11. 12 11
Monk's Gate 478, 565
11 12. 12 10
Nicaea 362
12 9. 12. 12 9
Wondrous Love 439
12 10. 12 10
Was lebet 568
12 11. 12 11
Kremser 423
12. 12. 12. 12 with Refrain
Mandatum 576
Ubi caritas 606
Ubi caritas (Murray) 577
13. 11 7 with Alleluias
Seek Ye First 711
14 14. 478
Lobe den Herren 390
14 14. 14. 15
St. Keverne 326
Irregular
Adeste fideles 83
Ascension 75
Ballad 673
Cherponi (Jesu, Jesu) 602
Christ is arisen 713
Cranham 112
Donna nobis pacem 712
Gott sei gelobet 319
Grand Isle 293
Hall 463
Ich ruf zu dir 634
In paradisum 354
Kontakion (Kievan Chant) 355
Lift Every Voice 599
Lytlington 694
National Anthem 720
New Dance 464
Now 333

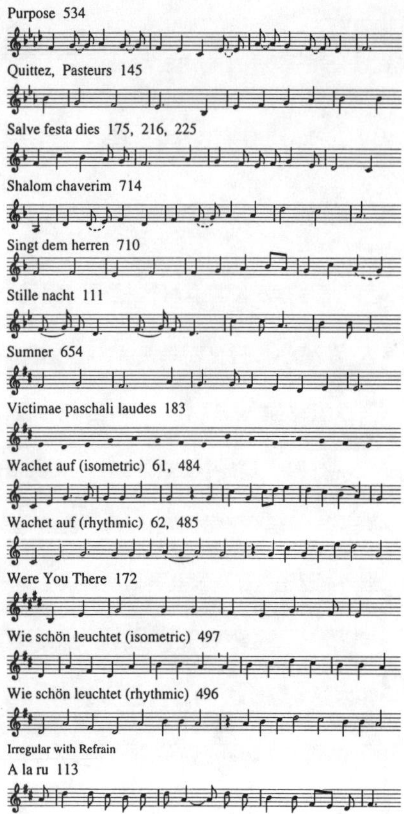
Purpose 534
Quittez, Pasteurs 145
Salve festa dies 175, 216, 225
Shalom chaverim 714
Singt dem herren 710
Stille nacht 111
Sumner 654
Victimae paschali laudes 183
Wachet auf (isometric) 61, 484
Wachet auf (rhythmic) 62, 485
Were You There 172
Wie schön leuchtet (isometric) 497
Wie schön leuchtet (rhythmic) 496
Irregular with Refrain
A la ru 113

Balm in Gilead 676
Beatitudes 560
Festival Canticle 417
Houston 490
I am the Bread of Life 335
Jacob's Ladder 453
Nova, nova 266
Poor little Jesus 468
Raymond 418
Simple Gifts 554
The First Nowell 109
Venite adoramus 110

Hymn 202

Page 406. Stanza 5, line 4, Latin text: The second word should be "sempiterna," not "sempliterna."

Hymn 203

Page 411. Attributions should be listed as LW/JeW

Hymn 207

Page 418. Example 1: The note "* misprinted as g" under the sixth stave should be under the third stave, and ranged to the right

Hymn 208

Page 419 f. Stanzas 2-4 of the Latin text: Add a final "Alleluia" to stanzas 2-4.

Page 420. Stanza 3, line 1, Latin text: The first word should be "surrexit."
In line 2 after the Latin text of the hymn, read "quat[t]uor."

Hymn 211

Page 425. Stanza 1, line 3, German text: The third word should read "Urstend."

Page 426 Stanza 5, line 1,German text: The fourth word should be "kommt."

Hymn 218

Page 441. Latin text: In the burden of the original text the words "pro" and "victoria" should be separated.

Hymn 226

Page 453 Stanza 4, line 2, Latin text: The last word should be "temperies."

Page 454. Stanza 8, line 2, Latin text: The first word should be "fove."

Hymn 270

Page 522. Stanza 1, line 3, Latin text: Words are divided incorrectly. The line should read, "semen Dei seritur."

Hymn 271

Page 525. Stanza 1, line 1, Latin text: Read "altus."
Stanza 2, line 1, Latin text: Read "cujus."
Stanza 5, line 1, Latin text: Read "Nec."
Stanza 6, line 1, Latin text: Read "Hic."
Stanza 7, line 3, Latin text: Read "ac."
Stanza 7, line 4, Latin text: For "Ner" read "Iter."

Hymn 273

Page 529. Stanza 5, line 4, Latin text: Sense requires "coeli."
Stanza 8, line 2, Latin text: Sense requires"Paule" for "Pauli."

Hymn 286

Page 552. Stanza 6, line 2, German text: The first word should read "Für."
Stanza 9, line 4, German text: The fourth word should be "geopfert" (e and o have been reversed).

Hymn 302

Page 577. The proper form of the Greek title for *The Teaching of the Twelve Apostles* is *Διδαχὲ τῶν δώδεκα ἀποστόλων.*

Hymn 319

Page 600. Stanza 2, line 3, German text: The fourth word should read "konnte."
Stanza 3, line 1, German text: The next to the last word should read "Gnade."

Hymn 339

Page 633. Stanza 1, line 2, German text: Read "Sündenhöhle" for the last word.
Stanza 7, line 3, German text: Read "würdiglich" for third word.

Hymn 355

Page 659. Read "Theophanes" in the text on words.

Hymn 362

Page 670. Example 1, A: The reciting note should be C, not B:

Hymn 366

Page 680. Line 2, German text: The last word should be "Stärke."

Hymn 376

Page 695. On the first line read "an der Wien."

Hymn 383

Page 717. Stanza 5, line 4, German text: Read "letzte."

Volume Three B

Hymn 390

Page 738. Stanza 1, line 1, German text: As in other stanzas, read "Herren" (upper-case H).

Hymn 408

Page 768. Stanza 2, line 1, German text: Read "geschaffen" for "Geschaffen."
Stanza 3, line 6, German text: The line should read, "Der Herr ist Gott, der Herr ist Gott!"

Hymn 413

Page 777. Stanza 2, line 7, French text: Read "espèrent."
Stanza 3, line 5, French text: Read "Le Seigneur va . . . ."

Hymn 420

Page 789. Change the attribution from RG to RS-W

Hymn 421

Page 790. Stanza 2, line 7, German text: The last word should be "Herren" (not "Herran").

Hymn 436

Page 819. Stanza 1, line 2 , German text: Read "Es kommt" (lower-case k).
Stanza 1, line 3, German text: Read "Königreich."

Hymn 111

Page 231. Stanza 3, line 5, German text: Read “in” for “un.”

Hymn 127

Page 264: The proper Greek on page 264 is *καθημερινόν.*

Hymn 132

Page 271. Music: The second sentence should read, “Believed by some authorities to be the work of Luther, the tune appears here in its original rhythmic form in a harmonization based on Hans Leo Hassler from the *Liedbook voor de Kerken* (The Hague, Netherlands, 1973), as well as in a harmonization of Johann Sebastian Bach [143. 297].”

Hymn 139

Page 281. Stanza 5, line 2, German text: The last word should be giessen.

Hymn 161

Page 328. Fifth and sixth lines of the first paragraph: Read “the intended shape was Ψ or Y.”

Page 329. Stanza 3, line 4, Latin text: The first word should read “regnavit.”

Page 330. Second full paragraph: The first line should read: “The present version by John Webster Grant was . . . .”

Hymn 162

Page 331. The Greek should read *ἀπο τοῦ ξύλοῦ.*

Hymn 164

Page 334. Stanza 4, line 3, Latin text: The last word should be “gratissimum.”
The title of Abelard’s hymnal is *Hymnarius Paraclitensis.*

Hymn 168

Page 339. Stanza 2, line 5, Latin text: Read “caeli” for “cael.”

Page 340. Stanza 6, line 3, Latin text: Read “tibi” for “titi.”

Page 341. Stanza 1, line 1, German text: The last word should be “Wunden.”
Stanza 1, line 8, German text: The third word should be “tausendmal.”

Hymn 170

Page 347. Change attribution from RG to RS-W.

Hymn 173

Page 350. Stanza 4, line 3, German text: Read “Ligt hie” (separate the words).

Hymn 194

Page 394. Stanza 2, line 2, German text: The first word should be “Über.”

Page 395. Stanza 5, line 4, German text: The next to the last word should be “kein”.

Hymn 201

Page 403. Stanza 6, line 2, German text: The second word should be written “Herr.”
Stanza 9, line 4, German text: The third word should be “das,” not “deas.”

Page 404. Stanza 13, line 4, German text: Read “der Welt-fürst.”

Page 69. The following corrections should be made in the Greek text of the the *Phos hilaron* (line numbers by page, not hymn text):

line 4: ἑσπερινὸν
line 5: Ὕμνοῦμεν
line 7: Ἄξιόν
line 10: Ζωὴν
line 11: Ὁ...δοξάζει

Hymn 49
Page 89. Fourth full paragraph: Read: . . . rendering God his own (*ta sa ek ton son, τὰ σὰ ἐκ τῶν σῶν*, as the Eastern rites put it).

Hymn 54
Page 98. Stanza 5, line 2, German text: The second word should read "kehrt."

Hymn 61
Page 116. Stanza 2, line 4, German text: Read "von" for "jvon."

Hymn 67
Page 125. Stanza 1, line 3, German text: Read "berüben" for "be."

Hymn 74
Page 139. The place of publication for *Cantate Domino* in the section on words should be Kassel, not Chicago.

Hymn 80
Page 151. Stanza 5, line 2, German text: Read "die."
Page 152. Stanza 13, line 3, German text: Read "zu rugen" for "zu rhen".

Hymn 83
Page 159. Stanza 2, line 3, Latin text: Read "gestant" for "getant".

Hymn 85
Page 165. The proper full title of the Sarum hymnary is *Hymnorum cum notis opusculum* (Paris, 1518).

Hymn 87
Page 168. Last stanza quoted, line 3: Read: To all Thyself impart.

Hymn 103
Page 202. Footnote 1: The title of the work cited should read, *"Das Deutsche Kirchenlied von der ältesten Zeit bis zu Angang des . . ."*

Hymn 107
Page 217. Example 1: D E F should read A B C and G H I should also read A B C.
Page 218. Example 2: Delete D, E, F to the left of the braces. Above the first stave, for "C^7" read "C^1."
Page 220. Example 5: For "Bach BXV" read "Bach BWV."

Volume One

"The Tunes of Congregational Song in Britain"

Page 354. In the ninth line of the first full paragraph after "four voices." add "(See figure 39.)".

Page 356. Switch the musical examples for figures 39 and 40 (page 360). The captions are correct as they appear.

Page 359. The reference to the figure in the middle of this paragraph should be to figure 40.

Page 360. See note on page 356 above.

Volume Three A

Hymn 6

Page 10. Paragraph 1, lines 4-5: Read: . . . "Sun of Righteousness"). Christ is "the true light" (Jn 1:9, 1 Jn 2:8), whose "glory" we have seen (Jn. 1:14).

Hymn 7

Page 12. Example 1 (Walter 1524): In the first system the breve before the repeat sign should be f, not g.

Hymn 8

Page 13. Insert in the blank space in the block quotation the metrical pattern for a dactyl and a trochee: – ⌣ ⌣ | – ⌣

Hymn 9

Page 19. Sixth line of text from the bottom of the page: For "same cadencial pattern as A (see Example 3)" read "same cadential pattern as the notes marked a in Example 3 below."

Hymn 26

Page 52. The proper full title of the Sarum hymnary is *Hymnorum cum notis opusculum* (Paris, 1518).

Hymn 27

Page 54. The proper title of the Sarum hymnary is *Hymnorum cum notis opusculum* (Paris, 1518).

Hymn 30

Page 58. The proper title of the Sarum hymnary is *Hymnorum cum notis opusculum* (Paris, 1518).

Hymn 33

Page 63. Line 16, Latin text: The first word should read "Splendeat."

Hymn 37

Page 68. The standard current spelling of the name of the editor of *de Symbolis* in ¶ 1 on words is Ussher.

ERRATA AND CORRIGENDA
in *The Hymnal 1982 Companion*,
Volumes One and Three A and Three B

The Church Hymnal Corporation
445 Fifth Avenue New York, New York 10016

Hymn 475

Page 894. Stanza 3, line 3, German text: Read, "Da liegt unser Wille, Seele, Leib, und Leben."

Page 896. In the narrative after the German text, the first words by which the hymn is cited should be "Gott ist gegenwärtig."

Hymn 478

Page 901. The letters and accents are correct for the Greek on page 478, but the words are divided incorrectly. πώ λων should be printed as one word: πώλων.

Hymn 498

Page 935. In the next to the last line on music, read "eighth."

Hymn 500

Page 938. The text on music is labelled "Words." Replace "Words" with "Music."

Hymn 504

Page 946. The entry on music should read: See hymn 502.

Hymn 515

Page 962. Stanza 2, line 2, German text: Read "Die ein Mensch nur nennen kann."

Page 963. In the entry on words on this page, delete the parenthetical statement at the end of the first paragraph. Delete also the parenthentical numbers attached to stanzas 2 and 3 on this page. The parenthetical statement at the bottom of the page should read, "Notice that sts. 2 and 3. are reversed."

Hymn 518

Page 971. Stanza 5, line 2, Latin text: Read the last word as "nectitur."
Stanza 7, line 3, Latin text: Read "infunde."

Hymn 522

Pages 975. Under Music: The Austrian national song began "Gott erhalte Franz den Kaiser".

Page 976. The German national anthem begins "Deutschland, Deutschland, über alles."

Hymn 533

Page 997. In the first line after Example 1, read "Giuseppi," not "Giovanni" for the Italian equivalent of Joseph.

Hymn 535

Page 1000. Line 2: For "Book of Revelations" read "Book of Revelation."

Hymn 540

Page 1006. Stanza 4, line 6 , German text: Read "Es wird doch endlich."

Hymn 560

Page 1035. In the first line of the section on words, read "genealogy."

Hymn 588

Page 1087. The entry on words should begin: The Rev. John Cawood's text, "Almighty God thy word is cast," . . . .

Hymn 606

Page 1119. Last paragraph, last line: For "the SCN General Report" read "the SCCM General Convention Report . . . ."

Hymn 621

Page 1142. Stanza 16, line 4, Latin text: Read "magnifica."

Hymn 623

Page 1144. Stanza 2, line 2, Latin text: Read "pax," for "pas."
Page 1145. Stanza 5, line 4, Latin text: Read "referet."

Hymn 687

Page 1282. Example 1 (music) : Replace Example 1 on this page with Example 1 below:

Example 1

Der xlvj. Psalm/ Deus noster refugium et virtus/ rc.

Martinus Luther.

Hymn 688

Page 1290. Footnote 1: The last title should be *Das protestantische Kirchenlied. . . .*

Hymn 695

Page 1301. Stanza 5, line 4, German text: The last word of stanza 5 should be written "Nacht" (upper case N).

Hymn 701

Page 1309. Stanza 1, line 5, German text: The third word should be "Hertzen."
Stanza 2, line 2, German text: The last word should be "Stürmen."
Stanza 2, line 8, German text: The third word should be "Sünd."
Page 1310. Stanza 5, line 4, German text: The last word should be "Sünden."